SIXTH CANADIAN EDITION

ESSENTIALS OF MANAGING HUMAN RESOURCES

EILEEN B. STEWART
British Columbia Institute of Technology

MONICA BELCOURT
York University

MELANIE PEACOCK
Mount Royal University

GEORGE W. BOHLANDER
Arizona State University

SCOTT A. SNELL
University of Virgina

NELSON EDUCATION

Essentials of Managing Human Resources, Sixth Canadian Edition

by Eileen B. Stewart, Monica Belcourt, Melanie Peacock, George W. Bohlander, and Scott A. Snell

VP, Product and Partnership Solutions:
Anne Williams

Publisher, Digital and Print Content:
Jackie Wood

Executive Marketing Manager:
Amanda Henry

Content Development Manager:
Toula Di Leo

Photo and Permissions Researcher:
Jessie Coffey

Production Project Manager:
Jaime Smith

Production Service:
Cenveo Publisher Services

Copy Editor:
Rodney Rawlings

Proofreader:
Cenveo Publisher Services

Indexer:
BIM Publishing Services

Design Director:
Ken Phipps

Managing Designer:
Franca Amore

Interior Design:
Trinh Truong

Cover Design:
Ken Cadinouche

Cover Image:
Diana Ong/Superstock/Getty Images

Compositor:
Cenveo Publisher Services

Printed and bound in the United States of America
1 2 3 4 18 17 16

For more information contact Nelson Education Ltd.,
1120 Birchmount Road, Toronto, Ontario, M1K 5G4. Or you can visit our Internet site at
http://www.nelson.com

Library and Archives Canada Cataloguing in Publication

Stewart, Eileen B., 1943-, author
Essentials of managing human resources / Eileen B. Stewart, Monica Belcourt, Melanie Peacock, George W. Bohlander, Scott A. Snell. — Sixth Canadian edition.

Includes index.
ISBN 978-0-17-657028-6 (paperback)

1. Personnel management—Textbooks. I. Belcourt, Monica, 1946-, author II. Peacock, Melanie, author III. Bohlander, George W., author IV. Snell, Scott, 1958-, author V. Title. VI. Title: Managing human resources.

HF5549.E85 2016
658.3 C2015-906531-3

ISBN-13: 978-0-17-657028-6
ISBN-10: 0-17-657028-4

To my son, Jason Robertson, his wife, Andrea Mclean, and my wonderful new grandson, Caleb Robertson, who continue to provide encouragement and support, and in memory of my husband Richard Robertson, who still is my inspiration—ES

To my husband, Michael, for making life so interesting—MB

To my darling husband Cam. I love the chapters of our life that we are writing during our journey together—MP

To my wife, Ronnie Bohlander, and to our children, Ryan and Kathryn—GB

To my wife, Marybeth Snell, and to our children, Sara, Jack, and Emily—SS

Brief Contents

Contents

PART 5: WORLD PERSPECTIVE 362

Preface

The previous edition of *Essentials of Managing Human Resources* was published just as the global economic scene appeared to be recovering from what has been called the "Great Recession." However, we seem to have: continuing global economic instability, skill shortages, mounting government debt, and intense global competition. Because of this, and the different expectations and values of the newer entrants to the workforce, organizations are very aware of the need to focus on their people: the people who make or break company success. Attracting and engaging scarce talent is not easy, but it must happen if the Canadian economy is to grow.

With this ongoing focus on the people in a company—the company's "human resources"—it is important to understand what types of people practices are needed to create the engaged workforce. This book is written to help you understand HR "language"—the practices, processes, and systems necessary for the success of the people in the organization, and therefore, the success of the organization. For example, one of the more important systems in an organization is recruiting and selecting capable and skilled people.

This textbook builds on concepts you have learned or been introduced to in either a general management or a general organizational behaviour course. It is written for students who will become (or are) employees, supervisors and line managers, and HR professionals. Since the text covers the major human resources management processes and systems, it will provide a good overview if you are thinking about moving into the HR profession.

The book has been authored by experienced instructors recognized by students for many years for their excellence in teaching and facilitating learning. The authors are also active HR practitioners who share business stories throughout the text to make the materials interesting for students.

Essentials of Managing Human Resources is a shorter and a more relevant book for general business students with simpler language. It is important, however, to remember that the field of HR has its own jargon, or specialized language. Therefore, one goal of this book is to help you learn the terminology so that you can deal with HR issues in a more informed way.

Finally, this book is designed to cover all the materials you will need for a good general understanding of all the HR activities in a company, as well as your role—whether you are an employee or a have the added responsibilities of a supervisor. It shows how theory applies to HR practices in the 21st century. Further, the book has stories about all types of organizations: profit, nonprofit/voluntary, and public-sector; unionized and non-unionized; and small and large.

WHAT'S NEW IN THE SIXTH EDITION

Building on the continued success of the fifth edition, and incorporating suggestions from users of the text, the following changes have been made:

- Each chapter has content and questions that illustrate the integrated and strategic nature of human resources management.
- The vast majority of references have been updated, with 95% since 2014.
- Figures, charts, and pictures in chapters have been updated.
- The chapter on health and safety has been redesigned to focus on building a culture of well-being with sections on organizational culture and employee engagement.
- HRM Close-ups appear in each chapter.
- At Work with HRM, HRM and the Law, and Ethics in HRM boxes are in each chapter and have been revised for students.
- There is updated content in all chapters to help students acquire the tools and skills to be successful employees.
- The text reflects current Canadian research from professional journals/periodicals and academic journals.
- New cases that focus on Canadian companies are presented in each chapter.
- Review Questions, Critical Thinking Questions, including ones relating to the HRM Close-up, and Developing Your Skills materials in each chapter have been updated.
- Additional websites are identified within each chapter.

FEATURES OF THE BOOK

Each chapter contains the following materials:

- Learning Outcomes are listed at the beginning of each chapter, with reference icons indicating the objective within the chapter.
- An **HRM Close-up** that relates a story about a supervisor's experience in human resources management opens each chapter.
- **Toolkit** boxes contain tools and resources for handling HR matters.
- **At Work with HRM** boxes feature real-world applications relating to a specific topic with critical thinking questions at the end.
- **HRM and the Law** boxes help explain the legal implications of HR.
- **Ethics in HRM** boxes highlight sensitive issues employees and supervisors might face.
- An **Emerging Trends** box provides information about trends in relation to each chapter theme.
- **Key Terms** appear in boldface and are defined in margin notes. The key terms are also listed at the end of the chapter and in the Glossary.
- **Figures with graphs** and **research information** appear throughout the chapters.
- **Illustrations** reinforce points and maintain reader interest.
- A **Summary** at the end of each chapter reinforces the learning objectives.
- A **Need to Know/Need to Understand** box at the end of each chapter helps to identify key topics.
- **Review Questions** and **Critical Thinking Questions** promote basic recall and stimulate critical thinking questions for discussion.
- **Developing Your Skills** contain both text-based and Web-based experiential exercises.
- Two **case studies** in each chapter present current HRM issues in real-life settings that allow for critical analysis.
- **Notes and References** are included for further research and information.
- **Website addresses**, indicated with an arrow symbol in the margin, are provided throughout the text.

SUPPLEMENTARY MATERIALS

Instructor Resources

The **Nelson Education Teaching Advantage (NETA)** program delivers research-based instructor resources that promote student engagement and higher-order thinking to enable the success of Canadian students and educators. Visit Nelson Education's **Inspired Instruction** website at **www.nelson.com/inspired** to find out more about NETA.

The following instructor resources have been created for *Essentials of Managing Human Resources*, Sixth Canadian Edition. Access these ultimate tools for customizing lectures and presentations at **www.nelson.com/instructor**.

NETA Test Bank

This resource was written by Barbara Lipton. It includes multiple-choice questions written according to NETA guidelines for effective construction and development of higher-order questions. Also included are context-specific questions, true/false, and essay questions.

The NETA Test Bank is available in a new, cloud-based platform. **Nelson Testing Powered by Cognero®** is a secure online testing system that allows instructors to author, edit, and manage test bank content from anywhere Internet access is available. No special installations or downloads are needed, and the desktop-inspired interface, with its drop-down menus and familiar, intuitive tools, allows instructors to create and manage tests with ease. Multiple test versions can be created in an instant, and content can be imported or exported into other systems. Tests can be delivered from a learning management system, the classroom, or wherever an instructor chooses. Testing Powered by Cognero for *Essentials of Managing Human Resources* also be accessed through **www.nelson.com/instructor**.

NETA PowerPoint

Microsoft® PowerPoint® lecture slides for every chapter have been created by Eileen Stewart, British Columbia Institute of Technology. There is an average of 25 slides per chapter, many featuring key figures, tables, and photographs from *Essentials of Managing Human Resources.* NETA principles of clear design and engaging content have been incorporated throughout, making it simple for instructors to customize the deck for their courses.

Image Library

This resource consists of digital copies of figures, short tables, and photographs used in the book. Instructors may use these JPEGs to customize the NETA PowerPoint or create their own PowerPoint presentations.

Videos

Instructors can enhance the classroom experience with the exciting and relevant videos provided directly to students through MindTap (see below). They are also available to instructors at **www.nelson.com/instructor.** These videos have been selected to accompany *Essentials of Managing Human Resources.*

NETA Instructor Guide

This resource was written by Eileen Stewart, British Columbia Institute of Technology. It is organized according to the textbook chapters and addresses key educational concerns, such as typical stumbling blocks student face and how to address them. Other features include lecture outlines, answers to end-of-chapters material, critical thinking questions, and notes of the end-of-chapter case studies.

MindTap

MindTap®

Offering personalized paths of dynamic assignments and applications, **MindTap** is a digital learning solution that turns cookie-cutter into cutting-edge, apathy into engagement, and memorizers into higher-level thinkers. MindTap enables students to analyze and apply chapter concepts within relevant assignments, and allows instructors to measure skills and promote better outcomes with ease. A fully online learning solution, MindTap combines all student learning tools—readings, multimedia, activities, and assessments—into a single Learning Path that guides the student through the curriculum. Instructors personalize the experience by customizing the presentation of these learning tools to their students, even seamlessly introducing their own content into the Learning Path.

STUDENT ANCILLARIES

MindTap

MindTap®

Stay organized and efficient with **MindTap**—a single destination with all the course material and study aids you need to succeed. Built-in apps leverage social media and the latest learning technology. For example:

- ReadSpeaker will read the text to you.
- Flashcards are pre-populated to provide you with a jump start for review—or you can create your own.
- You can highlight text and make notes in your MindTap Reader. Your notes will flow into Evernote, the electronic notebook app that you can access anywhere when it's time to study for the exam.
- Self-quizzing allows you to assess your understanding.

Visit **www.nelson.com/student** to start using MindTap. Enter the Online Access Code from the card included with your text. If a code card is *not* provided, you can purchase instant access at the Nelson Brain site, **NelsonBrain.com**.

ACKNOWLEDGMENTS

This edition could not have happened without the hard work of many people, particularly the users of earlier editions. We are grateful to the supervisors and HR practitioners who have shared their stories and helped influence the thinking, and to all the individuals who shared their stories with us.

Many thanks to Simon Vaughan and to the featured individuals for their work on the HRM Close-ups.

The efforts of the Nelson Education team were excellent. Thanks to Anne Williams, Jackie Wood, and Toula Di Leo for their guidance, wisdom, and patience.

The authors and publisher also wish to thank those who reviewed this project during its development and provided important insights and suggestions:

Sonya Hunt, College of New Caledonia

Grace O'Farrell, University of Winnipeg

Alexandra Panaccio, Concordia University

Carol Ann Samhaber, Algonquin College

Barbara Sharp, British Columbia Institute of Technology

Anne Zurowsky, Red River College

Our greatest thanks go to our families, particularly from those of the current co-authors: (Stewart and Peacock). Eileen Stewart is grateful to her son, Jason Robertson, daughter-in-law, Andrea McLean, and grandson, Caleb Robertson. They have provided help, support, research, and encouragement that were most welcome for the project to succeed. Melanie Peacock is thrilled by the support that her husband, Cam, and children have provided. And the previous authors' spouses—Michael Belcourt, Ronnie Bohlander, and Marybeth Snell—have also provided invaluable guidance and assistance. We are grateful to all of them for their enthusiasm and guidance.

Eileen B. Stewart
British Columbia Institute of Technology

Monica Belcourt
York University

Melanie Peacock
Mount Royal University

George W. Bohlander
Arizona State University

Scott A. Snell
The Pennsylvania State University of Virginia

ABOUT THE AUTHORS

Eileen B. Stewart

Eileen Stewart continues to teach part-time at the British Columbia Institute of Technology (BCIT), where she was program head, Human Resource Management Programs, for a number of years. She is a senior human resources professional with extensive experience in all areas of human resources management (HRM), including labour relations in both the public and private sectors. As the HR executive, she has managed human resources units in several of British Columbia's large public-sector organizations. With a diverse background that includes mining, banking, education, and municipal government, Ms. Stewart has a strong overall business orientation.

After receiving a B.A. in economics and commerce from Simon Fraser University, British Columbia, she joined Teck Mining as its first personnel manager. She then moved to BCIT, where she specialized in labour relations. She obtained her senior management experience at BCIT, as director of personnel and labour relations; the University of British Columbia, as director of human resources; and the City of Vancouver, as general manager of human resources.

While working full-time, Ms. Stewart completed her M.B.A. at Simon Fraser University. She currently teaches HRM courses at BCIT and continues to provide consulting services to private, public, and not-for-profit organizations.

Ms. Stewart is active in the HR community through her continued involvement with the Human Resources Management Association (HRMA). She was recognized by HRMA in 2012 with the Award of Excellence for the HR Professional of the Year and became an Honorary Life Member in 2015. She has also served as president of the HRMA, as well as in other executive roles, for several years. In addition to her professional involvement, she is Vice-Chair, Board of Directors, B.C. Women's Hospital and Health Centre Foundation, and is on the Board of Directors, Community Living BC. Previously, she was chair of the Board of Directors, YWCA of Vancouver, and sat on its Board for many years.

Melanie Peacock

Melanie Peacock is an Associate Professor at the Bissett School of Business at Mount Royal University and has been extensively involved in professional HR initiatives as a senior manager, independent HR Consultant, and educator. She obtained her Bachelor of Commerce degree from the University of Alberta, her M.B.A. from the Richard Ivey School of Business (University of Western Ontario), and her Ph.D. through the Faculty of Education at the University of Calgary.

As a senior manager in a variety of corporate environments, Dr. Peacock has led HR teams that create and implement numerous processes and systems that enable organizations to engage their employees and achieve strong results. As well, Dr. Peacock is an active media contributor and commentator.

Dr. Peacock enthusiastically promotes the value of the CHRP designation to business colleagues and has served on the Board of Directors for the Human Resources Institute of Alberta. As testimony to her exceptional work within the HR profession, Dr. Peacock was recognized with the HRIA's Distinguished Career Award in 2014. As well, in recognition of her instructional capabilities, Dr. Peacock was awarded the first Mount Royal Faculty Association Teaching Excellence Award in 2014.

Monica Belcourt

Monica Belcourt is a retired professor of Human Resources Management at York University. Her research is grounded in the experience she gained as director of personnel for CP Rail, as director of employee development, National Film Board, and as a functional HR specialist for the federal government. Dr. Belcourt alternated working in Human Resources Management with graduate school, obtaining an M.A. in Psychology, an M.Ed. in Adult Education, and a Ph.D. in management. She also holds the designation Certified Human Resource Professional. Dr. Belcourt has taught HRM at Concordia, UQAM, McGill, and York, where she founded and manages the largest undergraduate program in HRM in Canada. She created Canada's first degrees in human resources management: B.HRM, B.HRM (honours), and a Masters in HRM (www.atkinson.yorku.ca/mhrm).

As director of the International Alliance for HR Research, Dr. Belcourt manages these programs: the Research Forum in the *Human Resources Professional*; the Applied Research Stream at the annual conference; the *HRM Research Quarterly*; the best theses (M.A. and Ph.D.) awards program; and a funding program for HR research (www.yorku.ca/hrresall).

Dr. Belcourt is series editor for the Nelson Education Series in HRM, which includes nine texts to date: *Managing Performance Through Training and Development, Occupational Health and Safety, Recruitment and Selection in Canada, Strategic Compensation in Canada, Strategic Human Resources Planning, Research, Measurement and Evaluation of Human Resources, An Introduction to the Canadian Labour Market Industrial Relations in Canada,* and *International Human Resources: A Canadian Perspective*. Additionally, she is lead author of the best-selling book *Managing Human Resources*, published by Nelson Education, from which this text is adapted.

Active in many professional associations and not-for-profit organizations, Dr. Belcourt was the president (2003–2004) of the Human Resources Professionals Association of Ontario and serves on the national committee for HR certification. She is a past board member of CIBC Insurance and the Toronto French School. She is also a frequent commentator on HRM issues for CTV, *Canada AM*, CBC, *The Globe and Mail*, *The Canadian HR Reporter,* and other media.

George W. Bohlander

George W. Bohlander is professor emeritus of Management at Arizona State University (ASU). He teaches undergraduate, graduate, and executive development programs in the field of human resources and labour relations. His areas of expertise include employment law, training and development, work teams, public policy, and labour relations. He received his Ph.D. from the University of California at Los Angeles and his M.B.A. from the University of Southern California.

Dr. Bohlander is the recipient of six outstanding teaching awards at ASU and has received the Outstanding Undergraduate Teaching Excellence Award given by the College of Business at ASU. In 1996, Dr. Bohlander received the prestigious ASU Parents Association Professorship for his contributions to students and teaching.

Dr. Bohlander is an active researcher and author. He has published more than 40 articles and monographs covering various topics in the human resources area: these range from labour–management co-operation to team training. His articles appear in such academic and practitioner journals as Labor Studies Journal, Personnel Administrator, Labor Law Journal, Journal of Collective Negotiations in the Public Sector, Public Personnel Management, National Productivity Review, Personnel, and Employee Relations Law Journal.

Before beginning his teaching career, Dr. Bohlander served as personnel administrator for General Telephone Company of California. His duties included recruitment and selection, training and development, equal employment opportunity, and labour relations. He was very active in resolving employee grievances and in arbitration preparation. Dr. Bohlander has also worked with such organizations as the U.S. Postal Service, Kaiser Cement, McDonnell Douglas, Arizona Public Service, American Productivity Center, Rural Metro Corporation, and Del Webb. He is also an active labour arbitrator. He continues to be a consultant to both public- and private-sector organizations.

Scott A. Snell

Scott A. Snell is professor of Business Administration at the Darden Graduate School of Business at the University of Virginia. During his career, Dr. Snell has taught courses in human resources management, principles of management, and strategic management to undergraduates, graduates, and executives. He is actively involved in executive education and serves as faculty director for Penn State's Strategic Leadership Program as well as faculty leader for programs in human resources, developing managerial effectiveness, and managing the global enterprise. In addition to his teaching duties, Dr. Snell serves as director of research for Penn State's Institute for the Study of Organizational Effectiveness.

As an industry consultant, Professor Snell has worked with companies such as Arthur Andersen, AT&T, GE, IBM, and Shell Chemical to redesign human resources systems to cope with changes in the competitive environment. His specialization is the realignment of staffing, training, and reward systems to complement technology, quality, and other strategic initiatives. Recently, his work has centred on the development of human capital as a source of competitive advantage.

Dr. Snell's research has been published in the Academy of Management Journal, Human Resource Management Review, Industrial Relations, Journal of Business Research, Journal of Management, Journal of Managerial Issues, Organizational Dynamics, Organizational Studies, Personnel Administrator, Strategic Management Journal, and Working Woman. He is also co-author of Management: The Competitive Edge, with Thomas S. Bateman. In addition, Dr. Snell is on the editorial boards of Journal of Managerial Issues, Digest of Management Research, Human Resource Management Review, and Academy of Management Journal.

Dr. Snell holds a B.A. in psychology from Miami University, as well as M.B.A. and Ph.D. degrees in business administration from Michigan State University. His professional associations include the Strategic Management Society, the Academy of Management, and the Society for Human Resource Management.

1 Exploring Why HRM Matters to All Employees

LEARNING OUTCOMES

After studying this chapter, you should be able to

1 Define human resources management (HRM).

2 Identify the processes and practices of HRM.

3 Explain the importance of HRM to all employees.

4 Discuss the relationship between the line manager and the HR practitioner.

5 Describe current business topics and the impact on people in organizations.

6 Outline the key demographic and employee concerns.

7 Illustrate the link between business strategy and HRM strategy.

OUTLINE

HRM CLOSE-UP

"I need to help people understand the strategy and important business issues before new ideas can be implemented, all the time being positive and supportive of their need and ability to contribute with fresh thinking."

Tania Goodine always felt she'd like to manage people and develop a team. At university, she chose an undergrad degree in psychology, studied marketing, and then completed her M.B.A. Although her first job was as a marketing officer, Goodine soon headed up a team of her own and found herself doing two things she loves: marketing and people management.

At Libro Credit Union, with over 600 employees throughout southwestern Ontario, Goodine's title is Executive Vice-President, Engagement. She has oversight and responsibility for the brand of the credit union—its reputation in the community, its strategy and innovation, human resources, marketing, and communications.

In contrast to her early days at Libro, Goodine must now get work done through other people. Doing so means spending much of her day developing and coaching people, and helping to solve problems.

"It's always worth it," she says. "Investing time with people, no matter how challenging the conversation, is always worth the time and effort. In a service business, all you have are your people," she says. "They are earning business and keeping business. Therefore all the human resources processes and programs we have in place are critical to our success as a company."

Training at Libro is flexible, and employees complete programs at their own pace. Embracing individual differences and developing people to their full potential is Goodine's goal. "I believe people want to do a good job, and when they're not, there's almost always a legitimate reason. Sometimes, it's simply a training issue. It's almost never that they're unwilling," she explains.

The newest employees sometimes provide the greatest challenges for Goodine. They come to the organization with fresh ideas and eagerness, and it can be a fine balance to harness an employee's energy without shutting the person down.

"I need to help people understand the strategy and important business issues before new ideas can be implemented, all the time being positive and supportive of their need and ability to contribute with fresh thinking. Exploring social media is one example of that, where we work to establish business objectives and guidelines to manage risk, and then I get out of the way of creative ideas!"

Libro has a prescribed performance management process involving regular feedback with staff. As a result, there are no surprises when it comes to evaluating how a person is doing in their job. "I also look for opportunities to have people hold a mirror up to themselves," Goodine explains. "When employees can see a behaviour themselves, it makes learning and development so much easier."

Courtesy of Tania Goodine

Tania Goodine, vice-president, Brand, Libro Financial Group.

The most valuable advice Goodine received as a new manager was during a supervisory training session. A leader explained that everybody carries around a personal knapsack of issues they are dealing with. It is therefore important to recognize individual differences and vary your style accordingly. Sometimes a manager needs to be more direct, and sometimes a softer approach is needed. "Set the tone from day one," says Goodine. "To get trust, you have to give it. Take the time to know people and try to connect in a genuine way."

Source: Courtesy of Tania Goodine

INTRODUCTION

This book will introduce you to the field of human resources management. Human resources management is a business subject and it needs to be studied and understood within the business setting. It is possible that you are taking this course along with other business courses such as general management, economics, and organizational behaviour. All the information you learn in those courses will be applicable to your fuller understanding of human resources management.

Some of the important things to know and understand about business today are that we live in a global world, that there is constant change, and that any of a number of factors can impact the success of any business. The economy in Canada, and in the rest of the world as well, continues to struggle. And in Canada, competing forces affect the economy: a drop in the price of oil, a key export, sluggish consumer sales, and increases in housing and food.[1] What happens in the economy has a direct impact on how many employees any organization hires. Without a healthy and prosperous economy, businesses won't thrive and there will be fewer jobs available.

The managing of people in any organization remains key to the business agenda—perhaps even more so now. New phrases, such as "human capital," "intellectual assets," and "talent management," have crept into business jargon to emphasize the value that the people in the organization have.

As Tania Goodine says in the HRM Close-up, it is important to recognize the individual differences of each employee and to adapt her style accordingly. But what is human resources management (HRM) and why is it important?

Just for a moment, imagine an organization without people. No employees, no supervisors, no managers, executives, or owners. It's a pretty tough assignment. Without people, organizations would not exist. And while this idea may not be much of a revelation, it brings home the point that organizations are made up of people. Successful organizations are particularly good at bringing together different kinds of people to achieve a common purpose. This goal is the essence of human resources management. As students, you are the future of any organization—whether you become employees, supervisors, managers, or owners.

WHAT IS HUMAN RESOURCES MANAGEMENT?

LO1

What is human resources management (HRM)?

Human resources management (HRM)
An integrated set of processes, practices, programs, and systems in an organization that focuses on the effective deployment and development of its employees

Human resources management is more than hiring, paying, and training people. **Human resources management (HRM)** is an *integrated* set of processes, practices, programs, and systems in an organization that focuses on the effective deployment and development of its employees. And it is important to remember that a change in one HRM practice has an impact on the other processes, practices, programs, and systems.

The word "employee" is also intended to cover a contract worker, a person from another organization who is working on a project, or anyone in another, similar working relationship. This expansion of the term is indicative of the new workplace that is far more fluid and flexible than the workforce 10 to 20 years ago.

Managers use a lot of words to describe the importance of people to their organizations. The term "human resources" implies that people are as important to the success of any business as other resources, such as money, materials, machinery, and information.

WHAT ARE THE HRM PROCESSES AND PRACTICES?

LO2

What are the HRM processes and practices?

Before there can be a discussion about why to study HRM, let's look at the various individual systems and processes that fit together. While these will be examined individually, no process or practice is stand-alone, as there is overlap among all the areas.

1. *Creating a culture of a safe and healthy work environment.* Ensuring that the work environment creates a sense of well-being. Goodine and others in the company need to ensure their actions and behaviours create this.
2. *Defining, analyzing, and designing work.* Determining what tasks need to be done, in what order, with what skills, and how individual tasks fit together in work units. For example, in the HRM Close-up, Goodine has to ensure that the tasks are coordinated in a way to get the work done by her team. Creating high-performance work groups or teams is a form of defining and designing work.
3. *Planning for, recruiting, and selecting the workforce.* Ensuring that people in the organization are the right people with the right skills at the right time in the right place which means sourcing, attracting, and hiring the people with the necessary skills and background. In the HRM Close-up, Goodine has to plan when it is necessary to add more staff and then find and hire the people who can best represent the company and do the work as expected.
4. *Orienting, training, and developing employees.* Providing the resources to assist employees in developing the necessary knowledge and skills to do their job today and in the future. Goodine indicated that training is in a flexible format and that she spends a good portion of each day coaching and helping staff develop to their full potential. Organization development and learning is the total impact of individual learning.
5. *Managing employee performance.* Ensuring that there are appropriate mechanisms in place to provide feedback to employees regularly. To ensure that the business objectives are being met, Goodine and Libro provide regular feedback so that there are no surprises during review time.
6. *Rewarding and recognizing employees.* Developing and administering a variety of rewards and recognition components, including pay and benefits, that will attract, retain, and engage employees. Being in the financial services business, Libro will need to ensure that its compensation program can attract and retain the calibre of staff it desires.
7. *Relating to employees within diverse environments.* Ensuring that there are positive and constructive relations between the employees and their supervisors or managers and/or union representatives. Goodine notes that part of her job is to recognize individual differences in staff and adjust her management style accordingly.

These processes and activities and their relationship to the organization and the employees are shown in Figure 1.1. Throughout this text, you will also be provided with information that links organizational performance with the various people practices, thereby reinforcing the requirement to have HR processes that fit the organization. The collective set of these processes and activities, and how well they are linked with each other and the business, creates the setting for the business to be successful through its employees.

FIGURE 1.1 Overall Framework for HR

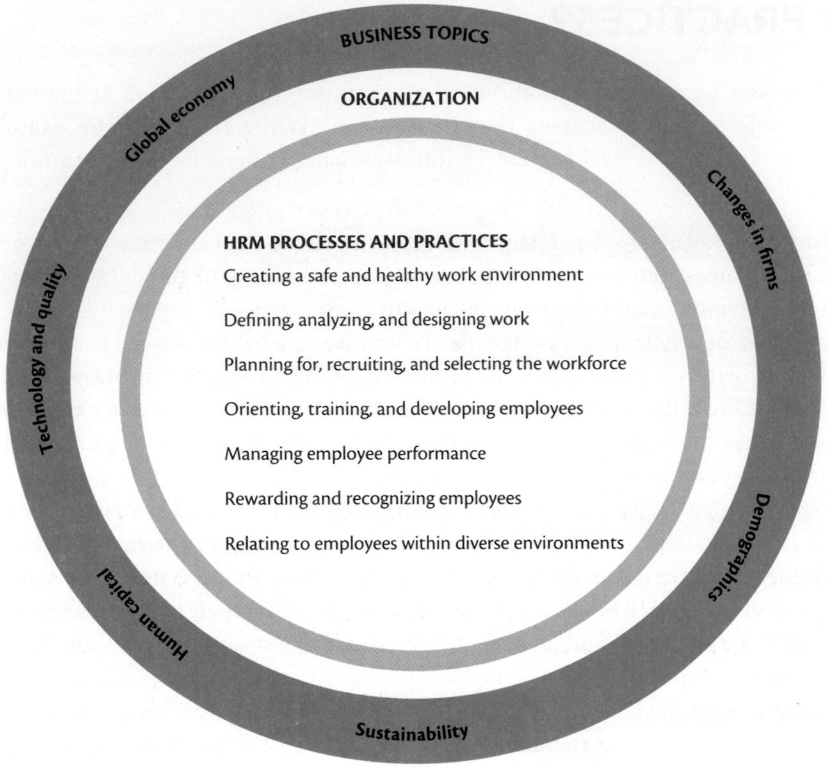

WHY STUDY HUMAN RESOURCES MANAGEMENT?

LO3

Why is HRM important to all employees?

To work with people in any organization, it is important to understand human behaviour and to be knowledgeable about the various systems and practices available to effectively use and build a skilled, knowledgeable, and motivated workforce. Managers must be aware of economic, technological, social, and legal issues that either help or hinder their ability to achieve organizational success. Employees need to understand what their work is, how they will be rewarded, and on what basis their performance will be measured.

You are the managers, team leaders, and employees of tomorrow: studying HRM will help you understand your roles and responsibilities in the organization and how your contribution makes the organizational successful.

In the process of managing human resources, increasing attention is being given to the individual needs of the employees. For example, Gen Y employees may be more motivated by money than Gen Z (or Millennials) employees.[2] Likewise, Gen Z employees are less likely to have work as their sole focus, whereas Boomers make work the primary focus.[3] Thus, this book will not only emphasize the importance of the contributions HRM makes to the organization but also show how, through good people management in an organization, the individual and our overall society are improved. Consider how you feel and behave if your work isn't enjoyable and you don't feel that you understand your role in the organization or that your work doesn't appear to be valued. You might respond in a variety of ways, including being unconcerned about a customer complaint. By acting in this way, you are not contributing to the success of the organization, which includes your own success. If enough people do this, our overall productive capacity as a society will decrease.

THE PARTNERSHIP OF LINE MANAGERS AND HR PROFESSIONALS

Role of the Line Manager

LO4

What is the relationship between the line manager and HR practitioner?

Managing people depends on effective leaders (supervisors and line managers). The leader is the key link between the employee and the organization. Therefore, the leader must have a thorough knowledge and understanding of contemporary HRM and how these practices influence the output of any organization. Although HR professionals may have responsibility for coordinating programs and policies pertaining to people-related issues, managers and employees themselves are ultimately responsible for making the organization successful. All line managers are people managers—not the HR professional or HR unit. It is through the effective leadership of the line manager or supervisor that the talent or "intellectual capital" of the organization is enhanced. Remember that it is the line manager who directly interacts with the employees and is responsible for their effective contribution to the organization. It is the manager's role to develop their employees and make work a great place.[4] Therefore, when an organization wishes to place an increased emphasis on the growth and development of its people, it is the line manager who is front and centre in identifying the gaps in any skill sets. It is only then that the HR practitioner can offer some ways and means of bridging the gap.

Readers of this book will become line managers, supervisors, and employees as well as HR professionals. This text is oriented toward helping people manage people more effectively and understanding the various HR processes, whether they become first-line supervisors, employees, or HR professionals. Students now preparing for careers in organizations will find that the study of HRM provides a background that will be valuable in any role. For example, an HR professional can assist the supervisor in developing steps to improve the performance of a particular employee. The consequences for the supervisor of developing a poor approach could result in the employee either not improving the performance or the employee feeling unsupported or criticized by the supervisor's approach. Likewise, it is important for the employee to know about managing their own performance and improving when necessary. In either situation, the primary objective of improving performance would not be achieved.

Role of the HR Professional

It is important for line managers to understand the role or function HR professionals play, whether these individuals are part of the organization or are external resources retained by the organization. HR practitioners are becoming more and more professional and are being trained with common bodies of knowledge and information. Besides knowing how to recruit and pay people appropriately, HR professionals need sound business knowledge, good problem-solving and influence skills, and personal credibility (trust and the ability to build personal relationships). The HR practitioner's primary role in today's organizations is to help equip the line manager with the best people practices so that the organization can be successful. HR professionals can provide service activities, such as recruiting and training. Further, they can be active in policy formulation and implementation in such areas as workplace harassment, healthy work environments, and change management. Lastly, an HR professional can be an employee advocate by listening to employee concerns and ensuring that the organization is aware of and responding to those concerns.

HR professionals are expected to fulfill their role by actively involving others in the organization, particularly the supervisors and managers, in the development and design of HR programs. For example, a company may want the HR professional to develop an overall recruitment approach to attract individuals with key skill sets. This approach would then generate a pool of applicants with the required skills. However, it would be the line manager who would actually select the best person from this pool.

In the tourism industry, it is important to hire and retain capable people.

Dmitry Kalinovsky/Shutterstock.com

Dave Ulrich,[5] a leading expert and author on human resources practices, states that an HR professional must be impactful and create value for the organization. Above all else, HR professionals must be able to integrate business skills, HR skills, and skills in helping employees handle change so that their organization can build and maintain a competitive advantage through its people.

The Ongoing Partnership

As we next look at the competitive and social challenges facing any business, it is important to reinforce the idea that managing people is not something done in a back room or by HR professionals alone. It is important to remember that HR doesn't tell managers what to do; and proactive managers know when to involve an HR professional. Managing people is every manager's responsibility and obligation, and successful organizations are those that equip their line managers with a thorough understanding of good HRM practices—either through having an HR unit or retaining expertise when needed. Even without an HR professional, the manager is still responsible for effective human resources management.

In organizations that have an HR unit, HR managers usually assume a greater role in top-management planning and decision making. There are, however, organizations that see HR as more an administrative matter than a key business section.[6] For HR to be seen as part of the business, it must have a solid understanding of the business and develop processes and practices that align with that business.[7] A recent study conducted by Aon Hewitt indicated that organizations that focus efforts on being a great employer have better business outcomes.[8] For additional information on this and other studies conducted by Aon Hewitt in this area, visit its website: **www.aon.com**.

Aon Hewitt
www.aon.com

Let's reconsider the comments made by Goodine in the HRM Close-up. The organization has more than 300 employees and an HR unit with an HR manager. But many smaller organizations often wonder when they should hire an HR professional. Frequently, when an organization has 75 to 100 employees, the owners or senior management may think it best to get professional assistance. Figure 1.2 shows what the relationship between HR and other business units might be in a small organization. Even smaller organizations, those with fewer than 75 employees, will frequently retain an independent HR practitioner; this is typically done through the owner or president, and the line manager may not have much interaction with the HR expert.

FIGURE 1.2 Relationship of HR to Other Business Units

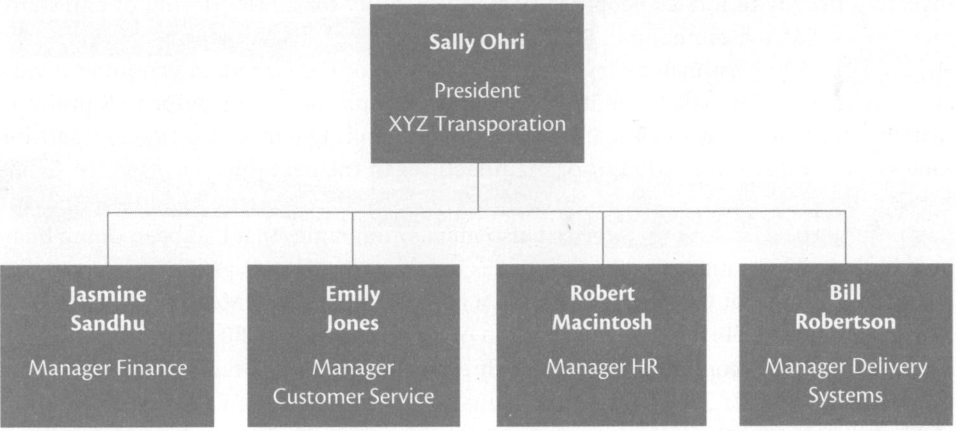

If Emily in Figure 1.2 needed to hire a customer service agent, she would work with Robert in confirming the job requirements, identifying possible recruitment sources, doing the final interviewing, and making the decision on which candidate to hire. Robert, on the other hand, would assist Emily as required, including the development of appropriate interview questions and conducting reference checks.

CURRENT BUSINESS TOPICS AND THE IMPACT ON PEOPLE IN ORGANIZATIONS

LO5

What are the current business topics?

Conference Board of Canada
www.conferenceboard.ca

Society for Human Resource Management (SHRM)
www.shrm.org

McKinsey & Company
www.mckinsey.com

Organizations such as the Conference Board of Canada (**www.conferenceboard.ca**), the Society for Human Resource Management (**www.shrm.org**), and McKinsey & Company (**www.mckinsey.com**) conduct ongoing studies of the most important competitive trends and issues facing firms. As we move forward in a new global environment, some of the business concerns are considerably different than they were just a few years ago.

1. global economy
2. changes in firms and business sectors
3. technology and quality
4. sustainability
5. developing human capital and talent management
6. demographic and employee concerns

Topic 1: Global Economy

The Canadian economy is primarily built on exports, including those in natural resources such as oil, gas, mining, and forestry. Because of this, for years many Canadian companies have been involved in the global markets. As Canada has moved into other goods and services to export, many companies have created global operations or worked collaboratively with foreign companies to sell Canadian products. Canadian exports were valued at close to $440 billion in late 2014.[9] This figure represents approximately 35% of Canada's gross domestic product (GDP).[10] At Work with HRM 1.1 provides insights about a number of Canadian companies that are successful in the global marketplace.

While many companies, such as Starbucks, Walmart, and Lowe's, are coming to Canada to do business, some Canadian companies have acquired firms in other countries. An example is Brookfield, headquartered in Toronto and one of the largest owners/managers of office properties and renewable energy generating facilities.[11]

The company recently acquired a large-scale gambling casino in Atlantic City and is investing heavily to induce people to come to that city for a full offering of entertainment as well as for gambling.[12] But **globalization** is not just something of interest to large firms. While estimates vary widely, 70 to 80% of the Canadian economy is now affected by international competition. This means, for a small distributor in Kamloops, British Columbia, or a small manufacturer in Alliston, Ontario, that the competition today is no longer the distributor or manufacturer in the next town or province. Trade agreements that allow a freer flow of goods and services mean competitors may be located anywhere around the world. It also means companies that had been doing business in Canada can move to other countries that may have lower production costs. For example, Ford Motor Co. decided to build a new engine plant in Mexico, rather than in Windsor, Ontario, eliminating the creation of approximately 1,000 jobs.[13]

Globalization
Moving local or regional business into global marketplace

Global growth continues to be sluggish even though it has been several years since the financial crisis of 2008. Specifically, Canada's growth is 1–2%; China is slowing; the EU is still soft; and the U.S. economy is only growing by 3%.[14] Slow growth hampers a vibrant Canadian economy. More recently, there have been other issues: Target leaving the Canadian market; the continued slide of price of crude oil; the default of Greece to the EU Bank in summer of 2015; and the large drop in the Chinese stock market.[15]

AT WORK WITH HRM 1.1

OUR GLOBAL SUCCESS: GREAT EMPLOYEES!

Many Canadian companies acknowledge that their success in the global marketplace is attributable to the people they have hired. Employers actively strive now to have work environments that make them eligible for "best employer" status. For example, Cactus Restaurants, a western Canada restaurant chain, received such an award for the largest in-house apprenticeship pursuing Red Seal Certification. Firms such as Avison Young, E.C.S. Electrical Cable Supply, Robotec, and Hunter Amenities were honoured in early 2015 for being in the top 50 Best Managed Companies in Canada.

Avison Young, a Canadian-owned commercial real-estate venture, is proud of its investment in people. It provides specialized training and workshops that allow its staff to provide exceptional service to the clients. Further, it highlights the importance of collaboration to achieve the best expertise and intellectual capital. It also believes that its culture of team orientation helps it keep the most talented in the commercial real-estate business.

With operations as far away as Dubai, E.C.S. Electrical Cable Supply provides wire and cable products to specialty markets, such as shipping, mining, and critical life support with portable cables. It is successful because its professionals have deep knowledge of the various industries and superb customer service capabilities. To help with the deepening of its knowledge base, the company provides personal development and encourages everyone to take an active part in the company's success.

Likewise, Robotec, a Quebec-based company that designs and manufactures innovative hydraulic systems that handle bulk solids or unusual items, provides equipment and service to projects in more than 20 countries. Because it employs people with specialized trades such as machinists, it actively recruits the best and then continues with their development to ensure that they stay.

Hunter Amenities, with headquarters in Burlington, Ontario, provides personal care products around the world. It attributes its success and growth to the dedication, creativity, and skills of its employees. Hunter's people are engaged because all the products are developed with the environment as part of the consideration.

CRITICAL THINKING QUESTIONS:

1. What other businesses in your geographic area have a global marketplace?
2. What types of skills might their employees need for them to continue being global players?

Sources: Adapted from "British Columbia's Top Employers 2014," *The Vancouver Sun*, February 2014; "Best Managed Companies 2015," March 2015, accessed July 8, 2015, www.bestmanagedcompanies.ca/en/meetourwinners/Pages/GoldStandardWinners.aspx; and "About Us," accessed July 9, 2015, www.hunteramenities.com/content/company.

Effect of Globalization on HRM

When managers start to "go global," they have to balance a complicated set of issues related to different geographies, cultures, laws, and business practices. Human resources issues underlie each of these concerns and include such things as identifying capable expatriate managers who live and work overseas; designing training programs and development opportunities to enhance the managers' understanding of foreign cultures and work practices; and adjusting compensation plans to ensure that pay schemes are fair and equitable across individuals in different regions with different costs of living.

So, while managing across borders provides new and broader opportunities for organizations, it also represents a quantum leap in the complexity of human resources management. Whether you are working for a large multinational company or a small parts distributor, HRM in other countries has an impact on you. Chapter 11 focuses on international human resources management.

Topic 2: Changes in Firms and Business Sectors

While Canada exports its oil and minerals, much of Canada's economy over the past several years has relied upon housing and consumer spending. For real growth, Canada will need to increase its exports.[16] Currently, Canada is heavily dependent on the economic health of the U.S., since approximately 75% of Canada's GDP is exported there.[17] Of significance is the fact that the amount of crude oil to the U.S. has now exceeded 3 million barrels per day.[18] However, the price of crude oil has been on a roller coaster—from a high of $110 in July 2014 to $78 in November 2014 to $33 in January 2016.[19]

Maintaining Canada's ability to export large quantities of oil and gas isn't easy, given the environmental concerns about extracting and shipping. There is huge public resistance to the Enbridge pipeline from Alberta to the British Columbia coast, and growing concern about TransCanada's Energy East project from environmentalists, farmers, ranchers, and ordinary people concerned about their livelihood in Atlantic Canada.[20]

Changes to company ownership has seen some interesting outcomes. Sobeys, a grocery chain with headquarters in Nova Scotia, bought Safeway in 2014, making Sobeys one of two national grocery retailers.[21] That same year, Hudson's Bay Company bought Saks, LifeLabs Medical Laboratory bought CML, and TD Bank Group bought 50% of CIBC's Aeroplan credit card portfolio.[22] As companies change, so do the requirements for the capabilities of employees. Dealing with the consequences of changes impacts all HRM practices.

Small and medium-sized businesses continue to be the lifeblood of a healthy economy. Gravity Pope, a specialty shoe and clothing store headquartered in Edmonton, has grown from a small store in Edmonton to having stores in Calgary, Vancouver, and Toronto.[23] A pub chain in Calgary that is noted for its craft beers recently announced it had entered into a joint venture to open a restaurant in Shanghai.[24]

Productivity and Managing Costs

Companies continually look at ways to lower costs and improve productivity to maximize efficiency in order to be globally competitive. Labour costs are one of the largest expenditures of any organization, particularly in service and knowledge-intensive companies. Organizations have tried a number of approaches to lower costs, particularly labour costs. These include downsizing, outsourcing, and the use of contract employees, each of which has a direct impact on HR policies and practices.

Downsizing is the planned elimination of jobs. There is no company or business sector that hasn't experienced downsizing at some point. More downsizing will occur when the economy is poor, but some might occur if the company decides to eliminate a product line or close a plant. For example, Saputo, a large dairy processor headquartered in Montreal, closed plants in both Alberta and the U.S. It moved the production elsewhere so that efficiencies could be increased and costs reduced.[25] Almost 200 jobs will be lost. And as

Downsizing
The planned elimination of jobs

BlackBerry (formerly Research in Motion—RIM) tried to find its balance, it downsized 65 employees when it changed its app strategy.[26]

A number of lessons were learned in earlier downsizing situations, so organizations are being much more careful about changing operations. For a number of years, the general approach was to do an across-the-board reduction or to eliminate individuals on the basis of performance. However, research has identified that the why and how a company downsizes can create negative views of how responsible the company is.[27] Other lessons include communicating what is going to happen as soon as possible, being honest regarding why the downsizing occurs, treating everyone with respect, and being sure downsizing is the right solution.[28]

If jobs and employees have to be eliminated, the manner in which the action is taken also has to be carefully planned. As much attention needs to be paid to those people who will still be employed as to departing employees. It is the people who are still employed who will will make the company successful, so it is important that they feel the company has treated everyone well. It is also important that the remaining employees feel as if they matter; a good way to achieve this is to provide additional training and development opportunities.[29]

When Target announced it was leaving Canada, it created a fund that would guarantee severance payments to its 17,500 employees—a fund that would be safe from bankruptcy proceedings.[30] Read HRM and the Law 1.1 to better understand the legal implications of shutting down a business.

Outsourcing and Contractors

Outsourcing
Contracting outside the organization for work formerly done by internal employees

Outsourcing means hiring someone outside the company or bringing in a company to perform tasks that could be done internally. Companies often hire the services of accounting firms, for example, to take care of financial services. Increasingly, activities such as maintenance, security, catering, and payroll are being outsourced in order to increase the organization's flexibility and to lower administrative costs. For example, organizations such as Telus, Accenture, and IBM have business units that provide outsourced services ranging from technology support, management, and telephone operator services.[31]

And outsourcing can be a niche market for some entrepreneurs. Mindfield, a recruiting company in Vancouver, provides hourly workers for companies such as Canadian Tire, Sport Chek, Overwaitea Foods, and Mark's Work Wearhouse. Its focus is on retail and small to medium-sized companies, and it uses state-of-the-art technology to recruit and assess skills for hiring and placement.[32]

While the use of outsourcing continues, there are examples of where outsourced work is returning to the home company. Sears Canada has established new call centres in Saskatchewan and Ontario, and brought the work back from the Philippines.[33] It has done so to provide an improved level of customer satisfaction, particularly for repair calls. Likewise, American Express Canada returned some activities to Canada from other countries. Furthermore, in some cases, using outsourced services can help with a business transformation, such as is occurring in Russia, where outsourcing has not traditionally been done.[34] However, since there is always a risk when outsourcing, here are some important things to examine:

1. What does the company want to outsource and why?
2. Who are the service providers and what will be the evaluation criteria?
3. What are the risks of outsourcing and how will the risks be mitigated?[35]

Contractor
A person hired by contract to perform a specific job and is not considered part of the employee base

In addition to downsizing and outsourcing, organizations will hire **contractors**. Generally speaking, contractors are hired to do a specific job for a specific period of time and have more flexibility in relation to hours of work, work location, and how the work is done. Contractors are not covered by mandatory employment deductions such as income tax and employment insurance premiums. However, contractors are still required to report all income and then to pay appropriate taxes.[36] The downside of using contractors is that they may not be as attached or committed to the work outcomes as an employee.

HRM AND THE LAW 1.1 CLOSING OPERATIONS AND TERMINATING 17,500 EMPLOYEES!

Headlines were made a few years ago when U.S. giant retailer Target moved into Canada and opened 133 retail stores in 2013. Then the shock occurred: in January 2015 Target announced that it had made a mistake by opening so many stores at once and had decided to close down its Canadian operations—all stores.

The financial and legal implications of the shutdown affected suppliers, customers, employees, investors, and creditors, and the decision was not made lightly. In making it, Target sought court-ordered protection from creditors with a $5.4 billion loss in its fourth quarter 2014. While employees knew that the business was not doing well, they were surprised that all stores would close. Many people, including customers, felt that only the ones doing poorly would close.

Only a few days after the announcement, Sears Canada publicly encouraged Target employees to apply for work with it. Sears also decided to do special events, such as local job fairs, to provide more opportunities for Target employees to consider it as an employer. An invitation was also extended to the Target head office people to meet with senior leaders of Sears. And within a few months, Lowe's announced that it would take over 13 of the Target stores that would create about 2,000 jobs.

Unfortunately, many of the employees only worked part-time at minimum wage, and that can be difficult for them. On the other hand, since turnover in the retail sector is fairly high, these employees will have skills that can be used in places such as Home Depot, Walmart, and others mentioned above.

What is different is that Target has pledged to create a $70 million trust that will provide a minimum of 16 weeks of wages and benefits. Although the amount of severance was required by law, the trust fund was not, since it was seeking creditor protection. However, it acknowledged that it couldn't make light of the decision and the impact on people, and felt it had to protect the employees. The courts approved the creditor protection, along with the trust. This was an unusual step; employees are frequently the last to be considered and the last to be paid in bankruptcy proceedings.

QUESTIONS:

1. Do you have a friend or family member who was working at Target? If so, what were their reactions?
2. Do you think Target ought to have paid more compensation than the minimum required by law for terminating all the employees? Explain your answer.

Sources: Adapted from Solarina Ho, "Target to Discontinue Canada Operation," *Canadian HR Reporter*, January 15, 2015, accessed July 9, 2015, www.hrreporter.com/articleview/23257-target-to-discontinue-canada-operation; Andrea Hopkins, "Target Workers, Shoppers, Dismayed at Canada Pullout," *Canadian HR Reporter*, January 15, 2015, accessed July 8, 2015, www.hrreporter.com/articleview/23265-target-workers-shoppers-dismayed-at-canada-pullout; Allison Martell, "Sears Offering Jobs, Discounts to Workers Affected by Target Exit," *Canadian HR Reporter*, January 19, 2015, accessed July 8, 2015, www.hrreporter.com/articleview/23276-sears-offering-jobs-discounts-to-workers-affected-by-target-exit; "Lowe's Gets 13 Target Canada Stores, Distribution Centre for $151 Million," *Canadian HR Reporter*, May 11, 2015, accessed July 9, 2015, www.hrreporter.com/articleview/24321-lowes-gets-13-target-canada-stores-distribution-centre-for-151-million; Mark Gollom, "Target Store Closures: What Will Happen to 17,600 Employees?" *CBC News*, January 20, 2015, accessed July 9, 2015, www.cbc.ca/news/business/target-store-closures-what-will-happen-to-17-600-employees-1.2913118; "Target Canada Closure: What You Can Expect," *CBC News*, January 15, 2015, accessed July 9, 2015, www.cbc.ca/news/business/target-canada-closure-what-you-can-expect-1.2911902; and Jeff Gray and Tim Shufelt, "Rare Move Protects Employees," *The Globe and Mail*, January 16, 2015, B7.

Topic 3: Technology and Quality

Advancements in technology have enabled organizations to improve processes (both production and administrative), reduce costs, and improve quality. With computer networks, unlimited amounts of data can be stored, accessed, and used in a variety of ways, from simple record keeping to controlling complex equipment. The effect is so dramatic that, at a broader level, organizations are changing the way they do business. Use of the Internet to transact business for both large and small companies is now a way of doing business and is transforming the way traditional brick-and-mortar companies operate. For example, Amazon's rise was based on its having only an online presence, with no storefront. It is now considered one of the tech giants of the world, as it not only sells books but also has developed electronic readers and Wi-Fi speakers.[37] Organizations are connected via computer-mediated relationships, and they are giving rise to a new generation of "virtual" workers who work from home, hotels, cars, or wherever their work takes them.

The implications for HRM are at times mind-boggling. For example, in the early years, HRM was more administrative and spent much of its time on processing forms. Technology is now found in all the HR practices; and many of you may have already experienced this, such as when applying online for a job. Support is also provided to all employees through technology, including intranets. Information is now also widely available to everyone regarding employment matters or anything to do with HRM. Toolkit 1.1 provides helpful current website addresses regarding HRM.

In addition, cloud computing is a growing trend impacting the way organizations handle data and whether or not the company has in-house IT employees. There is even a suggestion that cloud computing can create organizations that are more agile and produce better business outcomes.[38]

Telecommuning
Conducting work activities in different locations through the use of technology

Further, it is important to remember the impact technology and the Internet have had on the way people work. Specifically, people can live in one location and "work" in another, including their own home. This kind of work is called **telecommuting**, in which people may have their job structured to allow them to work from home and to work at any time. Staples Canada recently conducted a survey regarding how employees feel about telecommuting. The survey revealed that 71% of employees consider telecommuting an important benefit, as it enables employees to have a better work–life balance.[39] Staples' use of telecommuting gives it an advantage in recruiting talent.

Working in Canada
www.workingincanada.gc.ca

LinkedIn
www.linkedin.com

Monster.ca
www.monster.ca

Workopolis
www.workopolis.com

Eluta
www.eluta.ca

Due to the new technology, the skills necessary to be successful are different. For example, this text provides you with weblinks for additional information. You can access **www.workingincanada.gc.ca** for information on trends in jobs and occupations, earnings, and work prospects in Canada. Likewise, some of you will get work after you finish school by posting your profile and/or résumé online at websites such as **www.linkedin.com**, **www.monster.ca**, **www.workopolis.ca**, and **www.eluta.ca**.

Figure 1.3 provides information about the skills important for contributing to innovation in the workplace.

TOOLKIT 1.1 A GUIDE TO INTERNET SITES

The Internet offers employees and HR professionals a vast amount of resources for research, news, recruitment, and networking with people and organizations. Listed below are some Internet sites related to the HR field. Their addresses (URLs) are printed here for reference, but once you get started, it's easier to access the rest by following the links to related sites.

GENERAL HR SITES

www.workforce.com
This site posts articles regarding the latest trends and topics in human resources. It also provides links to HR specialist consultants.

www.hrreporter.com
An excellent Canadian resource for current news, information on the latest trends and practices, expert advice, experiences, and insights from HR practitioners, research, and resources.

www.hrVillage.com
An excellent source of up-to-date human resources information, featuring online articles, discussion forums, book reviews, and links to related sites.

SPECIALIZED SITES

www.canoshweb.org
This site offers a variety of information regarding safety and health in the workplace, reports and statistics, and industry trends. It also provides online access to the workers' compensation legislation in Canadian jurisdictions.

www.esdc.gc.ca/en/jobs/workplace/index.page?
This site provides online access to federal statutes and regulations, with links to provincial employment legislation.

www.statcan.gc.ca
The Statistics Canada site offers daily news updates, census information, and free tabular data on various aspects of the Canadian economy.

In addition to the above sites, this book's website, **http://www.nelson.com/student**, provides useful and up-to-date links to accompany this text.

FIGURE 1.3 Innovation Skills Profile 2.0

The Conference Board of Canada, as a nonprofit applied research organization, helps identify skills necessary to help organizations be more innovative and productive. Here are some of those skills:

Creativity, problem-solving, and continuous improvement skills—necessary to generate ideas

- Seeking different points of view and exploring options
- Being adaptable
- Asking questions
- Putting forward own ideas
- Looking for surprising connections

Risk assessment and risk-taking skills—necessary for being entrepreneurial

- Being comfortable when pursuing new opportunities
- Assessing and managing risk
- Keeping goals in sight
- Willing to experiment
- Learning from experiences

Relationship-building and communication skills—necessary to develop and maintain interpersonal relationships

- Engaging others
- Building and maintaining relationships in and outside the organization
- Sharing information
- Respecting and supporting other ideas

Implementation skills—necessary to turn ideas into capabilities, processes, products, and services

- Setting realistic goals
- Accessing and applying knowledge
- Using the right tools and technologies
- Using measurements to show the value of a solution
- Accepting feedback and learn from mistakes
- Being accountable

Source: Adapted from the Conference Board of Canada, *Innovation Skills Profile 2.0* found at http://www.conferenceboard.ca/cbi/innovationskills.aspx. Reproduced with permission from the Conference Board of Canada.

Quality

Meeting customer expectations and providing excellent customer service are essential for any organization. In addition to focusing on internal management issues, managers must also meet customer requirements of quality, innovation, variety, and responsiveness. These standards often separate the winners from the losers in today's competitive world. How well does a company understand its customers' needs? How fast can it develop and get a new product to market? How effectively has it responded to special concerns? "Better, faster, cheaper"—these standards require organizations to constantly align their processes with customer needs. Management approaches, such as quality management, Six Sigma, and Lean, outlined below, provide comprehensive approaches to responding to customers. These have direct implications for HR: the requirement to hire staff that can work in teams, the necessity of having compensation systems that support quality objectives, and the need to have performance management systems that recognize the importance of customer satisfaction and service excellence.

Lab technicians need technical skills as well as the ability to work with others.

Monkey Business Images Ltd/Thinkstock

The focus on quality began over 60 years ago with total quality management (TQM) and was based on a management philosophy that focused on understanding customer needs, involving employees, using fact-based decision making, communicating, doing things right the first time, and improving continuously.[40] A number of studies, pioneered by management expert W. Edwards Deming, have demonstrated the strong positive link between a focus on quality and higher customer satisfaction.[41]

Six Sigma
A process used to translate customer needs into a set of optimal tasks performed in concert with one another

Lean
Organizational system of improvements that maximize customer value and minimize waste

Companies such as Xerox, Hitachi, and Home Depot then adopted a more systematic approach to quality, called Six Sigma, which includes major changes in management philosophy and HR programs. **Six Sigma** is a statistical method of translating a customer's needs into separate tasks and defining the best way to perform each task in concert with the others. Six Sigma makes the improvements through measurement and data analysis.[42] The approach can also be used for internal organizational processes that deal with internal "customers." What makes Six Sigma different from other quality efforts is that it catches mistakes before they happen.

Lean is similar to Six Sigma, but it is a more inclusive organizational system of improvements that maximize customer value and minimize waste.[43] It was pioneered by Toyota as a way to look at not just individual machines but the overall flow of the production through the total process.[44] Since then, Lean has been used by many organizations from manufacturing to services. For example, the Saskatchewan healthcare system is using it to improve efficiency, quality, and customer service.[45] Another expert believes Lean builds trust and fosters employee engagement.[46]

Benchmarking
Finding the best practices in other organizations that can be brought into a company to enhance performance

Benchmarking looks at the "best practices" in other companies, whether competitors or not. By looking at other companies, managers and employees can assess if something might be used in their organization to improve overall performance. For example, the University of Calgary has benchmarked how the practice of law is changing and how adults learn so that its law school can create "excellence in lawyering."[47]

Key to all of these techniques are good and appropriate HR practices. One reason good HR practices are so essential to programs such as Six Sigma is that they help balance two opposing forces. Six Sigma's focus on continuous improvement drives the system toward disequilibrium, while Six Sigma's focus on customers, management systems, and the like provides the restraining forces that keep the system together. HR practices help managers balance these forces. Hence, the manager plays a key role in motivating employees to care about quality and helping the company foster a work environment that will allow employees to succeed in quality initiatives. Read At Work with HRM 1.2 to learn more about what organizations can do to become excellent at what they do.

The Baldrige Performance Excellence Program
www.nist.gov/baldrige

Excellence Canada
www.excellence.ca

AT WORK WITH HRM 1.2

BECOMING EXCELLENT AS A COMPANY!

As mentioned in the text, making use of initiatives that promote quality and efficiency is very dependent on the environment and culture of the company. So what can be done besides using Six Sigma and Lean?

Companies such as Apple and Amazon didn't become outstanding only by making sure their systems and processes were efficient—as one management author says, "Lean may eliminate waste but it doesn't help create value."

While there is no precise recipe, here are some things that can help:

- Ensure that the company's strategy and its actions work together and are measured to demonstrate success.
- Attract and retain the right people.
- Ensure that the environment supports and encourages collaboration and innovation at all levels.
- Get and keep customers that the company wants.

Arrow Electronics, a global company headquartered in British Columbia that provides services and solutions to commercial and industrial users of electronic components, has received awards for their focus on delivering solutions that fits its customer needs. Likewise, Ingram Micro Canada received a Microsoft award for its superior operational excellence.

And operational excellence isn't just in the for-profit sector. The University of Toronto makes sure its operations are aligned with the academic missions of the university. Further, the university makes sure its budgeting process is driven by the academic outcomes—not just a focus on financial constraints.

CRITICAL THINKING QUESTION:

Is use of any quality improvement initiatives just another management fad to get more work out of people? Explain the reasons for your answer.

Sources: Adapted from Andrew Miller, *Redefining Operational Excellence*, Amacon, 2014; Harvey Schachter, "Four Principles of Operational Excellence, *The Globe and Mail*, August 6, 2014, B11; Arrow Electronics, "About Arrow," accessed November 14, 2014, www.arrow.com/about_arrow; Michale Cusanelli, "Distribution Watch: Ingram Micro, Synnex, Arrow Electronics," *Distribution Watch*, accessed November 14, 2014, http://thevarguy.com/distribution-watch/111414/distribution-watch-ingram-micro-synnex-arrow-electronics; and James Flynn, "The Man Who Keeps the University Running," *The Varsity*, November 10, 2014, accessed November 14, 2014, http://thevarsity.ca/2014/11/10/meet-the-man-who-keeps-the-university-running.

Another approach to overall quality in an organization is the Baldrige Award for Performance Excellence, sponsored by the National Institute of Standards and Technology in the United States. This award looks at excellence from a systems perspective with detailed criteria in the areas of leadership; strategic planning; customer focus; measurement and knowledge management; workforce focus; process management; and results. In Canada, the Baldrige awards are managed through Excellence Canada. Organizations as small as Orono Public School in Ontario and as large as Bell have been recipients.[48]

Standards Council of Canada
www.scc.ca

Quality Digest
www.qualitydigest.com

ASQ
www.asq.ca

Visit the following sites for the most current information about quality initiatives: **www.scc.ca**, **www.qualitydigest.com**, and **www.asq.org**.

Topic 4: Sustainability

As the world progresses further into the 21st century, more and more attention is being paid to the health of our planet and the sustainability of economic growth. The world population is increasing, natural resources are declining, and the climate is changing. People are realizing there might be limits to how much humankind can be sustained. With this, businesses are examining the threats and opportunities presented by these concerns.

Some of the threats are in the oil and gas industry where, on the one hand, there is increased demand for its products, but, on the other, a desire to reduce the world's reliance on fossil fuels for energy. Canada's economy has benefited greatly from our ability to export oil and gas on the global markets. Changing that would dislocate both the employees and government revenues. A recent study done by *Corporate Knights*, a magazine dedicated to clean capitalism, indicates that Canada has a major opportunity to export clean energy generated by both wind and hydro power.[49]

On the other hand, with more focus on sustainability, there are new industries and companies on a global level looking at "clean" technology. Canada seems well positioned to move forward on the innovation front. For example, Westport Innovations, a Canadian company that specializes in natural gas engines and vehicles, has partnerships throughout the world to provide engine and vehicle technology that is better for the environment. It has recently developed an enhanced spark-ignited natural gas system with that is cost-competitive and provides the same levels of power and fuel economy as much larger engines.[50] Currently, the clean technology sector is the fastest-growing industry, with about 41,000 people in Canada, and it is projected to be worth $28 billion by 2022.[51]

Besides the environment, climate change is also on businesses' agenda. TD Bank Group achieved one of its environmental goals by creating TD Forests, which has increased the amount of forested lands by 10,500 hectares; more forests help reduce carbon dioxide.[52] Likewise, Mountain Equipment Co-op commits 1% of sales to conservation and outdoor recreation projects.[53]

As new business opportunities are created, new jobs and careers will also be created—environmental engineers and technologists, conservation biologists, environmental communications officers, etc.

To recognize the achievements of organizations that promote and take action for the "greening" of their businesses, *Corporate Knights* has been tracking, measuring, and ranking Canadian companies for several years. In this fashion, it has honoured a number of companies for being good corporate citizens in relation to the environment and the ability to be sustainable. Tim Hortons, Bombardier, Teck Resources Limited, and Bank of Montreal were in the 2014 Global 100 list of the most sustainable corporations.[54]

Topic 5: Human Capital and Talent Management

The idea that organizations "compete through people" highlights the fact that success increasingly depends on an organization's ability to engage its people. **Human capital** is an overall term used to describe the value of knowledge, skills, and capabilities that may not show up on a company's balance sheet but nevertheless have tremendous impact on an organization's performance. Scholars also suggest that looking at the total of the organization's people capabilities leads to higher satisfaction and performance of the employees that increases the performance of the organization.[55]

Human capital
The individual's knowledge, skills, and abilities that have economic value to an organization

Human capital is intangible and elusive, and cannot be managed the way organizations manage jobs, products, and technologies. One reason for this is that employees, not the organization, own their own human capital. If valued employees leave a company, they take their human capital with them, and any investment the company has made in training and developing those people is lost. Once again, it is important to emphasize that the supervisor/manager is the link between the organization and the employees. Therefore, managers are key in helping the organization maintain and develop its human capital.

To build human capital in organizations, managers must begin to develop ways of ensuring superior knowledge, skills, and experience within their workforce and to find ways to distribute this "capital" throughout the organization. In addition, employees need opportunities for development on the job. Therefore, managers have to do a good job of providing developmental assignments to employees and making certain that job duties and requirements are flexible enough to allow for growth and learning. To successfully develop people, supervisors and managers have to "let go."

Further, more and more organizations are recognizing that sets of knowledge capabilities—**core competencies**—are part of their human capital. These competencies are necessary in order to be different from their competition and provide ongoing value to their customers. For example, a core competency might be as follows: *Focus on customer*—ability to make an effort to identify internal and external customers and understand what adds value for them; to create an environment that appreciates delivery of good customer service.

Core competencies
A combination of knowledge, skills, and characteristics needed to effectively perform a role in an organization

While many core competencies, such as focus on customer or active listening skills, are similar from one organization to another, each organization will develop its own set and define the competency to fit that organization. Thus, the combination of competencies of all employees in that organization makes it stand out from its competition.

Once competencies are identified, organizations, through senior leadership, have to find ways of using and improving those competencies. Some organizations, such as Manulife Financial, encourage employees to volunteer in their local communities to gain additional skills.[56] Too often, employees have skills that go unused and thus skills become outdated. Some of this can be eliminated by leveraging what people have by sharing and helping others learn.[57] Efforts to empower employees and encourage their participation and involvement utilize the human capital available more fully. David Cronin, co-founder of DevFacto Technologies, a small firm specializing in creative technology solutions, says, "If you give them a purpose that's larger than themselves, you can lead them to results."[58]

And companies such as Hitachi have included a no-layoff policy as part of their talent management approach. Hitachi's manufacturing manager, Nick Montecchia, states, "There's a cost associated with trying to retrain and spending all that to get someone to become proficient."[59] Hitachi made the decision to ensure that there were no declines in productivity and quality.

Studies have consistently demonstrated that firms with a focus on building and enhancing human capital demonstrate higher profitability and stronger overall organizational performance.[60] Developmental assignments, particularly those involving teamwork, can also be a valuable way of facilitating knowledge exchange and mutual learning. Effective communications (whether face to face or through information technology) are instrumental in sharing knowledge and making it widely available throughout the organization. Dave Ulrich, considered one of the foremost management gurus of our time, noted:

> When employees find meaning at work, they care enough about it to develop their competence; they work harder and are more productive; they stay longer and are more positive about their work experience. But there is more: when employees are more positive, customers generally respond in kind. Employee attitude is a key lead indicator of customer attitude, and satisfied customers help the businesses they patronize to survive and thrive.[61]

As companies continue to focus on their human capital, the concept of **talent management** has evolved. Talent management is concerned with leveraging the competencies in the organization by first ensuring the competencies are in the right places in the organization and then measuring their impact against goals. Given the breadth of the concept, companies will look at various management and HR practices that have to be more clearly integrated than what might be found in many organizations. The practices that need to be considered in order to attract, keep, and engage employees include such things as:

Talent management
Leveraging competencies to achieve high organizational performance

- providing strong leadership
- providing opportunities for professional and personal development
- helping the employees work better
- communicating all the time and at all levels
- allowing the person to perform powerfully
- ensuring that the rewards and recognition are appropriate[62]

Human Capital Online
www.humancapitalonline.com

Inc. (Small Business Ideas and Resources for Entrepreneurs)
www.inc.com

Whether the organization is large or small, appropriate management and HR practices are necessary to attract and retain the talent today. For additional online resources that help small organizations develop their human capital, see **www.humancapitalonline.com** or **www.inc.com.**

LO6

What are the key demographic and employee concerns?

Topic 6: Demographic and Employee Concerns

In addition to the competitive challenges facing organizations, everyone in any organization needs to be concerned about changes in the makeup and expectations of employees. Some of these issues will be discussed here and others will be discussed in other chapters.

Statistics Canada
www.statcan.gc.ca

Among the most significant challenges in organizations, and more particularly affecting managers and supervisors, are the demographic changes occurring in Canada. You can find current information about the labour force through Statistics Canada (**www.statcan.gc.ca**). Because they affect the workforce of an employer, these changes—in employee background, age, gender, and education—are important topics for discussion.

Diversity of Backgrounds

Canadian workers will continue to be a diverse group. According to a recent report by Statistics Canada, it is predicted that by 2031, 33% of the labour force will be foreign-born and that 15% will belong to a minority group.[63] Most of the immigration is from Asia—a sharp contrast to immigration that occurred 50 years ago, which was primarily from European countries. Immigrants tend to settle in large urban areas such as Toronto, Montreal, and Vancouver. It has also been predicted that by 2031, one person in three in the labour force will be born outside Canada.[64] The majority of immigrants coming to Canada are from Asia and the Middle East.[65]

To ensure that skilled immigrants have access to employment opportunities, a number of partnerships have developed such as the Toronto Region Immigrant Employment Council (TRIEC) and the Assisting Local Leaders with Immigrant Employment Strategies (ALLIES, modelled after TRIEC). The purpose of these agencies is to help immigrants make use of their skills and talents in the workforce so that Canada can become more prosperous as a nation.[66]

Aboriginal Human Resources Council
http://aboriginalhr.ca

Aboriginal people make up 3.8% of the population and are predicted to be 5.3% by 2031.[67] Of note is the number of Aboriginal youths and the efforts of organizations to find ways to better involve Aboriginal people in the workforce. To assist with this, the Aboriginal Human Resource Council has a mandate to advance the full labour-market participation of Aboriginal people. Employers such as RBC, Syncrude, and IBM Canada are actively involved in the Council's programs and as advocates to other employers. To learn more, access the Council's website at **http://aboriginalhr.ca**.

More about the recruitment and selection of immigrants and Aboriginal people will be discussed in Chapter 4.

Generations at Work

The working-age population in Canada is getting older—there are more individuals than ever in the older age brackets (ages 45 to 64) and fewer than ever in the younger brackets. According to a 2014 report, there are more Canadians aged 55 to 64 than there are aged 15 to 24—meaning there are more older people still in the workforce, making less room for the new entrants.[68] Further, in a recent survey, over 50% of respondents said that they expected to work beyond age 65.[69]

The age distribution throughout the Canadian workforce means that there can be several generations working together—all with different values and expectations. It also means that organizations might not have the capacity to develop younger talent to prepare them to take on more significant roles when the older workers leave, or that more attention has been given to the youngest cohort of workers at the expense of development of other generations.[70]As a result, organizational leaders will need to manage a wide spectrum of workforce diversity.[71]

The generations at work are typically Boomers (born 1946–1964), Gen X (born 1965–1980) and Gen Y/Millennials (born 1981–2000). Figure 1.4 provides a summary of the generational differences in relation to a number of factors.

Culture
Consistent and observable pattern of behaviours in organizations

Companies are responding in a number of ways to this demographic shift. More attention is being paid to the corporate culture and ensuring that staff fit well with the **culture** and values of the organization. Culture has many definitions, but an easy one to remember is that it is the pattern of behaviours we see in an organization. (There will more about

FIGURE 1.4 Generations at Work

	Boomers (Born 1946–1964)	Gen X (Born 1965–1980)	Gen Y/Millennials (Born 1981–2000)
Work ethic values	Question authority Question work ethic of younger people Accept promotion before questioning impact on life	View boss as expert	Tech-savvy Want work to have a greater purpose Flexibility Achievement-oriented
Interactive style	Team player Optimistic	Individualistic	Group- or team-oriented Self-assured
Idea of work	Adventure	"Live to work" Structured	Good at multitasking Not concerned about job security Want challenging work
View of work rewards	Loyal Expect advancement	Independent Want trappings of success	Continuous feedback Input into decision making
Work and family life	Work is first	Conservative	Expect work–life balance

Sources: Adapted from Afton Smith Barber, "Exploring Generational Differences Between Generation Y and Baby Boomers in Work–Life Balance," University of Texas at Tyler, May 2014; Jennifer Kilber, Allen Barclay, and Douglas Ohmer, "Seven Tips for Managing Generation Y," *Journal of Management Policy and Practice* 15, no. 4 (2014): 80–91; Rob Asghar, "Gen X is from Mars, Gen Y Is from Venus: A Primer on How to Motivate a Millennial," *Forbes*, January 14, 2014, accessed November 12, 2014, www.forbes.com/sites/robasghar/2014/01/14/gen-x-is-from-mars-gen-y-is-from-venus-a-primer-on-how-to-motivate-a-millennial; Paul Taylor and George Gao, "Generation X: America's neglected 'middle child,'" *Fact Tank*, Pew Research Center, June 5, 2014, accessed November 12, 2014, www.pewresearch.org/fact-tank/2014/06/05/generation-x-americas-neglected-middle-child; and Stephen Cryne, "Millennials on the move," *Canadian HR Reporter*, June 1, 2014, 14.

organizational culture in Chapter 3.) And it is important, as it drives the company's performance and results. For example, Whole Foods Market, a recent entrant into Canada with a focus on organic food, provides a culture where employees can align their own personal values with those of the store.[72] Read At Work with HRM 1.3 to gain additional information about the importance of culture in an organization.

Skills and Labour Shortage

With the aging of the workforce and fewer new entrants, there is concern about shortages—and primarily for skilled workers. Although Canada has a relatively high unemployment rate, employers say that can't find workers. Some economists also suggest that what is really occurring is a mismatch between what skills people have and what employers really want. A recent report by the Conference Board of Canada indicates that certain industries call for skill sets that will see shortages: health-related occupations, skilled labour such as crane and tower operators, and work that requires scientific and mathematical skills.[73]

Some industries are more affected by shortages than others. The mining industry is expanding and will need more than 100,000 skilled workers over the next 10 years, as many of the existing employees will be leaving. In response to this situation, a recent report by the Organisation for Economic Co-operation and Development (OECD) titled "Employment and Skills Strategies in Canada" suggests the importance of making students better informed regarding the skills necessary to find work.[74] This has been accomplished by New Gold Mines. It entered into a partnership with the B.C. Aboriginal Mine Training

AT WORK WITH HRM 1.3

KNITTING A CORPORATE CULTURE

What is culture and why would it be important in the fashion industry?

As indicated in the chapter, culture is the consistent and observable patterns of behaviour in any organization. These patterns have great influence on what people do, say, and think whether the company is small or large. Culture is "the story" of what goes on in the organization.

Typically, the beginning of any culture starts with the actions and behaviours of the founder. When Matt Friesen started Wantering, a fashion-product search engine, he really wasn't thinking about culture. As with any start-up company, he was more concerned about whether he had the financial resources to build a successful business.

However, when Wantering acquired a Los Angeles fashion social network, he realized he had employees in Vancouver, New York, and Los Angeles. Even though still in the start-up phase, Friesen wanted to have a common culture, especially when the team in Los Angeles was very different from that in Vancouver. To help create a common culture, the team in Vancouver was sent to Los Angeles for a period to work and get to know the other employees.

But culture doesn't happen just because of bonding between employees. Other things Friesen is considering is gathering employee input about what to do to create a common culture, holding workshops in which commonalities of the original and now-merged companies can be identified, and developing a set of written values.

CRITICAL THINKING QUESTIONS:

1. How would you describe culture?
2. What other things might Matt Friesen do to create a common understanding of Wantering's culture?

Sources: Michael Watkins, "What Is Organizational Culture? And Why Should We Care?" *Harvard Business Review*, May 15, 2013, accessed November 13, 2014, https://hbr.org/2013/05/what-is-organizational-culture and Nick Rockel, "CEO Knits a Corporate Culture from Far-Off Threads," *The Globe and Mail*, October 22, 2014, B6.

Association and ensured that students knew what jobs would be available and what skills necessary, and provided apprenticeship opportunities.[75] Unfortunately, some organizations believe the problem can be addressed by more advertising or by dedicating more people to recruitment activities. However, as noted above, there are fewer new entrants due to fewer people being born.

To deal with these shortages, an employer can do a number of things—for example, provide more mentoring for Millennials, ensure that the management style in the organization is suitable for both tech-savvy and other workers, and make better use of the skills that immigrants bring.[76] As mentioned earlier, TRIEC in Toronto showcases and recognizes employers for their leadership in recruiting and keeping skilled immigrants as a way to better address the skills shortage.[77]

Gender Distribution of the Workforce

According to Statistics Canada, 62% of women over 25 are working.[78] Employers are under constant pressure to ensure equality for women with respect to employment, advancement opportunities, and compensation. And since the rate is so high during women's child-bearing years, employers also need to accommodate working mothers and fathers through parental leaves, part-time employment, flexible work schedules, job sharing, telecommuting, and childcare assistance. Employers are also finding that many working people are now faced with being caregivers to aging parents. Thus, the whole area of "dependent care" is creating issues in organizations that will require creative solutions. In addition, because more women are working, employers are more sensitive to the growing need for policies and procedures to eliminate sexual harassment in the workplace. Some organizations have special orientation programs to acquaint all personnel with the problem and to warn potential offenders of the consequences. Many employers are demanding that managers and supervisors enforce their sexual harassment policy vigorously.

Rising Levels of Education

The educational attainment of the Canadian labour force has steadily risen over the years. Not coincidentally, the most secure and fastest-growing sectors of employment over the past decade have been in those areas requiring higher levels of education. As organizations become more sophisticated and use more technology, there is less and less employment available for unskilled workers. The more education a person has, the greater the chances are of having work. Canada has a highly educated workforce with over 90% of the population having completed at least high school.[79] What is also notable is that more than 2/3 of Canadians in the 25-to-64 age bracket have completed postsecondary education.[80] Also, there is a strong link between level of education and employment. For example, 82% of people 25 to 64 with a university degree are employed.[81]

It is important to observe that while the educational level of the workforce has continued to rise, there is a widening gap between the educated and non-educated, leading to different types of work experiences. At the lower end of the educational spectrum, many employers are coping with individuals who are functionally illiterate—unable to read, write, calculate, or solve problems at a level that enables them to perform even the simplest technical tasks, such as reading an operating manual or following safety procedures. The topic of literacy will be discussed in more detail in Chapter 5, but it is important to know that only 20% of people with low literacy skills are employed and that a 1% increase in literacy could generate $18 billion in economic growth in Canada.[82]

The Changing Nature of the Job and Cultural Changes

The era of the full-time, ongoing job seems to have disappeared. Nearly half of all jobs created during the last two decades were non traditional—that is, part-time, temporary, or contract work. As job security erodes, so do pension plans and healthcare benefits, particularly for part-timers. And about 70% of part-time workers are women.[83] With the change in the traditional notion of "job for life," job-hopping is on the rise and employees

Bruce Rogovin/Photolibrary/Getty Images

Organizations are aware that different families need different types of work flexibility to balance demands of family and work.

are being forced to be more flexible. For example, Communitech Inc., a firm that helps laid-off employees in the tech industry find other work, says that today's workers need to be resilient, flexible, and unafraid of change.[84]

The attitudes, beliefs, values, and customs of people in a society are an integral part of their culture. Naturally, their culture affects their behaviour on the job and the environment within the organization, influencing their reactions to work assignments, leadership styles, and reward systems. Like the external and internal environments of which it is a part, culture is undergoing continual change. HR processes and systems, therefore, must be adjusted to accommodate and integrate these changes. McDonald's Canada, where 50% of the workforce is 18 years or younger, uses a special app it designed to connect with this younger demographic about new products and to recognize top-performing employees.[85]

Employee Rights, Ethics, and Privacy

Over the past few decades, legislation has radically changed the rules for managing employees by granting them many specific rights. Among these are laws granting the rights to equal employment opportunity, union representation if desired, a safe and healthy work environment, minimum working conditions (hours of work, wages, vacations, etc.), and privacy in the workplace. More information on employee rights will be presented in both Chapter 2 and Chapter 9.

With the various business scandals that continue to plague North America, increased attention is being paid to business ethics. This topic will be explored more fully in Chapter 9; however, Ethics in HRM 1.1 describes how some organizations respond to ethics violations.

HR managers and their staffs, as well as line managers, generally recognize the importance of discretion in handling all types of information about employees. The *Personal Information Protection and Electronic Documents Act* (PIPEDA) is a federal law that deals with the collection, use, and disclosure of personal information (note that Quebec is the only province with similar laws, although Ontario and others have draft legislation in place). This law requires federally regulated organizations holding personal information on customers or employees to obtain their consent before they use, collect, or disclose this information. Chapter 2 will describe more on privacy.

Changing Attitudes Toward Work

The different expectations of people, as shown in Figure 1.4, means there are also changing attitudes toward work and what will motivate people. Organizations that create supportive and inclusive cultures are seen as great workplaces where people want to do their best. For example, 360incentives, an information technology and software company in Ontario, was honoured as the #1 medium-sized employer in Canada's Best Workplaces.[86] The company treats new employees like rock stars by using a megaphone to announce their arrival as they are led through the offices. Likewise, Google Canada got the #1 ranking in large companies for the programs it offers to help employees cook and eat well at home.[87]

Another well-established trend is for employees to define success in terms of personal self-expression and fulfillment of potential on the job. They are frequently less obsessed with the acquisition of wealth and now view life satisfaction as more likely to result from balancing the challenges and rewards of work with those of their personal lives. Though most people still enjoy work and want to excel at it, they tend to be focused on finding interesting work and may pursue multiple careers rather than being satisfied with just "having a job." People also appear to be seeking ways of living that are less complicated but more meaningful.

These new lifestyles cannot help but have an impact on the way employees are motivated and managed. Employers are encouraged to provide mentoring (discussed further in Chapter 6) opportunities for younger employees so that they can receive acquire positive and constructive attitudes toward that employer.[88] Research has demonstrated that employees who are actively mentored report higher job and personal satisfaction and organizational commitment.[89] Further, with the continued slow economic growth around the world, it is important to look at the morale of the employees; mentoring is a way to help build morale.[90]

ETHICS IN HRM 1.1

ETHICS START AT THE TOP!

More and more focus is being put on leadership and ethics. No matter how much a company does to attract, retain, and engage employees, if the leaders do not conduct themselves ethically, people will not stay.

In mid-2014, current and former employees of the Toronto Transit Commission were arrested for violating purchasing policies. The TTC also indicated that the reputation and the public's trust in the TTC had also been harmed. And an employee at Sears Canada in Winnipeg was caught on video making racial slurs to a customer—which violated its code of ethics. The employee was fired.

Another aspect of ethics is ensuring that the organization has a whistle blower policy and that people are encouraged to bring concerns to senior managers. Further, it is important that all employees receive ethics training in their particular organization so that it can be clear what is expected regarding good ethical behaviour.

Some people believe that the explosion in social media is making people more accountable for ethical behaviour, as people are now concerned about being filmed doing something wrong. However, experts in the social media feel that any inappropriate behaviour is wrong and that people should do the right thing whether being filmed or not.

Ethics Resource Center, a nonprofit organization dedicated to improving ethical practices, has recently identified how leaders can enhance ethical practices. It indicated that Millennials are the most at-risk generation when it comes to ethics in the workplace, and that extra effort needs to occur when socializing them to the workplace. One of the reasons for this is that members of that generation can be daredevils and might think nothing of, for example, installing pirated software on company computers. Therefore, it is important that training occurs to help them understand the various business risks and how to behave.

CRITICAL THINKING QUESTION:

Do you have any other ideas for how leaders can enhance ethical practices? Explain your reasons.

Sources: Adapted from "TTC Workers Arrested, Charged with Theft," *Canadian HR Reporter*, June 12, 2014, accessed November 14, 2014, www.hrreporter.com/articleview/21466-ttc-workers-arrested-charged-with-theft; Sarah Dobson, "Ugly, Racist Altercation Caught on Video at Sears," *Canadian HR Reporter*, March 24, 2014, accessed November 14, 2014, www.hrreporter.com/articleview/20613-ugly-racist-altercation-caught-on-video-at-sears; Ethics Resource Centre, accessed November 14, 2014, www.ethics.org; and Ladan Nikravan, "Risky Business: Millennials at Work," *Chief Learning Officer*, November 13, 2014, accessed November 14, 2014, www.clomedia.com/blogs/1-ask-a-gen-y/post/5746-risky-business-millennials-at-work.

Balancing Work and Family

Work and the family are connected in many subtle and not-so-subtle social, economic, and psychological ways. Because of the new forms that the family has taken—for example, the two-wage-earner and the single-parent family—organizations find it necessary to provide employees with more family-friendly options. "Family-friendly" is a broad term that may include flexible work schedules, daycare, part-time work, job sharing, parental leave, executive transfers, spousal involvement in career planning, assistance with family problems, and teleworking. Another emerging issue is that of eldercare. Many employees not only balance work and childcare but also are responsible for aging parents. A recent study indicated that most employers want to help their employees with any caregiving responsibilities they might have.[91]

The Sunnybrook Health Sciences Centre and World Vision Canada were recently awarded Top Family-Friendly Employers for their initiatives supporting parents with young families. Some of the initiatives include alternative work arrangements, maternity and parental leave top-ups, and a strong focus on employee wellness.[92] Further, other studies have demonstrated that flexible work schedules create higher levels of job satisfaction.[93] For small business owners, a variety of flexible work options not only helps with balancing work–family responsibilities but also benefits the business: it can save money, reduce turnover, increase productivity, is an attractive benefit, and increases the talent pool.[94] However, it is important not to make assumptions about individual employee needs and to ensure that any type of mobile strategy works for them.[95]

Although flexible work options can help organizations, a recent survey also suggested that there were other reasons employees wanted such arrangements. While an improved work–life balance was the #1 reason (74% of respondents), the #2 reason was for health and exercise. Interestingly enough, 61% of those surveyed indicated that they would be more productive working from home because office politics would be reduced.[96]

For additional insights on trends and issues, read Emerging Trends 1.1.

EMERGING TRENDS 1.1

1. ***Continued development of clean technologies.*** More and more innovations are occurring with waste, and as a result, more "greening" is happening. The Centre for Alternative Wastewater Treatment in Ontario, for example, is working with GE Power & Water to find ways of recycling toxic industrial water. At EPCOR in Edmonton, bacteria are used to filter its wastewater. Some experts suggest that clean technology for cars might generate more growth than conventional cars.
2. ***Creating more environmentally friendly office environments.*** Along with the ongoing development of clean technologies, more offices are looking at acquiring LEED certification that the physical space has been designed and built to be as environmentally healthy and energy efficient as possible. For example, Earth Rangers in Ontario built a new building that uses close to 90% less energy than other similar-sized buildings.
3. ***Enhancing work flexibility.*** In response to the values and expectations of younger workers, and the pace of economic growth, different forms of work flexibility are occurring. Some of this shows up in the growth of part-time work in a global and competitive economy.
4. ***Learning to better engage Millennials.*** Millennials are the largest and most educated cohort in history, but they also look at things very differently. They are the most digitally experienced demographic, as they can't remember a time when there were no computers or other electronic devices. They are also more aware of social issues and expect employers to contribute to a better world in some way. Given the number of Millennials in the workforce, they are also key to how a company engages its employees. Corus Entertainment Inc., Toronto, understands the importance of this and was named one of Canada's 2015 Top Employers for Young People for its unique Innovative Storytellers Award at Ryerson University.
5. ***Focus on younger workers and better skills development.*** With a suggested skills shortage, investing in Gen Y/Millennials can provide the workforce skills necessary. Currently, many younger people are underemployed and have nonstandard work arrangements such as part-time and temporary. Some of this is being actively pursued through a new paid-training program developed by Canadian manufacturers. A good example is Cyclone Manufacturing Inc., now training its own machinists and paying them while they learn. It is also important to remember that Millennials are the leaders of the future.
6. ***Acceleration of social media technology.*** Social media has created both opportunities and threats within the business context. Companies use social media to inform its employees about business and ways to attract the type of employees they are looking for. However, it has also created a way for employees to vent frustration with their work. Likewise, employers can use social media to get additional information about potential applicants. For example, Facebook is developing a platform that can be used in the workplace that better connects everyone, and Plasticity Labs in Toronto has made use of social technologies to track and measure employee engagement.

Sources: Adapted from Tavia Grant, "Hiring for the Future," *The Globe and Mail*, November 17, 2014, B1; "Industry Learns How to Put Its Polluted Water Back to Work," *The Globe and Mail*, November 13, 2014, accessed November 14, 2014, www.theglobeandmail.com/partners/ge-innovation/industry-learns-how-to-put-its-polluted-water-back-to-work/article21571221/#dashboard/follows; Stephen Edelstein, "Clean Tech Could Generate More Growth Than Fossil Fuels: Study," *Green Car Reports*, November 12, 2014, accessed November 14, 2014, www.greencarreports.com/news/1095416_clean-tech-could-generate-more-growth-than-fossil-fuels-study; Earth Rangers Centre, accessed November 14, 2014, www.ercshowcase.com; Jessica Barrett, "The Death of Lifelong Jobs," *Vancouver Sun*, November 1, 2014, B6–7; Tavia Grant, "The 15-Hour Workweek," *The Globe and Mail*, October 4, 2014, B6–7; "Number of Employers Passing on Applicants Due to Social Media Posts Continues to Rise," *Career Builder*, June 26, 2014, accessed November 14, 2014, www.careerbuilder.ca/share/aboutus/pressreleasesdetail.aspx?sd=6%2F26%2F2014&id=pr829&ed=12%2F31%2F2014; Liz Bernier, "Hacking Happiness," *Canadian HR Reporter*, October 20, 2014, accessed November 14, 2014, www.hrreporter.com/articleview/22564-hacking-happiness-executive-series; *2014 Trends in Global Employee Engagement*, Aon Hewitt, 2014; Bernadette Smith, "Millennial Leaders: Are Organizations Ready," *PeopleTalk*, Spring 2015, 34–36; "Rise of the Millennials," *Corporate Knights*, Spring 2015, 32–36; *Canada's 2015 Top Employers for Young People, 2015*, 5; and Ivor Tossell, "Broken Social Scene," *Report on Business*, May 2015, 12.

BUSINESS STRATEGY AND HRM STRATEGY

What is the link between business strategy and HRM strategy?

As you can see, there are many issues facing supervisors and managers, as well as HR professionals, in today's business environment. In order to effectively manage these issues, an organization develops a business strategy to enable it to achieve a high level of performance. The strategy helps the organization determine what business or businesses it will be in, why it exists, what its key goals are, and what actions it needs to take to realize those goals.

It is important to recognize the distinction between *corporate strategy* and *business strategy*.

Corporate strategy deals with questions such as these: Should we be in business? What business should we be in? Corporate strategies are company-wide and focus on overall objectives, such as long-term survival and growth. There are two main types of corporate strategies. The first is a restructuring strategy, to ensure long-term survival. Under this option, we can find turnaround situations (Harmac Mill), divestitures (the Gillette empire getting rid of the Montreal Canadiens), liquidation (Circuit City), and bankruptcy (Magna Entertainment).

The second corporate strategy is growth. Organizations can grow incrementally (by adding new products or new distribution networks). For example, Procter & Gamble added skin care lotion and hair conditioners for babies, and began to distribute to drugstores and grocery stores. Organizations can gain new customers by expanding internationally, as Finning International Ltd. did when it started selling and renting Caterpillar equipment to the United Kingdom and Chile. Growth can also be achieved through mergers and acquisitions, such as when Rogers Communications acquired Fido and Best Buy Canada acquired Future Shop.

Unlike corporate strategy, business strategy focuses on one line of business and is concerned with the question "How should we compete?" Michael Porter has developed a classification system that helps us understand five ways a business unit can compete.[97] Let us illustrate his model by analyzing how hamburgers are sold. Restaurants can compete by being a low-cost provider (McDonald's); by trying to differentiate products in a way that will attract a large number of buyers (Burger King introducing the Whopper); by being a best-cost provider through giving more value for the money (East Side Mario's sells hamburgers, but on a plate in an attractive environment); by focusing on a niche market on the basis of lower cost to a select group of customers (offering fish burgers or vegetarian burgers); or by offering a niche product or service, that is, one customized to the tastes of a narrow market segment (MBRGR in Montreal sells a hamburger sprinkled with truffle shavings and fries for $100).

Part of any business strategy is to be competitive. However, to be competitive, an organization needs to think of its people as part of its competitive advantage. Thus, the people in the organization need to be managed in a manner that enables achievement of the strategy.

While people have always been central to organizations, today's employees are critical in helping to build a firm's competitive advantage. Competitive advantage is the capacity or quality that gives an organization an edge over its competition. The advantage might be productivity, price, quality, delivery, or service. Therefore, the focus of current HRM thinking and research is identifying and implementing people processes and systems that can make a particular firm stand out above the rest. The HR practices are expected to develop the employees' abilities and motivate them such that the organization is successful. For HR processes to lead to organizational success, the HR systems must be supported, used, and highly regarded.

An HR strategy aligned with the business strategy is particularly critical in organizations whose products or services rely upon the knowledge, skills, abilities, and competencies embedded in the employees—the knowledge workers. Further, if an organization thinks of employees as assets, there is a higher likelihood they will be invested in, supported, and nutured.[98] As a result, the HR areas of recruitment, learning and development, and retention—or "talent management"—become crucial to the attainment of the business goals.

For example, companies such as CIBC are intentionally designed to increase the value employees add to the bottom line and to customer satisfaction. CIBC actively involves employees in day-to-day decisions, such as determining what specific steps can be taken to reduce customer complaints. Further, companies such as Four Seasons Hotels invest a great deal to hire and train the best and brightest in order to gain advantage over their competitors.

Human resources management strategy Identifying key HR processes and linking those to the overall business strategy

What then is the link between business strategy and a human resources strategy? As stated earlier, a **human resources management strategy** involves the development and implementation of HR practices that enables the human capital (employees) to achieve the business objectives.[99] When one company buys another, often the success of the new business revolves around how well the people side of the merger was handled. Some of the people issues in the merger of two airlines in northern Canada, Canadian North and First Air, have delayed the actual merger. Both companies say that a tremendous amount of work remains to be done, including upping Inuit representation in senior staff, pilots, and flight engineers and increasing job stability as the merger occurs.[100]

Organizations of all sizes, public or private, should undertake a set of HR practices that enhance the employees' contribution to organizational success—as defined by the business strategy. All managers play a tremendous role in developing and maintaining effective HR practices and assisting the organization in creating a competitive advantage. If a manager believes employees have to be carefully monitored, when the business strategy suggests employees need to be empowered, it is highly unlikely the business will succeed. When a company (or a line manager) doesn't link the people processes and practices with the business objectives, the company will be unable to leverage its knowledge capabilities and will not be innovative enough to achieve the necessary competitive advantage.[101] For example, if a company wished to focus on providing superb customer service, the employee selection process would tend to hire people with those skills. It might also have a training and development program that reinforced the expectations regarding customer service, and a performance management system that rated how well the employees did in that regard.

Linking HR practices to the business strategy isn't just about customer service. For example, ATB Investor Services realized that it needed to build its leadership capacity in order to achieve its business results.[102] While this might be a natural outcome of slower business growth and fewer new employees, ATB identified it as a strategic gap. A recent survey by Mercer found that 64% of the respondents identified looking after the critical talent pool as key to their success. These same respondents also said they weren't doing as good a job as they might.[103] Likewise, Deloitte found that the relationship between employees and employers has shifted so that employees are more like business partners.[104] Loyalty for employees is now about more than money—they want to feel valued.[105]

While "competing through people" may be a key theme for human resources management, the idea remains only a framework for action. On a day-to-day basis, managers frequently focus on specific business challenges and issues, and may not always focus as critically on the people issues. You can see from Figure 1.1 that HRM helps blend many aspects of management–business pressures, such as technology and the global market, with the changing nature of the workforce. By balancing what are sometimes competing demands, HRM plays an important role in getting the most from employees for organizational success and providing a work environment that meets the employees' short- and long-term needs.

Summary

1. Define human resources management (HRM).
   - Integrated set of processes, programs, and systems that focus on effective deployment and development of employees.
2. Identify the processes and practices of HRM.
   - Defining and designing work
   - Planning for, recruiting, and selecting the workforce
   - Onboarding, training, and development
   - Managing performance
   - Recognizing and rewarding employees
   - Creating a safe and healthy work environment
   - Relating to employees within diverse environments
3. Explain the importance of HRM to all employees.
   - All employees are affected by HR practices.
   - Most employees have a supervisor that is the key link between employee and organization.
   - Helps everyone understand their roles and responsibilities in the organization.
   - People have always been central to organizations, but their strategic importance is growing in today's knowledge-based industries.
4. Discuss the relationship between the line manager and the HR practitioner.
   - Every manager's job is managing people.
   - Successful organizations equip their line managers with a thorough understanding of HRM.
   - HR professionals help the line manager be a good people manager by providing advice as well as direct services.
   - Combining expertise of HR professionals with the experience of line managers can develop and utilize the talents of employees to their greatest potential.
5. Describe current business topics facing organizations and the impact on people in organizations.
   - Globalization is creating pressure for managers to effectively manage people.
   - Change in firms and business sectors will focus on maximizing utilization of employees.
   - Technology has enabled organizations to focus on quality and customer.
   - Organizations use productivity improvements to help with sustainability.
   - Environment and climate change is creating both threats and opportunities.
   - Businesses are concerned about their human capital and talent management.
   - Demographics are creating challenges in managing people with different expectations and values.
6. Outline the key demographic and employee concerns.
   - There is a diverse and aging workforce with increased female participation.
   - Different generations are working side by side with differing values and expectations.
   - There is both a shortage of labour and a mismatch of skills required for work.
   - The work landscape is changing with more part-time and self-employed people.
   - Employees have more rights.
7. Illustrate the link between business strategy and HRM strategy.
   - Business strategy involves formulation of company's mission, goals, and action plans.
   - Part of any business strategy is to be competitive; to be competitive, an organization needs to think about its people as part of its "competitive advantage."
   - HRM strategy focuses on linking and aligning the HRM practices to the business strategy.
   - The HR practices and programs will reflect the particular strategy, such as growth.

Need to Know

- Definition of HRM
- Names of HR processes and practices
- Definition of strategic human resources management
- Nature of employee expectations and concerns

Need to Understand

- Impact of current business topics on HRM
- Link of business strategy and HRM strategy
- Role of line managers in responding effectively to the expectations and concerns of employees

KEY TERMS

benchmarking 16
contractor 12
core competencies 18
culture 20
downsizing 11
globalization 10
human capital 18
human resources management (HRM) 4
human resources management strategy 28
Lean 16
outsourcing 12
Six Sigma 16
talent management 19
telecommuting 14

REVIEW QUESTIONS

1. How would you define human resources management?
2. What are the HRM processes and practices discussed at the beginning of the chapter?
3. How would you describe each of the HRM processes and practices?
4. What is the relationship between team leaders (or supervisors and managers) and an HR practitioner?
5. Why is the link between a business strategy and the HR strategy important?

CRITICAL THINKING QUESTIONS

1. In the HRM Close-Up, Tania Goodine received some very valuable advice when she was a new manager. What was it and why would it be important?
2. What are the reasons that all employees need to know about and understand HRM?
3. How do current business concerns impact HRM?
4. You are a supervisor in a major chain of coffee bars. What might be your HR concerns in attracting and retaining employees who have an understanding of the importance of the customer?
5. There have been a number of news reports about Canada's Temporary Foreign Worker Program and the suggestion that foreign workers are taking jobs from Canadian residents. What would be the HR implications if Canada eliminated this program?
6. List at least three pros and three cons of having a more diverse workforce. Can Canada compete better globally with our diverse population? Why?
7. You and some of your classmates have been discussing the future of work flexibility in Canada. What is important to you regarding flexibility in a work setting? Why?

DEVELOPING YOUR SKILLS

1. Working in groups of three to four, discuss the statement: "Employers need to be more concerned about how employees feel about their work and how they are treated."
2. As discussed in this chapter, employers make use of social media to gather additional information about potential job applicants? Is this ethical? Why?
3. Using any search engine, search the phrase "Gen Z." Access each of the top 3 entries and create a list of 5 ways Gen Z's are described. Does the description sound like you? Why?
4. A number of jobs and careers are being created in the "clean technology" sector. Using any search engine, research "jobs in clean technology." Prepare a short summary of what you found.
5. Listed below are a number of websites that provide information about jobs. Look at each site. After doing so, identify which one(s) would be more useful to you when looking for work. Why?
6. Earlier in the chapter, you were introduced to the idea that certain skills, especially innovation skills, are required to be successful in today's organizations. To see how good your innovation skills aptitude is, access the General Innovation Skills Aptitude Test 2.0 through the Conference Board of Canada. Access the online tool at **www.conferenceboard.ca/Libraries/EDUC_PUBLIC/GISAT.sflb** and follow the instructions.

www.jobbank.gc.ca
www.monster.ca
www.linkedin.com
www.careerbuilder.ca
www.bcjobs.ca
www.jobs.ca
www.workopolis.com

CASE STUDY 1

Tim Hortons and Burgers—What's Going to Happen to a Canadian Icon?

In 2014, news feeds went wild with the announcement that Tim Hortons and Burger King were merging. But what does that mean for such a visible icon of Canada?

One of the more immediate concerns is what will happen to staff at both companies. Burger King is a subsidiary of a private Brazilian equity firm that has cut jobs at other companies when mergers have occurred. Currently, 3G Capital has said that no jobs will be lost yet it has said that there needs to be cost-cutting. Approximately 1500 employees work outside the individual restaurants and as many as 44% might be laid off. Both companies have said that the merger will allow expansion in the United States—which might mean additional jobs there but little growth of jobs in Canada.

Shareholders are also concerned that there will be pressure on individual franchisees to cut corners and that executive pay will be excessive. From previous mergers 3G has done, including Heinz and Labatt, cost reductions did occur to make the companies more profitable. Further, 3G's commitment to maintain staff levels at Tim Hortons only applies to the 16 corporate-owned restaurants.

Other critics say that food items at both stores will become interchangeable—thereby reducing the need for separate distribution systems or separate physical locations. Revenues at Canadian Burger King restaurants have been low whereas Tim Hortons outlets are highly profitable. There is some concern that any sharing of products may reduce the attraction consumers have for Tim Hortons, making it less profitable. Further, analysts have said that since Tim Hortons isn't in financial difficulty, any merger won't be a better deal for it.

Sources: Adapted from "Tim Hortons Takeover by Burger King May Be Bad for Canada: Study," CBC News, October 30, 2014, accessed November 15, 2014, www.cbc.ca/news/business/tim-hortons-takeover-by-burger-king-may-be-bad-for-canada-study-1.2818036; Dana Flavelle, "Shareholder Group Slams Tim Hortons Merger," *The Star*, November 13, 2014, accessed November

15, 2014, www.thestar.com/business/2014/11/13/shareholder_group_slams_tim_hortons_merger.html; Jamie Sturgeon, "Tim Hortons Coffee Coming to a Burger King Near You?" Global News, November 10, 2014, accessed November 15, 2014, http://globalnews.ca/news/1663426/tim-hortons-coffee-coming-to-a-burger-king-near-you; and Lucas Kawa, "It's Un-Canadian to Oppose the Tim Hortons–Burger King Tie-up," *Business in Canada*, October 31, 2014, accessed November 15, 2014, https://businessincanada.com/2014/10/31/tim-hortons-burger-king-merger-is-good-for-canada.

Questions:

1. What are the pros and cons of such a merger?
2. What are the HR implications?
3. Since the merger still has to be approved by the federal government, do you think it should? Why?

CASE STUDY 2

Controversy in the Oil Sands

With natural resources being a key economic driver of Canada, why is there so much controversy about extracting and shipping oil from Alberta?

The short answer is that it depends on whom you are speaking with. Many people in the resource industry support the extraction of oil while many other people such as farmers, environmentalists, and some First Nations oppose any expansion of oil production.

With the price of crude oil declining throughout the world in late 2014 and early 2015, it is also becoming more expensive to extract from certain areas in Alberta. Thus, the economic value in doing so is declining. Yet, as oil is a key export, the extraction of oil provides jobs for many thousands of Canadians. A recent study by the Canadian Energy Research Institute (CERI) indicated that even with oil trading at less than $80/barrel, revenue will still grow at a massive rate with approximately 3.7 million barrels/day by 2020 compared to about 2 million barrels today. And in another study by CERI, it is predicted that over the next 20+ years, investors will put over $514 billion into oil sands projects.

Even at today's rate of production in Alberta, approximately 20,000 people are directly employed in the oil and gas industry, 1,700 of those being First Nations. Employees are typically required to have a Grade 12 education with strong reading skills to read procedures and health and safety protocols. This is especially true if someone wishes to drive industrial vehicles, in which case they are required to take additional courses. Because the work is in remote areas of the province, a person can be away from home for a number of weeks with long workdays and physically demanding work. While at work, the employees live in camps built to accommodate all the staff. However, a person can earn $90,000–$120,000 depending on exactly what role.

People against additional development of the oil sands are usually concerned about the impact on the environment. Some studies have indicated that toxins can get into vegetation surrounding the area and also travel through waterways to other areas in Alberta. Others have indicated that some of the toxins can get to birds and animals and affect the food chain.

There are no right or wrong answers regarding any resource development. It is a matter of risk and reward.

Sources: Adapted from Jeff Lewis, "Is Oil Sands Development Still Worth It?" *The Globe and Mail*, October 28, 2014, accessed November 15, 2014, www.theglobeandmail.com/report-on-business/rob-magazine/is-oil-sands-development-still-worth-it/article21334385; Cameron French, "Canada's Oilsands Will Bring in Trillions Even at Depressed Oil Price: Study," *Yahoo Canada Finance*, November 11, 2014, accessed November 15, 2014, https://ca.finance.yahoo.com/blogs/balance-sheet/canadas-oil-sands-will-bring-in-trillions-even-at-202836032.html; Mike Obel, "Oil Sands Investment in Alberta, Canada, Expected to Surge in Next 24 Years—Study," *International Business Times*, November 11, 2014, accessed November 15, 2014, www.ibtimes.com/

oil-sands-investment-alberta-canada-expected-surge-next-24-years-study-1722067; Government of Alberta, "Alberta's Oil Sands: The Facts" (Edmonton: January 2014), accessed August 31, 2015, www.energy.alberta.ca/OilSands/pdfs/AlbertasOilSandsFactsJan14.pdf; Brenda Bouw, "I Want to Work in the Oil Sands. What Will My Salary Be?" *The Globe and Mail*, March 12, 2014, accessed November 16, 2014, www.theglobeandmail.com/report-on-business/careers/career-advice/life-at-work/i-want-to-work-in-the-oil-sands-what-will-my-salary-be/article17438086; Alexandra Paul, "Getting the Word Out," *Winnipeg Free Press*, November 15, 2014, accessed November 16, 2014, www.winnipegfreepress.com/local/getting-the-word-out-282801621.html.

Questions:

1. What are the opportunities and threats for continued extraction of oil from Alberta?
2. What HRM issues arise if oil is no longer a key resource for Canada?
3. What are the HR implications if some of the larger oil sands producers shut their operations?

NOTES AND REFERENCES

1. Barrie McKenna, "Bank of Canada Cites Oil Price, Hot Housing Market as Factors Roiling Rate Decisions," *The Globe and Mail*, accessed October 22, 2014, www.theglobeandmail.com/report-on-business/economy/plunging-crude-prices-could-delay-interest-rate-hikes-bank-of-canada/article21218167/#dashboard/follows.
2. Dan Schawbel, "Employers, Prepare to Meet Gen Z," *The Globe and Mail*, September 5, 2014, B11.
3. Bob Moritz, "How I Did It: The U.S. Chairman of PWC on Keeping Millennials Engaged," *Harvard Business Review*, November 2014, 41–44.
4. Suzanne Haywood, "Tom Peters on Leading the 21st-Century Organization," *McKinsey Quarterly*, September 2014, accessed October 27, 2014, www.mckinsey.com/insights/organization/tom_peters_on_leading_the_21st_century_organization.
5. Dave Ulrich, "6 Key Competencies for HR Professionals," presentation to the B.C. Human Resources Management Association, April 19, 2014.
6. Sarah Dobson, "Delving into HR's DNA," *Canadian HR Reporter*, October 20, 2014, 1.
7. Ibid.
8. "2014 Trends in Global Employee Engagement," Aon Hewitt, accessed October 25, 2014, www.aon.com/human-capital-consulting/thought-leadership/talent_mgmt/2014-trends-in-global-employee-engagement.jsp.
9. Statistics Canada, "Merchandise Trade of Canada on a Balance-of-Payments Basis," accessed October 27, 2014, www.statcan.gc.ca/tables-tableaux/sum-som/l01/cst01/trad45a-eng.htm.
10. Statistics Canada, "Gross Domestic Product at Basic Prices by Industry, July 2014," accessed October 27, 2014, www.statcan.gc.ca/tables-tableaux/sum-som/l01/cst01/gdps04a-eng.htm.
11. Barry Critchley, "Brookfield Gets Busy with $7.5 Billion of Acquisitions over Three Months," *The Financial Post*, October 10, 2014, accessed October 27, 2014, http://business.financialpost.com/2014/10/10/brookfield-gets-busy-with-7-5-billion-of-acquisitions-over-three-months.
12. Tara Perkins, "Atlantic City Bust," *The Globe and Mail*, November 1, 2014, B8-9.
13. Greg Keenan and Adrian Morrow, "Ford Picks Mexico over Windsor to Build New Engine," *The Globe and Mail*, October 25, 2014, B1.
14. "Turning Point," presentation by Hay Group Compensation Trends 2015, September 9, 2014.
15. Tamsin McMason, "Target's Canadian Retreat: A 20-Million Square Foot Hole," *The Globe and Mail*, January 16, 2015, B1; Barrie McKenna, "Crude Fallout Spreads Beyond Oil Patch," *The Globe and Mail*, April 7, 2015, B1; and Joanne Lee-Young and Chuck Chiang, "China's Banks Pump Funds in Effort to Quell Stock Market Panic," *The Vancouver Sun*, July 8, 2015, www.vancouversun.com/Business/asia-pacific/China+banks+pump+funds+effort+quell+stock+market/11197920/story.html.
16. John Shmuel, "Export Aversion: World Is Still a Daunting Challenge for Many Canadian Businesses," *Financial Post*, October 27, 2014, accessed October 27, 2014, http://business.financialpost.com/2014/10/27/export-aversion-world-is-still-a-daunting-challenge-for-many-canadian-businesses.
17. Statistics Canada, "Imports, Exports and Trade Balance of Goods on a Balance-of-Payments Basis, by Country or Country Grouping," accessed October 27, 2014, www.statcan.gc.ca/tables-tableaux/sum-som/l01/cst01/gblec02a-eng.htm.
18. "Canadian Crude Oil Exports to the U.S. Topped 3 Million Barrels per Day for First Time," *The Financial Post*, October 8, 2014, accessed October 27, 2014, http://business.financialpost.com/2014/10/08/oil-canada-exports-us/?__lsa=e1fd-943b.
19. Pete Evans, "Oil price will fall to $70US a barrel in 2015, Goldman Sachs says," CBC News, October 27, 2014, accessed October 27, 2014, www.cbc.ca/news/business/oil-price-will-fall-to-70-us-a-barrel-in-2015-goldman-sachs-says-1.2814041, Bloomberg, www.bloomberg.com/energy, accessed November 10, 2014; and Jeffrey Jones, "Oil Prices Fall Nearly 8%, Dashing Hopes for Recovery," July 6, 2015, www.theglobeandmail.com/report-on-business/industry-news/energy-and-resources/oil-crashes-8-per-cent-as-greek-vote-iran-talks-set-off-exodus/article25326141; and "Commodities," *The Globe and Mail*, January 8, 2016, B11.
20. Maude Barlow and Matt Abbott, "Three Myths About the Energy East Pipeline, *The Globe and Mail*, accessed November10, 2014, www.theglobeandmail.com/globe-debate/three-myths-about-the-energy-east-pipeline/article21518545.
21. "Helping Canadians Eat Better, Feel Better, and Do Better," Sobeys Corporate website, access October 27, 2014, www.sobeyscorporate.com/en/Our-Company/At-A-glance.aspx.
22. Ahmad Hathout, "Big Deals," *Report on Business*, June 2014, 30–39.
23. Geoffrey Morgan, "Edmonton Abuzz over Aspiring Entrepreneurs," *The Vancouver Sun*, October 21, 2014, E3.
24. Dan Barnes, "Yeast Meets East as Craft Beers Head to China," *The Vancouver Sun*, October 21, 2014, E4.
25. Ross Marowits, "Cheesemaker Saputo Closing Four Plants," Global News, March 26, 2014, accessed November 10, 2014, http://globalnews.ca/news/1232655/cheesemaker-saputo-closing-four-plants.
26. Amina Ligaya, "BlackBerry Ltd Cuts 65 More Jobs amid a Shift in App Strategy," *The Financial Post*, June 24, 2014, accessed November 10, 2014, http://business.financialpost.com/2014/06/24/

blackberry-ltd-cuts-65-more-jobs-amid-shift-in-app-strategy/?__lsa=e1fd-943b.

27. C. Lakshman, Aarti Ramaswami, Ruth Alas, Jean F. Kabongo, and J. Rajendran Pandian, "Ethics Trumps Culture? A Cross-National Study of Business Leader Responsibility for Downsizing and CSP Perceptions," *Journal of Business Ethics* 125, no. 1 (November 2014): 101–119.
28. Patricia M. Buhler, "Ten Tips for More Effective Downsizing," *Supervision*, August 2, 2014: 17–19.
29. Ibid.
30. Jeff Gray and Tim Shufelt, "Rare Move Protects Employees," *The Globe and Mail*, January 16, 2015, B7.
31. Telus International Outsourcing, accessed November 11, 2014, www.telusinternational.com/product_and_services/outsourcing, Accenture Outsourcing Services, accessed November 11, 2014, www.accenture.com/ca-en/outsourcing/Pages/index.aspx, and IBM Global Technology Services, accessed November 11, 2014, www-935.ibm.com/services/us/en/it-services/outsourcing.html.
32. Gail Johnson, "A Recruiting Niche Made This Company Recession-Proof," *The Globe and Mail*, October 15, 2014, H8.
33. Sean Silcoff, "Busy Signals: Why Call Centres Came Back," *The Globe and Mail*, March 14, 2012, B3.
34. Eugeny Sokolove, "Transformation Through Outsourcing," *The Moscow Times*, April 17, 2012, www.themoscowtimes.com/business/business_for_business/article/transformation-through-outsourcing/456840.html.
35. Smita Vasudevan, "Growing Outsourcing Risks," *Global Services*, May 27, 2011, www.globalservicesmedia.com/Strategies-and-Best-Practices/Risk-Management/Growing-Outsourcing-Risks/24/13/10964/GS110527859658.
36. Susan Ward, "Are You a Contractor or an Employee?" About.com, accessed November 11, 2014, http://sbinfocanada.about.com/od/taxinfo/a/contractor1.htm.
37. Hayley Tsukayama, "How Closely Is Amazon's Echo Listening?" *The Washington Post*, November 11, 2014, accessed November 11, 2014, www.washingtonpost.com/blogs/the-switch/wp/2014/11/11/how-closely-is-amazons-echo-listening.
38. "The Impact of Cloud," *The Economist Intelligence Unit*, accessed November 11, 2014, www.economistinsights.com/technology-innovation/analysis/impact-cloud.
39. "Telecommuting Offers Edge to Companies Looking to Recruit Talent: Survey," *Canadian HR Reporter*, June 2, 2014, accessed November 11, 2014, www.hrreporter.com/articleview/21331-telecommuting-offers-edge-to-companies-looking-to-recruit-talent-survey.
40. "Total Quality Management," ASQ, accessed November 11, 2014, http://asq.org/learn-about-quality/total-quality-management/overview/overview.html
41. Edwin Torres, "Deconstructing Service Quality and Customer Satisfaction: Challenges and Directions for Future Research," *Journal of Hospitality Marketing and Management* 23, no. 6 (August/September 2014): 652–677; and Po-Hsuan Wu, Ching-Yuan Huang, and Chen-Kai Chou, "Service Expectation, Perceived Service Quality, and Customer Satisfaction in Food and Beverage Industry," *International Journal of Organization Innovation* 7, no. 1 (July 2014): 171–180.
42. Matthew Daneman, "Xerox Cutting Back on Lean Six Sigma Program, Jobs," *Democrat & Chronicle*, October 13, 2014, accessed November 11, 2014, www.democratandchronicle.com/story/money/business/2014/10/13/xerox-cuts-popular-lean-six-sigma-program-jobs/17203841.
43. "What Is Lean?" Lean Enterprise Institute, accessed November 11, 2014, www.lean.org/WhatsLean.
44. "A Brief History of Lean," Lean Enterprise Institute, accessed November 11, 2014, www.lean.org/WhatsLean/History.cfm.
45. Janet French, "No Conflict in HQC's Lean Promotion, Monitoring Role, Chair Says," *The Star Phoenix*, November 6, 2014, accessed November 11, 2014, www.thestarphoenix.com/news/conflict+lean+promotion+monitoring+role+chair+says/10360087/story.html.
46. Josh Cable, "SLC 2014: Building a Safety Culture ... the Lean Way," *EHS Today*, November 5, 2014, accessed November 11, 2014, http://ehstoday.com/safety-leadership-conference-2014/slc-2014-building-safety-culture-lean-way.
47. Mallory Henry, "'Culture Change' Needed in Way Law Schools Assess, Revise Curriculum: Holloway," *Canadian Lawyer*, October 31, 2014, accessed November 11, 2014, http://canadianlawyermag.com/5339/Culture-change-needed-in-way-law-schools-assess-revise-curriculum-Holloway.html.
48. "2014 *Canada Awards for Excellence* Recipients," Excellence Canada, October 30, 2014, accessed November 11, 2014, www.excellence.ca/en/awards/2014-cae-recipients.
49. Tyler Hamilton, "Powering Up Canada's Exports," *Corporate Knights* 13, no. 4 (Fall 2014): 20–21.
50. "Westport Unveils Its Proprietary Enhanced Spark-Ignited Natural Gas System Targeting Medium-Duty Truck Applications," September 23, 2014, accessed November 11, 2014, www.westport.com/news/2014/enhanced-spark-ignited-natural-gas-system-targeting-medium-duty-truck-applications.
51. David Suzuki, "Clean Technology Fastest Growing Sector of Canadian Economy," *Net News Ledger*, October 26, 2014, accessed November 11, 2014, www.netnewsledger.com/2014/10/26/clean-technology-fastest-growing-sector-of-canadian-economy.
52. "Corporate Social Responsibility," *The Globe and Mail*, October 17, 2014, NCC1.
53. Ibid.
54. "Class of 2014, The Global 100," *Corporate Knights*, accessed November 11, 2014, www.corporateknights.com/wp-content/reports/2014_Global_100.pdf.
55. Dr. Muhammad Tariq Khan, Dr. Asas Afzal Humayun, and Dr. Muhammad Sajjad, "Connotation of 'Human Capital:' Concept, Effects and Benefits" (Review), *International Journal of Information, Business and Management* 7, no. 1 (2015): 19–35.
56. Paula Speevak Sladowski and Joanna Kaleniecka, "Employer-Supported Volunteering Builds Communities, Core Competencies," April 21, 2014, *Canadian HR Reporter*, accessed November 12, 2014, www.hrreporter.com/articleview/20880-employer-supported-volunteering-builds-communities-core-competencies.
57. Ibid.
58. "The 5 Do's and Don'ts of Successful Businesses," Business Development Canada, accessed November 12, 2014, www.bdc.ca/EN/small-business-week/Pages/five-dos-and-five-donts.html; and Kristene Quan, "How to Give Employees the Agency They Crave," *Profit Guide*, November 6, 2014, accessed November 12, 2014, www.profitguide.com/manage-grow/human-resources/meet-the-50-best-small-and-medium-employers-in-canada-71198/2.
59. Greg Keenan, "For Hitachi, Keeping Skilled Workers Is Key," *The Globe and Mail*, September 8, 2014, B7.
60. Ravi Bapna, Nishtha Langer, Amit Mehra, Ram Gopal, Alok Gupta, "Human Capital Investments and Employee Performance: An Analysis of IT Services Industry," *Management Science* 59, no. 3 (March 2013): 641–658.
61. Dave Ulrich and Wendy Ulrich, *The Why of Work* (New York: McGraw Hill, 2010), 5.
62. Karen Mishra, Lois Boynton, and Aneil Mishra, "Driving Employee Engagement: The Expanded Role of International Communications," *International Journal of Business Communication* 51, no. 2 (2014): 183–202, Harvey Schachter, "The Right HR Ingredients Can Boost Results," *The Globe and Mail*, August 18, 2014, B5; Ruth Holmes, "Talent Management 4.0: Engaging and Leading in HR's Brave New World," *Relocate Global*, October 6, 2014, accessed November 12, 2014, www.relocatemagazine.com/articles/rh102014talent-management-4-0-engaging-and-leading-in-hrs-brave-new-world; and "OMERS, Cisco, Keg Restaurants

Among Top 50 Employers for 2015," *Canadian HR Reporter*, November 7, 2014, accessed November 12, 2014, www.hrreporter.com/articleview/22740-omers-cisco-keg-restaurants-among-top-50-employers-for-2015.

63. Statistics Canada, "Study: Projected Trends to 2031 for the Canadian Labour Force," *The Daily*, August 7, 2011, accessed November 12, 2014, www.statcan.gc.ca/daily-quotidien/110817/dq110817b-eng.htm.
64. Ibid.
65. *Immigration and Ethnocultural Diversity in Canada*, 2011, accessed November 12, 2014, www.statcan.gc.ca/daily-quotidien/110817/dq110817b-eng.htm.
66. Allies Canada, accessed November 12, 2014, http://alliescanada.ca.
67. Statistics Canada, "Population Projections by Aboriginal Identity in Canada 2006 to 2031," accessed November 12, 2014, www.statcan.gc.ca/pub/91-552-x/2011001/hl-fs-eng.htm.
68. Statistics Canada, "Canada's Population Estimates: Age and Sex, 2014," accessed November 12, 2014, www.statcan.gc.ca/daily-quotidien/140926/dq140926b-eng.htm.
69. Tavia Grant, "Poll Shows Majority Plan to Work past Age 65," *The Globe and Mail*, February 18, 2015, B4.
70. Brian Kreissl, "Demographics and the Canadian Workforce," *Canadian HR Reporter*, October 15, 2014, accessed November 12, 2014, www.hrreporter.com/blog/HR-Policies-Practices/archive/2014/10/15/demographics-and-the-canadian-workforce.
71. Rick Lash, "Greying Work Force a Corporate Challenge," *The Globe and Mail*, March 13, 2015, B12.
72. Jessica Barrett, "Work in Progress: Good Job Versus Bad Job," *The Calgary Herald*, November 2, 2014, B2.
73. The Conference Board, "Growing Labour Shortages on the Horizon in Mature Economies," *The Chronicle Herald*, November 7, 2014, accessed November 13, 2014, http://thechronicleherald.ca/cream/home/1248944-growing-labour-shortages-on-the-horizon-in-mature-economies.
74. OECD, *Employment and Skills Strategies in Canada*, 2014, accessed November 14, 2014, www.keepeek.com/Digital-Asset-Management/oecd/employment/employment-and-skills-strategies-in-canada_9789264209374-en#page4; and "Canada Must Overcome Sector-Specific Skills Shortages," *Canadian HR Reporter*, June 12, 2014, accessed November 14, 2014, www.hrreporter.com/articleview/21469-canada-must-overcome-sector-specific-skills-shortages-oecd.
75. James Keller, "Labour Shortage Predicted for Mining Industry," *The Canadian Press*, accessed November 14, 2014, http://globalnews.ca/news/1031306/labour-shortage-predicted-for-mining-industry.
76. "Faced with Skills Shortage, Canadian Employers Are Recognizing the Value of Immigrants," *Canada Bound*, accessed November 14, 2014, http://canadaboundimmigrant.com/breakingnews/article.php?id=654.
77. Ibid.
78. Statistics Canada, "Labour Characteristics by Age and Sex, 2013," accessed November 14, 2014, www.statcan.gc.ca/tables-tableaux/sum-som/l01/cst01/labor20a-eng.htm.
79. Statistics Canada, "Education in Canada: An International Perspective, 2013," accessed November 14, 2014, www.statcan.gc.ca/daily-quotidien/140107/dq140107beng.htm.
80. Ibid.
81. Ibid.
82. "Literacy Statistics," accessed November 14, 2014, www.literacy.ca/literacy/literacy-sub.
83. Sarah Dobson, "Part-Time Work on the Rise," *Canadian HR Reporter*, October 6, 2014, 1.
84. Virginia Galt, "With Jobs for Life Dead, Workers Forced to Be Flexible," *The Globe and Mail*, July 15, 2014, B5.
85. "How McDonald's Keeps Its Young Workforce Engaged," *HRM Online*, November 12, 2014.
86. "Canada's Best Workplaces," *The Globe and Mail*, April 17, 2014, GPTW1.
87. Ibid.
88. Peter Cheese, "Get 'Em While They're Young," *People Management*, 5.
89. Ann Rolfe, "Taking Mentoring to the Next Level in Organisations," *Training and Development* 41, no. 2 (April 2014): 26–27.
90. Dan Carrison, "The Challenge of 2014: Sustaining Morale," *Industrial Management*, July 1, 2014, 6.
91. Gloria Galloway, "Employers Want to Help Caregivers," *The Globe and Mail*, January 20, 2015, A4.
92. "Canada's Top Family-Friendly Employers, 2014," accessed November 14, 2014, www.canadastop100.com/family.
93. Clare Koning, "Does Self-Scheduling Increase Nurses' Job Satisfaction?" *Nursing Management* 21, no. 6 (October 2014): 24–28.
94. Brittney Helmrich, "5 Ways Flexible Work Options Benefit Small Businesses," *Business News Daily*, October 23, 2014, accessed November 14, 2014, www.businessnewsdaily.com/7339-job-flexibility-benefits.html.
95. Leah Eichler, "Mobile Workspace Boon for Some, Not All," *The Globe and Mail*, February 28, 2015, B18.
96. Sarah Sutton Fell, "Your Workers Want More Flexibility but Companies Benefit Most," *Entrepreneur*, accessed November 14, 2014, www.entrepreneur.com/article/239111.
97. Michael E. Porter, *On Competition* (Boston: Harvard Business Press, 2008).
98. Brian Kreissl, "Human Capital Management Is Starting to Grow on Me," *Canadian HR Reporter*, August 11, 2014, accessed November 14, 2014, www.hrreporter.com/articleview/21938-human-capital-management-is-starting to grow-on-me.
99. Jeffrey A. Mello, *Strategic Human Resource Management*, 4th ed, (Independence, KY: Cengage Learning), 2015.
100. Jane George, "Canadian North: Merger with First Air Might Take Another Two Years," *Nunatsiqu Online*, September 24, 2014, accessed November 14, 2014, www.nunatsiaqonline.ca/stories/article/65674canadian_north_merger_with_first_air_might_take_another_two_years.
101. Mizuki Kobayashi, "Relational View: Four Prerequisites of Competitive Advantage," *Annals of Business Administrative Science*, 13 (2014): 77–90.
102. Sarah Dobson, "Few Successors Lined Up for Top Roles: Report," *Canadian HR Reporter*, August 11, 2014, accessed November 14, 2014, www.hrreporter.com/articleview/21951-few-successors-lined-up-for-top-roles-report.
103. Claudine Kapel, "How Do You Identify Critical Talent?" *Canadian HR Reporter*, July 14, 2014, accessed November 14, 2014, www.hrreporter.com/blog/Compensation-Rewards/archive/2014/07/14/how-do-you-identify-critical-talent.
104. Leah Eichler, "The Brave New World of 'On Demand' Work," *The Globe and Mail*, April 25, 2015, B16.
105. Romina Maurino, "Employee Loyalty about More Than Money," *The Vancouver Sun*, August 13, 2014, D4.

2 Operating Within the Legal Framework

LEARNING OUTCOMES

After studying this chapter, you should be able to

1. Explain the impact of laws on the behaviour and actions of supervisors and managers.
2. Discuss the legal framework of HRM in Canada.
3. Describe discrimination and harassment in the workplace.
4. Outline the line manager's role in creating a work environment that is free from harassment and discrimination.
5. Identify the general types of employment laws in Canada.
6. Explain the relationship between employment equity and diversity.
7. Discuss the concept of ethics in the management of human resources.

OUTLINE

HRM CLOSE-UP

"The lack of exposure to human resource realities can blindside you."

Outpost, launched in 1996, has carved a niche for itself in the travel magazine business. Adventure travel is its focus and the journalists write about off-the-beaten-track excursions to interesting and unusual places.

For the magazine's editorial director and publisher, most of today is spent reviewing a story about a 75 km trail hike on Vancouver Island, calling potential advertisers, and finalizing a deal with a tour company for coveted back-cover advertising space. But Matt Robinson must also set aside time for human resources management, because his responsibilities cover all aspects of the magazine's operation.

Though admittedly a "hands-off" manager, Matt does acknowledge that a good 15% of his time is spent interacting with the people who work for him. "We are small and therefore have to be nimble with staffing," explains Robinson. "The people who work for us are often part-time contract, freelance, or casual, and we also manage up to 12 student interns from colleges and universities annually."

Managing interns may seem straightforward, but there are things a manager has to be aware of when accepting interns. Robinson describes the legal considerations to do with workers' compensation, saying that if a magazine compensates an intern during their unpaid internship, that payment, although intended to show appreciation for the work, may interfere with that student's school insurance coverage, transferring liability back to the company. "Small companies with nominal staff wouldn't necessarily know about this," commented Robinson. "It's hard to stay on top of all the legalities of human resources. It's best to read up a little here and there so that you have the knowledge you need to avoid legal issues in the future."

Robinson has sought legal advice from time to time for help with tasks such as drawing up contracts. He says that other responsibilities related to managing people, for example, include maintaining a safe office environment, providing staff the proper tools to do their jobs, and ensuring everyone has time for a proper lunch. He also cautions that "the lack of exposure to human resource realities can blindside you."

Years ago, Robinson had an issue with an employee using a company computer inappropriately during work time. Although the laws are not entirely defined regarding use of the Internet during work hours, it is important to inform staff of company policies related to personal blogging, signing on to Facebook, texting, and twittering during business hours. It is also important to let staff know that the company's Web administrator has access to company electronic mail and that copies of that mail are saved as standard business practice.

Hiring the right person for the right job can be the best way to avoid legal problems down the road. "We're all salespeople," says Robinson, "especially in a job interview. It can take 60 days to start seeing things in terms of an employee's work performance." Doing research, asking for references, and spending quality time checking those references will pay off in the long run. "Be careful also about giving recommendations for past employees," he adds, "because that can come back to haunt you as well!"

For new people managers, Robinson has some solid advice: "Take the time to

Courtesy of Matt Robinson

Matt Robinson.

know something about human resources. It may be true that the strongest irons are forged in the hottest fires, but an HR issue can be a fire that's a little too hot!" He acknowledges that entrepreneurs are at the highest risk, because they want to get things done quickly and are not in the practice of prevention. "You want to offer a fair day's pay for a fair day's work and have fun doing it, but the proper parameters have to be there."

Source: Courtesy of Matt Robinson

INTRODUCTION

LO1

What is the impact of laws on the behaviour and actions of supervisors and managers?

As the HRM Close-up shows, there is no doubt that employment laws affect line managers and what they are expected to do to successfully manage the people they are responsible for. Laws have been written to protect the employer and the employees; these laws reflect the values of society, and in some situations, laws have been enacted because of poor management practices. Therefore, it is important for supervisors to understand the legal context in which they have to operate. Managers, supervisors, and employees can no longer behave and act in certain ways without severe consequences. When managers ignore the legal aspects of HRM, they risk incurring costly and time-consuming litigation, negative public attitudes, and damage to organization morale.

And some of the laws address not just legal issues, but also emotional ones. For example, human rights legislation is paramount over other laws, and concerns all individuals regardless of their gender, race, religion, age, marital status, disability, family status, sexual orientation, national origin, colour, or position in an organization. All employees, including supervisors and managers, should be aware of their personal biases and how these attitudes can influence their dealings with one another. It should be emphasized that whether supervisors act a certain way unintentionally or intentionally, they are responsible for any illegal actions they take. Being ignorant of the law is not a valid excuse. As Matt Robinson indicates, entrepreneurs are at highest risk, because they want to get things done quickly. This chapter will focus on the various employment laws at both the federal and provincial levels that affect how a manager practices human resources management.

Beyond legislation, there is also an expectation in today's society that treating employees in certain ways is just "good business." Thus, the concept of diversity management in a multicultural society has become part of business simply because it makes good business sense. It is important to remember that we have gone beyond what is required by law in our human resources management practices.

THE LEGAL BACKGROUND OF HRM

LO2

How does the legal framework in Canada work?

Canada has two distinct sets of laws that govern: federal and provincial. Federal laws apply to everyone who resides in Canada. For example, everyone must pay income taxes. Other laws are handled at the provincial level. For example, the provinces are responsible for determining who can get a driver's licence. While this chapter will discuss specific employment laws, other kinds of laws, such as common law (our body of law that has developed from judicial decisions), contract law (the laws that relate to legal and binding agreements, such as the purchase of a car), and government regulations (called statutory law), can also have an impact on HR. For example, common law establishes the basic employee–employer relationship of trust. Contract law governs a person engaged in a fee-for-service activity for a company. Statutory law creates employment conditions, such as providing minimum wages or holidays with pay (e.g., Canada Day on July 1).

There are a total of 14 different jurisdictions (government authorities), which means 14 different sets of laws.

Federal legislation applies to only about 10% of Canadian workers, those who are employed by any of the following: federal government departments and agencies, Crown corporations, and other businesses and industries under federal control such as banks, airlines, railway companies, and insurance and communications companies. Examples of companies governed by federal legislation are CIBC, Scotiabank, Air Canada, WestJet, Bell, and CBC.

In addition, each province and territory has its own legislation that covers employment standards, human rights, labour relations, and worker health and safety. Companies covered under provincial legislation include the corner 7-Eleven, the local McDonald's, and others such as Canadian Tire, RONA, and Walmart. Despite a great deal of similarity across provinces and territories, there are some notable variations in minimum wage and vacation entitlement, for example. Also, some aspects of human rights legislation differ from one jurisdiction to another. Some provinces and territories have employment equity legislation, and others do not. For example, Ontario and Quebec have stringent pay equity legislation. In Alberta and British Columbia, however, there is no such legislation. Therefore, any pay equity adjustments are the decision of the organization.

Although federal law regulates both Employment Insurance (EI) and the Canada Pension Plan (CPP), all employers and employees are covered, not just federal employees. EI provides for wage payment should you lose your job, and CPP provides for a small pension when you retire. Quebec has its own pension plan similar to the CPP. Changes to EI over the past several years have had an impact on human resources practices in organizations. For example, compassionate care benefits are available to employees who need time off to care for or support a family member who is gravely ill or at risk of dying within six months.[1] Further, a total of 35 weeks is available for parental leave, which can be used by either parent or shared between them.[2] In both these cases, the job is hold open for the person until the leave is over.

Federal Employment Laws

For companies that are federally regulated, there are two basic employment laws: the ***Canada Labour Code*** and the ***Canadian Human Rights Act.*** The *Canada Labour Code* covers basic employment conditions, labour relations, and health and safety in the federal sector. The Canada Industrial Relations Board administers this law.

Canada Labour Code
http://laws-lois.justice.gc.ca/eng/acts/L-2/index.html

Canadian Human Rights Act
http://laws-lois.justice.gc.ca/eng/acts/h-6

Personal Information Protection and Electronic Documents Act (PIPEDA)
http://laws-lois.justice.gc.ca/eng/acts/P-8.6/page-1.html

Like the *Canada Labour Code,* the *Canadian Human Rights Act* applies to all federal government departments and agencies, Crown corporations, and businesses and industries under federal jurisdiction, such as banks, airlines, railway companies, and insurance and communications companies. It is administered by the Canadian Human Rights Commission, which makes decisions on complaints involving discrimination and harassment. The concept of a certain level of basic human rights is part of the very fabric of Canadian society. It is also an area that is constantly expanding. For example, in late 2014 the person in charge of the Canadian Human Rights Commission spoke out against using genetic information to discriminate against employees for insurance coverage if their genetic profile indicated certain health risk factors such as diabetes.[3]

Of increasing concern for managers and HR professionals is privacy legislation. There are two primary laws—one that applies to only federally regulated companies (e.g., bank, airlines, etc.) and one that extends the federal legislation to provinces and businesses within the provinces. These laws are the ***Personal Information Protection and Electronic Documents Act (PIPEDA)*** and provincial legislation commonly called the "Personal Information Privacy Act." These acts have a direct influence on how companies and managers handle employee information and the rights of employees regarding this information. Both acts enhance the protection granted to employees on their personal information that a company retains. Organizations can use the information (such as social insurance number) only for its intended purpose (to remit premiums to the Canada Pension Plan). Organizations can no longer collect personal information without disclosing the full use to employees. Further, organizations must seek written permission from the employee to disclose personal information. For example, if you want to get a car loan, your employer is obliged to seek your written authorization to disclose your pay to the lending agency.

These acts have been most noted in the monitoring of e-mails, use of social media, and website visits of employees while at the worksite. More information on this will be covered in Chapter 9, "Dealing with Management Rights, Employee Rights, and Discipline."

As businesses look outside of Canada for new employees, they have become more familiar with the *Immigration and Refugee Protection Act* when they wish to recruit and hire people who are not citizens or permanent residents of Canada. This topic will be discussed in Chapter 5, "Planning for, Recruiting, and Selecting the Workforce."

Provincial Employment Legislation

Each province and territory has relatively similar legislation that provides certain rights and guarantees regarding employment. For example, each province has maximum limits regarding hours per day or hours per week that a person can work before the organization is obliged to pay overtime wages. Similarly, the health and safety of workers are also covered by provincial legislation. In addition, provinces and territories have legislation dealing with human rights and legislation that covers unions and their relationships with employers. In the following sections, you will get information about these major types of employment laws, whether provincial or federal. Figure 2.1 provides a summary of the various federal and provincial employment laws referred to in the previous two sections. In addition, websites for accessing the legislation can be found in the Appendix at the end of this chapter.

FIGURE 2.1 Major Employment Laws in Canada

Jurisdiction	Basic Employment Conditions	Labour Legislation	Occupational Health and Safety and Workers' Compensation	Human Rights
Federal	Canada Labour Code	*Canada Labour Code*	*Canada Labour Code*	Canadian Human Rights Act
Alberta	Employment Standards Code	Labour Relations Code	Occupational Health and Safety Code	Human Rights Act
British Columbia	British Columbia Employment Standards Act	Labour Relations Code	Workers' Compensation Act	Human Rights Code
Manitoba	Employment Standards Code	Labour Relations Act	Workplace Safety and Health Act/Workers Compensation Act	Human Rights Code
New Brunswick	Employment Standards Act	Industrial Relations Act	Occupational Health and Safety Act	Human Rights Act
Newfoundland and Labrador	Labour Standards Act	Labour Relations Act	Occupational Health and Safety Act	Human Rights Act
Nova Scotia	Labour Standards Code	Trade Union Act	Occupational Health and Safety Act	Human Rights Act
Nunavut	Labour Standards Act	Labour Standards Act	Safety Act/Workers' Compensation Act	Human Rights Act
Ontario	Employment Standards Act	Labour Relations Act, 1995	Occupational Health and Safety Act/Workplace Safety and Insurance Act	Human Rights Code
Prince Edward Island	Employment Standards Act	Labour Act	Occupational Health and Safety Act	Human Rights Act
Quebec	Act Respecting Labour Standards	Labour Code	Act Respecting Occupational Health and Safety	Charter of Human Rights and Freedoms
Saskatchewan	Saskatchewan Employment Act	Saskatchewan Employment Act	Saskatchewan Employment Act	Saskatchewan Human Rights Code

Note: Web sites for legislation can be found in the Appendix at the end of this chapter.

HUMAN RIGHTS LEGISLATION

The legislation that has had the most far-reaching impact on employment conditions has been the *Canadian Charter of Rights and Freedoms* and its impact in the area of human rights. The *Charter*, passed in 1982, guarantees certain rights and freedoms in our society. What it has done for employment legislation is to ensure that such legislation is consistent with its principles.[4] Rights under the Charter were reinforced when the first human rights legislation was passed. Although the original human rights legislation was at the federal level, all provinces have enacted similar laws.

The basic foundation of human rights legislation is that "all individuals should have an opportunity equal with other individuals to make for themselves the lives that they are able and wish to have and to have their needs accommodated, consistent with their duties and obligations as members of society, without being hindered in or prevented from doing so by discriminatory practices based on race, national, or ethnic origin, colour, religion, age, sex, sexual orientation, marital status, family status, disability, or conviction for an offence for which a pardon has been granted."[5] While the legislation is designed to protect individuals, it does not cover every situation. For example, "age" had been defined to be the ages between 19 and 65 in most jurisdictions. However, most jurisdictions have now eliminated the "65," which means that, in most cases, the notion of "mandatory retirement" would now be illegal. Employers now need to be vigilant regarding how older workers are treated so that organizations do not have complaints based on age discrimination.[6]

Human rights legislation is enforced through human rights commissions (or tribunals) and is achieved via a complaint process (explained in detail later). Since human rights legislation is paramount over other employment laws, the decisions of these commissions and tribunals have a huge influence over all types of employment issues. It is important to note that commission decisions have changed expectations regarding the proper treatment of employees. As a result, organizations now have higher standards to meet. For example, a recent human rights decision found that employers can be considered discriminatory if they fail to make accommodation for childcare responsibilities.[7]

Discrimination

LO3

What are discrimination and harassment?

The essence of human rights legislation, both federally and provincially, is to prohibit discrimination on the basis of race, religion, gender, age, national or ethnic origin, disability, or family or marital status. The majority of provincial human rights legislation also covers sexual orientation. Prohibited grounds continue to evolve as changes occur in Canadian society. For example, Alberta includes "transgender" in its definition of gender and includes "ancestry" which is broader than "national or ethnic origin."[8] Note that some jurisdictions include pardoned convictions (e.g., federal, British Columbia, Ontario, and Quebec) and records of criminal convictions (British Columbia, Quebec, Prince Edward Island, and Yukon Territory) as prohibited grounds. A person's political beliefs are protected in some jurisdictions, such as British Columbia, Manitoba, Now Scotia, New Brunswick, Newfoundland, Northwest Territories, Quebec, and Prince Edward Island. The complete list of prohibited grounds for each jurisdiction can be found by accessing the human rights agencies listed in Figure 2.2.

Systemic discrimination
The exclusion of members of certain groups through the application of employment policies or practices based on criteria that are not job-related

Many employment barriers are hidden, unintentionally, in the rules and procedures that organizations use in their various human resources management practices. These barriers, referred to as **systemic discrimination**, have prevented the progress of these designated groups. Inequity can result if these barriers discourage individuals on the basis of their membership in certain groups rather than their ability to do a job the employer needs done. An example of systemic discrimination would occur when an employer's workforce

FIGURE 2.2 Provincial and Territorial Human Rights Agencies

Organization	Website
Alberta Human Rights Commission	www.albertahumanrights.ab.ca
British Columbia Human Rights Tribunal	www.bchrt.bc.ca
Manitoba Human Rights Commission	www.gov.mb.ca/hrc
New Brunswick Human Rights Commission	www.gnb.ca/hrc-cdp
Newfoundland & Labrador Human Rights Commission	www.justice.gov.nl.ca/hrc
Northwest Territories Human Rights Commission	www.nwthumanrights.ca
Nova Scotia Human Rights Commission	www.gov.ns.ca/humanrights
Nunavut Human Rights Tribunal	www.nhrt.ca
Human Rights Tribunal of Ontario	www.hrto.ca
Human Rights Legal Support Centre	www.hrlsc.on.ca
Prince Edward Island Human Rights Commission	www.gov.pe.ca/humanrights
(Québec) Commission des droits de la personne et des droits de la jeunesse	www.cdpdj.qc.ca/en
Saskatchewan Human Rights Commission	www.shrc.gov.sk.ca
Yukon Human Rights Commission	www.yhrc.yk.ca

Source: "Your Guide to Understanding the Canadian Human Rights Act," Canadian Human Rights Commission, accessed January 10, 2015, http://www.chrc-ccdp.ca/eng/content/your-guide-understanding-canadian-human-rights-act-page2

represents one group in our society and the company recruits new employees by posting job vacancies within the company or by word of mouth among the employees. This recruitment strategy is likely to generate a candidate similar to those in the current workforce, thereby unintentionally discriminating against other groups of workers in the labour market. A better approach might be to vary recruitment methods by contacting outside agencies and organizations.

Bona fide occupational qualification (BFOQ)
A justifiable reason for discrimination based on business reasons of safety or effectiveness

Employers may be permitted to discriminate if employment qualifications are based on a **bona fide occupational qualification (BFOQ)** or *bona fide occupational requirement (BFOR)*. For example, Saskatchewan uses the example of a taxi driver who must be able to see in order to carry out the requirements of the work.[9] A BFOQ is justified if the employer can establish its necessity for business operations. Business necessity is a practice that includes the safe and efficient operation of an organization. In other words, differential treatment is not discrimination if there is a justifiable reason. However, it should be pointed out that it is difficult for many employers to establish legitimate BFOQs. A law firm lost its ability to retire partners when the B.C. Human Rights Tribunal determined that the individual was more like an employee and that no BFOQ existed. The law firm appealed the decision to the Supreme Court of Canada, and in 2014 the Court determined that the person was not an employee and so no discrimination existed.[10] Therefore, a supervisor will probably be asked to carefully examine job requirements and demonstrate that a certain characteristic is absolutely essential. The federal government, for example, has been allowed to hire only women as guards in prisons for women; however, a retail store specializing in women's fashions would not be allowed to hire only women. Frequently, the HR professional and the line manager would work together to review job requirements to determine if the qualifications met the BFOQ requirement. For recruitment and hiring purposes, it is important that job requirements not create a discriminatory situation. Likewise, even the process of hiring can be considered discriminatory if inappropriate questions are asked. This area will be discussed more fully in Chapter 5.

Most of the decisions made by the Supreme Court of Canada, human rights tribunals, and arbitrations have looked at whether the discrimination was "intentional" or "unintentional." Intentional discrimination is very clear and direct, such as a requirement that only males five-foot nine and taller could apply. On the other hand, some discriminatory employment situations are unintentional. Another example is the requirement that a firefighter be able to run a certain distance within a fixed amount of time.

A Supreme Court decision several years ago changed this approach from previous court decisions and the result remains the standard when determining BFOQ.[11] The case involved a female forest firefighter in British Columbia who was terminated after performing successfully on the job for 3 years. As a consequence of a coroner's report, new fitness standards had been instituted requiring that all firefighters be able to run 2.5 km in 11 minutes. The person failed the standard on 4 attempts and was terminated, even though she had been doing the work successfully. The Court decided that the test was discriminatory, since females have a lower aerobic capacity than males and would therefore be unable to meet the standard. The decision went on to establish a new approach to BFOQ. From now on, an employer is required to demonstrate that it is impossible to accommodate individuals discriminated against without undue hardship. This means that whatever the standard is, the employer must provide for individual accommodation, if possible.[12]

Another concept that has arisen from human rights decisions is that of reasonable accommodation. **Reasonable accommodation** involves adjusting employment policies and practices so that no individual is denied benefits, is disadvantaged with respect to employment opportunities, or is blocked from carrying out the essential components of a job because of race, colour, disability, or any of the other prohibited grounds of discrimination. This is a legal obligation, so as new prohibited grounds are added to any human rights legislation, they, too, become eligible for reasonable accommodation. When an accommodation request is made, an employer needs to thoroughly investigate and consider methods by which the employee's particular needs (e.g., family status, gender, disability) can be accommodated in the workplace, including whether the specific tasks can be organized in a way to deal with the need.

Reasonable accommodation
Attempt by employers to adjust the working conditions and employment practices of employees to prevent discrimination

It is important to remember that accommodation works both ways: both the employee and the employer must live up to the agreement. In an interesting case dealing with accommodation due to religious beliefs, the Canada Public Service Labour Relations Board determined that the employer had provided appropriate accommodation but that the employee was not entitled to "perfect accommodation," that the employer had provided several options, and that the employee had failed on their part of the accommodation.[13] Although reasonable accommodation is expected unless "undue hardship" is created for the employer, most midsized-to-large organizations would have difficulty saying that an accommodation request would create undue hardship. For example, if someone does not have the necessary eye-hand coordination to do detailed electronics work, the employer may be obliged to reconfigure the tasks so that the person can do the work. Whether an employer can accommodate the work to fit the individual needs is ultimately a decision made by human rights tribunals. Ethics in HRM 2.1 describes what happens when a federal agency denied an accommodation request as the person was not the only parent who could handle issues with childcare.

It is no longer acceptable for employers to assume that all employees will "fit in" no matter what their special needs. Employers must find the means to alter systems to meet the needs of their employees as long as this does not cause them "undue hardship" as mentioned in Ethics in HRM 2.1. However, undue hardship may be something different for a small organization compared with a larger organization. For example, it may be a hardship for a small firm to modify a washroom to accommodate a person in a wheelchair, but it may be reasonable to expect a large organization, with its own building, to renovate or install a washroom that can accommodate a wheelchair.

Reasonable accommodation may include redesigning job duties; adjusting work schedules; providing technical, financial, and human support services; and upgrading facilities. And with our aging workforce, people are working longer, which may mean employers will need to also accommodate older workers with age-related health issues.[14] It is also important to remember that being over 65 is a protected ground of discrimination.

Ability Society
www.abilitysociety.org

Abilities Magazine
www.abilities.ca

Canadian Council on Rehabilitation and Work
www.ccrw.org

Mental Health Works
www.mentalhealthworks.ca

The City of Toronto developed award-winning facilities in its Barrier Free Access program, which was designed to allow people with disabilities accessible passage throughout city facilities. Many not-for-profit organizations in Canada support and encourage employment opportunities for people with disabilities, among them Ability Society (**www.abilitysociety.org**), Abilities (**www.abilities.ca**), and Canadian Council on Rehabilitation and Work (**www.ccrw.org**). While many employers tend to think of accommodation in terms of physical disabilities, it is important to remember that the duty to accommodate includes all the prohibited grounds of discrimination, including mental illness. The focus on mental illness is becoming more prominent as its impact in the workplace is better understood. That is why the Ontario Human Rights Commission released a new policy in 2014 to help employers understand their responsibilities.[15] Other organizations such as Mental Health Works (**www.mentalhealthworks.ca**) can also provide advice and guidance regarding workplace issues. A further discussion on healthy workplaces will be in Chapter 3.

Reasonable accommodation benefits all employees. The provision of allowances for childcare expenses when employees take company-sponsored courses not only removes a barrier that blocks many women but also may assist any employee with sole parenting responsibilities. The flexible work schedules adopted by some companies in northern Canada benefit First Nations employees who are prepared to work unusual hours in exchange for significant breaks away from the worksite in order to take part in traditional hunting and fishing activities. Many other employees also benefit from these flexible work schedules. Further, with the cultural and religious diversity of the Canadian population, more and more employers are being asked for accommodation for religious purposes including religious dress (hijabs, kirpans, turbans, etc.) and prayer times.[16] At Work with HRM 2.1 provides two accommodation cases that were decided by an arbitrator and a tribunal.

Reverse Discrimination

Reverse discrimination
Giving preference to members of certain groups such that others feel they are the subjects of discrimination

In pursuing initiatives to avoid discrimination, employers may be accused of **reverse discrimination**, or giving preference to members of certain groups such that others feel they are being discriminated against. For example, if a company feels that it has too few women employees, it may take active steps to hire more women. By hiring more women, however, the company may hire fewer men, opening it up to criticism that it is discriminating against men. When these charges occur, organizations are caught between attempting to correct past discriminatory practices and handling present complaints that they are being unfair. If an organization is required to comply with any type of employment equity legislation (discussed later), it can be quite legal to discriminate and hire certain individuals.

In some cases, organizations may identify the need to hire a certain proportion of people from specific groups, such as visible minorities. While these organizations may state that they wish to find a larger pool of qualified applicants from a particular group, the organizations may, in fact, create a type of quota system for hiring. If it is perceived that there are hard numbers attached to hiring, then it is easy for individuals not in a targeted group to feel that they are being discriminated against. Charges of reverse discrimination have occurred in the fire and police services as those organizations try to achieve a workforce more reflective of the residents in their communities.

ETHICS IN HRM 2.1

WAS THE DENIAL REASONABLE?

In late 2014, the Canadian Human Rights Tribunal reaffirmed an earlier decision that the Canada Border Services Agency (CBSA) had discriminated against an employee on the grounds of "family status" when it denied the request for accommodation. Specifically, both the husband and wife worked for CBSA, had 2 small children, had unpredictable rotating work schedules, and were unable to get reliable childcare due to the schedule. CBSA refused the request, since both parents were full-time employees, but said it would accommodate if 1 of the parents went to part-time status. Part-time status also meant reduced benefits. CBSA stated that "family status" did not include childcare obligations. The CHRT decided that childcare obligations were legally required and not just a personal choice of a parent. Therefore, the work schedule problems were more than just trivial, that the parents had made serious efforts to find suitable childcare, and that CBSA had failed in its duty to accommodate. The decision cost CBSA lost wages, $15,000 for injury to dignity, and $20,000 special compensation since the agency's conduct was "willful and reckless."

CRITICAL THINKING QUESTION:

What is your opinion of the decision, including the monetary penalties? Why?

Source: *Blackstone v. Canada (Border Services)*, 2014 FCA 110, September 12, 2014, decisions.chrt-tcdp.gc.ca/chrt-tcdp/decisions/en/item/73292/index.do?r=AAAAAQAlSm9obnN0b25lIHYuIENhbmFkYSAoQm9yZGVyIFNlcnZpY2VzKQAAAAAB; *Johnstone and Canadian Human Rights Commission v. Canada Border Services*, 2010 CHRT 20, accessed January 12, 2015, http://decisions.chrt-tcdp.gc.ca/chrt-tcdp/archive/en/item/6537/index.do?r=AAAAAQAlSm9obnN0b25lIHYuIENhbmFkYSAoQm9yZGVyIFNlcnZpY2VzKQAAAAAB; and Fasken Martineau, "Blockbuster Annual Update," *Labour, Employment, Human Rights and Privacy 2014*, October 1, 2014.

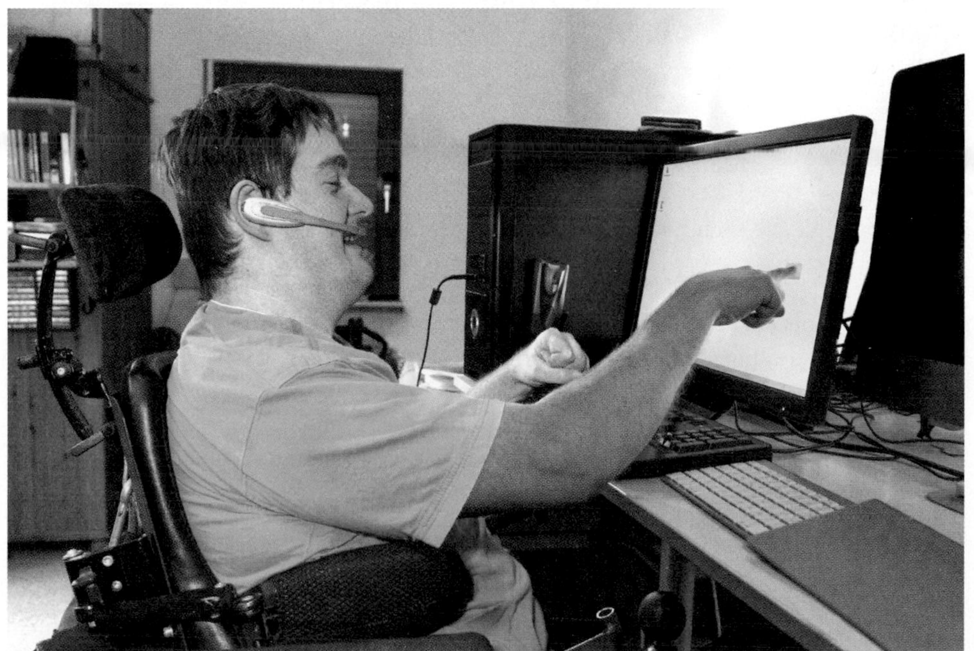

Belushi/Shutterstock.com

Organizations are looking for individuals with diverse skills and capabilities.

Harassment
Any unwanted physical or verbal behaviour that offends or humiliates the individual

LO4

What is the role of the line manager in creating a work environment that is free from harassment and discrimination?

Harassment

Besides prohibiting discrimination, human rights legislation prohibits harassment. Some provinces protect only against sexual **harassment**, while other provinces prohibit any type of workplace harassment. Harassment is any unwanted physical or verbal behaviour that offends or humiliates a person.[17] Harassment can take many forms and can be one incident or several incidents. It is not acceptable, for instance, for one co-worker to strike

AT WORK WITH HRM 2.1

WHAT ABOUT ACCOMMODATING SOMEONE WHO HAS A PHYSICAL INJURY?

Two recent decisions suggest that even if an employee does not have a permanent disability, they might have a case for discrimination.

A newspaper reporter in Ontario was accommodated after the reporter had seriously injured an ankle when not at work. The employee could not drive or take public transit, so the newspaper allowed the employee to work from home and only did stories that could be handled using a telephone. This went on for some time, until the newspaper was made aware that the employee was at maximum recovery, at which time the employer asked that work be done in the office.

The newspaper did not require the employee to go into the field. However, even though the person was recovered, the employee hobbled at work and complained of pain. The newspaper had heard comments about the employee's activities outside of work and did an investigation. It determined that the person was regularly driving and moving around much better than at work. When asked, the reporter couldn't explain the differences, and was terminated for lying.

At arbitration, the termination was upheld because the employee had lied to avoid more strenuous assignments. When accommodated, an employee is obligated to cooperate.

In a similar case at a daycare society, a full-time employee broke an ankle and was off work almost 5 months. The work required that the person be physically active when working with the children. Shortly after the employee returned, it was noted by the supervisor that the person was being cautious with movements and was sitting down a great deal. As a result, a fitness report was requested and the employee was not allowed to work until clearance had been obtained. The medical report stated that the duties needed to be modified and that no prolonged walking or standing could be done for another 2 months. Since the work requirements included a great deal of walking and standing, the day care concluded that the person couldn't do the required work and that with only 2 other staff it could not modify the work.

The employee complained of discrimination based on physical disability. Since the disability was not permanent and accommodation was not possible, the tribunal agreed that the employer decided correctly.

CRITICAL THINKING QUESTION:

Do you think these were appropriate decisions? Why or why not?

Sources: Jeffrey R. Smith, "When Dishonesty Overrides Disability," *Canadian HR Reporter*, June 2, 2014, accessed January 12, 2015, www.hrreporter.com/blog/Employment-Law/archive/2014/06/02/when-dishonesty-overrides-disability; Human Rights Tribunals of Alberta, *Perera v. St. Albert Day Care Society*, 2014 AHRC 10, accessed January 12, 2015, www.canlii.org/en/ab/abhrc/doc/2014/2014ahrc10/2014ahrc10.html?searchUrlHash=AAAAAQAYcmVhc29uYWJsZSBhY2NvbW1vZGF0aW9uAAAAAAE.

another, and it is not acceptable to make personal comments that are offensive to the other person. When dealing with harassment in the workplace, a manager needs to ask whether a "reasonable person" would consider a certain behaviour or action as harassment. If the answer is yes, then the supervisor is expected to act accordingly. It is interesting to note that what is considered harassment in today's workplace was sometimes considered acceptable behaviour not long ago. For example, it used to be acceptable to call someone a name that reflected the person's ethnic background.

While for some time, discussions of harassment have focused on sexual harassment, in the last several years the focus has been on general harassment in the workplace. Specifically, organizations have developed policy statements and guidelines for dealing with harassment in the workplace. Even with policies and guidelines, organizations may still not do enough to eliminate harassment. For example, in early 2015, CBC received a report (after it had terminated a popular radio host) describing a culture that appeared to condone inappropriate behaviour such as yelling, cruel jokes, and demeaning comments.[18] The report cost 2 executives their jobs for not doing enough to deal with the host, who had consistently breached the standards of conduct.[19]

The Canadian Human Rights Commission defines harassment as follows:

> Harassment is any unwanted physical or verbal behaviour that offends or humiliates you. Generally, harassment is a behaviour that persists over time. Serious one-time incidents can also sometimes be considered harassment.

Harassment occurs when someone:

- makes unwelcome remarks or jokes about your race, religion, sex, age, disability or any other of the 11 grounds of discrimination.
- threatens or intimidates you.
- makes unwelcome physical contact with you, such as touching, patting, pinching or punching, which can also be considered assault.[20*]

When considering whether the behaviour is harassing, the test used is: "Would a reasonable person know that the conduct was not welcomed by the other?" What this means for supervisors is that they are expected to work with employees to ensure they are behaving and acting acceptably. HRM and the Law 2.1 describes the impact of a harassment complaint in which the employer had a culture that allowed sexually explicit banter and jokes.

It is important for organizations to have policies dealing with harassment. For example, the Newfoundland and Labrador Government has an extensive one dealing with harassment and a discrimination-free workplace.[21] It includes definitions, responsibilities, and information about how complaints are filed and handled.

In another example, Humber College's human rights policy states:

> The Humber College Institute of Technology & Advanced Learning and the University of Guelph-Humber (hereafter referred to as "Humber" or "the College") has the right, as well as the legal and moral responsibility, to ensure that all its members are treated fairly, equitably, and respectfully, in order to provide a learning, living and working environment that is free from discrimination and harassment. This policy outlines Humber's position related to acceptable and unacceptable behavior with respect to human rights and the responsibilities of the College, students and employees.[22**]

Its policy defines harassment as:

> Harassment is defined by the *Ontario Human Rights Code, 1962,* as engaging in a course of vexatious comment or conduct that is known or ought reasonably to be

HRM AND THE LAW 2.1 DOES EMPLOYEE PARTICIPATING MAKE IT HARASSMENT?

A recent case between an employee and business, decided by the British Columbia Human Rights Tribunal, dismissed the complaint. The specifics of the case involved an individual who had worked for the company for a number of years and had worked at a number of different retail stores. It was well known throughout the company that all the work environments had a culture where "sexually explicit banter, jokes and innuendo were considered reasonable social interaction between employees and between employees and managers." The submissions by the employer and several employees indicated that the complainant had actively and willingly participated in the banter. The company stated that there was no adverse impact to anyone as all participated in the behaviours and no reasonable person would conclude that the conduct was unwelcome. The manager of the store in which the employee worked when the complaint was filed indicated that the person had never complained or expressed any concern about the environment and/or the actions.

The tribunal decided that the employee had been an active participant, and that no complaints had been made regarding what frequently occurred at work. However, the tribunal went on to say that if the employee had not participated, there was every likelihood that the conduct and actions could be deemed sexual harassment.

CRITICAL THINKING QUESTION:

What do you think of the decision? Why?

Sources: Extract from British Columbia Human Rights Tribunal, *Kafer v. Sleep Country Canada and Another*, 2013 BCHRT 289, December 3, 2013, accessed January 13, 2015, www.bchrt.gov.bc.ca/decisions/2013/pdf/dec/289_Kafer_v_Sleep_Country_Canada_and_another_No_2_2013_BCHRT_289.pdf; and Fasken Martineau, "Blockbuster Annual Update," Labour, Employment, Human Rights and Privacy 2014, October 1, 2014.

* Canadian Human Rights Commission, http://www.chrc-ccdp.ca/eng/content/what-harassment

** Courtesy of Humber College HRS

known to be unwelcome (Section 10 (1) (f)). The College interprets this to include any behaviour that is known or ought reasonably to be known to the perpetrator to be offensive, embarrassing or humiliating to other individuals. Such conduct may include visual representations, electronic messages, written messages, verbal and/or physical conduct, and may relate to any of the grounds of discrimination prohibited by the *Ontario Human Rights Code, 1962*, or other malicious grounds. Some examples of harassment are:

- unwelcome remarks, jokes, slurs innuendoes or taunting;
- hazing, stalking or shunning;
- the repeated mistreatment of one employee, targeted by one or more employees with a malicious mix of humiliation, intimidation and sabotage of performance (bullying);
- displaying derogatory or offensive pictures, graffiti or materials either through printed copy or personal computer;
- verbal abuse;
- insulting gestures or practical jokes which cause embarrassment or awkwardness;
- unauthorized and/or unnecessary physical contact;
- an impassioned, collective campaign by co-workers to exclude, punish and humiliate a targeted worker.

For the purposes of this policy, "harassment" also includes personal/psychological harassment.[23*]

Humber's policy is very far-reaching: it applies to students, faculty, staff, its governing body, visitors to the campus, and corporations and vendors who do business with the college.

For harassment policies to succeed, confidentiality is necessary, as is the need to do a thorough investigation. For example, a company was fined $5,000 for not taking the complaint seriously and doing a thorough investigation.[24] Without organizational commitment to zero tolerance of harassment, such policies are meaningless. It is also important to remember that harassment is against the law. As the Province of Saskatchewan reminds employers: "[I]t's against the law" and "If you violate the *Code* you could be liable for the harm caused … ."[25]

Toolkit 2.1 presents some suggestions for developing an effective harassment policy.

Psychological harassment
Repeated and aggravating behaviour that affects an employee's dignity, psychological, or physical integrity that results in a harmful work environment

The concepts of harassment in the workplace are being broadened to include **psychological harassment**, such as bullying, yelling at subordinates, excluding employees from certain activities, making derogatory comments, and other similar actions. Psychological harassment can create a poisoned work environment and a toxic culture that can also become quite costly through disability claims, increased stress, and turnover.[26] While the concept of psychological harassment is based on prohibited grounds in human rights legislation, several jurisdictions have also included psychological harassment in health and safety legislation, for example Ontario and British Columbia. Sometimes there is a fine line between bullying and strong management, but the difference appears to be whether feedback is constructive to help the employee with their work.[27] It is important to know that expressing differences of opinion or taking reasonable disciplinary action does not constitute bullying.[28] For additional information on psychological harassment in the workplace, resources can be found at the Psychological Harassment Information Association (**www.psychologicalharassment.com**).

Psychological Harassment Information Association
www.psychologicalharassment.com

Enforcement of Human Rights Legislation

The federal government and each province and territory have a commission or similar agency to deal with complaints concerning discriminatory practices covered by legislation. For example, the Canadian Human Rights Commission (CHRC) (**www.chrc-ccdp.ca**) deals with complaints from those employees and businesses covered by the *Canadian Human*

Canadian Human Rights Commission (CHRC)
www.chrc-ccdp.ca

* Courtesy of Humber College HRS

Rights Act. These commissions can act on their own if they feel that there are sufficient grounds for a finding of discrimination. The agencies also have the ability to interpret the act. Figure 2.3 presents a flowchart of the process used at CHRC to resolve complaints. You will note that the process includes a very early step of resolution and mediation. Other human rights commissions operate in a similar fashion.

The steps are as follows:

1. *Inquiry and screening.* An individual contacts the CHRC about launching a complaint.
2. *Early resolution and mediation.* A CHRC representative works with the complainant and tries to achieve an early resolution directly or through mediation.
3. *Formal complaint.* If the matter hasn't been resolved in step 2, and the individual wishes to pursue the matter, a formal complaint is filed.
4. *Notification.* The CHRC contacts the employer to determine its perspective. Then it decides whether the complaint is valid and the complaint proceeds to mediation or a hearing.
5. *Mediation.* Specialists are assigned by the CHRC to assist the parties in finding a mediated solution. This is a voluntary and confidential step.
6. *Investigation.* An investigation, which includes gathering any documents and other evidence, is made; a report analyzing the information, along with a recommendation as to the further handling of the case, is then prepared and submitted to the Commission. The Commission can dismiss the case, refer it to conciliation, or refer to the tribunal for a final and binding decision.
7. *Conciliation.* This is similar to mediation, except that it is mandatory. Even with conciliation, the parties are encouraged to resolve the case between themselves.
8. *Tribunal.* When a case is referred to a tribunal, there is no guarantee that the complaint will be upheld. Further, if the tribunal decides the complaint is valid, it can order corrective measures such as human rights training, a change in the human rights policies, or an actual payment for lost wages, pain, and/or suffering.[29]

FIGURE 2.3 Canadian Human Rights Commission Dispute Resolution Process

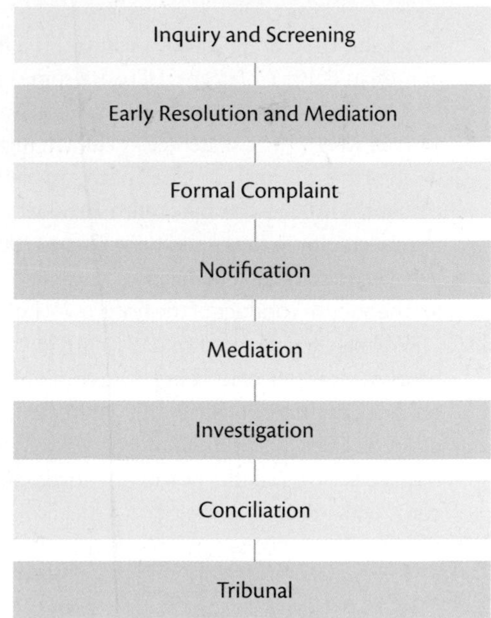

Source: Table developed from narrative at Canadian Human Rights Commission, "What can we expect?" accessed January 17, 2015, www.chrc-ccdp.ca/eng/content/what-can-we-expect.

TOOLKIT 2.1 GUIDELINES FOR HAVING AN EFFECTIVE ANTI-HARASSMENT POLICY

- Indicate in the policy that the organization is committed to a harassment-free environment.
- Encourage employees to come forward with complaints.
- Provide a clear definition of harassment.
- Provide guidelines for individuals about making a complaint.
- Provide a step-by-step procedure for making a complaint.
- Provide information about who will be involved in the investigation and when the complainant may expect the decision.
- Outline the responsibilities of management at all levels in the organization.
- Maintain confidentiality.
- Guarantee fair and prompt action.
- Policy is communicated and consistently enforced.

Additional resources from the various human rights commissions are available at the websites listed in Figure 2.2.

Source: Adapted from Brian Kenny, "When the Harassment Dust Settles," *Canadian HR Reporter*, December 1, 2014, accessed January 17, 2015, www.hrreporter.com/articleview/22947-when-the-harassment-dust-settles-toughest-hr-question; Michael Richards and Nicholas Sharratt, "Workplace Investigations Need to Be Thorough, Unbiased," *Canadian HR Reporter*, June 14, 2014, accessed January 17, 2015, www.hrreporter.com/articleview/21715-workplace-investigations-need-to-be-thorough-unbiased; and Alberta Human Rights Commission, "Sample Harassment Policy," accessed January 17, 2015, www.albertahumanrights.ab.ca/SampleHarassPolicy.pdf.

AT WORK WITH HRM 2.2 — WHY SO COSTLY?

Small and large organizations can feel the financial impact of human rights violations. Here are some examples.

The owner of a small hotel in Saskatoon was ordered to pay $44,900 when the Saskatchewan Human Rights Commission decided that a former clerk had been sexually harassed. Of the amount, $10,000—the maximum fine—was awarded to the former employee for harassment plus $31,900 in lost wages. What was also notable is that $3,000 was awarded to the court for the abusive conduct of the hotel owner during the hearing.

Walmart was ordered to pay $410,000 to an employee for harassment at one of its stores. The employee alleged that not only did harassment occur but Walmart ignored the complaint as it felt that the employee was trying to undermine the supervisor. Eventually the employee quit and sued for constructive dismissal. The trial for the dismissal resulted in an award of $1,450,000 against Walmart and the supervisor.

Both Walmart and the supervisor appealed this decision at the Ontario Court of Appeals. During the hearing, Walmart and the supervisor argued that the initial award contained an amount for aggravated damages that should be set aside. The appeals court determined that the employer had taken no steps to deal with the harasser's conduct that was flagrant and outrageous. This portion of the award amounted to $300,000—$200,000 against Walmart and $100,000 against the supervisor.

A restaurant in Toronto was ordered to pay almost $100,000 to three former employees who launched a human rights complaint based on harassment for religious beliefs. The Ontario Human Rights Tribunal determined that they had been forced to eat pork as well as breaking one of the religious fasts.

CRITICAL THINKING QUESTION:
Do you think these costs are reasonable? Why or why not?

Sources: "Saskatoon Hotel Owner Fined for Human Rights Breach," *Global News*, July 11, 2014, accessed January 17, 2015, http://globalnews.ca/news/1445492/saskatoon-hotel-owner-fined-for-human-rights-breach; Graeme McFarlane, "Harassment Too Costly to Ignore," *PeopleTalk*, Summer 2014, 44; and Stuart Rudner, "Discrimination in the Workplace," *Canadian HR Reporter*, May 5, 2014, accessed January 17, 2015, www.hrreporter.com/blog/Canadian-HR-Law/archive/2014/05/05/discrimination-in-the-workplace

Any person who obstructs an investigation or a tribunal, or fails to comply with the terms of a settlement, can be found guilty of an offence punishable by a fine and/or jail sentence. Provincial tribunals can also provide financial decisions against an employer. For example, the Ontario Human Rights Tribunal decided than an Ottawa company had discriminated against a foreign-born person when the company stated that it only hired "white men"; the complainant was awarded $8,000 plus interest.[30]

Provincial human rights laws are enforced in a manner similar to that used in the federal system. The majority of cases are resolved at the investigation stage. If no agreement can be reached, the case is presented to the province's human rights commission. The members of the commission study the evidence and then submit a report to the minister in charge of administering human rights legislation. The minister may appoint an independent board of inquiry, which has similar powers to a tribunal at the federal level. Failure to comply with the remedies prescribed by the board of inquiry may result in prosecution in provincial court. Individuals may be fined between $500 and $1,000, and organizations or groups between $1,000 and $10,000. These levies may vary across provinces.

The impact of fines can be particularly difficult on small businesses. For example, a tribunal recently awarded a record amount of damages ($200,000) to 2 sisters from Mexico working at an Ontario-based fish plant who were subjected to ongoing sexual harassment.[31] Read At Work with HRM 2.2 to gain a fuller understanding of the range of awards.

LO5

What are the general types of employment laws in Canada?

EMPLOYMENT STANDARDS LEGISLATION

All federal, provincial, and territorial jurisdictions have passed employment standards laws specifying the minimum obligations of employers. The names of the laws usually include the words "employment standards" or something similar. However, the minimum obligations for federal companies are covered under the *Canada Labour Code*.

Usually included in this type of legislation are items such as hours of work, minimum wages, overtime pay, vacation pay, public holidays, and who is covered by the legislation. Standards vary between provinces. In Alberta, for instance, certain provisions, such as keeping overtime records, do not apply to architects or engineers.[32]

Ontario Employment Standards
www.labour.gov.on.ca

Manitoba Employment Standards
www.gov.mb.ca/labour/standards

Saskatchewan Employment Standards
www.saskatchewan.ca/work/employment-standards

The legislation also typically reflects the views of the specific government with regard to its social policy. For example, British Columbia's legislation provides the right for a person to take a limited number of days off to tend to childcare needs; other jurisdictions, such as Ontario, have no such provision. Both British Columbia and Ontario have legislation that provides nine statutory or public holidays. There is usually a separate branch or agency that administers and interprets the legislation for both employers and employees. All the websites are listed in the Appendix at the end of this chapter, but you might want to look at several of the following: **www.labour.gov.on.ca**, **www.gov.mb.ca/labour/standards**, and **www.saskatchewan.ca/work/employment-standards.**

This legislation is important, as it applies to all employers, unionized or not. And because it specifies minimum obligations of employers, every employer—large or small—needs to be aware of the legislation. This is particularly true if the organization also uses contractors (see Chapter 1). There might be circumstances in which the contractor is really considered an employee. For example, if the company controls the hours of work, the tools and equipment used, and the actual performance of the work, the person might be deemed an employee and therefore covered by employment standards.[33]

An agency or commission that both interprets and enforces the law administers the legislation. For example, if employees feel that they are not receiving the right amount of vacation pay, they can contact the agency and find out what the right amount should be. If they are getting the wrong amount, then the agency can contact the employer and start an investigation. Further, other legislation may influence what standards must be met. A case involving a collective agreement that allowed the employer to adjust automatic wage adjustments during parental leave was deemed to be violating human rights legislation, and it was ruled that the employment standards requirement must be met.[34]

Sometimes organizations think a certain provision in these standards do not apply. For example, there have been many instances in which an employer thinks a manager paid by salary is not entitled to overtime. This only applies if the person is truly doing managerial work and isn't just titled "manager" while doing non-managerial work.[35]

LABOUR RELATIONS LEGISLATION

Labour relations legislation governs both the process by which a trade union acquires bargaining rights and the procedures by which trade unions and employers engage in collective bargaining.

In some jurisdictions, such as Ontario, the legislation (*Labour Relations Act*, 1995) applies primarily to workplaces in the private sector, but also covers certain parts of the public sector (e.g., municipal workers, hospital employees, school boards). Ontario has separate legislation for certain types of employers in the public sector, such as hospitals and Crown corporations.[36] However, in other jurisdictions, such as British Columbia, the legislation can apply to any workplace, whether in the public or the private sector.

Labour relations legislation applies only to unionized employees and to employers with unionized employees. Currently, approximately 4.6 million employees (or 30% of the Canadian workforce) belong to a union primarily in the public sector (75%) with less than 15% being in trades.[37] Unionization continues to decline in Canada.[38]

Labour relations legislation is usually administered through an agency called the Labour Relations Board, which is responsible for administering and enforcing the legislation. This board makes decisions on a variety of complaints from either a union or an employer. An employer might complain about the location of a trade union's picket, or union members might complain that the union has not fairly represented them. The board hires the people making these decisions and are usually lawyers or have some type of legal training.

More information on labour relations legislation will be given in Chapter 10.

HEALTH AND SAFETY LEGISLATION AND WORKERS' COMPENSATION

As you will see elsewhere in this book, the work environment and well-being of employees is a responsibility of employers. This responsibility is partially governed by legislation that describes the expected standards for health and safety in the workplace, as well as outlining the role and involvement of employees in health and safety.

The federal, provincial, and territorial governments regulate occupational health and safety. While statutes and standards differ slightly from jurisdiction to jurisdiction, attempts have been made to harmonize the various acts and regulations. Health and safety legislation has had an impact on workplace injuries and illnesses. The number of workplace accidents in Canada has declined even though there has been an increase in the number of workers.

All supervisors, managers, and HR professionals should become familiar with the occupational health and safety legislation governing the jurisdiction under which their organization operates. The fundamental duty of every employer is to take every reasonable precaution to ensure employee safety.

In addition to providing a hazard-free workplace and complying with the applicable statutes and regulations, employers must inform their employees about health and safety requirements. Employers are also required to keep certain records, to compile an annual summary of work-related injuries and illnesses, and to ensure that supervisors are familiar with the work and its associated hazards (the supervisor, in turn, must ensure that workers are aware of those hazards). In most jurisdictions, employers are required to ensure that the employees are knowledgeable about workplace health and safety.

Violations of health and safety statutes are administered through a government agency, frequently called the Workers' Compensation Board. As part of the legislation, workers can receive a monetary payment if they are injured or get a disease that can be attributed at work. Thus, the employer is responsible not only for the health and safety of the workplace but also for financial compensation if the worker is injured or gets a disease from the job. In all jurisdictions, employers are required to report any accidents that cause injuries and diseases to the Workers' Compensation Board. An accident resulting in death or critical injury must be reported immediately; the accident must then be investigated and a written report submitted. Finally, employers must provide safety training and be prepared to discipline employees for failing to comply with safety rules. Web addresses for the various provincial agencies are in this chapter's Appendix.

The legislation also identifies the duties of workers, which include complying with all applicable acts and regulations; reporting hazardous conditions or defective equipment; and following all employer safety and health rules and regulations, including those prescribing the use of protective equipment, such as wearing hard hats or steel-toed boots at a construction site or protective eyewear in a laboratory. Workers have many rights that pertain to requesting and receiving information about safety and health conditions. They also have the right to refuse unsafe work without fear of reprisal.

Occupational health and safety laws also require supervisors to advise employees of potential workplace hazards; ensure that workers use or wear safety equipment, devices, or clothing; provide written instructions where applicable; and take every reasonable precaution to guarantee the safety of workers. As you will read later in Chapter 3, the supervisor is key in creating a healthy and safe work environment. The supervisor is the point of contact for almost every question regarding health and safety. Further, the supervisor will reinforce safety and health training, and will be the person held accountable for the employees' understanding and behaviour regarding health and safety in the workplace.

Lastly, most jurisdictions require the formation of health and safety committees operated jointly by employee and management representatives. This arrangement is intended to create a nonadversarial climate in which labour and management work together to create a safe and healthy workplace.

Individuals doing construction work must follow safety procedures to avoid accidents and injuries.

Aigars Reinholds/Shutterstock.com

EMPLOYMENT AND PAY EQUITY

Central to Canada's economic growth and prosperity in a highly competitive global marketplace will be a barrier-free environment in which all Canadians can fully explore and develop their career potential. Labour force statistics, described in Chapter 1, indicate changing patterns of immigration, the rising labour force participation rates of women, and an aging population with a proportionately higher incidence of disabilities. Women, visible minorities, First Nations people, and people with disabilities are the designated groups under the federal employment equity legislation. These designated-group members entering Canada's labour pool constitute a vital resource, and their full participation in the workplace will be fundamental to an organization's ability to understand and respond to the needs of a rapidly changing marketplace.

Employment Equity

Equity by definition means fairness or impartiality. In a legal sense, it means justice based on the concepts of ethics and fairness and a system of jurisprudence administered by courts and designed primarily to decrease the rigidity of common law. The implementation of **employment equity** has involved the establishment of policies and practices designed to ensure equitable representation in the workforce and to redress past discriminations as they relate to employment and employment practices.

Employment equity
A distinct Canadian process for achieving equality in all aspects of employment

The Law on Employment Equity

The *Employment Equity Act* requires that the federal government, federal agencies, and Crown corporations with 100 employees or more and that are regulated under the *Canada Labour Code* must implement employment equity and report on their results. Some of the companies covered by the *Employment Equity Act* are Royal Bank, Rogers Foods Ltd., General Electric Canada, Brinks Canada Limited, and Metro Vancouver Port Authority. Under the act the employer is required to develop plans to better represent the **designated groups** as mentioned above. In creating the plan, the employer must identify and remove any employment barriers, such as a keyboarding test for jobs in which no keyboarding is required. Further, the plan must have a timetable for achieving these changes. Although this law does not extend to the provinces, the federal government, through its Federal Contractors Program, expects organizations that do business with the federal government, such as 3M Canada, General Electric Canada, GlaxoSmithKline, and PricewaterhouseCoopers, to implement employment equity principles.[39]

Designated groups
Women, visible minorities, Aboriginal peoples, and persons with disabilities who have been disadvantaged in employment

While there are no specific provincial acts pertaining to employment equity, the concept of employment equity is rooted in federal and provincial employment standards legislation, human rights codes, and the *Canadian Charter of Rights and Freedoms*. Employment equity involves the identification and removal of systemic barriers to employment opportunities that adversely affect designated groups. It also involves the implementation of special measures and reasonable accommodation (discussed earlier under "Discrimination"). The employment equity legislation identified 4 designated groups in Canada that had not received equitable treatment in employment—women, visible minorities, First Nations peoples, and people with disabilities—recognizing that they faced significant but different disadvantages in employment. Some of the disadvantages included high unemployment, occupational segregation, pay inequities, and limited opportunities for career progress. While there has been progress since the introduction of the legislation in the mid-1980s, some of the original concerns have not been advanced very far.

While women represent 48% of people employed,[40] the employment tends to be concentrated in education (70%), accommodation and food services (58%), and health care (82%).[41] On the other hand, women tend to be underrepresented in mining, oil and gas (20%), and manufacturing (26%). But they are close to being equally represented (44%) with men (56%) in recreation and cultural jobs.[42]

The number of Aboriginal people is only about 4.3%[43] of the population, with an increase of over 20% between 2006 and 2011.[44] The numbers of young Aboriginal workers will increase, and in western Canada they will account for a substantial portion of labour market growth. However, many Aboriginal people face major employment barriers, which may be compounded by low educational achievement and lack of job experience, as well as language and cultural barriers. In urban centres, many Aboriginal workers are concentrated in low-paying, unstable employment. Economic self-sufficiency and participation in the economy are seen as essential to Aboriginal development. At Work with HRM 2.3 describes the success of several organizations in assisting Aboriginal people to become an integral part of their workforces.

Visible-minority groups vary in their labour force profiles and in their regional distributions. Toronto and Vancouver have large visible-minority populations. Studies have shown that Latin Americans and Southeast Asians experience lower-than-average incomes, higher rates of unemployment, and reduced access to job interviews, even for those persons with the same qualifications as other candidates. Systemic barriers that have a negative employment impact on visible minorities can include culturally biased aptitude tests, lack of recognition of foreign credentials, and excessive levels of language requirements. Recent statistics indicate that the 19% of the Canadian population are visible minorities with that

AT WORK WITH HRM 2.3

CANADA'S TOP EMPLOYERS!

More and more organizations are being recognized for the work they are doing to enhance employment for First Nations people. Canada's Top 100 Employers 2015 honoured a number of companies for this work. Among the award recipients was Cameco Corporation for the large number of Aboriginal people it employs. Further, it has focused on recruiting people from northern Saskatchewan, most of whom are Aboriginal. In addition, it is working with an apprenticeship committee to employ over 600 Aboriginal people. Likewise, Manitoba Hydro was recognized for establishing an Aboriginal Sharing Circle and recruiting Aboriginal students for employment from the University of Manitoba's engineering and business schools.

Home Depot received its award for participating in a formal recruitment activity as well as joining a business roundtable that helps to create employment opportunities for Aboriginal youth in Toronto.

Canada Mortgage and Housing Corporation was recognized for its efforts in recruiting Aboriginals in partnership with Aboriginal Human Resource Council and for an internship program.

CRITICAL THINKING QUESTIONS:

1. What has the company you are working for (or have recently worked for) done to assist visible minorities, people with disabilities, and Aboriginal people in getting hired?
2. Is there more they could do? If so, please explain.

Source: Adapted from "Canada's Top 100 Employers 2014," February 10, 2014, accessed January 18, 2015, www.canadastop100.com/diversity.

number becoming over 31% in another 15 years.[45] It is also projected that Toronto and Vancouver will have 60% of their populations as visible minorities in the same timeframe.[46]

People with disabilities represent approximately 11% of the Canadian population, and only about one-half of them are employed, as against 79% of Canadians without a disability.[47] People with disabilities face attitudinal barriers, physical demands unrelated to actual job requirements, and inadequate access to the technical and human support systems that would make productive employment possible. It is encouraging to note that more and more small business owners are hiring people with a disability, which helps create a more inclusive and diverse workforce that leads to better business performance.[48]

The employment experiences of people with disabilities are also dependent on their level of education. In most cases, people with minor limitations and who are university graduates do not experience as many barriers as those with little education or more extreme limitations.[49]

As mentioned earlier in the chapter, these employment practices can unintentionally exclude certain segments of our population from employment opportunities. Toolkit 2.2 gives examples of suggested solutions to systemic barriers.

Benefits of Employment Equity

Employment equity makes good business sense, since it contributes to the bottom line by broadening the base of qualified individuals for employment, training, and promotions, and by helping employers to avoid costly human rights complaints. Most provinces now take an active approach to ensuring there is appropriate representation in their workforces. For example, the Manitoba Civil Service Commission believes a diverse employee base can better serve the citizens of Manitoba.[50] Likewise, organizations such as Loblaw Companies Limited in Ontario have created a dedicated network for female staff that helps with their development in the company.[51]

Employment and Social Development Canada, through its Labour Program, administers the federal *Employment Equity Act*, and through annual reports it provides statistical information about the successes of organizational initiatives in achieving a more representative workforce. In the most recent report, visible minorities' participation rate has been achieved, whereas women, people with disabilities, and Aboriginal peoples are still underrepresented.[52]

For additional information on the *Employment Equity Act*, visit ESDC's website at **www.esdc.gc.ca**.

Employment and Social Development Canada (ESDC)
www.esdc.gc.ca

TOOLKIT 2.2 EXAMPLES OF EMPLOYMENT PRACTICES

1. *Word-of-mouth recruiting*. While this is a common form of making job opportunities known to family and friends, it is better to have a formal job posting that can also be targeted to particular underrepresented groups.
2. *Job requirements*. Employers that require Canadian experience may be excluding visible minorities, particularly recent immigrants. It is important to assess all prior experiences and have culturally neutral qualifications.
3. *Training and development*. It is important to review the organization's approach to training of its employees and ensure that appropriate training is available to all.
4. *Promotion and advancement*. Opportunities for changes should be widely communicated in the organization. Also, when reviewing performance, all employees need to be measured using the same criteria.
5. *Organizational environment*. It is a good idea to have flexible work arrangements to handle work and family obligations.

Source: Adapted from Ontario Human Rights Commission, "Appendix—Workplace Policies, Practices and Decision-Making Processes and Systemic Discrimination," accessed January 18, www.ohrc.on.ca/en/policy-and-guidelines-racism-and-racial-discrimination/appendix-%E2%80%93-workplace-policies-practices-and-decision-making-processes-and-systemic-discrimination; and Manitoba Civil Service Commission, "Principles & Policies for Managing Human Resources: 1.5.2 Removing Employment Barriers," accessed September 3, 2015, www.gov.mb.ca/csc/policyman/removbar.html#one.

First Nations University is a unique Canadian university that creates a learning environment about First Nations culture and values.

First Nations University

Pay Equity

Pay equity
The practice of equal pay for work of equal value

As a result of a 1978 amendment to the *Canadian Human Rights Act*, **pay equity**—equal pay for work of equal value—became law. Federal pay equity law makes it illegal for federally regulated employers to discriminate against individuals on the basis of job content. The focus of pay equity legislation is to narrow the wage gap between men and women, on the basis that women's work historically has been undervalued and therefore underpaid relative to work primarily done by men. For example, the average hourly wage of males who worked full time in 2014 was $26.79, but only $23.10 for women.[53] One of the principles behind pay equity is gender neutrality, designed to reduce systematic discriminatory pay practices.[54]

Pay equity is based on two principles. The first is equal pay for equal work. Equal pay for equal work means that if a woman and a man are doing substantially the same work for the same organization or company, they must receive the same wage unless the difference is due to a formal seniority system, a temporary training assignment, or merit pay.[55] Equal pay for equal work is regulated through basic employment conditions legislation, usually titled *Employment Standards Act.*

The second principle of pay equity is equal pay for work that may be comparable in value to the organization. Pay equity compares the value and pay of different jobs. This means male and female workers must be paid the same wage rate for jobs of comparable value, such as nurse (historically female-dominated work) and electrician (historically male-dominated).

Implementation of pay equity is based on comparing jobs performed mostly by women with jobs performed mostly by males. Comparisons require the use of a gender-neutral job comparison system to evaluate the jobs in the organization.[56] The value of the work is based on the skills and effort required, the responsibilities of the job, and the conditions under which the work is performed. It is important to remember that the comparisons are made on job content, not on the performance of the employee. The comparison must be done in such a way that the characteristics of "male" jobs, such as stockroom attendants who lift and organize groceries, are valued fairly in comparison with the characteristics of "female" jobs, cashiers who lift and bag groceires.[57] For example, under pay equity, Canadian National Railways would need to compare the work of an accounts payable clerk with that of a person who repairs the train cars.

The federal pay equity legislation applies to the workforce under its jurisdiction and covers all organizations regardless of number of employees. The system is complaint-based, meaning that an employee, a group of employees, or a union can raise complaints. However, it can take years for complaints to be resolved.

For example, it took 28 years to resolve a pay equity case involving Canada Post! The case was originally filed with the Canadian Human Rights Tribunal in 1983 and involved pay comparisons with clerical workers (primarily female) to operations jobs, such as letter carriers (primarily male). The tribunal initially upheld the complaint, and then the issue went through years of various appeals. Finally in 2005, a decision that upheld the complaint was made, and it was appealed to the Supreme Court of Canada. In November 2011, the Court reinstated the original award, which will now cost Canada Post approximately $250 million.[58] However, as of 2015, Canada Post was still processing the payments as each employee file had to be thoroughly reviewed to ensure the 30-year information was accurate.[59]

Pay equity legislation is in 6 provinces: Manitoba, New Brunswick, Nova Scotia, Ontario, Prince Edward Island, and Quebec. While British Columbia, Newfoundland, and Saskatchewan have no legislation, they've developed frameworks for negotiations with some public sector unions. Alberta has no legislation.[60] There is not always a requirement that there be pay equity legislation in a province to launch a complaint there regarding pay issues. For example, a recent case was launched in British Columbia that claimed equal pay was denied due to gender discrimination. Three female pulp mill employees stated they were discriminated against in pay because of their gender because all the male employees in the same positions were paid more.[61]

Ontario Pay Equity Commission
www.payequity.gov.on.ca/en/index.php

Canadian Human Rights Commission
www.chrc-ccdp.ca

Nova Scotia Pay Equity Commission
http://novascotia.ca/lae/payequity

For more information on pay equity, check the following sites: **www.payequity.gov.on.ca/en/index.php, www.chrc-ccdp.ca, and http://novascotia.ca/lae/payequity**.

Even though there have been recent changes in some of the employment legislation described at these sites, changes will continue as Canadian social values change. See Emerging Trends 2.1 for things to watch.

EMERGING TRENDS 2.1

Several recent significant court decisions may have an impact on the rights of both employees and employers. Here are a few items to consider:

1. *Workplace accommodations.* With many young parents in the workforce, as well as individuals who are looking after aging parents and a workforce that is getting older, employers will need to pay careful attention to requests for accommodation—particularly those involving "family status." Requests due to mental illness and addictions might also increase. Further, more and more employers are recognizing that people with varying degrees of disability are ignoring the "dis-" and looking at abilities. In doing so, employers are making all aspects of the work environment and culture barrier-free.
2. *Psychological harassment and assaults.* With such high-profile cases as that of Ghomeshi, increased attention is being paid to what employers do regarding allegations of harassment and the health of the workplace. Employers have been penalized with large fines for not taking complaints seriously or for inadequate investigations. For example, one Toronto restaurant became well known in June 2015 when 3 female chefs filed sexual harassment charges. Other restaurants have reacted, and have used cases like this to have frank discussions with staff about the need to have a different culture and treat everyone with respect. Since sexual banter is such a part of the kitchen world, some chefs are having difficulty knowing what to say and do.
3. *Workplace culture.* With the inclusion of bullying in some provincial health and safety legislation, as well as bullying being considered harassment and therefore contrary to human rights, more court and tribunal cases are dealing with cases involving a toxic environment. Employers will need to be watchful to ensure that managers, supervisors, and employees conduct themselves appropriately at work.

continued

4. *Financial penalties for human rights violations.* In both human rights tribunals as well as civil courts, decisions against employers are having increased financial costs for back pay and damages. While there is a limit on how much can be assessed for fines, there is no limit on the amount for damages.
5. *Gender discrimination.* As more employees identify themselves as being part of the LGBT community, organizations that have tended to have a culture that is very male-oriented will need to take extra steps to ensure there are no challenges of discrimination and/or harassment. Further, organizations such as RBC identify that the culture of any organization must support and encourage all employees to embrace full diversity.

Sources: Adapted from Fasken Martineau, "Blockbuster Annual Update," Labour, Employment, Human Rights and Privacy 2014, October 1, 2014; Liz Bernier, "Human Rights Policy Clarifies Mental Health, Addiction," *Canadian HR Reporter*, July 14, 2014, 1; Daniel Chodos, "Accommodating Disability in the Workplace: The Trials and Tribulations," *Canadian HR Reporter Webinar*, access January 19, 2015, www.hrreporter.com/webinardisplay/167-accommodating-disability-in-the-workplace-the-trials-and-tribulations; Nicola Middlemiss, "CBC Accused of 'Looking the Other Way' over Workplace Harassment," *HRM Online*, December 3, 2014; Sarah Dobson, "Health Cultures, Reduced Costs," *Canadian HR Reporter*, November 17, 2014, accessed January 19, 2015, www.hrreporter.com/articleview/22808-healthy-cultures-reduced-costs; Geoffrey Breen, "Surprising Reinstatement Decision of the Human Rights Tribunal Upheld," October 10, 2014, accessed January 19, 2015, www.casselsbrock.com/CBNewsletter/Surprising_Reinstatement_Decision_of_the_Human_Rights_Tribunal_Upheld; "Top 10 Employment and Labour Law Cases & Trends in 2014," December 9, 2014, accessed January 19, 2014, www.casselsbrock.com/CBNewsletter/Top_10_Employment_and_Labour_Law_Cases___Trends_in_2014; Daniel Lublin, "Fallout Spreading from Big Workplace Cases," *The Globe and Mail*, January 28, 2015, B17; Liz Bernier, "Pursuing Their Fullest Potential," *Canadian HR Reporter*, January 26, 2015, 3; Tavia Grant, "The Disability Edge," *The Globe and Mail*, February 28, 2015, B6; Jennifer Lewington, "Builders, Landlords Adjust to Barrier-Free Rules," *The Globe and Mail*, April 7, 2015, B6; and Chris Nuttall-Smith, "Kitchen Fires," *The Globe and Mail*, June 20, 2015, A13.

DIVERSITY

LO6

What is the relationship between employment equity and diversity?

Diversity management
The combination of organizational policies and practices that supports and encourages employee differences in order to reach business objectives

Inclusion
Putting the concept of diversity into action

Managing diversity goes beyond any legislation in addressing the need to create a fair work environment. The terms "diversity management" and "employment equity" are often used interchangeably, but there are differences. **Diversity management** is voluntary; employment equity is not. Managing diversity is a broader concept encompassing such factors as religion, personality, lifestyle, and education. Frequently you will hear organizations talk about **inclusion** as part of diversity. While diversity refers to our differences, inclusion is putting into action all those differences to create a very successful organization.[62] An inclusive environment leads to enhanced employee engagement, provides a brand image of best place to work, and serves customers better.[63] In August 2014 Deloitte Canada, a professional services firm, released a report that noted a diverse workforce not only is better for our society but also increases organizational capacity and innovation to help the company succeed.[64] And further research conducted by McKinsey & Company determined that companies can be as much as 30% more likely to have financial results higher than their competition.[65]

According to Statistics Canada, much of the increase of our total population over the next 20 years will be due to immigration.[66] In this context, diversity management is not merely a legal obligation but rather a requirement for company success. It is also not just about racial and cultural background, but also about accepting and understanding differences. One of the more progressive firms is Sodexo Canada, a company that provides a variety of life services, and uses its diverse talents to both benefit clients and achieve its business objectives. As Dean Johnson, the Canadian president and CEO says, "It's vital from a business perspective."[67] Other organizations take inclusion a step further by supporting LGBT employees. See At Work with HRM 2.4 for a fuller description of TD Bank's leading-edge approach to inclusion.

Statistics show that the ethnocultural profile of Canada has been changing since the 1960s and will continue to change dramatically given the federal government's immigration policy. According to the most recent census data (2011), 20% of the Canadian population is visible minorities and over 4% are Aboriginal.[68] The top nonofficial languages (i.e., neither French nor English) spoken by Canadians are, in ranked order, Chinese (all dialects), Tagalog (Phillipines), Spanish, and Punjabi.[69]

AT WORK WITH HRM 2.4

TD BANK GOES A STEP FURTHER!

It has only been a few years, but already TD Bank is standing out among employers that truly endeavour to have an inclusive workplace. About 10 years ago, TD's CEO, Ed Clark, spoke out in support of gay rights; he is now advocating for full support for all LGBT in all communities. This seemed a natural progression, as TD Bank had been offering same-sex benefits since 1994.

However, TD is no longer the only financial institution expressing support for inclusion. RBC made headlines in Toronto in mid-2014 when it draped rainbow flags to support the WorldPride summit. Doing so gave a very visible representation to LGBT concerns in what might be considered a very conservative industry. BMO has similarly pushed for internal diversity for many years, and understands the impact it can have on business outcomes.

And it isn't in just the financial services that are becoming more aware of cultures that are not inclusive. Bay Street and its Type-A business environment is seeing more people feeling comfortable enough to publicly identify themselves within the lesbian, gay, bisexual, transgender (LGBT) community. Individuals working in places such as Acasta Capital and TD Asset Management are supporting the change and speaking openly about themselves. Likewise, the CEO of Accenture, who is openly gay, has indicated that business is lacking LGBT leaders and that organizations need to do more to support diversity that acknowledges LGBT leaders. He feels that such diversity is good for business.

As employers in Canada continue to seek qualified and experienced staff, more are looking at how inclusive their organizations really are. These companies are undertaking significant re-examination of their policies and how the words play out in actions in relation to LGBT individuals. Only through education and open conversation will employers realize an inclusive environment where differences are recognized and celebrated.

CRITICAL THINKING QUESTION:

Can you think of other initiatives that organizations can adopt to help create a positive work environment that supports diversity and inclusion?

Source: Adapted from Tim Kiladze, "Canada's Banks Take Pride in Message of LGBT Support," *The Globe and Mail*, June 26, 2014, B1; Tim Kiladze, "Being Gay on Bay Street," *The Globe and Mail*, June 28, 2014, A13; and Nicola Middlemiss, "We Need More LGBT Leaders—Says Accenture CEO," *HRM Online*, January 29, 2015.

CEOs in Canada recognize the importance of diversity in their overall business strategy. As Canadian companies compete in the global marketplace, it is important that they do more than just have a diverse workforce—they need to ensure that those employees are engaged and developed.[70]

The importance of having diversity and inclusion does not extend only to established organizations. The Pan Am Games, held in Toronto in 2015, have developed diversity policies that cover everything from governance to employees to volunteers to suppliers. These policies recognize the economic impact of the Games to people who might have been underrepresented in large projects in the past. As Bill Zakarow, Director of Procurement, TO2015, says, "Diversity is reflected in both our employee and supplier base because we know it's going to be reflected in our customer base."[71]

While CEOs may recognize the importance of diversity, there are still ample examples of immigrants struggling to gain employment opportunities in their chosen field of study or experience. There is, therefore, a continuing need to create programs and other ways to tap into a vital and talented component of our population and maximize the country's human capital. Canada's economic growth will be dependent on employers making use of the talent immigrants bring. That is why organizations such as Toronto Region Immigrant Employment Council (TRIEC) created the Immigrant Success Awards to recognize leadership in immigrant employment.[72]

It is important to remember that in Canada, diversity also includes Aboriginal peoples. A recent strategy was developed in New Brunswick to assist Aboriginals get jobs in the shipbuilding industry. It is designed to also create opportunities for Aboriginal communities to participate in building businesses that support that industry.[73] Another example of diversity success is described in At Work with HRM 2.5, which showcases the business successes of an Aboriginal group in the interior of British Columbia.

Creating an Environment for Success

Transforming an organizational culture into one that embraces diversity and is inclusive can be a complex and lengthy process. Diversity and inclusion initiatives should be taken slowly so that everyone can understand that this change is an evolutionary process and that expectations should be realistic.

Leadership is one of the most important variables in an organization's ability to successfully incorporate the value of diversity into its business strategy. Canadian businesses also have an opportunity to focus their strategies to evolve the cultures to continue on the path to inclusion.[74]

AT WORK WITH HRM 2.5

NOW THAT'S BUSINESS SUCCESS!

Chief Clarence Louie is very proud of the successes his community has achieved. As Chief of the Osoyoos Indian Band and CEO of Osoyoos Indian Band Development Corporation in British Columbia, he has provided leadership and vision for the band to excel in a number of enterprises. He has been recognized with numerous awards, including Chairman of the Aboriginal Business Canada Board.

During the last 30 years the band has created a large and successful business enterprise on the band's 13,000 ha of land, of which about a third is vineyards. The band businesses include Nk'Mip vineyards, Nk'Mip Gas & Convenience Store, Nk'Mip construction, Oliver Readi Mix, Nk'Mip Golf Course, Nk'Mip Campground & RV Park, the first Aboriginal winery in North America—Nk'Mip Cellars and Nk'Mip Desert Cultural Centre—an eco-cultural centre that promotes Okanagan Native heritage and culture, and Spirit Ridge Vineyard Resort and Spa. All of the band's business interests are handled through the Osoyoos Indian Band Development Corporation of which Spirit Ridge Vineyard Resort and Spa is its premium accommodation.

The variety of businesses provides the band with numerous jobs, countless career opportunities for its members, and $26 million in annual revenue. The Osoyoos Indian Band prides itself in having low unemployment rates, a healthy economic outlook, and the potential for more business development. Chief Louie is a strong believer in education that he sees as making Aboriginals employable. He also is a strong believer in individuals being independent and self-sufficient. He does speak out about the need to teach Aboriginals how to work, how to have a work ethic, and how to focus on the economy—not just handing out money.

Louis is also quick to say that the band hasn't just done everything on its own, but has partnered wisely with outside business leaders. He brought in experts to help the band develop financial controls and created the Nk'Mip Cellars as a joint venture with Vincor.

Osoyoos Indian Band Development Corporation

Chief Clarence Louie

The band's latest project? Leasing some of its land for the B.C. government to build a new provincial prison. Through the relationship, he is hoping there will be employment opportunities for band members. This new initiative has had its share of criticism, given the history many First Nations have with justice systems throughout Canada. His response: "We need our band members working in that prison as role models."

Sources: Adapted from Osoyoos Indian Band, accessed January 20, 2015, www.oibdc.com; Jake MacDonald, "How a B.C. Native Band Went from Poverty to Prosperity," *Report on Business*, June 23, 2014, 43–54; and Roy MacGregor, "The Best Native Leader Canada Never Had," *The Globe and Mail*, August 16, 2014, A6.

As part of its commitment to its staff and clients, KPMG, a global consulting firm, understands the importance of a diverse workforce, and was named one of Canada's best diversity employers in 2015 for its initiatives such as creating a diversity, equity, and inclusion team responsible for the company's diversity strategy and appointing a Chief Diversity Officer responsible for the company achieving its diversity goals.[75] Likewise, Corus Entertainment Inc. was honoured for its partnerships with local universities and colleges to provide financial awards to Aboriginal students and students with disabilities.[76] Cameco, one of the world's largest uranium producers, is distinctive among employers for employing 3 elders at its mine sites where any worker can consult about home or work issues.[77]

Training is essential to the success of diversity implementation. A number of companies, such as CIBC, have created training activities that focus on diversity. CIBC developed a Manager Diversity Toolkit that trains leaders on how to promote diversity throughout the career of an employee.[78] The managers are helped to create an environment where everyone feels included.

Breaking down barriers is also an important part of diversity initiatives. Enbridge in Alberta (one of the Top 100 Employers in Canada) has undertaken a number of initiatives to encourage women in science, technology, engineering, and math (STEM). Two of the more notable ones are Females in Engineering, an outreach program that encourages young, female Aboriginal students to consider STEM careers; and there is also Women@ Enbridge, a resources group at Enbridge to support women through their careers.[79]

An added advantage of establishing a diversity initiative is its impact on employee retention. Keeping well-qualified and skilled employees is an important goal, considering the amount of resources, both in time and money, spent on recruiting and hiring new employees. The above-mentioned report of Deloitte's also identified that Canada's talent shortages are forcing organizations to look new sources of prospective employees.[80]

When establishing diversity initiatives, an overall review of policies and employment practices must be considered. The use of an employee attitude survey may prove beneficial in finding areas of systemic or perceived discrimination. The success indicators used most often by Canadian organizations are turnover rates, representation rates at key levels throughout the organization, employee engagement, and promotion rates.[81]

A final element in successful diversity initiatives is a performance indicator so that progress can be measured and monitored and everyone, particularly managers, can be held accountable.[82] Measuring management's performance with regard to diversity initiatives will instill those values in the minds of all employees and demonstrate that valuing diversity is part of day-to-day business. Another key to success is setting an example and creating an atmosphere that respects and values differences. Many Canadian organizations have recognized the competitive advantage to be gained by embracing diversity, and this will continue to assist Canada in its economic sustainability.

ORGANIZATIONAL ETHICS

LO7

What is the role of ethics in the management of human resources?

Throughout this chapter the legal requirements of HRM are emphasized. Laws and court decisions affect all aspects of the employment process—recruitment, selection, performance appraisal, safety and health, labour relations, and testing. Managers must comply with governmental regulations to promote an environment free from litigation.

However, beyond what is required by the law is the question of organizational ethics and the ethical—or unethical—behaviour engaged in by all employees. **Ethics** can be defined as a set of standards of acceptable conduct and moral judgment. Ethics provides cultural guidelines—organizational or societal—that help decide between proper and improper conduct. Therefore, ethics, like the legal aspects of HR, permeates all aspects of the employment relationship. For example, managers may adhere to the organization's objective of hiring more members of designated groups, but how those employees are supervised and treated once

Ethics
Set of standards of conduct and moral judgments that help to determine right and wrong behaviour

employed gets to the issue of managerial ethics. Compliance with laws and the behavioural treatment of employees are two completely different aspects of the manager's job.

While ethical dilemmas will always occur in the supervision of employees, how employees are treated is what largely distinguishes the ethical organization from the unethical one. An ethical organization recognizes and values the contributions of employees and respects their personal rights. And certainly some of the cases mentioned earlier in this chapter are reinforcing this belief.

Many organizations have their own codes of ethics that govern relations with employees and the public at large. These codes are formal written statements of the organization's primary values and provide a basis for the organization's and individual managers' behaviours and actions. For example, the Canadian Centre for Ethics and Corporate Policy (**www.ethicscentre.ca**) is designed to promote and practice ethical decision making, and in doing so ensures that its members have codes that are widely publicized. Among its members are Investors Group, Loblaw Companies Limited, BMO Financial Group, Four Seasons Hotels, and Walmart Canada.[83] Organizations now have ethics committees and ethics ombudspersons to provide training in ethics to employees.

Canadian Centre for Ethics and Corporate Policy
www.ethicscentre.ca

In addition, the Government of Canada has an ethics commissioner, reporting directly to the prime minister. The role of the commissioner is to help appointed and elected officials prevent and avoid conflicts between their public and private interests.[84] Provincial governments such as Alberta and New Brunswick also have ethics commissioners. The ultimate goal of ethics training and ethics commissioners is to avoid unethical behaviour and adverse publicity; to gain a strategic advantage; but most of all, to treat employees in a fair and equitable manner, recognizing them as productive members of the organization.

WHISTLEBLOWING

Even with codes of ethics and ethics committees, people do not always behave ethically. Organizations such as Canada Post encourage high standards of business conduct by providing examples of actions and behaviours that might be unethical.[85] When something unethical happens, employees will sometimes report an organization's unethical practices outside the organization. This is referred to as **whistleblowing**. People will sometimes not report unethical actions or behaviours, as they are concerned about revenge from those involved; but sometimes the unethical actions are so high-profile that they cannot be ignored. For example, in 2014, the Toronto Transit Commission created a hotline and website for whistleblowers after an investigation led to the arrest and prosecution of 6 current and former employees for purchasing equipment for personal use.[86] It also ordered ethics training for all supervisory and management staff.

Whistleblowing
Reporting unethical behaviour outside the organization

In order to ensure that employees understand the importance of dealing with unethical behaviour, leaders play a crucial role in reinforcing ethical behaviour by their own actions, as well as playing a role in encouraging and supporting whistleblowing.[87] Whether an organization is small or large, there are basic guidelines to follow: (1) be trustworthy, (2) maintain confidences, (3) be impartial and objective, (4) be fair, and (5) avoid any real or potential conflict of interest.[88]

Summary

1. Explain the impact of laws on the behaviour and actions of supervisors and managers.
   - Accepted practices and behaviours of supervisors and managers toward their employees are governed through a variety of employment legislation at both the provincial and federal levels.
   - Various laws establish certain minimum requirements regarding working conditions as well as providing protection of basic human rights.

2. Discuss the legal framework of HRM in Canada.
   - There are two distinct sets of legislation—federal and provincial.
   - The *Canadian Charter of Rights and Freedoms* is the cornerstone of contemporary employment legislation.
3. Describe discrimination and harassment in the workplace.
   - Discrimination is denying someone something because of race, ethnic background, marital status, or other prohibited grounds under human rights legislation.
   - Harassment is any behaviour that demeans, humiliates, or embarrasses a person.
   - Discrimination and harassment are illegal under human rights legislation.
4. Outline the line manager's role in creating a work environment that is free from harassment and discrimination.
   - Supervisor or manager needs to ensure that unacceptable behaviours are dealt with.
   - Supervisor is expected to work with employees to ensure that they are behaving and acting in an acceptable fashion.
   - Line manager is key link in creating an appropriate work environment.
5. Identify the general types of employment laws in Canada.
   - Employment standards legislation describes the basic obligations of employers.
   - Labour legislation governs both the process by which a trade union acquires bargaining rights and the procedures by which trade unions and employers engage in collective bargaining.
   - Health, safety, and workers' compensation legislation describes the expected standards for health and safety in the workplace and the impact if an employee is injured.
   - Human rights legislation prohibits discrimination on the basis of such areas as race, ethnic origin, marital status, and gender.
   - Human rights legislation is paramount over other employment laws.
   - Human rights legislation also protects individuals from all types of harassment.
6. Explain the relationship between employment equity and diversity.
   - Managing diversity not only incorporates but also goes beyond employment equity.
   - The goal of diversity management is to make optimal use of an organization's multicultural workforce in order to realize strategic business advantages.
   - Inclusion is putting diversity into action.
7. Discuss the concept of ethics in the management of human resources.
   - Ethics in HRM extends beyond the legal requirements of managing employees.
   - Managers engage in ethical behaviour when employees are treated in a fair and objective way and when an employee's personal and work-related rights are respected and valued.

Need to Know

- Relationship of Canadian Charter of Rights and Freedoms to employment laws
- Names of employment laws and what they do
- Definition of harassment and discrimination
- Purpose and definition of employment and pay equity
- Definition of diversity
- Definition of ethics

Need to Understand

- Impact of legislation on managerial actions
- Relationship of bona fide occupational requirements to discrimination
- Impact of reasonable accommodation on managerial action
- Relationship of managerial behaviours to harassment and discrimination

- Harassment as a form of discrimination
- Impact of employment practices and managerial decisions on fair employment opportunities
- Link between diversity and business performance
- Relationship of manager's actions and organizational ethics

KEY TERMS

bona fide occupational qualification (BFOQ) 42
designated groups 53
diversity management 58
employment equity 53
ethics 61
harassment 45
inclusion 58
pay equity 56
psychological harassment 48
reasonable accommodation 43
reverse discrimination 44
systemic discrimination 41
whistleblowing 62

REVIEW QUESTIONS

1. What are the 2 primary federal employment laws?
2. What is discrimination? What is harassment?
3. What is the name of the federal law that protects employees from harassment and discrimination?
4. What are the names of the general employment laws?
5. What is pay equity and why is it related to discrimination?
6. What is diversity? What is inclusion?
7. How would you define ethics?
8. Explain a code of ethics.

CRITICAL THINKING QUESTIONS

1. In the HRM Close-up, Matt Robinson states that entrepreneurs are at a high risk when it comes to HR issues? Why do you think he says this? What has he done to help reduce his risk?
2. While people know that harassment and discrimination are illegal, why would an employee or potential employee be reluctant to complain?
3. There is much concern about how people behave in the workplace and use words like "respectful" to indicate how employees are to treat everyone. What does respectful look like to you?
4. You see a part-time job posted in your community for a tutor in a specific foreign language that also requires that the tutor be from the country of that language. Would being from a specific country be a justifiable BFOQ? Why or why not?
5. You are a new branch manager of a large financial institution located in a medium-sized town. You know the company has a code of ethics that specifically states client information is confidential and not to be discussed or disclosed. You become aware that some staff are talking among themselves about some financial problems a prominent resident is having. How would you handle this and why?
6. A friend of yours has heard you are taking a business course that focuses on human resources management and wants some help. Your friend, a parent of 2 small children, has learned that the daycare is changing the closing hours from 6:00 p.m. to 5:30 p.m. Your friend's work ends at 5:00 p.m. and it takes approximately 45 minutes to get to the daycare. The organization at which your friend works has a large office complex

with more than 1,000 employees. Is this a case for reasonable accommodation? Why or why not?

DEVELOPING YOUR SKILLS

1. Much attention is given to the issue of harassment and discrimination in the workplace. The cornerstone to addressing this is achieving organizational awareness. Training can help raise awareness. Working in groups of 3 or 4, develop the outline of a training session that would raise awareness for a small company with 75 employees. The outline should include (1) topics to be covered, (2) specific examples of harassment and/or discrimination, (3) how complaints are to be made and to whom, and (4) who would attend the training.
2. Companies are concerned about bullying at work and want to do what they can to prevent it. Watch the video "Bully Free At Work: The Facts on Workplace Bullying," at **www.youtube.com/watch?v=V-q2VRAxjh8**. Working in groups of 2 or 3, determine whether you have encountered bullying at work. If so, what did you do and why? Did your actions improve the workplace environment?
3. Working in pairs, list as many jobs as you can in which an employer could justify "female only" applicants based on a BFOQ.
4. Using any search engine, conduct a search on the phrase "workplace inclusion." Review the first 10 matches and determine if they would be helpful resources. Prepare a 1–2-page summary of the results of your search, indicating whether the sites were useful and how an employer might make use of the information.
5. Access the Fairmeasures Inc. site at **www.fairmeasures.com** and go to the "Workplace Issues" drop-down menu, and click on "Business Ethics." Read the various FAQs and pick one to explore further. Access each specific example and read the explanation. Prepare a 1-page analysis about why you picked the question and what you learned.
6. Using any search engine, search on the phrase "company codes of ethics." What are the top 10 listings? Are any companies included? If so, which ones? Find at least 3 different companies with codes of ethics and compare one to the other. Are there any similarities? If so, what? Prepare a short summary of your findings.
7. Working in a group of 4 to 5 students, identify the ethical dilemmas that might arise in the areas of selection, performance reviews, health and safety, privacy rights, and compensation.

Fair Measures Inc.
www.fairmeasures.com

CASE STUDY 1

Accommodation Using Google?

Using Google to search and research information is a way of life for most Canadians. And while that is a very good source of information, it may not be sufficient to demonstrate that an employer has thoroughly investigated a request for accommodation. An Ontario human rights case illustrates that an employer needs to do more than just Google.

The company had an employee who was terminated 3 months after being hired. The person claimed the company had discriminated on the basis of their attention deficit hyperactivity disorder (ADHD). They had met with the manager to inform the manager of the disorder. In order to see what tasks might be done, the manager did a Google search on

ADHD. While the manager could not find any information relevant to the work done by the employee, some general information was acquired. At the hearing, the company stated that the employee did not have the technical abilities to perform the job and was terminated for those reasons. It further stated that any more accommodation due to the ADHD would be an undue hardship.

The tribunal concluded that the company had failed in its duty to accommodate, as it had not made an individual assessment of the employee's needs by seeking information from a doctor but relied on only general information. Whether or not the job requirements were legitimate BFOQs had not been adequately investigated for the employee and therefore the employee had been discriminated against.

The employee was awarded $10,000 in damages and the employer was ordered to retain an expert in human rights to audit and fix any gaps in any of its human rights procedures.

Source: Adapted from Megan Rolland, "Google: Not a Replacement for Individualized Accommodation," Fasken Martineau site, January 31, 2015, www.fasken.com/en/google-not-a-replacement-for-individualized-accommodation.

Questions:

1. Do you think any request for accommodation has to be thoroughly considered from an individual employee's perspective? Why or why not?
2. What could the company do now to prevent this in the future?
3. If you were a manager and an employee requested accommodation due to a medical condition, what would you do first? Explain.

CASE STUDY 2

Is Genetic Testing for Work Purposes Ethical?

Chantale Leroux works as a clerk for Avco Environmental Services, a small toxic-waste disposal company.

The company has a contract to dispose of medical waste from a local hospital. During the course of her work, Chantale comes across documents that suggest that Avco has actually been disposing of some of this waste in a local municipal landfill. Chantale is shocked. She knows this practice is illegal. And even though only a small portion of the medical waste that Avco handles is being disposed of this way, any amount at all seems a worrisome threat to public health.

Chantale gathers together the appropriate documents and takes them to her immediate superior, Dave Lamb. Dave says, "Look, I don't think that sort of thing is your concern, or mine. We're in charge of record-keeping, not making decisions about where this stuff gets dumped. I suggest you drop it."

The next day, Chantale decides to go one step further, and talk to Angela van Wilgenburg, the company's operations manager. Angela, clearly irritated, says, "This isn't your concern. Look, these are the sorts of cost-cutting moves that let a little company like ours compete with our giant competitors. Besides, everyone knows that the regulations in this area are overly cautious. There's no real danger to anyone from the tiny amount of medical waste that 'slips' into the municipal dump. I consider this matter closed."

Chantale considers her situation. The message from her superiors was loud and clear. She strongly suspects that making any more noise about this issue could jeopardize her job. Further, she generally has faith in the company's management. They've always seemed like honest, trustworthy people. But she is troubled by this apparent disregard for public safety. On the other hand, she asks herself whether maybe Angela was right in arguing the danger was minimal. She looks up the phone number of an old friend who works for the local newspaper.

Source: Reprinted by permission of Chris MacDonald, Businessethics.ca.

Questions:

1. What should Chantale do?
2. What are the reasonable limits on loyalty to one's employer?
3. Would it make a difference if Chantale had a position of greater authority?
4. Would it make a difference if Chantale had scientific expertise?

APPENDIX

Web Sites for Employment Legislation

1. Federal Government
    - Canada Labour Code: **http://laws.justice.gc.ca/en/L-2**
    - Canadian Human Rights Act: **http://laws-lois.justice.gc.ca/eng/acts/h-6**
    - Worker's compensation agency: **www.canoshweb.org**
2. Province of Alberta
    - Employment Standards Code: **www.qp.alberta.ca/documents/Acts/E09.pdf**
    - Labour Relations Code: **www.alrb.gov.ab.ca/alrb_code.htm**
    - *Occupational Health and Safety Act*: **www.employment.alberta.ca/SFW/295.html**
    - Workers' Compensation Board of Alberta: **www.wcb.ab.ca**
    - *Alberta Human Rights Act*: **www.qp.alberta.ca/documents/Acts/A25P5.pdf**
3. Province of British Columbia
    - *EmploymentStandardsAct*:**www.bclaws.ca/Recon/document/ID/freeside/00_96113_01**
    - Labour Relations Code: **www.bclaws.ca/Recon/document/ID/freeside/00_96244_01**
    - *Workers' Compensation Act*: **www.bclaws.ca/Recon/document/ID/freeside/96492_00**
    - WorkSafeBc: **www.worksafebc.ca**
    - Human Rights Code: **www.bclaws.ca/EPLibraries/bclaws_new/document/ID/freeside/00_96210_01**
4. Province of Manitoba
    - Employment Standards Code: **www.gov.mb.ca/labour/standards/index.html**
    - *Labour Relations Act*: **http://web2.gov.mb.ca/laws/statutes/ccsm/l010e.php**
    - *Workplace Safety and Health Act*: **http://web2.gov.mb.ca/laws/statutes/ccsm/w210e.php**
    - Workers' Compensation Board of Manitoba: **www.wcb.mb.ca**
    - Human Rights Code: **http://web2.gov.mb.ca/laws/statutes/ccsm/h175e.php**
5. Province of New Brunswick
    - *Employment Standards Act:* **www.gnb.ca/labour**
    - *Industrial Relations Act:* **www.gnb.ca/labour**
    - *Occupational Health and Safety Act:* **www.gnb.ca/leg1_e.asp**
    - *WorkSafeNB:* **www.worksafenb.ca**
    - *Human Rights Act:* **http://laws.gnb.ca/en/ShowPdf/cs/2011-c.171.pdf**
6. Province of Newfoundland and Labrador:
    - All statutes accessible with links to each law: **www.assembly.nl.ca**
    - Workplace Health, Safety and Compensation Commission: **www.whscc.nf.ca**
7. Province of Nova Scotia:
    - All statutes accessible with links to each law: **http://nslegislature.ca/legc/index.htm**
    - Workers' Compensation Board of Nova Scotia: **www.wcb.ns.ca**

8. Province of Ontario:
   - All statutes accessible with links to each law: **www.e-laws.gov.on.ca/navigation?file=home&lang=en**
   - Workplace Safety and Insurance Board: **www.wsib.on.ca**
9. Province of Prince Edward Island:
   - Electronic versions of legislation accessible by downloading PDF files: **www.gov.pe.ca/law/statutes**.
   - Workers' Compensation Board of Prince Edward Island: **www.wcb.pe.ca**
10. Province of Quebec:
    - All statutes accessible with links to each law: **http://www2.publicationsduquebec.gouv.qc.ca**
    - Commission de la santé et de la sécurité du travail au Québec: **www.csst.qc.ca**
11. Province of Saskatchewan:
    - *Saskatchewan Employment Act*: **www.publications.gov.sk.ca/details.cfm?p=70351&cl=5**
    - Saskatchewan Workers' Compensation Board: **www.wcbsask.com**
    - Human Rights Code: **www.qp.gov.sk.ca/documents/English/Statutes/Statutes/S24-1.pdf**
12. Government of Nunavut:
    - All statutes accessible with links to each law: **www.justice.gov.nu.ca**
    - Workers' Safety and Compensation Commission: **www.wcb.nt.ca**

NOTES AND REFERENCES

1. Service Canada, "Employment Insurance Compassionate Care Benefits," accessed January 5, 2015, www.servicecanada.gc.ca/eng/ei/types/compassionate_care.shtml#protected.
2. Service Canada, "Employment Insurance Maternity and Parental Benefits," accessed January 5, 2015, www.servicecanada.gc.ca/eng/ei/types/maternity_parental.shtml#eligible.
3. "David Langtry Speaks About Genetic Discrimination Before the Senate Committee on Human Rights, December 11, 2014, accessed January 5, 2015, www.chrc-ccdp.ca/eng/content/11122014-david-langtry-speaks-about-genetic-discrimination-senate-committee-human-rights.
4. Canadian Heritage, "The Canadian Charter of Rights and Freedoms," accessed January 6, 2015, www.pch.gc.ca/eng/1355260548180/1355260638531.
5. *Canadian Human Rights Act*, Section 2, Purpose of Act, accessed January 5, 2015, http://laws-lois.justice.gc.ca/eng/acts/h-6/page-1.html#h-2.
6. Janice Rubin, "Ageism Not Easy to Circumnavigate," *Canadian HR Reporter*, June 2, 2014, accessed January 20, 2015, www.hrreporter.com/articleview/21318-ageism-not-easy-to-circumnavigate.
7. Sarah Dobson, "Childcare Obligations Clarified in Federal Decision," *Canadian HR Reporter*, June 16, 2014, accessed January 5, 2015, www.hrreporter.com/articleview/21487-childcare-obligations-clarified-in-federal-decision.
8. "Protected Areas and Grounds Under the *Alberta Human Rights Act*," Alberta Human Rights Commission, accessed January 10, 2015, www.albertahumanrights.ab.ca/publications/bulletins_sheets_booklets/sheets/history_and_info/protected_areas_grounds.asp.
9. "Bona Fide Occupational Requirement (BFOR)," Saskatchewan Human Rights Commission, accessed January 10, 2015, http://saskatchewanhumanrights.ca/+pub/documents/policies_guidelines/Bona-Fide-Occupational-Requirement.pdf.
10. *McCormick v. Fasken Martineau DuMoulin LLP*, Judgments of the Supreme Court of Canada, May 22, 2014, accessed January 10, 2015, http://scc-csc.lexum.com/scc-csc/scc-csc/en/item/13663/index.do.
11. Canadian Human Rights Commission, "Bona Fide Occupational Requirements and Bona Fide Justifications Under the *Canadian Human Rights Act*: The Implications of *Meiorin* and *Grismer*," accessed January 10, 2015, www.chrc-ccdp.ca/sites/default/files/bfore_0.pdf.
12. For students who wish to understand in more detail the *Meiorin* case, access http://scc-csc.lexum.com/scc-csc/scc-csc/en/item/1724/index.do.
13. Jeffrey R. Smith, "Holdout for 'Perfect' Accommodation Fails," *Canadian HR Reporter*, November 14, 2014, 5.
14. Trevor Lawson, "Accommodating an Aging Workforce," *Canadian HR Reporter*, June 1, 2015, 15.
15. Liz Bernier, "Human Rights Policy Clarifies Mental Health, Addiction," *Canadian HR Reporter*, July 14, 2014, 1.
16. Kenneth Krupat, "Accommodating Religion," *Canadian HR Reporter*, January 27, 2014, accessed January 13, 2015, www.hrreporter.com/articleview/20012-accommodating-religion.
17. "What Is Harassment?" Canadian Human Rights Commission, accessed January 13, 2015, www.chrc-ccdp.ca/eng/content/what-harassment.
18. Adrian Humphreys, "Report Flays Culture of 'Big Egos' at the CBC," *The Vancouver Sun*, April 17, 2015, B1.
19. Simon Houpt, "CBC Ousts Two Executives as Scathing Report Details Abuse in Workplace," *The Globe and Mail*, April 17, 2015, A1.
20. "What Is Harassment?"
21. Newfoundland and Labrador Human Resource Secretariat, "Harassment and Discrimination-Free Workplace Policy," January 14, 2015, www.exec.gov.nl.ca/exec/hrs/working_with_us/harassment.html.
22. Humber Policy, "Human Rights Policy," accessed January 14, 2015, http://hrs.humber.ca/assets/files/human_rights/humanrightspolicy.June.28.pdf.
23. Ibid.
24. Alix P. Herber, "Inadequate Workplace Investigation Can Be Costly, *The HR Space*, Fasken Martineau, July 17, 2014.
25. "A Guide to Human Rights for Employers," Saskatchewan Human Rights Commission, accessed January 14, 2015, http://

saskatchewanhumanrights.ca/+pub/documents/publications/SHRC_Rights_Employers%20Guide.pdf.

26. Sarah Dobson, "Healthy Cultures, Reduced Costs," *Canadian HR Reporter*, November 17, 2014, accessed January 17, 2015, www.hrreporter.com/articleview/22808-healthy-cultures-reduced-costs; and "Bullying in the Workplace," Canadian Centre for Occupational Health and Safety, accessed January 17, 2015, www.ccohs.ca/oshanswers/psychosocial/bullying.html.
27. "Bullying in the Workplace."
28. Ibid.
29. "What Can We Expect?" Canadian Human Rights Commission, accessed January 17, 2015, www.chrc-ccdp.ca/eng/content/what-can-we-expect.
30. Maria Babbage, "Company Fined After Saying It 'Only Hires White Men,'" *The Globe and Mail*, September 9, 2014, A8.
31. Nicola Middlemiss, "Record Damages Awarded in Canadian Sexual Harassment Case," *HRM Online*, June 16, 2015, accessed July 6, 2015, www.hrmonline.ca/hr-news/record-damages-awarded-in-canadian-sexual-harassment-case-192401.aspx.
32. Employment Standards Regulations, Province of Alberta, accessed January 17, 2015, www.qp.alberta.ca/1266.cfm?page=1997_014.cfm&leg_type=Regs&isbncln=9780779733927.
33. Jeffrey R. Smith, "Commitment Issues," *Canadian HR Reporter*, November 4, 2014, accessed January 17, 2015, www.hrreporter.com/blog/Employment-Law/archive/2014/11/04/commitment-issues.
34. Colin Gibson, "Employer Obligations for Maternity Leave," *Canadian HR Reporter*, October 20, 2014, accessed January 17, 2015, www.hrreporter.com/articleview/22557-employer-obligations-for-maternity-leave.
35. Ontario Ministry of Labour, "Laws—Labour Relations," accessed January 17, 2015, www.labour.gov.on.ca/english/lr/laws/index.php.
36. Stuart Rudner, "Entitlement to Overtime," *Canadian HR Reporter*, April 14, 2015, accessed July 6, 2015, www.hrreporter.com/blog/Canadian-HR-Law/archive/2015/04/14/entitlement-to-overtime?utm_medium=Email&utm_campaign=HRNewswire_20150414&utm_source=Act-On%20Software&.
37. Statistics Canada, "Average Usual Hours and Wages of Employees by Selected Characteristics," accessed January 17, 2015, www.statcan.gc.ca/pub/71-001-x/2014012/t017-eng.htm; "Labour Force Survey, Employees by Union Status, Establishment Size, Job Tenure, Type of Work and Job Permanency," accessed January 17, 2015, www5.statcan.gc.ca/cansim/pick-choisir?lang=eng&p2=33&id=2820224; and Statistics Canada, "Labour Force Survey, Employees by Union Status, North American Industry Classification System," accessed January 17, 2015, www5.statcan.gc.ca/cansim/pick-choisir?lang=eng&p2=33&id=2820223.
38. Statistics Canada, "Labour Force Survey, Employees by Union Status, North American Industry Classification System," accessed January 17, 2015, www5.statcan.gc.ca/cansim/pick-choisir?lang=eng&p2=33&id=2820223.
39. "List of Certified Employers—Federal Contractors Program," Labour Program, Government of Canada, accessed January 17, 2015, http://www.labour.gc.ca/eng/standards_equity/eq/emp/fcp/list/a_z.shtml#B.
40. Statistics Canada, "Labour Force Survey Estimates by Sex and Detailed Age Group," 2014, accessed January 17, 2015, www5.statcan.gc.ca/cansim/a26.
41. Statistics Canada, "Labour Force Survey Estimates, by North American Industry Classification System, Sex and Age Group, December 2014, accessed January 17, 2015, www5.statcan.gc.ca/cansim/a47.
42. Ibid.
43. Statistics Canada, *Aboriginal People in Canada*, March 28, 2014, 4.
44. Ibid.
45. Douglas Quan, "Have Canada's Changing Demographics Made It Time to Retire the Concept of 'Visible Minority'?" *The National Post*, June 27, 2014, accessed January 18, 2015, http://news.nationalpost.com/2014/06/27/have-canadas-changing-demographics-made-it-time-to-retire-the-concept-of-visible-minority.
46. Ibid.
47. Statistics Canada, "Study: Persons with Disabilities and Employment," December 3, 2014.
48. "4 in 10 Small Business Owners Hiring People with Disabilities," *Canadian HR Reporter*, October 7, 2014, accessed January 17, 2015, www.hrreporter.com/articleview/22469-4-in-10-small-business-owners-hiring-people-with-disabilities.
49. Statistics Canada, "Study: Persons with Disabilities and Employment," December 3, 2014.
50. "Diversity and Employment Equity," Manitoba Civil Service Commission, accessed January 18, 2015, www.gov.mb.ca/csc/employment/emplequity.html.
51. "Canada's Top 100 Employers 2014," February 10, 2014, accessed January 18, 2015, www.canadastop100.com/diversity.
52. "*Employment Equity Act*: Annual Report 2013," Labour Program, Employment and Social Development, accessed January 18, 2015, www.labour.gc.ca/eng/standards_equity/eq/pubs_eq/annual_reports/2013/index.shtml.
53. Statistics Canada, "Average Hourly Wages of Employees by Selected Characteristics and Occupation," December 2014, accessed January 18, 2015, www.statcan.gc.ca/tables-tableaux/sum-som/l01/cst01/labr69a-eng.htm.
54. "Guiding Principles for Interpreting the Act," Ontario Pay Equity Commission, accessed January 19, 2015, www.payequity.gov.on.ca/en/resources/guide/ope/ope_3.php.
55. "An Overview of Pay Equity in Various Canadian Jurisdictions," Ontario Pay Equity Commission, accessed January 19, 2015, www.payequity.gov.on.ca/en/about/pubs/genderwage/pe_survey.php.
56. "Frequently Asked Questions About Pay Equity," Labour Program, accessed January 19, 2015, www.labour.gc.ca/eng/standards_equity/eq/pay/faq.shtml.
57. "What Is Pay Equity?" Executive Council Office, New Brunswick, accessed January 19, 2015, www.gnb.ca/0012/Womens-Issues/wg-es/payequity-e.asp.
58. "Human Resources Year in Review," *Canadian HR Reporter*, January 13, 2014, accessed January 19, 2015, www.hrreporter.com/articleview/19898-human-resources-year-in-review.
59. "Canada Post Makes Pay Equity Payment Slowly," Public Service Alliance of Canada, September 24, 2014, accessed January 19, 2015, http://psacunion.ca/canada-post-makes-pay-equity-payments-slowly.
60. "Canadian Pay Equity Requirements," Hay Group, 2014.
61. Laura Kane, "Tribunal to Hear Case of Women Who Claim Pay Discrimination," *The Vancouver Sun*, January 24, 2015, A8.
62. T. Hudson Jordan, "Moving from Diversity to Inclusion," *Diversity Journal*, December 2014, accessed January 19, 2015. www.diversityjournal.com/1471-moving-from-diversity-to-inclusion.
63. Stacia Sherman Garr, Karen Shellenback, and Jackie Scales, *Diversity and Inclusion in Canada: The Current State*, Deloitte Canada, August 2014, 17–18.
64. Ibid.
65. Vivian Hunt, Dennis Layton, and Sara Prince, "Why Diversity Matters," McKinsey and Company, January 20151
66. "Population Projections for Canada (2013 to 2063)," Statistics Canada, accessed January 20, 2015, www.statcan.gc.ca/pub/91-520-x/2014001/c-g/c-g2.4-eng.htm.
67. Liz Bernier, "Diversity Not Just About Compliance," *Canadian HR Reporter*, March 10, 2014, accessed January 20, 2015, www.hrreporter.com/articleview/20474-diversity-not-just-about-compliance.
68. Statistics Canada, *Immigration and Ethnocultural Diversity*, May 8, 2013, 4; and Statistics Canada, *Aboriginal People in Canada*, March 28, 2014, 4.

69. Ibid.
70. Alona Puehse, "Diversity and Inclusion: Open Doors of Opportunity," *PeopleTalk*, Winter 2014, 37.
71. "Toronto 201 Pam Am/Parapan Am Games: Using Diversity Supports Economic Growth," DiverseCity, accessed January 20, 2015, http://diversecitytoronto.ca/leadership-stories/organization-success-stories/toronto-2015-pan-amparapan-am-games-using-diversity-supports-economic-growth.
72. Liz Bernier, "Connecting Talent with Opportunities," *Canadian HR Reporter*, May 19, 2014, accessed January 20, 2015, www.hrreporter.com/articleview/21202-connecting-talent-with-opportunities.
73. "Shipbuilding Strategy to Create Opportunities for Aboriginal Workers in New Brunswick," *Canadian HR Reporter*, April 3, 2014, accessed January 20, 2015, www.hrreporter.com/articleview/20712-shipbuilding-strategy-to-create-opportunities-for-aboriginal-workers-in-new-brunswick.
74. Stacia Sherman Garr, Karen Shellenback, and Jackie Scales, *Diversity and Inclusion in Canada: The Current State*, Deloitte Canada, August 2014, 38.
75. Canada's Best Diversity Employers, November 4, 2014, accessed January 20, 2015, www.canadastop100.com/diversity.
76. Ibid.
77. "Cameco Has Deep Roots in Aboriginal Communities," *2015 Canada's Best Diversity Employers*, 12.
78. "Diversity Not Just About Compliance."
79. Ibid.
80. Stacia Sherman Garr, Karen Shellenback, and Jackie Scales, *Diversity and Inclusion in Canada: The Current State*, Deloitte Canada, August 2014, 38.
81. Ibid., 36.
82. Ibid., 39.
83. "Current Membership," Canadian Centre for Ethics & Corporate Policy, accessed January 23, 2015, www.ethicscentre.ca/EN/membership/current_membership.cfm.
84. "Welcome to the Office," Office of the Conflict of Interest and Ethics Commissioner, accessed January 23, 2015, http://ciec-ccie.parl.gc.ca/EN/Pages/default.aspx.
85. Canada Post Code of Conduct, 2014, 6–7.
86. "TTC Workers Arrested, Charged with Theft," *Canadian HR Reporter*, June 12, 2014, accessed January 23, 2015, www.hrreporter.com/articleview/21466-ttc-workers-arrested-charged-with-theft.
87. Sheng-min Liu, Jian-qiao Liao, and Hongguo Wei, "Authentic Leadership and Whistleblowing: Mediating Roles of Psychological Safety and Personal Identification," *Journal of Business Ethics*, January 2015, accessed January 23, 2015, http://link.springer.com/article/10.1007/s10551-014-2271-z.
88. "A Framework for Universal Principles of Ethics," W. Maurice Young Centre for Applied Ethics, University of British Columbia, accessed January 23, 2015, http://ethics.ubc.ca/papers/invited/colero-html.

3 Creating a Culture of Well-Being

LEARNING OUTCOMES

After studying this chapter, you should be able to

1. Describe organizational culture.
2. Explain the impact of organizational culture on employees.
3. Discuss the relationship of organizational culture and employee engagement.
4. Describe the link between culture and health and safety in the workplace.
5. Cite the measures to use to reduce health and safety concerns.
6. Explain the importance of building a culture of well-being.
7. Describe the programs and services that help create well-being in the organization.

OUTLINE

HRM CLOSE-UP

"We're not just investing in the company, we're investing in individuals."

Dave Holmes has just returned from Cambodia. He hadn't ventured there on vacation, although he does admit that he had a good time. Instead, he went to lead 45 employees on what some companies might call a staff meeting or a team-building exercise, but which Canadian tour operator G Adventures calls a "Purpose Camp."

"We've run these Purpose Camps before," Holmes, G Adventures' mayor explains. "We bring staff together for a four-day session where we talk about why we do the things the way that we do and what sets us apart, as opposed to the nuts and bolts of their day-to-day job."

G Adventures is the largest small-group adventure travel company in the world. From humble origins 25 years ago, the Toronto-based company now transports more than 100,000 people a year with revenues of over $300 million.

Yet, for all the exotic destinations they offer, G Adventures recognizes that there is one thing separating them from their rivals in the competitive adventure travel market: their people. "What sets us apart as a company is our company culture," says Dave Holmes. "What we hear from our travellers time and time again is that we have the best people working here."

And that difference is not by accident, as G Adventures puts a great deal of time and expense into creating a work environment that not only attracts the best people, but also retains them.

As mayor of G Adventures, Dave Holmes is responsible for maintaining morale and developing the company's culture of well-being. Part of his job is as a spokesperson representing the company to the outside world, and part is as a member of G-Force, an internal team whose job it is to make the company's almost 2,000 employees in 109 countries happy.

"We put a huge emphasis on workplace happiness," Holmes says. "So it's up to me and my team to come up with ways to make sure that people are happy, that they're looking forward to coming to work every day, and that everything we do, no matter what level of the organization someone's in, reflects our company core values. Basically it's a lot of fun."

As nice as it may sound to make staff happy, the end goal is as grounded in good business sense as it is in seeing smiles.

"We want our employees to be as happy as possible for a few reasons," Holmes explains. "Firstly, it relays onto our travellers and potential customers. Secondly, we believe in the wholesome approach to well-being. There are studies that happy employees are less likely to burn out on the job. Happy employees are more likely to think of innovative and creative ways to solve problems. Happy employees are more likely to show up to work every day. Not only is it good for the company, but it's also good for our staff, and we do care about our people here at G Adventures."

Used by permission of Dave Holmes.

Dave Holmes, Mayor, G Adventures.

Beyond meetings in exotic locales, G Adventures' positive culture extends to flexible hours, options to work from home, an openness to suggestions, and a special Toronto head office that houses a staff of 200.

"We've got very unique meeting rooms. We make them fun, happy places to be in where people want to be," Holmes says. "We've got video games, free coffee, free ice cream, beer o'clock on Fridays when everyone toasts the week with beer, wine, or cider, and we create that social atmosphere so that people are going to want to be here, want to have a good time, and want to contribute beyond simply what their role is."

Although G Adventures' quest for staff happiness has a financial cost, Holmes believes that that investment is quickly recovered. "If we make people more engaged and more happy, that will pay forward to our travellers and anyone who comes in contact with our brand," Holmes says. It also helps the company to retain staff and thereby recoup on the investment made in hiring and training. "The standard employee attrition rate for the travel industry is about 30%," he says. "We're at about 5% for every year."

"We're not just investing in the company," adds Holmes. "We're investing in individuals."

Source: Used by permission of Dave Holmes.

INTRODUCTION

While this chapter provides a fuller discussion of healthy and safe work environments, it does so from the perspective of the culture of the organization and how that impacts the well-being of the work environment. The last chapter discussed the work environment that supports a more diverse and inclusive workforce. To have such an environment, the values, actions, and behaviours need to reflect that. The same is true for a healthy and safe work environment—the collective values, actions, and behaviours need to demonstrate that a healthy and safe work environment is key to the organization's success. As you continue in this chapter, you will note that job stress and concern about the mental health of employees are increasing, and that how these issues are dealt with will depend greatly on everyone in the organization. In Chapter 2 you also learned about the increasing attention to harassment, including psychological harassment and bullying. Again, how these concerns are handled will be a reflection of the work environment and its culture. You will note from the HRM Close-up that G Adventures is very serious about its culture and the work it takes to maintain a culture that keeps everyone engaged. It is through the attention to the well-being of staff in all the countries that ensures a healthy and safe work environment. And while there are sometimes hidden costs if the work environment allows harassment (turnover, loss of productive time), the costs associated with an unhealthy and/or unsafe work environment are direct and very tangible. For example, approximately 242,000 incidents of workplace injuries occurred in 2013 (most recent data available).[1]

Although the laws safeguarding employees' physical and emotional well-being are an incentive to provide desirable working conditions, many employers are motivated to create a culture of well-being as it makes good business sense. The more cost-oriented employer recognizes the importance of avoiding accidents and illnesses wherever possible. Costs associated with sick leave, disability payments, replacement of employees who are injured or killed, and workers' compensation far exceed the costs of creating a culture of well-being and having a healthy and safe work environment. Accidents and illnesses attributable to the workplace may also have pronounced effects on employee engagement and morale and on the goodwill that the organization enjoys in the community and in the business world.

Although managers at all levels are expected to know and enforce health and safety standards throughout the organization, in reality the supervisor has the biggest role. The supervisor must ensure a work environment that protects employees from physical hazards, unhealthy conditions, and unsafe acts of other personnel. Through effective safety and health practices, the physical and emotional well-being of employees may be preserved and even enhanced. In this chapter you'll also be presented with information about how to create a culture of well-being—a healthy and safe work environment and organizational culture.

ORGANIZATIONAL CULTURE AND ITS IMPORTANCE

Organizational Culture

LO1

What is organizational culture?

Organizational culture
Collective understanding of beliefs and values that guide how employees act and behave

For those of you who have had an organizational behavior course, you'll probably easily be able to answer the question: what is **organizational culture**. For those of you who have not, the simplest way to describe culture is the "personality" of the organization—the collective understanding of beliefs and values that guide how employees act and behave.

Culture doesn't just happen or appear overnight. It usually starts with the original business owner and then builds over time as new people come into the organization and interpret the beliefs and values of the original owner. Depending on how aligned newer actions are with established expectations, culture can change over time. Depending on the original founder's beliefs and values, it can take great effort to ensure that those beliefs and values remain over time.

A good example of ensuring the culture remains over time is SC Johnson, the worldwide company that produces a variety of household products such as Drano, Pledge, Raid, etc. It is a family-owned business that has built its reputation on trust for quality and excellence in its products. The fifth generation of family members continues that culture, even if it means discontinuing a highly profitable product due to safety concerns.[2] SC Johnson recently did this when it ceased making its top-selling Saran product when consumer advocates expressed grave concern about the product containing PVC. It didn't, but it did contain a product that could be confused with PVC, and so its owners decided to "act in the best interests of our customers, whose trust in our company is a primary reason they buy our products."[3]

Impact of Organizational Culture on Work Environment and Employees

LO2

How does culture impact employees?

Since culture influences actions and behaviours, culture really provides the compass for guiding what employees do and say. There are several dimensions of culture—all which contribute to the personality of the organization. For example, does management take into consideration the impact of decisions on employees or does it focus on getting the work done at all costs? Another dimension is whether rules and regulations are used to control employee behaviour or the organization supports empowerment. One further dimension is how much the organization focuses on team versus individual effort. One final one that will be mentioned is the willingness of the organization to encourage employees to be innovative and risk-taking.[4]

As mentioned earlier in this chapter, culture derives from the original founders' visions. And whether it changes over time is a function of how new leaders behave and act. A good example of this is when Steve Jobs, founder of Apple Inc., died and Tim Cook became CEO. Apple's culture was very much aligned with Jobs' vision yet Cook has created a more inclusive and open company. His particular style is more like a coach who trusts his staff and he isn't manipulative the way Jobs was.[5] Cook indicates that the culture is measured by excellence, helpfulness, ambition, innovativeness, ability to admit mistakes, and integrity, and is more important than just making money.[6]

Culture has a profound impact on the success of any organization. Specifically, when employees are empowered to innovate and failures are part of the learning, research has demonstrated that organizations are more successful.[7] Risks become a way that ideas become actions. But as you will see later in this chapter, there are some areas of the actual running of the business in which certain types of risks are not acceptable.

You will remember from Chapter 1 that the values and expectations of the different generations affect how employees relate to their companies. Likewise, the various components of culture also affect the attraction and retention of employees. For example, the co-founder of Klick Health, a digital marketing firm in Toronto, wanted a culture that was open and employee-centred, where people could be involved and engaged in the business.[8] This focus is kept at the forefront when new people are hired—it is necessary to have people who will fit into the culture and enable others to grow and succeed.

Read At Work with HRM 3.1 to learn more about how culture is exhibited and what it does for the organization.

AT WORK WITH HRM 3.1 — IS CULTURE REALLY THAT IMPORTANT?

Think about any work that you've done and what the work environment was like. Were you encouraged to learn from your mistakes? Were you encouraged to innovate? Were you asked to be and function as part of a team? Were you allowed to make decisions that helped the customer, or did you always have to ask a supervisor even when you knew the answer?

continued

These are all examples of what culture "looks like" every day in all organizations. Some of the most successful companies ensure that their cultures support innovation, learning, risk-taking, and being part of a team. They know that the culture has been a factor in their success.

The founder of Marriott Hotels understood the link between employee satisfaction, business outcomes, and customer satisfaction. In building a very successful enterprise, he ensured that the culture he encouraged could support those links. Among the things he did was to encourage cross-training (learning), trust, diversity, and inclusiveness. He also believed in open and frequent communication, and flexibility in working arrangements.

Likewise, Vancity, a credit union in British Columbia, has a culture that encourages employees to take care of their personal lives. Employee well-being is a focus—no matter what stage of life someone is at. The organization also feels very strongly that employee well-being drives both business results and employee engagement.

Both organizations also understand the importance of considering the organizational culture when managing different generations in the workforce. Since many employees want respect, understanding, and flexibility, how people are treated and how people act and behave demonstrate whether the culture can support those wants.

CRITICAL THINKING QUESTIONS:

1. If you're currently working or have worked, how would you describe the company's culture?
2. How would you describe the type of organizational culture you'd like to work in?

Sources: Adapted from "Isabelle St-Jean, "Flexible Thinking Drives Workplace Futures," *People Talk*, Winter 2014, 20-21; Robert Hackett, "KPMG's viral morale meme," *Fortune*, March 1, 2015, 26; and Brian Kreissl, "Managing a multigenerational workforce," *The Canadian HR Reporter*, April 6, 2015, 19.

EMPLOYEE ENGAGEMENT

LO3

What is the relationship between organizational culture and employee engagement?

Aon Hewitt
www.aon.com

Towers Watson
www.towerswatson.com

Employee engagement
Amount of commitment and dedication an employee has toward organization

More and more organizations are paying attention to the concept of **employee engagement**—employee commitment and dedication to the organization, in which the organization has truly captured the total person in achieving organizational outcomes. The concept has evolved from practical experience that requires further empirical research. Engagement is used to refer to the interplay of attitudes, behaviours, and dispositions that relate to organizational outcomes such as turnover and productivity. Several HRM consulting firms, such as Aon Hewitt and Towers Watson, conduct engagement surveys and publish studies identifying factors that drive employee engagement. These studies present a wide array of drivers and definitions that make the term "engagement" complicated. Some of the drivers include the organization's reputation for social responsibility, leadership, trust and integrity, nature of the job, and total rewards—all factors that are part of the organization's culture. Certain studies focus on particular drivers and their impact on specific organizational outcomes, such as employee turnover, absenteeism, tenure and retention, customer satisfaction, loyalty, sales, company productivity, and financial performance. Organizations become involved in top-employer surveys to have an independent external assessment of their employees' engagement as compared to other organizations.

Aon Hewitt, a global HR consulting and outsourcing solutions business of Aon Corporation, conducts an annual national Canadian workplace study that measures employee engagement. Cisco Canada has been recognized as one of Canada's top employers from 2009 to 2015 because of its focus on collaboration strong leadership and a commitment to providing challenging and interesting opportunites.[9] Aon also identified in a recent study that employers needed to focus on the specific behaviours and actions ("culture") that drove business success and created an engaged workforce.[10] Figure 3.1 illustrates what helps drive better employee engagement and the cultural factors that improve engagement.

FIGURE 3.1 Employee Engagement

Employee Engagement and Organizational Culture

Psychometrics Canada Inc. conducted a study on the perspectives of human resources professionals on employee engagement in the Canadian workplace. The recent study showed that when employees are engaged, they demonstrate higher levels of performance, commitment, and improved work relationships. Some themes for increasing engagement are identified below.

What Makes Employees Engaged?

- Positive work relationships with co-workers and management
- Good fit between skills, job requirements, and organization's culture
- Regular feedback on employee performance
- Opportunities to learn new skills
- Employees having control over their work
- Celebrations of progress
- Communication of direction and strategy of the organization
- Presence of a role model and/or mentor
- Trust and mutual respect among employees

What Can Leaders Do to Improve Employee Engagement?

- Design jobs to include employees' skills and strengths
- Listen to and incorporate employee opinions
- Communicate clear expectations
- Give recognition and praise
- Provide learning and career development opportunities
- Provide resources and support in finding solutions to problems
- Clarify roles and decision-making authority
- Provide flexible work schedules and workloads

Sources: Adapted from "Engagement Study: Control Opportunity & Leadership, 2011," with permission of Psychometrics Canada Ltd.; Karen Mishra, Lois Boynton, and Aneil Mishra, "Driving Employee Engagement," *International Journal of Business Communication* 51, no. 2 (2014): 183–202.

Another way for management to view engagement is by ensuring that workers are treated fairly and equitably. This idea supports the importance of such engagement drivers as leadership that cares about worker well-being, good relationships among managers and co-workers, and organizational pride. With increased organizational fairness, workers are likely to view their managers and organization more positively.

To achieve a high level of employee engagement, it is critical that leadership practices focus on key engagement drivers such as empowerment and not control.[11] But why do employees want to be engaged? A further study by Psychometrics Canada, a Canadian firm specializing in employee assessments, provided information about what makes employees engaged and what leaders can do to improve engagement. Figure 3.1 identifies a number of areas for consideration.

Further, engagement leads to less frustration at work, thereby creating greater impact at the work level, something that becomes increasingly important as employers strive to create a healthier work environment.

As you can see from Figure 3.1, the drivers for employee engagement and cultural components are the same ones necessary to foster a healthy and safe work environment.

CREATING A HEALTHY AND SAFE WORK ENVIRONMENT

Legal Framework

LO4

What is the link between culture and a healthy and safe work environment?

While the focus on creating a healthy and safe work environment will be from the perspectives of organizational culture, it cannot be ignored that there is a legal requirement to have healthy and safe work environment. As mentioned in the introduction to this chapter, close to 242,000 workplace injuries occurred in 2013. And of that number, over 24,000 created over 2 million person-years of lost time![12] Also, in that year, 901 employees died in work-related accidents.[13] The burden on the country's economy as a result of lost productivity and wages, medical expenses, and disability compensation is staggering. And there is no way to calculate the human suffering involved.

As described in Chapter 2, the federal, provincial, and territorial governments regulate occupational health and safety. While statutes and standards differ slightly from jurisdiction to jurisdiction, attempts have been made to harmonize the various acts and regulations. Health and safety legislation has had an impact on workplace injuries and illnesses. The number of workplace accidents in Canada has declined even though there has been an increase in the number of workers.

Occupational injury
Any cut, fracture, sprain, or amputation resulting from a workplace accident
Occupational illness
Abnormal condition or disorder resulting from exposure to environmental factors in the workplace
Industrial disease
A disease resulting from exposure relating to a particular process, trade, or occupation in industry

An **occupational injury** is any cut, fracture, sprain, or amputation resulting from a workplace accident or from an exposure involving an accident in the work environment. An **occupational illness** is any abnormal condition or disorder, other than one resulting from an occupational injury, caused by exposure to environmental factors associated with employment. It includes acute and chronic illnesses or diseases that may be caused by inhalation, absorption, ingestion, or direct contact. With regard to parts of the body affected by accidents, injuries to the back occur most frequently, followed by leg, arm, and finger injuries. An **industrial disease** is a disease resulting from exposure to a substance relating to a particular process, trade, or occupation in industry.

All supervisors, managers, and HR professionals should become familiar with the occupational health and safety legislation governing the jurisdiction under which their organization operates. The fundamental duty of every employer is to take every reasonable precaution to ensure employee safety. The motivating forces behind workplace legislation were effectively articulated in the landmark case *Regina v. Wholesale Travel Group*, which dealt with the legal liability and obligation of employers to behave in accordance with legislation:

> Regulatory legislation is essential to the operation of our complex industrial society; it plays a legitimate and vital role in protecting those who are most vulnerable and least able to protect themselves. The extent and importance of that role have increased continuously since the onset of the Industrial Revolution. Before effective workplace legislation was enacted, labourers—including children—worked unconscionably long hours in dangerous and unhealthy surroundings that evoke visions of Dante's inferno. It was regulatory legislation with its enforcement provisions that brought to an end the shameful situations that existed in mines, factories and workshops in the nineteenth century.

As discussed earlier in this chapter, there is a very strong link between the values and culture of the organization to employee behaviours. Culture sets the context for what employees do and don't do. When the culture supports cost cutting and getting the product out at all costs, employees will probably not take safety concerns seriously. At Work with HRM 3.2 describes how UPS focuses on employee involvement and a safety culture as the foundation of its health and safety program and not just a legalistic perspective of its responsibilities.

Much concern has been expressed about the high incidence of youth injuries. The statistics are alarming: teenagers are twice as likely as older workers to be injured on the job; young workers get hurt more than anybody else. This is usually attributable to lack of work experience and insufficient training. So it is even more important for organizations that employ young people to ensure that they are oriented to any dangers at work and to ensure that young people receive appropriate safety training. And it is important that young workers know that it is OK to say no if they are asked to do any work that is unsafe. But the biggest solution to helping young workers to stay safe is ensuring that safety is part of the company's culture.[14]

To help build the awareness of safety at work in young people, the Ontario agency responsible for safety, the Workplace Safety & Insurance Board (WSIB) has created a separate website as a resource for young people (**www.labour.gov.on.ca/english/atwork/youngworkers.php**). Its objective is to help younger workers protect themselves and others in the workplace. The poster in Toolkit 3.1 is targeted toward young people—making them aware of workplace risks.

Young Workers
www.labour.gov.on.ca/english/atwork/youngworkers.php

AT WORK WITH HRM 3.2

LOOK WHAT EMPLOYEE INVOLVEMENT CAN DO!

UPS Canada, an express carrier and package delivery company, has more than 1,100 stores, 11,000 employees, and 2,624 vehicles. The company was confronted with high injury rates, particularly sprains and strains from loading and unloading packages, and getting into and out of trucks. How did they reduce their injury rates?

UPS implemented the Comprehensive Health and Safety Process (CHSP) to improve health and safety by involving employees first. The results are impressive: lost-time injuries have been reduced by 35% since 2006. In addition, UPS has created a "Circle of Honor" to encourage road safety for its drivers. There are now over 7,200 employees in the Circle—each has driven 25 years or more and collectively they have all travelled more than 5.3 billion miles of road with a total of 198,000 years of safe driving. The Circle also has 394 members with 35 years or more with no roadside incidents.

How does CHSP work? For one thing, it provides a vast amount of training each year. For example, UPS tractor-trailer drivers received 80 hours of both computer-based and on-the-road training before ever going out on the road as equipment operators. For another, it also bases it on a culture of commitment to safety—creating values in which safety is first no matter what. This is especially true when drivers are faced with bad weather or package handlers with high production demands.

Employee involvement is the foundation of the health and safety process established by UPS. The company's approach can be illustrated as a pyramid of which the base consists of employees' personal values toward safety practices. The next level is built on management commitment and employee involvement. The remaining three tiers are worksite analysis, hazard prevention and control, and education and training. Worksite analysis is based on past data, prevention reports, audits, employee concerns, observation, and feedback. Hazard assessment and control utilizes an employee concern logbook as well as observation and feedback processes. And it is important to remember that CHSP is considered a process and not a program.

With both management and front-line employees involved and focusing jointly on safety, practices and values of placing safety above operational concerns are reinforced. And if an incident occurs, UPS conducts a formal investigation to look at possible root causes to eliminate a reoccurrence.

When a person walks through any of the distribution centres, it is obvious that safety is in company's DNA. Weekly communication meetings always end with a senior manager reminding drivers to be safe as they travel the various roadways and routes. With support like that, no wonder employees are involved and help reinforce the safety culture!

CRITICAL THINKING QUESTIONS:

1. If you're working or have worked, would this approach work at your company?
2. What characteristics of organizational culture are necessary for this approach?

Sources: Adapted from UPS Canada, "Fact Sheet," accessed April 17, 2015, www.ups.com/content/ca/en/about/facts/canada.html; UPS Canada, "Employee Safety," accessed April 17, 2015, www.community.ups.com/committed-to-more/employee-safety; Jayanth Jayaram, Jeff Smith, Sunny Park, and Dan McMackin, "A Framework for Safety Excellence: Lessons from UPS," *SupplyChain* 247 (October 20, 2013), accessed April 17, 2015, www.supplychain247.com/article/framework_for_safety_excellence_lessons_from_ups; and a tour of the Richmond B.C. distribution warehouse, April 22, 2015.

TOOLKIT 3.1 MAKING YOU THINK ABOUT SAFETY

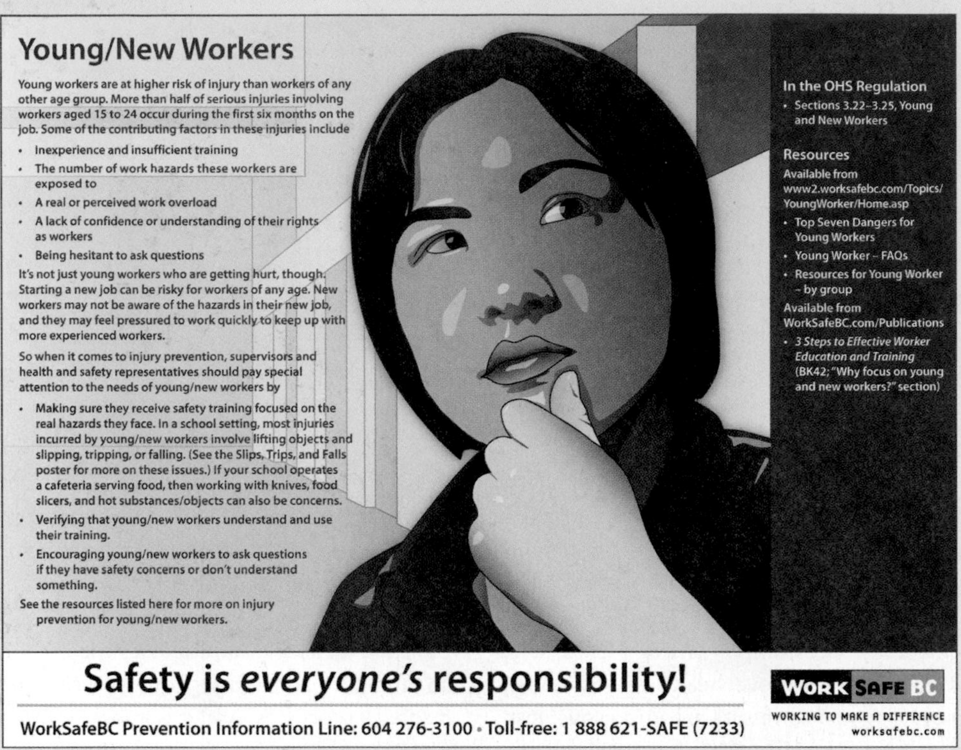

Used with permission of WorkSafeBC.

While Chapter 2 provided detail about the duties and responsibilities of employers, workers, and supervisors, Figure 3.2 summarizes the legally required duties and responsibilities of those directly involved in health and safety issues.

Safety becomes more critical as workplaces become more complex.

Lester Lefkowitz/Stone/Getty Images

FIGURE 3.2 Health and Safety Duties and Responsibilities

Employers

- Provide a hazard-free workplace.
- Comply with laws and regulations.
- Inform employees about safety and health requirements.
- Keep records.
- Compile annual summary of work-related injuries and illnesses.
- Ensure supervisors are familiar with work and associated hazards.
- Report accidents to WCB.
- Provide safety training.

Workers

- Comply with all laws and regulations.
- Report hazardous conditions or defective equipment.
- Follow employer safety and health rules.
- Refuse unsafe work.

Supervisors

- Advise employees of potential workplace hazards.
- Ensure workers use or wear safety equipment.
- Provide written instructions.
- Take every reasonable precaution to guarantee safety of workers.

Joint Health and Safety Committees

- Advise employer on health and safety matters.
- Create a nonadversarial climate to foster a safe and healthy work environment.
- Investigate accidents.
- Train others in safety obligations.

Even though this chapter is stressing the culture of the organization to create a healthy and safe work environment, it is important to remember that there are financial penalties for violations of occupational health and safety regulations. These penalties vary across provinces and territories. The Ontario *Health and Safety Act* provides for fines of up to $500,000, and offenders can be sent to jail. Manitoba has a similar provision.

Saskatchewan and Manitoba continue to have the 2 highest workplace injury rates in the country. Both provinces have proposed increased penalties to reflect the serious nature of violating laws that protect worker health and safety. The maximum fines under Manitoba's *Workplace Safety and Health Act* are $250,000 for the first offence and $500,000 for a second or subsequent offence and the possibility of jail time.[15] The province of Saskatchewan recently combined various employment laws, including occupational health and safety, into one law called the *Saskatchewan Employment Act*. The province also increased penalties for individuals causing a serious injury or fatality to $500,000 and $1,500,000 for corporations.[16] Financial penalties for federally regulated companies range from $100,000 to $1,000,0000.[17] Further, early in 2015, British Columbia introduced new workplace legislation that also expands a court's authority to bar the worst offenders from operating in a particular industry.[18] HRM and the Law 3.1 describes what happened to 2 companies in relation to safety violations.

HRM AND THE LAW 3.1 HOW MUCH IS THE PENALTY?

There are varying amounts of penalties when an employer is found to have violated safety protocols. But how much is appropriate when a person is burned?

Cabo Drilling Corporation, a company that specializes in drilling services in the mineral industry, received fines from the Newfoundland and Labrador Provincial Court for safety violations that resulted in severe burns to the hands and face of a worker on a drilling machine. Initially, the province's occupational health and safety division conducted an investigation and then eventually laid charges against the company. The investigation also identified that another worker was injured but the burns were less severe. The company was charged with failing to maintain a safe workplace, failing to provide equipment and tools that posed no risk to workers, and failing to provide sufficient training and supervision to keep the workers safe.

At court, Cabo pleaded to the charges and was fined $20,000 per person plus 15% for each victim as a surcharge. Further, it was ordered to contribute $10,000 to the occupational health and safety division for public education. The incident cost Cabo a total of $56,000 for the safety infractions.

In another case, an Ontario coroner's inquest into the death of a worker crushed by a building crane recommended that criminal charges be laid against the owner of the company. The company had already been fined $70,000 by the Ministry of Labour for the machine not being fully functional in the braking system. During the investigation that led to the charges, the Ministry determined that a capable worker would have noticed during a routine inspection that the brakes were unsafe.

CRITICAL THINKING QUESTIONS:

1. Do you companies should be fined for safety violations? Why or why not?
2. Do you think owners or key managers in companies should be charged under the *Criminal Code* when a death of a worker occurs and safety violations have been confirmed? Why or why not?

Sources: Adapted from "Corporate Profile," Cabo Drilling Corp., accessed April 18, 2015, www.cabo.ca/files/file/Fact%20Sheet/CaboCutSheetQ2_Feb272015.pdf; and "Nfld. Drilling Company Fined for 2013 Accident," *OHS Canada*, May 26, 2014, accessed April 18, 2015, www.ohscanada.com/compliance-enforcement/nfld-drilling-company-fined-for-2013-accident/1003080775/; and "Union Pleased with the Inquest into 2009 Crane Fatality," *OHS Canada*, May 20, 2014, www.ohscanada.com/compliance-enforcement/union-pleased-with-inquest-into-2009-crane-fatality/1003073202.

The federal government was so concerned about employers' responsibilities for workplace health and safety that the *Criminal Code* was changed to make it easier to bring criminal charges against co-workers, supervisors, executives, and employers when a worker is killed or injured on the job. The legislation was a direct result of a public inquiry into the Westray Mine disaster in 1992 that killed 26 workers. Numerous safety infractions occurred at Westray, and it was determined that senior managers and executives knew of the infractions but did nothing to fix them. There is no doubt that violations of health and safety laws can have significant consequences.

In addition to penalties for safety violations, workers' compensation provides financial benefits to injured workers or workers who become ill as a result of their work environment. These benefits can be in the form of a cash payout (if the disability is permanent) or wage-loss payments (if the worker can no longer earn the same amount of money). Unlimited medical aid is also provided, along with vocational rehabilitation, which includes physical, social, and psychological services. The goal is to return the employee to the original job (or some type of modification) as soon as possible. For example, the Nova Scotia Liquor Corporation recently received a safety award for its return-to-work program. The program has resulted in a reduction of lost days by 73% and reduced the premiums the corporation paid by 87%.[19]

Equally problematic is compensation for stress, which is discussed in more detail later in the chapter. Stress-related disabilities are usually divided into 3 groups: physical injuries leading to mental disabilities (e.g., clinical depression after a serious accident); mental

FIGURE 3.3 Ways to Reduce Workers' Compensation Costs

1. Perform an audit to assess high-risk areas within a workplace.
2. Prevent injuries by proper ergonomic design of the job (such as position of keyboard) and effective assessment of job candidates.
3. Provide quality medical care to injured employees by physicians with experience and preferably with training in occupational health.
4. Reduce litigation by effective communication between the employer and the injured worker.
5. Manage the care of an injured worker from the injury until return to work. Keep a partially recovered employee at the worksite.
6. Provide extensive worker training in all related health and safety areas.

stress resulting in a physical disability (ulcers or migraines); and mental stress resulting in a mental condition (anxiety over workload or downsizing leading to depression). Most claims, it should be pointed out, result from accidents or injuries.

Compensation has become a complex issue. Since workers can receive payment if they have contracted an industrial disease, cause and effect can be difficult to determine. Consider, for example, the case of a mine worker who has contracted a lung disease, but who also smokes heavily. While the number of Canadians injured at work every year is decreasing, there are still many people injured and the cost of these injuries is in the billions of dollars of compensation claims. This has left workers' compensation boards with a huge deficit to pay existing claims. To encourage employers to introduce better prevention and claims management practices, the emphasis of workers' compensation has been shifting from assessments and payments to the creation of a safety-conscious environment intended to reduce the number of work-related accidents, disabilities, and diseases. Figure 3.3 lists some ways employers can reduce their workers' compensation costs.

Promoting Workplace Health and Safety

LO5

What are the measures to use to reduce health and safety concerns?

Occupational health and safety legislation was clearly designed to protect the health, as well as the safety, of employees. Because of the dramatic impact of workplace accidents, however, managers and employees alike may pay more attention to these kinds of immediate safety concerns than to job conditions or work environments that may be dangerous to their health. It is essential, therefore, that health hazards be identified and controlled. Attention should also be given to non-work-related illnesses and injuries and their impact on the organization and its members. Special health programs may also be developed to provide assistance to employees with health problems.

Largely because of the growing public awareness of the efforts of environmentalists, factors in the work environment that affect health are receiving greater attention. Unprecedented air and water pollution throughout the world has made everyone more conscious of the immediate environment in which they live and work. Articles about workers who have been exposed to potential dangers at work can frequently be found in the newspapers. Pressure from the federal government and unions, and increased public concern, has given employers a definite incentive to provide the safest and healthiest work environment possible.

As part of Developing Your Skills at the end of this chapter, you will be asked to explore the website for the Canadian Centre for Occupational Health and Safety (**www.ccohs.ca**).

Canadian Centre for Occupational Health and Safety
www.ccohs.ca

As we've already learned, most employers have a formal safety program. The success of a safety program depends largely on managers and supervisors of operating departments, even though an HR department may have responsibility for coordinating the safety communication and training programs, and maintaining safety records required by occupational health and safety regulations. Above all else, the CEOs and other senior leaders in unique positions of influence set the tone for safe and healthy work practices. Bill Borger, president and CEO of the Borger Group of Companies, is very pleased and proud to have been awarded the 2014 Canadian Occupational Safety Gold Medal in the building and construction category. He states, "To me, safety is a leading indicator of the entire organization's health. That's how I measure it, so I put a lot of effort into it."[20] Borger feels that the weekly company-wide phone broadcast, with contests, jokes, safety tips, and company news, goes a long way to achieve its safety goals.

Organizations with formal safety programs generally have an employee—management safety committee that includes members from management, each department or manufacturing or service unit, and the pool of employees. Committees are typically involved in investigating accidents and helping to publicize the importance of safety rules and their enforcement.

Canada Safety Council
www.safety-council.org

Canadian Occupational Safety Magazine
www.cos-mag.com

Both the Canada Safety Council (**www.safety-council.org**) and Canadian Occupational Safety Magazine (**www.cos-mag.com**) provide resources to assist in the development of a safe work environment as does the Centre for Occupational Health & Safety mentioned above.

Health and Safety Awareness Programs

Probably the most important role of a safety program is motivating managers, supervisors, and subordinates to be aware of safety considerations. While there is a requirement by law to do this, success comes when a manager or supervisor willingly promotes a safe work environment. If managers and supervisors fail to demonstrate awareness, their subordinates can hardly be expected to do so. Unfortunately, most managers and supervisors wear their "safety hats" far less often than their "production, quality control, and methods improvement hats."

While discipline may force employees to work safely, the most effective enforcement of safety expectations occurs when employees willingly obey and champion safety rules and procedures. This goal can be achieved when management actively encourages employees to participate in all aspects of the organization's safety program, and the organization provides incentives to do so.

Protective clothing is required in some work settings.

Dmitry Kalinovsky/Shutterstock.com

As an example, Hydro One in Ontario has identified employee health and safety as one of its core values. It acknowledges that some of the work is done in hazardous situations and it wants its employees to go home safely every day. Hydro One promotes a strong safety culture by training staff and equipping them appropriately for any work hazards.[21]

Ontario Power Generation, the other electrical company in Ontario, also promotes a strong safety culture. It does so by ensuring that its leaders are committed to safety, are doing extensive employee training, and are using safety investigations for continuous learning and improvement.[22] It widely publishes that it has had a zero-injuries record for some years.

Toolkit 3.2 provides some steps in setting up a health and safety incentive program.

No matter what type of incentive programs are developed, the key to success is the employees' supervisor. One of a supervisor's major responsibilities is to communicate to every employee the need to work safely. Beginning at new-employee orientation (as discussed in Chapter 6), safety should be continually emphasized. Proper work procedures, the use of protective clothing and devices, and potential hazards should be explained thoroughly. Furthermore, employees' understanding of all these considerations needs to be verified during training sessions, and employees encouraged to take some initiative in maintaining a concern for safety. Since training by itself does not ensure continual adherence to safe work practices, supervisors must observe employees at work and reinforce safe practices. Where unsafe acts are detected, supervisors should take immediate action to find the cause. Supervisors need to foster a team spirit of safety among the work group. Again, it is important to identify that while this is a legal requirement, the success of any safety awareness depends on the willingness of the supervisor to actively support the employees in creating a safe work environment.

Many organizations advocate employee involvement when designing and implementing safety programs as well as ensuring that the top leaders support and promote a healthy and safe work environment.[23] Employees can offer valuable ideas regarding specific safety and health topics to cover, instructional methods, and proper teaching techniques. Furthermore, acceptance for safety training is heightened when employees feel a sense of ownership in the instructional program.

At Work with HRM 3.3 describes how ArcelorMittal Dofasco won an award for its health and safety approach.

TOOLKIT 3.2 CREATING A SUCCESSFUL HEALTH AND SAFETY INCENTIVE PROGRAM

- Obtain the full support and involvement of management by providing cost benefits.
- Review current injury and health statistics to determine where change is needed.
- Decide on a program of action and set an appropriate budget.
- Select a realistic safety goal, such as reducing accidents by a set percentage, improving safety suggestions, or achieving a period of time without a lost-time injury. Communicate your objectives to everyone involved.
- Select incentive rewards on the basis of their attractiveness to employees and their fit with your budget.
- Develop a program that is both interesting and fun. Use kickoff meetings, posters, banners, quizzes, and/or games to spark employee interest. Give all employees a chance to win.
- Communicate continually the success of your program. Provide specific examples of positive changes in behaviour.
- Reward safety gains immediately. Providing rewards shortly after improvements reinforces changed behaviour and encourages additional support for the safety program.

AT WORK WITH HRM 3.3

IT MAKES GOOD BUSINESS SENSE!

Does a healthy work environment help the company succeed? ArcelorMittal Dofasco, a steel manufacturer in Ontario that's been around for more than 100 years, thinks so, and it recently won an award for its accomplishments.

As described in Chapter 1, Excellence Canada recognizes and honours a variety of organizations for quality initiatives. It also has a special Healthy Workplace award granted from time to time to companies that have attained a high standard in creating a healthy work environment.

The company says that its success in creating such a workplace is due to maintaining a focus on its people. It has a stated value of: "Our Product Is Steel. Our Strength Is People."

One of the reasons for the award is its comprehensive workplace strategy that emphasizes wellness of the mind and body—at home and at work. The company believes that it makes good business sense to have healthy people. The criteria for the award include a broad-based approach to health and wellness in the workplace with specific factors of physical, environmental, mental, safety, and social issues. The overall goal of the award is to promote healthy employees, and there is evidence of a positive link between health and business growth, productivity, and business excellence.

CRITICAL THINKING QUESTION:

Do you think employers only create healthy workplaces to receive awards? Why or why not?

Sources: Adapted from "Commitment to Being a Healthy Workplace Garners Excellence Canada Award," ArcelorMittal Canada, October 30, 2014, accessed April 18, 2015, http://blog.arcelormittal.com/canada/2014/10/30/commitment-to-being-a-healthy-workplace-garners-excellence-canada-award; "Award Categories," *Excellence Canada*, accessed April 18, 2015, www.excellence.ca/en/awards/about-the-canada-awards-for-excellence/Award%20Categories; and "Canadian Health Workplace Criteria—Overview," *Excellence Canada*, accessed April 18, 2015, www.excellence.ca/en/knowledge-centre/products-and-tools/canadian-healthy-workplace-criteria2.

Monitoring and Investigating

Specific expectations and standards concerning health and safety are communicated through supervisors, bulletin-board notices, employee handbooks, and signs attached to equipment. Safety expectations are also emphasized in regular health and safety meetings, at new employee orientations, and in paper and online manuals of standard operating procedures. Such expectations typically refer to the following types of employee behaviours:

- using proper safety devices
- using proper work procedures
- following good housekeeping practices
- complying with accident and injury reporting procedures
- wearing required safety clothing and equipment
- avoiding carelessness or horseplay

Penalties for violation of health and safety rules are usually stated in the employee handbook. In a large percentage of organizations, the penalties imposed on violators are the same as those imposed for violations of other standards and expectations. They include an oral or written warning for the first violation, suspension or disciplinary layoff for repeated violations, and, as a last resort, dismissal. However, for serious violations—such as smoking around volatile substances—even the first offence may be cause for termination.

When an incident happens, the supervisor and a member of the safety committee should investigate, even if the incident is considered minor. Such an investigation may determine the contributing factors and reveal what preventive measures are needed, such as rearranging workstations, installing safety guards or controls, or, more often, giving employees additional training and ensuring they understand the importance of healthy and safe work practices.

Employers are also required to keep certain records and to compile and post an annual summary of work-related injuries and illnesses. From these records, organizations can compute their *incidence rate*, the number of injuries and illnesses per 100 full-time employees

Cylonphoto/Shutterstock.com

Best practices help with safety preparedness.

during a given year. Incidence rates are useful for making comparisons between work groups, between departments, and between comparable units within an organization. They also provide a basis for making comparisons with other organizations doing similar work. Occupational health and safety departments in each province and Human Resources and Skills Development Canada compile data an organization can use as a basis for comparing its safety record with those of other organizations. Progressive organizations can also use this information to benchmark "best practices."

Health and Safety Hazards

At one time, health and safety hazards were associated primarily with jobs found in industrial processing operations, such as coal mining. In recent years, however, hazards in jobs outside the plant, such as in offices, health-care facilities, and airports, have been recognized and preventive methods adopted. Substituting materials, altering processes, enclosing or isolating a process, issuing protective equipment, and improving ventilation are some common methods to prevent problems. General conditions of health with respect to sanitation, housekeeping, cleanliness, ventilation, water supply, pest control, and food handling are also important to monitor.

Believing that workers have the right to know about potential workplace hazards, industry, labour, and government joined forces several years ago to develop a common information system for labelling hazardous substances. The Workplace Hazardous Materials Information System (WHMIS) is based on three elements:

1. *Labels.* Labels are designed to alert the worker that the container holds a potentially hazardous substance. WHMIS class symbols and subclass designations are shown in Figure 3.4.
2. *The* **Material Safety Data Sheet (MSDS)**. The MSDS identifies the product and its potentially hazardous ingredients, and suggests procedures for the safe handling of the product.
3. *Training.* Employees must be trained to check for labels and to follow specific procedures for handling spills. As detailed in Chapter 6, training employees is part of the due diligence required of employers; it also becomes an important factor in the event of a lawsuit.

Material Safety Data Sheet (MSDS)
Documents that contain vital information about hazardous substances

FIGURE 3.4 WHMIS Class Symbols and Subclass Designations

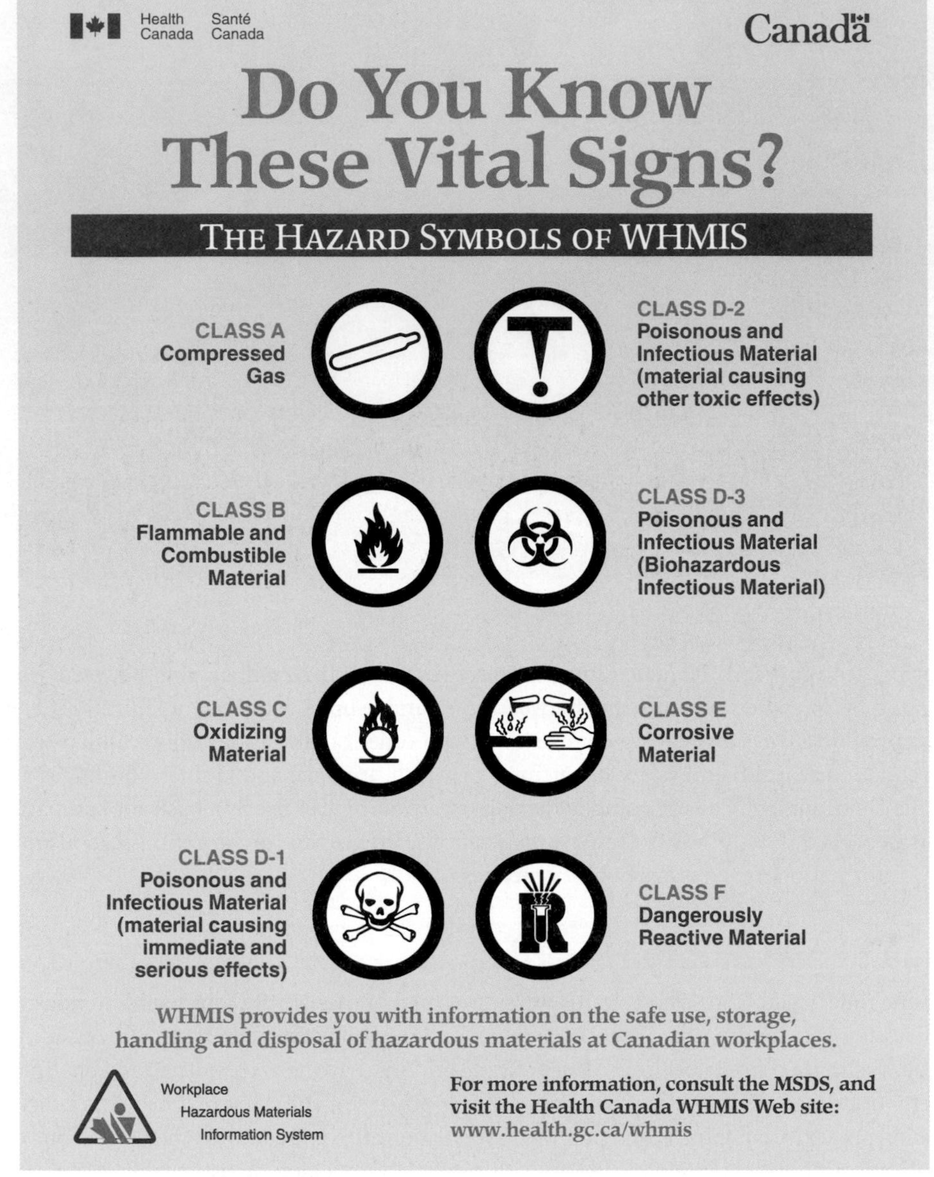

Source: © All rights reserved. Do You Know These Vital Signs?: The hazard symbols of WHMIS, Health Canada, 2005. Adapted and reproduced with permission from the Minister of Health, 2015.

While smoking in the workplace has been eliminated, there are still some concerns about people walking through smokers in front of buildings. Many provinces and municipal by-laws now restrict people from smoking too close to building entrances.

In addition, some employee health insurance plans charge a higher premium for smokers. However, most employers prefer positive reinforcement through wellness programs to encourage employees to stop smoking.

More attention is now given to keeping fragrances such as perfumes, colognes, oils, and other personal care products with scents, clear of the workplace. Many people can suffer painful reactions even if the scent is at a very low concentration. If an employee expresses concern about fragrances, it is important for the organization to treat the concern seriously, openly, and honestly.

The increasing use of technology has been associated with increased health risks ranging from musculoskeletal injuries caused by repetitive movements involved in computer and technical device use to reduced psychological well-being caused by isolation, reduced privacy, and increased surveillance, increased job demands, increased expectations for continuous learning, and frustration due to technical malfunctions.[24]

The constant use of e-mail can be another psychological strain on workers. Employers are beginning to reduce after-work use of company-issued smartphones, expressing concerns ranging from unpaid overtime to encroachment on family time. Further, people understand the need to escape their cell phones for thinking and relaxing—and getting away from data overload.[25]

Texting on your iPhone and listening to music on your iPad can be distracting, which may result in accidents or hearing loss. Can you resist the buzz-buzz-buzzing of your smartphone? Have you turned the volume down?

Meat cutters, cooks, dental hygienists, textile workers, violinists, flight attendants, office workers at computer terminals, and others whose jobs require repetitive motion of the fingers, hands, or arms are reporting injuries in growing percentages. These musculoskeletal disorders (MSDs), also known as **cumulative trauma disorders** or repetitive motion injuries, are injuries of the muscles, nerves, tendons, ligaments, joints, and spinal discs caused by repeated stresses and strains. One of the more common such conditions is *carpal tunnel syndrome*, characterized by tingling or numbness in the fingers occurring when a tunnel of bones and ligaments in the wrist narrows and pinches nerves that reach the fingers and base of the thumb.

Cumulative trauma disorders
Injuries involving tendons of the fingers, hands, and arms that become inflamed from repeated stresses and strains

Ergonomics attempts to design equipment and systems that can be easily and efficiently used by people. For example, some organizations are purchasing adjustable desks for employees who sit for long periods of time.[26] And recent research has confirmed that prolonged sitting correlates with bad health even when people exercise frequently.[27] Mini-breaks involving exercise and changing one's working position have been found helpful. Importantly, these kinds of injuries often go away if caught early. If they are not, they may require months or years of treatment, or even surgical correction.

Workplace Security, Violence, and Bullying

Perhaps the most significant event that has affected workplace security has been the events that occurred on September 11, 2001. From that day forward, organizations throughout Canada have put renewed emphasis on personal safety and security at work. On a recent study tour, one author of this book became acutely aware of the heightened security screenings one

M_a_y_a/E+/Getty Images

Employers are encouraging meetings to discuss preventing workplace violence.

had to go through to get into certain government buildings. In some cases, unless you were employed there, you could not enter. Further, if you were an employee, you had to go through substantive security checks, including metal detectors, prior to being authorized to enter.

Workplace Security

Terrorism, once largely confined to foreign countries, is now a major concern to many Canadian employers, such as airlines, sporting facilities, energy plants, high-tech companies, and financial institutions. Heightened security procedures include increased video surveillance, blast-resistant glass, tightened garage security, and off-site emergency backup offices.

And the concerns of employees are not restricted related to terrorism or bomb threats. In fact, changes to the *Canada Labour Code* have provided an expanded definition of the reasons employees can refuse work they perceive as dangerous. Employees can now refuse "any hazard, condition or activity that could reasonably be expected to be an imminent or serious threat to the life or health of a person exposed to it before the hazard or condition can be corrected or the activity altered."[28]

Workplace Violence

In Canada, some tragic incidents—such as that at L'École Polytechnique, in which 14 women were shot and killed, and the death of Grant De Patie, who was killed after chasing a car that drove away from the gas station without paying—have brought our attention to workplace violence.

Further, a recent study identified that only about 10% of employers are aware that domestic abuse impacts the safety of those at work, and that domestic violence can occur at work.[29] Since it costs Canadian employers almost $78 million every year due to direct and indirect domestic violence, employers are having to learn more about domestic violence and what can happen at work.[30]

The challenge of understanding workplace violence is that it has so many forms, not all of which are legislated against—for example, bullying, aggression, intimidation, ganging, and emotional abuse.

Many people think of workplace violence as a physical assault, but there are many forms, including these:

- threatening behaviour, such as shaking fists or throwing objects
- verbal or written threats
- harassment—any behaviour that demeans, embarrasses, or humiliates
- verbal abuse, including swearing, insults, or condescending language
- physical attacks, including hitting, shoving, pushing, or kicking[31]

Recent legislative changes have broadened the responsibility of employers to ensure their work environment is free of violence. Several provinces, including Alberta, British Columbia, Saskatchewan, Manitoba, Nova Scotia, Prince Edward Island, Quebec, Newfoundland, and Labrador, as well as federally regulated workplaces, have implemented regulations dealing with workplace violence as part of their occupational health and safety regulations. Among the requirements of these regulations are a risk assessment, development of policies and procedures to handle the risks identified, instruction and training of workers in handling violence, an emergency response plan, and a requirement that incidents be reported.[32] Most provinces have begun to expand legislation requiring procedures to be in place to eliminate or reduce the risks associated with working alone and at night.

Here are some of the risk factors in organizations that increase the risk of violence:

1. working with the public
2. handling valuables such as money or prescription drugs
3. carrying out enforcement duties, such as parking meter enforcement
4. working alone
5. working in a mobile environment, such as a taxicab
6. working during times of organizational uncertainty, such as strikes[33]

Exposure to workplace violence results in employees fearing more incidents of violence, leading to personal strains (such as stress) and organizational strains (such as reduced commitment). To implement some preventive measures, the Canadian Centre for Occupational Health and Safety suggests the following:

- workplace designs, such as locks or physical barriers, lighting, and electronic surveillance
- administrative practices, such as keeping cash register funds to a minimum, varying the time of day at which cash is emptied, and using a security firm to deliver cash
- work practices (particularly for those working alone or away from an office) that include having a designated contact, checking the credentials of a client, and having an emergency telephone source[34]

It is also important for all employees to be vigilant regarding potential workplace violence. For example, if an employee is agitated and shouting, others can respond by defusing the situation, establishing clear boundaries around appropriate behaviour, and accessing supervisory help. If an employee is shouting and swearing, others should remove themselves from the situation and alert security. Awareness of such threatening behaviours can provide an opportunity to intervene and prevent disruptive, abusive, or violent acts.

Finally, organizations can establish formalized workplace violence prevention policies, informing employees that aggressive employee behaviour will not be tolerated. Toolkit 3.3 lists violence prevention measures that organizations can take.

Organizations are also using a number of different ways to inform employees about security issues. For example, Seneca College in Ontario uses its intranet as a communication tool to inform employees of internal security as well as external security issues in the surrounding geographic area of the college. Another innovative approach to learning more about preventing workplace violence is the Canadian Initiative on Workplace Violence (**www.workplaceviolence.ca**). The Initiative is a research firm with partners from

Canadian Initiative on Workplace Violence
www.workplaceviolence.ca

TOOLKIT 3.3 "NO" TO VIOLENCE AT WORK!

There are some very specific things employers can do to minimize and prevent domestic violence in the workplace:

1. Establish violence, including domestic violence, prevention policy and standards.
2. Conduct a risk assessment.
3. Control violence hazards through workplace design and work practices.
4. Regularly inspect the workplace, and review the violence education program to ensure that standards are maintained.
5. Include domestic violence issues in workplace violence prevention policies and programs.
6. Educate employees on these policies and programs, appropriate actions to take, signs of domestic violence, how to prevent violence, and resources for victims of domestic violence.
7. Develop a workplace safety plan to help keep the workplace and all employees safe from threats of domestic violence.
8. Develop a personal safety plan, if an employee reports domestic violence, to ensure that the victim is protected while at the workplace.
9. Ensure that all employees are aware the employee assistance provider is available.
10. Encourage the victim to contact a professional.
11. Screen for the abuser (with the victim's permission) by providing a photo or description to reception and security.
12. Inform all workplace parties that they must report any abuse or violent behaviour.
13. Act upon any reports immediately.

Sources: Adapted from Public Services Health and Safety Association, "Addressing Domestic Violence in the Workplace: A Handbook," 2010, accessed April 20, 2015, www.pshsa.ca/products/addressing-domestic-violence-in-the-workplace; and from WorkSafeBC, "Addressing Domestic Violence in the Workplace: A Handbook for Employers," 2014.

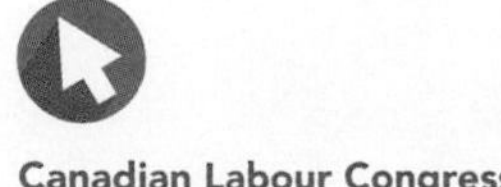

Canadian Labour Congress
www.canadianlabour.ca

universities, unions, and employers. It researches the impact of workplace violence and provides educational resources to help organizations eliminate such violence. Further, the Canadian Labour Congress (**www.canadianlabour.ca**) and University of Western Ontario undertook a comprehensive survey to gather data about the prevalence and impact of domestic violence at work that can better inform employers about the impact.

Workplace Bullying

Although bullying in the workplace was discussed in Chapter 2 as an example of psychological harassment, it also needs to be examined in the context of workplace safety and security. Bullying is prevalent in the workplace—and some estimates suggest that bullying at work impacts 25% of employees.[35] It is unclear whether bullying is more prevalent or that it is no longer acceptable anyplace in a civil society.

There is also the probability that ongoing bullying might create stress in the workplace and that the employee (or employees) might launch compensation claims. While most provincial agencies are rejecting claims for psychological stress, there have been a few cases in which claims have been accepted. For example, while WorkSafeBC has traditionally rejected mental health claims, it has recently accepted some for mental disorder that arose from "cumulative series of significant work-related stressors"[36]—and certainly regular and persistent bullying could qualify. Similarly, a tribunal in Ontario recently ruled that workplace-related stress might be a valid workers' compensation claim.[37] In this situation, it is also important to recognize that the word being used is "workplace" and not "work." What is being signalled is that it isn't necessarily the work the person is doing but the environment in which it is undertaken. Hence, the emphasis in this chapter is on the culture of the organization and the acceptable behaviours and actions.

And of growing concern is the emergence of cyber bullying in the workplace that is also a cause of stress in the workplace (to be discussed later). We don't often think of adults as vulnerable to it, but bullying is an extreme form of harassment and can happen anywhere. What is **cyber bullying**? It is a certain way of using information and technology. On such sites as Twitter, Instagram, and Facebook, most postings are benign. But what happens when the message is anonymous and a particular person is targeted with taunts, untruths, etc.? This form of harassment, depending on the severity, can cause stress, anxiety, depression, insomnia, and low self-esteem.[38] As Ethics in HRM 3.1 indicates, organizations that allow bullying in the workplace do face consequences.

Cyber bullying
Bullying by using communication technology and information

Some organizations have formal crisis management teams that conduct initial risk assessment surveys, develop action plans to respond to violent situations, and perform crisis intervention during violent or potentially violent encounters. For example, a crisis management team would investigate a threat reported by an employee. The team's mandate would be to gather facts about the threat, decide if the organization should intervene, and, if so, to determine the most appropriate method of doing so. Organizations, as part of their corporate social responsibility, have created emergency telephone lines for their employees and families in the event of a crisis, such as a blackout or severe weather conditions.

When violent incidents, such as the death of a co-worker, happen at work, employees can experience anxiety, shock, guilt, grief, apathy, resentment, cynicism, isolation, and a host of other emotions. Such incidents may require the violence response team to perform crisis intervention through positive counselling techniques. It is important also that employees are provided the opportunity and time to grieve.[39]

Stress in the Workplace

Stress
Any adaptive demand caused by physical, mental, or emotional factors that requires coping behaviour

According to a recent report on the main sources of workplace stress, Sun Life's Health Index found that 77% of those surveyed experienced excessive or uncomfortable stress at work.[40] People frequently talk about being stressed at work, yet are unable to explain what they mean. **Stress** is simply any demand on the physical or emotional self that requires a

ETHICS IN HRM 3.1

BULLIES GET OUT!

What is it like to be bullied at work? Ask Meredith Boucher, who went public in the summer of 2014. She worked at Walmart in Ontario, and saw great progress for herself after winning a number of awards for her work. But that all changed when she became a target of harassment and abuse by her manager. She states that the behaviour and actions started when she refused to falsify certain records, as the manager was concerned about a poor audit of the store. And then, she reports, the bullying behaviour started—and continued every day for 6 months. Ms. Boucher also noted that it took an emotional, mental, and physical toll over that time.

She documented the occurrences and provided the information to a senior manager, including confirmations from other employees. Eventually Walmart did an investigation and concluded that the complaint was unfounded which led to discipline for Boucher. She then quit and filed a lawsuit against both the manager and Walmart.

As the case went through the various stages, an appeals judge did conclude that the behaviour was abusive and that Boucher suffered a "visible and provable illness as a result." The judge awarded $1.4 million in compensation—which was later downgraded to $400,000. After the decision, Walmart reported that the manager had been moved to another store and there have been no further issues regarding the workplace behaviour.

Depending on the extent, harassment, and bullying in particular, can lead to a criminal charge under Canada's *Criminal Code*. There is a continuum of behaviours that range from harassment to assault. The actions can be overt, such as somebody saying something to someone, or less visible, such as someone texting something very hurtful about someone to someone else—for example, sending a picture altered with the intent to ridicule.

More attention is now being paid to bullying at work, particularly as various tribunals and courts continue to award money when complaints are upheld. There is also now the possibility that under workers' compensation further claims could be made for psychological injuries.

Clearly, more than ever, there is no place for bullies at work.

CRITICAL THINKING QUESTIONS:

1. Have you ever felt bullied at work or school? What did you do?
2. What would you now do if you faced the same situation?

Sources: Adapted from "Workplace Bullying a Major Concern in Canada, Says Woman Who Sued Wal-Mart," CBC News, June 14, 2014, accessed April 28, 2015, www.cbc.ca/news/business/workplace-bullying-a-major-concern-in-canada-says-woman-who-sued-wal-mart-1.2673109; Liz Bernier, "From the Schoolyard to the Office," *Canadian HR Reporter*, March 23, 2015, accessed April 28, 2015, www.hrreporter.com/articleview/23856-from-the-schoolyard-to-the-office; Michael P. Fitzgibbon, "Workplace Bullying and Harassment," *Addendum*, The Canadian Bar Association, accessed April 28, 2015, www.cba.org/cba/newsletters/addendum01-08/news.aspx; and Stuart Rudner, "Workers' Compensation for Harassment, Mental Distress?" *Canadian HR Reporter*, January 12, 2015, accessed April 28, 2015, www.hrreporter.com/blog/Canadian-HR-Law/archive/2015/01/12/workers-compensation-for-harassment-mental-distress.

person to cope. For example, while running 5 km, an individual may become short-winded after 3 km. Thus, the body is "stressed" as the individual deals with being short of breath. Likewise, a student may have just received a special award at school and be excited about the recognition. Again, the student has to cope with this. Stress can be either positive or negative, and each person handles stress differently.

In that Sun Life survey, respondents indicated that the top driver of excessive stress was personal finances and that the level of stress was impacting their work performance.[41] And a large-scale international study of 22,000 professionals in more than 100 countries confirmed that employees globally feel more stressed at work than they did 5 years ago.[42] So then, what work processes (the way work is designed and performed) and organizational practices are stressing the stressed at work? The international study found that technological advances are keeping employees connected 27/4 and that employees really do have more to do with less.[43] Angst and the feeling that things might be better someplace else are also fuelled by job postings on LinkedIn and other online job postings—further increasing stress levels.

Centre for Addiction and Mental Health
www.camh.ca

Stress can lead to mental health issues—which are increasing in the workplace. A 2015 survey conducted by the Centre for Addiction and Mental Health (CAMH) (**www.camh.ca**)

revealed that 40% of employees would not tell their manager if they had a mental health problem or similar problems that were impacting their performance.[44] Recognizing and dealing with the **workplace stressors** is the first step toward managing workplace stress. A corporate culture and work environment that promote a healthy, safe, and environmentally protected work environment can have a positive impact on worker stress.

Workplace stressor
A workplace event, process, or practice that has the potential to cause worker stress

To reinforce the concern that stress has on the health of the workplace, a research study was presented in 2014 to the Federal-Provincial-Territorial Ministers of Labour that indicated the economic costs of workplace stress in Canada is over $51 billion every year.[45] This study noted that laws weren't enough to improve the psychological well-being of the work environment and that it was the culture of the work environment that would improve the psychological environment of work. Toolkit 3.4 provides some suggestions about what employers can do to improve the psychological health of the workplace.

Several years ago a new National Standard on Psychological Health & Safety in the workplace was launched, giving organizations the tools to achieve measurable improvement in psychological health and safety of Canadian employees. It will help employers prevent the loss and liability associated with mental injuries—estimated at $11 billion a year in workplace losses alone—by nurturing psychologically safe working environments.[46]

Stress management programs involve employees and employers working together to take initiatives to reduce aspects of their work environments that result in negative impacts on employee health.

Many employers have developed stress management programs to teach employees how to minimize the negative effects of job-related stress. A typical program might include instruction in relaxation techniques, coping skills, listening skills, methods of dealing with difficult people, time management, and assertiveness. Organizational techniques, such as flexible work hours and reduced overtime, should not be overlooked in the process of dealing with stress in the workplace.[47]

TOOLKIT 3.4 WE NEED A PSYCHOLOGICALLY HEALTHY WORKPLACE!

Employers can develop a number of strategies to reduce stress in the work environment. Since stress is part of everyday life, it cannot be eliminated; but it can be reduced. Here are "best practices" from a 2014 research study to have a healthier workplace.

- Managers learning to be more responsive and supportive to employees, recognizing employee issues that need referral to an employee assistance program
- Managers communicating more openly about organizational changes
- Keeping workloads reasonable, controlling for overtime
- Allowing for more work flexibility
- Training front-line supervisors and employees on mental health so employees can discuss stress and mental health issues
- Assessing workplace stressors so that actions can be taken to mitigate
- Ensuring senior leaders affirm the need for a healthier work environment
- Becoming familiar with stress trigger factors such as job hazards, amount of overtime, and intensity of work
- Ensuring all efforts for an improved work environment are seamless—from occupational health and safety committees to wellness services, employee assistance programs, etc.
- Encouraging everyone to be accountable for better psychological health through performance management systems
- Ensuring that expectations regarding a healthier work environment is part of the culture.

Sources: Adapted from Dr. Ted Harvey and Neil Gavigan, "Minimizing Workplace Stress, Injuries and Violence in Canada: Towards a New Standard for Occupational Health and Safety," submission to the Mental Health Commission of Canada and Federal-Provincial-Territorial Ministers of Labour, September 2014; Sarah Dobson, "Health Cultures, Reduced Costs," *Canadian HR Reporter*, November 17, 2014, accessed April 22, 2015, www.hrreporter.com/articleview/22808-healthy-cultures-reduced-costs; and Sarah Dobson, "Manager Relationships Key to Mentally Healthy Workplace," *Canadian HR Reporter*, February 23, 2015, 2.

FIGURE 3.5 Tips for Reducing Job-Related Stress

- Build rewarding relationships with co-workers.
- Talk openly with managers or employees about job or personal concerns.
- Prepare for the future by keeping abreast of likely changes in job demands.
- Don't greatly exceed your skills and abilities.
- Set realistic deadlines; negotiate reasonable deadlines with managers.
- Act now on problems or concerns of importance.
- Designate dedicated work periods during which time interruptions are avoided.
- When feeling stressed, find time for detachment or relaxation.
- Don't let trivial items take on importance: handle them quickly or assign them to others.
- Take short breaks from your work area as a change of pace.

Even though the number and severity of organizational stressors can be reduced, everyone encounters situations that may be described as distressful. Those in good physical health are generally better able to cope with the stressors they encounter.

Before concluding this discussion, we should observe that stress harmful to some employees might be healthy for others. Most managers learn to handle distress effectively and find it can stimulate better performance. However, there will always be those unable to handle stress, who need help learning to cope with it. The increased interest of young and old alike in developing habits that will enable them to lead happier and more productive lives will undoubtedly be beneficial to them as individuals, to the organizations where they work, and to a society where people are becoming more and more interdependent. Progressive companies are also discovering that other interventions, such creating a culture of celebration and reinforcing values, help with the overall workplace environment.[48] Further, as discussed earlier in this chapter, employee well-being and health are more likely in organizations with highly engaged staff. Therefore, there is additional rationale to ensure work stressors are kept to a minimum. Figure 3.5 provides some suggestions on how individuals can reduce stress.

BUILDING A CULTURE OF WELL-BEING

LO6

Why is it important to build a culture of well-being?

Along with improving working conditions that are hazardous to employee health and safety, many employers provide a variety of services and support that encourage employees to improve their overall health. It is recognized that better health benefits not only the individual but also the organization through reduced absenteeism, increased efficiency, and better morale. An understanding of the close relationship between physical and emotional health and job performance has made broad health-building programs attractive to employers as well as to employees. And with recent research that suggests 5% of Canadians have mental health issues, unions are also getting involved in providing programs that encourages their members to be involved in making the work environment healthy and safe.[49] As public expectations for ethical business practices are increasing, organizations are beginning to follow through on their social and environmental commitment responsibilities, creating new opportunities to improve the quality of work life and organizational performance. These organizations are using individual health promotion programs as the first step toward a more comprehensive approach to employee well-being. Health services, alternative health care, wellness, disability management, and employee and family assistance programs can begin to address the underlying causes of presenteeism, absenteeism, stress, and work–life imbalance. Also critical is the understanding of the work environment and how work processes and practices can be improved to enhance employee health and organizational performance. Graham Lowe, a leading researcher on healthy organizations, states that a supportive culture that values employees, employee involvement, commitment from senior leadership, communication, an understanding of the strategic link of organizational goals and health outcomes are the building blocks of a healthy organization.[50]

Studies have demonstrated a strong link between high-performance work systems with employee well-being and a reduction in burnout.[51] In such a system, employees who are treated respectfully and experience quality interpersonal relationships tend to be more committed and to participate more fully.[52]

As described in At Work with HRM 3.4, two organizations have won awards for creating a healthy work environment.

LO7

What are the services and programs that help create well-being in the organization?

Health Services

One of the supports that an employer can provide is health services. The type of health services that an employer provides is primarily related to the size of the organization and the importance of such services. Small organizations have only limited facilities, such as those needed to handle first-aid cases, while many larger firms offer complete diagnostic, treatment, and emergency medical services. Since employers are required to provide medical services after an injury, the larger firms may have nurses and physicians on full-time duty or certainly have arrangements with local physicians for preferred attention. Medium-size and smaller organizations have one or more physicians on call.

Wellness Programs

Another support are wellness programs. Typical elements in a wellness program are access to flexible work hours, healthy food, fitness facilities, health professionals, health groups, activities, relaxation techniques, chiropractic, therapeutic massage, acupuncture, and homeopathy. Some suggest that wellness programs may not achieve the desired results, but recent research indicates that if the employer is clear about the goals and that the culture supports wellness, a well-designed and well-executed program can achieve both health and financial results.[53] Since Canada has a publicly funded health-care system, these same critics argue that employers ought not to do this. However, wellness programs can take a preventive approach that the Canadian health-care system mostly cannot. Also, it may now be the more socially responsible thing to increase the organization's stature as a good employer that attracts and retains staff and has high employee engagement.[54]

While early wellness programs attempted to develop a return-on-investment (ROI) metric to justify the expense, many organizations and benefits professionals suggest that an ROI isn't as important as seeing improved employee health and productivity.[55]

Disability Management

Disability management
Integrated approach to managing disability-related benefits

More and more organizations are taking an integrated approach to dealing with short- and long-term absences. Initially, **disability management** programs were linked to workplace injuries as a way to get employees back to work as soon as possible. These programs have now evolved to an approach that combines a strong organizational commitment centred on line supervisors, overseen by expert internal resources, and supported by clinical case management.[56] This means that the focus is also on creating a work environment where employees want to return to work as soon as they are medically able. Professionals have long known that being off work is unhealthy.[57] Part of an effective disability management program includes a graduated return to work in which the employee works fewer hours

AT WORK WITH HRM 3.4

A HEALTHY ORGANIZATION IS GOOD FOR BUSINESS!

Throughout this chapter, you've been provided with a number of reasons why it is important to have healthy organizations. But is this just a theory, or do businesses really believe it makes a difference?

Ask John Mannarino, who founded Mannarino Systems and Software Inc. in Montreal. As a company that sells safety-critical systems and software engineering services to a number of sectors including power generation, aerospace, and space, the organization believes it is important to have a culture that reflects the important of safety in their products. Not only must the work be of the highest quality, but the work environment must provide an atmosphere that enables employees to do and be their best. The senior managers focus on a team atmosphere, including allowing flextime to have a healthy work–life balance. The company believes strongly that a healthy work environment has enabled it to become a leader in its field.

Healthy work environments are not just for the private sector. Take the County of Wellington in Ontario. It won the 2014 Gold Award for Canada's Safest Employers—in both the safety and the public-sector category. Much of the credit for the work culture and environment goes to the county counsellors, senior management, and employees. All believe that a culture of respect is necessary for a psychologically healthy work environment. To help make this happen, employees are encouraged to "Walk the Talk"—that is, use face-to-face conversation instead of e-mail. Likewise, it has introduced mandatory training for all employees in recognizing and responding to mental health issues. The County also ensures that its programs build and maintain mental wellness and prevention before issues arise.

Its advice to other employers: Build the business case with hard data to demonstrate that a healthy and safe work environment does mean better business results.

CRITICAL THINKING QUESTION:

If a healthy work environment is good for business, why don't more organizations have them? Explain your answer.

Sources: Adapted from "Mannarino Flourishes amid the Aerospace Giants," Canada's 2015 Top Small & Medium Employers, *The Globe and Mail*, March 15, 2015, 43; "Safety Is in the Details," Mannarino Systems & Software website, March 15, 2015, accessed April 23, 2015, www.mss.ca/vns-site/newsletter/march2015/index.html; and Liz Bernier, "Making Mental Health a Priority at Work," *The Canadian HR Reporter*, December 1, 2014, accessed April 23, 2015, www.hrreporter.com/articleview/22959-making-mental-health-a-priority-at-work.

and, in some situations, is accommodated by being assigned to a different shift.[58] Even in difficult economic times, a carefully designed and well-managed program can be effective in getting capable staff back to work while communicating that the employer is interested in their well-being.[59]

Facilitating a return-to-work plan would include maintaining contact with the employee while they are on leave, providing organizational support to the supervisor and team by discussing implementation and anticipated challenges and solutions, understanding the tasks and responsibilities that need to be modified, and having a clear diagnosis and plan. This approach would reduce any anxiety, alienation, fears of re-injury and job loss, and stigma that the employee involved might feel.

Employee Assistance Programs

A broad view of health includes the emotional as well as the physical aspects of one's life. While emotional problems, personal crises, financial problems, and substance abuse are considered personal matters, they become organizational problems when they affect behaviour at work and interfere with performance. It is estimated that psychological problems, including depression, anxiety, mental illness, and stress in the workplace, cost the Canadian economy about $51 billion every year, about 30% of that attributed to productivity losses.[60]

Employee assistance programs (EAPs) or more inclusive ones called "employee and family assistance programs" (EFAPs) can provide a useful way to deal with problems,

Employee assistance program (EAP)
Program to provide short-term counselling and referrals to appropriate professionals

FIGURE 3.6 Employee Assistance Programs

Listed below are some of the usual services in EAPs:

- personal issues
- job stress
- relationship issues
- eldercare, childcare, and parenting issues
- harassment
- substance abuse
- separation and loss
- balancing work and family
- financial or legal
- family violence

In addition, and depending on the wishes of the company, there may be services for retirement and layoff assistance, wellness and health promotion, fitness, and disability issues. Also, depending on the service provider, training is provided for managers and supervisors.

Sources: "Employee Assistance Programs," Canadian Centre for Occupational Health and Safety, accessed May 14, 2015, www.ccohs.ca/oshanswers/hsprograms/eap.html; and ComPsych, accessed May 14, 2015, www.compsych.com/canada.

such as stress and depression, that might lead to more serious mental health problems. Supervisors are often given training and policy guidance in the type of help they can offer. Figure 3.6 outlines the types of EAP services offered to employees in Canada. While many companies do not offer programs due to concerns over the cost/benefits of such initiatives, research has shown that 80% of mental health problems can be successfully treated with early detection and treatment.

The Employee Assistance Trade Association
www.easna.org

For additional information on EAP and/or EFAP service providers, access **www.easna.org**.

The most prevalent problems among employees are personal crises involving marital, family, financial, or legal matters. Such problems often come to a supervisor's attention. In most instances, the supervisor can usually provide the best help simply by being understanding and supportive and by helping the individual find the type of assistance needed. In many cases, the person is referred to the EAP (or EFAP) program. Many organizations that have an EAP also have operations and offices that are in many different locations yet want to use the same EAP provider. Therefore, in recent years, many EAP providers have begun to offer 24/7 telephone access to bilingual expert counsellors, telephonic counselling sessions, and online assistance to support managers.[61] Managers would want to ensure that they leverage the online support services offered by EAP providers: these include training, guides, checklists, videos, assessment tools, and articles.

As mentioned earlier in this chapter, emotional and/or mental health issues are on the rise and creating direct and indirect costs to the Canadian economy. Mental health issues continue to be a leading cause of short-and long-term disability as well as costing the Canadian economy over $33 billion per year.[62] A persistent focus on awareness, communication, and education would begin to reduce the fear, stigma, and discrimination around mental illness.

And it is important to pay attention to the mental well-being of managers also. Too often the focus is always on the employees and not the leaders.[63] Whether leaders will be able to perform their jobs must be determined on an individual basis and by qualified professionals. In reviewing such situations, the organization should pay particular attention to workplace cultural factors, since there is general agreement that emotional disturbances are primary or secondary factors in a large proportion of workplace accidents and violence—whether the person is a leader or not.

Business and industry lose billions of dollars every year because of substance abuse. According to the most recent study by the Canadian Centre on Substance Abuse, the total cost is close to $40 billion yearly, or $1,267 for every Canadian. In addition, legal substances such as tobacco and alcohol account for 80% of the abuse. Specifically, the following losses occur:

- $14.6 billion from alcohol abuse
- $8.2 billion from illicit drugs
- $17 billion from tobacco[64]

In confronting the problem, employers must recognize that substance addiction follows a rather predictable course, and they can take specific actions to deal with employees showing its symptoms at particular stages of its progression. Substance abuse typically begins with social drinking or drug taking that gets out of control. As the abuse progresses, the person loses control over how much to use and when. The person uses denial to avoid facing the problems created by the substance abuse and often blames others for them. The first step in helping the abuser is to awaken the person to the reality of the situation.

To identify substance abuse as early as possible, it is essential that supervisors monitor the performance, attendance, and behaviour of all employees regularly and systematically. A supervisor should carefully document evidence of declining performance, behaviour, and/or attendance, and then bring the matter to the attention of the employee with evidence that the work is suffering. The employee should be assured that help will be made available without penalty. In fact, through court decisions concerning substance addiction, the courts have confirmed that substance addiction is a disability, and employers are legally obliged to deal with the problem. This means the employer can no longer terminate someone because of an abuse problem. Specifically, a supervisor needs to set clear expectations, be consistent, act, and follow any other health and safety regulations. Since the assessments are made solely with regard to poor job performance, attendance, or behaviour, a supervisor can avoid any mention of the abuse and allow such employees to seek aid as they would for any other problem. A supervisor cannot discipline an employee for suspicion of abusing a substance: discipline is dependent on the degree of problem with job performance, attendance, or behaviour. Between 70 and 80% of employees accept the offer to get help and resolve their problems. Therefore, it is important for supervisors and managers to recognize that any discipline, whether a verbal warning or a termination, has to be related to the job. Further, as mentioned in previous chapters, there are many constraints on employers to legally ensure that the workplace is safe, secure, and free of discrimination.

In conclusion, it is important to remember the role leaders play in creating a culture that supports well-being. Building organizational processes and systems is a difficult task at the best of times. They must be able to respond well to immediate needs and help propel the organization toward a desirable future. In addition, these processes and systems must be simple to manage and maintain. When this doesn't happen, the result is too much time, resources, and attention spent on ineffective activities. In a culture that enables good health and safety in the workplace, employees will work together to maintain it, and there will be less focus on the legislated requirements.

Consider Emerging Trends 3.1 for information about what is on the horizon for workplace health and safety.

EMERGING TRENDS 3.1

1. ***Increasing attention to culture of organization.*** More organizations are finding that the culture of the organization can have a large impact on employee engagement and the well-being of the organization. It is no longer enough to pay attention to the legal requirements of health and safety legislation; it is also necessary to focus on how people interact. It is through appropriate and acceptable workplace actions and behaviour that the culture can change to support a healthy and safe work environment. Research has demonstrated that employees who are empowered and engaged take more responsibility for their own health and safety and work.
2. ***Expanding employee and family assistance programs (EFAP).*** With the increasing demands on employees and their families, EAP services have expanded to include services and resources for the entire family—particularly financial and stress counseling.
3. ***Increasing attention to mental health in the workplace.*** Many organizations have worked with and supported the Mental Health Commission of Canada to have open dialogue about mental health and the impact on the work environment—everything from harassment to bullying and violence. It is also recognized that treatment alone won't solve the issues and that supportive work environments need to be involved.
4. ***Ensuring harassment and bullying are not present in the work environment.*** As noted earlier in this chapter, the culture of the organization influences what behaviours and actions are acceptable or unacceptable. Some organizations consider these elements as a form of workplace violence and are taking more proactive steps to eliminate them. Health and safety legislation is targeting the reduction and elimination of workplace violence, harassment, and bullying by modifying the laws requiring the investigation and compensation of incidents.
5. ***Ensuring appropriate processes are in place for monitoring substance and prescription drug abuse.*** For the workplace to be healthy and safe, individuals with substance abuse issues need to be encouraged to seek professional assistance. To do so requires interventions by the employer that are respectful which can include mandatory referrals and treatment. While some people might feel this is a violation of someone's privacy, if done appropriately, it will not.
6. ***Ensuring assessments are done to prevent violence in the workplace.*** As more attention is paid to preventing violence in the workplace, the Canadian government has created a special committee that has identified key areas for employers to pay attention to: organizational risk assessments, individual and customer (client) risk assessments, security assessment, and having a personal safety response team.

Sources: Marie-Gabrielle Belanger, "Drug Testing Does Not Always Violate Fundamental Rights," *The HR Space*, Fasken Martineau, April 24, 2015; Bruce Cheadle, "Budget Day: Black Ink for First Time in 7 Years," *Canadian HR Reporter*, April 21, 2015, accessed May 14, 2015, www.hrreporter.com/articleview/24125-budget-day-black-ink-for-first-time-in-7-years?utm_medium=Email&utm_campaign=HRNewswire-West_20150421&utm_source=Act-On%20Software&; J. Anitha, "Determinants of Employee Engagement and Their Impact on Employee Performance," *Journal of Productivity and Performance Management* 63, no. 3 (2014): 308–323; Mental Health Commission of Canada, "Changing Directions, Changing Lives: The Mental Health Strategy for Canada," accessed May 14, 2015; Association of Workers' Compensation Boards of Canada, "Emerging Trends," accessed May 14, 2015, http://awcbc.org/?page_id=91&lcp_page0=2#lcp_instance_0; Institute for Work & Health, "IWH Research on Vulnerable Workers Leads to Tool for Measuring Risk Factors," *At Work*, 80 (Spring 2015): 3; Nadine Wentzell, "Dealing with Prescription Drug Abuse in the Workplace," *Canadian HR Reporter*, September 8, 2014, 13; Derrick Penner, "Mental Illness Challenges Human Resources," *The Vancouver Sun*, April 29, 2015, C2; and Chloe Taylor, "Workplace Violence—Breaking the Silence," *HRM Online*, May 13, 2015, accessed May 18, 2015, www.hrmonline.ca/hr-news/workplace-violence--breaking-the-silence-191279.aspx.

Summary

1. Describe organizational culture and the impact it has on the work environment.
   - Organizational culture is the collective understanding of beliefs and values that guide how employees act and behave—the personality of the organization.
2. Describe the impact of organizational culture on employees.
   - Culture provides the compass or guide for actions and behaviours.
   - Supportive cultures enable a positive approach to a healthy and safe work environment.

3. Explain the relationship between organizational culture and employee engagement.
   - Cultures that focus on social responsibility, leadership, and trust tend to have more engaged employees.
   - Employees that are more engaged tend to have higher productivity, stay with the organization longer, and support the organization.
4. Describe the link between culture and health and safety in the workplace.
   - Culture guides actions and behaviours.
   - Cultures that openly demonstrate a commitment to a healthy and safe work environment will have employees who act and behave in a healthy and safe way.
5. Cite the measures to use to reduce health and safety concerns.
   - Inform and train employees about safety and health expectations in the organization.
   - Keep records and investigate any accidents.
   - Involve employees in identifying and eliminating health and safety issues.
   - Emphasize the importance of health and safety in the work environment.
6. Describe the programs and services that help create well-being in the organization.
   - Health services
   - Wellness programs
   - Disability management
   - Employee assistance programs
7. Explain the importance of building a culture of well-being.
   - Proactive leadership and management commitment enables a culture that supports workplace well-being.
   - Culture is conducive to health and safety.

Need to Know

- Definition of organizational culture
- Definition of employee engagement
- Types of health and safety services and programs in the workplace

Need to Understand

- Role of culture in the health and safety of an organization
- Responsibilities of all employees in creating a healthy and safe work environment
- A proactive approach to employee well-being
- Prevention and control of workplace violence
- Role managers can play in preventing workplace stress and creating a resilient workforce

KEY TERMS

cumulative trauma disorders 89
cyber bullying 92
disability management 96
employee assistance program (EAP) 97
employee engagement 76
industrial disease 78
Material Safety Data Sheet (MSDS) 87
occupational illness 78
occupational injury 78
organizational culture 74
stress 92
workplace stressor 94

REVIEW QUESTIONS

1. What is organizational culture?
2. How does culture impact employees?
3. What is employee engagement?
4. What is the legislation that covers health and safety in the workplace?
5. What are 2 ways an employer can reduce its workers' compensation costs?
6. What can employers do to reduce health and safety concerns in the workplace?
7. What are some of the safety expectations in a typical work environment?
8. What is cyber bullying?

CRITICAL THINKING QUESTIONS

1. In the HRM Close-up, Dave Holmes comments on the financial cost of investing in G's staff. What is his reason for making this investment?
2. You've just been hired by Rim Auto Parts as the manager of its largest store in a major city. Part of your responsibility is to continue to foster an organizational culture that focuses on a healthy and safe work environment. How would you approach this, and what might you do?
3. You have recently started working in a large retail store as a management trainee. You are asked to develop a series of actions to improve employee engagement. What might you consider and why?
4. You work in the medical equipment and pharmaceutical department at a local hospital. Your department is responsible for dispensing medical supplies and prescriptions to patients. There have been recent incidents in which patients have been quite vocal and threatening in their behaviour toward staff. As a consequence, you and 4 other staff have been appointed to a task group to undertake a workplace violence audit and then develop appropriate procedures. What steps might you take to do the audit, and what procedures might you use to minimize the possibility of workplace violence?
5. You have recently joined a community recreational centre that hires many young workers. You are told of a growing concern about the health and safety of these employees. What would you do and why?
6. As a senior manager at a large insurance company, you've been asked to explain the company's approach to wellness by commenting on its slogan, "Wellness is not just a program—it's a message and how you deliver it makes a difference." How would you explain the slogan's meaning?
7. You've recently joined a fast-food chain and have been asked to develop a comprehensive wellness program. What would you include and how would you ensure its success?

DEVELOPING YOUR SKILLS

Hofstede Centre
http://geert-hofstede.com

Excellence Canada
www.excellence.ca/en/awards/2014-cae-recipients/2014-caevideo-amd

1. On an individual basis, access Hofstede's organizational cultural model at **http://geert-hofstede.com/organisational-culture.html**. The model consists of 8 dimensions or variables of culture. Click on each to get an explanation of that particular dimension. Then click on the "Culture and Strategy Play and Learn App" and work through Level 1. Determine what was the most interesting dimension and why. Share your results with your classmates.
2. Using any search engine, search on the phrase "employee engagement." Look at each of the top 10 sites. Write a 1-page summary of your results, including which site provided the best information or most interesting information on employee engagement.
3. On an individual basis, access **www.excellence.ca/en/awards/2014-cae-recipients/2014-caevideo-amd** and watch the video about ArcelorMittal Dofasco and information about its healthy workplace. What one thing about the information impressed you? Why?

4. Working in small groups, access the Province of Alberta's interactive health and safety quiz at **http://work.alberta.ca/ohs-quiz/index.html**. Pick 2–3 categories and take the quiz. Identify which quiz was the most useful and why. Share your results with the rest of your classmates.
5. Access the following websites or your provincial workers' compensation site.
   - **www.safety-council.org** (Canada Safety Council)
   - **www.ccohs.ca** (Canadian Centre for Occupational Health and Safety)
   - **www.awcbc.org** (Association of Workers' Compensation Boards of Canada)
6. Identify 3 companies that have violated health and safety regulations in your province. Prepare a 1-page summary describing the losses to the organizations in work (hours), the dollar penalties, and any other considerations such as family impact.

Alberta Occupational Health and Safety
http://work.alberta.ca/ohs-quiz/index.html

Canada Safety Council
www.safety-council.org

Canadian Centre for Occupational Health and Safety
www.ccohs.ca

Association of Workers' Compensation Boards of Canada
www.awcbc.org

CASE STUDY 1

Culture and Healthy Organizations

It is easy to say that supportive and people-centred cultures typically have more engaged and productive employees. But does that mean that the organization has an environment of well-being? As with most answers, "it all depends."

Senior leaders in particular need to act and behave in a way that creates and maintains a great work environment—one that values and puts trust in its people and ensures there is open communication at all levels. But where are such leaders found?

Sun Life Financial, a financial services company with headquarters in Toronto, takes great pride in focusing employee health as the core to its positive work culture—one that it says makes the company so successful. Its health focus includes physical and psychological well-being for its employees and their families. In order to maintain this focus, managers are trained to recognize and be able to respond to unusual situations, to communicate effectively, and to engage employees in work activities that sustain the culture. The managers are also critical in helping the employees understand the company's values and what is important to everyone. Managers are also trained to acknowledge and thank employees on a regular basis—it isn't enough to just do this occasionally.

Another well-known company with a positive culture that has become a competitive advantage is IKEA. The company is known for creating and sustaining a culture that blends employees' individual qualities with its values. The company wants its employees to be down-to-earth and always prepared to contribute to its positive culture, proud to work there and be part of a team. IKEA's values of respect both for employees and for customers, leading by example, being willing to change, being cost-conscious, learning from mistakes, and working together with enthusiasm were instilled by its founder, Ingvar Kamprad.

Sources: Adapted from Jim Riley, "Ikea's Distinctive and Positive Organizational Culture," May 6, 2015, accessed May 19, 2015, http://beta.tutor2u.net/business/blog/would-you-fit-into-the-organisational-culture-at-ikea; Sarah Dobson, "Health Cultures, Reduced Costs," *Canadian HR Reporter*, November 17, 2014, 6; "Employee Health Is Core to Organizational Success," *Canadian HR Reporter*, November 17, 2014, 9; and "Our Values," Ikea.com, accessed May 19, 2015, www.ikea.com/ms/en_US/the_ikea_story/working_at_ikea/our_values.html#.

Questions:

1. If you are working or recently worked, how would you describe the culture of the organization?
2. Do you think you'd fit into Ikea's culture? To assess, go to **www.ikea.com/ms/en_US/the_ikea_story/working_at_ikea/our_values.html#** and answer the 10 questions. What did you learn about yourself?

CASE STUDY 2

Safety Concerns at the Grand Hotel

The Grand Hotel has received many awards for its customer experience. It has over 10,000 people staying at its hotel every year. Part of the success of the hotel has been its focus on providing its staff with all the tools to provide an exceptional experience for the hotel guest and by creating a "health and safety first" culture.

Recently the hotel general manager has noticed an increase in the number of reported accidents and workplace injuries. A hotel employee was so concerned about the number of back injuries and wrist strains that they contacted the local WCB officer and asked that there be a safety audit. However, the audit did not uncover anything unusual for the hotel industry. The general manager asked the employee why they had gone to the WCB instead of contacting their supervisor and manager.

The hotel has the following policy on the work environment:

> The Grand Hotel is committed to a culture of well-being which creates a healthy and safe work environment. The hotel endeavours to provide an environment that promotes health and safety practices that go far beyond the minimum required by law. The hotel expects that health and safety, of both employees and guests, is primary in every area of operation.

New employees get training on how to do their work safely, with special focus on lifting, carrying, and using items such as sheets and trash cans. Employees get reminders about safe work practices and how to stay healthy at monthly staff meetings. As new methods are identified to minimize the physical and mental impact of the work, there is training and regular coaching from supervisors.

Last week the general manager got a notification from the provincial agency that the hotel's workers' compensation premiums would be increased in the following calendar year as a result of the increased claims.

Questions:

1. Why might the accident and injury claims be increasing?
2. By law, workplace safety is the responsibility of the employer and employee. What else can the Grand Hotel do to ensure employees are doing their work in a safe and healthy way?
3. Do you think the hotel does have a culture of well-being? Explain your answer.

NOTES AND REFERENCES

1. Association of Workers' Compensation Boards of Canada, "2013 Injury Statistics," accessed April 15, 2015, http://awcbc.org/?page_id=14.
2. Fisk Johnson, "SC Johnson's CEO on Doing the Right Thing, Even When It Hurts Business," *Harvard Business Review*, April 2015, 33–36.
3. Ibid.
4. For those interested, a full description of the various dimensions of culture identified by Geert Hofstede can be found at The Hofstede Centre, http://geert-hofstede.com.
5. Adam Lashinsky, "Becoming Tim Cook," *Fortune*, April 1, 2015, 60–72.
6. Ibid.
7. Lindsay Macintosh, "Embrace Failure for Organizational Success," *PeopleTalk*, Spring 2015, 20.
8. Diane Jermyn, "Company Culture a Magnet for Talent, Not a Frill," *The Globe and Mail*, October 15, 2014, E3; and "Canada's Best Workplaces," *The Globe and Mail*, April 10, 2015.
9. "OMERS, Cisco, Keg Restaurants Among Top 50 Employers for 2015," *Canadian HR Reporter*, November 7, 2014, accessed April 17, 2015, www.hrreporter.com/articleview/22740-omers-cisco-keg-restaurants-among-top-50-employers-for-2015.
10. "2014 Trends in Global Employee Engagement," Aon Hewitt website, 2014, accessed September 12, 2015, www.aon.com/human-capital-consulting/thought-leadership/talent_mgmt/2014-trends-in-global-employee-engagement.jsp.
11. Amelia Chan, "Remove the Roadblocks to Engagement," *PeopleTalk*, Winter 2014, 14–15.

12. Province of Alberta, "Occupational Health and Safety Results 2013," accessed April 17, 2015, http://work.alberta.ca/documents/2013-OHS-Data.pdf.
13. Association of Workers' Compensation Boards of Canada, "2013 Number of Fatalities, by Gender and Jurisdiction," accessed April 17, 2015, http://awcbc.org/?page_id=14.
14. Liz Bernier, "Engaging Young Workers in a Safety Culture," *Canadian HR Reporter*, April 6, 2015, 13.
15. "The Workplace Safety and Health Act," Manitoba.ca, accessed April 17, 2015, http://web2.gov.mb.ca/laws/statutes/ccsm/w210e.php.
16. Government of Saskatchewan, "Understanding Occupational Health and Safety in Saskatchewan," 2015.
17. "Overview, *Canada Labour Code*, Part II," accessed April 17, 2015, www.labour.gc.ca/eng/health_safety/pubs_hs/overview.shtml#offences.
18. Gordon Hoekstra, "Liberals Introduce New Workplace Safety Laws," *The Vancouver Sun*, February 12, 2015, D1.
19. Workers' Compensation Board of Nova Scotia, "Employer Return-to-Work Award Nova Scotia Liquor Corporation," May 2014, accessed April 18, 2015, http://worksafeforlife.ca/Home/Programs-Awards/Mainstay/Winners.
20. "Building and Construction 2014: Borger Group of Companies," *Canadian Occupational Safety*, October 20, 2014, accessed April 18, 2015, www.cos-mag.com/safety/safety-stories/4160-building-and-construction-2014-borger-group-of-companies.html.
21. Hydro One, "Putting Safety First," accessed April 18, 2015, www.hydroone.com/OurCommitment/Safety/Pages/Default.aspx.
22. Ontario Power Generation, "Corporate Safety," accessed April 18, 2015, www.opg.com/about/safety/corporate-safety/Pages/corporate-safety.aspx.
23. Canadian Centre for Occupational Health and Safety, "Workplace Health and Wellness Program—Getting Started," accessed April 18, 2015, www.ccohs.ca/oshanswers/psychosocial/wellness_program.html.
24. Kevin Kelloway and Lori Francis, *Management of Health and Safety*, 5th ed. (Toronto: Nelson Education, 2011).
25. Marie Mawad and Cornelius Rahn, "Executives Recognize Importance of Taking a 'Digital Timeout,'" *The Vancouver Sun*, January 24, 2015, H5.
26. Doni Bloomfield, "Employees Take a Stand Against Being Desk Jockeys," *The Vancouver Sun*, January 24, 2015, H5.
27. Ibid.
28. "Definition of 'Danger,'" *Canada Labour Code*, October 2014, accessed April 18, 2015, www.labour.gc.ca/eng/resources/ipg/062.shtml.
29. Liz Bernier, "Domestic Violence Spills into Workplace," *Canadian HR Reporter*, January 26, 2015, accessed April 15, 2015, www.hrreporter.com/articleview/23333-domestic-violence-spills-into-workplace.
30. Canadian Labour Congress, "Domestic Violence at Work," accessed April 20, 2015, www.canadianlabour.ca/issues/domestic-violence-work; and Social Sciences and Humanities Research Council of Canada, "Can Work be Safe When Home Isn't?" 2014.
31. Canadian Centre for Occupational Health and Safety, "Violence in the Workplace," accessed April 18, 2015, www.ccohs.ca/oshanswers/psychosocial/violence.html.
32. "Canada Occupational Health and Safety Regulations," Justice Laws website, accessed April 20, 2015, http://laws.justice.gc.ca/eng/regulations/sor-86-304/page-114.html.
33. Canadian Centre for Occupational Health and Safety, "OSH Answers Fact Sheets: Violence in the Workplace," accessed April 20, 2015, www.ccohs.ca/oshanswers/psychosocial/violence.html.
34. Ibid.
35. Liz Bernier, "From the Schoolyard to the Office," *The Canadian HR Reporter*, March 23, 2015, accessed April 26, 2015, www.hrreporter.com/articleview/23856-from-the-schoolyard-to-the-office.
36. Erin Ellis, "Working in a Stressful Job Can Be Hard on an Employee's Head," *The Vancouver Sun*, June 21, 2014, D1.
37. Yamri Taddese, "Are You Ready for a Flood of Stress-Related Compensation Claims?" *The Canadian HR Reporter*, July 14, 2014, 5.
38. Jennifer Newman, "Bullies Aren't Restricted to the Schoolyard," *The Vancouver Sun*, February 21, 2015, D8.
39. Brenda Bouw, "Dealing with Death at Work," *The Globe and Mail*, October 8, 2014, B15.
40. Susan Stefura, "Money Issues Top Source of Stress: Survey," *Canadian HR Reporter*, September 8, 2014, 25.
41. Ibid.
42. Liz Bernier, "High Stress, High Stakes," *The Canadian HR Reporter*, April 6, 2015, 3.
43. Ibid.
44. Sarah Dobson, "Manager Relationships Key to Mentally Healthy Workplace," *Canadian HR Reporter*, February 23, 2015, 2.
45. Dr. Ted Harvey and Neil Gavigan, "Minimizing Workplace Stress, Injuries and Violence in Canada: Towards a New Standard for Occupational Health and Safety," submission to the Mental Health Commission of Canada and Federal-Provincial-Territorial Ministers of Labour, September 2014.
46. Mental Health Commission of Canada, "National Standard of Canada for Psychological Health and Safety in the Workplace," accessed April 22, 2015, www.mentalhealthcommission.ca/English/issues/workplace/national-standard.
47. Liz Bernier, "A Hard Day's Night," *Canadian HR Reporter*, April 6, 2015, 1.
48. Liz Bernier, "High Stress, High Stakes."
49. Katie Burrell, "Making Mental Health Mandatory," *Canadian HR Reporter*, April 20, 2015, 17.
50. The Lowe Group, "Ten Guiding Principles for Healthy Organizations," accessed April 22, 2015, http://grahamlowe.ca/documents/298/GLG%20Healthy%20Org%20Guiding%20Principles%20rev_Mar15.pdfGraham.
51. Di Fan, Lin Cui, Mike Mingqiong Zhang, Cherie Jiuhua Zhu, Charmine E.J. Hartel, & Chris Nyland, "Influence of High Performance Work Systems on Employee Subjective Well-Being and Job Burnout," *The International Journal of Human Resource Management* 25, no. 7 (2014): 931–950.
52. Ibid.
53. Ron Z. Goetzel et al., "Do Workplace Health Promotion (Wellness) Programs Work?" *Journal of Occupational & Environmental Medicine* 56, no. 9 (September 2014): 927–934.
54. Brian Kreissl, "Are Employee Wellness Initiatives Effective?" *Canadian HR Reporter*, December 16, 2014, accessed April 28, 2015, www.hrreporter.com/blog/HR-Policies-Practices/archive/2014/12/16/are-employee-wellness-initiatives-effective.
55. Bruce Jacobs, "RIP Wellness ROI?" *BenefitsPro*, February 10, 2014, accessed May 14, 2015, www.benefitspro.com/2014/02/10/rip-wellness-roi#.
56. Laurie Down, "The Disability Case Manager's Tool Box," *Canadian HR Reporter*, April 20, 2015, 14.
57. Nancy Gowan, "Defining 'Light Duties' in Return-to-Work Programs," *Canadian HR Reporter*, October 20, 2014, 12.
58. Ibid.
59. Ibid.
60. Mental Health Commission of Canada, "Making the Case for Investing in Mental Health in Canada," accessed May 14, 2015.
61. "GuidanceResources® Services in Canada," ComPsych, accessed May 14, 2015, www.compsych.com/canada.
62. Joan Burton, "The Business Case for a Healthy Workplace," IAPA (Industrial Accident Prevention Association) website, 2008, accessed September 12, 2015, www.iapa.ca/pdf/fd_business_case_healthy_workplace.pdf.
63. Nicola Middlemiss, "Too Little Attention Paid to Managers' Mental Health," *HRM Online*, April 27, 2015, accessed May 14, 2015, www.hrmonline.ca/hr-news/too-little-attention-paid-to-managers-mental-health-190639.aspx.
64. Canadian Centre on Substance Abuse, "The Costs of Substance Abuse in Canada," accessed May 14, 2015, www.ccsa.ca/Eng/topics/Costs-of-Substance-Abuse-in-Canada/Pages/default.aspx.

4 Defining, Analyzing, and Designing the Work

LEARNING OUTCOMES

After studying this chapter, you should be able to

1. Explain the manager's and the employee's role in defining and designing work.
2. Discuss the relationship between job analysis and HRM processes.
3. Explain the relationship between job analysis and a job description.
4. Define and describe the sections in a job description.
5. Describe the uses of information gained from job analysis.
6. Explain the relationship of job design to employee contributions.
7. Discuss the different types of work designs to increase employee contribution.

OUTLINE

HRM CLOSE-UP

"Narrowing the gap between the executives and the front line provided the employees with a sense that management does really care, and that's very important to them and also to us."

In 2006, the government of Ontario decided there needed to be a better way to provide the people of the province with access to government services and information. The result was ServiceOntario, a division of the Ministry of Government and Consumer Services that streamlines not just their own services, but those of most other ministries in an efficient one-stop-shopping experience.

Today, ServiceOntario is one of the largest government customer service operations in North America with more than 80 in-person service centres, over 200 privately operated service provider centres, a robust website, and telephone call centres located in Toronto, Oshawa, Thunder Bay, and Kingston. In one recent year, ServiceOntario handled more than 35 million transactions, and it now represents more than a dozen ministries assisting people with everything from health cards and driver's licences to acquiring government publications.

Mary Ben Hamoud is Director, Central Region Contact Centre Services, for ServiceOntario. Out of a total ServiceOntario staff of more than 2,000 people, the call centres within her responsibility account for approximately 220 employees, all of whom must undergo intensive training before handling enquiries.

"With so much falling under the ServiceOntario umbrella, our contact centres must not only be knowledgeable on the products and services that we provide to the broader public, but we're also mandated to be consistently fair and respectful," Ben Hamoud says. "We also must remain current with new legislation and government policies and this makes our environment very dynamic, both at the senior management level where requirements are constantly reviewed and assessed, and at the front line where the information is disseminated."

Prior to joining the government, Mary Ben Hamoud had more than 15 years of experience managing various state-of-the-art call centres, including those of one of the country's largest automotive manufacturers and a leading telecommunications company. ServiceOntario was her first venture into the public sector, however.

"As a public-sector service, I quickly learned that our service principles commit us to providing everyone with equitable and superior services and a clear explanation of our decisions, all while maintaining the utmost security of the public's private information," Ben Hamoud explains. "All of this must be done in the most efficient, cost-effective and time-sensitive manner as we know that when people contact us they need accurate answers or assistance quickly."

Meeting the needs of Ontarians and the requirements of the various ministries with their unique and multiple service offerings was a significant challenge for those who established ServiceOntario and its overall brand-awareness. But that wasn't the only difficulty encountered.

"Aside from defining the work, we had to consider how to create our own culture while respecting and maintaining the culture that was coming to us from our partner ministries," Ben Hamoud says. "I think that was one of the biggest challenges."

As ServiceOntario continues to evolve, there have been other changes, including a recent effort to promote more direct contact between upper management, the front-line staff and ultimately the customers.

"Our deputy minister was very much interested in what was happening on the front line," Ben Hamoud explains. "In an organization as large as ServiceOntario, the challenge was how best to do that while not overloading anyone."

Used by permission of Mary Ben Hamoud

Mary Ben Hamoud, Director, Central Region Contact Centre Services, ServiceOntario.

The chosen outcome was to restructure a layer of management. That redistribution of the work not only succeeded in immediately giving senior management and executives a better grasp of how things were at the front line, but it also achieved other valuable benefits.

"The redistribution exercise provided an opportunity to really get connected to the front line, and that experience allowed us to be more engaged with staff," Ben Hamoud says. "I think it was one of the most brilliant things that happened in the organization. I unfortunately didn't know too many of my front-line staff before because of that layer of management, but now I know almost all of my agents by first name".

"I'm intimately aware and involved with their success and their performance. That feels really good, and it also provides the employees with a sense that management does really care, and that's very important to them and also to us."

Source: Used by permission of Mary Ben Hamoud

INTRODUCTION

As Mary Ben Hamoud from ServiceOntario noted, work needs to be designed in a manner that enhances customer service, promotes communication, and supports the appropriate distribution of tasks. This being so, organizations are transforming themselves in an attempt to become more effective. Companies such as Karo, a Calgary-based branding agency, are paying attention to the structure and culture of their organizations. Karo practises what it preaches by creating teams—smaller and more interconnected groups within its organization—to deliver results to its clients.[1] There is an emphasis on smaller scale, less hierarchy, fewer layers, and more decentralized work units.

As organizations reshape themselves, managers want employees to operate more independently and flexibly to meet customer demands. To do this, managers require that decisions be made by the people who are closest to the information and are directly involved in the product or service delivered. The objective is to develop jobs and basic work units adaptable enough to thrive in a world of high-speed change.

This chapter will discuss how jobs can be analyzed and also designed to best contribute to the objectives of the organization while satisfying the needs of the employees who perform them. You will learn about the role of the line manager and the employee in defining and designing work, and the terminology used to describe how jobs are defined. Several innovative job design and employee contribution techniques that increase job satisfaction and employee empowerment while improving organizational performance are discussed. Teamwork and the characteristics of successful teams are highlighted. The chapter concludes with a brief discussion of the future design of organizational work.

DEFINING WORK

Job
A group of related activities and duties

Position
Specific duties and responsibilities performed by only one employee

Work
Tasks or activities that need to be completed

Role
The part played by an employee within an organization and the associated expected behaviours

Organizations are complex systems composed of numerous and varied tasks. A **job** consists of a group of related activities and duties. Ideally, the duties of a job should consist of natural units of work that are similar and related. They should be clear and distinct from those of other jobs to minimize misunderstanding and conflict among employees and to enable employees to recognize what is expected of them. For some jobs, several employees may be required, each of whom will occupy a separate position. A **position** consists of the specific duties and responsibilities performed by only one employee. In a city library, for example, four employees (four positions) may be involved in reference work, but all of them have only one job (reference librarian).

In many ways, the words "job" and "position" are relics of the industrial age. As organizations need to be more flexible and adaptable, and utilize their people resources well for a competitive advantage, managers also need to think in terms of "work." By thinking of **work**, employers have more flexibility to define what needs to be done and when, and to change employee assignments on a short-term basis.

You will recall from Chapter 1 that you were introduced to the concept of "competencies"—characteristics or behaviours necessary for successful work performance in an organization. Competencies become very important when focusing on "work" compared to job. For example, those individuals seeking a designation of Certified Human Resource Professional (CHRP) must display 44 professional competencies that are organized into nine functional areas of knowledge and five enabling competencies. Proficiency levels for each competency are outlined as well. Instead of organizations focusing on job descriptions, companies will use "work profiles" or "work agreements" to describe the work to be done. Further, the concept of "roles" is also linked to competencies. Your **role** is the part you play in the organization, and it will have certain expected behaviours. For example, your role as a customer service representative includes active listening as an expected behaviour. You will continue to see more references to work and work processes, project management, tasks, and task analysis than to "job." Further information regarding the competencies associated with the CHRP designation may be viewed at **www.chrp.ca/?page=chrp_competency**.

CHRP Designation
www.chrp.ca/?page=chrp_competency

Whether thinking in terms of "job" or "work," a manager needs to describe what tasks need to be done and in what order, the skills a person needs to successfully perform the work requirements, and the role a person plays in the company. This is the essence of organizational success. For all HR processes, you will need to have this type of information.

THE MANAGER'S AND THE EMPLOYEE'S ROLE IN DEFINING WORK

LO1

What is the manager's role in defining and designing work? How can an employee assist a manager in defining and designing work?

The line manager or supervisor is the primary individual who determines what tasks and activities need to be performed, and in what order, to reach the company's goals or objectives. Therefore, it is critical that the line manager understand what steps need to be implemented to design jobs in order to maximize organizational performance. While the line manager will take an active role in determining what skills and abilities are needed to successfully perform the work, often an employee (the **job incumbent**, the person actually doing the work) will be asked for information regarding the job and its requirements. The person performing the job is often able to contribute information regarding the work only they would know. Further, through job analysis, the line manager will play an integral role in developing and/or writing a job description and will rely upon input from the job incumbent to ensure that information regarding the job is accurately collected and documented.

Job incumbent
The employee hired to do a job

Job Analysis

LO2

What is the relationship between job analysis and HRM processes?

LO3

What is the relationship between job analysis and a job description?

Job analysis is referred to as the cornerstone of HRM, because the information it collects informs and supports so many HRM processes. **Job analysis** is the process of obtaining information about jobs (or work) by determining what the duties, tasks, or activities of those jobs are and the necessary skills, knowledge, training, and abilities to perform the work successfully. The procedure involves undertaking a systematic approach to gathering specific job information, including the work activities, worker attributes, and work context.[2] This being the case, when job information is accurate it will be easier to recruit, select, manage performance, plan for training and development and health and safety issues, and compensate an individual doing this work. The ultimate purpose of job analysis is to improve organizational performance and productivity. Figure 4.1 illustrates how job analysis is done and what the information is used for.

Job analysis is concerned with objective and verifiable information about the requirements of a job (compared to "job design," which reflects subjective opinions about the ideal requirements of the job). Job analysis is not done in a vacuum: it is important that the organization's goals and strategies be known and understood. Without the organizational context or an understanding of the organization as a whole, the requirements identified may not reflect foreseeable future requirements. A proactive strategic approach would link the jobs to the organization's performance.[3]

Job analysis
Process of obtaining information about jobs by determining the duties, tasks, or activities and the skills, knowledge, and abilities associated with the jobs

Job analysis is typically undertaken by trained HR people; however, a line manager with good analytical abilities and writing skills can also do it. The HR professional can provide assistance to the manager in gathering the relevant information by ensuring that appropriate questions are asked and that the job is not "inflated" (made to sound more difficult or important than it really is). Therefore, as previously noted, the employee performing the work also has a critical part to play to ensure that accurate information about the job is collected. It is also valuable to have the person doing the work (and the supervisor or team leader) review the data gathered to ensure that it is accurate and complete. Online resources providing job profiles are another source of information. For example, the government of Canada provides a resource of National Occupational Classification codes (NOC codes) that lists detailed information regarding various jobs. Regardless of the source of information, prior to any job analysis being conducted it is critical that the line manager

FIGURE 4.1 The Process of Job Analysis

WHERE YOU GET JOB INFORMATION

Employee
Supervisor
Online job profiles

HOW YOU OBTAIN JOB INFORMATION

Questionnaires
Interviews
Diaries
Observations

WHAT JOB INFORMATION IS COLLECTED

Tasks
Duties
Responsibilities
Equipment used
Skills required
Knowledge required
Experience required
Working conditions
Effort
Job context
Performance standards

WHERE THE INFORMATION GOES

Written Job Description, Including:
Job title
Summary of job
Job duties and responsibilities
Job specification (skills, knowledge, abilities)
Standards of performance

HOW INFORMATION IS USED

Recruitment
Selection
Performance management
Training and development
Health and safety
Compensation

and employees have received transparent communication to inform them of how the analysis will be conducted and what the information will be used for.

Job data can be collected in a range of ways. Individual interviews may be conducted (asking questions, such as "What duties do you perform every day?" or "What tools do you use to complete these duties?") with employees performing the jobs, or groups of employees who perform the same job may be interviewed to collect information. Alternatively, the incumbent may be observed in order to better understand the work required. Or they may be asked to keep a diary or log of work performed. In larger organizations a uniform approach is frequently used, such as asking people to fill out an electronic or hard-copy questionnaire that requests a list of work activities. Review Toolkit 4.1 for examples of questions that might be posed either in an interview or on a questionnaire.

When deciding which method of job analysis should be used, the time and money spent versus quality of information collected should be taken into consideration. Efficiency and effectiveness should be balanced. It is also important that the line manager review the information collected in order to ensure accuracy. Ethics in HRM 4.1 describes what can happen if a job is inflated.

For links to a variety of resources on job profiles, writing job descriptions, and conducting a job analysis, go to **www.job-analysis.net** and **http://alis.alberta.ca.**

Job Descriptions

LO4

What are the sections in a job description?

Once all the information on a particular job has been collected, it is organized into a **job description**—a written document. This description includes the types of duties or responsibilities, and the skills, knowledge, and abilities or competencies (job specifications; see below) needed to successfully perform the work. Since no standard format applies to job descriptions, they tend to vary in appearance and content from one organization to another. However, typical headings are the following:

I. *Job Title.* Provides an indication of the general nature of the job. For example, "night supervisor," "salesperson," "lab assistant," or "team leader."
II. *Reports To.* Listing of the position that this job is accountable to.
III. *Date.* Date that the description was written. Indicates currency of information.
IV. *Written By and Approved By.* Names and titles of individuals involved in writing the document. Provides points of contact for future questions or clarification.
V. *Summary.* Two or three sentences describing the overall purpose of the job. Answers the question "Why does this job exist?"
VI. *Duties and Responsibilities.* Individual statements, usually listed in order of importance, of the key duties and responsibilities. You would expect to see between 10 and 15 statements.
VII. *Job Specification.* The required knowledge, skills, and abilities.
VIII. *Performance Standards.* A prioritized list outlining several expected results of the job.

The specific skills, knowledge, and abilities required to successfully perform the job become the **job specifications**. Skills relevant to a job can include education and experience, specialized training, and specific abilities such as manual dexterity. If there are any physical demands, such as walking long distances or reaching high shelves, these would also be mentioned. Many organizations now view job specifications as including "employability" skills and knowledge, such as problem-solving abilities. An example of employability skills, as outlined by the Ontario Ministry of Training, Colleges and Universities, can be viewed at **www.tcu.gov.on.ca/pepg/audiences/colleges/progstan/essential.html**.

TOOLKIT 4.1 JOB ANALYSIS QUESTIONS

Here are some questions one might ask when conducting a job analysis:

1. In a brief statement (three to four sentences), describe the basic purpose of your position. Do it in a way that answers "Why does my position exist?"
2. What are the most important responsibilities of your position, and how much time do you spend on each of these? Please list each main responsibility in order of importance. Start each statement with an action verb such as "provides," "determines," "verifies."
3. What are the key tasks for each of the responsibilities? What percentage of your time each month do you spend on each task?
4. What are the physical surroundings and/or hazards of your position? (This can include travel, exposure, danger, and environmental risks.)
5. Describe the mental and physical effort you expend in performing your work. For example, do you have long periods of intense concentration? Is there a lot of routine? Is the position physically demanding? Please include the frequency of the effort.
6. What are the knowledge and basic skills required to successfully fulfill the responsibilities?
7. Describe two or three of the more difficult problems you must solve to your job done. Include situations that are a constant challenge and situations that require judgment and time to consider alternative solutions before problems can be resolved.

Job description
A document that lists the tasks, duties, and responsibilities of a job to be performed along with the skills, knowledge, and abilities or competencies needed to successfully perform the work

Toolkit 4.2 provides an example of a job description for the manager of retail operations at a sports arena. Note that this example includes specific HR responsibilities, as noted in the first section under "People Management." It includes both duties and specifications, and should satisfy most of the job information needs of managers while providing information for other critical HRM processes, as discussed later in this chapter.

Problems with Job Descriptions

While many managers consider job descriptions a valuable tool for performing HRM activities, several problems are frequently associated with these documents, including the following:

Job Analysis Homepage
www.job-analysis.net

Alberta Career Profiles
http://alis.alberta.ca

ETHICS IN HRM 4.1 INFLATING THE JOB

At some point in your working life, you will be asked to describe your job, perhaps when being interviewed by a job analyst or by answering questions on a form. Most employees have a reasonable expectation that their answers will affect their lives in significant ways. The information obtained may be used to reclassify the job to either a higher or lower pay level. Most employees believe that standards of performance may change, and the employer will expect them to work faster or to do more, although that is not the goal of job analysis. As a result of these beliefs and expectations, employees have a vested interest in "inflating" their job descriptions, by making the job sound very important and very difficult. Thus, night clerks in hotels become "auditors," and receptionists become "administrators." Job inflation might reflect an employee's sincere belief in the significance of his or her contribution, or it may be an attempt to lobby for higher pay.

CRITICAL THINKING QUESTIONS:

1. Do you believe employees intentionally inflate their jobs or do they genuinely believe their jobs to be significant, as per their descriptions?
2. As a manager, how can you ensure job information is correct if the employee and you view the job differently?

Essential Employability Skills
www.tcu.gov.on.ca/pepg/audiences/colleges/progstan/essential.html

1. They are poorly written, using vague rather than specific terms, so they provide little guidance to the jobholder (e.g., "other duties as assigned").
2. They are sometimes not updated as job duties or specifications change.
3. They may violate the law by containing specifications not related to job success (e.g., "must be single between the ages of 25 and 35").
4. They can limit the scope of activities of the jobholder.
5. They do not contain standards of performance, which are essential for selecting, training, evaluating, and rewarding jobholders.
6. When expected behaviours are not included, they can be the basis for conflict, including union grievances.

Writing Clear and Specific Job Descriptions

Job specifications
Statement of the needed knowledge, skills, and abilities of the person who is to perform the position

In writing a job description, it is essential to use statements that are concise, direct, and simply worded. Unnecessary words or phrases should be eliminated. Typically, the sentences that describe job duties begin with a present-tense and action-oriented verb, with the implied subject of the sentence being the employee performing the job. An example for an accounting clerk for a small company might read: "Deposits cheques on a daily basis" or "Prepares month-end financial statements by the 10th of the following month." (Note that these two statements include performance standards.) The term "occasionally" is used to describe those duties that are performed once in a while. The term "may" is used in connection with those duties performed by only some workers on the job. Other examples of action-oriented, present-tense verbs are "coordinates," "handles," "researches," "conducts," "generates," and "evaluates." You can obtain a list of verbs used in job descriptions at **www.job-analysis.net**.

Legal Considerations with Job Descriptions

Even when set forth in writing, job descriptions and specifications can still be vague. To the alarm of many employers, however, today's legal environment has created what might be called an "age of specifics." Human rights legislation requires that the specific performance requirements of a job be based on valid job-related criteria. Decisions that involve either job applicants or employees and that are based on criteria either vague or not job-related are increasingly being successfully challenged. Managers of small businesses, in which employees may perform many different job tasks, have to be particularly concerned about writing specific job descriptions. In a very small business, such as Aquinox Pharmaceuticals in British Columbia, the focus is not so much on writing a job description but on identifying the core activities and then describing the attributes needed to be successful.[4]

When preparing job descriptions, managers must be aware of human rights legislation. Written job descriptions must match the requirements of the job. Also, position descriptions may need to be altered to meet the standard of "reasonable accommodation." Reasonable accommodation is used most frequently to match religious or disability needs, although any prohibited ground for discrimination under human rights legislation would have to be considered for reasonable accommodation.

The 2010 case *Fiona Johnstone v. Canada Border Services* made it clear that reasonable accommodation for family-status reasons is valid.[5] In a judicial review in 2014, the Federal Court upheld this decision, reinforcing the requirement to fully consider the requirements for, and what constitutes grounds for, reasonable accommodation.[6]

Job descriptions written to match the needs for reasonable accommodation reduce the risk of discrimination. The goal is to match and accommodate human capabilities to job requirements. For example, if the job requires the jobholder to read extremely fine print, to climb ladders, or to memorize stock codes, these physical and mental requirements should be stated within the job description. Read HRM and the Law 4.1 to understand more about the legal implications of inappropriate job requirements.

TOOLKIT 4.2 SAMPLE JOB DESCRIPTION

Company Name
Job: Manager, Retail Operations
Reports To: Director, Retail Operations
Date: April 5, 2016
Written By:
Approved By:

SUMMARY

The manager, retail operations, is responsible for all aspects of retail operations for game nights and events. The manager ensures the store, booths, and kiosks are staffed with well-trained sales and service professionals and are visually attractive with appropriate merchandise for the customer environment. While staff development, sales, and service are primary focus areas, administrative activities such as payroll and scheduling are also part of this role.

ESSENTIAL DUTIES AND RESPONSIBILITIES

People Management

1. Recruit, train, motivate, and develop a professional and knowledgeable part-time and on-call service and sales workforce.
2. Coach and communicate with employees in a fair and consistent manner (e.g., mentoring sessions, performance evaluations).
3. Work closely with senior retail management and human resources regarding disciplinary and other sensitive employee issues.
4. Identify and implement employee recognition and incentive programs.
5. Ensure staff are trained in all key areas of the business.

Business Management

1. Ensure selling areas are open for business on time and are clean and visually attractive.
2. Identify opportunities for increasing revenue.
3. Create sales and promotional programs.
4. Work with marketing staff regarding event details, such as expected attendance levels, merchandise deals, internal and external event contacts.
5. Produce sales reports.

Administration

1. Schedule staff in a fair and consistent manner.
2. Input payroll information into payroll time -management system.
3. Monitor payroll against budget and sales.
4. Develop and maintain an employee manual.

REQUIRED EXPERIENCE AND QUALIFICATIONS (JOB SPECIFICATIONS)

1. Four to six years' retail experience, with at least two years' supervisory experience.
2. Degree or diploma in business administration or related field.
3. Excellent leadership skills with the ability to coach, mentor, and motivate a sales service team.
4. Excellent communication, interpersonal, and problem-solving skills.
5. A solid understanding of the business and customer environment.
6. Must be able to identify and implement new business opportunities and promotions.
7. Flexible and adaptable.
8. Computer-literate, with a working knowledge of MS Word, MS Excel, point-of-sale software, and electronic mail systems.
9. Must be able to work evenings and weekends.

STANDARDS OF PERFORMANCE

1. Meets on a weekly basis with all staff to review sales results.
2. Orients new staff during the first shift on customer -service requirements.
3. Meets or exceeds monthly sales targets.
4. Submits sales within 24 hours of each event.
5. Trains staff on any new procedures within one week.
6. Keeps customer satisfaction levels at 80% or above.

Digital Vision/Thinkstock

Specific job requirements must be based on valid job-related criteria such as airplane pilots having a certain level of eyesight.

USES OF INFORMATION FROM JOB ANALYSIS

LO5

What are the uses of information gained from job analysis?

As stated earlier in the chapter, a variety of HRM processes make use of the output of job analysis: recruitment, selection, performance management, training and development, health and safety, and compensation. These are discussed below.

Recruitment

Recruitment is the process of locating and encouraging potential applicants to apply for job openings. Because job specifications establish the qualifications required of applicants for a job opening, they serve an essential role in the recruiting function, as they define "who" will be successful doing the job and provide a basis for attracting qualified applicants. From a legal perspective, it is critical that the requirements listed for the job actually reflect necessary components. For example, requirements that labourers have a high-school diploma, that firefighters be at least six feet tall, and that truck drivers be male discriminate against members of certain designated groups, many of whom have been excluded from these jobs in the past. Further details will be discussed in Chapter 5.

Selection

After you have located individuals interested in working for you, you must now hire someone. Selection is the process of choosing the individual who has the relevant qualifications and who can best perform the job. Therefore, a manager will use the information collected through job analysis as a basis to compare the skills and abilities of each applicant.

Linking the organization's goals with work information gathered from the people who actually do the work is important when analyzing jobs.

michaeljung/Shutterstock.com

Given changes to our society and the various employment laws, employers must be able to show that the specifications used in selecting employees for a particular job relate specifically to the duties of that job. Because line managers usually help define the specifications, they must ensure that the job requirements recruit the best candidate and do not discriminate. Managers must be careful to ensure that they do not hire employees on the basis of "individualized" job requirements that satisfy personal whims but bear little relation to successful job performance.

Performance Management

The job requirements obtained from the job analysis provide the criteria for evaluating the performance of the job incumbent. These individual performance standards are linked to the business performance goals and strategies incorporated in the performance management systems, as discussed in Chapter 7. Evaluating an employee's ongoing performance is a major responsibility of the line manager. From the employer's standpoint, written job descriptions can serve as a basis for minimizing the misunderstandings that occur between managers and their subordinates concerning job requirements. They also establish management's right to take corrective action when the duties covered by the job description are not fulfilled as required by performance standards. As the workplace evolves due to rapid advances in digital communication technology and workers work in more distributed ways, performance reviews become an increasingly important method for managers to monitor and evaluate worker activities and performance. The results of the performance evaluation may reveal whether certain requirements, or **standards of performance** listed on a job description, for a job continue to be valid. For example, a job may require an employee to word-process at the rate of 30 words per minute (wpm), but the performance review may determine that 60 wpm is necessary. If the criteria used to evaluate employee performance are vague and not job-related, employers may find themselves being charged with unfair discrimination.

Standards of performance
Set out the expected results of the job

HRM AND THE LAW 4.1 JOB DESCRIPTION TENSIONS

Tensions may arise in the workplace out of family-related or disability-related limitations on an employee's availability and ability for work.

In 2012 an employee who had worked for an architecture service firm for 27 years was frequently late, absent, or requesting to be able to work from home, in order to care for an ailing mother. The employee was subsequently terminated due to failure to work out of the employer's office, and then claimed discrimination based upon family status. The legal question before the tribunal was if the employer's strict office attendance policy resulted in discrimination on the basis of family status. The tribunal found in favour of the employee, and the employer was ordered to pay the employee $15,000 for injury to dignity, feelings and self -respect; develop and implement a workplace human rights policy, that includes duty to accommodate and distribute policy to partners and staff; and provide mandatory human rights training, including duty to accommodate to supervisory and human resources staff.

As another example, in 2014 a case was decided in favour of the employee (Denise Seeley) seeking accommodation (due to family status and childcare responsibilities) from her employer, Canadian National Railway (CNR). CNR requested that Seeley temporarily relocate from Alberta to Vancouver to cover a staff shortage. CNR's request posed a problem for Ms. Seeley, as she was not able to arrange for adequate childcare during her absence. Initially, Ms. Seeley requested an extension of time to relocate to Vancouver and then eventually requested that she be exempted from having to relocate to Vancouver due to her childcare obligations. Although CNR granted Ms. Seeley an extension, she was eventually dismissed for failing to relocate to Vancouver. Ms. Seeley alleged the CNR had discriminated against her on the basis of her family status because her requests for accommodation were not granted even though other employees with medical conditions had been accommodated in the past.

CRITICAL THINKING QUESTIONS:

1. Do you think these decisions were appropriate? Provide and explain reasons for your answer.
2. Is it fair to other employees (i.e. single or childless people) if their co-workers are given accommodations due to family status, potentially resulting in more work and responsibilities for those not asking for accommodations?

Sources: *Devaney v. ZRV Holdings Limited*, 2012 HRTO 1590 (CanLII), August 17, 2012; and Canadian *National Railway Company v. Seeley*, 2014 FCA 111 (CanLII), accessed November 23, 2014, http://canlii.ca/t/g6sdq.

Job analysis can help determine the type and level of education and training necessary to successfully perform the work.

anyaivanova/Shutterstock.com

Training and Development

Any discrepancies between the knowledge, skills, and abilities (referred to as KSAs) demonstrated by a jobholder and the requirements obtained through job analysis provide clues to training needs. Also, if the job specification section contains competencies (such as "focuses on customer" or "demonstrates excellent customer service skills"), these competencies could provide the basis for training. As line managers are often responsible for training the new employee, accurate job specifications and descriptions are essential. Also, as career development is often a concern for both the manager and the employee, the formal qualification requirements set forth in higher-level jobs serve to indicate how much more training and development are needed for employees to advance to those jobs.

Health and Safety

The job analysis identifies the health and safety–related physical and mental capabilities required to perform the job, and the work environment conditions in which the job is performed. It describes the existing and potential safety and health hazards associated with workplace injuries or illnesses, which are particularly important in redesigning jobs to improve employee wellness and eliminate or reduce exposure to hazards. Creating a healthy organizational culture is discussed in Chapter 3.

In 2011 the Air Canada pilots' case of discrimination due to the mandatory retirement age of 60 was dismissed. The Canadian Human Rights Tribunal determined that extra staffing, scheduling, and health and safety requirements would constitute an undue hardship for the airline and that mandatory retirement of pilots at age 60 is a "bona fide occupational requirement" (BFOR).[7]

Compensation

Job analysis and the resulting descriptions are often used solely for compensation purposes. In determining the rate at which a job is paid, the relative worth of the job is one of the most important factors. This worth (*pay rate*) is based on what the job demands of an employee in skill, effort, and responsibility, and on the conditions and hazards under which the work is performed. Systems that measure the worth of jobs are called *job evaluation systems* (see Chapter 8). Job descriptions and job specifications are used as sources of information in evaluating jobs. Often, the HR department designs these job evaluation systems. Ultimately, however, it is the line manager who makes pay decisions based on performance relative to the standards of performance that have been established.

Job Analysis in a Changing Environment

The traditional approach to job analysis assumes a static job environment and large organization in which jobs remain relatively stable even though incumbents who might hold these jobs perform them differently. Here, jobs can be meaningfully defined in terms of tasks, duties, processes, and behaviours necessary for job success. This assumption, unfortunately, discounts technological advances that are often so accelerated that jobs as defined today may be obsolete tomorrow. Furthermore, downsizing, the adoption of teams, the demands of small organizations, or the need to respond to global change can alter the nature of jobs and their requirements. For organizations using "virtual" jobs or "virtual" teams, there is a shift away from independently performed jobs with narrow job specifications and descriptions to a focus on the relationships among workers and their work environments.[8] In a dynamic environment where job demands rapidly change, job analysis data can quickly become inaccurate, and outdated information can hinder an organization's ability to adapt to change. Job information must be regularly reviewed and adjusted as needs change.

For organizations that operate in a fast-moving environment, several novel approaches to job analysis may accommodate needed change.

First, managers might adopt a future-oriented or strategic-oriented approach to job analysis in which managers have a clear view of how jobs should be restructured to meet future organizational requirements.[9]

Second, organizations might adopt a competency-based approach in which emphasis is put on characteristics or behaviours of successful performers rather than on standard job duties and tasks and so on. As was described in Chapter 1, these competencies would be customized to the organization's culture and strategy, and include the tailoring of broad competencies such as communication skills, decision-making ability, project management, conflict resolution skills, adaptability, and self-motivation. Competencies are developed using a top-down rather than a bottom-up approach, with the goal of integrating organizational and human resources management objectives, strategies, and systems.[10]

Neither of the above two approaches are without concerns, including the ability of managers to predict future job needs accurately, and the need for job analysis to comply with human rights legislation.

A third and perhaps more practical method might be to have a "living job description" or a "role description" that is updated as the nature of the work changes. The line manager and employee would then ensure that substantial changes in duties, responsibilities, skills, and other work characteristics are documented on an ongoing basis. One type of living job or role description is a behavioural one that describes how the work is to be done and what results are expected. Often, these descriptions also address typical issues and problems that may occur and the results that can be expected in dealing with the issues. By doing this, the manager and employee can also establish standards of performance. These descriptive and evaluative job descriptions can be linked to the organization's online performance management system, allowing for continuous updating by all users.

As previously discussed, determining the work to be done involves an approach that links the organization's future goals with work information gathered from the people who actually do the work.

In order to have "the right people with the right skills at the right time," contemporary managers must take the time to think about the work and the skills required to do the work. Organizational success depends on capable people. Managers want to be sure that they have the correct number of employees and the correct skills mix. Clearly identifying the work duties and the skills needed to perform the work can help managers achieve that objective. It is important to remember that the purpose of identifying who does what is to bring all the talent together, in order to capitalize on synergy among employees and achieve the company's goals.[11] This leads to considerations of how work should be designed in order to most effectively achieve results while keeping employees motivated.

LO6

What is the relationship of job design to employee behaviours and contributions?

DESIGNING THE JOB

Job design
Process of defining and organizing tasks, roles, and other processes to achieve employee goals and organizational effectiveness

An outgrowth of job analysis, **job design** is the process of defining and arranging tasks, roles, and other processes to achieve employee goals and organizational effectiveness. For example, organizations engaged in self-management teams, continuous improvement, or process reengineering may revamp their jobs in order to eliminate unnecessary job tasks or find better ways of performing work. Job design should facilitate the achievement of organizational objectives and at the same time recognize the capabilities and needs of those who are to perform the job. Job design is concerned with appropriately altering and modifying the job so

FIGURE 4.2 Basis for Job Design

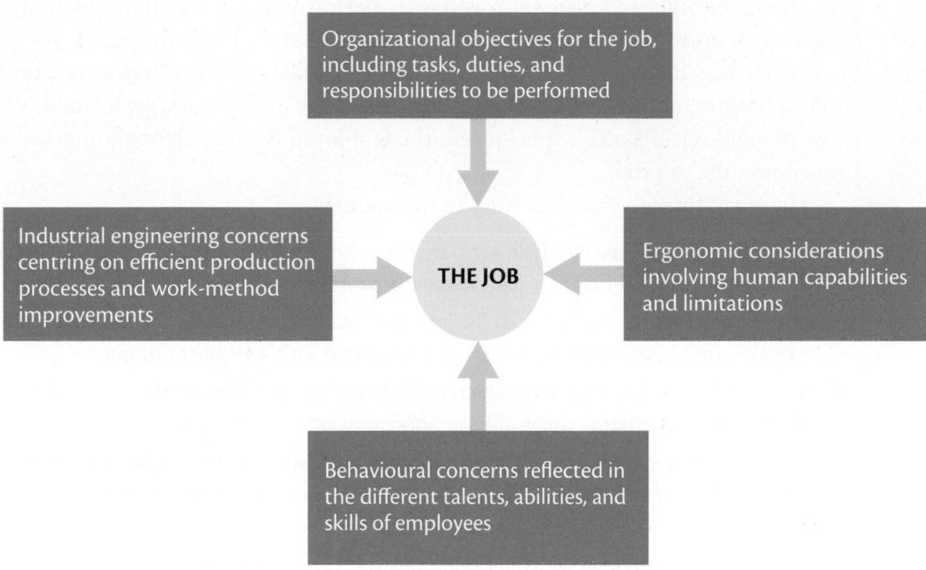

that there is a good person–job fit and person–organization fit. Improving the quality of work life facilitates positive worker attitudes and behaviours, leading to organizational effectiveness. Historically, the focus has been on analyzing and defining specific jobs within physical "brick and mortar" structures. Today, with the rapid advances of communication technology, the meaning of the word "job" is in flux with workers working in more distributed, unconstrained work environments.[12] These fundamental changes in the relationships between workers, the type of work they do, how they perform their work, when the work is scheduled, and the organizational environment are increasing the use of nonstandard employment forms and nontraditional strategies for job design. Job design strategies can include the following:

- job rotation (in which people move from one job to another to learn new tasks)
- job enlargement (in which a person's job expands in the types of tasks he or she is expected to perform)
- leadership teams (in which a leader takes on multiple responsibilities and activities rather than one well-defined functional leadership role)
- job enrichment (in which a person's job takes on higher-order responsibilities)
- job crafting (in which a person initiates, shapes, and customizes the work to enhance motivation and decrease boredom)[13]

Nontraditional and emerging employment forms are discussed later in this chapter. As Figure 4.2 illustrates, job design is a combination of four basic considerations: (1) the organizational objectives the job was created to fulfill; (2) industrial engineering considerations, including ways to make the job technologically efficient; (3) ergonomic concerns, including workers' physical and mental capabilities; and (4) employee attitudes and behaviours that influence their contributions. Employee contributions are reflected in the participation of employees in making job improvements or enhancing operational decisions.

Job Design and Job Characteristics

Job characteristics model
An approach to job design that recognizes the link between motivational factors and components of the job to achieve improved work performance and job satisfaction

Job design was further advanced when behavioural scientists focused on various job dimensions that would simultaneously improve the efficiency of organizations and the job satisfaction of employees. The **job characteristics model** proposes that three psychological states of a jobholder result in improved work performance, internal motivation, and lower absenteeism and turnover. The motivated, satisfied, and productive employee is one who (1) experiences meaningfulness of the work performed, (2) experiences responsibility for work outcomes, and (3) has knowledge of the results of the work performed. When these three psychological states are achieved, the employee is more strongly motivated to continue doing the job well.

There are five job characteristics in this model:

1. *Skill variety.* The degree to which a job entails a variety of different activities, which demand the use of a number of different skills and talents by the jobholder
2. *Task identity.* The degree to which the job requires completion of a whole and identifiable piece of work—that is, doing a job from beginning to end with a visible outcome
3. *Task significance.* The degree to which the job has a substantial impact on the lives or work of other people, whether in the immediate organization or in the external environment
4. *Autonomy.* The degree to which the job provides substantial freedom, independence, and discretion to the individual in scheduling the work and in determining the procedures to be used in carrying it out
5. *Feedback.* The degree to which carrying out the work activities required by the job results in the individual being given direct and clear information about the effectiveness of his or her performance

The job characteristics model seems to work best when certain conditions are met. One of these is that employees must have the psychological desire for the autonomy, variety, responsibility, and challenge of enriched jobs. When this personal characteristic is absent, employees may resist the job redesign effort. Job redesign efforts almost always fail when employees lack the physical or mental skills, abilities, or education needed to perform the job. Forcing enriched jobs on individuals who lack these traits can lead to their frustration. The advances in information technology resulting in increased flexible work arrangements have expanded the scope of these characteristics to employees doing front-line work.[14]

Designing Work for Enhanced Contributions

LO7

How can work be designed to increase employee contribution?

Although a variety of techniques have been developed to involve employees more fully in their organizations, all these techniques have two characteristics in common—enhancing collaboration and increasing synergy. By increasing the degree of collaboration in the work environment, these techniques can improve work processes and organizational decision making. By increasing synergy, they underline the adage that the contributions of two or more employees are greater than the sum of their individual efforts. Research has shown that greater involvement in their jobs and/or working in a group setting strengthens employee commitment to an organization's goals, increases employee acceptance of decisions, and encourages a co-operative approach to workplace tasks. Two collaborative techniques are discussed below: employee empowerment and employee teams.

Employee Empowerment

Employee empowerment
Granting employees power to initiate change, thereby encouraging them to take charge of what they do

Employee empowerment is a technique for involving employees in their work through a process of inclusion. It encourages employees to become innovators and managers of their own work, and involves them in their jobs in ways that give them more control.

Monkey Business Images Ltd/Thinkstock

Employees are empowered to work on a project to improve customer delivery times.

Empowerment has been defined as pushing down decision-making responsibility to those close to internal and external customers and is therefore a very intentional form of job design. *Job crafting* is one example of empowerment, by which workers do not wait for management initiatives but customize their work to meet both their own needs as well as the organization's goals.[15] Empowerment and job crafting strategies are more fluid in nature, a departure from other job design methods that are generally top-down and fixed in nature. Interviews with employees in both a small service organization and a large manufacturing organization found that senior employees felt more constrained than front-line employees in their ability to craft their jobs even though they had greater autonomy and power.[16]

While defining empowerment can become the first step to achieving it, in order for empowerment to grow and thrive, organizations must encourage these conditions:

- *Participation*. Employees must be encouraged to take control of their work tasks. Employees, in turn, must care about improving their work process and interpersonal work relationships.
- *Innovation*. The environment must be receptive to people with innovative ideas and must encourage people to explore new paths and to take reasonable risks at reasonable costs. An empowered environment is created when curiosity is as highly regarded as technical expertise.
- *Access to information*. Employees must have access to a wide range of information. Involved individuals make decisions about what kind of information they need to perform their jobs.
- *Accountability*. Empowerment does not involve being able to do whatever you want. Empowered employees should be held accountable for their behaviour toward others. They must produce agreed-upon results, achieve credibility, and operate with a positive approach.

Additionally, employee empowerment succeeds when the culture of the organization is open and receptive to change. An organization's culture is created largely through the philosophies of senior managers and their leadership traits and behaviours. In an empowered organization, effective leadership is exemplified by managers who are honest, caring, and receptive to new ideas, and who treat employees with dignity and respect and as partners in organizational success. Further, for empowerment to work, it must be aligned directly with the strategy of the organization and individual accountability throughout the enterprise.

Canadian Society for Quality
http://canadianqualitycongress.com

However, some organizations will have difficulty promoting empowerment, as managers are sometimes unwilling to give up power or give employees the authority to make decisions. For more information on how to encourage employee empowerment, access the resources and information at the Canadian Society for Quality (**http://canadianqualitycongress.com**). Toolkit 4.3 gives some additional examples of employee empowerment.

Employee teams
An employee-contributions technique in which work functions are structured for groups rather than for individuals, and team members are given discretion in matters traditionally considered management prerogatives, such as process improvements, product or service development, and individual work assignments

Employee Teams

During the past decade perhaps one of the more radical changes to how work is done has been the introduction of **employee teams**. These are a logical outgrowth of employee involvement and the philosophy of empowerment. While many definitions of teams exist, an employee team may be defined as a group of employees working toward a common purpose, whose members have complementary skills, whose work is mutually dependent, and who have discretion over tasks performed. Furthermore, a team seeks to make members of the work group share responsibility for the group's performance. Inherent in the concept of employee teams is that employees, not managers, are in the best position to contribute to workplace improvements.

TOOLKIT 4.3 EXAMPLES OF EMPLOYEE EMPOWERMENT

Many types of organizations have successfully empowered their employees. Examples include such diverse companies as DuPont, Walmart, Costco, and Home Depot. Empowered employees have improved product and service quality, reduced costs, increased productivity, and modified, or in some cases designed, products.

PURDYS CHOCOLATIER: MAKE INNOVATION A CONTEST

Like many firms, Vancouver-based Purdys Chocolatier puts a high value on its employees' suggestions to make it better, but the confectioner ups the ante by making innovation a competition. Through a program called "Make us better ideas," Purdys awards points to warehouse and production employees—redeemable for everything from coffee cards to paid days off—based on the impact of their suggestions. Once an idea is acted on, the firm measures the significance of the result. The more beneficial it is to the company, the more points the employee receives. The perks make people more inclined to think big-picture, and to speak up when they get a great idea. Best of all, the whole process gives employees a clear indicator of the importance of their work to the company as a whole.

CISCO SYSTEMS CANADA: LET THE INTERN MENTOR THE CEO

Smart companies know that it's not only those at the top of the organization chart who have something to share; great ideas, innovations and advice can come from even the most junior staffers. Cisco Canada has put in several practices to help facilitate a less top-down approach to information sharing, including a reverse-mentoring program in which corporate leaders turn to younger recruits for tips. In getting the opportunity to advise higher-ups, fresh faces feel valued and important, which makes them far more motivated to expend the effort needed to make the business better.

LULULEMON: EMPLOYEE GROWTH AND WELLNESS

In its capacity as a clothing retailer, Lululemon wants employees to read self-help books and attend self-empowerment training sessions. Employees are encouraged to promote a vision and a lifestyle to customers.

Sources: "Canada's Best Employers 2015: The Top 50 Large Companies," accessed November 23, 2014, www.canadianbusiness.com/lists-and-rankings/best-jobs/2015-best-employers-top-50; www.vancouversun.com/life/Companies+like+Lululemon+take+different+approach+relationships+with+employees/8562925/story.html; Bruce Constantineau, "Companies Like Lululemon Take Different Approach to Relationships with Employees," *Vancouver Sun*, June 25, 2013.

Two issues important in the design of work for teams are (1) the appropriate use of teams and (2) the types of teams.[17] Job tasks that require specialized individual expertise may be inappropriate for teams. Teams should be used when the work is amenable to teamwork and is adequately structured and supported, by both managers and employees.[18] Transitioning to distributed workplaces requires more effort on the part of managers to ensure that practices and processes capitalize on team communication, collaboration, and collective knowledge. Teams can operate in a variety of structures, each with different strategic purposes or functional activities. Figure 4.3 describes six different team forms.

One form, the **virtual team**, also called a *distributed team*, consists of dispersed team members who need to meet regularly but do not require high levels of interdependency among members. Communication technology is integrated so that workers are able to constantly consult each other. Managers must establish common communication processes and practices that work effectively as well as create a sense of collaborative communication. Virtual teams provide these organizations access to previously unavailable diverse and collective expertise and knowledge and may be especially useful in bringing geographically dispersed employee talent together.[19] More organizations are forming leadership teams to address the challenges faced by those in leadership roles. A cross-national study of senior leadership teams suggests that particular attention needs to be given to the design, dynamics, and performance of these senior-level teams.[20]

Virtual team
A team with widely dispersed members linked through computer and telecommunications technology

Regardless of the structure or purpose of the team, here are a few of the characteristics of successful teams:

- commitment to shared goals and objectives
- consensus decision making
- open and honest communication
- shared leadership
- climate of co-operation, collaboration, trust, and support

FIGURE 4.3 Work Design and Types of Teams

Surgical teams require coordinated interaction among all members in real time with the responsibility and accountability for outcomes lying primarily with one person. Appropriate for work that requires a high level of individual insight, expertise, and/or creativity but is too large or complex to be handled by any one member working alone.
Coaching groups are individual members who do not depend upon what the others do; the output of a group is simply the aggregation of members' individual contributions. Appropriate only when there is little need for interdependent work by group members.
Face-to-face teams have members with complementary expertise, experience, and perspectives who work together interdependently in real time to generate a product for which they are collectively accountable. Appropriate for a wide variety of tasks for which creating a high-quality product requires coordinated contributions in real time.
Virtual, or distributed, teams use communication technologies to exchange observations, ideas, and reactions at times of their own choosing. Teams are collectively responsible and accountable for work products and are useful when it is difficult for team members to meet regularly and the work does not require high levels of interdependence.
Leadership teams include all significant leaders who share responsibility for leading an entire organization or a large organizational unit. This kind of team addresses the expanding pace and scope of leadership.
Sand dune teams are dynamic and fluid social systems that change in number and kind of members as business requirements and opportunities change. Well suited for fast-changing environments.

Source: Adapted from Greg R. Oldham, J. Richard Hackman. "Not what it was and not what it will be: The future of job design research," *Journal of Organizational Behavior* 31 (2010): 463-479. Copyright © 2010 John Wiley & Sons, Ltd.

- valuing of individuals for their diversity
- recognition of conflict and its positive resolution

Unfortunately, not all teams succeed or operate to their full potential. Therefore, in adopting the work team concept, organizations must address several issues that could present obstacles to effective team function: these include authoritarian leadership and aggressive communication styles, inadequate resources and support, and poor work design.[21] For example, new team members must be retrained to work outside their primary functional areas, and compensation systems must be constructed to reward individuals for team accomplishments. Another consideration is that work teams alter the traditional manager–employee relationship. Managers often find it hard to adapt to the role of leader rather than supervisor and sometimes feel threatened by the growing power of the team and the need to hand over authority. Furthermore, some employees may have difficulty adapting to a role that includes traditional supervisory responsibilities. As team members become capable of carrying out processes, such as strategic planning, that were previously restricted to higher levels of management, managers must be prepared to design work that utilizes their newfound expertise. In designing work teams, special attention needs to be given to the more fluid relationships and communication among workers and their work activities.[22]

Role of Management

Leadership issues arise at several levels when employees are involved in decision making. At both the executive and management levels, there needs to be clear support for employee involvement and teams, as changes may be required in processes and actions to support this new way of doing business. For many years, managers and supervisors have played the role of decision maker. Thus, organizations will need to redefine the role of supervisor when employees are participating more in the operations of the company. For example, Mike Moore Construction works closely with its owners, subtrades, and partners to ensure that everyone from management to labourer is involved in workplace decisions and practices.[23] Decisions within the company are based on a process of inclusion.

Therefore, in order to capitalize on employee empowerment and employee teams it is critical that the organization be clear on what is expected of managers and supervisors and the skills necessary to be successful. Further, it needs to carefully consider its overall design and structure. Research has demonstrated that the organizational structure and context (size, centralization, and hierarchical levels) are key determinants of behaviours in the organization.[24] If the organization wants a more committed and engaged workforce, then the way it is structured—who reports to whom and who makes decisions—will greatly influence the effectiveness of the leaders.

Organizations have found that the success of employee involvement depends on first changing the roles of managers and team leaders. With fewer layers of management and a focus on team-based organizations, the role of managers and supervisors is substantially different. Managers are expected to be open to suggestions, actively support two-way communication, and encourage risk taking. Rather than autocratically imposing their demands on employees and closely watching to make sure that the workers comply, managers share responsibility for decision making with employees. Typically, "team leader" has replaced the term "manager."

In a growing number of cases, leadership is shared among team members. Some organizations rotate team leaders at various stages in team development. Alternatively, different individuals can assume functional leadership roles when their particular expertise is needed most.

A clear example of the role senior managers play in creating an involved organization is described in At Work with HRM 4.1.

AT WORK WITH HRM 4.1

BEST EMPLOYERS

Would you like to work for one of Canada's #1 companies? Most of us would answer yes.

Earls Restaurants Ltd. was included in the listing of Canada's Best Employers 2015 in a study conducted by Aon Hewitt. What led to this honour? Some of the reasons were as follows:

- Restaurant employees receive at least 24 hours of training every year; the company's Red Seal apprenticeship program pays the full cost of knives, books, and technical culinary training.
- All workers can participate in leadership or personal development courses.
- Company awards include food-and-wine tours to destinations such as Japan, Bordeaux in France, and California's Napa Valley.

CRITICAL THINKING QUESTIONS:

1. What would your current or past company need to do to go out of its way to meet the needs of the employees and be considered a top employer?
2. Given what you know or have heard about the restaurant business, would you want to work for Earls?

Source: "Canada's Best Employers 2015: The Top 50 Large Companies," accessed November 22, 2014, www.canadianbusiness.com/lists-and-rankings/best-jobs/2015-best-employers-top-50.

Future Design of Organizational Work

There have been changes in jobs and work contexts over the past few decades. Globalization, technology, and demographics have given rise to new questions about how, where, when, and what work is done. Organizations have been responding by replacing traditional (permanent full-time, full-year) jobs with a range of nontraditional employment forms and flexible arrangements such as these:

- contract or freelance work
- e-work
- temporary work
- job or work sharing
- telework
- compressed workweek
- mobile work
- home-based work
- flextime or flexyear
- time-limited projects
- partnership arrangements or talent
- pooling

The increasing use and convergence of social, mobile, and cloud computing technologies are creating unique ways to work—ways so new that their definitions have yet to be agreed upon. These contingent employment options are associated with improved work–life balance and increased job insecurity. Organizations are therefore being challenged to provide meaningful work to engage and motivate a diverse group of employees who structure their work in differing ways.[25] Future job design will shift its focus away from traditional jobs, in which individuals worked independently within bounded organizational structures, toward the more dynamic fluid relationships among workers and their work activities that utilize networked communication technology. Consequently, future job design practices will require more attention to job crafting, thereby allowing employees to utilize their strongest competencies and skills. This, in turn, will enhance employees' motivation while still achieving the organization's desired goals. In addition, the broader organizational context and culture (e.g., technology, work flow, decentralization, and control systems), distributed teams, the social and relational aspects and attributes of work, diversity, and the linking of competencies, work, and organizational strategy must continue to be considered when designing work.[26] For information about what might be in the future for job/work design, read Emerging Trends 4.1.

EMERGING TRENDS 4.1

1. ***Diversity and generational differences.*** Managers and supervisors will be continually challenged by the changing nature and mix of their workers. The Millennials are entering the workplace in significant numbers, and research suggests that they hold different work values and motivations from the Gen X and Baby Boom generations. For example, social values (building interpersonal relationships) and intrinsic values (having an interesting, results-oriented job) were rated lower by Millennials than by Boomers. Differing value systems have implications for how jobs are designed and what will motivate different groups of employees and how they can best work together. Most of the Canadian baby boom generation is continuing to work part-time, or members are returning to work during their retirement years. They are working in a wide range of employment forms and for diverse reasons, and therefore job design must be considered to entice them to continue participating in the workforce. In designing work, caution needs to be taken to ensure that generations are not viewed too narrowly as homogenous groups and that recognition is given to the broader aspects of human diversity.
2. ***Increasing use of competencies.*** As work becomes more fluid, organizations will incorporate the core competencies needed for success in each job. These competencies will be the skills, knowledge, abilities, and other behaviours (KSAOs) that lead to the organization's desired results. Competencies are developed top-down by senior managers to ensure that they are strategic, future-oriented, and linked to the organization's strategy. An attempt is made to distinguish the KSAOs of top performers while keeping employees motivated within their jobs.
3. ***The emergence of "job architecture."*** Managers will want to link strategic jobs with organizational performance outcomes, to put a focus on competitive advantage. As organizations change and evolve, there will be certain critical points that require a business-led view of the structure of the organization. By using a job architecture model, the roles, skills, and careers of the individuals can be effectively managed, and the various HR processes can be more clearly integrated while business processes are streamlined for efficiency and effectiveness.
4. ***Job crafting and organizational context.*** With the increased uncertainty and change in work environments and the workforce (in the form of more diversity), when designing future work special attention will need to be given to the social and collaborative aspects, the changing workplace contexts, and the process by which workers craft their jobs. Employees should be encouraged to play to their strengths and have input in how their roles are enacted.

Sources: Adapted from Jean Twenge, Stacy Campbell, Brian Hoffman, and Charles Lance, "Generational Differences in Work Values: Leisure and Extrinsic Values," *Journal of Management* 36 (2010): 1117–1142; Peter Bamberger and Samuel Bacharach, "Predicting Retirement upon Eligibility: An Embeddedness Perspective," *Human Resource Management* 53, no. 1 (2014): 1–22; Mo Wang and Kenneth Shultz, "Employee Retirement: A Review and Recommendations for Future Investigation," *Journal of Management* 36 (2010): 172–206; Statistics Canada, *Perspectives on Labour and Income*, accessed November 25, 2014, www.statcan.gc.ca/pub/75-001-x/75-001-x2012003-eng.htm; David Harrison and Stephen Humphrey, "Designing for Diversity or Diversity for Design? Tasks, Interdependence, and Within-Unit Differences at Work," *Journal of Organizational Behavior* 31 (2010): 328–37; Paul Sparrow and Lilian Otaye-Ebede, "Lean Management and HR Function Capability: The Role of HR Architecture and the Location of Intellectual Capital," *International Journal of Human Resource Management* 25, no. 21 (2014): 2892–2910; Brian Becker and Mark Huselid, "SHRM and Job Design: Narrowing the Divide," *Journal of Organizational Behavior* 31 (2010): 379–88; Adam Grant et al., "Putting Job Design in Context: Introduction to the Special Issue," *Journal of Organizational Behavior* 31 (2010): 145–57; Elizabeth Redmont, "Competency Models at Work: The Value of Perceived Relevance and Fair Rewards for Employee Outcomes," *Human Resource Management* 52, no. 5 (2013): 771–792; and Adam Grant and Sharon Parker, "Redesigning Work Design Theories: The Rise of Relational and Proactive Perspectives," *Academy of Management Annals*, accessed November 30, 2011, http://iwp.dept.shef.ac.uk/files/docs/GrantParker_WorkDesign-Annals.pdf.

Summary

1. Explain the manager's role in defining and designing work and how an employee can assist with this.
   - The manager or supervisor is the primary individual who determines what work needs to be done.
   - The manager takes an active role in determining what skills and abilities are needed to successfully perform the work.
   - As the person performing the work, an employee contributes knowledge and information regarding the elements within a specific job.
2. Discuss the relationship between job requirements and HRM processes.
   - HRM processes, such as recruitment or training, make use of information about the work or job.
   - A job consists of a group of related activities and duties.
   - A position consists of the specific duties and responsibilities performed by only one employee.
3. Explain the relationship between job analysis and a job description.
   - Job analysis is the process of obtaining information about jobs (or work) by determining what the duties, tasks, or activities are.
   - The outcome is a job description—a written document that contains a number of elements.
   - A job description is a written description listing the types of duties, responsibilities, and the skills (job specifications) needed to successfully perform the work.
4. Define and describe the sections in a job description.
   - Company name
   - Position title—indication of what the duties might be or the nature of the work
   - Date document is completed
   - Summary of job—two or three sentences describing the overall purpose of the job
   - List of duties and responsibilities—statements of the key duties and responsibilities
   - Job specifications—statement of the needed knowledge, skills, and abilities or competencies of the person who is to perform the work
   - Standards of performance
5. Describe the uses of information gained from job analysis.
   - Job specifications establish the qualifications required of applicants for a job opening and play an essential role in the recruiting function.
   - Information on the job description is used as a basis for comparing the skills and abilities of each applicant in the selection process.
   - Managers must be careful to ensure that they do not hire employees on the basis of "individualized" job requirements that satisfy personal whims but bear little relation to successful job performance. Performance management should align with the job requirements.
   - Requirements contained in the job description and specifications provide clues to training needs.
   - Job requirements highlight health and safety issues and necessities.
   - The pay of a job is based on what the job demands in skill, effort, and responsibility, and on the conditions and hazards under which the work is performed.
6. Explain the relationship of job design to employee behaviours and contributions.
   - Job design is the process of defining and arranging tasks, roles, and other processes to achieve the employee's goals and organizational effectiveness.
   - Job design strives to incorporate the behavioural needs of employees, which leads to improved performance.
   - Job design can enhance or take away from the employee's ability to participate in decision making.

7. Discuss the different types of work designs to increase employee contribution.
   - Employee empowerment is a method of involving employees in their work and encouraging them to take charge of what they do.
   - Employee teams are groups of employees who assume a greater role in the production or service process.
   - Nontraditional employment forms and arrangements are addressing employee and employer needs for work flexibility.

Need to Know

- Definition of job analysis, job description, job specification, standards of performance, and job design
- Definition of employee empowerment and employee and group contributions

Need to Understand

- Relationship of job requirements to recruitment, selection, performance management, training and development, health and safety, and compensation
- Relationship between job analysis, job descriptions, job specifications, and standards of performance
- Role of line manager in designing jobs for maximum employee contributions
- Ways to encourage employee empowerment and team work

KEY TERMS

employee empowerment 120
employee teams 122
job 108
job analysis 109
job characteristics model 120
job description 110
job design 118
job incumbent 109
job specifications 112
position 108
role 108
standards of performance 115
virtual team 123
work 108

REVIEW QUESTIONS

1. What job information would you collect when conducting a job analysis?
2. What is the difference between job analysis and a job description?
3. What are the problems associated with a written job description?
4. What are the uses of information from job analysis?
5. What are the types of employee and group contributions?
6. What are the different forms of teams?
7. What are two nontraditional employment forms?

CRITICAL THINKING QUESTIONS

1. You have just been hired as a customer service representative at a branch of a large bank. The branch manager is considering creating a nontraditional work schedule for everyone. The manager has asked for your advice about what to consider to ensure its success—and the continued strong performance of the branch. What would you say?
2. Assume that you are a new supervisor in a hotel and you have been asked to prepare a job description for room attendant. What would you include as five key duties and

what would you list as three key skills? Would you involve the current room attendant in the preparation of the job description? Why?

3. If a job incumbent inflates his/her work when submitting information for job analysis, why should this person be included in the process? Why shouldn't the information for job analysis only be collected from the job incumbent's supervisor or manager?
4. What are some of the pitfalls of employee teams? How can these be managed or lessened?
5. You are a small business owner in the catering business. What would you offer your employees in order to be considered a top employer in the business community?
6. How is the increasingly mobile workforce changing how, when, where, and what work is done? What opportunities and challenges face managers and mobile workers?

DEVELOPING YOUR SKILLS

1. In groups of four or five, identify the job specifications (knowledge, skills, and abilities) for the position of college or university instructor. (You will have approximately 20 minutes to complete the exercise.) Each group will then present its findings to the rest of the class. Discuss and compare the requirements and develop a single list of job specifications.
2. Access the Web page of the National Occupation Classification (NOC) system that is managed by Human Resources and Skills Development Canada (**www5.hrsdc.gc.ca/NOC/English/NOC/2011/AboutNOC.aspx**). Familiarize yourself with the various job classification information. Search through the various job titles and find a job description that interests you. Prepare a one-page summary describing the key duties and skills, and explain what training and experience you would need in order to be hired.
3. Use the job analysis questions in Toolkit 4.1 to interview someone, perhaps another student who is working, about his or her job position. What did you discover about the job analysis interview process and the information required?
4. For a job you currently have (or for a past job) list three new/different things that your employer might do to redesign your job to make you feel more empowered? How would you convince your employer to implement your ideas?
5. Access and use current research about a nonstandard work option (e.g., telework, mobile work, flexible schedules) that you would like your current or future employer to consider. Write a one-page proposal to your employer that illustrates the benefits of your chosen employment form (e.g., teleworkers are more satisfied than office workers).
6. Access the following website to review competing rights between employees and employers pertaining to requests for accommodation: **www.ohrc.on.ca/en/policy-competing-human-rights/appendix-d-case-examples-resolving-competing-rights**.
   In groups of four to six, discuss how you would deal with each of the scenarios presented.

CASE STUDY 1

But My Job Has Changed

Job descriptions are a critical tool used for job orientation and training and, importantly, in annual employee performance evaluations. When the duties and responsibilities listed in the job description do not reflect current job content, employee/management disagreements can arise, as this case illustrates.

Both employees and managers agree that Brenda Batten has been an exceptional employee. As a senior technical representative (STR) for Blackhawk Aironics, she is valued for her knowledge in airplane instrumentation. One manager described her as "simply an expert in the complex technology of satellite weather systems."

Recently, Blackhawk Aironics implemented a new work reorganization plan. STRs such as Brenda now work largely by telecommuting with managers and engineers at company headquarters and with customers scattered throughout North America. Additionally, under the new work plan, STRs were given more freedom to deal directly with customers and engineers without supervisory intervention. This greatly facilitated customer service needs and demands in an aviation market everyone considers highly dynamic.

Brenda's current job description reflects the technical dimensions of her position but not the telecommuting requirements now performed. Personal competencies such as decision making, self-motivation, problem solving, and communication skills are not covered.

Brenda met with her manager, Martin Eaton, for her annual performance review. Unfortunately, unlike past meetings, which were highly satisfactory, this meeting quickly developed into a disagreement. At the centre of the controversy were the factors to be used to measure Brenda's new job demands. Martin wanted to put major emphasis on the tasks and duties listed in her current job description. As he explained to Brenda, "I hardly see you anymore, and I have no objective criteria or performance data by which to measure those behaviours you now use." Brenda, in response, acknowledged that some things in the current job description were still important aspects of her job, but overall the description did not capture the full scope of her new duties and responsibilities. Brenda concluded that she was satisfied with Martin's evaluation of the technical aspects of her job, but that she was not pleased with the overall evaluation of her performance. As she told Martin, "It's simply not fair; you just don't know what I do now."

Questions:

1. Given the facts of this case, is it possible for Brenda and Martin to reach a satisfactory result? Explain.
2. How could an organization go about identifying and measuring the personal competencies of employees?
3. How might the company prevent this problem from recurring? Explain.

CASE STUDY 2

What Should a New Manager Do?

Jack Deppster arrived for his first day of work as store manager at the Buzz, one of the largest and most popular retail stores at a local mall. The Buzz, operating various locations throughout Canada, sold clothing and accessories targeted to people between 18 to 24 years old. Jack, taking a business administration degree, was seen as a motivated and self-directed person who got results. On the basis of his strong GPA, volunteer experience, and previous retail experience working as a salesperson for a grocery store, the management group at Buzz expected strong performance from him. Jack impressed the HR hiring manager and district manager during the interview process and they believed he would have no problem in achieving the target of increasing store sales by 5% over the next six months. Jack also believed he could achieve this goal, and was excited about the opportunity to take on his first management role.

However, the honeymoon did not even last a few hours. During the morning Jack noticed quite a bit of chaos in the store. Some of the cashiers did not know how to operate the registers; others seemed to be circumventing established processes and cashing people out in unique ways. When Jack questioned them about this, they said they had discovered different, easier methods to utilize the technology that allowed them to spend more time talking to customers as they paid, and that this was their favourite part of the job.

However, the sales staff did not seem interested in helping customers and seemed very bored. Jack noticed that many of the salespeople would spend time talking to each other, even when it was apparent that customers were in need of assistance. The situation in the inventory room was no better. The shelves were a mess, and items were pulled out of boxes by various employees in a random fashion whenever store displays began to look empty. The employees told Jack it was his job as store manager to order and track inventory, so the storage room was his responsibility. However, Jack felt that all employees should be involved in inventory management.

To further complicate matters, Jack knew that Buzz would soon be implementing new technology, which would impact the cash registers and the inventory tracking and ordering system. Jack was confused and disappointed. This was not what he had anticipated!

Questions:

1. How could Jack use the job characteristics model to redesign the job of salespeople in the store?
2. Explain how Jack might utilize employee teams to increase employee empowerment.
3. Should Jack allow some cashiers to determine how they cash people out? Is this a good idea, given that new technology will soon be implemented? What are the consequences of allowing, or not allowing, this to continue?

NOTES AND REFERENCES

1. "Work," Karo Persuasive Experiences, accessed March 25, 2012, www.karo.com/portfolio.
2. Juan I. Sanchez and Edward L. Levine, "The Rise and Fall of Job Analysis and the Future of Work Analysis," *Annual Review of Psychology* 63 (November 30, 2011).
3. Greg R. Oldham and Richard R. Hackman, "Not What It Was and Not What It Will Be: The Future of Job Design Research," *Journal of Organizational Behavior* 31 (2010): 463–79.
4. Jason Robertson (Director, Business Development, Aquinox), interview by the author, February 2015.
5. *Fiona Johnstone v. Canada Border Services*, File No. T1233/4507, Ottawa, August 6, 2010, accessed March 15, 2012, www.chrt-tcdp.gc.ca/aspinc/search/vhtml-eng.asp?doid=1021&lg=_e&isruling=0.
6. *Canada (Attorney General) v. Johnstone*, 2014 FCA 110 (Federal Court of Appeal, May 2, 2014).
7. *Vilven and Kelly v. Air Canada and Air Canada Pilots Association* (2011), Canadian Human Rights Tribunal, Files T1176/5806, T1177/5906, and T1079/6005, accessed October 12, 2011, http://chrt-tcdp.gc.ca/search/files/t1079_6005ed081110.pdf.
8. Oldham and Hackman, "Not What It Was and Not What It Will Be."
9. Ibid.
10. Michael A. Campion et al., "Doing Competencies Well: Best Practices in Competency Modeling," *Personnel Psychology* 64, no. 1 (Spring 2011): 225–62.
11. M. Armstrong, *Armstrong's Handbook of Human Resource Management Practice* (Philadelphia: Kogan Page, 2014).
12. Oldham and Hackman, "Not What It Was and Not What It Will Be."
13. Madelon L. van Hooff and Edwin van Hooft, "Boredom at Work: Proximal and Distal Consequences of Affective Work-Related Boredom," *Journal of Occupational Health Psychology* 19, no. 3 (2014), 248–259.
14. Oldham and Hackman, "Not What It Was and Not What It Will Be."
15. Hooff and Hooft, "Boredom at Work," 248–259.
16. Justin M. Berg, Amy Wrzesniewski, and Jane E. Dutton, "Perceiving and Responding to Challenges in Job Crafting at Different Ranks," *Journal of Organizational Behavior* 31, nos. 2–3 (February 2010): 158–186.
17. Oldham and Hackman, "Not What It Was and Not What It Will Be."
18. Maria Paasivaara and Casper Lassenius, "Communities of Practice in a Large Distributed Agile Software Development Organization," *Information & Software Technology* 56, no. 12 (2014): 1556–1577.
19. Rikkel Duus and Mudithal Cooray, "Together We Innovate: Cross-Cultural Teamwork Through Virtual Platforms," *Journal of Marketing Education* 36, no. 3 (2014): 244–257.
20. Oldham and Hackman, "Not What It Was and Not What It Will Be."
21. Barry Banther, "Five Qualities of a Lasting Leader," *Health Care Registration: The Newsletter for Health Care Registration Professionals*, 23, no. 7 (2014): 6–7.
22. Oldham and Hackman, "Not What It Was and Not What It Will Be."
23. "Moore Wins 2011 OGCA Doug Chalmers Award," *Daily Commercial News*, September 26, 2011.
24. Frederick P. Morgeson, Erich C. Dierdorff, and Jillian L. Hmurovic, "Work Design In Situ: Understanding the Role of Occupational and Organizational Context," *Journal of Organizational Behavior* 31, nos. 2–3 (February 2010): 351–60.
25. "Effective Engagement Strategies for an Increasingly Dispersed Workforce," *Public Manager* 43, no. 3 (2014): 62–65.
26. Oldham and Hackman, "Not What It Was and Not What It Will Be."

5 Planning for, Recruiting, and Selecting the Workforce

LEARNING OUTCOMES

After studying this chapter, you should be able to

1. Discuss the steps in human resource planning.
2. Describe the relationship between HR planning, recruiting, and selecting people to work with the organization.
3. Compare the advantages and disadvantages of recruiting from within the organization.
4. Outline the advantages and disadvantages of external recruitment.
5. Explain the objectives of the selection process.
6. Describe the typical steps in the selection process.
7. Identify the various sources of information used for selection decisions.
8. Discuss the different methods and types of questions for conducting an employment interview.
9. Illustrate the value of different types of employment tests.
10. Explain the legal and ethical considerations within recruitment and selection.

OUTLINE

HRM CLOSE-UP

"We are curious about what our customers are looking for, and we are curious about our employees and what they need to be successful. Knowing this is the best way for our company to succeed."

At Precision BioLogic Inc. (PBI), in Dartmouth, Nova Scotia, 60 employees fulfill traditional responsibilities of jobs in areas such as sales, manufacturing, product development, quality control, administration, and management. But the company's organization chart is far from traditional. On paper, it looks like a living organism with functional cells and pods and many offshoots showing relationships between job functions.

The organic structure is reflective of the company's business, that of developing and manufacturing products used by medical lab technicians to diagnose people with clotting or bleeding disorders. Employees work in teams in a non-hierarchical structure that recognizes that each person plays a key role in the customer relationship.

"You won't find terms like 'boss,' 'subordinate,' or 'direct report' at PBI," explained co-CEO Jennifer Mills. "I have broad responsibility for the operations of our company, but it doesn't mean I'm any more important than anyone else."

Bosses at PBI are referred to as "Primary Supports," as the term implies a two-way support relationship rather than a one-way "telling and directing" one. And when it comes to recruiting, the company takes much care and time in the process.

"When I myself was hired," said Mills, "the process took many months. It began with lunch with the CEO, and then I had meetings or lunches with members of the management team. I had so many meetings, lunches, and dinners that when I finally received the job offer, my husband quipped, 'Did he give you a job offer or a marriage proposal?'"

This kind of focus and care in recruiting and selection ensures that Precision BioLogic finds an ideal match. Many people are involved in the process, including team members, colleagues, and the primary support person, who all meet with the candidate before a decision is made.

"Hire for *fit!*" exclaims Mills. "Culture fit is the most important aspect. We have a unique culture and when people haven't worked out, it's rarely been that they do not have the right skills or knowledge–it's normally because they don't fit with the culture."

The culture at PBI is described as collaborative with lots of communication and good humour. At the centre of its values chart are the words 'trust, curiosity, and fun.'

When a job needs filling, the company prepares a role dimension, a compensation range, and a job profile that is essentially a "personality profile" for the role. Recruits then complete their own personality profile and the two are compared. Differences are explored in order to determine a fit. This profiling is designed to indicate qualities such as a person's level of sociability, whether the person is a multitasker or prefers a single focus, and whether the person is more likely to enjoy working with data or with people.

Of course, job skills, education, and experience count, but according to Mills, if "a role personality goes against the candidate's natural personality, it's not likely going to be a good fit. In fact, when we first adopted this system, we had all our staff complete the profiles. Nearly all of them said that the survey described them very accurately. And there's no judgment in the profiling. People's personalities are not right or wrong, just distinct and different."

If someone indicates unhappiness in a job, Mills refers again to the personality profiling. She once had an accountant who wasn't feeling fulfilled. "We discovered that she was highly sociable and put her on the office social committee," she said. "It gave her the ability to access this part of her personality without having to change her chosen career. Awareness is really helpful. We can make subtle shifts to help staff."

Courtesy of Jennifer Mills

Jennifer Mills, co-CEO, Precision BioLogic Inc.

For most of its hiring, Precision BioLogic works with a recruiting agency. The agency knows the company and its culture very well and does much of the groundwork to prepare a short list of candidates. The agency uses Internet, professional networking tools like LinkedIn, and other online posting sources to identify potential recruits.

Anticipating staffing requirements is a key part of the executive team's strategic planning process. This way, they can stay ahead of the curve and allow for the careful approach needed in hiring. And if they do encounter an unforeseen crunch, the company can reassign staff internally where possible. "Everyone is willing to chip in and help out," states Mills, "which also provides development opportunities."

Source: Courtesy of Jennifer Mills

INTRODUCTION

In earlier chapters we stressed that the structure of an organization and the design of the work within it affect the organization's ability to reach its objectives. These objectives, however, can be achieved only through the efforts of people. It is essential that work within the organization is done by people qualified to do the work and most likely to best perform the work. To achieve this, defining the core competencies for any work is critical to the recruitment and selection processes, and this starts with the line manager, who is also encouraged to think about current and future people requirements. Jennifer Mills clearly understands the importance of finding the right person for the company. Precision BioLogic uses a variety of ways to find (recruit) and then pick (select) the people who have the attitudes desired to make the firm successful. This being so, planning for human resources requirements is a critical first step.

Recruitment and selection continue to be one of the top concerns of all levels of management within an organization. Despite the economic challenges of the past several years, almost all organizations are finding it increasingly difficult to secure qualified and appropriate applicants to fill job openings. According to recent studies, most employers have entered a period in which jobs ranging from the unskilled to the professional and highly technical are harder to staff; this condition is not likely to improve in the near future, especially for small businesses.[1] Given legal requirements, ethical considerations, and the complex economic environment, managers cannot rely solely upon unsolicited applications to fill openings, nor can they be sloppy in making hiring decisions. This chapter will discuss the process of planning for staffing requirements and then finding, attracting, and selecting applicants.

HUMAN RESOURCE PLANNING

You will recall from Chapter 1 that a company becomes competitive by means of its people. Therefore, it is essential that an organization look strategically at its people and the skills they require to accomplish the strategic and operational goals of the organization.

But what is meant by "strategic"? While strategy has many definitions, we will use the one you might have learned in a management course. Strategic plans tend to be broader in scope and longer in time frames (two to three years), provide overall direction, and apply to the entire organization. Basically, a company's strategy lies in determining its key goals and the actions it needs to take to achieve those goals. The importance of strategic planning is highlighted by Target's failure in the Canadian marketplace; the company's inability to properly implement strategic planning had devastating consequences.[2]

Strategic HRM, as noted in Chapter 1, includes all the HR policies, processes, and practices that help the company achieve those goals through its employees. Therefore, it is important that the line manager link the goals of the company to the competencies of the people employed.

In linking goals to competencies, the line manager will need to anticipate the current and future needs of the company and develop the roadmap to get there. What the manager is really doing is ensuring that the company has people with the right competencies for the present and for future organizational growth.[3] This is called **human resource planning**—a process to ensure that the people required to run the company are being used as effectively as possible, where and when they are needed, in order to accomplish the organization's goals. Depending on the organization, the process might also be called "manpower planning" or "employment planning." No matter which phrase is used, the purpose is the same: to have the right people with the right skills in the right jobs at the right time. Given the economic uncertainty, organizations might sometimes want to ignore this. However, it is even more important in difficult financial circumstances to ensure they have the appropriate staff to achieve success both in the short term and into the future.[4]

Human resource planning
Process to ensure that an organization has people available (employed) who have the right competencies, and that these people are being effectively utilized in the right capacities in order for the company to achieve its desired objectives

Linking HR Planning to Strategic Planning

Organizations will undertake strategic planning where major objectives are identified and comprehensive plans are developed to achieve the objectives. Because strategic planning involves the allocation of resources, including the people resources of the organization, HR planning is aligned to ensure that the objectives are met. And from the overall organizational objectives, divisions and/or departments will also set subordinate objectives that support the attainment of organizational ones. Thus, the line manager will need to make plans not only for business objectives but plans for the necessary staffing resources. For example, if the organization has strategically decided to enter a new market, it needs to ensure that it has the people with the right skill sets to gain a foothold in that market. Consequently, the HR plan must have an activity that assesses the skill of current employees and possibly a recruitment activity that attracts new employees with the necessary skills.

Likewise, through HR planning, all HR processes, systems, and practices can be aligned to the overall business strategy. In doing this, the organization ensures that it has the people capabilities to adjust to changes in the environment. One area of strategic HR planning receiving much attention is succession planning. Organizations are concerned about developing leaders for the future and are focusing efforts on leadership development so that the leaders have the competencies necessary to keep pace with the direction and overall strategy of the organization.[5] In the best companies, such as Fairmont Hotels, BMO, and IBM, virtually no distinction exists between strategic planning and HR planning; the planning cycles are the same, and HR issues are seen as inherent in the management of the business.

Importance of HR Planning for Staffing Needs

Why is it important for the line manager to be involved in human resource planning? Consider these facts about the Canadian labour force, which highlight the requirement to understand the diversity (gender, age, geographic location) within this landscape:

- Canada has a population of about 35.5 million with an unemployment rate of 6.6% in January 2015.
- In January 2015, employment increased among women aged 55 and over, while there was little change in the other demographic groups.
- Employment rose in Quebec, Alberta, New Brunswick, and Prince Edward Island in January 2015 while it fell in Saskatchewan.
- The workforce is aging—by 2031 it is projected that 25% of the workforce will be 55 or older.
- By 2031 the percentage of foreign-born workers is expected to be 33%.
- Of Canadians who left their long-term jobs, defined as lasting 12 years or more, within the traditional retirement period between age 60 and 64, 44% were re-employed within a decade.
- Approximately 35% of workers are part-time or self-employed, with the self-employed around 15% of total employment.[6]

These dramatic shifts in the composition of the labour force require that managers become more involved in planning their staffing needs, since such changes affect not only employee recruitment but also methods of employee selection, training, compensation, and motivation. As illustration of the impact of changes in the workforce, companies such as the PTI Group in Alberta have determined that the hiring of Aboriginal people(s) is a strategic imperative. PTI supplies remote-site services such as food services and worker accommodations, particularly within the resource industry. Since much of its work in Canada occurs on or near Aboriginal land, the company decided it was in its long-term best interest to create employment opportunities for the local communities. In doing so, PTI has also partnered with Northern Alberta Institute of Technology to create training programs where it can employ the graduates.[7] Without doing its own workforce planning, PTI would not have known there was a problem.

An organization may incur several intangible costs as a result of inadequate or no people planning. For example, inadequate planning can cause vacancies to remain unfilled. The resulting loss in efficiency can be costly, particularly when lead time is required to train replacements. Situations also may occur in which employees are laid off in one department while applicants are hired for similar jobs in another department.

Realistically, planning occurs more systematically in medium-sized and larger organizations. Small, entrepreneurial organizations tend to approach HR staffing needs on a more short-term basis. These businesses tend to spend most time creating the business and give little time to creating staffing plans.[8]

An example of a small organization that does pay attention to its staffing needs is Brainworks Software. The company was given the 2014 small business excellence award within the Avaya and International Avaya User Group Customer Innovation Awards. Brainworks is a geographically distributed company with more than half its employees working remotely, and its ability to select staff on the basis of skills and expertise rather than location allows it to achieve the highest levels of customer satisfaction.[9]

HR Planning Approaches

LO1

What are the steps in human resource planning?

Since the overall outcome of HR planning is to have the right people with the right competencies at the right time in the right jobs, there is a need to forecast the demand for employees. Forecasting can be done through quantitative approaches, such as a **trend analysis**, or qualitative approaches, such as **management forecasts**.

A trend analysis will forecast employment requirements on some type of organizational index, such as sales or units of production. Previous years' experiences will be analyzed and projections will be made for the future. This type of numerical analysis is often accomplished through the use of software. In management forecasts, the opinions and judgments of people knowledgeable about the organization's future needs will develop scenarios that can be used for planning purposes. The Delphi and the Nominal Group technique are two forecasting methods in which managers' opinions regarding employment demands are obtained.

Trend analysis
Quantitative approach to forecasting labour demand on an organizational index

Management forecasts
Opinions and judgments of supervisors or managers and others knowledgeable about the organization's future employment needs

Staffing table
Graphical representations of organizational jobs along with the numbers of employees currently occupying those jobs and future employment needs

Markov analysis
Method for tracking the pattern of employee movements through various jobs

Skills inventory
Information about the education, experiences, skills, etc. of staff

Besides forecasting the demand for employees, an organization will also need to look at the supply of employees. This activity includes looking both internally, in the organization, and externally, to the larger labour market. Two techniques to assess the internal supply are the **staffing table** and **Markov analysis**. Staffing tables are graphical representations of all organizational jobs, along with the numbers of employees currently occupying those jobs (and perhaps also future employment requirements derived from demand forecasts). Markov analysis shows the percentage (and actual number) of employees who remain in each job from one year to the next, and the proportions of those promoted, demoted, or transferred or who leave the organization.

While staffing tables and Markov analysis focus on numbers of employees, another technique focuses on the skill mix or **skills inventory**. When assessing the organization's supply, organizations will identify the key skills or core competencies necessary for organizational success. Without knowing the core competencies required for business success, the other HR processes may not be successful. All other HR needs are based on the identified competencies of employees to ensure good organizational performance. Organizations such as Hewlett-Packard and DuPont Canada use HR information and enterprise systems to assist in this task. Figure 5.1 describes the steps in the planning process. Information taken from skills inventories assists an organization with succession planning, which will be discussed further in this chapter.

FIGURE 5.1 The HR Planning Steps

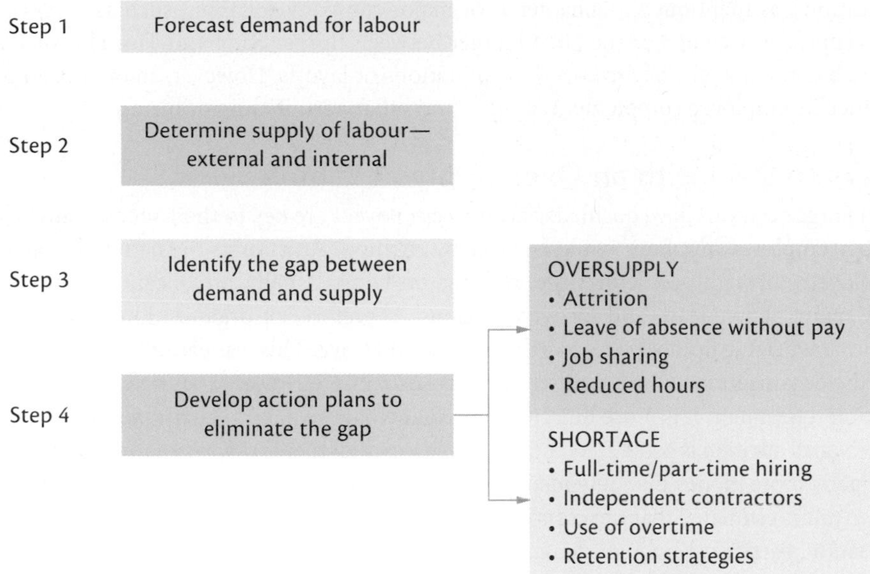

Results of HR Planning

The outcome of HR planning is to achieve a usable balance between the demand for and supply of employees. It is here that organizations can see the results of good HR planning.

The demand for and supply of labour is very much a function of the economic environment. The dynamics within the Canadian economy are complex, and it is often difficult to forecast impending changes. Global economies and the increasing Canadian household debt load are just two factors that need to be considered when examining national economic conditions (e.g., think of the financial crisis in Greece).[10]

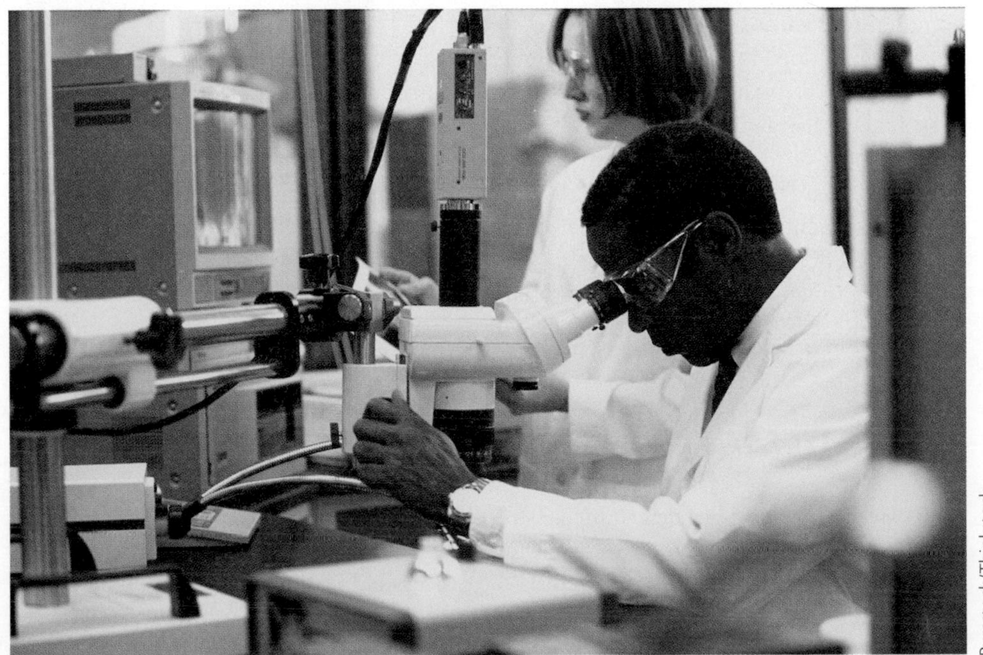

Purestock/Thinkstock

These scientists have knowledge and expertise that will enable the company to achieve its goals.

But HR planning is no guarantee the organization will never have too many employees for its immediate or long-term needs. This situation can be the result of severe economic conditions, as mentioned in Chapter 1, or major company collapses, such as Target's 2015 bankruptcy in Canada, or the 2014 merger between Burger King and Tim Hortons. In all cases, a company may be faced with terminations or layoffs. However, an organization can balance its employee complement in other ways than terminating or hiring.

Ways to Deal with an Oversupply of Labour

Some organizations have decided that since employees are key to their success, any need to reduce employee numbers would be done by attrition. Attrition is the natural departure of employees through people quitting, retiring, or dying. Usually, organizations can estimate how many people leave and for what reasons. Therefore, an organization may be able to avoid downsizing because it knows that people will leave. This was easier to do when people left the organization at the age of retirement—usually 65. However, with many people postponing retirement, it is more difficult to predict what the natural attrition rate will be.

Not all attrition is good. If too many people leave—if there is *high turnover*—it can cost the company more money than intended. Replacing an employee is a costly and time-consuming activity. It is estimated that the costs of turnover can be as high as two times the annual compensation, particularly in high-demand skill areas or professionals.[11] And the costs are not just financial: they can include the loss of key knowledge. One of the more serious business issues of the 21st century has been the concern with retaining key employees.

If the organization can predict that the excess supply of employees is more short-term, it may suggest that some employees take a leave of absence (without pay), job-share, or reduce working hours (and pay); or it can redeploy people to units that have a need.

Ways to Deal with Shortages of Labour

Even though human resource planning frequently focuses on the surplus of employees, currently much of the attention has been on projected labour shortages—particularly in certain occupations and industries. For example, British Columbia is projecting that there will be almost 62,000 more jobs than people to fill them by 2020, with a shortage of skilled trades much sooner.[12] Therefore, an organization may need to recruit from the outside the company. However, if the need might possibly be short-term or temporary, the organization will not want to hire for the longer term, and it may request that current employees work extra hours, such as during peak periods.

As mentioned in Chapter 1, the number of part-time employees has increased a great deal. Therefore, it is not unusual for companies to hire part-time staff to cover labour shortages. Likewise, organizations will utilize the services of a temporary employment agency to acquire short-term staff, particularly in areas where a certain type of expertise is required, such as software programming. In addition, an organization might enhance retention strategies, or as mentioned in Chapter 1, people might be hired as independent contractors for a set period of time.

The HRM Guide
www.hrmguide.net/canada

Once a manager knows what work is to be done and the skills required, the task of finding and selecting the right people begins. For more information on HR planning, see **www.hrmguide.net/canada**.

Recruitment
The process of locating and encouraging people to apply for jobs

RECRUITMENT

LO2

What is the relationship between HR planning, recruitment, and selection?

Once an organization has determined its needs, it must then recruit potential employees. The line manager, together with HR professionals, will identify where a company might look for these candidates. **Recruitment** is the process of locating and encouraging people to apply for existing or anticipated job openings. The purpose of recruitment is to have a sufficient pool of qualified applicants. Figure 5.2 provides an overview of the process.

The process informs the applicants about the qualifications required to perform the job and the career opportunities the organization can offer. **Employment branding** is another key consideration.[13] An organization's reputation in the employment landscape, and what applicants believe their employment experience will be like (i.e., work–life balance, fairness and equity, communication norms), influence their decision to apply to job opportunities. This being so, organizations should be aware of how they are perceived by those seeking employment.

Employment branding
An organization's reputation as an employer

Whether a vacancy will be filled by someone within the organization or from outside will, of course, depend on the availability of people, the organization's HR practices, and the requirements of the job.

Recruiting Within the Organization

LO3

What are the advantages and disadvantages of internal recruiting?

Most public-sector organizations, and many private-sector ones, try to follow a policy of filling job vacancies above the entry-level position through promotions and transfers from within. By filling vacancies in this way, an organization can capitalize on the investment it has made in recruiting, selecting, training, and developing its current employees. Promotion-from-within policies at CIBC and Canada Mortgage and Housing Corporation have contributed to the companies' overall growth and success.

Advantages of Recruiting from Within

Promotion serves to reward employees for past performance and is intended to encourage them to continue their efforts. Promoting from within makes use of the people who already know the organization and the contribution they have made. It also gives other employees reason to anticipate that similar efforts by them will lead to promotion, thus improving morale within the organization. This is particularly true for members of designated groups who have had difficulty finding employment and often faced even greater difficulty in advancing. Most organizations have integrated promotion policies as an essential part of their employment equity programs.

Transfers can also serve to protect employees from layoff or to broaden their job experiences. This strategy becomes more noticeable as organizations become flatter with fewer layers between front-line employees and executives. Furthermore, the transferred employee's familiarity with the organization and its operations can eliminate the orientation and training costs that recruitment from the outside would entail. Most importantly, the transferee's performance record is likely to be a more accurate predictor of the candidate's success than the data gained about outside applicants.

FIGURE 5.2 The Recruitment Process

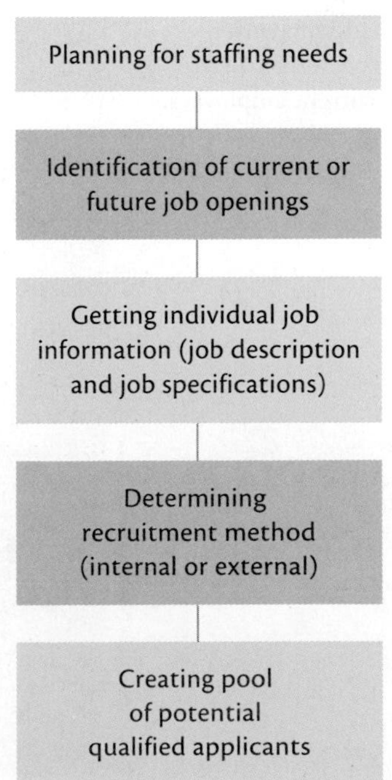

Methods of Locating Qualified Internal Job Candidates

The effective use of internal sources requires a system for locating qualified job candidates and for enabling those who consider themselves qualified to apply for the opening. Qualified job candidates within the organization can be located by using computerized record systems and internal job postings.

HUMAN RESOURCES MANAGEMENT SYSTEMS Information technology has made it possible for organizations to create databases that contain the complete records and qualifications of each employee. Using increasingly user-friendly search engines, managers can access this information and identify candidates for available jobs. Organizations have developed résumé-tracking systems that allow managers to query an online database of résumés. Companies such as Oracle and SAP Canada are leaders in developing technology for staffing and skills management.

Similarly to the skills inventories mentioned earlier, these systems allow an organization to rapidly screen its entire workforce to locate suitable candidates for an internal opening. This data can also be used to predict the career paths of employees and to anticipate when and where promotion opportunities may arise. Since the value of the data depends on its being up to date, the systems typically include provision for recording changes in employee qualifications and job placements as they occur.[14]

SUCCESSION PLANNING As mentioned earlier, many organizations conduct succession planning—the process of identifying, developing, and tracking key employees for future promotions or transfers. Therefore, when a job opening occurs in a particular part of the organization, it might make use of the succession plan and put the internal employee into the vacancy. Succession plans rely upon the organization identifying its long-term goals, outlining the competencies required to achieve those goals, and making sure that the employee is developed in order to assume other roles and take on other responsibilities in the future.

Internal job posting
Method of communicating information about job openings

INTERNAL JOB POSTING Organizations may advertise about job openings through a process referred to as **internal job posting**. In the past, this process has consisted largely of posting vacancy notices on company employment boards in an HR department or common area, such as lunchroom. In addition, internal advertising can also be done through a company's intranet, e-mails or other types of internal memos, and company newsletters. Increasingly, companies such as Xerox are developing computerized job posting systems and maintaining voluntary lists of employees looking for upgraded positions. As part of the overall approach to assessing internal staff and their skill sets, organizations will use technology, including Web-based solutions, to determine whether any staff have the necessary skills for a certain role.[15]

Internal job posting can provide many benefits to an organization. However, these benefits may not be realized unless employees believe the process is being administered fairly. Furthermore, it is more effective when internal job posting is part of a career development

Job vacancies filled from within the organization capitalize on the development of current employees.

Chris Ryan/Caiaimage/Getty Images

program in which employees are made aware of opportunities available to them within the organization. For example, the organization may provide new employees with literature on job progression that describes the lines of job advancement, training requirements for each job, and skills and abilities needed as they move up the job-progression ladder.

Limitations of Recruiting from Within

Sometimes, certain jobs that require specialized training and experience cannot be filled from within the organization and must be filled from outside. This situation is especially common in small organizations. Also, for certain openings it may be necessary to hire individuals from another organization who have gained the knowledge and expertise required for these jobs.

Even though the company may encourage job openings to be filled from within, outside candidates should be considered in order to prevent the inbreeding of ideas and attitudes. Applicants hired from the outside, particularly for certain technical and managerial positions, can be a source of new ideas and may bring with them the latest knowledge. Indeed, excessive reliance on internal sources can create the risk of "employee cloning." Furthermore, it is not uncommon for firms in competitive fields, such as high technology or retailing, to attempt to gain secrets and managerial talent from competitors by hiring away their employees.

Recruiting Outside the Organization

LO4

What are the advantages and disadvantages of external recruiting?

Frequently, organizations will decide to fill positions by bringing people in from outside the organization. Thus, when a mid-level manager of the organization leaves, a chain reaction of promotions may subsequently occur, creating other openings throughout the organization. The question, therefore, is not whether to bring people into the organization, but rather at what level to bring them in.

Usually, external recruitment is organized and coordinated by an HR department, with the line manager frequently giving suggestions about where to recruit, such as an ad in a newspaper or professional journal. However, if there is no HR department, these managers need to be aware of such things as labour-market conditions and where to recruit.

Organizations such as RONA, Scouts Canada, and the Bank of Montreal will often focus on external recruitment for senior management positions. In many of these cases, hiring someone from the outside is seen as bringing in new ideas, different styles, new energy, and earlier successes.[16]

Advantages and Disadvantages of External Recruitment

Like recruiting from within, external recruitment has advantages and disadvantages.

One advantage is that the individual brings certain unique skills the company needs now. Likewise, it is possible to bring in people with a variety of different experiences and perspectives.

A disadvantage is the lack of solid information about the person's performance on the job. That information is likely to be available only through second-hand sources, such as what the applicant volunteers and what references might say. Also, the person may not know the industry or organization, necessitating more extensive orientation and training. Further, there may be constraints in the organization, such as salary levels, that prevent the organization from accessing a large pool of applicants. Significant costs are usually associated with external recruitment. These include time, the cost of advertising (sometimes as much as $9,000 per newspaper), and the cost of familiarizing the person with the organization. Lastly, there may also be legislative requirements, such as employment equity, which lead to certain applicant pools.

The Labour Market

Labour market
Area from which applicants are recruited

The **labour market**, or the area from which applicants are recruited, will vary with the type of position to be filled, the amount of compensation to be paid, and, as mentioned earlier, the economic environment. Recruitment for executives and technical personnel who require a high degree of knowledge and skill may be national or even international in scope. Recruitment for jobs that require relatively little skill, however, may encompass only a small geographic area—such as within a city of within a province. The reluctance of people to relocate may cause them to turn down offers of employment, eliminating them from consideration beyond the local labour market.

The condition of the labour market may also help to determine which recruiting sources an organization will use. During periods of high unemployment, organizations may be able to maintain an adequate supply of qualified applicants from unsolicited résumés alone. A tight labour market, one with low unemployment, may force the employer to advertise heavily and/or seek assistance from local employment agencies. How successful an organization has been in reaching its employment equity goals may be still another factor in determining the sources from which to recruit. For a number of years, Canada has relied on immigration to assist in meeting the demand for labour. In addition, the department responsible for immigration, Citizenship and Immigration Canada, has worked with businesses to create processes that are more responsive to labour market shortfalls. In early 2012, the federal government announced that there would be a more flexible immigration system to enable people with skilled trades qualifications to enter Canada.[17] This change will, hopefully, reduce critical shortages in the trades, such as plumbers and electricians. The government has further stated that this revised system would allow employers to determine who has the skills necessary instead of the government.[18] These changes are intended to allow applicants into Canada that have the skills in short supply. Further, in 2015 some temporary foreign workers in Alberta were given more time to become permanent residents as they faced a deadline for leaving the country.[19] As mentioned in Chapter 1, Canada has an aging population with insufficient younger workers to fill the work requirements in the future. Further, as more and more individuals become part of a global talent pool, companies will seek a number of ways to recruit beyond one's home country.

The dynamics of the labour market mirror the general economy. When there is a poor economic climate with many people unemployed, there may be a larger pool of applicants; if the economy is strong with few unemployed, the pool of applicants may be much smaller. There are also training and education programs that aim to provide an appropriate number of skilled applicants so that most of those graduates can be hired—such as nurses and other medical specialists. This does not mean everyone is always hired, though, as the person may not have the skills needed by a particular employer. However, employers who make good use of their HR planning activities will continue to look for qualified applicants whether the economy is good or poor.

Outside Sources of Recruitment

LinkedIn
www.linkedin.com

Facebook
www.facebook.com

Twitter
http://twitter.com

The outside sources from which employers recruit will vary with the type of position to be filled. A software developer, for example, is not likely to be recruited from the same source as a retail service person. Trade schools can provide applicants for entry-level positions, though these recruitment sources are not as useful when highly skilled employees are needed. Networking, referrals from previous and existing staff, information from customers/clients, and involvement in the community are a few ways organizations seek outside people. A variety of new and creative recruitment approaches continues to evolve with the expanded use of social networks (see **www.linkedin.com**, **www.facebook.com**, and **http://twitter.com**).

Some of the major outside sources of recruitment are discussed below.

ADVERTISEMENTS One of the frequent methods of attracting applicants is through advertisements. Advertisements may be posted in websites, newspapers, or trade journals, or transmitted by radio, television, billboards, posters, and e-mail. And it is no longer unusual to see an ad on the side of a bus. Advertising has the advantage of reaching a large audience of possible applicants. Some degree of selectivity can be achieved by using newspapers and journals directed to a specific readership. Professional journals, trade journals, and publications of unions and nonprofit organizations fall into this category.

Well-written advertisements can highlight the major assets of the position while showing the responsiveness of the organization to the job and career needs of applicants. Advertisements in all types of media should follow the AIDA principle: provoke Attention, Interest, Desire, and Action in those seeing the ad.[20] Part of the information typically included is a statement that the organization is an equal-opportunity employer and that only those candidates selected to move forward in the process will be contacted.

Employment and Social Development Canada (ESDC) (**www.esdc.gc.ca**) is responsible for administering the Employment Insurance program through its Service Canada agency, found in most communities. Individuals who become unemployed must register at one of these offices and be available for "suitable employment" in order to receive their weekly employment insurance cheques. Service Canada has created a national job bank that lists information about jobs across the country province by province. The database can be searched by type of job and geographic area within the province (**www.jobbank.gc.ca**).

Employment and Social Development Canada
www.esdc.gc.ca/eng/jobs/lmi/publications/index.shtml

Service Canada Job Bank
www.jobbank.gc.ca

INTERNET The Internet is the most commonly used search tactic by job seekers; 60% of Canadians with Internet access have gone online in search of a job. Both companies and applicants find the approach cheaper, faster, and often more effective.

There is no doubt the Internet has had an impact on print advertising in the newspapers. Not too many years ago, a person would see five to ten pages of career ads in all the major newspapers. Now, you might find no more than one or two pages a week. Further, many companies use their websites to announce job openings. For example, Mountain Equipment Co-op posts detailed information about job openings at its site along with a savable application form. Likewise, WestJet and CIBC actively use their company sites to encourage people to consider working for them. Canadian recruiting sites include Monster.ca (**www.monster.ca**), Workopolis (**www.workopolis.ca**), Jobs.ca (**www.jobs.ca**), and Working.com (**www.working.com**), a site that provides information about job opportunities throughout Canada.

Monster
www.monster.ca

Workopolis
www.workopolis.ca

Jobs.ca
www. jobs.ca

Working.com
working.com

Employers say that the Internet is faster (some job applicants responding within 30 minutes of the job posting); that it generates higher-quality candidates; and that it is cheaper (by as much as 80%) than traditional advertising media. An Internet posting can be as low as $50 per month, as against a newspaper ad at $6,000 per day, with Monster and Workopolis being about $750 per job posting. There is also an interesting side benefit for the job seeker, given the difficult employment landscape: according to one study, a person is unemployed 25% less time by making use of Internet job postings.[21]

Both companies and job seekers find the approach is cheaper, faster, and potentially more effective. It is estimated that there are more than 4,000 websites where applicants can submit their employment backgrounds and potential employers can check for qualified candidates. A capability like this can help companies find the people with the competencies required in today's dynamic business environment.

CareerBuilder, an internationally focused online recruitment advertiser, recently stated that employers need to use current technology for effective recruitment. According to one of its studies, 28% of Canadian employers use social media sites to seek potential job applicants. Further, even though few people secure a job through these sites, 22% of job applicants actively use LinkedIn and Facebook to identify opportunities.[22] It is therefore important that employers develop a strategic approach to the use of social media as a recruitment tool.

But a Web-based ad is not sufficient. The organization must also have the means to easily and quickly process the large number of applications that can come from their own sites or other job search engines. To help with screening, companies have integrated front-end career websites with their own databases. This arrangement can pull the right data from all candidates and organize it to make the review more efficient; it can also provide recruitment statistics.[23] In addition, résumés are stored and the software is sophisticated enough to connect candidates directly to the hiring manager. Some of the technology in use, particularly in larger organizations, enables the application to be moved electronically from one step to another, ensuring that a good candidate isn't lost due to long delays.

Companies, such as RONA, Bombardier, Finning Canada, and Hydro One, and organizations, such as the federal government and the Ontario government, use the Internet to attract people. Employers indicate that the reason is to increase the opportunity to attract the people with the right skill sets for their organizations.

As mentioned at the beginning of the chapter, social media networking sites have been very much in the forefront for job seekers. For example, Facebook and LinkedIn have created apps where employers can post jobs inside the 800-million-member social network.[24] Such a situation has created an incredibly large labour pool at small recruitment cost.

EMPLOYMENT AGENCIES Employment agencies, including executive search firms and temporary employment agencies, attempt to match applicants with the specific needs of a company. A fee is charged to the employer for services that are tailored to the employer. By law, job seekers cannot be charged for help in finding work. It is common for such agencies to specialize in serving a specific occupational area, such as office staff or technical computer people. Private agencies usually focus on clerical, technical, and junior–middle management, whereas executive search firms tend to focus on senior and executive management. These agencies may charge an employer 25 to 30% of the annual salary if they find a candidate who gets hired. Since these agencies differ in the services they offer, job seekers would be wise to take the time to find a recruiter who is knowledgeable, experienced, and professional. When talking with potential recruiters, individuals should discuss openly their philosophies and practices with regard to recruiting strategies, including advertising, in-house recruiting, screening procedures, and costs for these efforts.

Boyden
www. boyden.ca

Korn/Ferry
www.kornferry.com

Executive search firms (also called "headhunters") are employment agencies that typically focus on senior-level and executive-level managerial positions. The search tends to be very focused to that employer. The fees charged the employer by the agencies may range from 30 to 40% of the annual salary for the position to be filled. The employer pays this fee.

To get a sense of the range of organizations that use executive search firms, access the sites of Boyden (**www. boyden.ca**) and Korn/Ferry (**www.kornferry.com**).

Agencies that provide temporary employees are one of the fastest-growing recruitment sources. Companies such as Imperial Oil Ltd., Home Depot, and SaskTel use temporary employees extensively. "Temps" are typically used for short-term assignments or to help when managers cannot justify hiring a full-time employee, such as for vacation fill-ins, for peak work periods, or during an employee's parental or sick leave.

Increasingly, temps are being employed to fill positions once staffed by permanent employees. At Hydro-Québec, for example, "long-term temporaries" have replaced permanent hires as a staffing practice. Employees are hired for one-to-three-year terms. This practice is growing, because temporaries can be laid off quickly, and with less cost, when work lessens. The use of temporaries thus becomes a viable way to maintain proper staffing levels. Also, the employment costs of temporaries are often lower than those of permanent employees, because temps are usually not provided with benefits and can be dismissed without the need to file employment insurance claims.

The drawbacks of contract employees are that their commitment to the company may be lower than that of full-time employees, and they may take confidential information to their next employer, possibly a competitor. Further difficulties may be encountered in getting full-time and contract employees to effectively work together.

Check out the websites of Angus One Professional Recruiters (**www.angusone.com**), Olsten Staffing Services (**www.olsten.com**), Adecco (**www.adecco.ca**), and Manpower, one of Canada's largest temporary agencies (**www.manpower.ca**), to find out more about employment agencies.

Angus One Professional Recruiters
www.angusone.com

Olsten Staffing Services
www.olsten.com

Adecco
www.adecco.ca

Manpower
www.manpower.ca

EDUCATIONAL INSTITUTIONS Educational institutions are typically a source of young applicants with formal training but relatively little full-time work experience. High schools are usually a source of employees for clerical and blue-collar jobs. Community colleges, with their various types of specialized training, can provide candidates for technical jobs. These institutions can also serve as a source of applicants for a variety of white-collar jobs, including those in the sales and retail fields. Some management-trainee jobs are staffed from this source. Humber College in Etobicoke, Ontario, and the B.C. Institute of Technology offer a Human Resource Management training program. For technical and managerial positions, universities are generally the primary source.

It is important for employers to be aware of what attracts students to employers. Universum, a global survey company, conducts research on students' perceptions of employers. Part of the survey asks about the ideal company. Some of the top "ideal companies" in Canada for 2014, as rated by Canadian business students, were Google, Ernst & Young, the Government of Canada, Apple, and Air Canada.[25]

OPEN HOUSES AND JOB FAIRS Organizations may also use open houses and job fairs to recruit new employees—particularly if the organization is expanding or is looking for particular types of skills. For example, with the shortage of skilled trades, an organization might participate in a job fair at an educational institution that graduates tradespeople. Or the organization might have an open house where potential applicants are encouraged to visit the company and see what might be available. Seasonal resort operations such as Whistler/Blackcomb in British Columbia use open houses at the start of each ski season as a way to attract people with a variety of skills, and Home Depot typically holds recruitment open houses at key points throughout the year.

As an innovative example, in 2011, combining the concept of an open house with the use of technology, a job fair was created in which 20 employers from a wide array of industries (e.g., financial services, insurance, and retail) attracted over 18,000 job applicants throughout Canada.[26] While the event had virtual employer booths describing the opportunities, job seekers could access the information at any time during the event, no matter where they lived or worked. This ability represents an example of the evolving use of technology in recruitment.

EMPLOYEE REFERRALS The recruitment efforts of an organization can be aided by employee referrals or recommendations made by current employees. Managers have found that the quality of employee-referred applicants is normally quite high, since employees are generally hesitant to recommend individuals who might not perform well. According to a management professor, 88% of employers rate employee referrals as their #1 source of quality candidates.[27] The effectiveness of this recruitment effort can be increased by paying commissions or bonuses to employees when they make a successful "recruitment sale." An organization, however, needs to ensure in utilizing employee referrals that it is not creating a situation of systemic discrimination.

UNSOLICITED APPLICATIONS AND RÉSUMÉS Many employers receive unsolicited applications and résumés from individuals who may or may not be good prospects. Even though the percentage of acceptable applicants from this source may not be high, the source cannot be ignored. Many job search strategies suggest that individuals use this method to introduce themselves to organizations that are of interest to them.[28]

Given that many employers now seek to use technology during the recruitment process, for such an approach to be successful for the job seeker, it might be useful to create a digital résumé. This tool can be exceptionally helpful if the work one is seeking is within the technology or digital world. For a digital résumé to be effective, it might contain visual information, video, and infographics.[29]

Good public relations dictate that any person who contacts an organization for a job be treated with courtesy and respect. If there is no possibility of employment in the organization at present or in the future, the applicant should be tactfully and frankly informed of this fact.

PROFESSIONAL ORGANIZATIONS Many professional organizations and societies offer a placement service to members as one of their benefits. For example, the Human Resources Institute of Alberta (HRIA) provides members with weekly e-mails of job opportunities. The system enables employers to connect with HR professionals and inform them of job prospects.

UNIONS If a company is unionized and has employees that belong to labour unions, those unions can be a principal source of applicants for blue-collar jobs (such as welders, electricians, and plumbers) and for some professional jobs. Some unions, such as those in the maritime, printing, and construction industries, maintain hiring halls that can provide a supply of applicants, particularly for short-term needs. Employers wishing to use this recruitment source should contact their local union for employer eligibility requirements and applicant availability.

David Paul Morris/Bloomberg via Getty Images

Job fairs are a good way to source applicants.

Recruitment Considerations

When recruiting applicants, organizations must ensure that all legal requirements, as addressed in Chapter 2, are met. For example, an advertisement should not specify height or weight requirements unless this is a bona fide occupational requirement within the role. As previously noted, systemic discrimination might occur if employee referrals are the only recruitment source used. Also, as organizations continue to develop diverse workforces, employers will often focus on attracting staff in communities of different ethnic and cultural backgrounds. Those employers that fall under the federal employment equity legislation (see Chapter 2) are expected to have a recruitment program that focuses on the designated groups of women, visible minorities, people with disabilities, and First Nations people. While Canada (unlike the United States) does not have a quota system, under employment equity legislation there is an expectation that over time those organizations that fall under the legislation will have a workforce reflective of the general population of Canada. Therefore, recruitment initiatives should take this into consideration, and it is important for line managers and supervisors to be knowledgeable about and supportive of their organization's objective to have employees with diverse ethnic and cultural backgrounds. Managers need to be held accountable for the success (or failure) of creating a more diverse workforce.[30] Managers may also be actively involved in recruitment "outreach" programs, where they speak at ethnic community centres to let people know about employment opportunities with their company. Other avenues are ethnic-community newspapers and TV stations. Maple Leaf Sports and Entertainment extended itself into the South Asian community by ensuring that hockey games were broadcast in Punjabi.[31]

A particularly effective organization in bridging the immigrant gap is the Toronto Region Immigrant Employment Council (TRIEC) (**www.triec.ca**). The Council represents an innovative partnership between employers, unions, postsecondary institutions, other community organizations, and government. The organization came into existence in 2003 when the city realized that to have well-settled and satisfied immigrants, it was necessary for immigrants to have successful employment opportunities. The mission of the organization is to create and facilitate solutions to better the integration of immigrants into the regional workforce.[32] It is unique in that it doesn't work directly with immigrants but provides a collaborative approach to engaging the various parties that can help immigrants get settled, find work, and succeed in Canada.

TRIEC
www.triec.ca

MOSAIC
www.mosaicbc.com

Costi Immigrant Services
www.costi.org

Diversity World
www.diversityworld.com

Canadian Abilities Foundation
www.abilities.ca

Aboriginal Careers
www.aboriginalcareers.ca

Nation Talk
www.nationtalk.ca

There are also several organizations that help new immigrants, people with disabilities, and First Nations people find work and employers to find potential employees. Among these are MOSAIC (**www.mosaicbc.com**), Costi Immigrant Services (**www.costi.org**), Diversity World (**www.diversityworld.com**), Canadian Abilities Foundation (**www.abilities.ca**), Aboriginal Careers (**www.aboriginalcareers.ca**), and Nation Talk (**www.nationtalk.ca**).

SELECTION

LO5

What are the objectives of selection?

Once the recruitment process has yielded applicants whose qualifications appear to fit the organization's requirements, organizations have to assess those qualifications and make decide whom to hire. This is usually the line manager's responsibility. If there is an HR department, it will usually play a supporting role by arranging interviews, doing reference checking, administering employment tests, and so on. However, if no HR professional is there to help, the line manager needs to know these steps and their importance.

Matching People and Jobs

Selection
The process of choosing individuals who have relevant qualifications and who will best perform on the job to fill existing or projected job openings

Making hiring decisions is not a scientific process, and so it cannot be structured to achieve perfect results. However, being systematic increases the possibility of acquiring staff committed to the vision and business plans.[33] **Selection** is the process of choosing individuals who have relevant qualifications to fill existing or projected job openings. Those responsible for making selection decisions should have adequate information about the jobs to be filled, and as much relevant information as possible about the applicants themselves, in order to be able to predict the candidate's job performance.

Prior to the selection process, it is important to reconfirm the necessary knowledge, skills, and abilities for the job. As mentioned in Chapter 4, these requirements are identified through job analysis. Managers can then use selection methods, such as interviews, references, psychological tests, and the like, to assess the applicant's competencies and match these against the requirements of the job and the needs of the organization.[34]

Ordinarily, managers are well acquainted with the requirements pertaining to skills, physical demands, and other factors for jobs in their respective departments. If the interview step includes professionals from the HR department, the HR professional will need to maintain a close liaison with the various departments to become thoroughly familiar with the jobs and its needed competencies.

The Selection Process

LO6

What are the steps in the selection process?

In most organizations, selection is a continuous process. Turnover inevitably occurs, leaving vacancies to be filled by applicants from inside or outside the organization or by individuals whose qualifications have been assessed previously. In some situations, organizations will have a waiting list of applicants who can be called when permanent or temporary positions become available.

The number of steps in the selection process and their sequence will vary, not only with the organization but also with the type and level of job to be filled. Each step should be evaluated on its contribution. The steps that typically make up the selection process are shown in Figure 5.3. Not all applicants will go through all these steps. Some may be rejected after a review of their application form or résumé, or after a preliminary interview.

FIGURE 5.3 Steps in the Selection Process

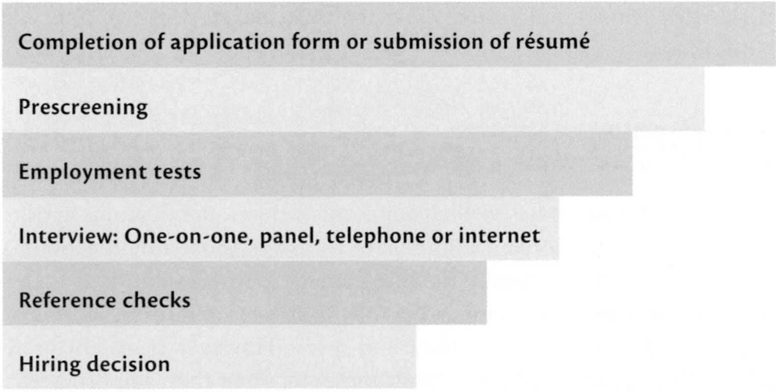

Note: Steps may vary. An applicant may be rejected after any step in the process.

As shown in Figure 5.3, organizations use several different means to obtain information about applicants. These include application forms and résumés, interviews, tests, and reference checks. Regardless of the method used, it is essential that it conform to accepted ethical standards, including privacy and confidentiality, as well as legal requirements. Above all, it is essential that the information obtained be sufficiently reliable and valid.

Obtaining Reliable and Valid Information

The degree to which interviews, tests, and other selection procedures yield comparable data over time is known as **reliability**. For example, unless interviewers would judge the capabilities of a group of applicants to be the same today as they did yesterday, their judgments are unreliable—that is, unstable. Likewise, a test that gives widely different scores when administered to the same individual a few days apart is unreliable.

Reliability
The degree to which interviews, tests, and other selection procedures yield comparable data over time and by alternative measures

Validity
How well a test or selection procedure measures a person's attributes

In addition, information pertaining to a person's suitability must be as valid as possible. **Validity** refers to what a test or other selection procedure measures and how well it measures it. In the context of employee selection, validity is essentially an indicator of the extent to which data from a procedure (interview or test, for example) predict job performance. However, whether something is valid depends upon the selection tool's overall reliability. The bullseye scenario is a helpful way to remember these important concepts. Someone may hit the same area of a target every time a dart is thrown (very reliable), but if the dart continues to land outside of the targeted area, the desired results are not achieved (not valid). Therefore, whatever selection procedures or tools are used—whether an interview or an employment test—they must be both reliable and valid in order to provide useful information about predicting the applicant's performance in the organization. The procedure or tool used may need to be modified (or not used), or the results carefully evaluated due to cultural differences. For example, companies that only screen job applicants for values will not get good information about a person's overall capability to perform the job successfully; the best overall predictor for job performance (and training success) is the person's general mental abilities.[35]

While it is important that all information be both reliable and valid, organizations are most concerned about the reliability and validity of any employment tests they might conduct. This topic will be discussed further in the section "Employment Tests."

Sources of Information About Job Candidates

LO7

What are the various sources of information when making a selection decision?

Many sources of information are used to provide as reliable and valid a picture as possible of an applicant's potential for success on the job. This section looks at the usefulness of application forms and résumés, interviews, employment tests, and reference checks.

Application Forms

Many organizations require application forms to be completed, because they provide a fairly quick and systematic means of obtaining a variety of information about the applicant. Application forms serve several purposes:

- They provide information for deciding whether an applicant meets the minimum requirements for experience, education, and so on.
- They provide a basis for questions the interviewer will ask about the applicant's background.
- They also offer sources for reference checks. For certain jobs, a short application form is appropriate.

Many managers remain unclear about the questions they can ask on an application form. While most know they should steer clear of such issues as age, race, marital status, and sexual orientation, other issues are less clear. The following are some suggestions for putting together an application form:

- *Application date.* The applicant should date the application. This piece of information helps managers know when the form was completed and gives them an idea of the time limit (e.g., one year) that the form should be on file.
- *Educational background.* The applicant should also provide grade school, high school, college, and university attendance—but not the dates attended, since that can be connected with age.
- *Experience.* Virtually any questions that focus on work experience related to the job are permissible.
- *Arrests and criminal convictions.* Questions about arrests, convictions, and criminal records are to be avoided. If bonding is a requirement, ask if the individual can be bonded.
- *Country of citizenship.* Such questions are not permitted. It is allowable to ask if the person is legally entitled to work in Canada.
- *References.* It is both permissible and advisable that the names, addresses, and phone numbers of references be provided. (References are covered in more detail below.)
- *Disabilities.* Employers should avoid asking applicants if they have physical disabilities or health problems, if they have ever received psychiatric care or have been hospitalized, or if they have ever received workers' compensation.

As mentioned in the section on Internet sourcing, many organizations are no longer using paper applications and are having job seekers apply for work directly online. In some cases, there is an electronic application and in other cases job seekers send their résumé to an e-mail address.

Résumés

A résumé is a document that summarizes and highlights relevant information about an individual who is seeking employment. Contact information, education, previous work experiences, volunteer experiences, and personal interests are typical components. However, individuals frequently exaggerate or overstate their qualifications on a résumé; in a tight labour market, candidates sometimes even delete advanced qualifications. One survey indicated that 45% of individuals in the 18-to-34 age range "stretch" the truth on their résumés,[36] in spite of legal consequences (including termination) and ethical considerations.[37] Ethics in HRM 5.1 discusses some of these issues.

While résumés should be accurate, applicants can still ethically display creativity in how they present themselves.

Students can practise reading and analyzing résumés online at **www.resumecompanion.com**, **www.livecareer.com**, **www.careermag.com**, and **jobstar.org/tools/resume/index.php**.

Look at Emerging Trends 5.1 for the latest techniques used in developing résumés.

ResumeCompanion
www.resumecompanion.com

Live Career
www.livecareer.com

Career Magazine
www.careermag.com

JobStar
jobstar.org/tools/resume/index.php

The Employment Interview

Traditionally, the employment interview has played a very important role in the selection process—so much so that it is rare to find an instance where an employee is hired without some sort of interview. Depending on the type of job, applicants may be interviewed by one person, by members of a work team, or by other individuals in the organization. While researchers have raised doubts about its validity, the interview remains a mainstay of selection because (1) it is especially practical when there are only a few applicants, (2) it serves other purposes, such as public relations, and (3) interviewers maintain great faith and confidence in their own judgments.

ETHICS IN HRM 5.1

WHEN DOES "STRETCHING" BECOME LYING?

Most candidates for white-collar jobs prepare a résumé and submit it to prospective employers. They also complete the application form, answering questions required by employers for comparison purposes. Some recruitment agencies noticed during the last recession that résumé padding increased. Applicants were "stretching" the dates of their employment, misleading employers about the nature of their duties, and misrepresenting their salaries. When you are writing a résumé, adding three months to your previous employment, saying you were a night auditor instead of clerk, and adding $950 to your last salary might seem relatively harmless.

But what are the facts? Studies of "creative" résumé writing indicate that about 30% of résumés report incorrect dates, 11% misrepresent reasons for leaving, and others exaggerate education attainments or omit criminal records. The probability is that about two-thirds of employers check references. Some former employers give only dates of employment and previous salary ranges.

Most organizations require you to sign a statement saying that the information you supply is true and that if it is not, you will be dismissed. Some cases of résumé padding have been heavily publicized. A Toronto Stock Exchange manager was dismissed for lying about having a master's degree. A member of Parliament listed an ILB on his résumé, which normally stands for International Baccalaureate of Law, but which he claimed stood for Incomplete Baccalaureate of Law. In one heart-wrenching case, a person who was ready to retire was found to have lied about his age decades earlier to get a job. On discovery, he was dismissed and lost his pension. In another case, a Canadian businessman was sentenced to eight months in jail in New Zealand for lying on his résumé: he had listed false qualifications, such as an MBA.

Falsifying a résumé doesn't just happen with "white-collar" jobs. In 2011, a football coach was forced to resign for allegedly overstating his experience as a head coach, and in 2012 a political figure overstated a relationship with the board of trustees at a community college.

In a labour market where too many people are chasing too few jobs, candidates will also lie on their résumés, but do so by dropping experience and educational qualifications. This practice, called "stripping," is used because job seekers are ready to take any job in order to survive or to hold them over until the jobs they really want are available.

Here are some tips for employers when reviewing résumés:

1. Watch for ambiguity—probe on use of general or vague terms.
2. Ask more than once—rephrase similar questions and compare answers.
3. Be factual—ask references to confirm basic information such as employment history.

CRITICAL THINKING QUESTION:
Have you ever overstated information on your résumé? Explain your reason.

Source: Adapted from "Almost One-Half of Workers Know Someone Who Lied on Resume," *Canadian HR Reporter*, September 27, 2011, accessed January 9, 2012, **www.hrreporter.com/articleview/11315-almost-one-half-of-workers-know-someone-who-lied-on-resum**.

Nevertheless, interviews are plagued by problems of subjectivity and personal bias. Some interviewers' judgment is more valid than others'. Remember, the purpose of the interview is to gather relevant information to determine whether the candidate has the skills, abilities, and knowledge to be successful on the job in the organization. However, it is also critical that the interview questions be based on the work requirements (as determined through the job analysis) and specific knowledge required. Interviewers need to have been appropriately trained to ensure they are not influenced by candidates' appearance or how well-spoken they are.[38]

LO8

What are the different methods and questions for conducting employment interviews?

Interviewing Methods

Employment or selection interviews differ according to the methods used to obtain information and to find out an applicant's attitudes, feelings, and behaviours. Organizations have a variety of methods to choose from. Further, depending on the number of interviews, more than one method may be used.

EMERGING TRENDS 5.1

1. ***Quick response codes (QR).*** While the marketing field has used barcodes in linking ads to consumers, organizations can also make use of QR to target applicants with information not easily conveyed in print. Such a tool will move the mobile smartphone to the platform of choice for recruitment.
2. ***Mobile platforms.*** Both job seekers and employers are making use of apps. Job seekers can apply wherever they happen to be and manage their job search process from anywhere, and employers can manage postings through mobile apps.
3. ***Video résumés.*** With the evolution of so many different technologies, job seekers, especially those in creative fields, are using video technology to present their résumés. While there can be a number of legal issues associated with this for the potential employer, it has had some appeal for certain organizations. Employers also have tools that allow them to assess the candidates' by using pop-up video comments while reviewing the résumé.
4. ***Video interviewing.*** Given the potential for geographic diversity among applicants, video interviewing will allow employers to "meet" candidates in an efficient (both from a time and a cost perspective) manner.
5. ***Increased use of social networks.*** More and more job seekers are using their contacts on social networks both to get recommendations and to post their résumés. For example, a LinkedIn profile might be used in lieu of a résumé when applying. Likewise, many organizations will search the various social network sites to gather information about applicants.

Sources: T. Raphael, "For Adidas, QR Codes Are Already a Big Thing," December 7, 2011, accessed March 18, 2015, **www.ere.net/2011/12/07/for-adidas-qr-codes-are-already-a-big-thing**; "Emerging Trends in Recruitment," March 3, 2015, accessed March 18, 2015, **www.allaboutpeople.net/emerging-trends-in-recruitment**; J. Freeborn, "How to Master Social Media Recruitment in 2015," February 5, 2015, accessed March 19, 2015, **www.social-hire.com/social-recruiting-advice/5103/how-to-master-social-media-recruitment-in-2015**.

One-on-One

Most often, the first face-to-face interview occurs between the applicant and an interviewer. The interviewer could be an HR professional or a supervisor. Questions are asked and observations are made of both the interviewer and the applicant. The structure of the questions could be behavioural description interview (BDI), situational, or non-directive. (The different types of questions are explained below.)

Panel or Group Interview

Panel (group) interview
An interview in which a board of interviewers questions and observes a single candidate.

This type of interview involves a panel of interviewers who question and observe a single candidate. In a typical **panel** (or **group**) **interview**, the candidate meets with several interviewers who take turns asking questions. After the interview, the interviewers pool their observations to reach a consensus about the suitability of the candidate.[39] During the interview, the panel may use structured questions, situational questions, BDI questions, or a combination of all three.

Telephone Interview

Generally, organizations are doing more interviews today than they have done in the past. Much of this is caused by the need to make a better hire decision than in the past. Companies have assessed that a poor decision can be very costly and want to minimize the costs. Therefore, many companies use a telephone interview as the first interview in the screening process. This interview can be conducted by someone from the company, or with the advent of technology, companies can use software where applicants are asked to respond to questions by touching a keypad.

Internet-Based Interview

Increased use of technology has not only helped in creating a way to recruit job applicants, but also enabled organizations to pre-screen or assess applicants online. A growing number of organizations have been using online assessment tools to help with the interview process. Some companies will assess online using the GMA (general mental ability) tool or personality profiles. Sometimes the candidates are asked to answer a series of multiple-choice questions tailored to the job. The answers are compared either with an ideal profile or with profiles based on other candidates' responses. Using computer-based technology can also assist in filtering out unqualified candidates. Monster makes use of online interviewing; given that its business is Web-based services, this practice is consistent with its use of technology.[40] Depending on the company and software in use, a computer interview conducted in conjunction with online tests can measure everything from contradictory responses and time delays related to answering to the applicants' keyboarding skills.

In addition to the benefits of objectivity, some research evidence suggests that applicants may be less likely to engage in "impression management" in computerized interviews than in face-to-face interviews. Such technology is typically used at the initial stages of the interview process.[41]

Types of Interview Questions

Regardless of the type of interview method used, questions must be asked of the applicant. In addition, for an interview to be reliable, the questions must be stated in such a way that the same questions are asked of each applicant. The questions can be very specific to get specific answers (structured), or they can be less structured where broad and open-ended questions are asked. Listed below are the types of interview questions typically used.

STRUCTURED QUESTIONS Since the objective of an interview is to gather data for making a decision, companies will look at the interview process as an investment and therefore create structured questions to determine if the person has the competencies to do the work.[42] Because structured questions are based on job requirements and an established set of answers against which applicant responses can be rated, they provide a more consistent basis for evaluating job candidates. Structured questions are more likely to provide the type of information needed for making sound decisions. They also help to reduce the possibility of legal charges of discrimination. Employers must be aware that any interview is highly vulnerable to legal attack and that more challenges (human rights and grievances) in this area can be expected in the future. The two main types of structured questions are discussed below.

The leading type of structured interview question being used is a **behavioural description interview (BDI)**. A BDI question focuses on real work incidents, not hypothetical situations as a situational interview question does. The BDI format asks job applicants what they did in a given situation. For example, to assess a potential manager's ability to handle a problem employee, an interviewer might ask, "Tell me about the last time you disciplined an employee." Or the format might be this sequence:

Behavioural description interview (BDI)
Question about what a person did in a given situation

1. Describe a situation when you disciplined an employee.
2. What was the action taken?
3. What were the results?

Toolkit 5.1 provides an example of a BDI question and approach for interviewing someone for a front-desk position in a hotel.

Such an approach to interviewing is based on solid research that past performance is the best predictor of future performance. You will notice that with this type of interview, the questions can produce a variety of responses. The interviewer will usually clarify or ask further questions to get the necessary information. Many more organizations are using BDI questions to better assess the applicant's ability to perform successfully in the organization's environment. If you have recently looked for work, you may have encountered BDI questions.

TOOLKIT 5.1 SAMPLE BDI INTERVIEW QUESTION

You are being considered for work in our hotel. As we encounter difficult situations with our customers, please describe a time you had to tell a customer that there was no reservation for a room. What action did you take? What were the results?

Some additional clarification might be gained from the following questions:

1. Was there any aspect of your decision that you were uncertain about?
2. Did the customer have information that you didn't have?
3. Could anyone overhear the customer?
4. What decision did you finally make?

This type of interview question is being used more for a number of reasons:

1. Answers can provide a rich source of information. Questions are based on the job requirements directly related to the skills and competencies needed to successfully perform the work.
2. Responses provide a clear view of the candidate's past behaviour and results.
3. Responses provide consistency to selection process due to format of questions.
4. Answers are noted and rated on the basis of previously established guidelines.
5. Such questions provide a high degree of validity when done properly.[43]

Situational question
Question in which an applicant is given a hypothetical incident and asked how he or she would respond to it

Another variation is the **situational question**, in which an applicant is given a hypothetical incident and asked to respond. The response is evaluated relative to pre-established benchmarks. Interestingly, many organizations are using situational questions to select new college graduates. Toolkit 5.2 shows a sample situational question used to select systems analysts at a chemical plant.

UNSTRUCTURED QUESTIONS These types of questions are broad and open-ended and allow the candidate to talk freely with little interruption from the interviewer. For example, an interviewer might ask: "Tell me more about your experiences on your last job." The applicant is allowed a great deal of latitude in guiding the discussions. Generally, the interviewer listens carefully and does not argue, interrupt, or change the subject abruptly. The interviewer also uses follow-up questions to allow the applicant to elaborate, makes only brief responses, and permits pauses in the conversation—this last technique is the most difficult for the beginning interviewer.

A study conducted by the University of Western Ontario indicated that unstructured questions might result in inconsistent and subjective responses that can disadvantage minority candidates, particularly for those organizations with employment equity programs.[44,45]

TOOLKIT 5.2 SAMPLE SITUATIONAL INTERVIEW QUESTION

Question
You work in an environment where deadlines are part of everyone's work. The project you are working on has a deadline that you feel is not realistic. What would you do in this situation?

Record Answer

____
____
____

Scoring Guide
Good. "I would discuss the situation with my teammates to get feedback on whether my conclusion is accurate."
Good. "I would bring my concern to the project manager and work out a suitable solution."
Fair. "I would let the team know of my concerns but do the best I can."
Poor. "I would ignore my concerns."

WHICH TYPE OF QUESTIONS TO USE? The greater freedom afforded to the applicant in the non-directive interview is particularly valuable in bringing to the interviewer's attention any information, attitudes, or feelings that may often be concealed by more structured questioning. However, because the applicant determines the course of the interview and no set procedure is followed, little information that comes from these interviews enables interviewers to cross-check agreement with other interviewers.

Thus, the reliability and validity of the non-directive interview may be expected to be minimal. Based on experiences in hiring, it is probably a better approach to use both types of questions—structured to get good information about skills and competencies to do the work and unstructured to help in determining the candidate's fit in the organization.[46]

Guidelines for Employment Interviewers

Studies on the employment interview tend to look at questions such as "What traits can be assessed in the interview?" and "How do interviewers reach their decisions?" The purpose of the studies is to assess how an interview can be structured to improve the overall process. Toolkit 5.3 presents some of the major findings of these studies. It shows that information is available that can be used to increase the validity of interviews.

Training has been shown to dramatically improve the competence of interviewers. If it is not done on a continuing basis, training should at least be done periodically for managers, supervisors, and HR representatives who conduct interviews. Interviewer training programs should include practice interviews conducted under guidance. Some variation in technique is only natural. However, the following list presents ten ground rules for employment interviews that are commonly accepted and supported by research findings.

TOOLKIT 5.3 WHAT ARE SOME OF THE FINDINGS FROM RESEARCH STUDIES ON THE INTERVIEW?

1. Understand that there is difficulty in gathering the right information and in making an informed decision.
2. Use appropriate and good questions to get the necessary information. Structured interviews are more reliable than unstructured interviews.
3. Review candidate information (such as résumé) after the interview. To do so before the interview can lead to certain impressions and therefore certain conclusions, such as where the person went to school.
4. Impressions and judgments need to come from the interview and applications or résumés.
5. Take time to come to a conclusion—don't make early judgments.
6. Observe the behaviour and actions of the candidate during the interview. Sometimes, candidates will behave in a way intended to strengthen their credentials, for example, name-dropping or projecting an image of the ideal candidate.
7. Look for information outside the interview to confirm conclusions and perceptions.
8. Practise asking questions before the interview.
9. Ask questions to determine fit with the organization—particularly about interpersonal skills and motivation.
10. Allow the applicant time to talk, which provides a larger behaviour sample.
11. Be aware that nonverbal as well as verbal interactions influence decisions.

Sources: Adapted from Allen Hullcutt, "From Science to Practice," *Canadian HR Reporter*, June 6, 2011, accessed January 10, 2012, **www.hrreporter.com/articleview/10442-from-science-to-practice**; Scott Erker, "Do's and Don'ts of Recruitment," *Canadian HR Reporter*, November 15, 2010, accessed January 10, 2012, **www.hrreporter.com/articleview/8457-dos-and-donts-of-recruitment**; and Brian W. Swider, Murray R. Barrick, T. Brad Harris, and Adam C. Stoverink, "Managing and Creating an Image in the Interview," *Journal of Applied Psychology* 96, no. 6 (2011): 1275–1288.

1. *Establish an interview plan.* Determine the areas and specific questions to be covered. Review job requirements, application or résumé data, test scores, and other available information before seeing the applicant.
2. *Establish and maintain rapport.* Greet the applicant pleasantly, explain the purpose of the interview, display sincere interest in the applicant, and listen carefully.
3. *Be an active listener.* Strive to understand, comprehend, and gain insight into what is only suggested or implied. A good listener's mind is alert, and facial expressions and posture usually reflect this fact.
4. *Pay attention to nonverbal cues.* An applicant's facial expressions, gestures, body position, and movements often provide clues to that person's attitudes and feelings. Interviewers should be aware of what they themselves are communicating nonverbally. However, be cautious in your interpretation of nonverbal cues, as some cultures, such as First Nations, are more comfortable with silence.
5. *Provide information as freely and honestly as possible.* Answer the applicant's questions fully and frankly. Present a realistic picture of the job.
6. *Use questions effectively.* To obtain a truthful answer, questions should be phrased as objectively as possible, giving no indication of what response is desired.
7. *Separate facts from inferences.* During the interview, record factual information. Later, record inferences or interpretations of the facts. Compare inferences with those of other interviewers.
8. *Recognize biases and stereotypes.* One typical bias is for interviewers to consider strangers who have interests, experiences, and backgrounds similar to their own to be more acceptable. Stereotyping involves forming generalized opinions of how people of a given gender, race, or ethnic background appear, think, feel, and act. Also, interviewers will sometimes rate one competency, such as leadership, very high and assume that all other competencies are equally as high (halo effect). Likewise, an interviewer may consider all competencies average even though there is evidence of either poor or excellent job performance (central tendency).
9. *Control the course of the interview.* Stick to the interview plan. Provide the applicant with ample opportunity to talk, but maintain control of the situation in order to gather the information required.
10. *Standardize the questions asked.* To increase reliability and avoid discrimination, ask the same questions of all applicants for a particular job. Keep careful notes; record facts, impressions, and any relevant information, including what was told to the applicant. As noted earlier, structured questions and preparation are good ways of ensuring you obtain the information you are seeking.

Employers have found it advisable to provide interviewers with instructions on how to avoid potentially discriminatory questions in their interviews. The examples of appropriate and inappropriate questions shown in Figure 5.4 may serve as guidelines for application forms as well as pre-employment interviews. Complete guidelines may be developed from current information available from the office of the Canadian Human Rights Commission (or check **www.chrc-ccdp.gc.ca**). Once the individual is hired, the information needed but not asked in the interview may be obtained if there is a valid need for it and if it does not lead to discrimination.

Canadian Human Rights Commission
www.chrc-ccdp.gc.ca

As a final helpful hint for interviews, applicants need to be provided with information on all aspects of the job, both desirable and undesirable (this is called a *realistic job preview*), so that they may opt out of the selection process if they feel they would not be satisfied with the job. This reality check helps avoid production losses and costs associated with low job satisfaction that can result in the person leaving the organization.

FIGURE 5.4 Appropriate and Inappropriate Interview Questions

Type of System	Appropriate Questions	Inappropriate Questions
National or ethnic origin	Are you legally entitled to work in Canada?	Where were you born?
Age	Have you reached the minimum or maximum age for work, as defined by the law?	How old are you?
Sex	How would you like to be referred to during the interview?	What are your childcare arrangements?
Marital status	As travel is part of the requirement of our position, would you foresee any problems meeting this obligation?	What does your spouse do for a living? Is there travel involved? Who takes care of the children when you are away?
Disabilities	Do you have any conditions that could affect your ability to do the job?	Do you use drugs or alcohol?
Height and weight	(Ask nothing.)	How tall are you? How much do you weigh?
Address	What is your address?	What were your addresses outside Canada?
Religion	Would you be able to work the following schedules?	What are your religious beliefs?
Criminal record	Our job requires that our employees be bonded.	Are you bondable? Have you ever been arrested?
Affiliations	As an engineer, are you a member of the engineering society?	What religious associations do you belong to?

Employment Assessments

An employment assessment is an objective and standardized way to assess a person's KSAs (knowledge, skills, and abilities), competencies, and other characteristics in relation to other individuals.[47] When an organization decides to use a particular employment assessment or test, it is critical that the attribute or skill being tested is used in the work. For example, if someone's keyboarding skills are tested and yet the job doesn't have any tasks that require keyboarding, it would be inappropriate to use that test. Again, the purpose of tests is to gather additional information on the candidate so that job performance in the organization can be predicted.

As mentioned earlier in this chapter, there continue to be concerns about the reliability and validity of employment tests. The concern is focused on whether these tests are biased and appropriate for the job under consideration.[48] In a court decision in 2010, the court held that the written examination of applicants for a firefighter position adversely affected certain minority groups.[49] While an organization is certainly able to design and use any test it so chooses, without ensuring the validity and reliability of the test through on-the-job performance over time employers are creating legal challenges for themselves.[50]

Aptitude tests
Measures of a person's capacity to learn or acquire skills

Achievement tests
Measures of what a person knows or can do right now

Organizations use assessments/tests to gather more in-depth information on applicants.[51] However, the information from the assessment will not be useful if there are challenges of bias and discrimination. To better understand the legal implications of pre-employment testing, read HRM and the Law 5.1.

What is the value of different types of employment tests?

Types of Employment Assessments/Tests

Employment assessments/tests may be classified in different ways. Generally, they are viewed as measuring either **aptitude** (capacity to learn or acquire skills) or **achievement** (what a person knows or can do right now).

HRM AND THE LAW 5.1 WAS THIS DISCRIMINATION?

When making a hiring decision, managers must ensure that the use of pre-employment assessments does not create a complaint of discrimination. In a case involving the Toronto District School Board and an applicant, it was determined by the Ontario Human Rights Tribunal that while the assessment was valid and reliable, pre-employment accommodation needed to be done with that particular applicant.

Specifically, the applicant, with a diagnosed learning disability and attention-deficit disorder, applied for a part-time caretaker role. As part of the screening process, the employer used literacy and numeracy assessments. The applicant informed the school board of the learning disability and asked that there be some accommodation to write the test: "specifically, to write in a separate room, to have someone break down the questions so that they could be understood, and to use a calculator. The applicant was informed that the board does not accommodate. The person administering the tests suggested that the applicant just write the tests, see what the results were, and then further consider any accommodation needs. The applicant felt that this was being "set up to fail."

At the time of the application, the job seeker was working with an agency that assists adults with learning disabilities. The executive director of the agency contacted the school board, confirmed the need for accommodation, and indicated that medical documentation could be provided. Even after the documentation was received and reviewed, the school board refused to provide accommodation.

In making its decision, the tribunal first determined that the applicant had been discriminated against in the application process. The tribunal indicated that the applicant had a documented learning disability that makes it difficult to perform on written tests without assistance and that to be forced to do so would mean that the applicant would perform poorly. The tribunal concluded that the applicant had fulfilled the responsibility by informing the school board that accommodation was required. While the tribunal accepted that to do so for a pre-employment screening test would be difficult, such accommodation could have occurred. Finally, the tribunal confirmed that the employer did not seek information about the nature of the disability, as it was required to.

And the consequence of this decision to the Toronto District School Board? The tribunal awarded $7,500 in compensation to the job applicant for injury to dignity.

CRITICAL THINKING QUESTIONS:

1. Given what you were informed about in Chapter 2 on accommodation, do you think the decision is reasonable? Why?
2. What are some of the potential issues with other candidates who do not or may not be aware of the ability to seek accommodation when being assessed for a job?

Source: *Human Rights Tribunal of Ontario, David Mazzei, Applicant, and Toronto District School Board, Melanie Stoughton and Silvana Filice, Respondents,* February 24, 2011, TR-0527-09, 2011 HRTO 400.

COGNITIVE ABILITY TESTS Cognitive ability tests measure mental capabilities, such as general intelligence, verbal fluency, numerical ability, and reasoning ability. A variety of tests—both paper-and-pencil- and computer-administered—measure cognitive abilities, including the General Aptitude Test Battery (GATB), the Graduate Management Aptitude Test (GMAT), the Bennett Mechanical Comprehension Test, and the Wonderlic Cognitive Ability Test. Figure 5.5 shows some items that might be used to measure different cognitive abilities.

Although cognitive ability tests can be developed to measure specialized areas such as reading comprehension and spatial relations, many experts believe that the validity of cognitive ability tests simply reflects their connection to general intelligence. Measures of general mental abilities have been shown to be good predictors of performance, as well as career success and job satisfaction.[52] Generally speaking, while cognitive ability tests are highly predictive of the applicants' performance on the job, frequently these tests are viewed as unfair—by both managers and candidates.[53] Further, there is evidence suggesting that cognitive ability tests may create lower levels of minority representation.[54]

FIGURE 5.5 Sample Measures of Cognitive Ability

Verbal

1. What is the meaning of the word "surreptitious"?
   a. covert c. lively
   b. winding d. sweet

2. How is the noun clause used in the following sentence? "I hope that I can learn this game."
   a. subject c. direct object
   b. predicate nominative d. object of the preposition

Quantitative

3. Divide 50 by 0.5 and add 5. What is the result?
   a. 25 c. 95
   b. 30 d. 105

4. What is the value of 144^2?
   a. 12 c. 288
   b. 72 d. 20736

Reasoning

5. ________ is to boat as snow is to ________.
   a. Sail, ski c. Water, ski
   b. Water, winter d. Engine, water

6. Two women played 5 games of chess. Each woman won the same number of games, yet there were no ties. How can this be?
   a. There was a forfeit. c. They played different people.
   b. One player cheated. d. One game is still in progress.

Mechanical

7. If gear A and gear C are both turning counterclockwise, what is happening to gear B?
   a. It is turning counterclockwise. c. It remains stationary.
   b. It is turning clockwise. d. The whole system will jam.

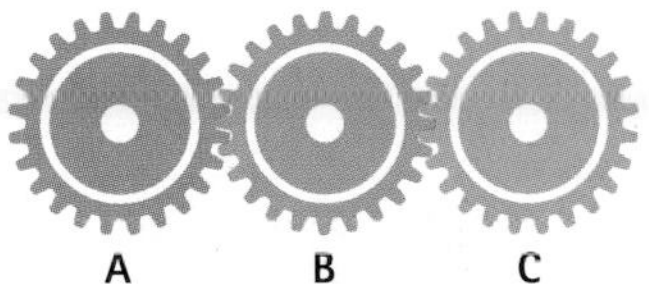

A B C

Answers: 1. a, 2. c, 3. d, 4. d, 5. c, 6. c, 7. b

One of the more interesting uses to which measuring general mental ability has been put is the National Football League's administering the Wonderlic to measure the brainpower of its recruits to ensure that they can keep up with both the physical and the mental demands of the game.[55]

PERSONALITY AND INTEREST INVENTORIES Whereas cognitive ability tests measure a person's mental capacity, personality tests measure personal characteristics such as extroversion, agreeableness, and openness to experience. While the ability of such tests to predict job performance has been quite low, recent research indicates that people tend to blame themselves and react inappropriately when something goes wrong. This type of awareness can be useful when assessing candidates for managerial roles.[56] Personality tests can be problematic if they inadvertently discriminate against individuals who would otherwise perform effectively. Therefore, although it is generally not recommended that personality tests be used for background information when selecting employees, they can be very useful as part of a career development program and for enhancing team work.[57]

EMOTIONAL INTELLIGENCE/EMOTIONAL AND SOCIAL COMPETENCE One of the newer, and greatly debated, types of employment tests measures the *emotional intelligence* of the applicant—particularly for leadership roles. Emotional intelligence (EI) has many definitions, but the one most commonly used describes it as a set of personal qualities distinct from cognitive ability and important for success.[58] Researchers, including those who originally developed the concept, believe there is more to success at work than mere intellect. This being so, the concept of EI is evolving into *emotional and social competence* (ESC), which consists of a range of personality characteristics and is not just a single measurement.[59] Emerging from the research is a question whether any one type of employment assessment can measure ESC and the idea that what might be better is a set of different tests that measure the broad spectrum of personality and social competence. The research also suggests that emotional and social competence is more appropriately assessed for leadership roles.[60]

PHYSICAL ABILITY TESTS In addition to learning about a job candidate's mental capabilities, employers may need to assess a person's physical abilities. Particularly for demanding and potentially dangerous jobs like those held by firefighters and truck drivers, physical abilities such as strength and endurance tend to be good predictors of performance on the job, but possibly also of ability to minimize injury.[61] A physical ability test is not the same as a medical exam. Some organizations may still require a medical exam before actually starting employment to ensure there is no medical condition that might preclude the employee from successfully performing the work. However, many organizations are no longer doing medical exams due to privacy issues or potential challenges of discrimination.

JOB SAMPLE TESTS Job sample tests, or work sample tests, require the applicant to perform tasks that are a part of the work required on the job. Like job knowledge tests, job sample tests are constructed from a carefully developed outline that, experts agree, includes the major job functions; the tests are thus considered content-valid. They are often used to measure skills for office and clerical jobs. Job sample tests have been devised for many diverse jobs: a map-reading test for traffic control officers, a lathe

dolgachov/Thinkstock

Assessments, such as the applicants' keyboarding skills, can provide additional information in the selection process.

test for machine operators, a complex coordination test for pilots, an in-basket test for managers, a group discussion test for supervisors, and a judgment and decision-making test for administrators, to name a few.

SUBSTANCE ABUSE (DRUG AND ALCOHOL) TESTING The Canadian Human Rights Commission and some of its provincial counterparts have issued policies on employment-related drug testing. Generally speaking, an employer in Canada, in contrast to its U.S. counterparts, cannot do random substance abuse testing, even in safety-sensitive work environments, and if it does so the employer is at risk of challenges.[62] Addiction to drugs or alcohol is considered a disability, and the employer is to be guided by legislation and by practices such as workplace accommodation. For example, when Suncor Energy attempted to implement random drug and alcohol testing of employees, this was contested by the union, and the legal judgment supported the union, indicating that this type of testing is unreasonable exercise of Suncor's management rights.[63]

Even if the employer has established that drug testing is job-related—typically, this involves safety issues—the candidate must be informed that job offers are conditional on the successful passing of a drug test and that this test will be required during the course of employment. To comply with legal issues in Canada, any policies in relation to substance abuse testing must have a clear and legitimate purpose. As well, the policies must be administered in a reasonable manner, including not being invasive or done in a discriminatory fashion.[64]

LO10

What are legal and ethical considerations within recruitment and selection?

Reference Checks

Organizations use a variety of ways to check references, including electronic and telephone. But while references are commonly used to screen and select employees, they have not proved successful for predicting employee performance. Written letters of reference are notoriously inflated, which limits their validity. Generally, telephone checks are preferable because they save time and provide for greater candour. At Intuit, the Edmonton, Alberta, software company that produces Quicken, managerial applicants are asked to provide between five and nine references who are then called and asked specific questions.

An employer has no legal obligation to provide a former employee with a reference. To avoid liability, many employers are providing a perfunctory letter of reference, which supplies only the name, employment dates, last position with the company, and final salary. It is important for employers to be understanding of the handling of reference information so that the employer does not create legal issues for itself. The best way to do this is to have a consent form that the applicant signs that provides the reference names and contact information.[65] By using sources in addition to former employers, organizations can obtain valuable information about an applicant's character and habits. Telephone interviews are most effective, and one key question that is particularly effective in screening is to ask, "Would you rehire this employee?" Some employers prefer to outsource reference checking to professional firms, such as Intelysis Employment Screening Services in Toronto, to obtain as accurate information as possible. A survey conducted by Robert Half International, an employment agency, identified that 21% of job seekers were eliminated from consideration after reference checks.[66]

Those individuals supplying references must do so in a responsible manner without making statements that are damaging or cannot be substantiated. To aid employers in ensuring that appropriate reference checks are done, a number of companies provide screening services. Among these are Informed Hiring (**www.informedhiring.com**), BackCheck (**backcheck.net**), and Hire Performance (**www.hireperformance.ca**). With an increasing number of companies providing pre-employment screening, the National Association of Professional Background Screeners (**www.napbs.com**) was formed to create and promote standards when screening job applicants.[67]

Informed Hiring
www.informedhiring.com

BackCheck
backcheck.net

Hire Performance
www.hireperformance.ca

National Association of Professional Background Screeners
www.napbs.com

Cleaning up after a devastating windstorm can create dangerous situations for employees.

© Reuters/CORBIS

Inadequate reference checking can contribute to high turnover or difficulties with the employee. Further, organizations might face legal liability issues if inadequate checks were done. It is important to remember, though, that such investigation needs to be in relation to the work. For example, Mark's Work Wearhouse in Alberta was banned from having credit checks done on candidates for sales positions.[68] The company indicated that credit checks were important to see whether the salesperson could handle financial responsibilities and identify risk for store theft. The Alberta commission disagreed and determined that this was an invasion of privacy.

A final caution on reference checks: accessing social media sites to see what candidates have posted not only may be inaccurate but also might be considered an invasion of privacy.[69] There has been sufficient concern on this latter point that the Privacy Commissioner of Alberta issued guidelines for employers using social media for background checks.[70]

Toolkit 5.4 provides some sample questions to use when doing reference checks.

Reaching a Selection Decision

Although all steps of the selection process are important, the most critical one is the decision to accept or reject applicants. Because of the cost of placing new employees on the payroll, the short probationary period in many organizations, and human rights considerations, the final decision must be as sound as possible. Thus it requires systematic consideration of all the relevant information about applicants. Commonly summary forms and checklists are used to ensure that all the pertinent information has been included.

Summarizing Information About Applicants

Fundamentally, an employer is interested in what an applicant both can and will do. An evaluation of candidates on the basis of assembled information should focus on these two factors, as shown in Figure 5.6. The "can-do" factors include knowledge, skills, and aptitude (the potential) for acquiring new knowledge and skills. The "will-do" factors include motivation, interests, and other personality characteristics. Both factors are essential to successful performance on the job. The employee who has the ability (can do) but is not

TOOLKIT 5.4 SAMPLE REFERENCE CHECK QUESTIONS

1. How long has the person been employed in your organization?
2. Describe their attendance pattern.
3. Can you give me some examples of how the candidate demonstrated initiative?
4. What are the person's strengths?
5. How did the person get along with others in the work unit?
6. What are some areas the person needs to develop?
7. Was the person successful in their role?
8. Why did the person leave your employment?
9. Would you rehire?
10. Describe the person's ability to work with others or in a team.

Sources: "Checking References: Top 10 Questions to Ask," *Hcareers.com*, August 7, 2014, accessed February 22, 2015, **www.hcareers.com/us/resourcecenter/tabid/306/articleid/298/default.aspx**; adapted from Public Service Commission, "The Right Choice!" accessed January 13, 2012, **www.psc-cfp.gc.ca/ppc-cpp/acscmptnc-evl-cmptnc/chck-ref-eng.htm**; "Sample Reference Check Questions," Best-Job-Interview, accessed January 13, 2012, **www.best-job-interview.com/reference-check-questions.html**; and "Conducting Effective Reference Checks," go2hr, accessed January 13, 2012, **www.go2hr.ca/ForbrEmployers/Recruitment/ReferenceandBackgroundChecks/tabid/103/Default.aspx**.

motivated to use it (will not do) is little better than the employee who lacks the necessary ability. Consequently, motivation-based interviewing questions may be used as part of the selection process in order to determine a candidate's "attitude" and desire to do what is required to succeed in a job.[71]

Specific criteria must be established under the various factors, especially for the "can-do" factors. For example, if a person is being hired as a call-centre agent, one ability might be to "input data quickly on a computerized system" or the competency of "ability to present a positive voice image." In most call-centre environments, there are performance standards regarding the time it would take to input the average call-centre information and the number of customer complaints. The standards would also identify extremely poor performance. This would then be a specific level below which an applicant would not be deemed suitable for the job.

It is also helpful to remember that summarizing the information about the candidates is not a mechanical process. The decision maker needs to be sure that any employment assessments are appropriate for the work and that any challenges to their use can be defended, that the weighting of any criterion is done consistently for all applicants, and that job performance indicators are appropriate for all stages of the job.[72]

Of primary importance is ensuring that the entire process is well structured. Recent research indicates that by improving the overall structure of the decision process, including structured interview questions, the validity and reliability of the process improves.[73]

A useful approach to ensuring that the criteria are appropriate and conform to legal requirements is the OUCH test: Objective, Uniform in application, Consistent in effect, and Has job-relatedness.

FIGURE 5.6 "Can-Do" and "Will-Do" Factors in Selection

"CAN-DO" FACTORS		"WILL-DO" FACTORS		
Knowledge Skills Aptitudes	×	Motivation Interests Personality characteristics	=	JOB PERFORMANCE

Making a selection decision is no different than making any other type of management decision: identifying criteria and weighting of the criteria needs to be done. For practice on this, see the exercise at the end of this chapter in Developing Your Skills.

It is much easier to measure what individuals can do than what they will do. The can-do factors are readily evident from test scores and verified information. What the individual will do can only be inferred. Responses to interview and application-form questions may be used as a basis for obtaining information for making inferences about what an individual will do.

Decision Strategy

The strategy used for making personnel decisions for one category of jobs may differ from that used for another category. The strategy for selecting managerial and executive personnel, for example, will differ from that used in selecting clerical and technical personnel. While many factors are to be considered in hiring decisions, the following are some of the questions that managers must ask themselves:

1. Should the individuals be hired according to their highest potential or according to the existing needs of the organization?
2. At what grade or wage level should the individual be started?
3. Should initial selection be concerned primarily with an ideal match of the employee to the job, or should potential for advancement in the organization be considered?
4. To what extent should those who are not qualified but "qualifiable" be considered?
5. Should overqualified individuals be considered?
6. What effect will a decision have on meeting employment equity plans and diversity considerations?

In addition to the above, people will typically approach the hiring decision in one of two ways.

- A "clinical approach," in which each person involved will give different weights to the applicants' background. This approach can lead to different decisions and frequently demonstrates biases and stereotypes, as it is based on personal judgment.
- A "statistical approach," in which criteria for successful job performance are listed and weighting factors are assigned. Information gathered from interviews and assessments are then combined, with the person receiving the highest score being offered the job. In this approach, it is important to identify any threshold or cutoff—the point at which a person is no longer considered.

Studies have demonstrated that the statistical approach provides a far better outcome—in terms of hiring the best person for the job—than the clinical approach.[74]

It is of interest to note that even when all legal, ethical, and procedural considerations are taken into account, bad hiring decisions may still occur. A study by Career Builder revealed that approximately "68% of employers fell victim to bad hires" at one point.[75] This being so, the processes of recruitment and selection will continue to evolve and advance.

The Final Decision

The line manager decides who gets hired. Therefore, it is important that this person understand the importance of the steps necessary to make a good decision. In large organizations, notifying applicants of the decision and making job offers is often the responsibility of the HR department. This department will confirm the details of the job, working arrangements, wages, and so on, and specify a deadline by which the applicant must reach a decision. In smaller organizations without an HR practitioner, the manager will notify the candidates. Therefore, if there is an HR department, it is valuable to forge a strong partnership with HR in order to gain their valuable technical and legal assistance.

Summary

1. Discuss the steps in human resource planning.
   - Forecast demand for labour in the organization.
   - Determine the supply of labour—both external and internal to the organization.
   - Identify the gap between demand and supply.
   - Develop action plans to close or eliminate the gap.
2. Describe the relationship between HR planning, recruiting, and selecting people to work with the organization.
   - As organizations plan for their future, supervisors and managers at all levels must play an active role in planning for future people requirements.
   - It is critical that the organization have the right number and types of employees available to ensure that the organization meets its short and long-term strategic goals.
   - Managers play a key role in planning for the human resources necessary to achieve the business plan.
3. Compare the advantages and disadvantages of recruiting from within the organization.
   - By recruiting from within, an organization can capitalize on previous investments made in recruiting, selecting, training, and developing its current employees.
   - Internal promotions can reward employees for past performance and send a signal to other employees that their future efforts will pay off.
   - A disadvantage can be the inbreeding of ideas and attitudes.
4. Outline the advantages and disadvantages of external recruitment.
   - External recruitment can bring in new ideas and acquire people with specialized skills.
   - Constraints on the organization, such as a legislated employment equity plan, may lead to a different pool of applicants than what the manager may want.
5. Explain the objectives of the selection process.
   - The selection process attempts to get the right person with the right skills at the right time in the right job.
6. Describe the typical steps in the selection process.
   - Typical steps start with the receipt of an application (form and/or resume), then an initial interview, possible employment tests, an interview with the supervisor, reference checks, and then a hiring decision.
7. Identify the various sources of information used for selection decisions.
   - Application forms or résumés
   - Employment tests
   - Interviews
   - References
8. Discuss the different methods and types of questions for conducting an employment interview.
   - One-on-one, in which there is only the candidate and one interviewer
   - Panel or group, in which more than one interviewer is present
   - Telephone, in which an initial screening is done
   - Internet, in which a variety of technologies, including video streaming, is used
   - Unstructured, in which the interviewer is free to pursue whatever approach and sequence of topics might seem appropriate
   - Structured, in which each applicant receives the same set of questions, which have pre-established answers
   - Situational, in which candidates are asked about hypothetical situations and how they would handle them
   - Behavioural descriptions of previous work experiences
   - Motivational, in which candidates' attitudes and desires to achieve certain outcomes are assessed

9. Illustrate the value of different types of employment tests.
   - More objective than the interview.
   - Can provide a broader sampling of behaviour and skills.
10. Explain the legal and ethical considerations within recruitment and selection.
    - Reference information needs to be accurate and fair.
    - Inadequate reference checking an contribute to turnover or problems with the employee.
    - Important to establish selection criteria.
    - Ensure selection process is well-structured.

Need to Know

- Purpose of human resource planning
- Ways to deal with labour shortages and oversupply
- Definition of recruitment
- Various recruitment sources
- Definition and purpose of selection
- Typical steps in selection process
- Types of interview methods and questions

Need to Understand

- Advantages and disadvantages of internal or external recruitment
- Use of tests and interviews in selection decision
- Applications and interview questions in relation to human rights legislation
- Importance of good decision making in hiring
- Legal and ethical considerations in recruitment and selection

KEY TERMS

achievement tests 157
aptitude tests 157
behavioural description interview (BDI) 153
employment branding 139
human resource planning 134
internal job posting 140
labour market 142
management forecasts 136
Markov analysis 136
panel interview 152
recruitment 138
reliability 149
selection 148
situational question 154
skills inventory 136
staffing table 136
trend analysis 136
validity 149

REVIEW QUESTIONS

1. Why is human resource planning important?
2. What are the various approaches to planning?
3. What are the comparative advantages and disadvantages of filling openings from internal sources? From external sources?
4. If you were looking to hire for the following jobs, where might you recruit? (List both internal and external sources.)
   - Call centre operator
   - IT data administrator
   - Sales associate for retail
   - Construction worker
   - Massage therapist
   - Electrician

5. Discuss some of the employment problems faced by new immigrants to Canada.
6. What are the interviewing methods described? Which method would you prefer and why?
7. Describe the guidelines for a successful employment interview.
8. What are the criticisms of employment testing?

CRITICAL THINKING QUESTIONS

1. You have recently applied for work at a medium-size clothing retails store as an full-time sales person. Part of the screening process will include a group interview with some of the people you would be working with. What questions do you think they will ask you? What questions would you ask of them?
2. When a labour shortage is experienced a company may ask current employees to work overtime. What are legal and ethical considerations of this strategy? How long would this type of strategy be sustainable?
3. A candidate may be unwilling to relocate due to family obligations and considerations. This being so, is it viable for an organization to offer employment to both spouses in order to employ the chosen candidate? What are the strategic, ethical, and legal considerations?
4. You have recently applied for a barista position in a local coffee shop and have been asked to supply the names of references. What would the references say about you for this work?

DEVELOPING YOUR SKILLS

1. Here is your opportunity to take personality tests. Access the Jung Typology Test at Human Metrics (**www.humanmetrics.com/cgi-win/JTypes2.asp**) and access the Big Five Personality Test (**www.outofservice.com/bigfive**). Complete each online assessment. Review the results. Is this consistent with your understanding and awareness of yourself? Are there any surprises? If so, what are they?
2. Working in groups of four or five, list three recent times you have been interviewed. Working with this list, identify the type of interview conducted. Determine whether the interview questions were appropriate for the work and whether the interview was effective in attracting you to work for the organization.
3. The opening HRM Close-up describes the importance of hiring "for fit." Also, Richard Branson often speaks to the importance of "hiring for attitude." Design three questions you would ask a candidate in order to assess their "fit" within an organization. What legal and ethical considerations were important in designing these questions?
4. Working in pairs, one person will access **easyjobresumebuilder.com** and click on "Resume Samples," and the other person will access **resume-now.com** and click on "Create Resume." For EasyJob Resume Builder, pick one of the related links with sample résumés. Review the sample résumé and then prepare your own. For Resume-Now, follow the instructions and prepare a résumé. Bring your résumé to class. Working in your pair, critique each other's résumés, and identify what is similar and what is different in their formatting. Share your findings with the rest of the class.
5. Access the corporate website for Bombardier, one of Canada's premier aerospace and transportation companies, at **bombardier.com** and click on "Careers." Watch the short video and read the rest of the information about working at Bombardier. Prepare a one-to-two-page summary explaining why you would or would not want to work there. Comment on how effective the video was in helping you make your decision.

Jung Typology Test
www.humanmetrics.com/cgi-win/JTypes2.asp

The Big Five Personality Test
www.outofservice.com/bigfive

EasyJob Resume Builder
www.easyjobresumebuilder.com

Resume-Now
resume-now.com

Bombardier
bombardier.com

CASE STUDY 1

Why Aren't They Interested?

Joseph Bloom was confused and disappointed. As HR director for a medium-sized technology firm, he had convinced senior management that attending the local career fair was a strategic approach to generating interest in the company and acquiring résumés from students who would be graduating in the near future. The costs (registration fee, booth materials, salaries of employees who attended) were substantial and yet the response from students was dismal. Only about 20 people stopped by the booth and of those who did, only 4 handed over a résumé. Joseph did not understand what went wrong.

The city's one university and employers from all sectors had hosted the fair. Joseph did note that representation from employers was lower than in previous years, but thought that this might be due to the poor economy and that there would be fewer employment opportunities for new graduates. However, Joseph's company would still be actively hiring new graduates, and in addition he liked to have various résumés on hand should opportunities arise on little notice. Joseph thought that students would know this and therefore be keen to stop by his company's booth.

Joseph noticed that some companies were giving away items (pens, cell-phone holders) at their booths and this seemed to attract more students. "Well, this is just silly promotion and a waste of money" thought Joseph, but at the same time he did wonder why the booths with items to be given to students seemed more popular. "Technology is such an exciting and dynamic profession so we shouldn't need to entice people to stop by and hand over a résumé. Who wouldn't want to work for such a great company as ours?" Joseph knew that senior management would not be pleased when he reported the outcome from the career fair, and wondered what might be done differently if the company decided to attend again next year.

Questions:

1. Why didn't many students stop by the booth? List 3 key reasons that can be determined based upon information provided in the case.
2. Based upon the three reasons you have selected, what might Joseph do differently to address each issue if the company were to attend a career fair again?
3. What would entice you to approach people at a booth during a career fair?

CASE STUDY 2

It Isn't Rocket Science!

Pizza Barn provides upscale takeout pizzas and has locations in major cities all across Canada. Miranda Jones, an HR analyst working at the corporate offices in Vancouver, was concerned as she reviewed statistics pertaining to the workforce during the past six months.

She noted that over the past half-year, pizza makers (known as "dough masters" within the company) had a high turnover rate. Miranda compared Pizza Barn's numbers to those of other companies in the industry and found that employees were leaving at three times the industry average. Further, pizza makers were staying with the company for an average of only three weeks.

To better understand what was happening, Miranda began talking to managers at various locations across the country. Eric Anders, the manager of the Regina location, could not understand why he had such difficulty keeping staff. "Being a pizza maker is such a simple and basic job. It isn't rocket science! However, people just don't seem to like working here. When they quit, the pizza makers keep telling me that this just "isn't their scene," whatever that means. It seems like dough experts think this is going to some type of exciting job and dynamic place to work and are then disappointed once they actually start doing the job." When Miranda asked about Eric's recruitment and selection process, he told her that he places advertisements at the local high schools and universities, goes through the résumés that come in, and selects the best candidates to interview. To save time, he invites four or five people to meet with him at the same time and spends about 20 minutes asking each a few behavioural questions. Eric asks for one or two references, which he does check before hiring anyone. The interview also involves a test for manual skills, as pizza makers need to be coordinated. Conversations with managers at different locations across Canada yielded the same results. All managers followed processes similar to those Eric had outlined and were experiencing high levels of turnover.

Miranda was perplexed. The recruitment and selection processes were thorough and yet something wasn't working.

Questions:

1. What changes would you suggest to the recruitment and selection processes for "dough masters"? Why?
2. Should all Pizza Barn locations across Canada use the same recruitment and selection processes? Do geographic diversity and differences in the labour market mean these processes should differ on the basis of location? Why or why not?
3. Should Miranda be concerned about the turnover of pizza makers? Why or why not?

NOTES AND REFERENCES

1. "Top Talent Getting Harder to Find: Survey, *Canadian HR Reporter*, December 12, 2011, www.hrreporter.com/articleview/11936-top-talent-getting-harder-to-find-survey;" and "Data Bank Focus: Hiring Future Leaders," *Workforce*, November 16, 2011, www.workforce.com/article/20111116/NEWS02/111119978/data-bank-focus-hiring-future-leaders.
2. Phil Wahba, "Why Target Failed in Canada," January 15, 2015, accessed February 8, 2015, http://fortune.com/2015/01/15/target-canada-fail.
3. P.A. Bamberger, *Human Resource Strategy: Formulation, Implementation, and Impact*, 2nd ed. (New York: Routledge, 2014).
4. Harvey Deutschendorf, "5 Ways to Boost Employee Engagement and Satisfaction in Tough Times," April 5, 2014, accessed February 19, 2014, www.business2community.com/human-resources/5-ways-boost-employee-engagement-satisfaction-tough-times-0781213#vksH8gChAsKybV1w.99.
5. Karen Pastakia, "Leadership No Game of Chance," *Canadian HR Reporter*, June 6, 2011, accessed January 3, 2012, www.hrreporter.com/articleview/10440-leadership-no-game-of-chance.
6. Statistics Canada, accessed February 19, 2015, www.statcan.gc.ca/start-debut-eng.html; Statistics Canada, "Labour Force Survey, January 2015," accessed February 15, 2015, www.statcan.gc.ca/daily-quotidien/150206/dq150206a-eng.htm;ArminaLigaya,"Most Older Workers Who Leave Career Jobs Return to Work Within a Decade: Statistics Canada," January 28, 2014, accessed February 10, 2015, http://business.financialpost.com/2014/01/28/most-older-workers-who-leave-career-jobs-return-to-work-within-a-decade-statistics-canada; Statistics Canada, "Study: Projected Trends to 2031 for the Canadian Labour Force," *The Daily*, August 17, 2011, accessed February 19, 2015, www.statcan.gc.ca/daily-quotidien/110817/dq110817b-eng.htm.
7. Shannon Klie, "Aboriginals a 'Strategic Imperative,'" *Canadian HR Reporter*, April 25, 2011, accessed January 4, 2012, www.hrreporter.com/articleview/10088-aboriginals-a-strategic-imperative.
8. "Three-Quarters of Small Businesses Lack Succession Plans," *Canadian HR Reporter*, October 17, 2011, accessed January 4, 2012, www.hrreporter.com/articleview/11461-three-quarters-of-small-businesses-lack-succession-plan-survey.
9. Deb Kline, "Avaya and International Avaya User Group Announce Winners of the 2014 Customer Innovation Awards," April 30, 2014, accessed February 9, 2015, www.avaya.com/usa/about-avaya/newsroom/news-releases/2014/pr-140430.
10. "Here Are the Top 4 Risks Facing Canada's Economy, According to the Bank of Canada," *National Post Wire Service*, July 17, 2013, accessed February 19, 2015, http://business.financialpost.com/2013/07/17/bank-of-canada-economy-risks.
11. "Employee Turnover—How Much Is It Costing You?" *BC Jobs*, accessed January 4, 2012, www.bcjobs.ca/re/hr-resources/human-resource-advice/recruitment-and-retention/employee-turnover—how-much-is-it-costing-you.
12. Tara Carman, "B.C. Faces Vast Labour Shortages Unless It Can Attract More Workers," *The Vancouver Sun*, February 3, 2102.
13. J. Rokkaa, K. Karlssonb, and J. Tienarib, "Balancing Acts: Managing Employees and Reputation in Social Media," *Journal of Marketing Management* 30 nos. 7–8 (2014), 802–827.

14. Interested readers can check out the websites of these companies at www.oracle.com/applications/peoplesoft-enterprise.html and www.sap.com/canada/index.epx.
15. David Burlington, "Unified Talent Management: The Platform Is the Service," *Workforce Management*, accessed January 22, 2009, www.workforce.com.
16. Robert Cyran, "Yahoo's Hire Is Slap for eBay," *The Globe and Mail*, January 5, 2012, B11.
17. Robert Hiltz, "New Rules to Open Border to Skilled Trades," *The Vancouver Sun*, January 30, 2012, B3.
18. Joe Friesen, "Immigration Overhaul to Let Employers Choose Prospects," *The Globe and Mail*, March 2, 2012, A5.
19. "Some Temporary Foreign Workers in Alberta to Get Reprieve," *CBC*, February 3, 2015, accessed February 21, 2015, www.cbc.ca/news/canada/calgary/some-temporary-foreign-workers-in-alberta-to-get-reprieve-1.2943184.
20. Lois Geller, "The AIDA Principle: Roadmap for a lot of Great Advertising," *Forbes*, June 2, 2014, accessed February 23, 2015, www.forbes.com/sites/loisgeller/2014/06/02/the-aida-principle-roadmap-for-a-lot-of-great-advertising.
21. Leigh Goessl, "Study Finds Internet Job Search Reduces Time Spent Unemployed," *Digital Journal*, October 5, 2011, accessed January 6, 2012, http://digitaljournal.com/article/312400.
22. Ian Sullivan, "Recruiting via Social Media? Be Honest, Direct," *Canadian HR Reporter*, October 10, 2011, accessed January 6, 2012, www.hrreporter.com/articleview/11413-recruiting-via-social-media-be-honest-direct.
23. Susan Grant, "Technology Streamlines Recruitment," *Canadian HR Reporter*, April 11, 2011, accessed January 7, 2012, www.hrreporter.com/articleview/9962-technology-streamlines-recruitment.
24. Michelle V. Rafter, "Six Facebook Recruiting Apps," *Workforce Management*, December 9, 2011, accessed January 6, 2012, www.workforce.com/article/20111209/NEWS02/111209953/six-facebook-recruiting-apps.
25. "2014 Canada Top 100 Ideal Employer Ranking—Business," accessed February 21, 2015, www3.universumglobal.com/2014-canada-ideal-employer-ranking-business/#.VOjAZS5BkgY.
26. Robin Waghorn, "Internet Puts Spin on Traditional Career Fair," *Canadian HR Reporter*, November 21, 2011, accessed January 6, 2012, www.hrreporter.com/articleview/11769-internet-puts-new-spin-on-traditional-career-fair.
27. Jennifer Salopek, "Employee Referrals Remain a Recruiters Best Friend," *Workforce*, December 6, 2010, accessed January 7, 2012, www.workforce.com/article/20101206/NEWS02/312069996.
28. "Job Search Strategies," accessed January 7, 2012, www.kellyservices.ca/web/ca/services/en/pages/tip_mar10_search_strategies.html; "Job Search Strategies," SaskNetWork, accessed January 7, 2012, www.sasknetwork.gov.sk.ca/html/JobSeekers/lookingforwork/searchstrategies.htm; Career and Employment Services, University of Manitoba, "Job Search Strategies," accessed January 7, 2012, www.umanitoba.ca/student/employment/media/job_search_workbook.pdf; and other, similar resources on job search techniques.
29. Tina Mansfield, "Looking for a Job? Building a Digital Resume," *Backbone*, October 15, 2011, 15–17; Eileen Chadnick, "Giving Your CV a Fresh Boost," *The Globe and Mail*, November 23, 2011, B20. For additional sources on writing résumés, see BCJobs.ca; Youth Canada, "Writing a Resume," www.youth.gc.ca/eng/topics/jobs/resume.shtml; Monster.ca; and "Canada's #1 Online Resume Builder," accessed January 9, 2012, www.resume-now.com/default.asp?lp=rnarsmsm31&cobrand=RSMN&tag=12020816290992 1&hitlogid=91663265&ref=9061&utm_source=PPCg&utm_medium=SEMK&utm_term=writing+resumes&utm_campaign=Canada&match_type=e&ad=11378631331.
30. Amanda Silliker, "Making Managers Accountable for Diversity," *Canadian HR Reporter*, August 15, 2011, accessed January 7, 2012, www.hrreporter.com/articleview/10997-making-managers-accountable-for-diversity.
31. Marina Jiménez, "Scoring Points with Newer Canadians," *The Globe and Mail*, March 13, 2009, L1.
32. "About Us," TRIEC, accessed January 7, 2012, http://triec.ca/about-us.
33. John Ewing, "The First Steps to Growing Your Company," *Green Industry PRO* 10 (October 2011): 11–12.
34. Farah Naqvi, "Competency Mapping and Managing Talent," *Journal of Management Research* 8, no. 1 (2009): 85–94.
35. Christopher M. Berry, Malissa A. Clark, and Tara K. McClure, "Racial/Ethnic Differences in the Criterion-Related Validity of Cognitive Ability Tests," *Journal of Applied Psychology* 96, no. 5 (2011): 881–906.
36. Anne Fisher, "Are Young Job Seekers Less Ethical or Just Desperate?" *Fortune*, July 12, 2011, accessed January 9, 2012, http://management.fortune.cnn.com/2011/07/12/are-young-job-seekers-less-ethical-or-just-desperate.
37. Kate Rogers, "Why Lying on Your Resume Is Never Worth It," *Fox Business*, September 13, 2013, accessed February 22, 2015, www.foxbusiness.com/personal-finance/2013/09/13/why-should-never-lie-on-your-resume.
38. "Bias-Free Hiring and Assessment: Removing the 'Canadian Experience' Barrier," September 24, 2013, accessed February 25, 2015, www.hireimmigrants.ca/resources-tools/webinars/register-now-bias-free-hiring-and-assessment-removing-the-canadian-experience-barrier.
39. Don Georgevich, "Panel Interview Tips—Five Essential Steps to a Great Panel Interview," accessed February 25, 2015, www.jobinterviewtools.com/blog/panel-interview-tips-five-essential-steps-great-panel-interview.
40. Tim Halloran, Director of Recruiting, Monster.com, video accessed January 10, 2012, through YouTube and GreenJobInterview.com.
41. Nita Wilmott, "Interviewing Styles: Tips for Interview Approaches," About.com: Human Resources, accessed January 10, 2012, http://humanresources.about.com/cs/selectionstaffing/a/interviews.htm.
42. Murray R. Barrick, Brian W. Swider, and Greg L. Stewart, "Initial Evaluations in the Interview," *Journal of Applied Psychology* 95, no. 6 (2010): 1163–1172.
43. Hanna Dunn, "Behavioural Interviews Deserve Accolades," *Canadian HR Reporter*, July 12, 2010, accessed January 10, 2012, www.hrreporter.com/articleview/8031-behavioural-interviews-deserve-accolades.
44. "Interview Format Influences Perception of Hiring Fairness: Study," *Canadian HR Reporter*, May 21, 2010, accessed January 10, 2012, www.hrreporter.com/articleview/7872-interview-format-influences-perception-of-hiring-fairness-study.
45. "Bias-Free Hiring and Assessment: Removing the 'Canadian Experience' Barrier," September 24, 2013, accessed February 25, 2015, www.hireimmigrants.ca/resources-tools/webinars/register-now-bias-free-hiring-and-assessment-removing-the-canadian-experience-barrier.
46. Wallace Immen, "Want Better Employees? Ask Better Questions," *The Globe and Mail*, January 6, 2012, B14.
47. For additional resources on employment testing, see Robert M. Guion, *Assessment, Measurement and Prediction for Personnel Decisions*, 2nd ed. (New York: Routledge, 2011).
48. Jana Szostek and Charles J. Hobson, "Employment Test Evaluation Made Easy," *Employee Relations Law Journal* 37, no. 2 (Autumn 2011): 67–74.
49. Arthur B. Smith Jr. and Michael H. Cramer, "Supreme Court Rules on Pre-employment Tests and Disparate Impact," *Texas Employment Law*, July 2010, 6.
50. Yanseen Hemeda and Joan Sum, "Understanding Pre-employment Testing," *Canadian HR Reporter*, November 21, 2011, accessed January 10, 2012, www.hrreporter.com/articleview/11765-understanding-pre-employment-testing.

51. Ashley Shadday, "Assessments 101: An Introduction to Candidate Testing," *Workforce Management*, January 5, 2010, accessed January 10, 2012, www.workforce.com/article/20100105/NEWS02/301059990.
52. Timothy A. Judge, Ryan L. Klinger, and Lauren S. Simon, "Time Is on My Side: Time, General Mental Ability, Human Capital, and Extrinsic Career Success," *Journal of Applied Psychology* 95, no. 1 (2010): 92–107.
53. John J. Sumanth and Daniel M. Cable, "Status and Organizational Entry: How Organizational and Individual Status Affect Justice Perceptions of Hiring Systems," *Personnel Psychology* 64 (2011): 963–1000.
54. Eddy S.W. Ng and Greg J. Sears, "The Adverse Impact in Selection Practices on Organizational Diversity: A Field Study," *The International Journal of Human Resource Management* 21, no. 9 (July 2010): 1454–1471.
55. David W. Freeman, "Wonderlic Test on Tap for NFL Hopefuls: What It Is and Who Has Highest Score?" *CBC News*, February 24, 2011, accessed January 13, 2012, www.cbsnews.com/8301-504763_162-20035953-10391704.html?tag=mncol;lst;7.
56. Ben Dattner and Robert Hogan, "Can You Handle Failure?" *Harvard Business Review*, April 2011, 117–121.
57. Rick Smith, "Building on Your Strengths," *HR Professional* 27, no. 1 (January 2010): 22–25.
58. Cary Cherniss, "Emotional Intelligence: New Insights and Further Clarifications," *Industrial and Organizational Psychology* 3 (2010): 183–191.
59. Ibid.
60. Frank Walter, Michael S. Cole, and Ronald H. Humphrey, "Emotional Intelligence: Sine Qua Non of Leadership or Folderol?" *Academy of Management* (February 2011): 45–59.
61. Norman D. Henderson, "Predicting Long-Term Firefighter Performance from Cognitive and Physical Ability Measures," *Personnel Psychology* 3 (2010): 999–1039.
62. Danielle Harder, "Courts Clarify Unresolved Issues in 2009," *Canadian HR Reporter*, February 19, 2010, accessed January 13, 2012, www.hrreporter.com/articleview/7564-courts-clarify-unresolved-issues-in-2009; and Jeffrey R. Smith, "Right Idea, Wrong Application for Drug, Alcohol Policy," *Canadian HR Reporter*, August 15, 2011, www.hrreporter.com/articleview/11001-right-idea-wrong-application-for-drug-alcohol-policy-legal-view.
63. John Cotter, "Suncor Drug Testing: Oil Giant Loses Another Bid to Randomly Test Workers," *The Canadian Press*, May 26, 2014, accessed February 20, 2015, www.huffingtonpost.ca/2014/03/26/suncor-drug-testing_n_5037680.html.
64. David Whitten, "Deconstructing Random Drug, Alcohol Testing," *Canadian HR Reporter*, November 21, 2011, accessed January 13, 2012, www.hrreporter.com/articleview/11775-deconstructing-random-drug-alcohol-testing-legal-view.
65. Ken Cahoon, "Pre-employment Screening—What Is Necessary?" *Canadian HR Reporter*, July 18, 2011, accessed January 16, 2012, www.hrreporter.com/articleview/10784-pre-employment-screening-what-is-necessary.
66. "Survey 21 Percent of Job Seekers Dropped After Reference Checks," *Workforce Management*, June 23, 2010, accessed January 16, 2012, www.workforce.com/article/20100623/NEWS01/306239996.
67. The National Association of Professional Background Screeners, accessed January 16, 2012, www.napbs.com.
68. Shannon Klie, "Tread Carefully with Credit Checks: Privacy Commissioner," *Canadian HR Reporter*, March 22, 2010, accessed January 16, 2012, www.hrreporter.com/articleview/7670-tread-carefully-with-credit-checks-privacy-commissioner.
69. Michael Overell, "Reference Checks and Social Media: On Shaky Ground?" *Recruitloop*, November 10, 2011, accessed February 22, 2015, http://recruitloop.com/blog/reference-checks-and-social-media-on-shaky-ground.
70. Paul R. Sackett and Filip Lievens, "Personnel Selection," *Annual Review of Psychology* 59 (2008): 16.1–16.32.
71. "Be Prepared for Motivation-Based Interviews; They Are Tough and Get to the Core of the Applicant," January 8, 2013, accessed February 23, 2015, http://thingscareerrelated.com/2013/01/08/be-prepared-for-motivation-based-interviews-they-are-tough-and-get-to-the-core-of-the-applicant.
72. Robert M. Guion, *Assessment, Measurement and Prediction for Personnel Decisions*, 2nd ed. (New York: Routledge, 2011), 427.
73. Amanda Silliker, "Tread Carefully with Social Media Checks," *Canadian HR Reporter*, January 30, 2012, 1.
74. Ibid.
75. "Be Prepared for Motivation-Based Interviews; They Are Tough and Get to the Core of the Applicant," January 8, 2013, accessed February 23, 2015, http://thingscareerrelated.com/2013/01/08/be-prepared-for-motivation-based-interviews-they-are-tough-and-get-to-the-core-of-the-applicant.

6 Orienting, Training, and Developing Employees

LEARNING OUTCOMES

After studying this chapter, you should be able to

1. List characteristics of an effective orientation process.
2. Describe the benefits of employee orientation.
3. Discuss the systems approach to training and development.
4. Describe the components of a training-needs assessment.
5. Identify the principles of learning and how they facilitate training.
6. Identify the types of training and development methods used for all levels of employees.
7. Describe training programs that are currently popular and emerging trends.
8. Explain how a career development program integrates individual and organizational needs.
9. Discuss how an employee's career development can be enhanced.

OUTLINE

HRM CLOSE-UP

"It's really about continuous learning and trying to create the energy and the belief that people should strive to be lifelong learners in order to maximize their success."

In 2006, BC Ferries' ***Queen of the North*** sank south of Prince Rupert. Although 99 passengers and crew were saved, two passengers disappeared and were presumed drowned. The accident precipitated an overhaul of every aspect of BC Ferries that has resulted in the company becoming an industry leader not just in Canada, but around the world.

Prior to the accident, BC Ferries' onboarding process was the same as that in many other organizations. "If you were new to the company, were moving to another vessel or being promoted, you would be hooked up with someone and follow that person around, observe, and listen and eventually try things out under that person's oversight," explains Jeff Joyce, Director of Fleet Operations. "When it was reasonably felt that you were capable of safely doing the job yourself, you were given a clearance for that position."

As customary as that was at the time, it was too reliant on the skills of the person being shadowed. If that staff member wasn't sufficiently experienced, was too busy, or just didn't enjoy being shadowed, the results could be inconsistent. While it had worked well enough for 45 years, it became apparent that a more standardized training system might produce more consistent results.

The outcome was BC Ferries' Standardized Education and Assessment program (SEA) and its Simulator Training Centres (STC).

"What we do now in almost all of our entry-level positions is put them through a bit of training before we even decide to hire them, just to see how they perform," says Joyce. That pre-hiring training is the first phase of SEA and requires candidates to immerse themselves in an online self-study workbook. Only once they have passed a multiple-choice exam can they advance further in the hiring process.

"It really ups the ante for the candidate recognizing that we're serious about our training and that we want to make sure that we have effective people and safe people with the right qualities," says Joyce.

Once hired, new employees undergo a day-long orientation program. From there they advance to the second phase of SEA, onboard or on-site education.

"The third phase of the program is the clearance phase, which includes the exam as well as demonstrative activities that they have to do," Joyce explains. "It's sort of like a board approach where they have to respond to scenarios that are given to them verbally. Employees have to be successful in every phase in order to be cleared and officially allowed to work."

SEA continues well beyond hiring, however. The fourth phase focuses on skill enhancement and career progression, providing BC Ferries' more than 4,000 employees with the constant opportunity for professional advancement. "It's a process that ensures that for those that want it, there's always hope and a career path," Joyce says. "It's about continuous learning and trying to create the energy and the belief that people should strive to be lifelong learners in order to maximize their success."

As mentioned, along with SEA, BC Ferries also rolled out their state-of-the-art Simulator Training Centres.

"The simulation training program started as an idea to improve bridge team effectiveness, and we went through a planning and procuring process to eventually start delivering curriculum in October 2011," Joyce says. Today, the company has three bridge simulators, and during the summer when all hands are literally on deck carrying customers, the centres' instructors head out to the fleet to observe the bridge teams in action and to evaluate if the STC lessons are being incorporated into daily use.

Courtesy of Jeff Joyce

Jeff Joyce, Director, Fleet Operations, BC Ferries.

Not only have SEA and STC improved the company's safety record, but since their introduction there has been a drop in absenteeism, an improvement in staff retention levels, and an increase in the number of staff involved in delivering training from 67 to 425. In addition, other marine service providers have expressed an interest in using BC Ferries' excess capacity in the simulators, providing the company with a possible extra revenue stream.

"We've also had two international awards presented to us as a result of both the SEA program and the STC," Joyce adds with quiet pride. "Due to our practice of involving front-line employees in the development of SEA material and STC curricula, both have proven to be powerful employee engagement tools as well. The sustainment of both is largely due to our employees' efforts in continuously improving the products."

Source: Courtesy of Jeff Joyce

INTRODUCTION

The ability of an organization to ensure its people continue to learn, grow, and develop has become critical to business success. As noted in Chapter 1, organizations often compete on competencies—the core sets of knowledge and expertise that give them an edge over their competitors. Frequently, they refer to "intellectual capital," the combination of the "human capital" (the competencies) and the organizational support that enables human capital to flourish.[1] Further, as individuals learn (e.g., the human capital increases), the organization has the potential to learn. Only through individuals does the organization gain knowledge.[2] **Orientation**, **training**, and **development** play a central role in enabling, nurturing, and strengthening the human capital in the organization. As shown in the HRM Close-up, BC Ferries understands the strategic importance of this and actively supports learning, growth, and development of employees.

Orientation
Formal process of familiarizing new employees with the organization, their jobs, and their work unit; critical to socialization which is the embedding of organizational values, beliefs, and accepted behaviours

Training
The acquisition of skills, behaviours, and abilities to perform current work

Development
The acquisition of skills, behaviours, and abilities to perform future work or to solve an organizational problem

Further, as will be discussed in this chapter, it is critical that organizations approach their orientation, training, and development needs in a systematic way. Doing so will ensure a clear linkage to the organization's strategic direction. Rapidly changing technologies require that employees continuously hone their KSAs (knowledge, skills, and abilities), or "competencies," to cope with new processes and systems. A carefully designed program can also be a key lever in attracting and retaining people with the key competencies that will keep the organization's competitive advantage. Jobs that require little skill are rapidly being replaced by ones that require technical, interpersonal, and problem-solving skills. And, as described, the business world is constantly changing, requiring improved skills and abilities.

The manager or supervisor plays a key role in ensuring that the orientation, training, and development efforts are appropriate and reinforced for the individuals for whom they are responsible. Without the managers' involvement, organizational growth, success, and sustainability might be at risk. Other trends toward empowerment, total quality management, teamwork, and globalization make it necessary for managers as well as employees to develop the skills that will enable them to handle new and more demanding assignments.

ORIENTATION

LO1

What are the characteristics of an effective orientation process?

LO2

What are the benefits of employee orientation?

Orientation, or employee onboarding, is a very particular type of training. The first objective in the process is to get new employees off to a good start. This is generally achieved through a formal orientation program. Orientation is the formal process of familiarizing new employees with the organization, their job, and their work unit. Socialization, or the embedding of organizational values, beliefs, and accepted behaviours, is also a key outcome. The benefit for new employees is that it allows them to get "in sync" so that they become productive members of the organization. Orientation is a process—not a one-day event. Further, it is important to remember that how employees are treated when they first come on board makes a huge impact on their views of supervisors, managers, and the organization.

Benefits of Orientation

In some organizations a formal new-hire orientation process is almost nonexistent, or, when it does exist, is performed in a casual manner. Some employees may show up for the first day on a new job, being told to work, and receiving no instructions, introductions, or support. This situation is unfortunate, since a number of practical and cost-effective benefits can be derived from conducting a well-run orientation. Benefits frequently reported by employers include the following:[3]

1. lower turnover
2. increased productivity
3. improved employee morale and identification with the company

4. lower training costs
5. facilitation of learning
6. reduction of anxiety

The more time and effort an organization devotes to making new employees feel welcome, the more likely they are to identify with the organization and the more quickly to become productive. Unlike training, which emphasizes the "what" and the "how," orientation stresses the "why." It is designed to develop in employees a certain attitude about the work and their role in the organization. It defines the philosophy behind the rules and provides a framework for their work in that organization.

Continuous Process

Since an organization is faced with ever-changing conditions, its plans, policies, and procedures must change with these conditions. Unless current employees are kept up to date with these changes, they may find themselves embarrassingly unaware of activities to which new employees are being oriented. While the discussion that follows focuses primarily on the needs of new employees, it is important that all employees be continually reoriented to changing conditions.

Co-operative Endeavour

For a well-integrated orientation process, co-operation between line and staff is essential. The HR department is ordinarily responsible for coordinating orientation activities and for providing new employees with information about conditions of employment, pay, benefits, and other areas not directly under a supervisor's direction. However, the supervisor has the most important role in the orientation process. New employees are interested primarily in what their supervisor says and does and what their new co-workers are like. Before the arrival of a new employee, the supervisor should inform the work group that a new worker is joining the unit. It is also common practice for supervisors or other managerial personnel to recruit co-workers to serve as volunteer "sponsors" or "buddies" for incoming employees. In addition to providing practical help to newcomers, this approach conveys an emphasis on teamwork.

AndreyPopov/Thinkstock

Video conferencing is used to help orient new employees in remote locations.

Careful Planning

An orientation process can make an immediate and lasting impression on an employee that can mean the difference between the employee's success and failure. Thus, careful planning—with emphasis on goals, topics to be covered, and methods of organizing and presenting them—is essential. Successful orientation processes emphasize the individual's needs for information, understanding, and a feeling of belonging. To avoid overlooking items that are important to employees, many organizations devise checklists for use by those responsible for conducting the orientation. Orientation information can also be printed and given to the new employee. Companies are also beginning to use their intranets to make the information more readily available to their employees.

Toolkit 6.1 suggests items to include in an orientation checklist for supervisors. Orientation should focus on matters of immediate concern, such as important aspects of the job and organizational behaviour expectations (e.g., attendance and safety). Since orientation focuses on helping the new employee become familiar, comfortable, and productive, it is important not to overwhelm or provide too much information at one time. Those planning an orientation process should take into account the anxiety employees feel during their first few days. Anxiety is natural, but if employees are too anxious, training costs, turnover, absenteeism, and even production costs may increase. Anxiety reduction can be accomplished by establishing specific times at which the supervisor will be available for questions or coaching. Furthermore, reassuring newcomers that the performance levels they are observing among their co-workers will be attained within a predetermined time frame, based on experiences with other newcomers, can decrease anxiety. This reassurance is particularly important for employees with limited work experience who are learning new skills.

Okanagan College
www.okanagan.bc.ca/administration/human-resources/Joining_Okanagan_College.html

Husky Energy
http://huskyorientation.com/region

Current Developments in Orientation

Many companies are using intranets (internal websites) and online orientation modules to keep new and current employees up-to-date, among them Okanagan College (**www.okanagan.bc.ca/administration/human-resources/Joining_Okanagan_College.html**) and Husky Energy (**http://huskyorientation.com/region**).

Also, as discussed in Chapter 3, organizations need to pay special attention to the health and safety of employees. This being so, online resources are often used to orient new

TOOLKIT 6.1 SUPERVISORY ORIENTATION CHECKLIST

1. formal greeting, including introduction to colleagues
2. explanation of job procedures, duties, and responsibilities
3. training to be received (when and why)
4. supervisor and organization expectations regarding attendance and behaviour norms
5. job standards and production and service levels
6. performance appraisal criteria, including estimated time frame to achieve peak performance
7. conditions of employment, including hours of work, pay periods, and overtime requirements
8. organization and work unit rules, regulations, and policies
9. overview of health and safety expectations, as well as when specific training will occur
10. those to notify or turn to if problems or questions arise
11. chain of command for reporting purposes
12. an overall explanation of the organization's operation and purpose
13. a review of the organizational chart or structure indicating departments and work flow
14. offers of help and encouragement, including a specific time each week (in the early stages of employment) for questions or coaching

HRM AND THE LAW 6.1 KEEPING EMPLOYEES SAFE THROUGH MANDATED TRAINING

While occupational health and safety (OH&S) legislation in Canada outlines the general rights and responsibilities of the employer, the supervisor, and the worker, there is special "right to know" legislation that applies specifically to hazardous products. It actually comprises several pieces of legislation collectively called the Workplace Hazardous Materials Information System (WHMIS).

WHMIS training is legally required for all employees exposed or likely to be exposed to a hazardous material or controlled product at the workplace, and employers must establish an education program for their workers to ensure that workers understand WHMIS and the hazards of the controlled products they work with or near. Education programs about WHMIS must be followed up with job-specific training in safe work procedures for handling, storing, and disposing of these products. Workers must also be trained in procedures to follow in the event of an accident or spill.

As further evidence of the criticality of this type of training, in 2015 the federal government incorporated the GHS, an internationally consistent approach to classifying chemicals and communicating hazard information though labels and safety data sheets.

If employers are not providing this required training, inspectors have the authority to stop the use of a particular controlled product, which of course can result in unproductive downtime. Penalties for non-compliance may also include a fine of up to $25,000 and/or a term of up to 12 months in jail.

CRITICAL THINKING QUESTIONS:

Are the penalties for not providing WHMIS training too harsh? Is jail time a reasonable punishment for not providing legislated training?

Source: Adapted from "OH&S Legislation in Canada—Introduction," accessed April 4, 2015, **www.ccohs.ca/oshanswers/legisl/intro.html**; "Why you need WHMIS," WHMIS.net Online Learning and Training, accessed April 17, 2015, **www.whmis.net/why-you-need-whmis.htm**; Canadian Centre for Occupational Health and Safety, accessed April 17, 2015, **www.ccohs.ca/oshanswers/legisl/intro.html**.

employees to health and safety expectations and protocol. As previously noted, employees must be made aware of their rights and responsibilities regarding workplace health and safety. HRM and the Law 6.1 provides a specific example and further information. Younger employees (defined as those 15–24 years old) are more at risk for workplace accidents, and so government-sponsored online resources are available.[4] The general legislation states that health and safety orientation and training must occur before employees begin working, and that the supervisor must continue to coach and train the new workers after the initial orientation and training. As examples, the Alberta (**http://work.alberta.ca/occupational-health-safety/bloodylucky.html**) and British Columbia governments (**www2.worksafebc.com/Topics/YoungWorker/Home.asp**) have created websites specifically addressing workplace health and safety for younger employees. (Warning: Examples on these sites are quite graphic!)

Alberta.ca
http://work.alberta.ca/occupational-health-safety/bloodylucky.html

Work Safe BC
www2.worksafebc.com/Topics/YoungWorker/Home.asp

TRAINING AND DEVELOPMENT: A SYSTEMS APPROACH

Training typically refers to skills, behaviours, and abilities employees can apply to their current work; *development* is typically focused on assisting employees fulfill future job requirements or solve an organization's problems. These terms tend to be combined into a single phrase—"training and development"—to recognize the combination of activities used by organizations to increase the abilities and capabilities of their employees.

You often hear the word *learning* as well. Learning refers to an ongoing change in behaviour and thinking: ultimately the goal of training and development.

LO3

What are the four phases of the systems approach to training?

The primary reason organizations train new employees is to bring their KSAs up to the level required for satisfactory performance. As these employees continue on the job, additional training and development provide opportunities for them to acquire new knowledge and skills. As a result of this training, employees may be even more effective on the job and may be able to perform other jobs in other areas or at higher levels.

For help in understanding the importance of training in today's business environment, refer to Figure 6.1, which lists the skills many employers seek.

The primary goal of training and development is to contribute to the organization's overall goals; therefore, programs and opportunities should be structured with an eye to attaining desired organizational outcomes and strategies. Unfortunately, many organizations never make the connection between their strategic objectives and their training and development programs. Instead, fads, fashions, or "whatever the competition is doing" sometimes drives the agenda. As a result, much of an organization's investment can be wasted—training and development programs are often misdirected, poorly designed, inadequately evaluated—and these problems directly affect organizational performance.

FIGURE 6.1 Workplace Skills and Capabilities

Employees want to know what employers are looking for today in skill sets. The Conference Board of Canada has researched this topic and prepared the following broad list. While all employers do not look for all of these skills, many employers look for many of these skills.

Fundamental Skills

- read and understand information presented in different forms (e.g., words, graphs)
- write and speak so that others understand
- use relevant knowledge and skills (scientific, technological) to explain and clarify
- identify the root cause of a problem
- evaluate solutions to make a decision
- use numbers to complete tasks, such as making estimates and verifying calculations
- manage information by locating, gathering, and organizing information using appropriate technology and systems

Personal Management Skills

- be flexible and adaptable
- be honest and ethical
- be responsible for setting goals
- be able to work safely
- demonstrate positive attitudes and behaviours, such as dealing with people with honesty and integrity
- be willing to keep learning

Teamwork Skills

- understand and contribute to the organization's goals
- understand and work within the dynamics of the group
- plan and make decisions with others and support the outcomes
- respect the thoughts and opinions of others
- adapt to changing requirements
- understand the role of conflict in group dynamics and resolve as appropriate

Source: Adapted from *Employability Skills 2000+ PDF 2000 E/F* (Ottawa: The Conference Board of Canada, 2000, pdf file). Reproduced with permission from the Conference Board of Canada.

Many new employees come equipped with most of the skills and capabilities needed to start work. Others may require extensive training before they are ready to make much of a contribution to the organization. All employees need some type of training and development on an ongoing basis to maintain effective performance or to adjust to new ways of work. Therefore, to ensure that investments in training and development have the maximum impact on individual and organizational performance, a systems approach should be used. (*Note:* This systems approach is also applicable to employee orientation programs). The systems approach involves four phases: (1) needs assessment, (2) program design, (3) training delivery, and (4) evaluation of training. While the word "training" will be used in the discussion on the systems approach, all elements refer to orientation and development as well. Figure 6.2 illustrates the systems model.

Each phase of the systems approach will now be reviewed.

Phase 1: Conducting the Needs Assessment

LO4

What are the components of a training-needs assessment?

Managers and HR professionals should stay alert to the kinds of training needed, where the training is needed, who needs the training, and which methods will best deliver increased abilities to employees. If workers consistently fail to achieve productivity objectives, this might be a signal that training is needed. Likewise, if organizations receive an excessive number of customer complaints, this might suggest inadequate training.

To make certain that training is timely and focused on priority issues, and that training is the right solution for the concern, managers should approach a needs assessment systematically. You might think of this as trying to identify the training problem. The needs assessment can occur at the organizational level (examining the environment and strategy of the company to see where to put training emphasis); the task level (reviewing the activities of the work to determine the competencies needed); and the person level (reviewing which employees need training).

A needs assessment can be done by asking (and answering) four questions:

1. How important is this issue to the success of the organization? If it is important, proceed to questions 2, 3, and 4.
2. What competencies or knowledge, skills, and abilities do employees *need*?

FIGURE 6.2 Systems Model of Training

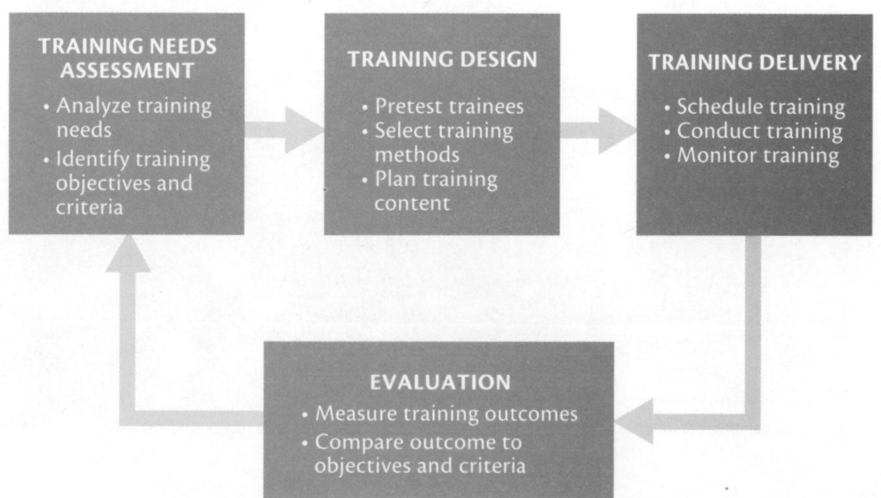

3. What competencies or knowledge, skills, and abilities do the employees currently *have*?
4. What is the gap between the desired (need) and the actual (have)?

Once answers have been determined, then specific action plans can be developed to address the gap. For example, since the September 11, 2001, attacks, training of airport security personnel has increased substantially. It has also increased for flight crews of airlines, employees in the transportation industry, workers in nuclear power plants, and even security staff at theme parks.

Toolkit 6.2 provides some suggestions for an approach to identifying training needs.

Other training issues tend to revolve around the strategic initiatives of an organization. Mergers and acquisitions, for example, frequently require that employees take on new roles and responsibilities and adjust to new cultures and ways of conducting business. Nowhere is this more prevalent than in grooming new leaders within organizations. Other issues, such as technological change, globalization, reengineering, and total quality management, all influence the way work is done and the types of skills needed to do it. Still other concerns may be more tactical but no less important in their impact on training. Organizational restructuring, downsizing, empowerment, and teamwork, for example, have immediate training requirements.

Finally, trends in the workforce itself have an impact. As mentioned in Chapter 1, employees increasingly value self-development and personal growth, and with this has come an enormous desire for learning. At the same time, as older workers may decide to postpone retirement, training will need to be done for a variety of different generations. Because no company in the private sector can count on stable employment levels, organizations as diverse as Inco and Boeing are facing situations in which they need to prepare the next generations of employees as the current groups approach retirement.

Before someone does any training, it is important to determine specific training needs.

diego_cervo/Thinkstock

TOOLKIT 6.2 IDENTIFYING TRAINING NEEDS

The following steps may be taken to discover an organization's requirements for training:

1. Invite key stakeholders (i.e. job incumbents, supervisors, managers) to a brainstorming session. Be sure to advise attendees of the purpose of the meeting in advance and have a trained facilitator lead the discussion.
2. With the group, review the organization's strategic plans and desired outcomes.
3. Through discussion, conduct a gap analysis and identify training opportunities would assist employees to these key goals. Determine the training priorities. This step may be done using the nominal group technique.
4. Training priorities and outcomes should be as detailed as possible. For example, do not list "communication skills" as a desired outcome. Instead, as examples, list oral presentation skills or report writing skills.
5. Encourage attendees to suggest ways to conduct the training and ensure that support and resources are available to ensure successful implementation.

It is important that the supervisor or manager be knowledgeable about the organization's needs, the requirements of the work, and the capabilities of the person in order to assess that training is the right solution. Training efforts (and dollars) can be wasted if the supervisor has not adequately determined whether training is appropriate. The question to ask here is something like: "If Joe receives more training on how to handle customer complaints, will his performance improve?" If performance issues are due to ability problems, training may likely be a good intervention. However, if performance issues are due to poor motivation or factors outside an employee's control, training may not be the answer. Ultimately, managers have to sit down with employees to talk about areas for improvement so that they can jointly determine the training and developmental approaches that will have maximum benefit.[5]

Phase 2: Designing the Training Program

Once the training needs have been determined, the next step is to design (or buy) appropriate training programs. The success of training programs depends on more than the organization's ability to identify training needs. Success hinges on taking the information gained from the needs analysis and utilizing it to design first-rate training programs. Experts believe that training design should focus on at least four related issues: (1) instructional objectives, (2) trainee readiness and motivation, (3) principles of learning, and (4) characteristics of instructors.

Instructional Objectives

As a result of conducting organization, task, and person analyses, managers will have a more complete picture of the company's training needs. On the basis of this information, they can more formally state the desired outcomes of training through written **instructional objectives**. Generally, instructional objectives describe the desired outcomes of the training: the skills and knowledge the company wants people to have and the behaviours employees should acquire or change. For example, a stated objective for one training program might be "Employees trained in team methods will be able to demonstrate the following skills within six months: problem-solving, conflict resolution, and effective team meetings."

Instructional objectives
Desired outcomes of a training program

Frequently, managers will seek external resources to design the training program and write the learning objectives. However, they will contribute help and guidance. It is therefore important for managers to be able to describe what they want the person to do or how they want the person to act after completing a training program.

Trainee Readiness and Motivation

Trainee readiness
The consideration of a trainee's maturity and experience when assessing him or her

Two preconditions for learning affect the success of those who are to receive training: readiness and motivation. Trainee readiness refers to both maturity and experience factors in the trainee's background. Prospective trainees should be screened to determine that they have the background knowledge and the skills necessary to absorb what will be presented to them. The other precondition for learning is trainee motivation. For optimum learning to take place, trainees must recognize the need for new knowledge or skills, and they must maintain a desire to learn as training progresses. **Trainee readiness** will also be impacted by previous success, or lack of success, encountered in previous training situations. By focusing on the trainees rather than on the trainer or training topic, managers can create a training environment that is conducive to learning. Six strategies can be essential:

1. Use positive reinforcement.
2. Eliminate threats and punishment.
3. Be flexible.
4. Have participants set personal goals.
5. Design interesting instruction.
6. Break down physical and psychological obstacles to learning.

While most employees are motivated by certain common needs, they differ from one another in the relative importance of these needs at any given time. Training objectives that are clearly related to trainees' individual needs will increase the motivation of employees to succeed in training programs. Again, the manager plays a vital role in ensuring that the training is suitable for the person and that the person is ready to take on the training initiative.

Principles of Learning

LO5

What are the principles of learning and how do they facilitate training?

Ultimately, training has to build a bridge between employees and the organization. One important step in this transition is giving full consideration to the psychological principles of learning, that is, the characteristics of training programs that help employees grasp new material, make sense of it in their own lives, and transfer it back to the job.

Because the success or failure of a training program is frequently related to certain principles of learning, managers as well as employees should understand that different training methods or techniques vary in the extent to which they utilize these principles. When investing in effective and efficient training programs, it is important that they incorporate the following principles of learning (see Figure 6.3):

1. *Goal setting.* It is important that the goals and objectives for the training are clear.
2. *Individual differences.* People learn at different rates and in different ways.
3. *Active practice and repetition.* Trainees should be given frequent opportunity to practise their job tasks in the way that they will ultimately be expected to perform them.
4. *Whole-versus-part learning.* Most jobs and tasks can be broken down into parts that lend themselves to further analysis. Determining the most effective manner for completing each part then provides a basis for giving specific instruction.
5. *Massed-versus-distributed learning.* Another factor that determines the effectiveness of training is the amount of time devoted to practice in one session. Should trainees be

given training in five two-hour periods or ten one-hour periods? In most cases, it has been found, spacing out the training will result in faster learning and longer retention.

6. *Feedback and reinforcement.* Can any learning occur without feedback? Some feedback comes from self-monitoring while other feedback comes from trainers, fellow trainees, and the like. As an employee's training progresses, feedback serves two related purposes: (1) knowledge of results and (2) motivation.
7. *Meaningfulness of presentation.* The material to be learned must be presented in as meaningful a manner as possible so that the trainees can connect the training with things that are already familiar to them.
8. *Modelling.* The old saying "A picture is worth a thousand words" applies to training. Quite simply, we learn by watching.

FIGURE 6.3 Principles of Learning

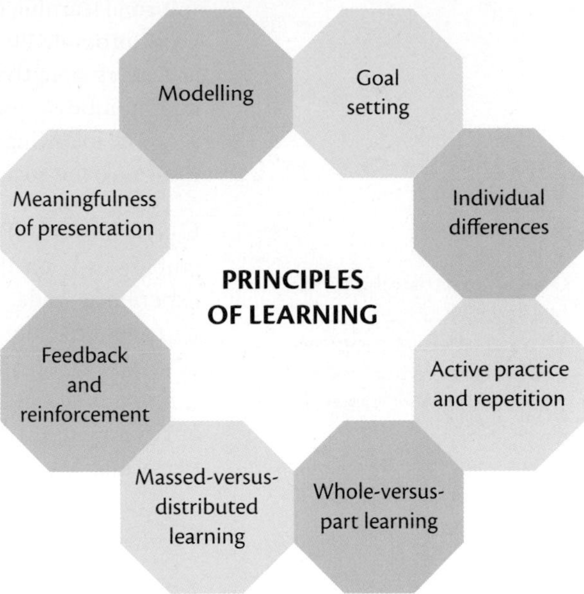

In recent years some work organizations have used **behaviour modification**. This technique operates on the principle that behaviour that is rewarded—positively reinforced—will be exhibited more frequently in the future, whereas behaviour that is penalized or unrewarded will decrease in frequency. For example, in safety training it is possible to identify "safe" behavioural profiles—actions that ensure fewer accidents—as well as unsafe profiles. As a follow-up to training, or as part of the training, managers can use relatively simple rewards to encourage and maintain desired behaviour.

Behaviour modification
Technique that if behaviour is rewarded, it will be exhibited more frequently in the future

Characteristics of Trainers

The success of any training activity will depend in large part on the skills and personal characteristics of those responsible for conducting the training. Good trainers, whether staff persons, line managers, or external facilitators, need to be knowledgeable about the subject, be well-prepared, have good communication skills, and be enthusiastic about the subject matter.

Phase 3: Implementing the Training Program

Despite the importance of *needs assessment, instructional objectives, principles of learning,* and the like, choices regarding instructional methods are where "the rubber meets the road" in implementing a training program. A major consideration in choosing among various training methods is determining which ones are appropriate for the KSAs to be learned. For example, if the material is mostly factual, methods such as lecture, classroom, or programmed instruction may be fine. However, if the training involves a large behavioural component, other participative methods, such as on-the-job training, simulation, or interactive virtual training, might work better.

Training and Development Methods

LO6

What are the types of training and development methods used for all levels of employees?

A wide variety of methods can be implemented for training and developing employees at all levels. Some of the methods have a long history of usage. Newer methods have emerged as the result of a greater understanding of human behaviour, particularly in the areas of learning, motivation, and interpersonal relationships. More recently, technological advances, especially in Web 2.0 technologies and social media from blogs to virtual collaboration environments, have resulted in emerging learning approaches that, in many instances, are more effective and economical than the traditional training methods. It is now becoming increasingly common for organizations to use several different delivery methods, and it is expected that the way people learn and receive training will continue to evolve as learning becomes increasingly learner-driven and collaborative.[6] The awareness and prevalence of informal learning (e.g., seeking information from co-workers or the Internet) continues to grow, prompted by the increased need of organizations to transfer and retain knowledge as leaders from the Baby Boom cohort approach retirement.[7] Informal e-learning through communities of practice, sharing of experiences, and self-learning is growing rapidly.[8]

The following are various types of training methods that can more or less blend formal, informal, and social learning.

On-the-job training (OJT) Method by which employees are given hands-on experience with instructions from their supervisor or other trainer

ON-THE-JOB TRAINING One of the most common methods used for training employees is **on-the-job training (OJT)**. OJT has the advantage of providing hands-on experience under normal working conditions and an opportunity for the trainer—a manager or senior employee—to build good relationships with new employees. Although all types of organizations use it, OJT is often one of the most poorly implemented training methods. Three common drawbacks are (1) the lack of a well-structured training environment, (2) poor training skills of managers, and (3) the absence of well-defined job performance criteria.

Toolkit 6.3 describes some basic steps that can be taken to address the drawbacks of OJT programs.

Apprenticeship training System of training in which a worker entering the skilled trades is given thorough instruction and experience, both on and off the job, in the practical and theoretical aspects of the work

APPRENTICESHIP TRAINING **Apprenticeship training** is used extensively when individuals entering an industry, particularly in the skilled trades such as machinist, laboratory technician, or electrician, are given thorough instruction and experience, both on and off the job, in the practical and theoretical aspects of the work. Many former fishers left the declining East Coast fishery to join in a seafarers' training program funded by several companies, the federal government, and the Nova Scotia government to learn new skills working in the engine rooms of larger vessels. Magna International, the auto parts giant, pays students to train as millwrights and tool-and-die makers. Learning is offered variously in shops, laboratories, and classrooms. Employers in the oil industry in Alberta

TOOLKIT 6.3 THE PROPER WAY TO DO ON-THE-JOB TRAINING

P *Prepare.* Decide what employees need to be taught. Identify the best sequence or steps for training. Decide how best to demonstrate these steps. Have materials, resources, and equipment ready.

R *Reassure.* Put each employee at ease. Learn about his or her prior experience, and adjust accordingly. Try to get the employee interested, relaxed, and motivated to learn.

O *Orient.* Show the employee the correct way to do the job. Explain why it's done this way. Discuss how it relates to other jobs. Let the employee ask lots of questions.

P *Perform.* When employees are ready, let them try the job themselves. Give them an opportunity to practise the job and guide them through rough spots. Provide help and assistance at first, then less as they continue.

E *Evaluate.* Check the employees' performance, and question them on how, why, when, and where they should do something. Correct errors, repeat instructions.

R *Reinforce and review.* Provide praise and encouragement, and give feedback about how the employee is doing. Continue the conversation, and express confidence in the employee's work.

have established an apprenticeship approach to ensure that oil-patch workers have the appropriate training. The Banff World Media Festival and Shaw Media have developed a Global Writers Apprentice Program that provides emerging Canadian writers with the opportunity to gain experience by apprenticing in the story department of a prime-time series.[9]

CO-OPERATIVE TRAINING AND INTERNSHIP PROGRAMS Similarly to apprenticeships, **co-operative training** and **internship programs** combine practical on-the-job experience with formal education. Typically, co-op programs are offered at colleges and universities where students work for an entire semester as part of their education. While they don't get course credit, they do earn a salary for their work and graduate with an indication that they have been involved in a co-op program. They can thereby demonstrate to prospective employers that they have work experience. The pioneer in co-op education is the University of Waterloo, but there are now co-op programs throughout Canada. Syncrude Canada, Harley-Davidson, and Canadian Microelectronics Corporation are among the many companies that have formed partnerships with education. Further, organizations benefit by getting student-employees with new ideas, energy, and eagerness to accomplish their assignments. Humber College in Toronto, British Columbia Institute of Technology (BCIT) in Burnaby, and many other colleges and universities allow students to earn credits on the basis of successful job performance and fulfillment of established program requirements.

Co-operative training
Training program that combines practical on-the-job experience with formal education

Internship programs
Programs jointly sponsored by colleges, universities, and other organizations that offer students the opportunity to gain real-life experience while allowing them to find out how they will perform in work organizations

Internship programs have recently received considerable attention, due to the legal and ethical considerations of having interns work for no pay with the promise of providing valuable work experience.[10] Guidelines for interns are governed by employment standards legislation, and employers must pay careful attention to these requirements in order to determine if a person qualifies to be classified and treated as an intern.[11]

CLASSROOM INSTRUCTION This method lends itself particularly to training in areas where information can be presented in lectures, demonstrations, films, and videotapes or through computer instruction. A special type of classroom facility is used in "vestibule training." Trainees are given instruction in the operation of equipment like that found in operating departments. The emphasis is on instruction. For example, a checkout clerk in a supermarket first learns how to use the cash register.

SELF-DIRECTED LEARNING Self-directed learning occurs when individuals work at their own pace at programmed instruction. Such learning typically involves the use of books, manuals, or computers to break down subject-matter content into highly organized, logical sequences that demand continuous response on the part of the trainee.

AUDIO-VISUAL Audio-visual methods are used to teach the skills and procedures required for a number of jobs. An example would be golf and tennis coaches using video recorders or camcorders so that their students can see their mistakes. Telehealth, a shared B.C. Ministry of Health video-conferencing system, connects patients through live video conferencing to clinical, administrative, and educational consultations in more than 100 communities across the province. Video conferencing can deliver faster service, allow for desktop conversations and meetings across distances, and enhance the management, sharing, and archiving of digital content.[12,13]

SIMULATION Simulation is used when it is either impractical or unwise to train employees on the actual equipment used on the job. An obvious example is training employees to operate aircraft, spacecraft, and other highly technical and expensive equipment. The simulation method provides realism in equipment and its operation. For example, before the launch of its first edition, the *National Post* used simulations to train a new workforce by requiring them to produce a mock newspaper with real content and headlines.

E-learning
Learning that takes place through electronic media

E-LEARNING The simpler, audio-visual, programmed, and computer-oriented training methods just discussed are evolving into what trainers today describe as e-learning. **E-learning** covers a wide variety of applications, such as Web-based and computer-based training (CBT) and virtual classrooms. It includes delivery of content via the Internet, intranets and extranets, audiotape, videotape, satellite and broadcast interactive TV, DVD, and CD-ROM. E-learning makes it possible to provide drill and practice, problem solving, simulation, gaming forms of instruction, and certain sophisticated forms of individualized instruction in a way that is more engaging for learners than traditional classroom instruction. It is also cheaper for employers to administer because, in many instances, it can be delivered directly via the employees' computers.

E-learning has become firmly established as a delivery method within organizations: 78% are self-paced, 48% are instructor-led, 34% are blended, and 27% are collaborative, becoming an alternative to, not a replacement for, classroom delivery methods.[14] Further, with the use of mobile devices, e-learning provides the opportunity for training in multiple locations and at times suited to learners' schedules and preferences.[15] There are also systems that can track the progress of learners. For example, go to **http://moodle.org** to see how e-learning systems are used in educational institutions to track student progress.

Moodle
http://moodle.org

E-learning also allows employees to search through a virtual sea of information in order to customize their own learning in their own time and space. More companies are demanding access to individual training components for employees to use when and where they need them. This approach helps alleviate the boredom trainees can experience during full-blown training courses, and employees are more likely to retain the information when they can immediately put it to use. It is also important to ensure that the strategies and culture of the organization support and encourage e-learning.

Although e-learning systems can be very sophisticated, they need not be overly expensive. Many e-learning training programs use existing applications that employees are familiar with—for example, PowerPoint, Word, and Adobe Acrobat—and convert them into Flash programs so they can be easily viewed online with any browser. Web-based training can also be revised rapidly, thereby providing continuously updated training material. This capability not only makes it easier and cheaper to revise training curricula, but also saves travel and classroom costs. When combined with other communications technology such as e-mail, teleconferencing, video conferencing, and groupware, Web-based training can be even more effective.

SPECIAL PROJECTS OR TASKS On-the-job experiences present employees opportunities to perform under pressure and to learn from their mistakes. Such experiences are some of the most powerful and commonly used techniques. However, just as on-the-job training for first-level employees can be problematic if not well planned, on-the-job experiences should be well organized, supervised, and challenging to the participants. Methods of providing on-the-job experience include the following:

A. *Coaching* involves a continuing flow of instructions, comments, and suggestions from the manager to the subordinate.
B. *Understudy assignments* groom an individual to take over a manager's job by helping the individual gain experience in handling important functions of the job.
C. *Job rotation* provides, through a variety of work experiences, the broadened knowledge and understanding required to manage more effectively.
D. *Lateral transfer* involves horizontal movement through different departments, along with upward movement in the organization.
E. *Special projects* and *junior boards* provide an opportunity for individuals to become involved in the study of current organizational problems and in planning and decision-making activities.

F. *Action learning* gives managers release time to work full-time on projects with others in the organization. In some cases, action learning is combined with classroom instruction, discussions, and conferences.
G. *Planned career progressions* utilize all these different methods to provide employees with the training and development necessary to progress through a series of jobs requiring higher and higher levels of knowledge and/or skills.

SEMINARS AND CONFERENCES Seminars and conferences are useful for bringing groups of people together for training and development. In management development, seminars and conferences can be used to communicate ideas, policies, or procedures, but they are also good for raising points of debate or discussing issues (usually with the help of a qualified leader) that have no set answers or resolutions. In this regard, seminars and conferences are often used when attitude change is a goal. Check out **http://cmcoutperform.com** for a variety of conferences geared toward managers.

Canadian Management Centre
http://cmcoutperform.com

CASE STUDIES Case studies use documented examples, which may have been developed from the actual experiences of participants in their own organizations. Cases help managers learn how to analyze (take apart) and synthesize (put together) facts, become conscious of the many variables on which management decisions are based, and in general improve their decision-making skills.

This textbook uses case studies as a way for students, with the help of the instructor, to better understand and integrate the information covered in each chapter.

MANAGEMENT GAMES Management games are valuable for bringing a hypothetical situation to life and provide experiential learning. Many games have been designed for general use. For example, TD Bank uses a simulation called Desert Kings to encourage more open communication, to increase levels of team performance, and to increase commitment to both internal and external customer service.

ROLE PLAYING Role playing consists of assuming the attitudes and behaviour—that is, playing the role—of others, often a supervisor and a subordinate who are involved in a particular problem. By acting out another's position, participants in the role playing can improve their ability to understand and cope with others. Role playing can also help participants learn how to counsel others by helping them see situations from a different point of view. Role playing is used widely in training health-care professionals to be empathetic and sensitive to the concerns of patients. It is also used widely in training managers to handle employee issues relating to absenteeism, performance appraisal, and conflict situations.

Phase 4: Evaluating the Training Program

Training, like any other HRM process, should be evaluated to determine its effectiveness. A variety of methods are available to assess the extent to which training and development programs improve learning, affect behaviour on the job, and have an impact on the bottom-line performance of an organization (e.g., business results and cost–benefit analysis). Unfortunately, few organizations adequately evaluate their training programs. In many ways, this lack of evaluation goes beyond poor management; it is poor business practice. Given the substantial monetary stake that organizations have in training, it would seem prudent that managers would want to maximize the return on that investment.

Donald Kirkpatrick developed four basic methods to evaluate training: (1) reactions, (2) learning, (3) behaviour, and (4) results.[16] Recently, he has presented a fifth level, return on investment, though others believe this is considered within the "results" evaluation or fourth level.[17] Some of these levels are easier to measure than others, but each is important because it provides different information about the success of the programs. The combination of these can give a total picture of the training program in order to help the organization determine if business results are improving, and for managers to decide where problem areas lie, what to change about the program, and whether to continue with a program.[18] Organizations' learning evaluation efforts are becoming more challenging with the growth in different learning techniques and the diversity of participants.[19] At Work with HRM 6.1 provides an example of how a Saskatchewan company uses four levels to evaluate its training.

Method 1: Reactions

One of the simplest and most common approaches to training evaluation is assessing participant reactions. Happy trainees are more likely to focus on training principles and to utilize the information on the job. However, participants can do more than say whether they liked a program or not. They can give insights into the content and techniques they found most useful. They can also critique the instructors or make suggestions about participant interactions, feedback, and the like.

While evaluation methods based on reactions are improving, too many conclusions about training effectiveness are based on broad satisfaction measures that lack specific feedback. Furthermore, it should be noted that positive reactions are no guarantee that the training has been successful. Collecting glowing comments from trainees may be easy; but, gratifying as this information is to management, it may not be useful to the organization unless it somehow translates into improved behaviour and job performance.

Method 2: Learning

Beyond what participants *think* about the training, it might be a good idea to see whether they actually learned anything. Testing knowledge and skills before a training program provides a baseline standard on trainees that can be measured again after training to determine improvement. This approach also means that whatever the person is learning must be used at work. For example, if an employee was learning new software and the employee's computer did not have the software, the employee's inability to perform was a result of inadequate resources, not of an absence of learning.

AT WORK WITH HRM 6.1

MOVING TOWARD A FOUR-LEVEL EVALUATION

Conexus is the largest credit union in Saskatchewan, with assets of $5.2 billion. According to Laurie Johnson, EVP Human Resources, the credit union's training and development budget for its 984 employees is 3% of payroll.

This number does not include the value of the internal training programs offered by the organization or the developmental opportunities offered through monthly one-on-one coaching sessions, mentoring, the emerging leaders program or the women's network. The organization's formal training budget is spent on university education and external training programs. Its largest internal training program develops financial service representatives (their title is to be changed to "relationship managers"). The training consists of several steps and each is measured.

The training is a blended delivery approach with online training followed by classroom-based modules. Content covered includes things such as understanding the banking system, cash duties, and introduction to Conexus's products and services. As employees progress and take on more complex situations, more advanced training is available, on topics such as consumer lending practices, TFSAs, and RRSPs.

In the training, there are many exercises in which employees apply the learning. When employees have completed the training and return to their branches, they practise applying the skills.

continued

Conexus is progressing toward the fourth level of evaluation of the effectiveness of training as per this classification:

1. *Reaction.* A very small component of the evaluation is focused on this. Questions are asked about the training environment and other contributing factors. The organization has found the need to move to a more advanced evaluation of the training to get more detail on our training.
2. *Learning/comprehensive review.* The online module has a testing component to the learning. In these evaluations, participants are asked to assess their knowledge of the content before the training and after training to get a sense of what has been learned. A yearly review of the organization's curriculums is conducted by meeting with leaders and participants to understand the effectiveness of the training, identify any gaps, and make changes based on this evaluation. The focus is on asking questions regarding the participant's learnings coming out of the session and how quickly they master the learning curve.
3. *Behavior/employee performance competencies.* The behavioural components of performing a job are assessed in monthly one-on-one coaching sessions and in observational coaching sessions with employees. These sessions are conducted by the employee's leader. The process in place is for employees to take the training and go back to their branch where observational coaching and one-on-one coaching meetings will take place. There is a coaching guide to assist. A performance management system is in place by which 50% of all employees and leader's performance scores are based on "how" they do their job. Corporate competencies and values are in place to perform this assessment.
4. *Results and return on investment.* The organization is in the midst of gathering business intelligence in order to track the measures of effective performance in all areas of the organization. Once these measures are in place, Conexus will be able to identify how providing training can lead to more effective results.

CRITICAL THINKING QUESTIONS:

1. If the annual payroll for Conexus is $18,750,000, what is the annual dollar amount budgeted for training and development?
2. Are there other ways Conexus can ensure that the training and development expenditures are worthwhile?

Source: Reprinted with permission from Laurie Johnson

Method 3: Behaviour

Much of what is learned in a training program never gets used on the job. It's not that the training was necessarily ineffective. In fact, on measures of employee reactions and learning, the program might score quite high. But for any of several reasons, trainees may not demonstrate **transfer of training** (also called *transfer of learning*)—effective application of principles learned. While measuring the extent of the behaviour change may not be necessary, it is important for the supervisor to expect the behaviour change and to reinforce it.

Transfer of training
Effective application of principles learned to what is required on the job

Ultimately, the success or failure of any training is whether there has been a transfer of that training. To maximize the transfer, managers can take several approaches:

1. feature identical elements of the job in the actual training
2. focus on general principles that can be adapted to fit situations in the work environment
3. establish a climate for transfer, with the manager being supportive and ensuring that the employee uses the new skills[20]

Method 4: Results (Return on Investment)

Both the people responsible for training and the managers are under continual pressure to show that their programs produce "bottom line" results. Most organizations measure their training in terms of its return on investment (ROI). This measure becomes even more important during economic downturns. Organizations want to know that the training has increased business results, whether they be profit, customer satisfaction, or decreased costs.[21]

Figure 6.4 illustrates an example of the costs and benefits of a training program and how to calculate the ROI. The Business Development Bank of Canada takes ROI very seriously,

FIGURE 6.4 Measuring the Costs/Benefits of Training

In assessing the value of training (or learning), organizations will look at the costs and benefits of training and assign a dollar value.

Typical Costs Included

- trainer's salary/cost
- trainees' salary/wages
- materials for training
- expenses for trainers/trainees (e.g., travel)
- cost of facilities and equipment
- lost productivity (opportunity cost)

Typical Benefits Included

- increase in productivity
- decrease in errors
- decrease in turnover
- behaviour changes
- improved safety record

For example, a revised safety training program might have the following costs: trainer time ($10,000), trainees' time ($20,000), materials ($5,000), and facilities ($1,000) for a total of $36,000. If the training covered two years and during that time the company saved $50,000 in workers' compensation insurance and the costs of other, related safety infractions, the benefits outweigh the costs.

spending 5% of its payroll on training with the goal to improve business outcomes. A meta-study conducted by Investing in People found that the Business Development Bank achieved a 74% ROI on training efforts to improve branch managers' coaching skills.[22]

Toolkit 6.4 provides background on a special project in Canada to better measure training results as well as some resources to determine the ROI.

Increasingly, organizations with sophisticated training systems look to training to support long-term strategy and change more than they look for short-term financial returns from their investments. For example, WestJet believes that investment in good training helps create an atmosphere in which people can do their best work.[23]

As training and development are viewed more and more from a strategic standpoint, there is heightened interest in benchmarking developmental services and practices against those of recognized leaders in industry. While no single model for exact benchmarking exists, the simplest models are based on the late W. Edwards Deming's classic four-step process. The four-step process advocates that managers do the following:

1. *Plan*. Conduct a self-audit to define internal processes and measurements, decide on areas to be benchmarked, and choose the comparison organization.
2. *Do*. Collect data through surveys, interviews, site visits, and/or historical records.
3. *Check*. Analyze data to discover performance gaps and communicate findings and suggested improvements to management.
4. *Act*. Establish goals, implement specific changes, monitor progress, and redefine benchmarks as a continuous-improvement process.

Benchmarking
Process of measuring one's own services and practices against the recognized leaders in order to identify areas for improvement

To use **benchmarking** successfully, managers must clearly define the measures of competency and performance and must objectively assess the current situation and identify areas for improvement.

The B.C. Human Resources Management Association has established projects that allow organizations to measure and benchmark training and development activities against each other. These projects compare data such as costs, staffing, administration, design, development, and delivery of training programs.[24]

Canadian Society for Training and Development
www.cstd.ca

Other helpful articles and publications on training and development can be found through the Canadian Society for Training and Development at **www.cstd.ca**.

THE TRAINING LANDSCAPE

The context in which training occurs is ever-evolving. Therefore, it is important to review the amount of time, energy, and resources (both financial and non-financial) that companies commit to training employees and the types of training considered to provide the most valuable results.

Investments in Training

According to a Conference Board of Canada survey, in 2013 Canadian businesses spent about $705 per employee on training. While that's up $17 from 2010, it's down nearly 40% from a peak of $1,207 in 1993. Meanwhile, only about 31% of Canadians participated in some type of non-formal job-related education or training in 2009. That's slightly better than the OECD average of 28%, but still below the 33% in the United States.[25]

With the relative lack of priority Canadian organizations are giving to learning and development, combined with Canada's economic downturn and lagging global competitiveness and innovation, the issue of whether training should be legally enforced arises.[26] Ethics in HRM 6.1 describes the debate surrounding decisions to force organizations to provide training and employees to take training.

Conference Board of Canada
www.conferenceboard.ca

However, organizations that make "Best Employers in Canada" lists tend to put a much higher value on the continued learning and development of their employees. A study conducted by the Conference Board of Canada (**www.conferenceboard.ca**) showed that organizations with strong learning cultures invest more in their learning and development and are realizing greater returns for their investment. Leaders in these companies put a high priority on employee engagement and communication. Overall, these organizations have superior employee performance, have higher levels of customer satisfaction, and provide higher-quality products and services to their customers.[27]

More and more organizations are also providing training on an "as needed" basis and ensuring it is linked to work experiences. For example, team training would be done as part of a team project on designing a new product. The types of training range from computer application skills to customer service.

The question organizations always ask is: Will training improve organizational performance? Even though the effectiveness of training initiatives on the KSAs of employees must be measured to ensure their positive impact on the organization's performance, most organizations still struggle to evaluate training effectiveness.[28] According to Linda Duxbury, a professor at Carleton University, there is going to be a group of people who don't have the skills the labour market wants or needs and therefore will be unemployable.[29] The costs and benefits beyond performance and productivity, such as recruitment and retention, need to be assessed. For training to be effective and transferred to the workplace, it is important that employers provide support—whether it be paying for the training, ensuring the use of the new KSAs on the job, or encouraging workers to increase their skill set.

ETHICS IN HRM 6.1 LEGISLATING LEARNING?

In recent years, widespread public concern has led to the development and passing of more laws that require workplace training in areas such as health and safety, the environment, and human rights. Although legislation enacted to date deals with strict minimal standards, enforcement, and penalties to employers that do not comply with the training requirements, the larger purpose of the legislation is to widely educate owners, managers, and workers about acceptable safe and non-discriminatory workplace behaviours.

In June 2010, Bill 168, which amended the Ontario *Occupational Health and Safety Act* to deal with the prevalence of, impact of, and risks associated with workplace violence and harassment, came into effect. It requires organizations to provide training in employer and employee obligations and related workplace policies and programs. Most recently, other provinces are requiring training that addresses violence in the workplace, including assessment of the risks of a domestic violence situation spilling over into the workplace. As an example of a response to this type of mandated training, the University of Western Ontario provides a variety of online courses that faculty, staff, and volunteers have to take in order to learn how to create a safe, healthy, diverse, and respectful workplace.

CRITICAL THINKING QUESTIONS:

1. Do you think mandatory training is right? Why or why not?
2. How would you react if your employer wanted you to participate in a training program that you thought was a waste of time? Why?

Sources: Adapted from "OH&S Legislation in Canada—Introduction," accessed April 4, 2015, **www.ccohs.ca/oshanswers/legisl/intro.html**; "Workplace Hazardous Materials Information System (WHMIS)," Health Canada, accessed April 7, 2015, **http://hc-sc.gc.ca/ewh-semt/occup-travail/whmis-simdut/index-eng.php**; "Workplace Violence and Workplace Harassment," Ontario Ministry of Labour, accessed April 3, 2015, **www.labour.gov.on.ca/english/hs/sawo/pubs/fs_workplaceviolence.php**; and "Domestic Violence in the Workplace," WorkSafe BC, accessed April 7, 2015, **www2.worksafebc.com/Topics/Violence/Resources-DomesticViolence.asp#Readmore**; "Human Resources—Required Training," University of Western Ontario, accessed April 17, 2015, **www.uwo.ca/hr/learning/required/index.html**.

TOOLKIT 6.4 INVESTING IN PEOPLE

Organizations spend a considerable amount of money and hours on training every year. However, with the economic challenges, organizations want to be sure that value is received from the training.

This desire led to an innovative project sponsored by Human Resources and Skills Development Canada and undertaken by the Canadian Society of Training and Development. The purpose was to have organizations determine the business impact of the training as the training was being developed, not after the training had been done. The project, called Investing in People, designed tools and methods for monitoring and assessing the effectiveness of the training as it was implemented. The focus of the monitoring was to determine the change in business results. Twelve Canadian organizations participated in these "training ROI" case studies.

Five programs determined that there was a positive relationship between formal training expenditures and performance indicators, such as employee productivity and company productivity. Additional ways to evaluate training and best training practices that organizations can use to measure ROI were found.

In the seven case studies in which a positive return did not occur, it was found that training was not aligned to the business strategies, initial program design was ineffective, and participants were unable to apply their new skills to their workplace. It was also found that many training programs and practices were ineffective and that ROI evaluation was challenging due to limited house resources and expertise.

Several recently researched tools and resources to measure training are available at the site Investing in People (www.cstd.ca/?IIP_Tools). Another useful tool for developing Return on Training Investment (ROTI) can be found at FutureEd Inc. (**www.futured.com/audited/returned.htm**).

Sources: Adapted from Canadian Society for Training and Development, "Investing in People," accessed April 7, 2015, **www.cstd.ca/?page=IIP**; and Lynette Gillis and Allan Bailey, "Investing in People—Meta Study of Evaluation Findings," Centre for Learning Impact, CSTD, March 2010, accessed April 7, 2015, **www.cstd.ca/resource/resmgr/iip/metastudy.pdf**.

Types of Training

LO7

What are some current popular training programs?

Although this chapter has focused almost exclusively on the processes underlying a systems model of training (needs assessment, principles of learning, implementation methods, and evaluation), it may be useful to discuss some of the more popular topics covered in these training programs. As noted in Figure 6.1, a wide variety of skills and capabilities is required in today's workplace. In addition to the training that addresses the competencies associated with a particular job, many employers develop training programs to meet the needs of a broader base of employees. This section summarizes some of these programs, including basic skills training and team training. Emerging Trends 6.1 provides information regarding evolving training issues.

Basic Skills Training

Experts define an illiterate individual as one having a sixth-grade education or less. Working adults who improve their literacy gain better pay and more promotions and are employed for longer periods of time. Further, people of low literacy tend to have lower rates of employment, and they tend to work in occupations with lower skill requirements.[30] Employers launch literacy training in order to improve productivity. Dofasco Steel in Ontario provides not only training in basic English and computer-related skills, but also advanced computer courses and business writing.[31]

These figures on literacy have important implications for society at large and for organizations that must work around these skill deficiencies. This is especially true given labour market considerations on the one hand and increasing skill requirements (related to advances in technology) on the other. Basic skills have become essential occupational qualifications, having profound implications for product quality, customer service, internal efficiency, and workplace and environmental safety.

In the past several years, the number of businesses that require a high-level of knowledge has grown due to globalization and a knowledge-based economy.[32] A recent study by the Canadian Chamber of Commerce found that Canada's slipping global competitiveness is due to the shortage of skilled and educated workers.[33] Canadian employers report that the top five skills they need in employees today are the ability to

- read and understand information
- listen, ask questions, and understand
- work in teams
- assess situations and identify problems
- communicate effectively, both in writing and verbally

But adults don't learn the way children do, so many of the traditional basic skills training techniques are not successful with adults. To implement a successful program in basic and remedial skills, managers should do the following:

1. Explain to employees why and how the training will help them in their jobs.
2. Relate the training to the employees' goals.
3. Respect and consider participant experiences, and use these as a resource.
4. Use a task-centred or problem-centred approach so that participants "learn by doing."
5. Give feedback on progress toward meeting learning objectives.

Teamwork Training

As discussed in Chapter 4, organizations rely on teams to attain strategic and operational goals. Whether the team is an air crew, a research team, or a manufacturing or service unit, the contributions of the individual members of the team are a function not only of the skills and capabilities (competencies) of each individual but also of the interaction of the team members. To give an example of how important this can be to an organization, Dofasco had 6,700 employees participate in four-day workshops on interpersonal and group skills over a three-year period. The company wanted all its employees to learn to work with one another in new and different ways.

Teamwork skills fall under two broad categories: task-related and relationship-related. Teamwork skills that characterize effective teams include a balance between the use of technical skills, such as time management and problem solving, and interpersonal skills, such as conflict resolution and collaboration. As noted earlier, Figure 6.1 highlights the importance of teamwork skills in today's workplace. Teams need to evaluate themselves periodically to ensure that the goal(s) is being achieved and that there are no concerns about interpersonal relationships.

Managers who want to design team training for their organization should keep the following points in mind:

1. Team building is a difficult and comprehensive process. Since many new teams are under pressure to produce, there is little time for training. Everything cannot be covered in a 24-hour blitz. Team training works best when it is provided over time and parallels team development.
2. Team development is not always a linear sequence of "forming, storming, norming, and performing." Training initiatives can help a team work through each of these stages, but managers must be aware that lapses can occur.
3. Additional training is required to assimilate new members. Large membership changes may result in teams reverting to a previous developmental stage.
4. Skills need to be acquired through practice and reviewing and rewarding the performance of the teams.[34]

EMERGING TRENDS 6.1

As investment in training evolves, so will the type of training that organizations focus on. Not only the "what" will be offered is changing, but "how" training is delivered continues to be altered. This being so, the following key trends are emerging.

1. ***Leadership development.*** The unexpected retirement of several high-profile CEOs continues to raise concern about the loss of organizational leadership experience and knowledge as the Baby Boom generation prepares to withdraw from the workplace. Hence, it is critical that organizations take time to develop leaders and allow them to grow and adapt to future needs and demands. Leadership development will continue to be a top priority and employers and individuals will share the responsibility of training and learning to sharpen skills.[35,36]
2. ***Change management.*** Increasingly, employees are expected to be able to adapt to and thrive in changing work conditions and requirements. Training opportunities of how to plan and enact successful transition, as well as how to address the potential barriers or points of resistance to change, enable organizations to grow and thrive in dynamic environment.[37]
3. ***Learning 2.0.*** Learning 2.0 is a term used to describe the reinvention of learning and development in the 21st century. It represents the paradigm shift from face-to-face and/or online instructor–controlled, structured, one-way adaptive training to the learner-driven, collaborative, and problem-focused learning made possible by Web 2.0 technologies that provide a massive forum for sharing information and working collaboratively.[38]
4. ***Online and mobile learning.*** Social, mobile, and cloud-computing technological advances, convergence, and the increase in collaborative work have led to changes in how organizations approach learning. They have also expanded the breadth and diversity of delivery methods: blogs, communities of practice, podcasts, instant messaging, wikis, and team learning. Tablets and emerging mobile technology tools will allow employees to manage their professional development digitally. *MOOCs* (massive open online courses) are an example of how thousands of people may enroll in one online course offering. As well, combining in person and online learning, known as blended delivery, will be utilized to a greater extent.[39]
5. ***Just-in-time training.*** The concept of training and development has evolved into the concept of "talent management." It means looking at the people in the organization as "talent" and then creating a plan to have the people at the appropriate skill level when needed.[40]

CAREER DEVELOPMENT—INDIVIDUAL AND ORGANIZATIONAL NEEDS

LO8

How does a career development program integrate individual and organizational needs?

Career development programs, with their greater emphasis on the individual, introduce a personalized aspect to the term "development." Most training and development programs have a career development component. Most career development programs should be viewed as a dynamic process that attempts to meet the needs of managers, their employees, and the organization.

Career planning, on the other hand, is a systematic approach in which you would assess your values, interests, abilities, and goals, and identify the path(s) you would need to take to realize your career goals. John Holland posited six personality types, or career anchors, into which people could be categorized: realistic, investigative, artistic, social, enterprising, and conventional.[41] Along these lines, Schein believed there were eight career anchors or considerations: autonomy/independence, security/stability, technical-functional competence, general managerial competence, entrepreneurial creativity, service or dedication to a cause, pure challenge, and lifestyle.[42] Through a deeper understanding of your type, or favourite activities that aligned with these anchors, you could then determine which careers would provide the best matching to your values and preferences. Through career development programs, you would then journey along the career path.

Ultimately, in today's organizations, individuals are responsible for initiating their own career planning. It is up to individuals to identify their knowledge, skills, abilities, interests, and values, and seek out information about career options in order to set goals and develop career plans. Managers should encourage employees to take responsibility for their own careers, by offering continuing assistance in the form of feedback on individual performance, and making available information about the organization, the job, and career opportunities that might be of interest.

The organization should be responsible for supplying information about its mission, policies, and plans, and for providing support for employee self-assessment, training, and development. Significant career growth can occur when individual initiative combines with organizational opportunity. Career development programs benefit managers by giving them increased skill in managing their own careers, greater retention of valued employees, increased understanding of the organization, and enhanced reputations as people developers.

Some organizations make use of leadership career development programs. Enbridge, an Alberta-based company in the energy transportation and distribution business, changed how it provided leadership development. For several years it sent a few executives every year to Queen's University for a three-week residential program. However, in assessing ways to maximize the training budget, the organization decided it could provide leadership training to a larger number of employees by custom-developing a program that could be delivered in-house. By changing the approach to delivery, Enbridge is now able to offer a leadership development program to employees every year instead of every five years. In recognition of their strategic approach, Enbridge got the 2014 WOW! Award for their program.[43]

The Banff Centre
www.banffcentre.ca

Center for Creative Leadership
www.ccl.org

For more information about the types of programs available for leadership development, visit the Banff Centre at www.banffcentre.ca and the Center for Creative Leadership at **www.ccl.org**.

As shown in Figure 6.5, organizational needs should be linked with individual career needs in a way that joins personal effectiveness and satisfaction of employees with the achievement of the organization's strategic objectives.

FIGURE 6.5 Balancing Individual and Organizational Needs

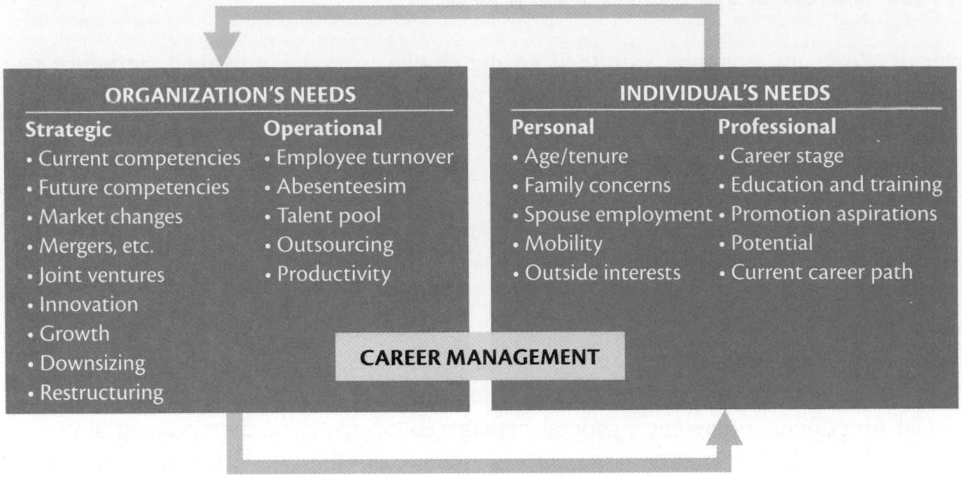

Creating Favourable Conditions

While a career development program requires many special processes and techniques, some basic elements must be present if it is to be successful, ones that create favourable conditions for the program.

Management Support

If career development is to succeed, it must receive the complete support of top management. The system should reflect the goals and culture of the organization, and a "people philosophy" should be woven throughout. A people philosophy can provide employees with a clear set of expectations and directions for their own career development. For a program to be effective, managerial staff at all levels must be trained in the fundamentals of job design, performance appraisal, career planning, and coaching.

Goal Setting

Before individuals can engage in meaningful career planning, they must have not only an awareness of the organization's philosophy but also a clear understanding of the organization's more immediate goals. Otherwise, they may plan for personal change and growth without knowing if or how their own goals match those of the organization.

For example, if the technology of a business is changing and new skills are needed, will the organization retrain to meet this need or hire new talent? Is there growth, stability, or decline in the number of employees needed? How will turnover affect this need? Answers to these kinds of questions are essential to the support of individual career planning.

HRM Practices to Enhance Career Development

To ensure that its career development program will be effective, an organization can implement various HRM practices. For example, a practice of job rotation can counteract obsolescence and maintain employee flexibility. Another practice that can aid development involves job transfers and promotions. A **transfer** is the placement of an employee in another job for which the duties, responsibilities, status, and remuneration are approximately equal to those of the previous job (or work requirements). A transfer may require the employee to change work group, workplace, shift, or organizational unit; it may even

Transfer
Placement of an individual in another job for which the duties, responsibilities, status, and remuneration are approximately equal to those of the previous job

necessitate moving to another geographical area. Transfers make it possible for an organization to place its employees in jobs where there is a greater need for their services and where they can acquire new knowledge and skills. A downward transfer, or demotion, moves an individual into a lower-level job that can provide developmental opportunities, but such a move is usually viewed unfavourably by the person demoted.

A **promotion** is a change of assignment to a job at a higher level in the organization. The new job (or work) normally provides an increase in pay and status and demands more skill or carries more responsibility. Promotions enable an organization to utilize the skills and abilities of its staff more effectively, and the opportunity to gain a promotion serves as an incentive for good performance. The two principal criteria for determining promotions are merit and seniority. Often, the problem is to determine how much consideration to give to each factor.

Promotion
Change of assignment to a job at a higher level in the organization

As organizations continue to change, including their structure and number of employees, it is becoming more difficult to promote people as part of career development. The issues of balancing work and family, mentioned in Chapter 1, can become paramount when considering a promotion. Even though there has been growth in the number of women working, the proportion of women in senior management positions has not changed over the past two decades. A report by the Conference Board of Canada outlined practices organizations are using to encourage the advancement of women: succession planning, mentoring, coaching, job rotation, and training.[44] Canadian Pacific Railway, Manitoba Lotteries Corporation, and TD Financial Group use a range of these practices to recruit and retain diverse talent, supporting their organizational goals of equity and performance.[45]

LO9

How can an employee's career development be enhanced?

Mentorship to Enhance Career Development

As mentioned earlier in this chapter, "development" is a long-term approach for acquiring and utilizing new skills. Since the purpose of a development program is to give employees enhanced capabilities, there are a number of ways this can occur. The responsibility to develop the talent lies with all managers in the organization—not just the person's immediate supervisor or team leader.

When one talks with men and women about their employment experiences, it is common to hear them mention individuals at work who influenced them. They frequently refer to immediate managers who were especially helpful as career developers. But they also mention others at higher levels who provided guidance and support. These managers (and executives) who coach, advise, and encourage less experienced employees are called **mentors**.

Mentors
Managers who coach, advise, and encourage less experienced employees

Generally, the mentor initiates the relationship, but sometimes an employee will approach a manager for advice. Most mentoring relationships develop over time on an informal basis. However, many organizations emphasize formal mentoring plans that assign a mentor to those employees considered for upward movement in the organization. A good mentorship is a reciprocal relationship, both the *mentee* and the mentor learning from each other. In recent years there has been a growth in the different types of mentoring relationships, from reverse mentoring (in which the roles are switched) to peer and team mentoring. Done well, the process is beneficial for both parties.

It is important to remember that a mentor relationship is very personal. Toolkit 6.5 provides guidelines for establishing and maintaining successful mentor and mentee relationships.

Organizations with formal mentoring programs include Shell International, Sun Microsystems, Johnson & Johnson, and the Bank of Montreal. Alternatively, given the importance of the issue, a number of mentoring organizations have begun to spring up. A new form of mentoring, sponsored by the Ms. Foundation for Women, provides an opportunity for both girls and boys, 8 to 18 years old, to spend a day with parents or friends on the job. The program is designed to give young people more attention and provide them with career role models. American Express, Chevron, and Estée Lauder participate in this program.

Purestock/Thinkstock

Mentoring is important to help develop people at all levels in an organization.

Not surprisingly, mentoring is also being done electronically. *E-mentoring* brings experienced business professionals together with individuals needing advice and guidance. Participants in e-mentoring typically never meet, but many form long-lasting e-mail connections that can be very beneficial. Still, most participants see these connections as supplements to—rather than substitutes for—in-person connections.

There are a number of resources for mentoring. A few examples include the following:

- *Society for Canadian Women in Science and Technology (SCWIST)* is an association that has assembled thousands of women in technology fields who act as online mentors to visitors to its website (**www.scwist.ca**).
- *National Mentoring Partnership* (**www.mentoring.org**) is an online site for a variety of different resources for mentors and mentees, including information about how to find a mentor.
- *Women's Enterprise Centre* (**www.womensenterprise.ca**) is an organization that encourages, helps, and supports women in British Columbia who want to own, operate, and grow their own business.

Society for Canadian Women in Science and Technology
www.scwist.ca

National Mentoring Partnership
www.mentoring.org

Women's Enterprise Centre
www.womensenterprise.ca

TOOLKIT 6.5 MENTORING GUIDELINES

Successful mentoring is built on a common understanding of interests and "ground rules." Here are some to consider before establishing a mentor–mentee relationship:

1. Formalize the expectations with a written agreement that outlines the behaviours of each person.
2. Monitor progress. Understand that either party can withdraw from the relationship at any time, and it is not necessary to provide an explanation.
3. All documents exchanged, such as company plans or résumés, will be treated as confidential.
4. The mentor cannot be solicited for a job. Doing so is grounds for breaking the relationship. There must be dedication to the process.
5. Respect each other's time. Arrive on time and prepare with a list of questions or topics to be discussed.
6. Provide feedback honestly. For example, the mentee might state, "This is not the kind of information I need at this stage," or the mentor might advise, "You should not skip meetings just because they are tedious; it is an important part of this company's culture to be visible at these meetings."

Keeping a Career in Perspective

It is important in any training and development program to keep everything in perspective. While work is a very important part of someone's life, it is only a part. Organizations want people who maintain an appropriate balance between their work life and their personal life, and therefore can continue to grow and develop for personal satisfaction and success for the organization.

Some of the other areas of life that must be considered are the following:

1. Off-the-job interests can provide a break from the demands of a career while allowing employees to gain satisfaction from non-work-related activities.
2. Family life can be negatively affected if the organization does not provide recognition of a person's life outside of work. Conflict between work and family may arise over such issues as number of hours worked per week, the need to relocate for career advancement, and the amount of overtime that may be required.
3. Planning for retirement is an important consideration given the aging workforce. Many companies are now providing pre-retirement programs to allow an employee to be productive in the organization while minimizing problems that can arise in the retirement years.
4. Dual-career families are a factor in the contemporary business world. Therefore, career development and progress may need to take the goals of the partner into consideration.

As mentioned in Chapter 1, the workforce of today is very different from that of yesterday. The organization might have as many as four generational cohorts—each with its own view and expectations about career development. Therefore, it will be important to maintain a balanced perspective on career development and to structure opportunities to fit the needs of both the diverse employee base and the organization.

Summary

1. List some characteristics of an effective orientation process.
   - Familiarizing new employees with the organization, their job, and their work unit.
   - Embedding organizational values, beliefs, and accepted behaviours.
   - Active involvement and participation from the supervisor.
2. Describe the benefits of employee orientation.
   - Lower turnover.
   - Increased productivity.
   - Improved employee morale and identification with the company.
   - Lower training costs.
   - Facilitation of learning.
   - Reduction of anxiety.
3. Discuss the systems approach to training and development.
   - Training and development need to be linked to the organization's goals and objectives.
   - A systems approach to training and development creates this link.
   - A systems approach consists of four phases: needs analysis, training program design, implementation, and evaluation.
4. Describe the components of a training-needs assessment.
   - Organizational-level, task- or job-level, and person-level assessments.
5. Identify the principles of learning and how they facilitate training.
   - Goal setting
   - Individual differences
   - Active practice and repetition
   - Whole versus part learning
   - Mass versus distributed learning
   - Feedback and reinforcement
   - Meaningfulness of presentation
   - Modelling

6. Identify the types of training and development methods used for all levels of employees.
   - On-the-job
   - Apprenticeship
   - Co-operative and internship programs
   - Classroom instruction
   - Self-directed
   - Audio-visual
   - Simulation
   - E-learning
   - Special projects or tasks
   - Seminars and conferences
   - Case studies
   - Role playing and management games
7. Describe the training programs that are currently popular.
   - Basic skills training (such as literacy), in which people learn the basics of reading and math
   - Teamwork training, in which people learn new behaviours and skills to work in teams
8. Explain how a career development program integrates individual and organizational needs.
   - It blends employee effectiveness and satisfaction with the achievement of the organization's strategic objectives.
   - HRM practices must fit so that both individual and organizational needs can be achieved.
   - Mentorship can enhance career development for employees.
9. Discuss how a employee's career development can be enhanced.
   - Mentoring.
   - Helping employees keep an appropriate work-life balance.

Need to Know

- Definition of orientation, training, development, and learning
- The steps within a systems approach to training
- Principles of learning and how they facilitate training
- Variety of training methods
- Ways to reinforce training in the work environment
- Methods to enhance career development

Need to Understand

- Strategic link between orientation, training, development, and organizational outcomes and objectives
- Importance of the line manager in identifying training needs
- Importance of ensuring appropriate method is used to enhance learning
- Role supervisor or line manager plays in helping the trainee use the new skills and behaviours
- Organizational and individual responsibility in a person's career development

KEY TERMS

apprenticeship training 184
behaviour modification 183
benchmarking 190
co-operative training 185
development 174
e-learning 186
instructional objectives 181
internship programs 185
mentors 197
on-the-job training (OJT) 184
orientation 174
promotion 197
trainee readiness 182
training 174
transfer 196
transfer of training 189

REVIEW QUESTIONS

1. What are the components and benefits of a well-designed orientation process?
2. What are the phases in a systems approach to training?
3. What are the principles of learning?
4. What are the various methods for implementing training and development?
5. What are four ways to evaluate training programs? Describe why each is important.
6. Why is there an increased emphasis on career development programs?
7. How can managers create favourable conditions for career development?
8. What is mentorship and how can it be used to enhance a person's career development?

CRITICAL THINKING QUESTIONS

1. What have been the biggest changes that you have noticed in how you learn as a post-secondary student? What do you think has been the key driver of these changes?
2. Would you be willing to take a blended delivery (partially in-person and partially online) postsecondary course? Why or why not? What would be some of the potential benefits and problems that you foresee?
3. Your employer has approached you to assume a supervisory role. While flattered, you are also concerned about your ability to carry out the role successfully. What type of training or development might you want to help you succeed? What would be the "hard skills" and "soft skills"?
4. Discuss this statement: Effective 21st-century organizational learning is a blend of formal, informal, and social learning strategies.
5. You have been asked to assist in developing an e-learning orientation program. Debate the advantages and limitations of using e-learning for "onboarding" new employees. How would you ensure the effective design, implementation, and transfer of learning?
6. What are some creative, and low-cost/no cost, ways that an organization could make a new employee feel welcome?
7. Access the site **http://moocs.com**. Do you think MOOCs are sustainable and will be a prominent feature in the postsecondary education landscape? Would you be interested in signing up for a MOOC? Why or why not? For another perspective, please read David Blake, "Think Massively, MOOC Musings," February 25, 2015, accessed April 9, 2015, http://moocs.com.
8. You work in an organization that focuses on wine sales and marketing. Recently, there have been a number of complaints about a particular customer service representative in terms of accuracy of wine knowledge shared with customers and timeliness of work orders. Complete the four steps in the systems approach to training and development. Specifically, consider: (1) How will you determine whether training is the answer? (2) What is a possible learning or training objective you could identify? (3) What methods would you use to implement training? (4) How would you evaluate if the training was effective?

DEVELOPING YOUR SKILLS

1. In groups of three or four, develop a list of behaviours or skills that would improve your performance as a team member. For each behaviour or skill, identify one or two training methods that would be appropriate for learning that behaviour or skill.
2. Providing training to employees is a significant retention tool in a tight labour market. In groups of four to five, discuss the benefits of training for individuals and organizations. Prepare a response, including the ethical considerations, to the following statement: "Employees should be required to repay the cost of any training if they leave the organization before one year."
3. In groups of three or four, prepare a new student orientation program for your campus. How long would the orientation program be and who would be involved? What would be included before, during, and after the formal orientation?

4. Access the Tony Bates' website, **www.tonybates.ca/2014/01/12/2020-vision-outlook-for-online-learning-in-2014-and-way-beyond**. Do you agree with Dr. Bates' comment that lecture-based learning will disappear or at least become less common? What do you believe will be the most common format for learning in postsecondary institutions within the next decade?
5. Some YouTube videos have been created as teaching resources. Find one and critique its effectiveness in assisting learning. Discuss whether it utilized the four components of the systems approach to the training and development model. Choose one aspect of the model you observed in the video and deliver a presentation about it to the larger class.

CASE STUDY 1

Welcome to the Jungle

Jason was excited about his first day of work at Jimmy's Jungle Gym. As a second-year kinesiology student, this job would provide Jason with the opportunity to work with young children and teach them about active and healthy play.

Jimmy's Jungle Gym was a play centre targeting three-to-six-year-olds and provided numerous types of "play pits" and equipment for these youngsters to use. A café was also located on-site where parents could visit with each other, grab a snack, and wait for their children to burn off some energy. Located in a local strip mall, the Jungle Gym had opened three months ago and employed one manager and twelve general employees. During each shift there would be five or six employees on-site, with each person expected to welcome guests, collect cash, manage the café, and interact with the children in the play pits.

Jason arrived for his first day and introduced himself to Bob, another employee who had been working at the Jungle Gym since it opened. The manager, Todd, eventually arrived and appeared surprised to see Jason. Todd then told Jason to go into the back staff room and spend an hour or so reading through manuals that described safety protocol and explanations about how the equipment in the play pits worked. Jason was concerned about this, as he was more of an active learner and found it difficult to learn new material merely by reading. However, as a new employee he did not want to rock the boat. After about 90 minutes Bob told Jason that he "was on" and to join the other five employees working.

Things were chaotic, to say the least. The children (over 50 of them) were loud and boisterous. As well, there was a long lineup in the café and parents were becoming agitated as they had to wait for some service. Jason asked Bob about how to use some of the ropes on the climbing wall and was told, "Figure it out. We are all expected to be competent and you were hired for your knowledge." Todd was also yelling at Jason to get to the café and help serve coffee to the adults. Jason had no idea of how to use the special coffee maker, and when serving a latte burnt his hand on the steam. For the rest of his six-hour shift he ran back and forth between the play pits and the café trying to keep children and parents happy. Ten minutes before his shift ended, a child was "lost" and all employees ran around in a panic trying to locate the youngster, who was eventually found hiding under a table in the café.

As he was leaving, Jason wanted to talk to Todd, but Todd was in his office and there was a "Do not disturb" sign posted on the door.

Jason walked home. His hand and head hurt! This was not what he had envisioned, and he wondered whether he should even bother showing up for his next shift tomorrow.

Questions:

1. Who should be in charge of orienting new employees at the Jungle Gym? Why?
2. What tools and resources might be used in lieu of manuals to orient new employees?
3. Outline an effective orientation process that Jimmy's Jungle Gym should use. Consider what should be done prior to, on, and after the first day of employment.
4. What possible legal liabilities is the company facing? Why?

CASE STUDY 2

Learning 2.0 at East Coast Tech Inc.

After ten years of managing one of the leading sales departments, Jan O'Brien was excited about her promotion to the position of learning and development manager for East Coast Tech Inc. (ECT). She had always been able to deploy new sales practices to keep the company ahead of their competitors and felt that her knowledge and experience would be valuable to her new position as the company restructured its workforce. This shift toward a more flattened organizational structure and distribution of leadership to the lower levels of the organization had created her new position.

ECT, a global telecommunications provider with more than 8,000 employees, was experiencing increased competition, requiring the company and employees to "work smarter" and "produce results." The recessionary impacts on their business resulted in a decline in finances to all departments, one of which was budget cuts to the learning and development department. In strategic planning meetings with the leadership team, it was clear to Jan that ECT was not decreasing its commitment to learning, but needed a new, more cost-effective learning strategy able to meet the "on demand" learning needs of all employees and managers at distant locations. The employees' roles were increasingly complex, requiring collaboration and teamwork to effectively meet client needs. The president of ECT clearly stated that that one of her first tasks was to conduct a thorough review of the learning and development function within the organization. The president wanted hard evidence, a "return on investment," to back up learning and development initiatives.

Being in the telecommunications industry, Jan was aware of how social media were catching on among the public, especially ECT employees. ECT had adopted policies that banned the use of social media in the workplace and had installed blocking software so that employees could not access Facebook, MySpace, and LinkedIn. Most of the managers had expressed concern that employees were spending countless hours on social media. Issues ranged from inappropriate use of them in meetings to worries about confidential organizational information being divulged.

Through her reading, Jan knew that a few competitors had introduced a learning approach and philosophy called Learning 2.0. This approach represented a shift from face-to-face or online instructor–controlled, structured, one-way adaptive training to the learner-driven, collaborative, problem-focused learning made possible by Web 2.0 technologies—which provide a massive forum for sharing information and working collaboratively. Jan felt that although this approach was radical, it might realize the president's productivity goals. She thought the introduction of social media capabilities would encourage employee innovation and engagement. Jan did not want to miss the opportunity but did not have the confidence and support within her department. Most employees expressed resistance.

Questions:

1. How would you approach the development of Learning 2.0 at ECT to ensure its success?
2. What key factors would enable ECT to implement its new learning approach?
3. Does ECT have the culture, leadership, and resources necessary to support this change?
4. How would you make a case for this direction to the leadership team?

NOTES AND REFERENCES

1. E. Fragouli, "Intellectual Capital & Organizational Advantage: An Economic Approach to Its Valuation and Measurement," *International Journal of Information, Business and Management* 7, no. 1 (2015): 36–57.
2. Ibid.
3. A. Ferdous and M. Polonsky, "The Impact of Frontline Employees' Perceptions of Internal Marketing on Employee Outcomes," *Journal of Strategic Marketing* 22, no. 4 (2014): 300–315, doi:10.1080/0965254X.2013.876077.
4. "Live Safe, Work Smart," accessed March 29, 2015, www.livesafe-worksmart.net/english/fast_facts/index.htm.
5. Susan M. Heathfield, "Performance Development Planning," About.com, accessed April 1, 2015, http://humanresources.about.com/cs/perfmeasurement/a/pdp.htm.
6. Tony Bates, "2020 Vision: Outlook for Online Learning in 2014 and Way Beyond," January 12, 2014, accessed April 2, 2015, www.tonybates.ca/2014/01/12/2020-vision-outlook-for-online-learning-in-2014-and-way-beyond.
7. "Learning and Development Outlook 2011: Are Organizations Ready for Learning 2.0?" The Conference Board of Canada, October 2011.
8. Tony Bates, "2020 Vision."
9. "Global Writers Apprentice Program," Banff World Media Festival, accessed March 30, 2015, http://banffmediafestival.com/competitions/shaw-media-writers-apprentice-program.
10. Ezra Stoller and Lily Sugrue, "Unpaid Internships: A Priceless Experience?" *The Harvard Crimson*, April 3, 2014, accessed April 5, 2015, www.thecrimson.com/article/2014/4/3/unpaid-internships-experience.
11. Canadian Intern Association, "What Is the Law?" accessed April 3, 2015, www.internassociation.ca/what-is-the-law.
12. "Embracing Opportunities for Better Patient Care," *News Canada's Healthcare Newspaper*, April 3, 2012, www.hospitalnews.com/embracing-opportunities-for-better-patient-care.
13. Katerina Kastritou, "Innovative Ways to Use Web Conferencing," March 24, 2015, accessed April 3, 2015, www.3cx.com/blog/webrtc/innovative-ways-web-conferencing.
14. "Learning and Development Outlook 2011: Are Organizations Ready for Learning 2.0?" The Conference Board of Canada, October 2011.
15. James Ramussen, "Why e-Learning on Tablets?" *Upside Learning*, March 19, 2015, accessed March 28, 2015, www.upsidelearning.com/blog/index.php/2014/03/19/why-elearning-on-tablets.
16. Jim Kirkpatrick and Wendy Kirkpatrick, "The Kirkpatrick Philosophy," Kirkpatrick Partners, accessed March 30, 2015, www.kirkpatrickpartners.com.
17. "More on Re-evaluating Evaluation—Jack Phillips and ROI," August 19, 2011, accessed April 4, 2015, www.dashe.com/blog/evaluation-2/more-on-re-evaluating-evaluation-jack-phillips-and-roi.
18. Jim Kirkpatrick and Wendy Kirkpatrick, "The Kirkpatrick Philosophy."
19. A. Vasconcelos, "Older Workers: Some Critical Societal and Organizational Challenges," *The Journal of Management Development* 34, no. 3 (2015): 352, http://search.proquest.com/docview/1664767789?accountid=1343.
20. Monica Belcourt, George Bohlander, and Scott Snell, *Managing Human Resources*, 6th Canadian ed. (Toronto: Nelson Thomson, 2011), 298.
21. Lynette Gillis and Allan Bailey, "Investing in People—Meta Study of Evaluation Findings," Canadian Society for Training and Development, March 2010, accessed April 6, 2015, www.cstd.ca/?page=IIP.
22. Lynette Gillis and Allan Bailey, "Business Development Bank of Canada: Measuring the ROI of a Coaching Program for Banking Branch Managers," Canadian Society for Training and Development, accessed April 6, 2015, www.cstd.ca/resource/resmgr/iip/bdc_report_final_english.pdf.
23. "WestJet Once Again Canada's Most Attractive Employer," May 3, 2013, accessed April 7, 2015, http://westjet2.mediaroom.com/index.php?s=43&item=769.
24. HR Metrics Service, accessed April 7, 2015, www.hrmetricsservice.org.
25. Chris Sorensen, "The Myths About Canada's Skills Gap," *Maclean's*, September 30, 2014, accessed April 7, 2015, www.macleans.ca/work/jobs/the-myths-about-canadas-skills-gap.
26. Douglas Watt, "Treading Water: Canada Is Gradually Losing Its Competitive Edge," The Conference Board of Canada, September 2011.
27. Colin Hall, "Learning and Development Outlook 2014: Strong Learning Organizations, Strong Leadership," Conference Board of Canada, February 18, 2014, accessed April 7, 2015, www.conferenceboard.ca/e-library/abstract.aspx?did=5734.
28. "Learning and Development Outlook 2011: Are Organizations Ready for Learning 2.0?" The Conference Board of Canada, October 2011.
29. "Linda Duxbury: Demographics Indicate Skilled Labour Shortage Will Increase in Decades Ahead," *GTA Construction Report*, March 10, 2015, accessed April 7, 2015, www.gtaconstructionreport.com/linda-duxbury-demographics-indicate-skilled-labour-shortage-will-increase-in-decades-ahead/?doing_wp_cron=1428249564.7206029891967773437500.

30. "Adult Literacy Facts," Life Literacy Canada, accessed April 7, 2015, http://abclifeliteracy.ca/adult-literacy-facts.
31. "In for the Long Run," ABC Life Literacy Canada, accessed April 7, 2015, http://abclifeliteracy.ca/long-run-0.
32. Watt, "Treading Water."
33. Canadian Chamber of Commerce, "Top 10 Barriers to Competitiveness," Skills Development Discussion Paper, March 2012.
34. Susan M. Heathfield, "How to Build a Teamwork Culture," accessed April 7, 2015, http://humanresources.about.com/od/involvementteams/a/team_culture.htm.
35. Mike Myatt, "The #1 Reason Leadership Development Fails," *Forbes*, December 19, 2012, accessed April 6, 2015, www.forbes.com/sites/mikemyatt/2012/12/19/the-1-reason-leadership-development-fails.
36. Right Management, "Leadership Development Trend for 2015: Shift Toward Shared Responsibility," *Human Capital* 28 (April 2015).
37. "Change Management," Queens University, accessed April 7, 2015, http://irc.queensu.ca/training/change-management-training-courses-management-of-change-process-organizational-change-management-plan.
38. "Learning and Development Outlook 2011: Are Organizations Ready for Learning 2.0?" The Conference Board of Canada, October 2011.
39. Tony Bates, "2020 Vision."
40. Sandy Dutkowsky, "Trends in Training and Development—The New Economy, Training in U.S. Companies, Who Does the Training in Corporations?" accessed April 6, 2015, http://careers.stateuniversity.com/pages/852/Trends-in-Training-Development.html.
41. Dawn Rosenberg McKay, "The Holland Code," accessed April 8, 2015, http://careerplanning.about.com/od/selfassessment/a/holland-code.htm.
42. Edgar H. Schein, *Career Anchors (Discovering Your Real Values)* (San Francisco: Jossey-Bass Pfeiffer, 1990).
43. "Employee Development," Enbridge, accessed April 6, 2015, www.enbridge.com/WorkwithEnbridge/CareersatEnbridge/Why-Enbridge/EmployeeDevelopment.aspx.
44. "Women in Senior Management: Where Are They?" Conference Board of Canada, August 2011.
45. Ibid.

7 Managing Employee Performance

LEARNING OUTCOMES

After studying this chapter, you should be able to

1 Define a performance management system.

2 Explain the purpose of a performance management system.

3 Describe the management practices necessary for a good performance management system.

4 Identify the steps in an effective performance management system.

5 Describe the different sources of performance review information.

6 Explain the various methods used for performance reviews.

7 Outline the characteristics of an effective performance review interview.

OUTLINE

HRM CLOSE-UP

"To see someone reach a goal or receive a promotion is the biggest compliment to a manager."

In his role as manager at the GoodLife Fitness Club in Saskatoon, Saskatchewan, Tyler Gorrell leads a team of personal trainers, membership development staff, customer service representatives, and team leaders who have direct responsibility for the front-line staff. It's a large group to oversee, but he's dedicated to ensuring a quality performance management process and sees it as integral to his staff's success. "Their success reflects on my success," he says. "To see someone reach a goal or receive a promotion is the biggest compliment to a manager."

Corporately, GoodLife Fitness supplies guidelines and templates to use in personal development plans and performance management discussions. These are all found on the company's intranet site. "I also rely on the People Department at GoodLife who are available to help with any specific circumstances I have. Other club managers and colleagues are also there to support me," explains Gorrell.

GoodLife's performance management process begins with a goal-setting exercise in which employees articulate personal, professional, development, and financial goals. "All of these goals tie together," says Gorrell. "An employee might be motivated by saving money for a personal trip, and they might want to know what they can do to improve performance and earn more money."

To gather information on how employees are doing, Gorrell uses a combination of tools and techniques. Managers, in particular, receive "360-degree feedback," whereby direct reports and peers provide input on their performance. Customer feedback is an important source of information as is systems data, such as numbers of new memberships, numbers of personal training sessions, revenue generated, and product sales. "I also look for a self-evaluation from staff. I like to understand the strengths and successes that the employee perceives and compare that to my own observations," says Gorrell.

Gorrell practises "Ten Minute Meetings" with his team leaders, and the team leaders do the same for their employees. These short coaching sessions are used to ask how a shift went yesterday, what risks or opportunities were presented, and what support staff need to reach specific goals. Even when the club is busy and there's lots to do, Gorrell makes sure he takes time to do this. "It's a matter of priority," he says. "It only takes an hour to go through this process with all of your employees and it's worth it."

Managers at GoodLife submit performance reviews electronically. Scores are captured in the system, giving the corporate office a way to ensure that reviews are being conducted. "But they also do 'Caring Audits' where the actual file is inspected," explains Gorrell. "Quality and integrity is important, and the company wants to ensure the employee is being cared for in terms of goal setting and performance management. It ties in with staff retention and the employee's ability to grow with the company. This matters to GoodLife," he adds.

Finding the time to coach staff and follow through on performance management commitments can be challenging, but Gorrell knows this has to be done regularly and consistently. "Once a year is never enough," he says. "As a manager, you have to be prepared. Know the metrics. Know what the employee needs to do to

Courtesy of Tyler Gorrell

Tyler Gorrell.

improve. Look at 'skill versus will' in order to understand reasons for poor performance. Ask if they are willing to try, and find out if they might be hindered by a lack of skill in a certain area."

"How you meet is important," stresses Gorrell. "Ensuring there are no distractions helps the employee know that the meeting is important and that they are special." Gorrell feels that connecting with the employee this way should take precedence over everything else a people manager does.

Personally, Gorrell enjoys working through the performance management process with his staff. He even enjoys being on the receiving end. "I like feedback," he says. "For me, performance reviews are the best opportunity to hear how I'm doing and to discover what I can improve."

Source: Courtesy of Tyler Gorrell

INTRODUCTION

In the preceding chapters, we discussed how an organization hires and develops a productive workforce. In this chapter, we turn to performance management, which is one of the most critical processes that managers use to maintain and enhance productivity and facilitate progress toward strategic goals. While we will focus mainly on a formal system, the processes of managing and reviewing performance can be informal as well. All managers monitor the way employees work and assess how this matches organizational needs. Supervisors and managers form impressions about the relative value of employees to the organization and seek to maximize the contribution of every individual. Yet while these ongoing informal processes are vitally important, most organizations also have a system that includes a formal review of the person's performance once or twice a year, or on an ongoing basis. In the HRM Close-up, Tyler Gorrell explains the successes of regular and continuous feedback, and coaching.

The success or failure of a performance management system depends on the philosophy underlying it, its connection with business goals, the attitudes and skills of those responsible for using it, and the individual components of the system. A performance management system is more than the actual review—it is an overall approach to getting the maximum contribution from each individual.

A PERFORMANCE MANAGEMENT SYSTEM

LO1

What is a performance management system?

LO2

What is the purpose of a performance management system?

Performance management system
A set of integrated management practices

A **performance management system** is a set of integrated management practices. While the formal review of employees' performance is a key component, a good performance review program does not make a good performance management system. A systems approach to performance management (1) allows the organization to integrate the management functions in order to maximize employee potential and (2) helps increase employees' satisfaction with their work and with the organization.

Formal programs for reviewing performance are by no means new to organizations. Performance review programs are used in large and small organizations in both the public and private sectors. Advocates see these programs as among the most logical means to review, develop, and thus effectively utilize the knowledge and abilities of employees as well as monitor the healthiness of the work culture. A senior manager at Softchoice, a technology company in Toronto, feels that performance management issues can be related to a toxic work environment.[1] Robert Bacal, a long-time observer of performance management systems, reminds us that the primary purpose for performance reviews is to improve future performance.[2]

It is important that the organization be clear about the purpose, but this is not always the case. Sometimes, companies want systems to communicate what work is valued; at other times, performance management systems are used to base pay decisions. For example, an organization that employs a team-based structure might have a performance management system that focuses on reviewing individual performance. This focus gives mixed messages about who owns the responsibility for the results and what is being valued in the performance review. Performance management needs to align everyone's work toward organizational goals and objectives and to ensure that employees are not working at cross-purposes.[3]

There is no doubt that managing performance is not always easy. Managers and supervisors frequently avoid discussing employee performance—good or poor. Yet, when reviews are candid, the organization improves and the individual's development is enhanced.[4]

Managing performance is not an added activity in the busy supervisor's life—it is central to the everyday work of managers. For years managers have struggled with the performance process, as have employees. However, as companies look for better ways of keeping and motivating employees, more managers are finding that the process is evolving and one of the keys to success is providing praise and other positive feedback.[5] Whether the company is small or large, praising efforts is a valuable tool to encourage great performance.[6]

A number of different research studies in a variety of industries, including engineering, health care, and education, demonstrate the strong link between performance management systems and organizational success. These studies consistently demonstrate, however, that the employee's performance needs to be connected to achieving the larger goals of the organization and that it is critical to have measurable performance criteria that is applied to everyone in the work unit.[7] Further, there is evidence that an effective system includes leadership behaviours where the supervisor is more concerned with the employee's job performance than their own.[8] With such clear evidence of the value of performance management systems, it will be useful for managers and HR practitioners to use these research findings when building a business case for the implementation of such a system.

MANAGEMENT PRACTICES

LO3

What are the management practices for a good performance system?

The following management practices are essential for an effective performance management system:

1. Setting and communicating clear performance expectations for all work and all jobs
2. Ensuring clear and specific performance objectives (or standards of performance) for all work
3. Providing supportive and helpful coaching by the supervisor to enable staff to reach their objectives
4. Focusing on the accomplishment of objectives during performance reviews
5. Recognizing and celebrating good performance
6. Creating action plans to improve performance, if necessary

As shown, the actual review step (item 4) is only one component of the system. However, the vast majority of performance management systems focus primarily on the review and typically use that step for making compensation decisions or making decisions about the continued employment of people. On the other hand, there are companies such as a hotel chain in Western Canada that is using a Web app called 15five (**www.15five.com**). The app provides the managers with a simple way to ask employees questions every week and then the managers respond to any issues quickly.[9]

15five
www.15five.com

Purposes of Managing Performance

Performance reviews have several purposes, all intended to benefit both the organization and the employee and to ensure that any decisions are based on objective information.

Compensation Purposes

The most frequent use of performance management systems is to make compensation decisions. If the organization indicates that it is paying for performance, then it is necessary that pay and performance is linked. Further, it will also be necessary to ensure that differences in performance levels can be measured and then converted into the pay decisions.[10]

Administrative Purposes

A performance management system also integrates a number of other major HR processes, such as promotion, transfer, and layoff decisions. Further, it can be used as part of HR planning—particularly when the organization has a succession plan. As well, the system provides a "paper trail" for documenting HRM processes that may result in legal action. For example, if a person were being disciplined regarding very poor customer service, the system would be able to identify what the goals were, how well the person met the goals, and what discussions and coaching sessions took place to improve performance in relation to customer service. And by having regular one-on-one meetings, discussions on performance can be held with less tension.[11]

Measurement of Performance

In order to assess the overall success of the organization, it is important to be able to measure the employees' accomplishments. Thus, you want to know how the employees performed compared to the established goals. A well-designed performance management system will be able to measure the performance of the organization and the employees. However, some recent studies suggest that the manner in which so many performance reviews are conducted may actually cause performance to decline.[12]

It is also important that the measures be reliable and valid. You were introduced to these concepts in Chapter 4 in relation to assessing skills in potential employees. These same concepts apply to measuring accomplishments. Performance measures must be consistent (reliable) and able to measure the performance (valid).[13] This issue will be explored further in the section "Complying with the Law" below.

Developmental Purposes

From the standpoint of individual development, a performance system provides the feedback essential for discussing strengths and areas where performance needs improving—at both the individual and organizational levels. In this way, training and development needs can be highlighted. For example, if, through setting objectives, many supervisors identify that people have to improve their computer literacy skills, then the organization can provide a solution that meets those needs. From this information, the organization may set up a formal training program for all employees. This approach can be better than having each supervisor deal with each person on an individual basis. Without such a step in the system, the manner in which developmental needs are identified can be hit-and-miss.

Regardless of the employee's level of performance, the system provides an opportunity to identify issues for discussion, eliminate any possible problems, and work on ways of achieving high performance. Newer approaches to performance management emphasize training and development and growth plans for employees. A developmental approach recognizes that the purpose of a manager is to support and help the person (or team) achieve results for good organizational performance. Having a sound basis for identifying performance goals, coaching, reviewing, and recognizing performance leads to successful organizations.

Figure 7.1 provides a summary of the purposes of managing performance.

Why Performance Management Systems Sometimes Fail

In actual practice, formal performance management systems sometimes yield disappointing results. Figure 7.2 shows that some of the reasons include the manager believing that it is only for the HR department, or that it is used to punish employees, or it isn't clear what is expected. Further, if a review is used to provide a written assessment for salary action and at the same time to motivate employees to improve their work, the administrative and developmental purposes may be in conflict. As a result, the actual review interview may become a discussion about salary in which the manager seeks to justify the action taken. In such cases, the discussion might have little influence on the employee's future job performance.

As with all HR processes and systems, if the support of top management is lacking, the system will not be successful. Even the best-conceived process will not work in an environment where managers are not encouraged and expected by their superiors to take

FIGURE 7.1 Purposes of Managing Performance

Compensation

- salary increases
- bonuses and pay-for-performance awards

Administrative

- promotion decisions
- transfer decisions
- layoff decisions
- succession planning
- paper trail for documenting HRM actions

Measurement of Performance

- determine accomplishment of goals
- influence employee behaviour
- improve organizational performance

Developmental

- feedback for discussing strengths and areas for improvement
- elimination of potential problems
- identify training needs

their responsibilities seriously in managing performance. To underscore the importance of this responsibility, top management should ensure that managers and supervisors are also part of the overall performance management system and that their performance will be reviewed for how well they are managing their employees' performance.

FIGURE 7.2 Reasons Performance Management Systems Can Fail

1. Performance management is not well defined and may not encourage outcomes.
2. Objectives are not prioritized.
3. The process is complex and not connected to the company strategy.
4. The system is not aligned with business performance.
5. The system isn't designed to adapt as needs change.
6. The system focuses on blame rather than helping employees.
7. Not enough time is spent on planning and communicating.
8. Performance management has competing and different purposes.
9. The focus is on annual review and insufficient ongoing feedback.
10. The performance process does not help employees develop skills and abilities.

Sources: Adapted from Scott Engler, "5 Reasons Your Performance Management Is a Failure," *Executive Board*, February 4, 2014, accessed February 15, 2015, **www.executiveboard.com/blogs/5-reasons-your-performance-management-is-a-failure**; "Why Does Most Performance Management, or Appraisal, Fail?" Performance Management Help Centre, Bacal & Associates, accessed February 14, 2015, **http://performance-appraisals.org/faq/failure.htm**; and Susan M. Heathfield, "Problems with Performance Appraisals: Where Do Managers Go Wrong?" accessed February 14, 2015, **http://humanresources.about.com/od/performance management/f/performance-appraisal-problems.htm?utm_term=performance%20appraisal%20failures&utm_content=p1-main-2-title&utm_medium=sem-sub&utm_source=google&utm_campaign=adid-5816e5a3-ec6d-4835-a574-afc43729d491-0-ab_gsb_ocode-4582&ad=semD&an=google_s&am=broad&q=performance%20appraisal%20failures&dqi=&o=4582&l=sem&qsrc=1&askid=5816e5a3-ec6d-4835-a574-afc43729d491-0-ab_gsb**.

Other reasons performance management systems can fail include the following:

1. Managers feel that little or no benefit will be derived from the time and energy spent on the process.
2. Managers dislike the face-to-face discussion and performance feedback.
3. Managers are not sufficiently adept in setting goals and performance measures, in coaching and supporting, or providing performance feedback.
4. The judgmental role of a review can conflict with the helping role of developing employees.

In many organizations performance management is a once-a-year activity in which the review interview becomes a source of friction for both managers and employees. An important principle of performance management is that continual feedback and employee coaching must be a positive regular activity—be it daily or hourly. The annual or semiannual performance review should be a logical extension of the day-to-day supervision process. For example, Mead Johnson Canada, a subsidiary of Bristol-Myers Squibb, a large pharmaceutical firm, changed its performance management system so that employees receive ongoing reviews. This system now has a future growth and expectations focus with immediate and specific feedback. Furthermore, other companies are encouraging frequent feedback sessions instead of only annually. At Work with HRM 7.1 describes how some companies are making use of more frequent reviews.

One of the main concerns of employees is the fairness of the performance management system, since the process is central to so many HRM decisions. Employees who believe the system is unfair may consider the review interview a waste of time and leave the interview feeling anxious and frustrated. They may also view compliance with the system as mechanical and thus play only a passive role during the interview process. By addressing these employee concerns during the planning stage of the system, the organization will help the performance management system succeed in reaching its goals. Employees can help ensure that the review is fair by being well prepared. This can include keeping track of positive (and negative) feedback from the supervisor and keeping records of courses, workshops, and any other training activities.

Finally, managers can have biases even in a well-run system.[14] For example, managers may inflate reviews because they desire higher salaries for their employees or because higher ratings make them look good as managers. Alternatively, managers may want to get rid of troublesome employees, passing them off to another department by inflating their ratings. Supervisors and managers have to be watchful for the same types of errors in performance reviews as in selection interviews. The supervisor may make decisions about a person's performance based on recent events (the recency error) or judge performance favourably or unfavourably overall by putting emphasis on only one area that is important in the supervisor's mind (the halo error). Likewise, the supervisor may be unwilling to give either extremely low or extremely high assessments and decide to rate everyone as "above average" (the central tendency). A supervisor can also be biased by comparing one employee's performance to another's (the contrast error) instead of assessing the employee against a set of standards.

It is not just biases that can create problems with performance management. Organizational politics and how the manager wants to be perceived can also creep into performance reviews. For example, managers may base the assessment on how they feel about the employee—whether they like the person or not.[15] Or they may want to maintain as much discretion as possible and therefore not use the performance management system as intended. Likewise, they may want to avoid any conflict and therefore delay the annual review for months.[16]

AT WORK WITH HRM 7.1

ISN'T YEARLY GOOD ENOUGH?

Employees and managers frequently indicate their frustration with only doing annual performance reviews. So what is the answer?

Much of the frustration could be reduced if managers spent more time meeting with their staff so that the manager knows what is going on and providing assistance to keep the employees focused on what needs to be accomplished. This can be as simple as asking, "How are things going?" and "What do you need from me?" It is also important to ask probing questions.

Some experts suggest that a manager set aside an hour a day for meeting one-on-one with 3 or 4 employees. It is also suggested that the manager prepare for the meeting and expect employees to do the same. Keep the discussions focused on what is within the employees' control. The manager also needs to use a coaching-type feedback approach.

And while it is important for the manager to provide feedback, it is also necessary to ensure there is more positive than negative feedback. The feedback needs to be ongoing and include praise and thanks for a job well-done.

Managers need to be trained to provide more ongoing coaching and feedback. They do not just automatically know. When managers take the time to check in with employees, it also provides the employee an opportunity to discuss any issues in relation to work, the organization, or even other employees. When managers are appropriately trained on providing effective feedback, both the manager and the employee learn that performance feedback is not a yearly form-driven process, but a management process that keeps everyone's eyes on the ball.

It is also important to be aware of the demographics of the employee population. For example, PricewaterhouseCoopers understands that its young professionals want frequent feedback—annually isn't good enough and won't keep them at the firm.

CRITICAL THINKING QUESTIONS:

1. If you've had work experience, how frequently did your supervisor or manager provide you feedback? Did you feel it was often enough? Why?
2. What other ideas do you have for encouraging managers to provide more frequent feedback to employees?

Sources: Adapted from Harvey Schachter, "The Solution to All Management Problems? Talk with Your Staff," *The Globe and Mail*, January 6, 2015, accessed February 14, 2015, **www.theglobeandmail.com/report-on-business/careers/management/the-solution-to-all-management-problems/article22168929**; Michelle Ray, "The Five Biggest Mistakes Leaders Make with Their Staff," *The Globe and Mail*, November 16, 2014, accessed February 14, 2015, **www.theglobeandmail.com/report-on-business/careers/leadership-lab/the-five-biggest-mistakes-leaders-make-with-their-staff/article21606639**; Brian Kreissl, "Ongoing Performance Management," *Canadian HR Reporter*, September 22, 2014, accessed February 14, 2015, **www.hrreporter.com/articleview/22323-ongoing-performance-management**; and David Ciccarelli, "Why the Annual Performance Review Doesn't Work," *The Globe and Mail*, October 8, 2014, accessed February 14, 2015, **www.theglobeandmail.com/report-on-business/careers/leadership-lab/why-the-annual-performance-review-doesnt-work/article20980895**.

STEPS IN AN EFFECTIVE PERFORMANCE MANAGEMENT SYSTEM

LO4

What are the steps in a performance management system?

The HR department ordinarily has primary responsibility for overseeing and coordinating the performance management system. HR may also design or select a performance management system to use. Managers from the operating departments must also be actively involved, particularly in helping to establish the objectives for the system. Furthermore, employees are more likely to accept and be satisfied with the performance management system when they have the chance to participate in its development. Their concerns about fairness and accuracy in determining raises, promotions, and the like tend to be alleviated somewhat when they have been involved at the planning stage and have helped develop the performance standards. This section describes the key steps for an effective performance management system. Other useful information on performance management can be found at About.com (**http://humanresources.about.com**), Free Management Library (**http://managementhelp.org**), and Development Dimensions International (**www.ddiworld.com**).

About.com
http://humanresources.about.com

Free Management Library
http://managementhelp.org

Development Dimensions International
www.ddiworld.com

Clarifying the Work to Be Done

Before any goals can be established or performance standards identified, it is important to clarify the work to be accomplished. And this is done by identifying the expected outcomes or results and determining how those results will be measured. For example, an expected result for a cook at a fast-food restaurant might be "no food wastage." The supervisor and cook would then decide how this would be measured. It might be measured by determining the number of kilograms of food in the garbage pail or the number of voided customer orders. Note that the clarification step is done jointly with the supervisor and the employee. The key to a good performance management system is the involvement of the employee in the entire process.

Setting Goals and Establishing a Performance Plan

Once the supervisor and employee (or team) are clear on expected results and how those results will be measured, goals must be set. And for the system to really work, these goals must be linked to overall business objectives. For example, an overall business objective for the fast-food restaurant is to reduce costs. Since food costs are a large proportion of overall costs, the restaurant may decide to focus on reducing food costs. Therefore, for the individual employee, cutting down on wasted food will contribute to this, so the goal may be "to reduce food waste by 10% within the next three months." You will note that this is a very specific goal that includes a time frame.

To ensure a strong link to business goals, the supervisor may also need to establish performance measures that are qualitative, such as customer relations, rather than quantitative (e.g., revenue).[17] With the use of both financial results (e.g., cost of food) and soft measures (e.g., customer satisfaction), the results are more strongly linked to the overall restaurant outcomes. This step also involves discussion between both the supervisor and the employee, which leads to greater involvement and commitment to the specific goals.

With the ongoing concern about business ethics, more and more organizations are including standards of performance related to ethics and reviewing ethical behaviour

A key step in performance management is setting specific and measurable goals.

imtmphoto/Shutterstock.com

as part of the performance management system. Ethics in HRM 7.1 discusses what can happen if ethical behaviour/action isn't included in the performance management system.

There are other types of methods, such as trait and behavioural, in addition to goals, which can be used in establishing the performance plan. These will be discussed later in the chapter.

Regular and Frequent Coaching

Coaching sessions are designed to help employees achieve their results. Coaching should not involve fault-finding or blaming. Most people want to do a good job, and, therefore, it is important that a supervisor approach coaching in a helpful and supportive way. If the employee is having difficulty reaching a goal, the supervisor and employee can explore together the reasons why and what can be done to fix the difficulty.

Coaching is also a good way to avoid costs of firing employees and hiring new employees. It is difficult for employees to improve on mistakes if the supervisor does not take the time to help them understand what they need to do. For coaching to be effective, the supervisor needs to listen carefully and ask probing open-ended questions so that conversation and dialogue can occur.[18] Encouraging and supporting an environment where coaching is a partnership, the employee is more likely to develop and gain from the coaching relationship. Read Toolkit 7.1 for some coaching tips.

ETHICS IN HRM 7.1 — WHAT ABOUT THE ETHICS OF OUR SYSTEM?

Most organizations use some type of performance management system to assess the performance of employees. And most of us assume that any system supports ethical behaviours and decisions. But what if it doesn't?

As part of any performance management system, employees have established goals geared to help the company succeed in its business performance. Many of the goals are quantitative measures such as number of items sold in a retail store or number of transactions in a financial institution. Goals such as these often are linked to bonuses—in which an employee earns more when they sell more products or the value of the sales is higher than the goal. Does this always mean the employee is doing the right thing for the customer?

Unfortunately not. For example, when Lloyds Banking employees were encouraged to sell certain financial products, some were inappropriately sold so that the employees would be eligible for higher bonuses. An investigation uncovered the fact that the bank had a culture of employees feeling obligated to achieve short-term goals, even at the expense of behaving ethically.

While it is necessary that employees be assessed on what they accomplish, it is also critical that they be assessed on how the work is accomplished. To make this happen, the performance management system needs to be grounded in the company's values and ethics.

To make ethics part of the system, everyone needs to be trained on what ethical and unethical behaviour and actions look like and then managers need to be trained on how to assess behaviours and actions appropriately. And above all, employees need to feel that the system is fair and that the performance discussions are beneficial to their ongoing development.

A recent incident at Sears Canada in Winnipeg demonstrated the need to ensure a company's code of ethics is linked to the training of employees. An employee was observed making a racial slur against a customer, and Sears' investigation confirmed it could have done more to ensure behaviours toward customers were part of its training and part of its performance system.

CRITICAL THINKING QUESTIONS:

1. What type of performance management system have you experienced?
2. Do you feel that the system incorporated the organization's values and ethics?

Sources: Adapted from Ruth Steinholtz, "Is Your Performance Management System Supporting or Undermining an Ethical Culture?" *HR Bullets*, November 26, 2014, accessed February 15, 2015, **www.hrbullets.co.uk/blog/is-your-performance-management-system-supporting-or-undermining-an-ethical-culture.html**; and Sarah Dobson, "Ugly, Racist Altercation Caught on Video at Sears," *Canadian HR Reporter*, March 24, 2014, accessed February 16, 2015, **www.hrreporter.com/articleview/20613-ugly-racist-altercation-caught-on-video-at-sears**.

Conducting a Formal Review of Performance

Most performance management systems include an annual formal review of the employee's overall performance. This occasion allows both supervisor and employee to consider the employee's accomplishments and to discuss development areas for the next year. It is also usually at this point that the organization uses the results of the annual performance review for salary adjustments.

Since the employee was involved in the original goal setting, and since there has been regular and frequent feedback and coaching, this step is more of a review—there shouldn't be any surprises.

Recognizing and Rewarding Performance

No system will be effective without recognition of accomplishments. Although we usually think of recognition in monetary terms, some non-financial rewards for the employee include the following:

1. being considered for a promotion
2. being given the opportunity to work on a special project
3. being praised by the supervisor
4. being profiled in a business journal about a particular achievement or receiving an award of excellence

These types of rewards cost little or no money. People like to know that their good work and achievements are noticed. For example, employees in a recent study indicated that they've not received any verbal or written appreciation from their supervisor.[19] By careful use of praise and positive feedback, the manager can energize the individual, and the employee can feel that they are making a difference.[20]

TOOLKIT 7.1 EFFECTIVE COACHING

1. Coaching is between two people.
2. Coaching is based on a relationship of trust and respect between the two, not on control.
3. Coaching is about personal development for the person being coached.
4. Coaching is designed to fit the individual needs of each person.
5. Both people must want to be involved in the coaching relationship.
6. The coach asks open-ended questions and doesn't "tell."
7. Coaching draws out the person's potential.
8. Coaching is about helping the person come to their own conclusions: the coach does not impose a solution.
9. Coaching requires active listening and full participation for both people.
10. Coaching is helping the other person learn and become self-sufficient.
11. Coaching is enabling—not training.
12. Coaching is about reflection and conversation.
13. Coaching builds accountability and creates stronger bonds between supervisor and employee.
14. Coaching focuses on real-world situations so that the person can learn and act or behave differently.
15. Coaching provides specific and timely feedback—and includes both positive and constructive comments.
16. Align coaching outcomes with business outcomes.

Sources: Adapted from Susan M. Heathfield, "Tips for Effective Coaching," *About.com*, accessed February 16, 2015, **http://humanresources.about.com/od/coachingmentoring/a/coaching.htm**; Monique Valcour, "A Great Manager Must Be a Great Coach: Here's 5 Tips to Get You Started," *Financial Review*, July 25, 2014, accessed February 17, 2015, **www.brw.com.au/p/leadership/great_manager_must_you_great_coach_vmJ9hRBE5Qie0laWwi3D0L**; "Introduction to Coaching," Society for Industrial and Organizational Psychology, accessed February 17, 2015, **www.siop.org/Workplace/coaching/introduction.aspx**; Jennifer Osborn, "Developing Workplace Coaching Skills," LIScareer.com, accessed February 17, 2015, **www.liscareer.com/osborn_coaching.htm**; and "How Do We Demonstrate Coaching's Effectiveness?" *Workforce*, July 31, 2014, accessed February 17, 2015, **www.workforce.com/articles/20670-how-do-we-demonstrate-coachings-effectiveness**.

Creating an Action Plan

While many performance reviews—formal as well as informal—would not need a structured improvement action plan, there are always situations in which there needs to be a clear understanding between the manager and the employee regarding what is necessary to improve performance. For such a plan to be helpful, any behaviours requiring change need to be clearly identified, expectations about what change looks like need to be clear, and clear time lines need to be set. It is also important that both the manager and employee are clear on what types of supports will be available.[21]

PERFORMANCE REVIEWS

Complying with the Law

Since performance assessments are used as a basis for HRM actions, they must meet certain legal requirements. The legality of any performance management system is measured against criteria of reliability, fairness, and validity. *Reliability* refers to whether performance is measured consistently among the employee participants. *Fairness* refers to the extent to which the system avoids bias caused by any factors unrelated to performance. *Validity* refers to the extent to which the system is job related and accurate. Under the *Charter of Rights and Freedoms*, and other federal and provincial human rights requirements, performance management systems must be, above all, valid. Worker performance must be assessed on the basis of job requirements to ensure legal compliance.

Although currently there are few lawsuits pertaining to performance management systems in Canada, the spillover effect of lawsuits in the United States has prompted organizations to try to eliminate vagueness in descriptions of traits, such as attitude, co-operation, dependability, initiative, and leadership. For example, the trait "dependability" can be made much less vague if it is spelled out as absence of employee tardiness or unexcused absences. In general, reducing room for subjective judgments will improve the entire process.

Employers might face legal challenges to their performance management systems when reviews indicate acceptable or above-average performance but employees are later passed over for promotion, disciplined for poor performance, discharged, or laid off. In these cases, the reviews can undermine the legitimacy of the subsequent decision. And legal challenges can be very costly. For example, if an organization terminated someone due to a downsizing, but then subsequently said it was for poor performance, the company would not be successful in defending its action if the personnel file did not contain a performance review backing that up. More information regarding performance reviews and discipline is discussed in Chapter 9.

Performance reviews should therefore meet the following guidelines:

- Performance ratings must be job-related, with performance standards related to the work as identified through job analysis.
- Employees must be given a written copy of their performance standards in advance of any formal performance review.
- Managers who conduct the review must be able to observe the behaviour they are assessing. This implies having a measurable standard with which to compare employee behaviour.
- Managers and supervisors should be trained to understand their role in managing performance, specifically on (1) how to set goals and performance standards, (2) how to coach and conduct a formal review session, and (3) how to write a review report or use any other written materials associated with the performance system.
- Reviews should be discussed openly with employees and coaching or corrective guidance offered to help poor performers improve their performance.
- An appeals procedure should be established to enable employees to express disagreement with the formal evaluation.

HRM AND THE LAW 7.1 DOES POOR PERFORMANCE INCLUDE ACTIONS AND BEHAVIOURS?

Most people think that poor performance is only about work output. However, poor performance can include any aspect of one's performance—including behaviours and actions.

This was demonstrated very clearly when a truck driver employed by a liquor distribution centre was terminated for harassment and bullying of co-workers. Initially, when the matter was first brought to the attention of the employer, an investigation was conducted. The truck driver had been employed for over 24 years and had had a good work record. When the company hired a female truck driver, the employee began to make derogatory remarks about her in her role as a union committee chair, which escalated to attempted shoving and threats. When both the union and the employer investigated, the employee confirmed that he had been trying to intimidate her and that he had made vulgar comments.

While he did apologize for his behaviour, he continued with this type of comments and actions, not only to the same worker but also to other female workers. He was warned that his performance was unacceptable and that further incidents could lead to termination. Things did not improve and he was eventually terminated.

The union filed a grievance about the employer's action, and the arbitrator concluded that the employee's actions constituted the most serious form of inappropriate workplace behaviour and upheld the dismissal.

On the other hand, in a case involving a railroad, the employer terminated an employee for harassing and verbally abusing other workers in phone calls. An investigation by the employer concluded that while the complaints had no merit, the conduct of the employee was confrontational and adversarial. Again, the union filed a grievance, and the arbitrator concluded that while the insults were inappropriate, they were not threats, and therefore didn't warrant termination. The employee was reinstated with back pay and ordered to undertake anger management.

Source: Adapted from Jeffrey Smith, "B.C. Employer Puts an End to Worker's Ongoing Harassment," *Canadian HR Reporter*, February 15, 2015, accessed February 21, 2015, **www.hrreporter.com/articleview/23592-bc-employer-puts-an-end-to-workers-ongoing-harassment-legal-view**; and Jeffrey Smith, "Worker's Angry Phone Calls Not Just Cause," *Canadian HR Reporter*, February 9, 2015, accessed February 21, 2015, **www.hrreporter.com/articleview/23470-workers-angry-phone-calls-not-just-cause-legal-view**.

Employers must ensure that managers and supervisors document reviews and reasons for subsequent HRM actions. This information may prove decisive should an employee take legal action. An employer's credibility is strengthened when it can support performance results by documenting instances of poor performance. Read HRM and the Law 7.1 to gain an understanding of some other dimensions of poor performance.

Deciding Who Should Provide Performance Information

LO5

Who should provide performance review information?

For many years, the traditional approach to reviewing an employee's performance was to base it solely on information the supervisor had gathered first-hand. However, given the complexity of today's jobs, it is often more realistic to gather information directly from those best acquainted with the person's performance, such as supervisors, the employee being reviewed, peers, team members, subordinates, and customers. The Canadian Institute of Chartered Accountants and the Ontario Ministry of Northern Development and Mines have begun using this approach.

Since supervisors spend much of their time gathering data for and conducting the review, the remainder of this section will focus on that portion of the performance management system.

Manager and/or Supervisor Review

Manager and/or supervisor review
Performance review done by the employee's supervisor

Manager and/or supervisor review has been the traditional approach to assessing an employee's performance. In most instances, supervisors are in the best position to perform this function, although it may not always be possible for them to do so. Managers often complain that they do not have the time to fully observe the performance of employees. These managers must then rely on performance records to review an employee's performance. For example, American Express Canada uses telephone monitors to assess the quality of the communication between a service centre representative and a customer. Employees are aware that they are being monitored for developmental purposes. If such reliable and valid measures are not available, the review may be less than accurate.

Where a supervisor reviews employees independently, the supervisor's superior often makes provision for an analysis of the reviews. Having reviews examined by a supervisor's superior reduces the chance of superficial or biased reviews. Reviews by superiors generally are more objective and provide a broader perspective of employee performance than do reviews by immediate supervisors.

Self-Review

Sometimes employees are asked to assess themselves on some or all aspects of their performance. **Self-review** is beneficial when managers seek to increase an employee's involvement in the review process. Such an approach may require an employee to complete a review form prior to the performance interview. At minimum, this gets the employee thinking about strengths and areas for improvement and may lead to discussions about barriers to effective performance. During the performance interview, the manager and the employee discuss job performance and agree on a final assessment. This approach also works well when the manager and the employee jointly establish future performance goals or employee development plans.

Self-review
Performance review done by the employee being assessed, generally on a form completed by the employee prior to the performance interview

Critics of self-review argue that employees are more lenient than managers in their assessments and tend to present themselves in a highly favourable light. However, one of the authors has found through personal experience that people tend to underrate their own overall performance. Managers might even boost employees' views of themselves.

Subordinate Review

Some organizations use **subordinate review** to give managers feedback on how their subordinates view them. Subordinates are in a good position to provide feedback on their managers, since they are in frequent contact with them and occupy a unique position from which to observe performance-related behaviours such as leadership, oral communication, delegation of authority, coordination of team efforts, and interest in subordinates. However, aspects of performance related to managers' specific job tasks, such as planning and organizing, budgeting, creativity, and analytical ability, are not usually appropriate for subordinate feedback.

Subordinate review
Performance review of a superior by an employee, which is more appropriate for developmental than for administrative purposes

Since subordinate feedback gives employees power over their bosses, the managers themselves may be hesitant to endorse such an approach, particularly when it might be used as a basis for compensation decisions. However, when the information is used for developmental purposes, managers tend to be more open to the idea. Available evidence suggests that when managers heed the advice of their subordinates, their own performance can improve substantially. To ensure that subordinate feedback is as objective as possible, it is important that everyone understand how feedback is written and collected.[22]

Peer Review

Individuals of equal rank who work together are increasingly asked to assess each other. A **peer review** provides information somewhat different from that provided by a superior, since peers often see different dimensions of performance. Peers can readily identify leadership and interpersonal skills along with other strengths and weaknesses of their co-workers. A superior asked to provide input about a server in a restaurant on a dimension such as "dealing with the public" may not have had much opportunity to observe it. Fellow servers, on the other hand, have the opportunity to observe this behaviour regularly.

Peer review
Performance reviews done by one's fellow employees, generally on forms compiled into a single profile for use in the performance interview conducted by the employee's manager

Many believe one advantage of peer input is that it furnishes more accurate and valid information than assessments by superiors. The supervisor often sees employees putting their best foot forward, while those who work with their fellow employees on a regular basis may see a more realistic picture. With peer input, co-workers are asked to provide input on specific areas, usually in a structured, written format.

Despite evidence that peer reviews are possibly the most accurate method of judging employee behaviour, often they are not used. Some of the reasons commonly cited are:

1. Peer reviews can be biased toward or against the employee.
2. Too much pressure is put on reviewers to meet time deadlines.
3. Too many people are involved.
4. Anonymous ratings can be less objective.[23]

When peers are in competition with one another (e.g., sales associates), peer reviews may not be advisable for administrative decisions, such as those relating to salary or bonuses. Also, employers who use peer reviews must make sure to safeguard confidentiality in handling the review forms. A breach of confidentiality can foster interpersonal rivalries, hurt feelings, or hostility among fellow employees.

Team Review

Team review
Performance review, based on TQM concepts, that recognizes team accomplishment rather than individual performance

An extension of the peer assessment is the **team review**. While peers are on equal standing with one another, they may not work closely together. In a team setting, it may be nearly impossible to separate out an individual's contribution. Advocates of team review argue that, in such cases, individual reviews can be dysfunctional since they detract from the critical issues of the team. To address this issue, organizations will occasionally use team reviews to assess the performance of a team as a whole.

A company's interest in team reviews is frequently motivated by its commitment to total quality management (TQM) principles and practices. At its root, TQM is a control system that involves setting standards (based on customer requirements), measuring performance against those standards, and identifying opportunities for continuous improvement. In this regard, TQM and performance reviews are perfectly complementary. However, a basic tenet of TQM is that performance is best understood at the level of the system as a whole, whereas performance reviews have traditionally focused on individual performance.

Customer Input

Customer input
Performance review that, like team review, is based on TQM concepts and seeks information from both external and internal customers

Also driven by quality and customer satisfaction concerns, an increasing number of organizations use internal and external **customer input** as a source of performance review information. While external customers' information has been used for some time to review restaurant, hotel, and car rental company personnel, companies such as FedEx, UPS, and Sears have begun utilizing external customers as well. For example, Sears' customers receive a coupon asking them to call a 1-800 number within the next week. In exchange for answering prerecorded questions on a touchtone phone, they receive $5 off their next purchase. Each call can be linked to a particular transaction (and sales associate) based on the receipt number. With 468 million transactions a year, enough survey data are generated for each sales associate to provide meaningful feedback on such performance measures as service and product knowledge. Customer information can also tell an organization if employees are following procedures. As one example, secret shoppers at the Radisson Hotel Saskatoon provided feedback to hotel management that employees were failing to provide accurate accounting on some customers' bills.

Managers establish customer service measures (CSMs) and set goals for employees that are linked to company goals. Often, the CSM goals are linked to employee pay through incentive programs. Customer survey data are then incorporated into the performance evaluation. By including CSMs in their performance reviews, managers focus on what is important and business results improve. For example, AMF Canada, a manufacturer of automated bakery equipment, uses customer feedback to drive the technology behind its success.[24]

In contrast to external customers, internal customers include anyone inside the organization who depends on an employee's work output. For example, managers who rely on the HR department for recruitment and training services would be candidates for seeking internal customer feedback of that department. For both developmental and administrative purposes, internal customers can provide extremely useful feedback about the value added by an employee or team of employees.

Putting It All Together: 360-Degree Review

As mentioned previously, many companies are combining various sources of performance appraisal information to create multi-person—360-degree—appraisal and feedback systems. Jobs are multifaceted, and different people see different things. As the name implies, *360-degree feedback* is intended to provide employees with as accurate a view of their performance as possible by getting input from all angles: supervisors, peers, subordinates, customers, and the like. Although in the beginning, 360-degree systems were purely developmental and restricted mainly to management and career development, they have migrated to performance appraisal and other HR purposes. Over 90% of Fortune 1000 companies have implemented some form of 360-degree feedback for career development, performance review, or both.

Because the system combines more information than a typical performance appraisal, it can become administratively complex. To handle the amount of information, software has been developed. For example, PerformancePlus and Competency Plus, developed by Exxceed, allow managers and employees to develop performance plans, goals, and objectives, and then track their progress over time. Managers can see all of an employee's goals and action steps on a single screen, and self-appraisals and multiple-rater reviews can be combined into a 360-degree format. After rating an employee's performance on each goal, raters can provide summary comments in three categories: victories and accomplishments, setbacks and frustrations, and general comments. To ensure security, a user ID and password are required, and all the data are captured and saved in the employee's history file. And with the introduction of social media, organizations are making use of the technology to seek input from a variety of sources.[25]

Halogen Software
www.halogensoftware.com

SurveyConnect
www.surveyconnect.com

Figure 7.3 is a graphical depiction of 360-degree input sources.

Software used to help prepare 360-degree feedback systems is available from a number of companies. Among these are Halogen Software (**www.halogensoftware.com**) and SurveyConnect (**www.surveyconnect.com**), which not only give a list of resources for anyone interested in using 360-degree systems but also provide information about "best practices."

FIGURE 7.3 360-Degree Review Information

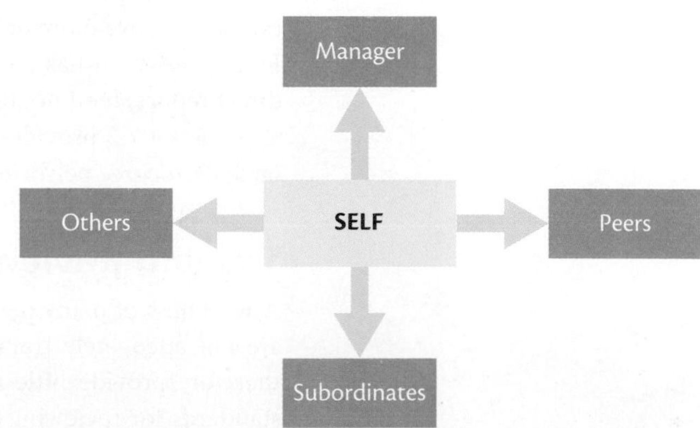

Figure 7.4 lists the pros and cons of 360-degree feedback.

Although 360-degree feedback can be useful for both developmental and administrative purposes, most companies start with an exclusive focus on development. Employees may be understandably nervous about the possibility of everyone "ganging up" on them in their evaluations. If an organization starts with only developmental feedback—not tied to compensation, promotions, and the like—employees will become accustomed to the process and will likely value the input they get from various parties.

Grand Challenges Canada, an organization that focuses on global health projects, makes use of social media to assist in its 360-degree performance review system. The advantage of this,

FIGURE 7.4 Pros and Cons of 360-Degree Feedback

Pros

- Climate of feedback fosters individual growth.
- Input is kept confidential.
- Based upon organizational goals and values.
- Provides behavourial observations from a variety of sources.
- Allows employees to view how others see them.
- Allows different perspectives to be compared.
- Provides ability to assess performance of organization as a whole.
- Helps more with employee development given the different perspectives.

Cons

- System is complex.
- Employees not sufficiently trained to use effectively.
- Employees are biased.
- Doesn't align with organizational culture or goals.
- Employees can have negative feelings.
- Feedback may not be honest.
- Information may not be interpreted consistently from one time to another.

Sources: Adapted from Terri Linman, "360-Degree Feedback: Weighing the Pros and Cons," accessed March 21, 2015, **http://edweb.sdsu.edu/people/arossett/pie/Interventions/360_1.htm**; Mary N. Vinson, "The Pros and Cons of 360-Degree Feedback: Making It Work," accessed March 21, 2015, **www.star360feedback.com/the-pros-and-cons-of-360-degree-feedback-making-it-work**; Neil Kokemuller, "The Pros & Cons of Performance Appraisal Methods," *Houston Chronicle*, accessed March 21, 2015, **http://smallbusiness.chron.com/pros-cons-performance-appraisal-methods-39497.html**; Neil Kokemuller, *eHow.com*, August 14, 2014, accessed March 21, 2015, **www.ehow.com/info_7747937_advantages-disadvantages-360-degree-feedback.html**; and "Kids in the Hall," *Report on Business*, March 2015, 32.

according to one of its program managers, is that input can be collected throughout the year and not just at performance review time. The company also found that it could "tag" people and projects that allowed it to compare the person's self-assessment with the manager's assessment.[26]

Based on the experiences of companies such as Celestica, Allstate Insurance, and Canadian Tire, it appears that 360-degree feedback can provide a valuable approach to performance review. Its success, as with any performance review method, depends on how managers use the information and how fairly employees are treated. Further, it is important to remember that there may be inconsistencies in the feedback depending on the rater. For example, the rater may not have worked with the employee long and so may rate differently than raters who have known the person longer. Research has also indicated that if the rating isn't kept confidential from the employee, the rating might be inflated. In addition, raters may have more or less confidence in the accuracy of their rating if the rating is lower. Finally, research has indicated that the most "accurate" of raters is the boss whereas any direct reports tend not to see much difference between high and low performers.[27]

Toolkit 7.2 provides sample competency descriptors and how they might be assessed on a 360-degree performance review.

Training Reviewers

A weakness of many performance management systems is that managers and supervisors are not adequately trained for setting performance goals or assessing performance and therefore provide little meaningful feedback to subordinates. Because they lack precise standards for reviewing subordinates' performance and have not developed the necessary

TOOLKIT 7.2 SAMPLE 360-DEGREE STATEMENTS WITH DESCRIPTORS

Based on interaction that you have had with the individual, select the level that best describes the individual's performance in each competency area.

Level 4. Consistently demonstrates the behaviour.

Level 3. Usually demonstrates the behaviour.

Level 2. Sometimes demonstrates the behaviour.

Level 1. Rarely demonstrates the behaviour.

Competency 1—Teamwork. Works effectively with others within own department and across departments for benefit of company. Specifically, displays an openness to ideas, works collaboratively with team members, participates in development of the team, celebrates team successes, and treats team members with respect.

Competency 2—Customer service. Shows a commitment to understanding customer needs and strives to exceed their expectations. Specifically, displays knowledge of customer needs, provides exceptional service to customers, exhibits knowledge of products, and shows steady gains in response time without sacrificing positive interaction.

observational and feedback skills, their reviews often become general, unspecific, and meaningless. Therefore, training people who will conduct performance reviews can vastly improve the overall performance management system. Thus it is important that supervisors and managers be trained in how to conduct performance reviews. The training needs to help remove the barriers of time constraints, lack of knowledge, and interpersonal conflicts. Overcoming these barriers makes the review process more effective.

As mentioned earlier (see "Why Performance Management Systems Sometimes Fail"), people may not be made aware of some of the rater errors that can occur. Part of the training needs to include such information as well as the ability to practise giving feedback.

PERFORMANCE REVIEW METHODS

LO6

What are the various performance review methods?

Since the early years of their use by the federal government, methods of reviewing staff have evolved considerably. Old systems have been replaced by new methods that reflect technical improvements and legal requirements and are more consistent with the purposes of a performance management system. In the discussion that follows, you will be introduced to those methods that have found widespread use; methods that are used less frequently will be touched on briefly. Performance review methods can be broadly classified as measuring traits, behaviours, or results; many organizations may incorporate all three into their system.

Trait Methods

Trait approaches to performance reviews are designed to measure the extent to which an employee possesses certain characteristics—such as dependability, creativity, initiative, and leadership—that are viewed as important for the job and the organization in general. Trait methods are popular as they are easy to develop but can be notoriously biased.

Frequently in the trait method, the supervisor is asked to numerically rate the person on the specific characteristics. For example, on the characteristic of "dependable," the supervisor might be asked to rate the person on a scale of 1 to 5, with 1 being unsatisfactory and 5 being exceptional. This is called a **graphic rating scale**, a sample of which is shown in Toolkit 7.3. The supervisor may also be asked to provide a short paragraph commentary on the person's dependability.

Graphic rating scale
A trait approach to performance review whereby each employee is rated according to a scale of characteristics

Behavioural Methods

As mentioned above, one potential drawback of a trait-oriented performance review is that traits tend to be vague and subjective. Behavioural methods have been developed to specifically describe which actions should (or should not) be exhibited on the job. Since behavioural methods are becoming more common, this section describes three approaches that use them: the behavioural checklist method, the behaviourally anchored rating scale (BARS), and behaviour observation scales (BOS).

Behavioural Checklist Method

This method consists of having the supervisor check those statements on a list that are believed to be the characteristics of the employee's performance or behaviour. A checklist developed for computer salespeople might include a number of statements like these:

_____ Is able to explain equipment clearly

_____ Keeps abreast of new developments in technology

_____ Tends to be a steady worker

_____ Reacts quickly to customer needs

_____ Processes orders correctly

Behaviourally anchored rating scale (BARS)
A behavioural approach to performance review that consists of a series of vertical scales, one for each important dimension of job performance

Behaviourally Anchored Rating Scale (BARS)

The **behaviourally anchored rating scale (BARS)** approach consists of a series of five to ten vertical scales—one for each important dimension or component of performance. These components are then given a numerical scale based on critical incidents of on-the-job performance. Toolkit 7.4 displays an example of this for an employee in a service-based industry such as hospitality.

Alina Solovyova-Vincent/E+/Getty Images

A customer service representative may be reviewed on being helpful when using the trait method of performance review.

TOOLKIT 7.3 GRAPHIC RATING SCALE WITH PROVISION FOR COMMENTS

Appraise employee's performance in PRESENT ASSIGNMENT. Check (✔) most appropriate square. Appraisers are *urged to freely use* the "Remarks" sections for significant comments descriptive of the individual.

1. KNOWLEDGE OF WORK: Understanding of all phases of his/her work and related matters	Needs instruction or guidance ☐ ☐ / Has required knowledge of own and related work ☐ / ✔ ☐ Has exceptional knowledge of own and related work Remarks: *Is particularly good on gas engines.*
2. INITIATIVE: Ability to originate or develop ideas and to get things started	Lacks imagination ☐ ✔ / Meets necessary requirements ☐ / ☐ ☐ Unusually resourceful Remarks: *Has good ideas when asked for an opinion, but otherwise will not offer them. Somewhat lacking in self-confidence.*
3. APPLICATION: Attention and application to his/her work	Wastes time Needs close supervision ☐ ☐ / Steady and willing worker ✔ / ☐ ☐ Exceptionally industrious Remarks: *Accepts new jobs when assigned.*
4. QUALITY OF WORK: Thoroughness, neatness, and accuracy of work	Needs improvement ☐ ☐ / Regularly meets recognized standards ☐ / ☐ ✔ Consistently maintains highest quality Remarks: *The work he turns out is always of the highest possible quality.*
5. VOLUME OF WORK: Quantity of acceptable work	Should be increased ☐ ☐ / Regularly meets recognized standards ✔ / ☐ ☐ Unusually high output Remarks: *Would be higher if he did not spend so much time checking and rechecking his work.*

Behaviour Observation Scales (BOS)

A behaviour observation scale (BOS) is similar to a BARS in that both are based on critical incidents. The value of BOS is that it enables the reviewer to play the role of observer rather than judge. In this way, he or she can more easily provide constructive feedback to the employee.

Results Methods

Rather than look at the traits of employees or the behaviours they exhibit on the job, many organizations review employee accomplishments—the results they achieve through their work. Advocates of results methods argue that they are more objective and empowering for employees. Looking at results, such as sales figures, production output, and the like, involves less subjectivity and therefore this method may be less open to bias. Furthermore, this approach often gives employees responsibility for their outcomes, while giving them

TOOLKIT 7.4 EXAMPLE OF BARS FOR SERVICE-BASED INDUSTRY

High	7	Consistently demonstrates exceptional verbal and written communication skills. Demonstrates exceptional sensitivity and empathy. Improves lines of communication throughout hotel.
	6	
	5	Frequently demonstrates exceptional verbal and written communication skills. Correctly assesses and responds to sensitive situations.
Average	4	Facilitates the clear, concise communication of information in appropriate forms in a timely fashion. Adapts communication style to meet the needs of others.
	3	Inconsistent ability to communicate effectively or in a timely manner. Does not always adapt communication style to meet the needs of others.
Low	2	
		Receives and imparts information inaccurately.
	1	

discretion (within limits) over the methods they use to accomplish them. This is empowerment in action. And with ongoing concerns about business ethics, more and more organizations are including standards of performance related to ethics and reviewing ethical behaviour as part of the performance management system. Ethics in HRM 7.1 (earlier in this chapter) discusses how this might be done.

Productivity Measures

A number of results measures are available to use in reviewing performance. Salespeople are reviewed on the basis of their sales volume (both the number of units sold and the dollar amount in revenues). Production workers are reviewed on the basis of the number of units they produce and perhaps the scrap rate or number of defects that are detected. Customer service people are reviewed on the number of customers handled. Executives are frequently reviewed on the basis of company profits or growth rate. Each of these measures directly links what employees accomplish with results that benefit the organization. In this way, results reviews can directly align employee and organizational goals.

Results methods may inadvertently encourage employees to look good on a short-term basis, while ignoring the long-term ramifications. Line supervisors, for example, may let their equipment suffer to reduce maintenance costs. Further, in any job involving interaction with others, it is not enough to simply look at production or sales figures. Factors such as co-operation, adaptability, initiative, and concern for human relations may be important to job success. If these factors are important job standards, they should be added to the review. For productivity measures to be successful, what is being measured must relate to business outcomes.[28]

Management by Objectives

A method that was very popular for a number of years attempted to overcome some of the limitations of results-oriented reviews. Management by objectives (MBO), pioneered by management guru Peter Drucker, focused on employees establishing objectives (e.g., production costs, sales per product, quality standards, profits), through discussion and communication with their superiors and related to the business objectives of the company.[29]

TOOLKIT 7.5 SAMPLE GOAL-SETTING WORKSHEET

Performance Management System

Name		**Performance Period**	
Key Results	Measure	Goal	By When

Over time, as organizations became more mature and management styles actively involved employees in making decisions, the concept of MBO evolved into that of the Balanced Scorecard (see below). However, depending on the maturity and management style of the organization, the principles of MBO can be helpful in involving employees in setting objectives.

Even without an MBO approach, an organization can create a simple goal-setting system. Toolkit 7.5 presents a sample goal-setting worksheet used in organizations. Note the column "Key Results." This is a description of what the goal will look like once it has been achieved. For example, a key result might be "Increased customer satisfaction." That would be measured by the percentage of satisfied customers, and the goal might be "To increase the customer satisfaction level from 75 to 80%."

The Balanced Scorecard

One of the most enthusiastically adopted performance management innovations over the past decade has been the **Balanced Scorecard (BSC)**, developed by Harvard professors Robert Kaplan and David Norton. The BSC is a measurement framework that helps managers translate strategic goals into operational objectives. The generic model, shown in Toolkit 7.6, has four related categories: (1) financial, (2) customer, (3) processes, and (4) learning. The logic of the BSC is that learning and people management help organizations improve their internal processes. These internal processes—product development, service, and the like—are critical for creating customer satisfaction and loyalty. Customer value creation, in turn, is what drives financial performance and profitability.

Balanced Scorecard
A measurement framework that helps managers translate strategic goals into operational objectives

The BSC—which, as mentioned above, evolved from the MBO—enables managers to translate broad corporate goals into divisional, departmental, and team goals in a cascading fashion. The value of this is that each individual can see more clearly how his or her performance ties into the overall performance of the firm.

The effectiveness of a BSC framework is also highly dependent on the culture of the organization. A recent study concluded that organizations that have a high degree of integration among work units, good communication, linkage with employee's performance, and continual review and revision of BSC metrics improve the effectiveness of BSC.[30]

TOOLKIT 7.6 THE BALANCED SCORECARD

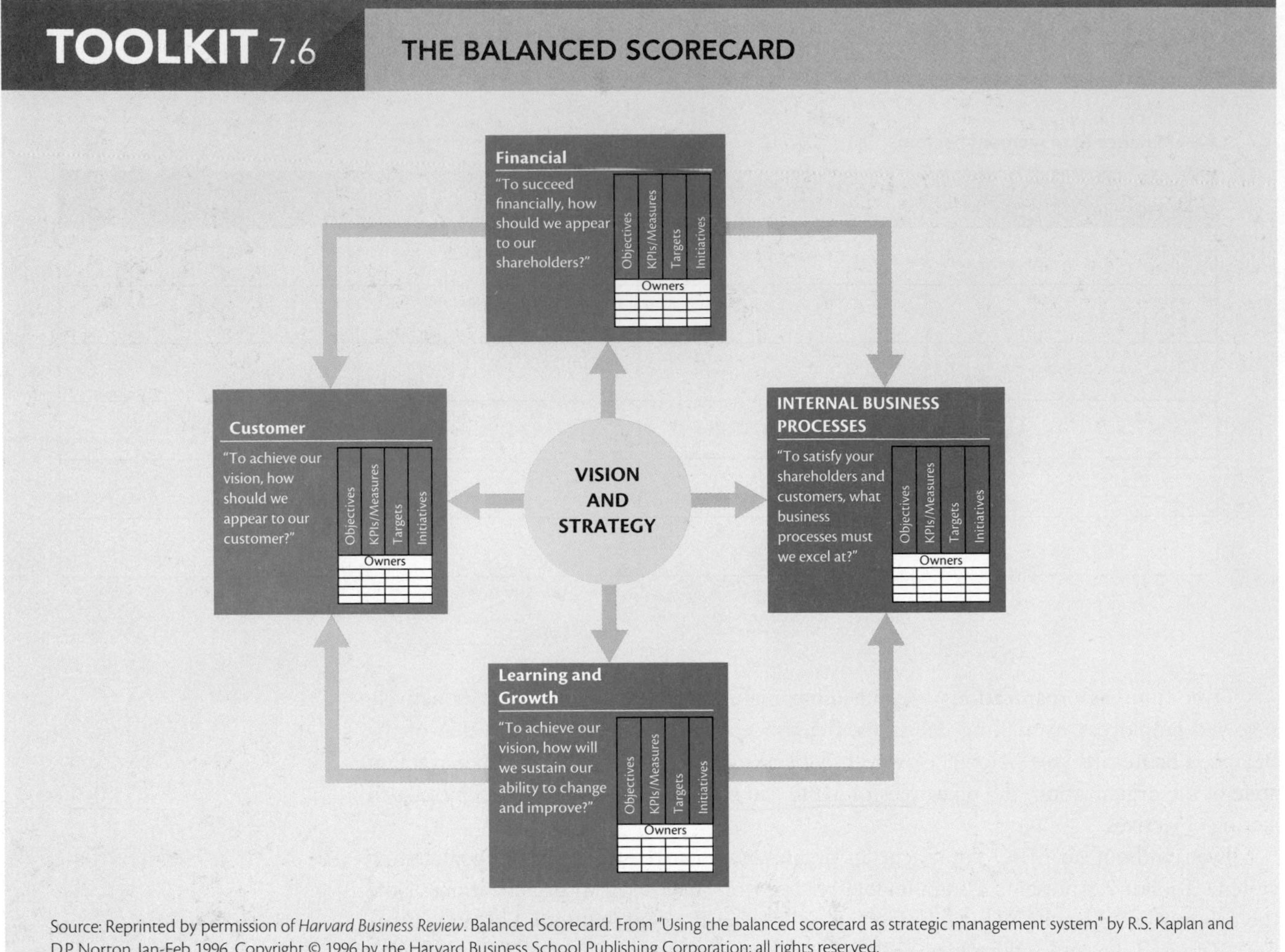

Source: Reprinted by permission of *Harvard Business Review*. Balanced Scorecard. From "Using the balanced scorecard as strategic management system" by R.S. Kaplan and D.P Norton, Jan-Feb 1996.

Which Performance Review Method to Use?

The approach used should be based largely on the purpose of the system. Figure 7.5 provides a helpful summary of the advantages and disadvantages of the specific performance review methods discussed in this section. Note that the simplest and least expensive techniques often yield the least accurate information and focus only on the actual review. While there has been a lot of discussion about which approach to use, whatever method is chosen needs to fit the organization's culture and values.[31] For example, designing and producing a form for supervisors to use in reviewing an employee's performance is relatively simple and inexpensive. On the other hand, implementing a 360-degree performance management system may require a change in management thinking and philosophy. This could take a long time, with many meetings and the involvement of expensive consultants.

The bigger picture here focuses on how the performance management system is used. Having a first-rate approach does no good if the manager simply shoves it in a drawer. Alternatively, even a rudimentary system, used properly, can initiate a discussion between managers and employees that genuinely gives rise to superior performance. These issues are discussed next under the topic of performance review interviews.

While you are being presented with all the positive reasons to have a formal performance management process, some organizations believe such processes are ineffective and are therefore eliminating what has become a once-a-year activity. Read At Work with HRM 7.2 to learn more.

For additional information on current trends in performance management, read Emerging Trends 7.1.

FIGURE 7.5 Summary of Various Review Methods

	Advantages	Disadvantages
Trait Methods	1. are inexpensive to develop	1. have high potential for rating errors
	2. use meaningful dimensions	2. are not useful for employee counselling
	3. are easy to use	3. are not useful for allocating rewards
		4. are not useful for promotion decisions
Behavioural Methods	1. use specific performance dimensions	1. can be time-consuming to develop/use
	2. are acceptable to employees	2. can be costly to develop
	3. are useful for providing feedback	3. have some potential for rating error
	4. are fair for reward and promotion decisions	
Results Method	1. have less subjectivity bias	1. are time-consuming to develop/use
	2. are acceptable to employees and superiors	2. may encourage short-term perspective
	3. link individual performance to organizational performance	3. may use contaminated criteria
	4. encourage mutual goal setting	4. may use deficient criteria
	5. are good for reward and promotion decisions	

AT WORK WITH HRM 7.2

OUT WITH PERFORMANCE APPRAISALS!

As was mentioned earlier, there has been much criticism about performance reviews. Because of this, some organizations, such as Microsoft, PricewaterhouseCoopers, and Juniper Networks have started doing something different.

In a recent study, over 58% of organizations said that performance management processes were not effective use of time. Further, in the same study, leading organizations indicated that they were eliminating the annual cycle and ensuring that managers provide ongoing feedback and coaching for continuous development of employees.

Some of the criticism has been both that meaningful feedback only occurs once a year and that managers were having to force-rank their staff. Critics believe that making sure there is a bell curve on performance rankings undervalued top performers and pushed average performers to the bottom—creating some amount of demotivation. Further, neuroscience research suggests that numerical ranking generates an automatic "fight or flight" response, and any constructive discussions or actions do not register with the employee.

continued

Another reason for the changed view of performance appraisal is that today's workforce, especially certain generations within it, expects regular feedback, coaching, and development. Moving toward a model of continuous coaching and development also means a different role for managers and leaders as well as ensuring that they have the skills to execute this new role. It also means that senior leaders need to have a different mindset regarding employee development. They need to be clear how the model fits into the strategy and the importance of the manager's role in employees' achievement.

CRITICAL THINKING QUESTIONS:

1. Should organizations eliminate the annual performance review? Why or why not?
2. How would you feel about continuous feedback and development? Explain your answer.

Sources: Adapted from Peter Cappelli, "Why We Love to Hate HR ... and What HR Can Do About It," *Harvard Business Review*, July/August 2015, 59; Alex Nabaum, Lisa Barry, Stacia Garr & Andy Liakopoulos, "Performance Management Is Broken," Deloitte University Press, March 4, 2014, accessed July 3, 2015, **http://dupress.com/articles/hc-trends-2014-performance-management**; Julie Bort, "Why Some Microsoft Empoyees Still Fear the Controversial 'Stack Ranking' Employee Review System," *Business Insider*, August 27, 2014, accessed July 3, 2015, **www.businessinsider.com/microsofts-old-employee-review-system-2014-8**; Lucie Mitchell, "Are Annual Appraisals Losing Impact?" *HR Magazine*, November 25, 2014, accessed July 3, 2015, **www.hrmagazine.co.uk/hr/features/1148344/annual-appraisals-losing-impact**; and David Rock, Josh Davis, and Beth Jones, "Kill Your Performance Ratings," *Strategy + Business* 76 (August 2014), accessed July 3, 2015, **www.strategy-business.com/article/00275?gko=c442b**.

EMERGING TRENDS 7.1

1. ***Changes in mindsets regarding managing performance.*** As organizations evolve in their structure and culture, people are re-examining how performance is measured. One of the refreshed thinking is looking at performance management as part of a talent management strategy. As organizations have a multitude of employees and other types of workers (contractors, business process providers, consultants, etc.) more attention is being given to how these individuals have their performance reviewed. This includes ensuring that there are key performance indicators and that there is appropriate oversight.
2. ***Re-examining components of feedback.*** Companies have for some time looked at all components of 360 feedback as the same. However, organizations are questioning whether everyone involved in the 360 is necessary or whether certain key people, such as team leaders, are more critical. Further, organizations are asking different questions to better get at performance-related behaviours.
3. ***Better aligning performance management system with organizational objectives.*** Many companies are reviewing their systems to ensure that the overall organizational objectives are being helped versus hindered by the existing system. The review is looking at not just what is achieved, but "how" to make sure that the company's values are reflected.
4. ***Confirming the strategic importance of managing performance.*** Coupled with a better alignment of any performance management system with the organizations' objectives, companies are reaffirming the strategic performance of managing performance as part of its talent strategy. There is a need to have the necessary capabilities for organization growth and evolution, and one way of identifying and enhancing capabilities is through a well-designed and executed performance management system.
5. ***Putting more emphasis on performance management as an ongoing process.*** As managers become better equipped to coach and mentor, the focus of the

continued

review will be on continual feedback to the employee. Managers will focus on having good conversations with all their staff.

6. ***Using analytical tools***. Just as metrics are used to measure organizational performance, more and more organizations are understanding the importance of using data analysis to measure the link of individual employee performance to organizational performance.

Sources: Adapted from Jennifer Gerves-Keen, "Reimagining Performance Management," *PeopleTalk*, Spring 2015, 16–17; Dorien Van De Mieroop and Eveline Vrolix, "A Discourse Analytical Perspective on the Professionalization of the Performance Appraisal Interview," *Journal of Business Communication* 51, no. 2 (April 2014): 159–182; Ruth Steinholtz, "Is Your Performance Management System Supporting or Undermining an Ethical Culture?" *HR Bullets*, November 26, 2014, accessed April 12, 2015, **www.hrbullets.co.uk/blog/is-your-performance-management-system-supporting-or-undermining-an-ethical-culture.html**; "Fresh Thinking Needed to Fix Performance Management," *Canadian HR Reporter*, April 15, 2014, accessed March 24, 2015, **www.hrreporter.com/blog/Compensation-Rewards/archive/2014/04/15/fresh-thinking-needed-to-fix-performance-management**; Brian Kreissl, "Ongoing Performance Management," *Canadian HR Reporter*, September 22, 2014, **www.hrreporter.com/articleview/22323-ongoing-performance-management**; Laura Wendt, "From Measurement to Ownership: The Evolution and Organizational Implications of Modern Performance Management," *Cornell HR Review*, November 2014: 1–11; Khaled Medini, Catherine Da Cunha, and Alain Bernard, "Tailoring Performance Evaluation to Specific Industrial Contexts," *International Journal of Production Research*, 53, no. 8 (April 2015): 2439–2456; Todd Hunter, "Fixing the Broken Performance Review," *Canadian HR Reporter*, March 23, 2015, 6; Nicola Middlemiss, "Legal Advice—Implementing Performance Objectives," *HR Online*, January 5, 2015; and Marcus Buckingham and Ashley Goodall, "Reinventing Performance Management," *Harvard Business Review*, April 2015, 40–50; and "Building Capabilities for Performance," *McKinsey Insights*, January 2015, accessed April 12, 2015, **www.mckinsey.com//insights/organization/building_capabilities_for_performance**.

PERFORMANCE REVIEW INTERVIEWS

The coaching and review discussions are perhaps the most important parts of the entire performance management process. These discussions give a manager the opportunity to discuss a subordinate's performance record and to explore areas of possible improvement and growth. They also provide an opportunity to identify the subordinate's attitudes and feelings more thoroughly and thus to improve communication.

The format for the coaching sessions and the formal performance review interview will be determined in large part by the purpose of the interview, the type of system used, and the organization of any interview form. Most performance interviews attempt to give feedback to employees on how well they are performing their jobs and on planning for their future development. Interviews should be scheduled far enough in advance to allow the interviewee, as well as the interviewer, to prepare for the discussion. Usually 10 days to 2 weeks' lead time is sufficient.

Conducting the Formal Performance Interview

LO7

What are the characteristics of an effective performance interview?

While there are no hard-and-fast rules for how to conduct a formal review, certain guidelines may increase the employee's acceptance of the feedback, satisfaction with the interview, and intention to improve in the future. Many of the principles of effective interviewing, discussed in Chapter 4, apply to performance review interviews as well. Here are other guidelines that should also be considered.

1. *Ask for a self-assessment*. As noted earlier in the chapter, it is useful to have employees review their own performance prior to the interview. Recent research evidence suggests that employees are more satisfied and view the performance management system as providing more procedural justice when they have input into the process. The interview can then be used to discuss those areas where the manager and the employee have reached different conclusions—not so much to resolve the "truth," but to work toward a resolution of problems.
2. *Invite participation*. The basic purpose of a performance interview is to initiate a dialogue that will help employees improve their performance. Research evidence suggests that participation is strongly related to an employee's satisfaction with the review

feedback as well as that person's intention to improve performance. It is also important to link performance to organizational objectives.[32] During the conversation, it is important that the supervisor actively listen to the employee's comments and responses to questions.

3. *Express appreciation.* Praise is a powerful motivator, and in a performance interview, particularly, employees are seeking positive feedback. Start the interview by expressing appreciation for what the employee has done well. In this way, the employee may be less defensive and more likely to talk about aspects of the job that are not going so well.
4. *Minimize criticism.* If an employee has many areas in need of improvement, managers should focus on those few objective issues that are most problematic or most important to the job.
5. *Change the behaviour, not the person.* Avoid suggestions about personal traits to change; instead, suggest more acceptable ways of performing. For example, instead of focusing on a person's "unreliability," a manager might focus on the fact that the employee "has been late to work seven times this month."
6. *Focus on solving problems.* In addressing performance issues, it is frequently tempting to get into the blame game, in which both manager and employee enter into a potentially endless discussion of why a situation has arisen. The interview should be directed at devising a solution to the problem.
7. *Be supportive.* One of the better techniques for engaging an employee in the problem-solving process is to ask, "What can I do to help?" By being open and supportive, the manager conveys to the employee that the manager will try to eliminate external roadblocks and work with the employee to achieve higher standards.
8. *Establish goals.* Since a major purpose of the performance review is to make plans for further growth and development, it is important to focus the interviewee's attention on the future rather than the past.
9. *Follow up day to day.* Ideally, coaching and ongoing feedback should be a regular part of a manager's job. Feedback is most useful when immediate and specific to a particular situation.
10. *Meeting setup.* Providing feedback is better when done in private and scheduled when both people can take the time to focus on the review.

TrainingABC
trainingabc.com

Sometimes the performance interview may be very difficult—either because the manager is uncomfortable or the employee is unwilling to take responsibility. Therefore, it is very important that the supervisor remain calm and be very clear on what the problem is and what specifically needs to be done differently. You might enjoy the YouTube video "Do's and Don'ts of an Appraisal," which provides some tips in a humorous way (**www.youtube.com/watch?v=WVPpNoRdoEk&feature=related**). For further resources on handling this type of interview, check out the various video clips produced by TrainingABC at **trainingabc.com**.

Improving Performance

In many instances, the performance interview will provide the basis for noting deficiencies in employee performance and for making plans for improvement. Unless these deficiencies are brought to the employee's attention, they are likely to continue until they become quite serious. Sometimes, underperformers do not understand exactly what is expected of them. However, once their responsibilities are clarified, they are in a position to take the corrective action needed to improve their performance.

michaeljung/Shutterstock.com

Retail service people are frequently reviewed on the basis of their interactions with customers.

Identifying Sources of Ineffective Performance

There are many reasons why an employee's performance might not meet the standards. First, everyone has a unique pattern of strengths and weaknesses. In addition, other factors—such as the work environment, the external environment (including home and community), and personal problems—have an impact. See Figure 7.6 for a comprehensive list of possible sources of ineffective performance related to these environments.

It is recommended that a diagnosis of poor employee performance focus on three interactive elements: skill, effort, and external conditions. For example, if an employee's performance is not up to standard, the cause might be a skill problem (knowledge, abilities, technical competencies), an effort problem (motivation to get the job done), some problem in the external conditions of work (poor economy), or some combination of these.

Managing Ineffective Performance

Once the sources of performance problems are known, a course of action can be planned. This action may lie in providing training in areas that would increase the knowledge and/or skills needed for effective performance. A transfer to another job or department might give an employee a chance to become a more effective member of the organization. In other instances, greater attention may have to be focused on ways to motivate the individual.

If ineffective performance persists, it may be necessary to transfer the employee, take disciplinary action, or discharge the person. Whatever action is taken, it should be done with objectivity, fairness, and a consideration for the employee's feelings. More information on dealing with ineffective performance is covered in Chapter 9.

FIGURE 7.6 Sources of Ineffective Performance

Organizational Policies and Practices

- ineffective placement
- insufficient job training
- ineffectual employment practices
- permissiveness with enforcing policies or job standards
- heavy-handed management
- lack of attention to employee needs or concerns
- inadequate communication within organization
- unclear reporting relationships

Job Concerns

- unclear or constantly changing work requirements
- boredom with job
- lack of job growth or advancement opportunities
- management–employee conflict
- problems with fellow employees
- unsafe working conditions
- unavailable or inadequate equipment or materials
- inability to perform the job
- excessive workload
- lack of job skills

Personal Problems

- marital problems
- financial worries
- emotional disorders (including depression, guilt, anxiety, fear)
- conflict between work demands and family demands
- physical limitations, including disabilities
- low work ethic
- other family problems
- lack of effort
- immaturity

External Factors

- industry decline or extreme competition
- legal constraints
- conflict between ethical standards and job demands
- union–management conflict

Summary

1. Define a performance management system.
   - Set of integrated management practices.
2. Explain the purpose of a performance management system.
   - Allows the organization to get the right things done.
   - Helps increase employees' satisfaction with their work and the organization.

3. Describe the management practices necessary for a good performance management system.
   - Setting and communicating clear performance expectations.
   - Clear and specific performance objectives.
   - Supportive and helpful coaching by the supervisor.
   - Focusing on accomplishment of objectives during performance appraisals.
   - Recognizing and celebrating good performance.
4. Identify the steps in an effective performance management system.
   - Clarifying the work (job) to be done.
   - Setting goals and establishing a performance plan.
   - Regular and frequent coaching.
   - Conducting formal review of performance.
   - Recognizing and rewarding performance.
   - Creating an action plan.
5. Describe the different sources of performance review information.
   - Manager or supervisor—able to provide feedback on contribution.
   - Self—provides a personal review of accomplishments.
   - Subordinate—provides a perspective on certain behaviours such as leadership.
   - Peers and team members—able to describe how the person works with others.
   - Customers—provide input about the quality of service.
6. Explain the various methods used for performance reviews.
   - Trait approaches are designed to measure the extent to which an employee possesses certain characteristics.
   - Behavioural methods specifically describe which actions should (or should not) be exhibited on the job.
   - Productivity measures look at results or outputs.
   - The Balanced Scorecard (BSC) is a measurement framework that helps managers and employees translate strategic goals into operational objectives.
7. Outline the characteristics of an effective performance review interview.
   - Ask the employee to review and assess own performance prior to the interview.
   - Invite and encourage active participation by employee in the discussion of performance.
   - Express appreciation for what the employee has done well.
   - Minimize criticism.
   - Change the behaviour, not the person.

Need to Know

- Definition of performance management system
- Purpose and reasons for introducing a performance management system
- The characteristics of an effective performance management system
- Various methods used to gather performance information
- Advantages and disadvantages of various performance review methods
- Guidelines for conducting a performance appraisal interview

Need to Understand

- Link of management practices with performance management systems
- Relationship of organizational performance with performance management systems
- Role the supervisor or line manager plays in the effectiveness of any system
- Relationship of methods to the overall system and the style of management
- Importance of good coaching and interviewing skills for appraising overall performance

KEY TERMS

balanced scorecard 227
behaviourally anchored rating scale (BARS) 224
customer input 220
graphic rating scale 223
manager and/or supervisor review 218
peer review 219
performance management system 208
self-review 219
subordinate review 219
team review 220

REVIEW QUESTIONS

1. Describe the purposes of a performance management system.
2. What are the relationships among performance management systems and selection, training, and development?
3. What are the steps of an effective performance management system?
4. What guidelines are necessary so that performance reviews are legally defensible?
5. Who could provide input on the performance of people working in the following jobs?
   A. Server in a restaurant
   B. Customer service representative in a financial institution
   C. Bus driver
   D. Childcare worker in daycare centre
   E. Grocery store cashier
6. Describe the pros and cons of each of the performance review methods.
7. How do you conduct an effective performance review?

CRITICAL THINKING QUESTIONS

1. In the HRM Close-up, Tyler Gorrel describes the performance management system at GoodLife. How do the steps compare with what is listed in Outcome 4? Is (are) there any step(s) missing? If so, which?
2. Your study group at college has been asked to develop a set of performance standards for use in providing input on the performance of your instructor. What would you include and why?
3. You have just been hired as a customer service representative at a major retail chain store. The branch manager has asked that you work with a small task force to develop an appropriate set of performance standards and an appropriate review method. What would you recommend and why?
4. The delivery department at an organic produce company is responsible for all deliveries to area restaurants, including rush deliveries. Recently the person who assigned the trucks and drivers failed to identify that an urgent order of fresh seafood needed to go to a key client. When this was discovered by the supervisor after the client complained, the person confirmed that this urgent order was not noted. This was not the first time a shipment had not been properly checked. The supervisor was also aware that during the employee's vacation, the replacement worker had been able to perform all the duties without any difficulty. Explain how a performance management system might have prevented such a situation.
5. You've just started working at a high-end grocery store in a large city. The store manager wishes to develop a graphic rating scale for cashiering staff. Identify three critical areas of the job (e.g., "interactions with customers") and develop an appropriate descriptive scale for each area.
6. Your friend works as a supervisor in a small credit union and has asked your advice on how to give feedback to a staff member who did not handle a customer request particularly well. What suggestions would you give?

DEVELOPING YOUR SKILLS

1. Working in groups of 2 or 3, develop a list of suggestions for use when involved in a coaching situation. When done, review your list with another group. What was similar? What was different?
2. On an individual basis, use the worksheet shown in Toolkit 7.5 to establish at least 2 goals in relation to this course. After completing the worksheet, pair up with another student. Review and critique each other's work. In particular, look for realistic measurements and dates of completion.
3. Working in pairs, access the performance appraisal site of Business Balls at **www.businessnewsdaily.com/5366-performance-review-tips-for-bosses.html**. Click on the sample performance appraisal form template. Review the form and determine if you would use it and why.
4. Working in groups of 4, review the following descriptions of 3 different employees. Describe the possible causes of poor performance in each case. Then pair off and create a role-playing scenario to practise giving performance feedback. (For assistance, review the role-playing information in Chapter 6.) While one pair conducts the performance feedback session, the other pair is asked to observe and then provide feedback to the role-playing pair.
   A. *Carl Spackler* is the assistant greens keeper at Bushwood Country Club. Over the past few months, members have been complaining that gophers are destroying the course and digging holes in the greens. Although Carl has been working evenings and weekends to address the situation, the problem persists. Unfortunately, his boss is interested only in results. Because the gophers are still there, he contends Carl is not doing his job. He has accused Carl of slacking off and threatened his job.
   B. *Sandeep Dhillon* works in research and development for a chemical company that makes non-nutritive food additives. His most recent assignment has been the development of a non-stick aerosol cooking spray, but the project is way behind schedule and seems to be going nowhere. CEO Frank Shirley is decidedly upset and has threatened that if things don't improve, he will suspend bonuses this year just like he did last year. Sandeep is dejected, because without the bonus he won't be able to take his family on vacation.
   C. *Soon Tan* is the host of a local television talk show called *Morning Winnipeg*. Although she is a talented performer and comedian, Soon has an unacceptable record of tardiness. The show's producer, David Bellows, is frustrated, because the problem has affected the quality of the show. On several occasions, Soon was unprepared when the show went on the air. Bellows has concluded that Soon is not a morning person and has thought about replacing her.
5. Access **www.surveyconnect.com**. Click the link "ActiveView 360 Demos" and watch the long-version demo and the 360-feedback process demo. Would such a system be easy or difficult to implement in an organization? Why?
6. Access the *Business News Daily* "Employee Performance Reviews: Tips for Bosses" at **www.businessnewsdaily.com/5366-performance-review-tips-for-bosses.html.** Write a one-page summary of the key tips and how those tips compare to any in the textbook.
7. Access the HR Council site for nonprofit organizations (**www.hrcouncil.ca**) and click "HR Toolkit," then "Keeping the Right People" and "Performance Management." Review the information and prepare a one-page summary explaining how the information would help a small nonprofit or small business owner deal with performance management.

SurveyConnect
surveyconnect.com

Business News Daily
www.businessnewdaily.com

HR Council
www.hrcouncil.ca

CASE STUDY 1

Results Count!

What if all organizations focused their performance approaches to results? Would that work in all cases?

It does work at Mabel's Labels, an Ontario company that designs, manufactures and sells waterproof labels for identifying personal belongings. In its brief 13 years in business, it has expanded into Walmart in both Canada and the United States. Recognizing that people have many priorities in their lives—personal and work—the company has ensured that its business success is measured by results. This means that individual performance is also measured by results. In this way, Mabel's people can work at almost any location. To quote one of them, "Work is what you do, not where you go."

Every week, staff determine where they will work. In making the decision, consideration is given to whether the team's needs are being met, and whether the person's own goals and deliverables can be met. One individual indicates that their best design work is done when alone; however, this same person expressed the value of office collaboration in coming up with design ideas.

Does such a focus create a culture of results only? Not according to the employees. People get together outside of work for socializing as well as volunteering for such things as food drives and helping at a local charity for seniors.

The company's approach to performance and employee engagement earned it an award in Canada's Top 100 Small & Medium Employers for 2015.

Sources: Adapted from "2015 Canada's Top Small & Medium Employers," *The Globe and Mail*, March 2015; and Mabel's Labels, **www.mabelslabels.com**.

Questions:

1. Would a results focus work in a financial services institution? Why or why not?
2. If Mabel's Labels decided to use a different approach to performance, what approach would you suggest? Why?

CASE STUDY 2

Will a New Performance System Work?

At the beginning of 2014, a large graphics and printing company in Winnipeg decided that its current performance management system was not meeting its expectations. The company had 5 sites throughout the Winnipeg area and 175 employees providing services to individuals to and small and medium-sized companies.

The existing system had the following components:

1. The review was done once per year.
2. The employee had to develop a written document outlining accomplishments.
3. The manager reviewed the employee's accomplishments, made an assessment, and assigned a rating from 1 to 5, with 5 being "superior" and 1 being "unsatisfactory."

4. Pay adjustments were tied to the rating.
5. Feedback to the employee about performance was done at the same time as the pay adjustment.

While this approach had been acceptable for a number of years, the company began to get complaints from both managers and employees. Managers were restricted in what they could reward for superior performance, and as a result everyone got the same pay adjustment. In fact, in a recent employee engagement survey, the issue of the company's approach to performance management was severely criticized.

The company decided it needed a new system, and put together a task force representing managers and employees from all its different sites. Everyone wanted a system that would provide ongoing feedback and that included goals and developmental plans.

With members of the task force communicating with all the employees regularly, the new performance management system became a reality and was ready for implementation in early 2015. The components of the new system included

- a meeting between the manager and employee to develop and agree to performance goals and personal and professional development plans at the beginning of each calendar year
- reviews of performance goals on a quarterly basis with feedback from the manager on accomplishments as well as discussions on the progress of development plans
- a formal review of the goals, accomplishments, and development plan at the end of the year, also the completion of the performance cycle

The formal review also includes the preparation of a written assessment by both the manager and the employee that is discussed at the review meeting. If there are differences regarding the manager's and employee's perceptions of accomplishments, the meeting is also used to develop a common understanding. Personal and professional development plans are reviewed with a preliminary discussion about plans for the next performance year.

Discussions regarding pay adjustments occur in a separate meeting about a month later, when the manager can better explain the reasons behind the adjustments.

Is the new system working? The answer seems to be yes. According to the most recent employee engagement survey, 85% of employees thought the new system was fair; 80% felt that they better understood on what basis pay adjustments were made; and 82% believed their career development was effectively handled.

Questions:

1. How do you think managers have responded to the new system and why?
2. What is key to the effectiveness of this new system?
3. What might be some negative aspects of this new system?
4. What might the emphasis on development plans mean for promotions?

NOTES AND REFERENCES

1. Sarah Dobson, "Healthy Cultures, Reduced Costs," *Canadian HR Reporter*, November 17, 2014, accessed February 14, 2015, www.hrreporter.com/articleview/22808-healthy-cultures-reduced-costs.
2. Robert Bacal, "What Is the Point of Performance Appraisal," accessed February 14, 2015, http://work911.com/articles/pointperformance.htm.
3. Brian Kreissl, "Ongoing Performance Management," *Canadian HR Reporter*, September 22, 2014, accessed February 14, 2015, www.hrreporter.com/articleview/22323-ongoing-performance-management.
4. Ron Ashkenas, "Stop Pretending That You Can't Give Candid Feedback," *Harvard Business Review*, February 28, 2014.
5. Ken Blanchard, Vicki Stanford, and David Witt, "Singing the Praises of Praises," *Workforce*, April 20, 2014, accessed February 14, 2015, www.workforce.com/articles/print/20375-singing-the-praises-of-praises.
6. Ibid.
7. Zanina Kirovska and Nedzmije Qoku, "System of Employee Performance Assessment, Factor for Sustainable Efficiency of Organization," *Journal of Sustainable Development* 5, no. 11 (December 2014): 25–51.
8. Robert C. Liden, Sandy J. Wayne, Chenwei Liao, and Jeremy D. Meuser, "Servant Leadership and Serving Culture: Influence on Individual and Unit Performance," *Academy of Management Journal* 57, no. 5 (2014): 1434–1452.

accessed February 14, 2015, http://smallbusiness.chron.com/form-reliability-affects-employee-performance-17633.html and Shane Thornton, "The Importance of Reliability in Performance Appraisals," *eHow*, accessed February 14, 2015, http://www.ehow.com/about_5445066_importance-reliability-performance-appraisals.html.

9. Michelle Berg, "The demise of the annual review, "*Canadian HR Reporter*, December 1, 2014, accessed February 14, 2015, www.hrreporter.com/articleview/22954-the-demise-of-the-annual-review.
10. Claudine Kapel, "Getting your compensation programs back on track," *Canadian HR Reporter*, January 6, 2014, accessed February 14, 2015, www.hrreporter.com/blog/Compensation-Rewards/archive/2014/01/06/getting-your-compensation-programs-back-on-track.
11. Brian Kreissl, "Ongoing performance management," *Canadian HR Reporter*, September 22, 2014, accessed February 14, 2015, www.hrreporter.com/articleview/22323-ongoing-performance-management.
12. Ray Williams, "Why performance appraisals need to be scrapped," *Financial Post*, February 22, 2014, accessed February 14, 2015, http://business.financialpost.com/2014/02/22/why-performance-appraisals-need-to-be-scrapped/.
13. Amanda L. Webster, "What Form of Reliability Affects Employee Performance?" Houston Chronicle, accessed February 14, 2015, http://smallbusiness.chron.com/form-reliability-affects-employee-performance-17633.html and Shane Thornton, "The Importance of Reliability in Performance Appraisals," *eHow*, accessed February 14, 2015, http://www.ehow.com/about_5445066_importance-reliability-performance-appraisals.html.
14. Zabeen Hirji and Stephen Shea, "Overcoming Hidden Biases at Work," *Canadian HR Reporter*, May 5, 2014, accessed February 14, 2015, www.hrreporter.com/articleview/21034-overcoming-hidden-biases-at-work.
15. Dane Jensen, "How Do You Manage Someone You Don't Like?" *Canadian HR Reporter*, February 9, 2015, accessed February 15, 2015, www.hrreporter.com/articleview/23468-how-do-you-manage-someone-you-dont-like.
16. Susan M. Heathfield, "Performance Appraisals Don't Work," *About.Com*, accessed February 15, 2015, http://humanresources.about.com/od/performanceevals/a/perf_appraisal.htm.
17. Jill Avery, Susan Fournier, and John Wittenbraker, "Unlock the Mysteries of Your Customer Relationships," *Harvard Business Review*, July/August 2014, HBR Reprint R1407E.
18. Monique Valcour, "A Great Manager Must Be a Great Coach: Here's 5 Tips to Get You Started," *Financial Review*, July 25, 204, accessed February 17, 2015, www.brw.com.au/p/leadership/great_manager_must_you_great_coach_vmJ9hRBE5Qie0IaWwi3D0L.
19. Claudine Kapel, "Lack of Acknowledgement Eroding Job Satisfaction," *Canadian HR Reporter*, October 15, 2014, accessed February 17, 2015, www.hrreporter.com/blog/Compensation-Rewards/archive/2014/10/15/lack-of-acknowledgement-eroding-job-satisfaction.
20. Claudine Kapel, "Are Your Employees Feeling the Love," *Canadian HR Reporter*, March 31, 2014, accessed February 17, 2015. www.hrreporter.com/blog/Compensation-Rewards/archive/2014/03/31/are-your-employees-feeling-the-love.
21. Nicole Fallon, "Employee Performance Reviews: Tips for Bosses," *Business News Daily*, January 1, 2015, accessed February 17, 2015, www.businessnewsdaily.com/5366-performance-review-tips-for-bosses.html.
22. Teresa Ewington, "Poor Performance," *Training Journal*, October 2014, 27–30.
23. T.H.P. Gould, "Do We Still Need Peer Review? An Argument for Change," *Journal of the Association for Information Science and Technology* 65, no. 1 (2014): 209–213.
24. Janice Hoppe, "Mixing it Up," *Food & Drink*, Spring 2015, 108–109.
25. Edie L. Goldberg, "Performance Management Gets Social," *HR Magazine*, August 2014, 35–38.
26. Liz Bernier, "5 Areas Where Social Media Shines," *Canadian HR Reporter*, January 27, 2014, accessed March 21, 2015, www.hrreporter.com/articleview/20016-5-areas-where-social-media-shines.
27. Robert W. Eichinger and Michael M. Lombardo, "Patterns of Rater Accuracy in 360-Degree Feedback," accessed March 21, 2015, www.star360feedback.com/patterns-of-rater-accuracy-in-360-degree-feedback.
28. Nikhat Afshan, Diganata Chakrabarti, and J.S. Balaji, "Exploring the Relevance of Employee Productivity-Linked Firm Performance Measures," *Journal of Transnational Management* 19, no. 1 (2014): 24–37.
29. Marife C. Posadas, "Converlogical Management Theory: Towards the Development of the Communicative Competence in an Organization," *DLSU Business & Economics Review* 24, no. 1 (July 2014): 45–58.
30. Yuanhong Chen, Zengbiao Yu, and Thomas W. Lin, "How Zysco Uses the Balanced Scorecard," *Strategic Finance* 97, no. 1 (January 2015): 27–36.
31. "Performance Management Orientation Guide 2014," *Workforce*, March 11, 2014, accessed March 21, 2015, www.workforce.com/roadmaps/151-performance-management/155-plan/20325-performance-management-orientation-guide-2014
32. "Building Capabilities for Performance," McKinsey Insights, January 2015, accessed March 21, 2015, www.mckinsey.com//insights/organization/building_capabilities_for_performance.

8 Rewarding and Recognizing Employees

LEARNING OUTCOMES

After studying this chapter, you should be able to

1. Explain an organization's strategic concerns in developing a strategic rewards program.
2. Identify the various factors that influence the setting of pay levels.
3. Describe the major job evaluation systems.
4. Illustrate the compensation structure.
5. List the types of incentive plans.
6. Explain the employee benefits that are required by law.
7. Describe voluntary benefits.

OUTLINE

HRM CLOSE-UP

"There's nothing more rewarding to any leader than managing to build a winning team."

At her Walmart store in New Westminster, British Columbia, manager Rajwinder Nijjer has a knack for recognizing and rewarding talent. On occasion, she even comes into the store at 4:00 a.m. to make personal contact with employees on the night shift so that she can get to know them and how they contribute to the store's success. Even with seven assistant managers who have direct responsibility for staff, Nijjer still feels strongly about making personal contact. "I didn't realize, until I was a store manager, how much I impact people directly and indirectly," says "RJ," as she's known by staff.

In a retail environment, where many employees are making minimum wage, reward and recognition programs play a key role in retaining a good workforce. With recognition programs, Nijjer says, "You can feel and sense your team's excitement. People will care and show more interest in profitability of the business. Rewards and recognition offer a solid foundation for building a winning team."

"People like to be recognized for a good job," Nijjer continues. "And I strongly believe that the quicker performance is recognized, the more impact it will have on your business and on the associate's personal development." To do this, Nijjer makes a point of spending at least 10 to 15 minutes per day with five different employees every day. She will work alongside them and get to know them as they get to know her. Then, a couple of days later, she will approach each of them and offer words of encouragement that recognize their effort and contribution on the job.

Walmart has corporately sponsored recognition programs such as Shining Star, in which staff can nominate fellow staff members via e-mail. Submissions are read aloud at meetings held three times daily to accommodate all work shifts. Once monthly, a star is recognized with a $75 gift card. Nijjer says this is a simple way to recognize staff and share success stories. It's especially effective for staff who work hard but might not yet be interested in making a career in retail. It helps to motivate staff and increase the ownership they take in the store's success. It may even influence their interest in a future at the company.

Nijjer also implements her own programs at the store, such as Coffee with the Coach, in which she dedicates time one-on-one to further recognize and reward staff. "Reward people who show initiative, who experiment, and who pursue innovation," she advises. "And be very specific when appreciating someone."

Several years ago, Nijjer hired a man for the part-time job of unloader. At his 90-day evaluation, she let him know how confident she was in his work ethic and his potential for a future with the company. He went on to master four key positions and is now her administrative manager. When Nijjer sent a congratulatory note to her management team after a store-wide initiative, the employee approached Nijjer and said "RJ, I am going to frame this e-mail of yours. I cannot believe that I am a part of management today only because you recognized my ability and helped me develop my skills. Now I'm in a position to afford a car and better living standards."

Courtesy of Rajwinder Nijjer

Rajwinder Nijjer.

Recognizing team effort is also important to Nijjer. "You need to keep the team together," she says, recalling the store's recent expansion and reopening. "In a project like that, we had two teams of 15 people overseeing the expansion and it was really important to recognize everyone together." She adds, "There's nothing more rewarding to any leader than managing to build a winning team."

Source: Courtesy of Rajwinder Nijjer

INTRODUCTION

You will note from the HRM Close-up that rewards and recognition are big issues not just for employees but also for the managers of those employees. Although companies may set guidelines about how much each position or job is worth, it is the manager who has to implement those guidelines. It is the manager who will make decisions about who gets paid what. And it is the manager's everyday interactions with the employees that influence how the employees feel about the organization. Therefore, it is important for the manager and the supervisor to have an understanding of rewards and recognition, and its link to the success of the organization. It is also important for the manager to understand how compensation is derived and what factors influence the setting of the wage and benefits structure.

Literature and research indicate that important work-related variables leading to job satisfaction—besides interesting work, alignment of employee goals and organizational goals, participative management, and flexibility in work practices—are rewards and recognition, particularly in the form of wages and benefits, supportive work environment, demonstrated appreciation from supervisor, and the ability to enhance skills and capabilities.[1] While other things might contribute, not many employees would continue working were it not for the money they earn. Employees want reward and recognition systems that are fair and commensurate with their skills and expectations. Compensation, therefore, is a major consideration in HRM. As mentioned earlier, the effectiveness of the manager has a large impact on an employee's job satisfaction, and it is usually the manager who is first to deal with any concerns or issues regarding compensation. While an HR professional might be responsible for gathering compensation information and developing approaches to how the organization approaches compensation, the manager typically makes decisions on how much a person is compensated. Further, with the continuing sluggish economy, the Conference Board of Canada indicates that due to falling oil prices and economic uncertainty many Canadian organizations have lowered their base salary increases.[2]

Direct compensation
Employee wages and salaries, incentives, bonuses, and commissions

Indirect compensation
All other forms of rewards such as extended health and dental plans, and other, similar programs and plans

Both managers and scholars agree that the way rewards are allocated among employees sends a message about what management believes is important and the types of activities it encourages. Furthermore, for an employer, total rewards (direct and indirect) constitute a sizable operating cost. In manufacturing firms, compensation is seldom as low as 20% of total expenditures, and in service enterprises it often exceeds 80%. A strategic rewards program, therefore, is essential so that compensation can serve to motivate employee production sufficiently to keep labour costs at an acceptable level.

While the focus of this chapter is on pay and benefits, it is important to state that many organizations think about and create "reward strategies." The thrust of this approach is to develop an organizational mindset to recognize and reward people with links to the business strategy.[3] In doing so, organizations will tend to have components of the rewards program, particularly direct compensation, that are tied to the success of the organization and to the contributions of that success through individual (or team) performance.

Conference Board of Canada
www.conferenceboard.ca

REWARDS AS PART OF COMPANY STRATEGY

LO1

What are the strategic organizational concerns when developing a rewards program?

It is important to know that employee recognition and rewards include all forms of pay, rewards, and recognition received by employees for the performance of their jobs. **Direct compensation** encompasses employee wages and salaries, incentives, bonuses, and commissions. **Indirect compensation** comprises the many benefits supplied by employers, such as extended health and dental plans, life insurance coverage, and *non-financial compensation* that includes employee recognition programs, rewarding jobs, and flexible work hours to accommodate personal needs. Direct and indirect compensation are collectively referred to as "total compensation" or **total rewards**. This latter phrase helps communicate to employees that their compensation doesn't have just a monetary value, but that it includes other forms of recognition and reward.

Total rewards
Everything that the employee feels is of value in the employment relationship

Companies structure their rewards in ways that enhance employee motivation and growth while aligning the employees' efforts with the objectives, philosophies, and culture of the organization. Designing the rewards and recognition system goes beyond determining what direct and indirect compensation to provide employees. Research has shown that companies that make the rewards strategy a part of the overall organizational framework have better performance than those that don't.[4] This finding is a compelling argument for the organization to take into consideration what employees see as important in the reward equation.

Looking at the reward system in a strategic fashion serves to mesh the overall rewards for employees with specific business objectives. Such a strategic approach can help the organization remain competitive.[5] For example, in the recruitment of new employees, the overall rewards for jobs can increase or limit the supply of applicants. Employers have adopted special reward strategies to attract job applicants with highly marketable skills, such as high-tech workers, and engineers and scientists with financial knowledge and good people skills. Organizations also use rewards to retain people with scarce skills. According to the 2015 report from the Hay Group (**www.haygroup.com**) regarding reward trends, there was still concern about retaining people with critical skills no matter what the economic climate.[6] This problem was further reinforced by a study conducted by Deloitte: it identified that the #2 issue facing Canadian business was the capability gaps that exist in the workforce.[7]

Hay Group
www.haygroup.com

If rewards are high, creating a large applicant pool, then organizations may choose to raise their selection standards and hire better-qualified employees. This, in turn, can reduce training costs for the employer. When employees perform at exceptional levels, their performance assessments may justify an increased pay rate. For these reasons and others, an organization should ensure that it has a systematic way to manage employee rewards that is linked to business performance. Recent research has demonstrated a strong link between a longer-term perspective on reward systems (for that particular organization) and achieving strong business results.[8]

It is important to remember that the concept of "total rewards" is a broader set of elements and includes not only the tangible rewards of pay, benefits, etc., but also factors such as career and development opportunities, work climate/culture, and work–life balance.[9] It is also important that the total rewards system be transparent to all employees. For example, McDonald's redesigned its program so that there was a closer link to rewards and performance and that all employees were aware of the change and why.[10] At Work with HRM 8.1 discusses the importance of communicating the total rewards program and its various components.

Linking Rewards to Organizational Objectives

Rewards have been revolutionized by heightened domestic competition, globalization, increased employee skill requirements, and new technology. Therefore, an outcome of today's dynamic business environment is that managers are needed to change their reward philosophies from paying for a specific position or job title to rewarding employees on the basis of their individual competencies or group contributions to organizational success. A recent study showed that 81% of responding organizations listed *improving employee's focus on achieving business goals* as a significant objective influencing reward changes (see Figure 8.1). A total rewards program, therefore, must be tailored to the needs of the organization and its employees. And in doing so, it is important to ensure that employees feel they are being rewarded.

AT WORK WITH HRM 8.1

DOES THE REWARD SYSTEM MAKE SENSE?

Many organizations structure their rewards systems to ensure employees are satisfied and motivated. But is that good enough? What about something as simple as the actual pay amount?

These are not easy questions, nor are the answers simple. Many factors go into structuring a company's reward system. A study by the Hay Group in 2015 indicated that it is important for the organization to actually benchmark its reward system to ensure a variety of factors are considered. Among them are:

- How aligned is the reward system with the business strategy?
- Are the total rewards above or below your competition?
- What is the number of employees compared to your competition?
- How motivated are your employees by the reward system?
- How aligned is your performance management system with the rewards system?

While a total rewards system can go a long way in satisfying employees, if the base salary isn't at a certain level, no amount of additional items in a reward system can make up for it. A number of studies and polls have determined that if the amount in 2015 dollars is $50,000 per year, employees are satisfied and feel successful. And it is also important that the organization be open and transparent about the rewards structure. This includes ensuring that employees know what the salary ranges are for any particular position. In this way, employees can be aware of opportunities for career advancement. Further, by being more open about the rewards structure, employees may feel more trusting of the employer.

CRITICAL THINKING QUESTIONS:

1. If you are working, do you know the value of your total rewards? Would you think differently about the organization if you did?
2. Do you think that being provided with information about your total rewards would encourage you to remain with an employer? Why or why not?

Sources: Adapted from David Hoad and Nathalie Olds, "Finding Value in Rewards," *Canadian HR Reporter*, January 26, 2015, 23; Liz Bernier, "Putting a price tag on employee satisfaction, *Canadian HR Reporter*, November 3, 2014, 6; and Karl Aboud, "How much do you pay staff," *Canadian HR Reporter*, May 5, 2014, 11.

Recent research suggests that there are five components of a total rewards program: compensation, benefits, work–life balance, recognition of performance, and learning and development and opportunities.[11]

Fundamental to the framework of total rewards is the compensation component. It is not uncommon for organizations to establish specific goals for aligning their objectives with their compensation program.[12] Formalized compensation goals serve as guidelines for

FIGURE 8.1 Significant Goals Driving Pay and Reward Changes

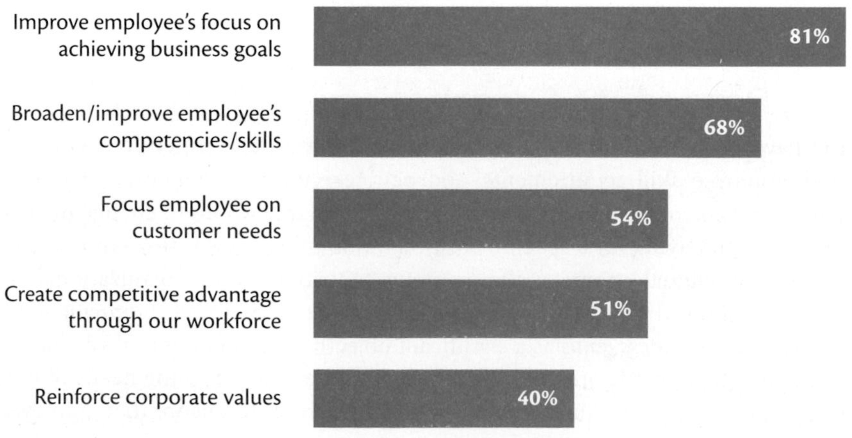

managers to ensure that wage and benefit policies achieve their intended purpose. Some of the more common goals are the following:

1. To reward employees' past performance.
2. To remain competitive in the labour market.
3. To maintain salary equity among employees.
4. To mesh employees' performance with organizational goals.
5. To control the compensation budget.
6. To attract, motivate, and retain staff.[13]
7. To influence employee work behaviours and job attitudes.[14]

To achieve these goals, specific actions or steps must be taken. Three areas of action are discussed below.

The Motivating Value of Compensation

Pay is a quantitative measure of an employee's relative worth. For most employees, pay has a direct bearing not only on their standard of living, but also on the status and recognition they may be able to achieve both on and off the job. Since pay represents a reward received in exchange for an employee's contributions, it is essential that the pay be equitable in relation to those contributions. It is also important that an employee's pay be equitable in relation to what other employees are receiving for their contributions.

Equity can be defined as anything of value earned through the investment of something of value. Equity theory is a motivation theory that explains how employees respond to situations in which they feel they have received less (or more) than they deserve.[15] Central to the theory is the role of perception in motivation and the fact that individuals make comparisons. The theory states that individuals form a ratio of their inputs (abilities, skills, experiences) in a situation to their outcomes (salary, benefits) in that situation. They then compare the value of that ratio with the value of the input/output ratio for other individuals in a similar class of jobs either internal or external to the organization. If the value of their ratio equals the value of another's, they perceive the situation as equitable and no tension exists. However, if they perceive their input/output ratio as inequitable relative to others', tension is created and they are motivated to eliminate or reduce the inequity. The strength of their motivation is proportional to the magnitude of the perceived inequity. If a person feels that someone is getting more compensation for similar work, this perception can negatively affect that employee's view of the value of the employee's own work. HR practitioners who specialize in compensation systems are particularly concerned not only that employees are paid fairly for the work they do, but also that they are paid equitably relative to other people in the organization.

For employees, compensation pay is **equitable** when it is perceived to be equal to the value of the work performed. Research clearly demonstrates that employees' perceptions of equity, or inequity, can have dramatic effects on their work behaviour and productivity, and therefore the employees' perception of the overall rewards system.[16] Although line managers do not design compensation systems, they do have to respond to employee concerns about being paid equitably. Compensation policies are internally equitable when employees believe that the wage rates for their jobs approximate the worth of the jobs to the organization. Perceptions of external equity exist when the organization is paying wages and benefits that are relatively equal to what other employers are paying for similar types of work. At Work with HRM 8.2 provides an interesting perspective on pay-for-performance and equity in today's economic climate.

Equitable compensation
Compensation received is perceived to be equal to the value of the work performed

Variable Pay and Incentives

A **pay-for-performance standard** serves to raise productivity and lower labour costs in today's economic environment. It is agreed that managers must tie at least some reward to

Pay-for-performance standard
Standard by which managers tie direct compensation to employee or organizational effort and performance

AT WORK WITH HRM 8.2

AM I MOTIVATED?

Much has been written over the last several years about the use of incentives—particularly as a way to link employee performance to the overall success of the organization. Do incentives work and will they motivate people?

The answer in recent studies suggests "yes" and "no," or "it all depends." Whether it is as a result of the economic turmoil over the last few years or the changing expectations of the workforce, there is no simple solution, and one size does not fit all. The real issue is whether or not people are satisfied with their compensation and whether it motivates them to perform well.

According to a recent study by the Conference Board of Canada, 79% of employers indicated that they have incentive awards for their top performers. Further, almost 50% indicated that the payouts exceeded targets. But it isn't always easy to ensure that the metrics used to measure performance can be tied to corporate objectives. However, it is important not to overstate the link as employees may not always be able to see the link between their performance and that of the organization. The use of incentive pay as a way to provide more compensation than modest changes to base salary is increasing in all industries.

However, there is also contrary evidence that suggests while pay is important, recognizing achievement is more memorable and creates a more engaged employee. Recognition has been shown to motivate employees to work harder.

What appears to be equally important when designing a pay-for-performance component is why the company is doing it. While such plans don't give rewards unless performance results are achieved, the design has to fit the organization. This includes whether there is a threshold of performance before any additional payments are made and tracking payments over years to ensure that the costs are providing the retention and motivation as expected.

CRITICAL THINKING QUESTIONS:

1. Would you like to have your pay tied directly to your performance? Why or why not?
2. Would pay-for-performance motivate you? Why or why not?

Sources: Adapted from Claudine Kapel, "Short-Term Incentive Plans Delivering Pay for Performance," *Canadian HR Reporter*, November 25, 2014, accessed March 1, 2015, **www.hrreporter.com/blog/Compensation-Rewards/archive/2014/11/25/short-term-incentive-plans-delivering-pay-for-performance**; Anne Fisher, "How to Get More Than a 3% Raise This Year," *Fortune*, February 20, 2015, accessed March 1, 2015, **http://fortune.com/2015/02/12/salaries-raises-promotions**; Claudine Kapel, "Use of Variable Pay on the Rise, Finds Study," *Canadian HR Reporter*, October 4, 2014, accessed March 1, 2015, **www.hrreporter.com/blog/Compensation-Rewards/archive/2014/10/06/use-of-variable-pay-on-the-rise-finds-study**, and Jo Faragher, "Show Me The Money," *People Management*, January 2015, 20–25.

employee effort and performance. Employees need to see and understand the link between their performance and the business performance.[17]

The term "pay for performance" or "variable pay," as described by many consulting firms such as Mercer and Towers Watson, refers to a wide range of direct compensation options, including merit-based pay, bonuses, salary commissions, and team or group incentive programs. Each of these compensation systems seeks to differentiate between the pay of average performers and that of outstanding performers. And some companies may decide to focus on a specific corporate objective such as energy conservation. For example, Co-Operative Food created a group incentive to achieve a reduction in its energy costs. It decided to do this to achieve a direct impact on its financial results.[18] Interestingly, productivity studies show that employees will increase their output by 15 to 35% when an organization institutes a pay-for-performance program.

Unfortunately, designing a sound pay-for-performance system is not easy. Considerations must be given to how employee performance will be measured, what monies will be allocated for compensation increases, which employees will be covered, what payout method will be used, and when payments will be made. A critical issue concerns the size of the monetary increase and its perceived value to employees, as a pay-for-performance program will lack its full potential when pay increases only approximate the rises in the cost of living.

Deloitte
www2.deloitte.com

A recent study by Deloitte (**www2.deloitte.com**), an international consulting firm, identified that one of the key issues for organizations is not just the need to

FIGURE 8.2 Advantages and Disadvantages of Pay-for-Performance Systems

Type of System	Advantages	Disadvantages
Individual	• Simple to compute • Clearly links pay to organizational outcomes • Motivates employees • Employees focus on clear performance targets • Distributes success among those responsible for producing success	• Standards of performance may be difficult to establish • May not be an effective motivator • Difficult to deal with missed performance targets • Available money may be inadequate • Employees may be unable to distinguish merit pay from other types of pay increases
Team	• Supports group planning • Builds team culture • Can broaden scope of contribution that employees are motivated to make • Tends to reduce jealousies and complaints • Encourages cross-training	• Individuals may perceive efforts contribute little to group success • Intergroup social problems can limit performance • Can be difficult to compute and therefore difficult to understand
Organization	• Creates effective employee participation • Can increase pride in organization • Can be structured to provide tax advantages • Has variable costs	• Difficult to handle if organization's performance is low • Can be difficult to compute and therefore difficult to understand • More difficult for individual effort to be linked to organizational success

have variable pay, but that total rewards must attract and keep top talent.[19] Further, with the ongoing economic uncertainty, some academics and practitioners have been advocating that the link between pay and performance be stopped. The basis for this criticism lies in the number of employees—particularly at senior management levels—who undertake business risk-taking actions that may actually harm the company. In addition, these individuals make reference to the incredibly high CEO compensation packages; that business challenges emerge daily and therefore tying pay to performance isn't realistic; and that people will manipulate the criteria to achieve better results.[20] Figure 8.2 provides a summary of the advantages and disadvantages of different pay-for-performance systems.

The Bases for Compensation

Work performed in most private, public, and not-for-profit organizations has traditionally been compensated on an hourly basis. This is referred to as **hourly work**, in contrast to **piecework**, in which employees are paid according to the number of units they produce. Hourly work, however, is far more prevalent than piecework as a basis for compensating employees.

Hourly work
Work paid on an hourly basis
Piecework
Work paid according to the number of units produced

Employees compensated on an hourly basis are classified as *hourly employees*, or wage earners. Those whose compensation is computed on the basis of weekly, biweekly, or monthly pay periods are classified as *salaried employees*. Hourly employees are normally paid only for the time they work. Salaried employees, by contrast, are generally paid the same for each pay period, even though they occasionally may work more hours or fewer than the regular number of hours in a period. They also usually receive certain benefits not provided to hourly employees.

DETERMINING COMPENSATION

LO2

What are the factors when determining pay levels?

A combination of *internal* and *external* factors can influence, directly or indirectly, the rates at which employees are paid, as shown in Figure 8.3.

FIGURE 8.3 Factors Affecting the Wage Mix

Internal Factors

The internal factors that influence wage rates are the employer's compensation policy, the worth of a job, an employee's relative worth in meeting job requirements, and an employer's ability and willingness to pay.

Employer's Compensation Strategy

Organizations will usually state objectives regarding compensation for their employees. For example, a public-sector employer may wish to pay fairly and at the market average. (Remember, "market" means the geographical area in which the organization typically finds qualified candidates for work.) On the other hand, a software development company may wish to pay fairly but be the industry leader to attract and retain high-calibre staff.

Usually, both large and small employers set pay policies reflecting (1) the internal wage relationship among jobs and skill levels, (2) the external competition or an employer's pay position relative to what competitors are paying, (3) a policy of rewarding employee performance, and (4) administrative decisions concerning elements of the pay system, such as overtime premiums, payment periods, and short- or long-term incentives.

Worth of a Job

As discussed in Chapter 3, the design of work or of a job leads to the organization being able to achieve its objectives. Organizations without a formal compensation program generally base the worth of jobs on the subjective opinions of people familiar with the jobs. In such instances, pay rates may be influenced heavily by the labour market or, in the case of unionized employees, by collective bargaining. Organizations with formal compensation programs, however, are more likely to rely on a system of job evaluation to aid in rate determination. Even when rates are subject to collective bargaining, job evaluation can assist the organization in maintaining some degree of control over its wage structure.

Job evaluation
Systematic process of determining the relative worth of jobs in order to establish which jobs should be paid more than others within an organization

Job evaluation is the systematic process of determining the *relative* worth of jobs in order to establish which jobs should be paid more than others within the organization. Job evaluation helps to establish internal equity between various jobs. Job worth is usually measured by the following criteria: level of skill, effort, responsibility, and working conditions of the job, no matter which particular formal system is used. The relative worth of a job is then determined by comparing it with others within the organization using these criteria. Furthermore, each method of comparison may be made on the basis of the jobs as a whole or on the basis of the parts that constitute the jobs. Refer to the four methods of comparison explored in the section "Job Evaluation Systems," below.

Employee's Relative Worth

In both hourly and salaried jobs, employee performance can be recognized and rewarded through promotion and with various incentive systems. Superior performance can also be rewarded by granting merit raises on the basis of steps within a rate range established for a job class. If merit raises are to have their intended value, however, they must be determined by an effective performance appraisal system that differentiates between those employees who deserve the raises and those who do not. This system, moreover, must provide a visible and credible relationship between performance and any raises received. Unfortunately, too many so-called merit systems provide for raises to be granted automatically. As a result, employees tend to be rewarded more for just being present than for being productive on the job.

In some situations, supervisors will also compare the performance of one employee to another. While proponents of performance stress that a person is to be assessed against standards of performance, there is a tendency to compare employees against each other. This is particularly true in the absence of any performance management system.

Employer's Ability and Willingness to Pay

In the public sector, the amount of compensation (pay and benefits) employees can receive is limited by the funds budgeted for this purpose and by the willingness of taxpayers to provide them. Federal government employees had their pay frozen for six years, in response to the drive to balance the budget and because of the public's perception of highly paid government workers. In the private sector, profits and other financial resources available to employers often limit pay levels. Economic conditions and competition faced by employers can also significantly affect the rates they are willing to pay. Competition and recessions can force prices down and reduce the income from which compensation payments are derived. In such situations, employers may have little choice but to reduce wages and/or lay off employees, or, even worse, go out of business. However, the manner in which an employer does this can have an impact on how the employees feel about their employer.

For example, in mid-2015 Loblaws restructured some of its grocery stores, and provided some employees with an option to receive a one-time payment in exchange for agreeing to a reduction in wages and benefits. Unfortunately, Loblaws overpaid these employees. When it asked for the overpayments to be returned, the manner in which it did so—demanding immediate repayment or it would take legal action—made the employees angry and generated distrust. Eventually Loblaws dropped the demand, but it no longer had the loyalty and trust of these employees.[21]

External Factors

The major external factors that influence wage rates are overall economy, labour-market conditions, area wage rates, cost of living, collective bargaining if the employer is unionized, and legal requirements.

Economy

Although Canada's economic woes are not as bad as elsewhere, given that it is an export-driven economy, businesses have to be sensitive to business projections. To deal with a possible labour shortage, particularly in key skill areas, companies are adopting a number of approaches. Recent surveys by the various consulting firms mentioned earlier have identified the following actions:

- designing variable pay to fit the organization and its industry
- providing meaningful pay increases even in a cost reduction environment
- providing non-cash benefits
- improving workplace health and well-being
- aligning total rewards with the business strategy[22]

Labour-Market Conditions

The labour market reflects the forces of supply and demand for qualified labour within an area. These forces help to influence the wage rates required to recruit or retain competent employees. It must be recognized, however, that counterforces can reduce the full impact of supply and demand on the labour market. The economic power of unions, for example, may prevent employers from lowering wage rates even when unemployment is high among union members. Employment laws may also prevent an employer from paying at a market rate less than an established minimum.

Area Wage Rates

A formal wage structure should provide rates that are in line with those being paid by other employers for comparable jobs within the area. Data pertaining to area wage rates may be obtained at minimal cost from local-area wage surveys. Wage-survey data may also be obtained from consulting firms, such as Towers Watson and the Hay Group. Smaller employers use government or local board of trade surveys to establish rates of pay. Many organizations conduct their own surveys. Others engage in a co-operative exchange of wage information or rely on various professional associations, such as the Professional Engineering Association of Ontario or British Columbia, for these data.

Statistics Canada
www.statcan.gc.ca

Cost of Living

Because of inflation, compensation rates tend to be adjusted upward periodically to help employees maintain their purchasing power. To do this, organizations frequently use the **consumer price index (CPI)**. The CPI is a broad measure of the cost of living in Canada and it measures the change in consumer prices over time.[23] The index is based on prices in a "shopping basket" and the contents of this basket can change over time depending on people's spending choices. Among the close to 600 items typically measured are food, clothing, shelter, and fuels; transportation fares; charges for medical services; and prices of other goods and services that people buy for day-to-day living. Statistics Canada collects price information monthly and calculates the CPI for Canada as a whole and for various Canadian city averages. Figure 8.4 illustrates wage increases for unionized and non-unionized employees, compared with the inflation rate.

Consumer price index (CPI)
Measure of the average change in consumer prices over time in a fixed "market basket" of goods and services

Using the CPI to determine changes in pay rates can also compress pay rates within a pay structure, creating inequities among those who receive the wage increase. For example,

FIGURE 8.4 Inflation and Wage Increases (1994–2015)

Inflation vs. Increases, 1994–2015
(percentage change)

f: Forecast.

*Wage increases for unionized employees from 1994 to 2013 are actuals as reported by Employment and Social Development Canada, Workplace Information Directorate. Wage increases for unionized employees for 2014 (actual) and 2015 (projected) are from the Compensation Outlook 2015 survey.

Source: From *Compensation Planning Outlook 2015* (Chart 1), October 30, 2014. Reprinted by permission of The Conference Board of Canada.

Ingram Publishing/Thinkstock

Employees' contributions (relative worth) are used when making decisions on pay.

an increase of 50 cents an hour represents a 10% increase for an employee earning $5 an hour, but only a 5% increase for someone earning $10 per hour.

Collective Bargaining

As you will see in Chapter 10, one of the primary functions of a labour union is to bargain collectively over conditions of employment, the most important of which is compensation. The union's goal in each new agreement is to achieve increases in **real wages**—wage increases larger than the increase in the CPI—thereby improving the purchasing power and standard of living of its members. This goal includes gaining wage settlements that equal if not exceed those established by other unions within the area.

Real wages
Wage increases larger than rises in the consumer price index; that is, the real earning power of wages

The agreements negotiated by unions tend to establish rate patterns within the labour market. As a result, wages are generally higher in areas where organized labour is strong. To recruit and retain competent personnel and avoid unionization, non-union employers must either meet or exceed these rates. The "union scale" also becomes the prevailing rate that all employers must pay for work performed under government contract. The impact of collective bargaining therefore extends beyond that segment of the labour force that is unionized.

Legal Requirements

As discussed in Chapter 2, legislation that either influences or requires certain pay rates is in place. For example, most provinces have a legislated minimum hourly wage, meaning that an employer cannot pay any worker less than the per-hour rate. In addition, pay equity legislation obliges certain companies to pay the same wage rate for jobs of a dissimilar nature and is based on comparing jobs performed mostly by men to jobs performed mostly by women. Under pay equity, a company must use a "gender-neutral" system, comparing jobs based on the amount and type of skill, effort, and responsibility needed to perform the job and on the working conditions in which the job is performed. Some provinces also consider male–female pay rates under human rights legislation. Read HRM and the Law 8.1 for a pay equity decision that took almost 30 years to resolve and payments are still outstanding.

HRM AND THE LAW 8.1

WHY IS IT TAKING SO LONG?

The Supreme Court of Canada has upheld a decision by the Canadian Human Rights Tribunal regarding pay equity at Canada Post. This case started in 1983 and was finally resolved in late 2011! However, as of 2015, very few payments have been made. Why?

The initial complaint was launched by the Public Service Alliance, the union representing about 2,300 employees who were mostly women. The complaint was in relation to pay equity—a claim that the clerical workers (primarily women) were paid less than comparable workers such as operations staff or letter carriers (primarily men). The claim was for $300 million.

While the case was not decided at the Canadian Human Rights Tribunal until 2005, that tribunal ruled in favour of the employees. Canada Post, however, appealed, and the Federal Court heard the case in 2008, overturning the tribunal decision. This decision was in turn appealed by the Public Service Alliance, and the case went to the Federal Court of Appeal, which also upheld the lower court's decision and ruled in favour of Canada Post. All parties eventually applied to have the case heard at the Supreme Court of Canada.

The initial complaint indicated that there was a 50% wage gap and this is what the union is seeking. During the intervening 28 years, Canada Post modified its wage structure so that, in 2002, the basis of the complaint was eliminated. The Supreme Court noted this, so it awarded $150 million instead of the $300 million sought. The decision does mean, however, that anyone working in clerical roles at Canada Post between 1982 and 2002 is eligible to receive pay equity adjustments. There are no further appeals available, and Canada Post must distribute the amount awarded. However, the union and Canada Post continued to argue about how much interest would be paid on the $150 million settlement. It wasn't until 2013 that Canada Post agreed to pay interest on $135 million.

No one knows what the final cost may be; some union members believe that as much as $250 million could be paid out. Canada Post has indicated that about 10,000 people have received cheques but that many more may be eligible. To ensure that potential claimants are contacted, it will be placing ads to find others.

The laws governing pay equity for federal employees were changed in 2009 so that public employees can no longer use the court system to obtain settlements in pay equity cases. The law now requires that any challenges regarding wages be handled through collective bargaining.

CRITICAL THINKING QUESTION:
What do you think?

Sources: Adapted from Vanessa Lu, "Canada Post Says 10,000 Have Received Pay Equity Cheques," *The Star*, January 13, 2015, accessed March 2, 2015, **www.thestar.com/business/2015/01/13/canada_post_says_10000_have_received_pay_equity_cheques.html**; Hugh Adami, "Most Pay-Equity Claimants Still Waiting for Canada Post Reimbursement, *Ottawa Citizen*, June 3, 2014, accessed March 2, 2015, **http://ottawacitizen.com/news/local-news/less-than-half-of-pay-equity-claimants-reimbursed-by-canada-post-so-far**; Public Service Alliance of Canada and Canada Post Corporation and Canadian Human Rights Commission, Nos. 33668, 33669, 33670, November 17, 2011; and "Canada Post Makes Pay Equity Payments Slowly," Public Service Alliance of Canada, September 24, 2014, accessed March 2, 2015, **http://psacunion.ca/canada-post-makes-pay-equity-payments-slowly**.

Job Evaluation Systems

LO3

What are the major job evaluation systems?

As mentioned earlier in this chapter, job evaluation is a way to determine the relative worth of jobs in an organization. The most typical job evaluation systems are described below.

Job Ranking System

The simplest and oldest system of job evaluation is the job ranking system, which arrays jobs on the basis of their relative worth. Job ranking can be done by a single individual knowledgeable about all jobs or by a committee composed of management and employee representatives. The basic weakness of the job ranking system is that it does not provide a very refined measure of each job's worth, and therefore it is not used frequently except in smaller organizations.

Job Classification System

In the job classification system, jobs sufficiently alike with respect to duties and responsibilities are grouped and will have a common name and common pay. Jobs that require increasing amounts of job responsibility, skill, knowledge, ability, or other factors used to compare jobs would then be grouped with a different common name and a different common pay. For example, the "social science services group" classification of the federal government's Public Service Commission uses nine different factors, including "very unpleasant working conditions" such as interactions with abusive individuals and possible threat to personal security.[24]

The descriptions of each of the job classes constitute the scale against which the specifications for the various jobs are compared. Managers then evaluate jobs by comparing job descriptions with the different wage grades in order to "slot" the job into the appropriate grade. While this system has the advantage of simplicity, it is less precise than the *point* and *factor comparison* systems (discussed next) because the job is evaluated as a whole.

Point System

The point system is a quantitative job evaluation procedure that determines a job's relative value by assigning points to various factors, such as amount of decision making, and then calculating the total points assigned to it. It has been successfully used by high-visibility organizations, such as Boeing and Honeywell, and by many other public and private organizations, both large and small. Although point systems are rather complicated to establish, once in place they are relatively simple to understand and use. The principal advantage of the point system is that it provides a more refined basis for making judgments than either the ranking or the classification system. It thereby can produce results that are more valid and harder to manipulate.

The point system permits jobs to be evaluated quantitatively on the basis of factors or elements—commonly called *compensable factors*—that constitute the job. The skills, efforts, responsibilities, and working conditions that a job usually entails are the more common major compensable factors that serve to evaluate the worth of a job as more or less important than another.

Factor Comparison System

The factor comparison system, like the point system, permits the job evaluation process to be accomplished on a factor-by-factor basis. A factor comparison system is typically used for legislated pay equity purposes. It differs from the point system, however, in that the compensable factors of the jobs to be evaluated are compared against the compensable factors of key jobs within the organization that serve as the job evaluation scale.

Key jobs are evaluated against five compensable factors—skill, mental effort, physical effort, responsibility, and working conditions—resulting in a ranking of the different factors for each key job. An example of a factor comparison system can be found on the University of British Columbia website (**www.hr.ubc.ca**), where the HR unit has posted its job evaluation program. You will note that things such as the type and amount of independent decision making are sub-factors of responsibility.

University of British Columbia
www.hr.ubc.ca

Regardless of the methodology used, be sure to remember that all job evaluation methods require varying amounts of judgment made by individuals. Supervisors or managers make decisions on the components of any job. Supervisors will also make decisions on how much responsibility and authority any particular job may have. Therefore, as careful an organization is in having objective ways of measuring the value of a job, subjective decisions are made regarding the content of the job. As mentioned previously, organizations frequently use a committee or panel for job evaluation assessments to help ensure objectivity.

Whatever system a company uses, employees and managers will ask why it is used. To better understand the reasons behind having some type of job evaluation system, look at the considerations in Toolkit 8.1.

What type of job evaluation system would be appropriate when determining the worth of rescue work?

TFoxFoto/Shutterstock.com

LO4

What does a compensation structure look like?

THE COMPENSATION STRUCTURE

Job evaluation systems provide for internal equity and serve as the basis for wage-rate determination. *They do not in themselves determine the wage rate.* The evaluated worth of each job based on its rank, class, points, or monetary worth must be converted into an hourly, daily, weekly, or monthly wage rate. The compensation tool used to help set wages is the wage and salary survey.

Wage and salary survey
Survey of the wages paid to employees of other employers in the surveying organization's relevant labour market

Wage and Salary Surveys

The **wage and salary survey** is a survey of the wages paid by employers in an organization's relevant labour market—local, regional, or national, depending on the job. The labour market is frequently defined as that area from which employers obtain certain types of

TOOLKIT 8.1 IS IT NECESSARY TO USE A JOB EVALUATION SYSTEM?

Organizations that have formal job evaluation systems are often questioned about the reasons behind a particular system. It is helpful for managers to review the considerations companies give when making such a decision.

- Using a few salary ranges is easier than managing hundreds of individual salary ranges.
- A job evaluation system is a structured way to ensure internal equity.
- The system can inform employees about career requirements.
- A system can ensure pay equity considerations under legislated requirements.
- A job evaluation system can provide validity of market data.

Sources: Adapted from Karl Aboud, "How Much Do You Pay Staff?" *Canadian HR Reporter*, May 5, 2014, 11; and Claudine Kapel, "Job Evaluation: The Unsung Hero of HR Processes," *Canadian HR Reporter*, October 20, 2014, accessed March 2, 2015, **www.hrreporter.com/blog/Compensation-Rewards/archive/2014/10/20/job-evaluation-the-unsung-hero-of-hr-processes**.

workers. The labour market for office personnel would be local, whereas the labour market for engineers would be national. It is the wage and salary survey that permits an organization to maintain external equity—that is, to pay wages to its employees that are equivalent to those of similar employees in other establishments.

Collecting Survey Data

Although many organizations conduct their own wage and salary surveys, a variety of "pre-conducted" wage and salary surveys are available to satisfy the requirements of most public, not-for-profit, or private organizations. For example, you might want to see what the average hourly rate is for an accounting clerk in the Toronto area. Or you might want to know the average hourly rate for a Web designer anywhere in Canada. Companies such as Towers Watson (**www.towerswatson.com**), Aon (**www.aon.com**), Mercer (**www.mercer.ca**), and Hay Group (**www.haygroup.com**) conduct annual surveys.

Towers Watson
www.towerswatson.com

Aon
www.aon.com

Mercer
www.mercer.ca

Hay Group
www.haygroup.com

The Wage Curve

The relationship between the relative worth of jobs and their wage rates can be represented by means of a wage curve. This curve may indicate the rates currently paid for jobs within an organization, the new rates resulting from job evaluation, or the rates for similar jobs currently being paid by other organizations within the labour market. Figure 8.5 provides an example of a wage curve for the administrative services group working with the federal government in 2015.

Pay Grades

From an administrative standpoint, it is generally preferable to group jobs into **pay grades** and to pay all jobs within a particular grade the same rate or rate range. When the classification system of job evaluation is used, jobs are grouped into grades as part of the evaluation process. When the point and factor comparison systems are used, however, pay grades must be established at selected intervals that represent either the point or the evaluated monetary value of these jobs.

Pay grades
Groups of jobs within a particular class that are paid the same rate or rate range

FIGURE 8.5 Wage Curve: Administrative Services Group, Federal Government, 2015

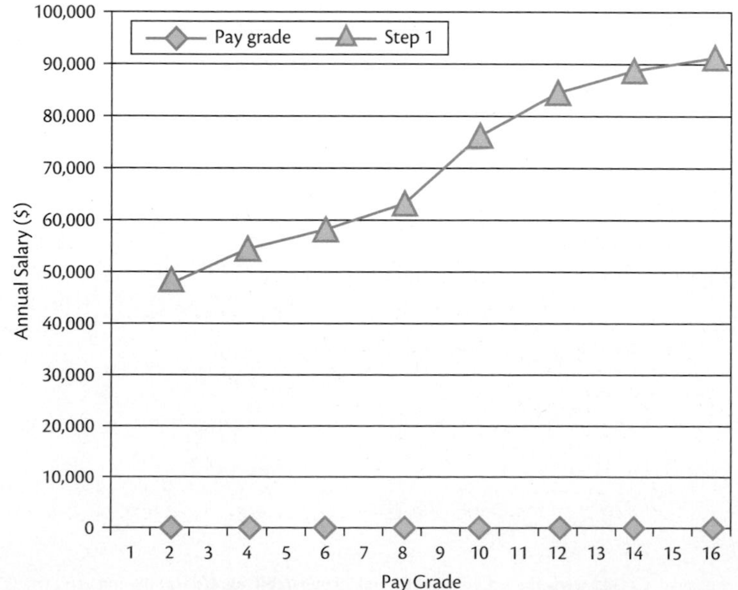

Rate Ranges

Although a single rate may be created for each pay grade, it is more common to provide a range of rates for each pay grade. The ranges may be the same for each grade or proportionately greater for each successive grade, as shown in Figure 8.6 using the same information for all the pay grades associated with the administrative services group. Rate ranges constructed on the latter basis provide a greater incentive for employees to accept a promotion to a job in a higher grade.

Other Ways to Determine Wages

The predominant approach to employee compensation is still the job-based system. Unfortunately, such a system often fails to reward employees for their skills or the knowledge they possess or to encourage them to learn a new job-related skill. Additionally, job-based pay systems may not reinforce an organizational culture stressing employee involvement or provide increased employee flexibility to meet overall production or service requirements. Therefore, many organizations have introduced competency-based or skill-based pay plans.

Competency-based pay
Pay based on how many capabilities employees have or how many jobs they can perform

Competency-based pay—also referred to as *knowledge-based pay*, *skill-based pay*, *pay-for-knowledge*, or *multiskilled-based pay*—compensates employees for the different skills or increased knowledge they possess or the collective behaviours or characteristics that they demonstrate rather than for the job they hold in a designated job category.[25] Regardless of the name, these pay plans encourage employees to earn higher base wages by learning and performing a wider variety of skills (or jobs) or displaying an array of competencies that can be applied to a range of organizational requirements. For example, in a manufacturing setting, new tasks might include various assembly activities carried out in a particular production system or a variety of maintenance functions.

Competency-based pay systems represent a fundamental change in the attitude of management regarding how work should be organized and how employees should be paid

FIGURE 8.6 Salary Structure with Increasing Pay Ranges: Administrative Services Group, Federal Government, 2015

Pay Grade	Step 1	Step 2	Step 3	Step 4
1	48,796	50,652	52,576	54,575
2	54,374	56,440	58,586	
3	58,281	60,495	62,794	
4	63,663	66,082	68,793	
5	76,002	78,876	82,171	
6	84,658	87,876	92,328	
7	89,112	92,503	96,014	98,898
8	92,014	108,305		

Source: Treasury Board of Canada, **www.tbs-sct.gc.ca/pubs_pol/hrpubs/coll_agre/pa/pa08-eng.asp**.

for their work efforts. The most frequently cited benefits of competency-based pay include distinguishing top from average performers, better ability to tie performance to business objectives, more flexibility in organizing work, and attraction and retention of a flexible workforce.[26] Competency-based pay also encourages employees to acquire training when new or updated skills are needed by an organization. Therefore, when considering the introduction of competency-based pay, it is important to

- link competencies to business objectives
- identify which jobs or types of work could benefit
- identify competencies that demonstrably affect performance
- devise methods to measure achievement of each competency
- determine appropriate amount of pay for acquired skill
- provide mechanisms to review overall effectiveness[27]

The Government of Canada has developed a competency framework for talent management in the Office of the Comptroller General. Competency is defined as "measurable and observable skills, abilities or knowledge that enable an employee to perform satisfactorily in a position."[28] For example, the complete competency profile for those in the finance area can be accessed through the Treasury Board of Canada Secretariat at **www.tbs-sct.gc.ca/fm-gf/tools-outils/guides/tm-gdt/tm-gdtpr-eng.asp**.

Treasury Board of Canada Secretariat
www.tbs-sct.gc.ca/fm-gf/tools-outils/guides/tm-gdt/tm-gdtpr-eng.asp

Broadbanding

Organizations that adopt a skill-based pay system frequently use *broadbanding* to structure their compensation payments to employees. This method simply collapses many traditional salary grades into a few wide salary bands. Broadbands may have midpoints and quartiles, or they may have extremely wide salary ranges or no ranges at all. Broadbanding encourages lateral skill building while addressing the need to pay employees performing several jobs with different skill-level requirements. Additionally, broadbands help eliminate the obsession with grades, and instead encourage employees to move to jobs in which they can develop in their careers and add value to the organization. Paying employees through broadbands enables organizations to consider job responsibilities, individual skills and competencies, and career mobility patterns in assigning employees to bands.

INCENTIVE PLANS

LO5

What are the various types of incentive plans?

For several years, a trend in rewards has been the use of incentive plans, also called *variable pay programs*, for employees throughout the organization. However, with the continuing economic concerns, many companies are re-examining whether these are appropriate in the current circumstances. A study by Deloitte Consulting found that 38% of employers responding were focusing on variable pay as part of redesigning their rewards program. However, this same study also indicated that 19% of employers were also re-examining their base pay.[29]

Another study, by Towers Watson, identified that employers do not necessarily always understand that base pay and career advancement may be more important than other types of rewards in attracting and retaining employees.[30] And while incentive plans create an operating environment that champions a philosophy of shared commitment through the belief that every individual contributes to organizational performance and success, it is important that the components of such plans be well communicated.

By linking rewards with organizational objectives, managers believe that employees will assume "ownership" of their jobs, thereby improving their effort and overall job performance. Incentives are designed to encourage employees to put out more effort to complete their job tasks—effort they might not be motivated to expend under hourly and/or seniority-based compensation systems. Financial incentives are therefore offered to improve or maintain high levels of productivity and quality that, in turn, improve the market for Canadian goods and services in a global economy.

Do incentive plans work? Various studies have demonstrated a measurable relationship between incentive plans and improved organizational performance. It is important to remember that a one-size incentive plan does not fit all organizations. For such plans to work, the plan must be designed to fit that particular organization and that employees must understand the impact of their performance on business results.[31]

A variety of individual and group incentive plans exists for both hourly and salaried employees. These include the following:

1. *Individual bonus*—an incentive payment that supplements the basic pay. It has the advantage of providing employees with more pay for exerting greater effort, while at the same time giving employees the security of a basic wage. Bonuses are common among managerial employees but as indicated earlier, organizations are increasingly providing bonuses to front-line staff.
2. *Team- or group-based incentive*—a plan that rewards team members with an incentive bonus when agreed-upon performance standards are exceeded. Figure 8.7 provides the pros and cons of team incentive plans.
3. *Merit raises*—an incentive, used most commonly for salaried employees, based on achievement of performance standards. One problem with merit raises is that they may be perpetuated year after year even when performance declines.
4. *Profit-sharing*—any plan by which an employer pays special sums based on the profits of the organization.
5. *Employee stock ownership plans (ESOPs)*—stock plans in which an organization contributes shares of its stock to an established trust for the purpose of stock purchases by its employees. With the recent economic turmoil, stock and stock options have not been as popular. And there is also always the issue of what happens to stock ownership when there is a change in ownership.

But do incentive plans work? At Work with HRM 8.3 provides some insights.

FIGURE 8.7 The Pros and Cons of Team Incentive Plans

Pros	Cons
Team incentives support group planning and problem solving, thereby building a team culture.	Individual team members may perceive that "their" efforts contribute little to team success or to the attainment of the incentive bonus.
The contributions of individual employees depend on group co-operation.	Intergroup social problems/pressure to limit performance (e.g., team members are afraid one individual may make the others look bad) and the "free ride" effect (one individual puts in less effort than others but shares equally in team rewards) may arise.
Unlike incentive plans based solely on output, team incentives can broaden the scope of the contribution that employees are motivated to make.	Complex payout formulas can be difficult for team members to understand.
Team bonuses tend to reduce employee jealousies and complaints over "tight" or "loose" individual standards.	
Team incentives encourage cross-training and the acquiring of new interpersonal competencies.	

AT WORK WITH HRM 8.3

ARE INCENTIVE PLANS WORKING?

Companies will use incentive pay as a strategic tool to attract, motivate, and retain employees, and to improve organizational performance. And with the ongoing economic issues, organizations want to keep key talent while keeping costs down. Is this goal achievable with incentive plans?

Yes, but careful attention has to be paid in the objectives, design, and implementation.

1. Companies will need to reward the most valued employees, which means that the organizations need to know who matters to business performance.
2. Companies need to determine the mix of short-term and long-term incentives.
3. Effective programs usually pay more to those who demonstrate better results.
4. Components need to be examined periodically to ensure that outcomes are being achieved.
5. To be effective, incentives must be linked to corporate goals, such as increased sales.
6. Plan design needs to address both short-term and long-term business performance.
7. The plan design needs to consider if there will be a threshold performance before any payouts are done.

For example, WestJet is proud to provide an employee share purchase plan for its employees—and refers to its staff as "owners." It feels that this type of recognition and reward has enabled it to be the most profitable North American airline.

CRITICAL THINKING QUESTION:

Would you like to have an incentive plan? Why or why not? Explain your reasons.

Sources: Adapted from Claudine Kapel, "Incentive Plans Alive and Well," *Canadian HR Reporter*, May 6, 2014, accessed March 2, 2015, **www.hrreporter.com/blog/Compensation-Rewards/archive/2014/05/06/incentive-plans-alive-and-well**; Claudine Kapel, "Use of Variable Pay on the Rise, Finds Study," *Canadian HR Reporter*, October 6, 2014, accessed March 2, 2015, **www.hrreporter.com/blog/Compensation-Rewards/archive/2014/10/06/use-of-variable-pay-on-the-rise-finds-study**; Claudine Kapel, "Short-Term Incentive Plans Delivering Pay for Performance," *Canadian HR Reporter*, November 25, 2014, accessed March 2, 2015, **www.hrreporter.com/blog/Compensation-Rewards/archive/2014/11/25/short-term-incentive-plans-delivering-pay-for-performance**; and "The Downside of Financial Incentives," June 30, 2014, *HRM Online*; and "Great jobs," WestJet, accessed March 2, 2015, **www.westjet.com/guest/en/jobs.shtml**.

EMPLOYEE BENEFITS

Employee benefits constitute an indirect form of compensation intended to improve the quality of the work and personal lives of employees. The cost of benefits can be as high as 40% when you include premiums for health and welfare, government-mandated coverage such as workers' compensation, vacation, and paid sick leave. In return, employers generally expect employees to be supportive of the organization and to be productive. Since employees have come to expect an increasing number of benefits, the motivational value of these benefits depends on how the benefits program is designed and communicated. Once viewed as a gift from the employer, benefits are now considered rights to which all employees are entitled.

Too often, a particular benefit is provided because other employers are doing it, because someone in authority believes it is a good idea, or because there is union pressure. However, the contributions that benefits will make to the compensation package (and therefore, to organizational performance) depend on how much attention is paid to certain basic considerations.

Linking Benefits to the Overall Rewards Program

Like any other component of the compensation plan, an employee benefits program should be based on specific objectives. The objectives an organization establishes will depend on many factors, including the size of the firm, its profitability, its location, the degree of unionization, and industry patterns. Most importantly, these objectives must be compatible with the organization's strategic rewards and recognition plan, including its philosophy and policies.

The chief objectives of most benefits programs are to

- improve employee work satisfaction
- meet employee health, security, and environment concerns and requirements
- attract and motivate employees
- retain top-performing employees
- maintain a favourable competitive position

For example, Open Text Corporation, a software development company in Ontario, recognizes that there are many components in a benefits program. Its inclusion of sheltered bicycle parking and shower facilities resulted in the company being listed in Canada's Top 100 Employers for 2015.[32]

But it is important to remember that not all benefits work for everyone. As a result, it is important that organizations design their benefits program to fit the unique demographics of the company.[33] As with other good HR practices, it is a good idea to consult with employees when a new benefit is being considered. Many organizations establish committees composed of managers and employees to administer, interpret, and oversee their benefits policies. Opinion surveys are also used to obtain employee input. Having employees participate in designing benefits programs helps to ensure that management is satisfying employee wants.

Cost Concerns

Organizations can typically spend about 35% to 45% of their annual payroll costs on benefits such as group health plans, pension contributions, EI premiums, CPP premiums, and workers' compensation premiums. The increasing costs, particularly of health-care provisions, have made more and more organizations strive to manage those costs.

Since many benefits represent a fixed rather than a variable cost, management must decide whether it can afford this cost under less favourable economic conditions. As managers can readily attest, if an organization is forced to discontinue a benefit, the negative effects of cutting it may outweigh any positive effects that accrued from providing it.

To minimize negative effects and avoid unnecessary expense, many employers enlist the co-operation of employees in evaluating the importance of particular benefits. For example, Saint John Energy, the electrical distribution agency for the City of Saint John, decided that it needed to find a more cost-effective pension plan. Its existing plan had been around for 80 years and was potentially unsustainable in the future. Since pension plans can be quite important to employees, it involved both current and retired employees in the redesign that not only met its cost concerns but also was endorsed by everyone.[34]

The escalating cost of health-care benefits is a major concern to employers, who must strike an appropriate balance between offering quality benefits and keeping costs under control. Recent evidence suggests that organizations that take a more strategic and holistic approach to the design of its benefits can effectively keep costs down and employees well.[35]

Increasing use of data analysis regarding the most utilized drug or medical service enables employers to find tactics to reduce the costs or help employees with a different approach to managing the health issue.[36] Part of the reason for this is the use of generic drugs and the results of wellness programs initiated a number of years ago. In addition, some organizations are approaching their costs of health-care benefits from a value-based perspective. Specifically, "value-based health care" is a systematic and holistic approach to creating a culture of health for employees. It does this promoting a healthier lifestyle that can lead to better productivity and lower benefits costs.[37] For additional articles on managing the cost of health care, check out the Web site of Benefits Canada (**www.benefitscanada.com**).

Benefits Canada
www.benefitscanada.com

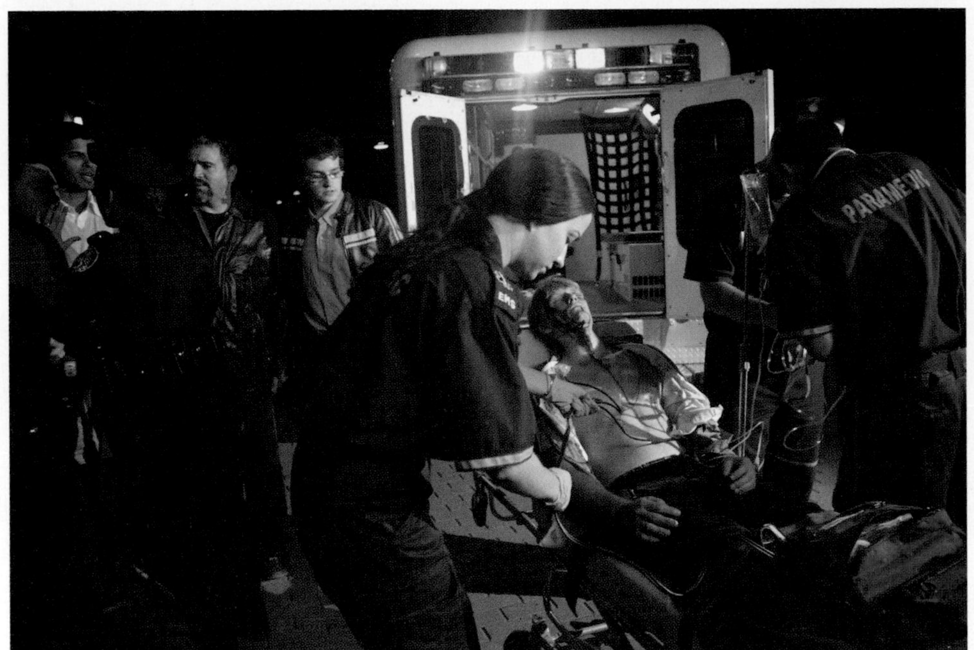

© Blue Images Online/Masterfile/Corbis

The increasing cost of medical benefits to employees continues to be an issue for employers.

At Work with HRM 8.4 describes what some companies have done to provide an innovative approach to benefits that is cost-effective.

AT WORK WITH HRM 8.4

WHAT A DIFFERENT BENEFIT!

What have both Deloitte and EllisDon done to rate an "innovation" comment when they were named in Canada's Top 100 Employers for 2015? Deloitte is an international consulting firm with offices in Canada's major cities and EllisDon is one of Canada's foremost construction firms. Both have offered a discount program to its employees—and the design is unique.

Basically, the companies have worked with a specific vendor—Venngo WorkPerks—who has provided a web portal designed for each organization that allows employees to access a selection of discount deals with local businesses and brand-name retailers.

Both companies have received high praise from their employees for the benefit. And for those offices in larger cities, the value the employees can receive can be significant. Employees feel they are really getting value for the money.

How does it work? The employers provide an annual fee, based on the number of employees in each organization, to Venngo for the service. Venngo then takes over and provides newsletters and communiqués to the employees to alert them to offers and specials. It has also developed a mobile app that has allowed employees to check often to see what might be available.

The biggest attractions for the discounts accessed by employees have been restaurants, shopping, and travel. Employees continue to indicate that they take advantage of the offerings and appreciate that their companies have provided a different benefit, which is similar to a concierge service and allows employees to use their dollars more effectively.

How much is the service used? EllisDon indicates that it has 1,200 active accounts with high usage. The company states that it is important to monitor usage to ensure that employees are getting value and that they enjoy the access.

CRITICAL THINKING QUESTIONS:

1. Do you think it is important for an employer to provide innovative or unique benefits? Why or why not?
2. If you had access to such a benefit, would you make use of it? Why or why not?

Sources: Adapted from Sarah Dobson, "Discount Programs a Popular Benefit," *Canadian HR Reporter*, December 15, 2014, accessed March 7, 2015, **www.hrreporter.com/articleview/23083-discount-programs-a-popular-benefit**; "Canada's Top 100 Employers 2015, accessed March 7, 2015, **www.canadastop100.com/national**; and Kenneth MacDonald, "Employers embracing flexibility," *Benefits Canada*, May 29, 2014, accessed March 7, 2015, **www.benefitscanada.com/benefits/health-benefits/employers-embracing-flexibility-53217**.

LO6

Which benefits does the law require?

BENEFITS REQUIRED BY LAW

Legally required employee benefits can cost over 15% of an organization's annual payroll. These benefits include employer contributions to the Canada or Quebec pension plan, employment insurance, workers' compensation (discussed in Chapter 3), and, in some provinces, provincial medicare.

Canada and Quebec Pension Plans (CPP/QPP)

The Canada and the Quebec Pension Plan cover almost all Canadian employees between the ages of 18 and 70. Both plans require employers to match the contributions made by employees. The revenues generated by these contributions are used to pay three main types of benefits: retirement pensions, disability benefits, and survivors' benefits. With Canada's population aging, funds from the CPP will not be able to meet the needs of retirees unless those currently working, and their employers, significantly increase their contributions.

Employment Insurance (EI)

Employment insurance (EI) benefits have been available for more than 50 years and were provided as income protection to employees who were between jobs. Employees and employers both contribute to the EI fund. The amount of benefit paid is a formula (which can change) based on the number of hours of employment in the past year and the regional unemployment rate. EI is also accessed for employees on parental leave. However, in addition, almost 40% of Canadian employers provide additional paid parental leave.[38]

Provincial Hospital and Medical Services

Most provinces fund health-care costs from general tax revenue and federal cost sharing. Ontario, Quebec, and Newfoundland also levy a payroll tax, while other provinces, such as Alberta and British Columbia, charge premiums payable by the resident or an agent, usually the employer (subsidies for low-income residents are provided).

The cost of the government providing health care has escalated to the point where major reform in Canada's health-care system is occurring. As of 2015, 29% of the Canadian population was over 55 with those over 80 comprising over 4%.[39] As has been discussed by policymakers, politicians, and journalists, the increasing longevity of people and the major health problems that do occur mean that our health-care system will need significant redesign to be sustainable.[40]

Leaves Without Pay

Most employers grant leaves of absence to employees who request them for personal reasons. In some provinces, legislation mandates that these types of leaves must be granted. These leaves are usually taken without pay, but also without loss of seniority or benefits.

Other Required Benefits

In addition to the benefits described, through provisions in employment standards legislation, provinces do require employers to pay for statutory holidays, minimum vacation pay, premiums when people work overtime, and in some provinces a severance payment when employees are terminated.

VOLUNTARY EMPLOYEE BENEFITS

In addition to the benefits required by legislation, employers can choose to provide more benefits as part of the overall compensation package. Organizations do this to ensure they can attract and retain the kinds of employees they want. These benefits are called "voluntary benefits." While there can be many types of these benefits, we will look at the more typical ones. You can review some of the other voluntary benefits at the International Foundation of Employee Benefit Plans site (**www.ifebp.org**).

LO7

What are some of the voluntary benefits?

Health and Welfare Benefits

Due to sharply rising costs and employee concern, the benefits that receive the most attention from employers today are health-care benefits. In the past, health insurance plans covered only medical, surgical, and hospital expenses. Today, employers include prescription drugs as well as dental, optical, and mental health-care benefits in the package they offer their workers. As mentioned earlier in this chapter, employers are attempting to ensure that the benefit provided will be of value to the person. Listed below is a brief description of typical health and welfare benefits.

International Foundation of Employee Benefit Plans
www.ifebp.org

Dental Coverage

Dental plans are designed to help pay for dental-care costs and to encourage employees to receive regular dental attention. Typically, the insurance pays a portion of the charges and the employee pays the remainder.

Extended Health Coverage

This benefit provides for additional payments beyond the basic provincial medical coverage. It typically provides such things as semiprivate or private hospital rooms, prescription drugs, private nursing, ambulance services, out-of-country medical expenses that exceed provincial limits, and vision care.

It should be noted that there could be duplication of coverage if both partners in a relationship have access to health coverage. In some cases, if there is better coverage in one plan than in another, the partner with the better coverage will enroll and include the partner.

One aspect of extended health coverage that is increasing greatly is the cost of prescription drugs. This situation becomes worse when provincial health plans reduce coverage or make use of generic drugs as private plans typically pick up the costs.[41] To counter this increase, many plans make use of generic drugs as well, but this only goes so far. Another way to help reduce costs is to ensure that employees can make informed decisions regarding their health care and to provide easy access to lower-priced pharmacies.[42] Employers and benefits carriers are also watching the increased use of genetic testing and its impact on all forms of insurance coverage. The concern is that as it becomes more widely available, the insurance companies would deny coverage simply because there might be a genetic marker indicating the "potential" of a certain health risk that might never materialize.[43]

Life Insurance

One of the oldest and most popular employee benefits is group term life insurance, which provides death benefits to beneficiaries and may also provide accidental death and dismemberment benefits.

Retirement and Pension Plans

Retirement is an important part of life and requires sufficient and careful preparation. In convincing job applicants that theirs is a good organization to work for, employers usually emphasize the retirement benefits that can be expected after a certain number of years of employment.

Other benefits coverage, such as dental, is often available to employees and their families.

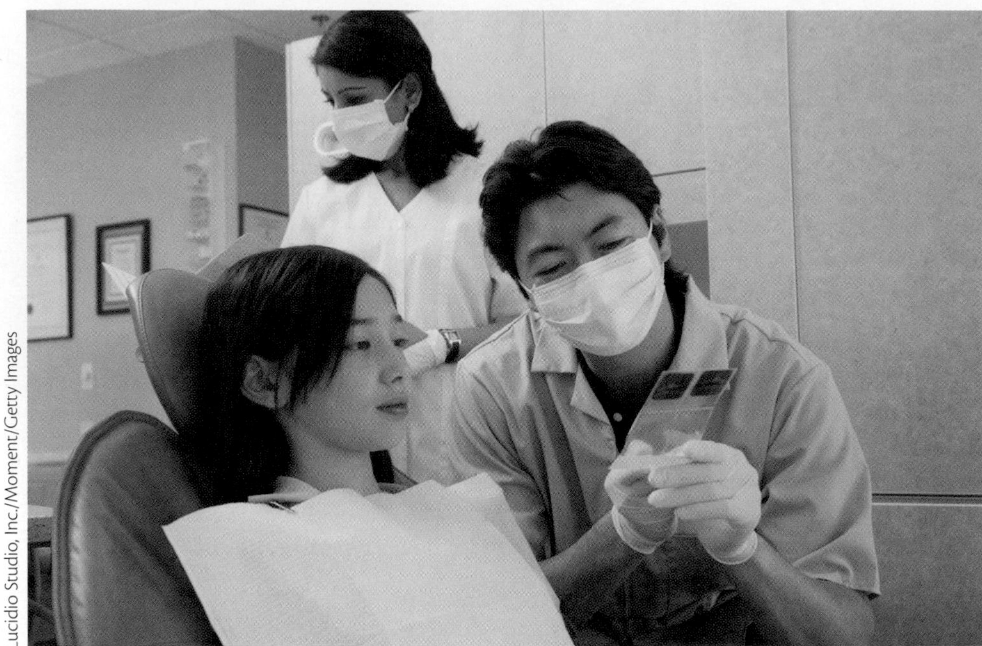

Lucidio Studio, Inc./Moment/Getty Images

Pension plans are classified into two primary categories: defined benefit and defined contribution. In a *defined benefit plan (DBP)*, a person receiving benefits receives a specific amount (usually based on years of service and average earnings), regardless of the amount of contributions. In a *defined contribution plan (DCP)* the person gets an amount based on the accumulated funds and how much those funds can purchase (at the time of retirement) for retirement benefits.

Since defined benefit plans have to provide the specific payment whether or not the employee has made sufficient contributions, the organization becomes liable for the difference. With the aging workforce, more and more organizations and employees are expressing concern about whether their plan will be able to fund what has been promised. The continued economic uncertainty has increased the concern about the viability of companies having a defined benefit plan. This concern has been magnified as the Ontario government considers implementing legislation that would create a government-run required registered pension plan.[44] For example, more than 75% of employers in a recent survey indicated that if there was such a plan, they would reduce contributions and 2/3 of the same employers said that they would eliminate their existing plans.[45]

Unfortunately, the concerns about the value of pension plans are not new. For some time, Canadian organizations have been faced with the dilemma of potentially having insufficient resources in the future to pay pensions to the people who will be retiring in the future. These concerns have led some employers to consider changing pension plan design from defined benefit to defined contribution. Within the private sector, companies are better understanding that the true cost of a defined benefit plan is much higher than employees would voluntarily wish to participate in.[46] Other suggestions to keep defined benefit plans viable are to have multi-employer pension plans, such as the Many Nations Pension Plan sponsored by 160 First Nations organizations or the Teamsters Canadian Pension Plan.[47]

There is also concern from various levels of government that the overall pension system needs to improve; hence, a number of reports have called for new models that are more flexible and appealing to employers and employees. To address this, the federal government in 2014 proposed a new voluntary pension plan option that would be available to employees of government-owned companies and of private-sector companies that were federally regulated.[48] While labour unions will be discussed more fully in Chapter 10, it is worthwhile to note that many major labour unions are not in support of the federal government's proposal, as they fear that employers will unilaterally reduce benefits if the funds do not do well financially.[49]

Given the current volatility of the stock market and the concern about future payments from pension plans, it is no wonder that there is a push to improve the performance of all pension plans, including government-funded ones. Further, Air Canada recently discontinued a pension agreement with the federal government that is expected to save Air Canada about $300 million over 2 years.[50] Ethics in HRM 8.1 discusses the dilemma of pension plans when companies are faced with cost pressures.

Pay for Time Not Worked

The "pay for time not worked" category of benefits includes statutory holiday pay, vacation pay (above any legislated minimum), bereavement leave, rest periods, coffee breaks, sick leave, and parenting benefits (salary continuance). These benefits typically account for a large portion of overall benefit costs.

Vacations with Pay

It is generally agreed that vacations are essential to the well-being of an employee. Eligibility for vacations varies by industry, locale, and organization size. A recent study indicated that most organizations provide more paid vacation than is required by law.[51] To qualify for longer vacations of three, four, or five weeks, one may expect to work for 7, 15, and 20 years, respectively. However, some organizations may not tie paid vacation to any years of service. For example, Netflix provides unlimited vacation for its employees.[52]

ETHICS IN HRM 8.1

BUT I THOUGHT MY RETIREMENT DOLLARS WERE SAFE!

Those people who have enjoyed working for employers who provide pension plans have assumed that these plans would always continue and that their retirement income would be secure based on the design of the pension plan. But that isn't always the case.

One of the longstanding court cases regarding pension benefits has been with Nortel. Remember when Nortel was the brand of successful Canadian businesses? Remember when it filed for bankruptcy in 2009? Since that time, the company has been sold off in parts with the proceeds being divided among its creditors through the law courts. However, in mid-2014, about 1/3 (30,000) of the pensioners reached a settlement regarding the $7.3 billion claim against Nortel. But even though the trial has finished, no decision is expected until sometime in late 2015. In the meantime, the pensioners have received no payment in relation to what they thought they would have in their retirement years.

The problem isn't just with extreme situations such as the impact of bankruptcy on pension plans. As retiree benefits become more expensive, employers are looking at a variety of ways to reduce their costs. To do so does pose legal risks to the employers. For example, Weyerhaeuser, a forest products company with extensive operations in Canada, decided to reduce its contribution to the cost of medical benefits to its retirees. Several of the retired staff launched a claim based on the idea that through their years of employment and what had been promised, they were entitled to continue to have the cost of premiums paid for totally by the company. And the trial judge agreed. The judge determined that the premium costs were a type of deferred compensation and that the retirees were entitled to as part of their retirement benefits.

In another case, GM Canada reduced health care and life insurance coverage for its retirees. The court judge ruled similarly to the judge in the Weyerhaeuser case, concluding that GM was contractually obligated to provide the original coverage.

CRITICAL THINKING QUESTIONS:

1. Is it ethical for companies to reduce retirement benefits? Why or why not?
2. What might employees do to ensure that this doesn't happen to them?

Sources: Adapted from "Partial Settlement Reached in Nortel $7.3 Billion Pension Debate," *HRM Online*, July 9, 2014; and Josee Dumoulin, "Grey Power," *Canadian HR Reporter*, June 2, 2014, accessed March 5, 2015, **www.hrreporter.com/articleview/21319-grey-power**.

Paid Holidays

Both hourly and salaried workers can expect to be paid for statutory holidays as designated in each province. The standard statutory holidays in Canada are New Year's Day, Good Friday, Canada Day (Memorial Day in Newfoundland and Labrador), Labour Day, and Christmas Day. Other holidays recognized by various provinces are Victoria Day, Thanksgiving Day, Remembrance Day, and Family Day. Additionally, each province may designate special holidays important to that province only. Many employers give workers an additional one to three personal days off.

With the increasing diversity in culture and religions in the workforce, situations may arise in which governments feel a need to change the number and type of statutory holidays so that there are more general kinds of observations rather than holidays tied to any one faith. However, it creates a more inclusive and accepting environment, as well as not creating a discriminatory environment, if organizations provide opportunities for people to recognize their religious days.[53]

Sick Leave

Employees may be compensated in several ways during periods when they are unable to work because of illness or injury. Most public employees, as well as many in private firms (particularly in white-collar jobs), receive a set number of sick-leave days each year to cover such absences. Where permitted, sick leave that employees do not use can be accumulated to cover prolonged absences. Accumulated vacation leave may sometimes be used as a source of income when sick-leave benefits have been exhausted. Group insurance that provides income protection during a long-term disability is also becoming more common. As discussed earlier in the chapter, income lost during absences resulting from job-related injuries may be reimbursed, at least partially, through workers' compensation insurance.

According to Statistics Canada, workplace absences have remained stable over the past several years. In 2014, an average of nine work days (almost 2% of the work year) were lost due to illness or family responsibilities.[54] Much of this amount is due to the aging workforce. Workers aged 55 and over missed 13 days of work on average each year, while workers aged 25 to 34 missed only 7 days.[55]

Wellness Programs

In recent years, new types of services have been offered to make life at work more rewarding and to enhance employee well-being. Excellence Canada (formerly the National Quality Institute) provides annual awards for organizations that have outstanding wellness programs. ArcelorMittal Dofasco, a Hamilton, Ontario, producer of steel, won a gold-level award for Healthy Workplace because it encourages each employee to support and participate in a variety of wellness activities.[56] While there is uncertainty about the exact return on the investments in these types of programs, some employers have demonstrated there is dollar value in them. For example, Bruce Telecom, a telecom services company in Ontario, convinced both employees and its union that having employees participate in a wellness program would be beneficial to everyone. And in doing so the company analyzed a number of metrics such as health claims, drug claims, and sick days and concluded that it saved over $136,000 in one year.[57]

Employee Assistance Programs

To help workers cope with a wide variety of problems that interfere with the way they perform their jobs, organizations have developed employee and family assistance programs (EFAPs). These programs typically provides diagnosis, limited counselling, and referral for advice or treatment when necessary for problems related to substance abuse (alcohol, drug), emotional difficulties, and financial or family difficulties. (EFAPs were discussed in detail in Chapter 3.) The main intent of these programs is to help employees and their families solve their personal problems or at least to prevent problems from turning into crises that affect their ability to work productively. A recent study determined that for every $1 invested in an EFAP that almost $9 was returned through less absence from work and improved productivity.[58]

Educational Assistance Plans

One of the benefits most frequently mentioned in literature for employees is the educational assistance plan. The primary purpose of this plan is to help employees keep up to date with advances in their fields and to help them get ahead in the organization. Usually, the employer covers—in part or totally—costs of tuition, books, and related fees, while the employee is required to pay for meals, transportation, and other expenses. Depending on the organization, some companies are willing to pay for courses not directly related to a specific job. Employers feel that by providing educational assistance it enables them to attract and retain the key employees they need to be successful.[59]

Childcare and Eldercare

Consider these statistics:

- Over 16% of the Canadian population is 65 or older.[60]
- One-third of employees are caregivers.[61]
- Annual lost productivity due to caregiving costs $1.3 billion.[62]
- The number of seniors requiring some type of help will double in the next 15 years.[63]

In the past, working parents had to make their own arrangements with sitters or with nursery schools for preschool children. Today, benefits may include financial assistance, alternative work schedules, and family leave. For many employees, on-site or near-site childcare centres are the most visible, prestigious, and desired solutions.

A growing benefit offered employees with children experiencing a short illness is called "mildly ill childcare." Medical supervision is the primary difference between these facilities and traditional daycare arrangements.

Responsibility for the care of aging parents and other relatives is another fact of life for more and more employees. The term **eldercare**, as used in the context of employment, refers to situations in which an employee provides care to an elderly relative while remaining actively at work. Most caregivers are women. According Statistics Canada, at the end of 2014 almost 6 million Canadians were 65 or older.[64] By 2033, it is estimated that 23%, will be 65 and older; and 7% of the population will be 80 or older.[65] As a consequence of the expected shortfall in eldercare facilities, the responsibility for the care of these seniors will be borne by their children and other relatives. The majority of caregivers are women.

Eldercare
Care provided to an elderly relative by an employee who remains actively at work

To reduce the negative effects of caregiving on productivity, organizations may offer eldercare counselling, educational fairs and seminars, printed resource material, support groups, and special flexible schedules and leaves of absence.

Interest in and demand for eldercare programs is increasing dramatically as the Canadian population ages and lives longer. One author of this text (Stewart) found herself in just this situation: raising a young child and having to care for aging parents at a distance.

It is important to consider the impact of childcare on the Canadian workplace, as well. Most people who are responsible for childcare are female. Given that the labour force is approximately 48% female,[66] significant issues can occur in the workplace when childcare duties need attention. Of the women working, 69% had children under six years old.[67] As mentioned earlier in this section, $1.3 billion is lost annually due to caregiving absences—a huge loss to the Canadian economy.

Organizations have been involved in a number of initiatives to improve this situation. For example, BMO is working with its EAP supplier to develop a program for caregivers in which employees participate in support sessions facilitated by trained professionals. In this way, employees can feel and understand that many others have the same difficulties and that they can rely upon each other to provide support.[68] Experts in the field state that companies who do not have programs to help employees be caregivers are at risk of losing talent or having increased absenteeism.[69]

Other Services

The variety of benefits and services that employers offer today could not have been imagined a few years ago. Some are fairly standard which we have briefly covered. Some are unique and obviously grew out of specific concerns, needs, and interests. Some of the more creative and unusual benefits are group insurance for employee pets, free baseball tickets for families and friends, and summer boat cruises. At Work with HRM 8.5 describes a unique benefit at a software firm.

There are many emerging trends in relation to rewards and recognition. See Emerging Trends 8.1 for some of the more prominent ones.

AT WORK WITH HRM 8.5

MY BEST FRIEND!

Have you thought about bringing your dog to work? Have you done so?

If you work at Salesforce.com, you might have done so. It started some time ago when someone had a problem with how their dogs would be cared for during the day. And the company has always considered itself different when it came to providing its employees with an uncommon work environment. The employees are very mobile using smartphones and laptops at long tables instead of individual offices.

When the idea came up, discussions occurred among employees via social media. While not everyone was keen for dogs at work, the company decided to run a trial program. It created a separate space—soundproof and with rubber flooring—with a fixed number of spaces for dogs. Reservations were required.

People with dogs find that they can be more productive when they don't have to worry about pet care. And people who don't have dogs also make use of the perk. The director of marketing has a busy travel schedule that doesn't allow for having a dog. However, if he feels particularly in need of canine support, he arranges to walk and spend time with a friend's dog. There is also evidence that people who bring their dogs to work are less stressed.

So many people think that it's such a great idea that the company is considering establishing similar facilities in its other offices.

CRITICAL THINKING QUESTIONS:

1. Do you think these special benefits are attractive? Why or why not?
2. Would the inclusion of unusual perks draw you to a specific employer? Why or why not?

Sources: Adapted from Christopher Tkaczyk, "Bring Your Best Friend to Work," *Fortune*, August 11, 2014, 26; and Chris Morris, "10 Companies That Let You Bring Your Dog to Work," *CNBC Online*, February 14, 2014, accessed March 9, 2015, **www.cnbc.com/id/101396437#**.

Monkey Business Images Ltd/Thinkstock

Given the number of working parents, many companies want employees to have access to childcare.

EMERGING TRENDS 8.1

1. ***Incentives and innovative programs for adopting a healthier lifestyle.*** As costs of health care—both publicly funded and through work benefits—continue to rise, employers are encouraging and supporting employees to be healthier. This includes providing health-risk assessments and specialized interventions such as smoking-cessation aids. Employers are concerned not just about the rising costs to health plans, but also about a less productive workforce. More attention is also being paid to improving mental health in the workplace.
2. ***Increased use of and unusual nonfinancial rewards.*** Organizations are looking at new ways to reward and recognize employees in order to encourage creativity and innovation. Some of these include allowing employees to work remotely from anywhere in the world, providing for eldercare assistance, and helping employees complete their degrees.
3. ***Creating different approaches to compensation.*** Organizations are being unorthodox as they look at the value of rewards and their overall purpose: to attract and retain employees. Some are ensuring they create rewards programs that are meaningful to the different demographic groups. Likewise, organizations are ensuring that all aspects of their compensation plans are transparent. As part of a retention strategy, some are paying full salary while female staff are on maternity leave.
4. ***Increasing base pay.*** Despite economic problems, organizations remain concerned about attracting and retaining staff at all levels in the organization but particularly those with high potential. It is for this reason that base pay, and not just other types of financial compensation, are being re-examined to ensure the amount is appropriate to reach the companies' goals.
5. ***Increased analysis of benefits costs.*** Primarily to deal with the changing demographics, employers will be looking at ways to ensure the drug plan costs are reasonable and that they are getting good value. Another way employers can improve the cost of benefits is by ensuring that the overall program is integrated including use of sick leave, any injuries at work, etc.
6. ***Designing benefits plans for multiple generations.*** Companies are recognizing that a "one size fits all"

continued

approach is no longer working, with the range of generations in today's workplace. This also includes looking at benefits as part of a comprehensive rewards and recognition program, and not just as "perks." The focus is on the individual, and not just the group, and thinking of the benefits program as an investment in their employees.

Sources: Nicola Middlemiss, "Could Eldercare Be the Next Employee Benefit?" *HRM Online*, February 10, 2015, accessed February 14, 2015, **www.hrmonline.ca/hr-news/could-eldercare-be-the-next-employee-benefit-187989.aspx**; Erin Anderssen, "Travel the World and Still Get a Paycheque: The Allure of a Results-Only Workplace," *The Globe and Mail*, August 1, 2014, L1; Morneau Shepell, "Survey on Compensation & Trends in Human Resources," September 2014; Claudine Kapel, "Leverage Career Development in Your Talent Strategy," *Canadian HR Reporter*, April 29, 2014, accessed March 9, 2015, **www.hrreporter.com/blog/Compensation-Rewards/archive/2014/04/29/leveraging-career-development-in-your-talent-strategy**; Caitlin Nobes, "Latest Employee Incentive: Free College Degrees," *HRM Online*, June 17, 2014; "Push for Differentiation for Performance Yields Positive Results," *Compensation Strategies* 21, no. 8 (August 2014): 8–9; Elena Belogolovsky and Peter A. Bamberger, "Signaling in Secret," *Academy of Management Journal* 57, no. 6 (2014): 1706–1733; "Benefits and Compensation Orientation Guide," *Workforce*, September 4, 2014; "The Downside of Financial Incentives," *HRM Online*, June 30, 2014; Towers Watson, "2014 Global Talent Management and Rewards Study," accessed September 26, 2015, **www.towerswatson.com/en-US/Insights/IC-Types/Survey-Research-Results/2014/08/2014-global-talent-management-and-rewards-study-making-the-most-of-employment-deal**; Suzanne Lepage, "Drug Plan Trends in Canada," *Benefits Canada*, March 1, 2015, accessed March 10, 2015, **www.benefitscanada.com/benefits/health-benefits/drug-plan-trends-in-canada-62988**; Jena McGregor, "An Unusual New Policy for Working Mothers," *The Washington Post*, March 6, 2015, accessed March 10, 2015, **www.washingtonpost.com/blogs/on-leadership/wp/2015/03/06/an-unusual-new-policy-for-working-mothers/**; Mike Kennedy, "How to Help Employees Manage Drug and Disability Claims," *Benefits Canada*, February 1, 2015, accessed March 10, 2015, **www.benefitscanada.com/benefits/health-benefits/how-to-help-employees-manage-drug-and-disability-claims-62245**; and Kevin Jeffrey, "Flexible Benefits for a New Generation(s)," *PeopleTalk*, Spring 2015, 44–45.

Summary

1. Explain an organization's strategic concerns in developing a strategic rewards program.
   - Companies structure compensation in ways that enhance employee motivation and growth
   - Compensation must be tailored to fit the needs of the company and its employees
   - Companies are concerned that employees believe the compensation to be equitable
2. Identify the various factors that influence the setting of pay levels.
   - There are internal and external factors
   - Internal factors include the organization's compensation policy, the perceived worth of the job, the performance of the employee, and the employer's willingness to pay
   - The external factors include labour-market conditions, cost of living, collective bargaining, and legal considerations
3. Describe the major job evaluation systems.
   - Job ranking system, which groups jobs on the basis of their relative worth
   - Job classification system, in which jobs are grouped according to a series of predetermined grades based on a number of factors
   - Point system, which determines a job's relative worth by using a quantitative system of points
   - Factor comparison system, in which a job is evaluated on a factor-by-factor basis; this type of system is typically used for legislated pay equity purposes
4. Illustrate the compensation structure.
   - Wage and salary survey, which provides information about average wage rates external to the organization
   - Development of a wage curve, which indicates the rates currently paid for jobs within the organization
   - Development of pay rates for paying individuals based on the job
5. List the types of incentive plans.
   - Individual bonus
   - Team- or group-based
   - Merit raises
   - Profit-sharing
   - Employee stock ownership plan

6. Explain the employee benefits required by law.
   - Canada and Quebec pension plans, which provide for a pension for all employees working in Canada
   - Employment Insurance, which provides income protection to employees who are between jobs
   - Workers' compensation insurance, which pays people for work-related accidents or illnesses
7. Describe voluntary benefits.
   - Benefits considered indirect compensation
   - Benefits an organization chooses to provide
   - Can include health and welfare coverage, pay for time not worked (vacation, sick leave), wellness programs, and childcare assistance

Need to Know

- Definition of rewards, compensation, and compensation management
- Internal and external factors that affect compensation
- Types of incentive plans
- Types of voluntary and mandatory benefits

Need to Understand

- Relationship of rewards and organizational objectives
- Complexity of factors in relation to compensation decisions
- Role of line manager in making individual employee reward decisions
- Impact of benefits costs on costs of running business

KEY TERMS

REVIEW QUESTIONS

1. How would you describe the goals of a total rewards strategy?
2. Why are rewards considered motivational?
3. What are the internal and external factors used in determining compensation levels?
4. What are the various methods of job evaluation?
5. How would you describe an incentive plan?
6. What is the purpose of a compensation structure?
7. Name the benefits required by law.
8. Name some of the voluntary benefits offered by employers.

CRITICAL THINKING QUESTIONS

1. In the HRM Close-up, Rajwinder Nijjer comments on the importance of rewards and recognition. What does she do in addition to what Walmart does?

2. A large-chain retail store in your community has many part-time employees, primarily in the 18-to-25-year age range. The corporate office is considering providing a modest benefits program for part-time employees. The local manager knows that you are taking an introductory course in human resources management and has approached you to give some ideas about what to include. What items would you suggest and why?
3. You have recently been promoted to a supervisor. Your company is in the retail grocery business and has a policy that supervisors are paid a salary instead of on an hourly wage basis. What are the advantages and disadvantages to you and your company?
4. You work for a yoga studio in your community as an instructor. The manager has approached you about your thoughts on introducing a bonus based on the number of classes taught and the total number of students who regularly attend. How would you respond and why?
5. Would it be better to grant pay increases on a percentage basis or by a fixed amount? Why? Explain your reasoning.
6. If you could design your total rewards package, what components would you include and why?
7. You are the owner-operator of a bicycle rental company in a large city. You have decided that you need to hire someone who can assist you, particularly in taking telephone reservations and working with customers. However, you're not sure how much you might have to pay someone for this work. Where would you get the information and what other factors might you need to consider?

DEVELOPING YOUR SKILLS

Monster
www.monster.ca

1. Think about your dream job. Do you know how much it pays? Working in pairs, go to Monster.ca (**www.monster.ca**) and use its Salary Wizard to find out how much that job would earn in the nearest large city to you. Is information about the methodology used provided? What would you need to do to determine whether the information was good data? Share your results with your classmates.
2. Assume you have just been hired as the store manager for a high-volume discount store in Winnipeg. Other stores in Alberta are owned by the same person. The previous manager has recently hired 10 part-time employees. The store has more than 50 full-time employees. While the part-time employees in Alberta have a benefits program, the employees in Winnipeg do not. The store owner wants to know whether there should be consistency on benefits across the country. What would you need to consider in your response? Prepare a one-page summary of your thoughts for the store owner.

Treasury Board of Canada Secretariat
www.tbs-sct.gc.ca/gui/cmgs-eng.asp

3. Working in groups of three or four, access the Competency Profile for Supervisors in the federal government at **www.tbs-sct.gc.ca/gui/cmgs-eng.asp**. Read the descriptions and the detail for each of the nine competencies listed. Once you have reviewed them, discuss whether pay ought to be based on these competencies, and, if pay is to be based on each competency, how you would weight each and why.
4. Working in groups of four or five, develop a rewards objective to match the following organization and its business goals. Luxor Corporation has 400 employees and a dynamic business strategy. It wishes to employ a high-quality workforce capable of responding to a competitive business environment. Share your results with the class, including an explanation of your results.

Exercise

Since pay for performance is an important factor governing compensation increases, managers must be able to defend the compensation recommendations they make for their employees. Merit raises granted under a pay-for-performance policy must be based on objective performance ratings if they are to achieve their intended purposes of rewarding outstanding employee performance. As managers know, however, they must deal with other factors that can affect compensation recommendations. These may include the opinions of the employee's peers or extenuating circumstances, such as illness or family responsibilities. The purpose of the following exercise is to provide you with the experience of granting salary increases to employees on the basis of their work performance and other information.

Following are the work records of five employees. As their manager, you have just completed their annual performance reviews, and it is now time to make recommendations for their future salaries. Your department budget has $10,000 allocated for salary increases. Distribute the $10,000 among your employees based on the descriptions for each person.

1. *Jas Ayand* currently earns $50,000. His performance review rating was very high. He is respected by his peers and is felt to be an asset to the work group. He is single with three young children to support.
2. *Jean Jones* earns a salary of $35,000. Her annual performance review was average. Several members of the work group have spoken to you about the difficulty involved in her job. They feel that it is a tough and demanding job and that she is doing her best.
3. *Tamara Tran* earns $38,000. Her performance review rating was below average, and she seems to have difficulty with other members of her team. Tanara has had a difficult time this past year. Both her parents, with whom she lived, have died recently.
4. *Simon Chan* earns $40,000. His performance review rating was above average. He is respected by his co-workers and is generally considered to be helpful and outgoing.
5. *Ray Bennett* earns $60,000. His performance review rating was very high. His peers resent him because he comes from a very wealthy family and they feel that he is trying to impress everyone.

Share your results with other class members. Be prepared to explain your allocation of money.

CASE STUDY 1

But Do Legislated Wage Rates Work?

All provinces in Canada have legislated minimum wage rates. Nova Scotia raised its rate to $10.60 in April 2015 and British Columbia raised its rate to $10.45 in September 2015. Most of the provinces have similar rates—ranging from $10 in the Northwest Territories to $11 in Ontario and Nunavut.

Governments do this because they want to provide workers with a guaranteed minimum income that will enable them to support themselves and their families. Setting rates is also intended to help the general economy—the more people are able to support themselves with increased incomes, the more tax revenues as well as an improved standard of living for the family there will be. In some places, such as with Nova Scotia and British Columbia, the governments are making the adjustments to align with an changes in the CPI.

However, critics of the change in B.C. say that 120,000 workers will still be below the poverty line. For example, the B.C. Federation of Labour is concerned that 6.4% of the workforce will not earn enough to rise above poverty. Even some workers feel that the change is an insult. There is also concern that since so much of the Canadian economic scene is based on small business, only larger firms are more likely to keep the same number of employees and raise the minimum. Other smaller organizations may cut hours or reduce staff to ensure that the total labour costs with the increased minimum do not change.

Manitoba has also been concerned about the impact on small businesses, which is why it eliminated the small business tax in 1999, stating that the savings to each small business owner is about $55,000, which means that small businesses can easily absorb an increase in the minimum wage.

On the other hand, many small employers pay more than the minimum wage to retain key staff. For example, only 1.5% of those employed in Alberta are paid the minimum wage; the percentage in Ontario is 9.1% of employees.

Sources: Adapted from "Minimum Wage by Province," Retail Council of Canada, accessed March 14, 2015, **www.retailcouncil.org/quickfacts/minimum-wage**; Justine Hunter and Maura Forrest, "B.C. to Tie Minimum Wage to Inflation," *The Globe and Mail*, March 13, 2015, S1; "Large Employers Much More Likely to Pay Minimum Wage," *Canadian HR Reporter*, December 2, 2014, accessed March 14, 2015, **www.hrreporter.com/articleview/22980-large-employers-much-more-likely-to-pay-minimum-wage**; "Manitoba Increasing Minimum Wage in October," *Canadian HR Reporter*, June 18, 2014, accessed March 14, 2015, **www.hrreporter.com/articleview/21527-manitoba-increasing-minimum-wage-in-october**; and "Alberta's Minimum Wage Increasing to $10.20 Sept. 1," *Canadian HR Reporter*, May 28, 2014, accessed March 14, 2015, **www.hrreporter.com/articleview/21292-albertas-minimum-wage-increasing-to-1020-sept-1**.

Questions:

1. Is it good economic policy or just politics when provinces legislate minimum wage rates? Why or why not?
2. Why would employers want to pay more than the minimum wage? Explain your reasons.
3. Do you feel that small businesses are at risk of reducing staff hours when the minimum wage increases? Explain your reasons.

CASE STUDY 2

What Are the Right Ingredients for a Recognition and Rewards Program?

The answer to the question ought to be simple and straightforward. But it isn't. Depending on where someone might be in their career, or depending on their family status, people might want very different things in any recognition and rewards program. So how do employers make decisions?

One answer is to ask employees. While there might be concern that by asking employees will have raised expectations as to what should be included. However, by not doing so, a company may put together a total rewards approach that is not meaningful to the employees and therefore may not achieve the total rewards strategy of the company. For example, a group of chief financial officers recently were asked to rate the total three components of a total rewards program. They listed: better benefit plan, more flexibility, and more vacation days. When a group of employees were asked the same question, their response was: more vacation days, more flexibility, and a better benefit plan. If the company could do only the first choice, it is possible that it would have missed the mark by following the views of the chief financial officer instead of the employees. And it is also possible that the costs might have been more.

If a company focuses on providing more work flexibility as part of the rewards and recognition program, it needs to make it happen. Recent research found that while flexible work arrangements were available in many organizations, only about one-third of those organizations allowed more than 50% of the employees to use flexible work arrangements.

Companies indicated that there was limit on the amount of flexibility due to service delivery and adequate coverage of work activities. The same study also found that not all managers are comfortable with having employees on flexible arrangements, believing that better levels of productivity would be achieved at work, rather than employees working from home.

Even though it is important to look at all ingredients in the total rewards package, companies need to ensure that their pay levels are competitive with the market if they want to attract and retain top talent. And depending on the geographic location of the company, the competitive pressures may be more severe. While the decline in oil prices has led to a number of staff reductions in Alberta, it hasn't allowed Alberta companies to ease up on watching the salaries of their employees.

Whether it is one component or the entire total rewards program, organizations need to periodically review and ensure they are meeting the needs of the employees and the organization.

Sources: Adapted from Claudine Kapel, "Remaining Market-Competitive Top Reward Priority," *Canadian HR Reporter*, November 17, 2014, accessed March 14, 2015, **www.hrreporter.com/blog/Compensation-Rewards/archive/2014/11/17/remaining-market-competitive-top-reward-priority**; "Other Than Better Pay, Workers Want More Vacation, Flexibility," *Canadian HR Reporter*, March 11, 2015, accessed March 14, 2015, **www.hrreporter.com/articleview/23762-other-than-better-pay-workers-want-more-vacation-flexibility**; Claudine Kapel, "Employers Still Struggling with Workplace Flexibility," *Canadian HR Reporter*, March 3, 2015, accessed March 14, 2015, **www.hrreporter.com/blog/Compensation-Rewards/archive/2015/03/03/employers-still-struggling-with-workplace-flexibility**.

Questions:

1. If you could build your own total rewards program, what would be the components? Explain your answer.
2. How might employers ask employees about components of a total rewards program without creating unrealistic expectations?

NOTES AND REFERENCES

1. Lookman Buky Folami, Kwadwo Asare, Eillen Kwesiga, Dennis Bline, "The Impact of Job Satisfaction and Organizational Context Variables on Organizational Commitment," *International Journal of Business & Public Administration* 11, no. 1 (Summer 2014): 1–18; Abdulmonem AlZalabani and Rajesh S. Modi, "Impact of Human Resources Management Practice and Perceived Organizational Support on Job Satisfaction: Evidence from Yanbu Industrial City, KSA," *IUP Journal of Organizational Behavior* 13, no. 3 (July 2014): 33–52; Valerie J. Vales, "Hawaii Government Employee Unions: How Do Salary, Benefits, and Environment Affect Job Satisfaction?" *Organization Development Journal* 32, no. 3 (Fall 2014): 41–55; and Claudine Kapel, "Lack of Acknowledgement Eroding Job Satisfaction," *Canadian HR Reporter*, October 20, 2014, accessed February 23, 2015, www.hrreporter.com/articleview/22558-lack-of-acknowledgement-eroding-job-satisfaction.
2. "Employers Lower Salary Increases amid Economic Uncertainty: Survey, *Canadian HR Reporter*, February 17, 2015, accessed February 23, 2015, www.hrreporter.com/articleview/23530-employers-lower-salary-increases-amid-economic-uncertainty-survey.
3. David Hoad and Nathalie Olds, "Finding Value in Rewards," *Canadian HR Reporter*, January 26, 2015, accessed February 23, 2015, www.hrreporter.com/articleview/23321-finding-value-in-rewards.
4. Teresa M. Amabile and Steven J. Kramer, "The Power of Small Wins," *Harvard Business Review* 89, no. 5 (May 2011): 70–80; and Gretchen Spreitzer and Christine Porath, "Creating Sustainable Performance," *Harvard Business Review* 90, no. 1 (January/February 2012): 92–99.
5. David Hoad and Nathalie Olds, "Finding Value in Rewards," *Canadian HR Reporter*, January 26, 2015, 23, accessed September 26, 2015, digital.hrreporter.com/i/446801-january-26-2015/22#.
6. "Compensation Trends and Strategies for 2015," presentation by Hay Group, September 9, 2014.
7. Deloitte, "Human Capital Trends, 2014—Proceed with Action, Challenges Ahead," 2014.
8. James F. Waegelein, "The Influence of Long-Term Performance Plans on Corporate Performance & Investment," *Journal of Applied Financial Research* 1 (2014): 88–95.
9. "What Is Total Rewards?" *WorldAtWork*, accessed February 24, 2015, www.worldatwork.org/aboutus/html/aboutus-whatis.jsp.
10. "Push for Differentiation for Performance Yields Positive Results," *Report on Salary Surveys* 21, no. 8 (August 2014): 8–9.
11. Towers Watson, "2014 Global Talent Management and Rewards Study," 3.
12. David Hoad and Nathalie Olds, "Finding Value in Rewards," *Canadian HR Reporter*, January 26, 2015, 23.
13. Elliot N. Dinkin, "Dust Off the Historical Approach to Total Compensation," *Benefits Quarterly*, First Quarter 2015, 43–50.
14. Richard E. Kopelman, Naomi A. Gardberg, and Ann Cohen Brandwein, "Using a Recognition and Reward Initiative to Improve Service Quality," *Public Personnel Management* 40, no. 2 (Summer 2011): 133–149.
15. Michaeline Skiba and Stuart Rosenberg, "The Disutility of Equity Theory in Contemporary Management Practices," *Journal of Business & Economic Studies* 17, no. 2 (Fall 2011): 1–19.
16. Ibid.
17. "Compensation Trends and Strategies for 2015," presentation by Hay Group, September 9, 2014.
18. Robert Crawford, "Co-operative Food Rewards Staff for Saving Energy," *Employee Benefits*, January 22, 2015, 1.

19. "2014 Global Top Five Total Rewards Priorities Survey, Deloitte.
20. Bruno S. Frey and Margit Osterloh, "Stop Tying Pay to Performance," *Harvard Business Review*, January/February 2012, 51.
21. "Loblaws Demands Workers Pay Back Thousands After Payment Error," *CBC News*, June 12, 2015; and Laura Wright, "Loblaws Overpayment Blunder: 3 Lessons Learned," *CBC News*, June 27, 2015, accessed July 7, 2015, www.cbc.ca/news/business/loblaws-overpayment-blunder-3-lessons-learned-1.3120116.
22. "2014 Global Top Five Total Rewards Priorities Survey," Deloitte; "2015 Survey on Compensation and Trends in Human Resources," Morneau Shepell; and Subeer Bakshi, "Is Your Variable Plan Working?" Towers Watson, 2014.
23. Statistics Canada, "Consumer Price Index," February 26, 2015, accessed March 1, 2015, www23.statcan.gc.ca/imdb/p2SV.pl?Function=getSurvey&SDDS=2301.
24. "Classification Standard, Economics and Social Science Services Group," Treasury Board of Canada Secretariat, accessed March 2, 2015, www.tbs-sct.gc.ca/cla/snd/ec-eng.asp#Toc159814569.
25. Katerina Kashi, "Employees Training and Development: What Competencies Should Be Developed the Most?" *Proceedings of the European Conference on Management, Leadership and Governance* (2014): 452–459.
26. Candace L. Hawkes and Bart L. Weathington, "Competency-Based Versus Task-Based Job Descriptions: Effects on Applicant Attraction," *Journal of Behavioral and Applied Management* (2014): 190–211.
27. Vikram Singh Chouhan & Sandeep Srivastava, "Understanding Competencies and Competency Modeling," *Journal of Business and Management* 16, no. 1 (January 2014): 14–22.
28. "Talent Management for the Finance Community—Employee Guide to Competency-Based Management," Treasury Board of Canada, Secretariat, accessed March 2, 2015, www.tbs-sct.gc.ca/fm-gf/tools-outils/guides/tm-gdt/tm-gdtpr-eng.asp.
29. "2014 Global Top Five Total Rewards Priorities Survey," Deloitte.
30. "2014 Global Talent Management and Rewards Study," Towers Watson, 3.
31. Subeer Bakshi, "Is Your Variable Plan Working?" Towers Watson, 2014.
32. "Canada's Top 100 Employers 2015," accessed March 6, 2015, www.canadastop100.com/national.
33. Kevin McFadden, "Benefits Trends: 3 Choices to Make Your Employee Benefits More Flexible," *Benefits Canada*, March 1, 2015, accessed March 6, 2015, www.benefitscanada.com/benefits/health-benefits/benefits-trends-3-choices-to-make-your-employee-benefits-more-flexible-62989.
34. Mel Bartlett and Paul Lai, "Collaboration Leads to Affordable Pension Plan Solution," *Benefits Canada*, February 20, 2014, accessed March 6, 2015, www.benefitscanada.com/pensions/db/collaboration-leads-to-affordable-pension-plan-solution-49757.
35. Chris Bonnett, "Making Connections to Improve Health Benefit plans," *Canadian HR Reporter*, September 5, 2014, accessed March 6, 2015, www.hrreporter.com/articleview/22178-making-connections-to-improve-health-benefit-plans.
36. Ibid.
37. Kim Siddall, "Making Wellness More Meaningful," *Benefits Canada,* August 21, 2014, accessed March 7, 2015, www.benefitscanada.com/benefits/health-wellness/making-wellness-more-meaningful-55976.
38. "Time Off in Canadian Workplaces," *Canadian HR Reporter*, 2015, 15.
39. Statistics Canada, "Population by Sex and Age Group," accessed March 7, 2015, www.statcan.gc.ca/tables-tableaux/sum-som/l01/cst01/demo10a-eng.htm.
40. Information gathered by the current author from a senior manager at Vancouver Coastal Health Authority, February 12, 2015.
41. Michael Biskey, "Reducing Drug Costs Using Behavioural Science," *Canadian HR Reporter*, April 7, 2014, accessed March 7, 2015, www.hrreporter.com/articleview/20751-reducing-drug-costs-using-behavioural-science.
42. Ibid.
43. Jacqueline Nelson, "Insurers Pressured over Genetic Tests," *The Globe and Mail*, July 11, 2014, B3.
44. Adrian Morrow, "Ontario Takes First Steps in Setting Up New Provincial Pension Plan," *The Globe and Mail*, December 8, 2014, accessed March 7, 2015, www.theglobeandmail.com/news/politics/ontario-takes-first-steps-in-setting-up-new-provincial-pension-plan/article21989145; and "Ontario Pension Plan Could Cost Jobs, Hurt Economy: Survey," *Canadian HR Reporter*, February 19, 2015, accessed March 7, 2015, www.hrreporter.com/articleview/23576-ontario-pension-plan-could-cost-jobs-hurt-economy-survey.
45. "Many Employers Would Reduce Contributions Under Existing Plans with ORPP: Survey," *Canadian HR Reporter*, February 12, 2015, accessed March 7, 2015, www.hrreporter.com/articleview/23514-many-employers-would-reduce-contributions-under-existing-plans-with-orpp-survey.
46. Fred Vettese, "The Biggest Myth About Defined Benefit Pensions Is How Much They Cost," *Financial Post*, September 6, 2014, accessed March 7, 2015, http://business.financialpost.com/2014/09/06/the-biggest-myth-about-defined-benefit-pensions-is-how-much-they-cost/.
47. "Pension Plans," *Many Nations Financial*, accessed March 7, 2015, http://manynations.com/pension-plans; and "The SMEP Advantage, Teamsters Canadian Pension Plan, accessed March 7, 2015, http://pension.teamsters-canada.org/section.php?id=20&lang=en.
48. "Canada Unveils New Pension Plan Proposal," *Canadian HR Reporter*, April 24, 2014, accessed March 7, 2015, www.hrreporter.com/articleview/20928-canada-unveils-new-pension-plan-proposal.
49. "Federal Framework for Target Benefit Pension Plans," Unifor, October 14, 2014, accessed March 7, 2015, www.unifor.org/en/federal-framework-target-benefit-pension-plans; and "Pension Innovation for Canadians: The Target Benefit Plan," Canadian Union of Public Employees, June 23, 2014.
50. Frederic Tomesco, "Air Canada Pension Exit Creates Potential Savings of About $310 Million," *The Globe and Mail*, May 28, 2015, B2.
51. "Time Off in Canadian Workplaces," 4.
52. "Not All Perks Are Created Equal," *HRM Online*, August 5, 2014.
53. Stuart Rudner, "Holiday Season Requires Finesse," *Canadian HR Reporter*, October 20, 2014, www.hrreporter.com/blog/Canadian-HR-Law/archive/2014/10/20/holiday-season-requires-finesse.
54. Statistics Canada, "Work Absence Statistics of Full-Time Employees," Table 279-0029, accessed March 9, 2015, www5.statcan.gc.ca/cansim/a26?lang=eng&retrLang=eng&id=2790029&pattern=279-0029..279-0039&tabMode=dataTable&srchLan=-1&p1=-1&p2=31.
55. Statistics Canada, "Work Absence Statistics of Full-Time Employees by Sex and Age Group," Table 279-0032, accessed March 15, 2015, www5.statcan.gc.ca/cansim/a26?lang=eng&retrLang=eng&id=2790029&pattern=279-0029..279-0039&tabMode=dataTable&srchLan=-1&p1=-1&p2=31.
56. "2014 Canada Awards for Excellence," Excellence Canada, accessed March 15, 2015, www.excellence.ca/en/awards/2014-cae-recipients/2014-cae-profiles/2014-caeprofile-amd.
57. Alyssa Hodder, "Strategy: How Bruce Telecom's Focus on Wellness Saved $136,000," *Benefits Canada*, February 1, 2015, accessed March 9, 2015, www.benefitscanada.com/benefits/health-wellness/strategy-how-bruce-telecoms-focus-on-wellness-saved-136000-62330.

58. "Employers See Significant ROI in EFAPs," *Canadian HR Reporter*, November 18, 2014, accessed March 15, 2015, www.hrreporter.com/articleview/22836-employers-see-significant-roi-in-efaps.
59. "Flex Hours, Education, T & D Top Retention Strategies: Survey," *Canadian HR Reporter*, August 28, 2014, accessed March 9, 2015, www.hrreporter.com/articleview/22089-flex-hours-education-td-top-retention-strategies-survey.
60. Statistics Canada, "Population by Sex and Age Group" accessed March 15, 2015, www.statcan.gc.ca/tables-tableaux/sum-som/l01/cst01/demo31a-eng.htm.
61. Liz Bernier, "Do Employers Care About Caregivers?" *Canadian HR Reporter*, February 9, 2015, accessed March 9, 2015, www.hrreporter.com/articleview/23469-do-employers-care-about-caregivers.
62. "Report from the Employer Panel for Caregivers," Employment and Social Development Canada, February 10, 2015, accessed March 9, 2015, www.esdc.gc.ca/eng/seniors/reports/cec.shtml.
63. Ibid.
64. Statistics Canada, "Population Projections for Canada (2013 to 2063)," Table 2.4, accessed March 9, 2015, www.statcan.gc.ca/pub/91-520-x/2014001/tbl-eng.htm.
65. Ibid.
66. Statistics Canada, "Employment by Age, Sex, Type of Work, Class of Worker and Province," January 2015, accessed March 9, 2015, www.statcan.gc.ca/tables-tableaux/sum-som/l01/cst01/labr66a-eng.htm.
67. Employment and Social Development Canada, "Indicators of Well-Being in Canada," updated March 9, 2015, www4.hrsdc.gc.ca/.3ndic.1t.4r@-eng.jsp?iid=13.
68. Liz Bernier, "Do Employers Care About Caregivers?" *Canadian HR Reporter*, February 9, 2015, accessed March 9, 2015, www.hrreporter.com/articleview/23469-do-employers-care-about-caregivers.
69. Suzanne Bowness, "Caring for the Caregivers," *The Globe and Mail*, August 19, 2015, B12.

Dealing with Management Rights, Employee Rights, and Discipline

LEARNING OUTCOMES

After studying this chapter, you should be able to

1. Describe statutory rights, contractual rights, due process, and legal implications of those rights.
2. Identify the job expectancy rights of employees.
3. Explain the process of establishing disciplinary practices, including the proper implementation of organizational rules.
4. Discuss the meaning of discipline and how to investigate a disciplinary problem.
5. Outline the differences between progressive and positive discipline.
6. Identify the different types of alternative dispute-resolution procedures.

OUTLINE

HRM CLOSE-UP

"Safeguarding employee privacy is really part and parcel of good employee relations."

John Jacak is a busy man. As the privacy officer for Calgary-based Agrium Inc., the leading global agricultural solutions provider and one of the largest distributors of fertilizer in the world, Jacak is responsible for staying on top of the constantly evolving world of personal information privacy. With 16,000 employees worldwide and the issue of privacy protection being a relatively new and constantly changing field, it's no mean feat.

"It is very much a fluid and dynamic environment and it's an area of the law that's still evolving," Jacak explains. "I try to keep my finger on the pulse of developments and evolving areas of the law."

Although government legislation at both federal and provincial levels mandates what personal information can be collected and just what can be done with that information, Agrium's robust and detailed Employee Privacy Policy has been driven by more than just legal compliance.

"Really, the bottom line behind it and the guiding principle is to maintain trust both of our employees and our customers," Jacak says. "The process is to build their trust and confidence by respecting their privacy and their personal information. It's part of the trust process and the respect process."

And respect is something that Agrium, founded in 1931, have always taken very seriously.

"Respect is a principle that really formed the bedrock to our employee relations practice and it just carries right across into privacy and maintaining privacy," Jacak explains. "Safeguarding employee privacy is really part and parcel of good employee relations."

He adds: "The privacy policy gives people a good sense of what information we collect. It's a clear statement that we have a commitment to safeguard their personal information and retain it for only as long as needed. And in doing that, I think we build trust and confidence. It's a clear statement to our employees, prospective employees, and former employees of what we do with their personal information. What it's used for, how we protect it, how long we retain it, and it gives them an indication that if they'd like to access it they can do so. By doing that I think it takes any questions out of their minds or potential concerns they may have."

Privacy and the retention of personal information are topics of concern for many people in society today, whether employees or customers. From the very outset of electronic record gathering, Agrium believed that the best approach with personal information was to be transparent and open. The company maintained that such an approach not only was the optimal way to help head off conflicts that might arise from a lack of understanding, but also helped express respect for their employees and a genuine concern for their well-being.

Used with permission by John Jacak

Agrium Inc.

"It's better from our standpoint to be transparent and just to lay it out on the table so everybody knows what the framework is for privacy practice," Jacak explains. "By embracing a transparent approach you really diffuse many concerns that people may otherwise have. When you don't address issues of safeguarding or retention, or when you don't have a clear statement that information collected will only be used for the purpose that was originally intended and consented to and in fact needed, [you open yourself up to problems]. So [transparency] just diffuses a whole lot of questions."

John Jacak believes that when it comes to the hazardous area of employee privacy, the only advisable route is honesty and openness about your privacy practices.

"Starting from a point of transparency translates into a more positive feeling on the part of the employee from the outset, as opposed to having these lingering questions and perhaps concerns that you don't need and you can nicely sidestep."

Source: Used by permission of John Jacak

INTRODUCTION

In this chapter, employee rights, management rights, workplace privacy, and employee discipline are discussed. Managers note that these topics have a major influence on the activities of both employees and supervisors. Managers are discovering that the right to discipline and discharge employees—a traditional responsibility of management—is more difficult to exercise in light of the growing attention to employee rights. In addition, disciplining employees is a difficult and unpleasant task for most managers and supervisors; many of them report that taking disciplinary action against an employee is the most stressful duty they perform. Balancing employee rights and employee discipline may not be easy, but it is a universal requirement and a critical aspect of good management. John Jacak, privacy officer at Agrium, describes in the HRM Close-up that openness and transparency are critical when it comes to gathering employee information.

Because the growth of employee rights issues may lead to an increase in the number of lawsuits filed by employees, this chapter includes a discussion of alternative dispute resolution as a way to foster a less legalistic approach to solving disagreements. As managers are the people who take disciplinary actions that are subject to challenge and possible reversal through governmental agencies or the courts, they should make a positive effort to prevent the need for such action.

When disciplinary action becomes impossible to avoid, however, that action should be taken in accordance with carefully developed HR policies and practices. Most of this chapter applies to both non-unionized and unionized workplaces. Where a concept applies only to a non-union workplace, this will be mentioned.

MANAGEMENT RIGHTS AND RESPONSIBILITIES

All companies have people, usually called "managers," who make fundamental decisions such as how the business is run or how much the company should charge for its products or services. In making these decisions, they have both rights and responsibilities. One of the more basic rights is that the company can hire or terminate whomever it wants.

However, as discussed both in this chapter and in Chapter 10, those rights now have to be exercised in certain ways, and managers now have more responsibility for how those rights are exercised. Managers function as representatives of the organization and therefore have the legal responsibilities and liabilities that go with that role.

In addition, employees and the public at large are demanding that employers demonstrate greater social responsibility in managing their people. Complaints that some jobs are deadening the spirit and injuring the health of employees are not uncommon. Complaints of discrimination against women, visible minorities, the physically and mentally challenged, and the elderly with respect to hiring, training, advancement, and compensation are being levelled against some employers. Issues such as comparable pay for dissimilar work, the high cost of health benefits, daycare for children of employees, and alternative work schedules are ones that many employers must address as our workforce grows more diverse.

One illustration of this is "negligent hiring," in which a person is hired and then involved in job-related misconduct that might have been determined if the person's previous work background and behaviours had been referenced.[1] While any claim would be against the employer, it is the action (or lack of action) of the manager that led to the situation. An example would be a long-term residential care facility in which a resident is physically assaulted by an employee with a long, verifiable history of physical violence.

In addition, supervisors and managers are expected to behave and act in ways that acknowledge that employees also have certain rights. Managers are no longer able to make decisions or take actions without being aware of their obligations with respect to how an employee must be treated in today's workplace.

EMPLOYEE RIGHTS

Various human rights laws, wage and hour regulations, and safety and health legislation have secured basic employee rights and brought numerous job improvements to the workplace. Now employee rights litigation has shifted to such workplace issues as employees' rights to protest unfair disciplinary action, to refuse to take drug tests, to have access to their own personnel files, to challenge employer searches and surveillance, and to prevent employers from using social media activity to gather information about potential employees.[2] All these things make it very important that managers act and behave in fair and objective ways.

The current emphasis on employee rights is a natural result of the evolution of societal, business, and employee interests. The term **employee rights** refers to the expectation of fair treatment from employers in the employment relationship. These expectations become rights when they are granted to employees by the courts, legislatures, or employers. Employee rights frequently involve an employer's alleged invasion of an employee's right to privacy. Unfortunately, the difference between an employee's legal right to privacy and the moral or personal right to privacy is not always clear. The confusion is due to the lack of a comprehensive and consistent body of privacy protection, whether from laws or from court decisions.

Employee rights
Expectations of fair treatment from employers

There can be a perceived invasion of privacy when the employer uses electronic monitoring or surveillance to observe or monitor employees while they are doing their work. Although such action is not illegal, employers are well advised to let employees know when and why they are doing it. For example, companies that have a call-centre operation frequently will use electronic means to monitor customer calls. However, employees are provided full information about the purpose and, in some situations, given guarantees that the data will be used only to help the employees learn and improve their customer-service skills.

Balanced against employee rights is the employer's responsibility to provide a safe workplace for employees while guaranteeing safe, high-quality goods and services to consumers. An employee who uses drugs may exercise a privacy right and refuse to submit to a drug test. But should that employee produce a faulty product as a result of drug impairment, the employer can be held liable for any harm caused by that product. Employers must therefore exercise *reasonable care* in the hiring, training, and assignment of employees to jobs. As mentioned earlier, without the exercise of reasonable care, employers can be held negligent by outside parties or other employees injured by a dishonest, unfit, or violent employee.[3] In law, **negligence** is the failure to use a reasonable amount of care where such failure results in injury to another person. Several years ago, the federal government established occupational health and safety negligence as a criminal offence. In 2014, three employees of the Montreal, Maine and Atlantic Railway were charged with criminal negligence causing death when a train derailed and killed 47 people in Lac-Mégantic, Quebec.[4]

Negligence
Failure to provide reasonable care where such failure results in injury to consumers or other employees

It is here that employee rights and employer responsibilities can come most pointedly into conflict. The failure of an employer to honour employee rights can result in costly lawsuits, damage the organization's reputation, and hurt employee morale. But failure to protect the safety and welfare of employees or consumer interests can invite litigation from both groups. At Work with HRM 9.1 discusses the practical implications for managers of the balance between employee rights and employer responsibilities. The remainder of this section will discuss various rights that employees have come to expect from their employers.

Employment Protection Rights

It is not surprising that employees should regard their jobs as an established right—a right that should not be taken away lightly. Without the opportunity to hold a job, personal well-being would be greatly curtailed. This line of reasoning has led to the emergence of three legal considerations regarding the security of one's job: statutory rights, contractual rights, and due process.

LO1

What are the various rights of employees and employers and the implications of these?

Statutory rights
Rights that derive from legislation

Statutory Rights

Statutory rights are rights that derive from legislation. As we saw in Chapter 2, human rights legislation protects employees from discrimination on the basis of such grounds as age, sex, and race, and from harassment.

For example, an arbitrator ruled that Brewers Distributors was justified in terminating a long-service employee for his ongoing harassment and bullying of a female worker. The situation occurred over some period of time and various actions included the employee making vulgar comments and threatening actions with machinery. At one point the union was allowed to speak to the worker about the misconduct, but nothing changed. The employer knew that the intimation and harassment had to stop. The arbitrator determined that the employee did not accept responsibility for his actions and that his continued employment made the workplace "unsafe and toxic."[6]

AT WORK WITH HRM 9.1

WHY DID IT COST SO MUCH?

For a number of years, two court cases[5] demonstrated the special recognition to the employer–employee relationship given through decisions of the Supreme Court of Canada. These decisions focused on the fair and individual treatment of each person. This meant that managers should pay greater attention to individual employees before, during, and at the end of employment.

One of the cases, *Wallace v. United Grain Growers*, pointed up the need for employers to pay more attention to how people are terminated. Besides compensation for lack of notice, employees were seeking damages if they felt they were poorly treated during the actual termination. This perspective meant that the manager's behaviour during the process could have a bearing on how much the termination would cost the employer.

However, a significant case decided by the Supreme Court in mid-2008 changed this approach. In *Honda Canada Inc. v. Keays*, the Court determined that earlier decisions had been inappropriate. In lower court decisions, the employee had been awarded $100,000 in punitive damages for the manner in which Honda conducted itself in the termination. The employee had been diagnosed with chronic fatigue syndrome, resulting in his eventually being placed in Honda's disability program. That program required employees to provide Honda with medical information from a physician that absences were due to the medical condition. What the employee's physician provided was insufficient, so Honda requested that the employee meet with an occupational medical specialist. The employee refused.

Honda then terminated the employee. The employee sued for wrongful dismissal, stating that Honda had demonstrated bad faith. The Court disagreed, saying that the employee had not been treated poorly—either in terms of compensation or behaviour.

This case eliminated a number of principles established through the *Wallace* case. The most significant was that employees were not entitled to additional severance or punitive damages, only to receive compensation for "actual" damages—that is, loss of wages. But the case maintained that employers must act in good faith when dismissing employees, and the employees must be treated respectfully. Any additional financial costs would only occur if the employee could prove that the way in which the employer terminated caused mental distress.

In a recent Newfoundland and Labrador court decision, the judge concluded that the Newfoundland and Labrador Legal Aid Commission failed to meet its obligations when it terminated an employee. Specifically, it did not act with fairness in the dismissal. The judge concluded that the employee's mental health was impacted far beyond normal stress and that the employer ought to have known this

continued

would happen. The judge went on to indicate moral damages were appropriate given the tone and content of the letter of dismissal. Judge LeBlanc further states, "This award recognizes, and compensates for, the bad faith actions ... considering the professional nature of the employment involved. In this case, I find that an award of $30,000 appropriate addresses the actions of the employer...." This is one of the highest awards in Canada for bad behaviour of an employer when terminating an employee.

CRITICAL THINKING QUESTIONS:

1. Do you believe that employees have too many rights? Why or why not?
2. What would you have decided in these cases and why?

Sources: Adapted from Darren Stratton, "Bad Faith & Unfair Dealing in Employee Dismissal: 7 Lessons in 7 Years," *CanLII Connects*, February 2, 2015, accessed March 28, 2015, **http://canliiconnects.org/en/commentaries/35631**; Todd Humber, "Parting Is Such Sweet, Pricey Sorrow," *Canadian HR Reporter*, February 10, 2015, accessed March 28, 2015, **www.hrreporter.com/blog/Editor/archive/2015/02/10/parting-is-such-sweet-pricey-sorrow**; and *Turner v. Newfoundland and Labrador Legal Aid Commission*, December 16, 2014, 2014 NLTD(G) 156.

Provincial employment standards acts establish basic rights for such things as overtime pay and minimum vacation pay. However, these laws were developed at a time when use of technology, such as e-mail and smartphones, was not blurring work and personal life. Not paying attention to this and the impact of the requirements for overtime pay has created issues for large organizations such as Scotiabank and CIBC.[7] One of the more interesting cases dealing with statutory rights are the various class-action suits against Scotiabank and CIBC in relation to unpaid overtime. Employees at retail branches who thought they were eligible for overtime pay initiated these lawsuits. The focus of the lawsuits revolves around whether any of the employees were considered exempt from overtime provisions. "Overtime" refers specifically to employees. People in certain occupations, such as accountants and engineers, are exempt. Likewise, positions such as manager are exempt. So, if a person isn't a manager or in a profession, the person is entitled to overtime. For many years organizations have considered employees who are paid a salary exempt from overtime; however, according to the law, this thinking is not correct. In late 2014, Scotiabank negotiated a $95 million settlement on claims of overtime. CIBC is defending its claim, while Canada Cartage, a trucking firm, has had a $100 million claim launched against it.[8]

Occupational health and safety legislation aims to ensure safe and healthy working conditions, while labour relations laws (discussed in Chapter 10) give employees the right to form and belong to unions and to bargain for better working conditions. All these laws are statutory and grant certain rights to people.

Contractual Rights

Contractual rights
Rights that derive from contracts

While law establishes statutory rights, **contractual rights** are derived from contracts. A *contract* is a legally binding agreement; if one party breaches the contract, a remedy can be sought through an appeal to the courts. Although formal contracts between employers and full-time employees are rare, they are standard practice when it comes to contingent workers, a growing segment of the Canadian labour force. Such a contract, referred to as the *employment contract*, will deal with such items as the type of work, length of work, the amount of pay for the work including any benefits, and whether there is any obligation on the employer if the employee is terminated.

Not all contracts are written. An implied contract can occur when an employer continues to employ someone after a fixed-term contract has ended. Implied contractual rights can be based on either oral or written statements made during the pre-employment process or subsequent to hiring. Sometimes information contained in employee handbooks, HR manuals, or employment applications can be considered to establish an implied right. Whether explicitly or implicitly, if an employee continues to work after the end of a fixed-term contract, and no new contract has been entered into, or if multiple fixed-term contracts occur, courts will generally consider that the person continues to be an employee.

A recent case revolved around an employer's attempt not to provide appropriate notice and/or compensation when the employment was terminated. An administrative person had been employed in Ontario on 16 one-year fixed contracts. While the court said that it was acceptable to have multiple fixed-term contracts, it also said that the underlying employment relationship was continuous and that the person was entitled to reasonable notice.[9]

The following are circumstances in which an implied contract may become binding:

- telling employees their jobs are secure as long as they perform satisfactorily and are loyal to the organization
- stating in the employee handbook that employees will not be terminated without the right of defence or access to an appeal procedure (i.e., due process)
- urging an employee to leave another organization by promising higher wages and benefits, and then reneging after the person has been hired

To lessen their vulnerability to implied-contract lawsuits, employers can do the following:

1. Train supervisors and managers not to imply contract benefits in conversations with new or current employees.
2. Include in employment offers a statement that an employee may voluntarily terminate employment with proper notice, and the employer may dismiss the employee at any time and for a justified reason (just cause). The language in this statement must be appropriate, clear, and easily understood while conveying a tone of welcome to the company.
3. Explain the nature of the employment relationship in documents—for example, employee handbooks, employment applications, and letters of employment.
4. Have written proof that employees have read all documents pertaining to the employment relationship. This proof can be in the form of an offer-of-employment letter that the person signs or another type of sign-off document.

It is important to remember that in a contractual situation employees also have obligations and responsibilities. For example, an employer in Quebec terminated an employee for refusing to participate in a harassment investigation. A subordinate made a harassment complaint about the employee. When the employer started the investigation into the complaint, the employee refused to answer certain questions stating that privacy rights were paramount. Even when the employee brought a lawyer to attend any investigative meetings, the employee persisted in refusing to answer questions. As a result, the employer dismissed the person. The tribunal concluded that the employee had an obligation to participate in the investigation and answer questions that might be useful. To refuse is grounds for discipline, specifically termination.[10]

Due Process

Due process
Employee's right to a fair process in making a decision related to employment relationship

Management has traditionally had the right to direct employees and to take corrective action when needed. Nevertheless, many individuals also believe that a job is the property right of an employee and that the loss of employment has such serious consequences that an employee should not lose employment without the protection of due process. Managers normally define **due process** as the employee's right to fair treatment in the handling of an employment matter.[11] While due process is not a legal obligation, it does flow from common law history of fair treatment. As a result, proactive employers will additionally incorporate the following principles—or rights—in their interpretation of due process:

1. the right to know job expectations and the consequences of not fulfilling those expectations
2. the right to consistent and predictable management action for the violation of rules

3. the right to fair discipline based on facts, the right to question those facts, and the right to present a defense
4. the right to appeal disciplinary action
5. the right to progressive discipline—to be informed about an incident and be given a chance to improve

Employment Rights Not a Guarantee

It should be understood that although employees might have cause to regard their jobs as an established right, there is no legal protection affording employees a permanent or continuous job. Furthermore, in general, the concept of due process does not guarantee employees any assurance of employment. However, the concepts of due process and of job as a right do obligate management to act in a consistent and fair manner.

Employees *do* have the right to expect sound employment practices and to be treated respectfully as individuals. In Canada, in absence of a formal contract specifying the duration of employment, the employment relationship can be construed as ongoing. While employment is not considered necessarily permanent, the employer must provide reasonable notice and grounds for termination. Thus, Canada functions under statutory and common (contract) law.[12]

Job Expectancy Rights

LO2

What are the job expectancy rights of employees?

Once hired, employees expect certain rights associated with fair and equitable employment. Employee rights on the job include those regarding substance abuse and drug testing, privacy, plant closing notification, and just-cause disciplinary and discharge procedures.

Substance Abuse and Drug Testing

In Canada, the social costs of substance abuse, including lost productivity, as well as the health-care costs, have been estimated at more than $39 billion.[13] Most human rights legislation considers substance abuse to be a disability and therefore needs to be accommodated.[14]

According to a recent survey by Statistics Canada, 24% of men and 11% of women aged 19 to 70 reported consuming more than five alcoholic drinks per occasion at least 12 times a year.[15] The trend in the general population continues to find daily and heavy drinking significantly higher for males than for females, highest marijuana use levels in the 18-to-39 age group, and approximately twice as many males as marijuana users as females. Since illicit drugs are available and increasingly available in high quality throughout Canada, studies are finding cannabis use is up among Canadian adults. Recent student surveys in Ontario find use patterns increasing for most drug categories. Various studies have indicated that alcohol and other drug use (both prescription and non-prescription) contribute to issues of job performance, work productivity, absenteeism, increased workplace accidents, and problems with interpersonal relationships.[16]

As mentioned earlier in this chapter, the failure of an employer to ensure a safe and drug-free workplace can result in astronomical liability claims when consumers are injured because of a negligent employee or faulty product. Because of this, Canadian companies are ensuring that they have policies and programs on all types of potential substance abuse, including prescription drugs.[17] Although the Canadian government has not introduced legislation on drug testing, such legislation exists south of the border. Companies with drug-testing policies report reductions in absenteeism, sick days, and accidents. Some of the issues surrounding drug and alcohol testing are discussed in At Work with HRM 9.2.

Canadian Centre on Substance Abuse
www.ccsa.ca

Employee Privacy

Consider these practices:

- General Electric installs fish-eye lenses behind pinholes in walls and ceilings to observe employees suspected of crimes.
- DuPont uses long-distance cameras to monitor its loading docks.
- An Alberta IDA drugstore requires cashiers to place their fingers on a pad that scans their fingerprints and allows them access to the cashiering system.

While these examples may seem a violation of privacy rights, it is not uncommon for employers to monitor employee conduct through surveillance techniques. Most retailers use some form of monitoring, and almost all of us have made a phone call in which we are informed that our call might be monitored.

Employees have no reasonable expectation of privacy in places where work rules that provide for inspections have been put into effect. They must comply with probable-cause searches by employers. And they can be appropriately disciplined, normally for insubordination, for refusing to comply with search requests. It is advisable that employers inform new employees, at either the final employment interview or an orientation session, that mandatory or random searches are done. See Figure 9.1 for the tools and techniques for monitoring employees.

Managers must be diligent when conducting employee searches. Improper searches can lead to employee complaints under various privacy legislation (see Chapter 2) and possible lawsuits claiming defamation of character and negligent infliction of emotional distress.

It is not uncommon for employers to monitor the conduct of employees through surveillance techniques. One of the most common means of electronic surveillance by employers is telephone surveillance to ensure that customer requests are handled properly or to prevent theft.

With the *Personal Information Protection and Electronic Documents Act* (PIPEDA), there is an expectation that employers be reasonable in their use of any type of surveillance

FIGURE 9.1 Tools and Techniques for Monitoring Employees

Performance	Output, keystrokes, telephone call content
	Use of resources
	Communications content: e-mail, social media
	Location: Cards, CCTV, GPS, RFID
	Covert: Mystery shoppers
Behaviours	Communications content: E-mail and social media
	Location: Cards, pages CCTV, GPS, RFID
	Software to track computer usage
	Covert: Mystery shoppers
	Psychometric, testing, drug testing, biometrics
	Lie detector tests
	Video surveillance
	Creating open work spaces
Personal characteristics	Covert: Mystery shoppers
	Psychometric, testing, drug testing, biometrics
	Lie detector tests
	Predisposition to health risk, genetic testing
	Video surveillance
	Creating open work spaces

Source: Adapted from Morgan Sims, "7 Ways to Monitor Employee Performance and Behavior," March 24, 2014, *Imedia Connection*, accessed April 3, 2015, **http://blogs.imediaconnection.com/blog/2014/03/24/7-ways-to-monitor-employee-performance-and-behavior**; Stuart Rudner and Natalie Macdonald, "The Law, Surveillance and Employee Privacy," *The Globe and Mail*, June 10, 2014, accessed April 3, 2015, **www.theglobeandmail.com/report-on-business/careers/career-advice/experts/what-privacy-rights-to-do-you-have-at-work/article19079506**; and Liz Bernier, "When Workers Feel Watched," *Canadian HR Reporter*, November 3, 2014, accessed April 3, 2015, **www.hrreporter.com/articleview/22674-when-workers-feel-watched**.

AT WORK WITH HRM 9.2

WHAT CAN EMPLOYERS DO TO DEAL WITH WORKPLACE DRUG AND ALCOHOL CONCERNS?

Many employers express concern about the impact of an employee being impaired at work. The concerns range from loss of productivity to safety for customers and employees. While legislation exists in the United States to allow random and regular drug testing, no such legislation exists in Canada. Further, since most human rights tribunals see drug or alcohol abuse as a disability, any testing for these substances can be a form of discrimination or a challenge on the rights to privacy.

What can employers do? Some recent cases across Canada will shed some light.

Suncor, an oil extractor and producer, has operations in the Alberta oil sands using heavy equipment in sometimes dangerous circumstances. It implemented a random drug and alcohol testing policy using urinalysis for safety-sensitive positions. In introducing the policy, the union grieved the policy, stating that it was a violation of the employees' privacy rights and human rights. The arbitration board noted that on the basis of a previous decision, urinalysis was not an effective test nor had Suncor demonstrated a problem that needed to be addressed, nor had Suncor proved that the incidents for which testing was done was the result of any substance abuse.

In another case, Canadian Pacific Railway terminated a long-service (36 years) employee for being at work "under the influence of alcohol." The employee had put in a longer shift than usual because of working on a derailment and also to be available for any emergency. The employee went home, had a beer, took a nap, had dinner with another beer. A couple of hours later the employee was called in to help with a freight car. When the employee arrived for work, the supervisor smelled alcohol on the mechanic's breath. When asked, the employee confirmed that beer had been consumed several hours before. The supervisor decided to remove the employee from work and ordered a substance test. While attempts were made to arrange for testing, it took so long that the testing experts said that any testing would not be accurate. Although the employee showed no signs of impairment during the incident, CPR determined that the employee had breached both the collective agreement and company policy for having any alcohol while on call. The union grieved the termination and the arbitrator concluded that the company had not been fair in its investigation and quick dismissal of an employee was only months away from retiring with a full pension.

CRITICAL THINKING QUESTIONS:

1. Do you think employers ought to have the right to test for drug or alcohol use? Why or why not?
2. How would you feel if your employer did random drug and alcohol tests? Explain your answer.

Sources: Adapted from *Unifor, Local 707A and Suncor Energy Inc., Oil Sands* (March 18, 2014), Tom Hodges—Chair (Alta. Arb.), *Communications, Energy and Paperworkers Union of Canada, Local 30 v. Irving Pulp & Paper Ltd., 2013 SCC 34* (S.C.C.); Jeffrey R. Smith, "Random Drug, Alcohol Testing Struck Down at Suncor," *Canadian HR Reporter*, April 21, 2014, accessed April 3, 2015, **www.hrreporter.com/articleview/20887-random-drug-alcohol-testing-struck-down-at-suncor-legal-view**; Jeffrey R. Smith, "Flimsy Evidence Not Enough to Knock CP Mechanic Off Track," *Canadian HR Reporter*, August 7, 2014, accessed April 3, 2014, **www.hrreporter.com/articleview/20754-flimsy-evidence-not-enough-to-knock-cp-mechanic-off-track-legal-view**.

technique. However, even surveillance outside the work environment can create problems, for both employers and employees. For example, the CEO of a catering company was forced to resign after he was videoed on an elevator abusing a dog. The incident occurred in Vancouver, but soon went viral when a local news station obtained a copy of the footage. The company investigated, had the CEO apologize, and even contributed $100,000 to an animal protection charity. Further, the CEO also agreed to do 1,000 hours of community service to support animal welfare. Unfortunately, there continued to be such a public negative reaction to the original incident that the company was concerned about its own economic survival if the CEO continued to be employed.[18] When an employer is considering using surveillance, it is suggested that the following "best practices" be used:[19]

1. Establish, communicate, and enforce written policies.
2. Have up-to-date policies that include social media and any other technology that can be perceived as intruding on one's privacy.

Employees in a number of different organizations are video-monitored—sometimes for their own protection.

J.R. Bale / Alamy

3. Ensure that only information relating to employment is collected.
4. Ensure that personal information is kept secure.
5. Apply policies consistently.

Employers have the right to keep all types of information, but its access and use has to be handled very carefully. This is highlighted by recent breaches of private health records involving high-profile people whose personal health information was disclosed inappropriately. Specifically, the Ontario Information and Privacy Commissioner stressed that as hospitals were moving toward electronic records, that it was essential that employees understand that inappropriate disclosures of patient information was a serious breach of privacy.[20] As technology continues to change, privacy commissioners are requested to examine the appropriateness of the technology. Recently, the Canadian Privacy Commissioner was asked to consider whether employers could monitor an employee's social network sites.[21] The Commissioner indicated that depending on the privacy settings of an individual user, many people and organizations could have access including co-workers, future employers, and recruitment firms. Ethics in HRM 9.1 highlights some of these issues.

ETHICS IN HRM 9.1 IS THIS AN INVASION OF PRIVACY?

Many employers use a variety of electronic surveillance techniques to monitor employee activities in the workplace—everything from attendance reporting to controlling employee access to certain areas of work. Organizations with off-site assets use GPSs (global positioning systems) to monitor the use of company vehicles or video cameras to monitor employees on extended sick leave. There is the monitoring of a person's profile on any of the social networking sites such as Twitter, Facebook, or LinkedIn, too. But when does this become an invasion of one's privacy? The answer is usually "It all depends."

continued

Crown Packaging, a manufacturer of a variety of cardboard and other similar paper products, terminated a long-service employee for abusing sick leave. In making the decision, it relied upon video surveillance provided by a private investigator.

The employee had requested vacation for a certain period of time that was denied because too many other employees would also be away. Subsequently, the employee called in to say that he had a back problem and wouldn't be reporting to work. As the time period was the same as that of the vacation request, the employer was suspicious and hired the investigator. In the video surveillance, the employee was seen doing certain activities that clearly showed he didn't have a back problem.

The union grieved the termination, and during the hearing the arbitrator determined that Crown Packaging had been too hasty in using video surveillance and that it had a duty to use less intrusive means to gather information. The employee was reinstated.

And with the introduction of "wearable technology" such as activity monitors, there are more possibilities of needing to balance an employer's right with the employee's privacy. For example, hockey teams use wearable monitors to assess fatigue and the potential for an increased risk of accidents. Mining companies use wearable technology that can provide critical alerts and warnings directly to employees. Then there are other activity monitors used to help an employee improve their overall health.

CRITICAL THINKING QUESTIONS:

1. Would you work differently if you knew your performance was continually monitored?
2. Is it ethical for employers to monitor employees this way? Why or why not?

Sources: Adapted from Clayton Jones, "Jumping the Gun on Employee Surveillance Can Shoot Down Your Case," *The HR Space*, Fasken Martineau, 2014; Jess Sloss, "New Tools, New Rules," *Canadian HR Reporter*, November 3, 2014, accessed April 3, 2015, **www.hrreporter.com/articleview/22683-new-tools-new-rules**; Brian Kreissl, "Surprise—You're on Camera," *Canadian HR Reporter*, September 16, 2014, accessed April 3, 2015, **www.hrreporter.com/blog/HR-Policies-Practices/archive/2014/09/16/surprise-youre-on-camera**; and Leah Eichler, "Hey, CEOs, Social Media Is Watching You," *The Globe and Mail*, September 12, 2014, accessed April 3, 2014, **www.theglobeandmail.com/report-on-business/careers/career-advice/life-at-work/hey-ceos-social-media-is-watching-you/article20522852**.

Access to Employee Files

The information kept in an employee's official employment record or employee file can have a significant impact—positive or negative—on career development. The personnel file, typically kept by the HR department, can contain performance reviews, salary information, investigatory reports, credit checks, criminal records, test scores, and family data.

In compliance with legislation, most employers give their employees access to their employment files. Virtually no organization is exempt from privacy legislation. PIPEDA also entitles employees to examine their own personnel file—including any information stored electronically.

In addition, any personal information cannot be used or disclosed without the prior knowledge and consent of the employee. For example, if you are seeking a car loan and the company wants confirmation of your employment, only you can authorize release of that information. The most important legal principle with regard to data privacy is the concept of consent—ahead of time—from the employee. Under PIPEDA, the person must be notified of the following before any information can be provided:

- that he or she is about to provide personal data
- the purposes for which the information is to be processed
- the people or bodies to whom the information might be disclosed
- the proposed transfer of information to other countries
- the security measures protecting the information

It is also important to remember that any medical information is not only personal but also confidential and potentially sensitive. Such information is to be accessed only by authorized people when required.[22]

Likewise, it is important to ensure that appropriate items reside in the employee file. For example, in its revised Employment Standards Code, Manitoba is allowing individual flextime agreements. The employer will need to have the employee sign the agreement, which will need to remain in the employee file until any changes occur. Employment professionals recommend that organizations develop a policy on employee files that includes, as a minimum, the points noted in Toolkit 9.1.

Electronic Privacy

The benefits of electronic communication, including e-mail, voice mail, and social media, are many: they allow for collaboration on projects, enable the sharing of ideas, and provide a way for employees to give input to the organization on any number of items.[23]

Unfortunately, the growth of management and financial information systems can create privacy problems by making personnel information more accessible to those with prying eyes, or to "hackers," who might use the information inappropriately. Even deleted messages can be accessed.

Further, there is the issue of an employee using a company-owned computer for inappropriate purposes. A landmark decision by the Supreme Court regarding a teacher and the school's laptop confirmed that there is some expectation of privacy even when something unacceptable is found accidentally on computer files.[24]

Technology creates the need for a critical balance between employee privacy and the employer's need to know. Employees might assume that their right to privacy extends to e-mail and voice-mail messages, but it does not. The *Freedom of Information and Protection of Privacy Act* (federal legislation) applies only to records in the custody or control of public bodies, such as a Crown corporation, a school board, or a government ministry. In many organizations it does not apply to the employment relationship. That means employers have the right to monitor materials created, received, or sent for business-related reasons.[25] Employers are strongly encouraged to develop clear policies and guidelines that explain to employees how any form of electronic communication is to be used, including when and under what conditions employees can be monitored (see Toolkit 9.2). In addition, employees should be reminded of their responsibilities under the company's policy every time they log on to the company's computer system. More and more decisions by courts and arbitrators are reaffirming the organization's right to monitor e-mail or any other electronic transmission on company-owned computers. This trend holds true for companies that monitor employee use of the Internet.

Therefore, it is important for managers and supervisors, as well as employees, to understand that employers have the right to monitor any and all electronic transmissions at work. Where e-mail and voice-mail policies do exist, employees should be required to sign a form

TOOLKIT 9.1 POLICY GUIDELINES ON HANDLING PERSONNEL FILES

- Ensure compliance with legislation.
- Define exactly what information is to be kept in employee files.
- Ensure informed consent has been received from employees regarding types of information that will be collected and stored.
- Develop different categories of personnel information, depending on legal requirements and organizational needs.
- Specify where, when, how, and under what circumstances employees may review or copy their files.
- Ensure appropriate security measures are in place to safeguard information.
- Identify company individuals allowed to view personnel files.
- Prohibit the collection of information that might be viewed as discriminatory or form the basis of an invasion-of-privacy suit.
- Audit employment records regularly to remove irrelevant, outdated, or inaccurate information.

Image Source White/Thinkstock

Employees do not necessarily have a right to privacy on the organization's telephone.

indicating that they have read and understand the policy. In most cases, courts will find disciplining an employee for Internet abuse to be a reasonable action. However, as mentioned earlier in this chapter, they can decide that even when inappropriate materials are found on a work computer, the manner in which they are found can have a bearing on issues of privacy.

Employee Conduct Outside the Workplace

Consider the following case. On Monday morning the owner of ABC Corporation reads in the newspaper that a company employee has been charged with robbery and assault on a local convenience store owner. The employee has been released pending trial. A phone call to the employee's supervisor reveals that the employee has reported to work. What should the owner do?

New technologies enable employers to monitor staff very closely, even on their personal time. As well, with the widespread use of smartphones, pictures and videos can be taken, posted in blogs and on Facebook, and become very public. While most courts uphold the right of the employer to monitor employees at the workplace, particularly if there is a justifiable reason to collect evidence, the question of monitoring employees outside the workplace is more complex.

For example, perhaps one of the more high-profile cases involved former CBC *Q* host Jian Ghomeshi. He was initially suspended from work while CBC investigated certain allegations. However, Mr. Ghomeshi made the termination very public when he posted on his Facebook account that he had been let go due to his sexual predilections.[26] CBC also confirmed that his private life had intruded on the image he was portraying to the public. Another company in British Columbia terminated someone for using profanities on social media posts about the boss, embarrassing the employer and others in the industry.[27]

Organizations that want to discipline employees for off-duty misconduct must establish a clear relationship between the misconduct and its negative effect on other employees or the organization. This link might be established, for example, in cases where off-duty criminal misconduct (e.g., child molestation) creates a disruptive impact on the workplace. Another example might be where the public nature of the employee's job (e.g., police or fire department personnel) creates an image problem for the organization.

Canadian Legal Information Online
canadaonline.about.com/cs/ law/a/legalinfo.htm

Law Central
www.lawcentralalberta.ca/en/canadian-public-legal-education-ple-organizations

Ultimately, whether an employer can terminate someone for activities outside work will depend on the profession, the profession's code of conduct, and what role the profession plays in our general society.

Read At Work with HRM 9.3 to consider what happens when someone impersonates a member of the armed forces.

Further legal resources on the topics discussed in this chapter can be found at Canadian Legal Information Online (**canadaonline.about.com/cs/law/a/legalinfo.htm**) or Law Central (**www.lawcentralalberta.ca/en/canadian-public-legal-education-ple-organizations**).

TOOLKIT 9.2 E-MAIL, INTERNET, SOCIAL MEDIA, AND VOICE-MAIL POLICY GUIDELINES

- Decide on whether policy will promote use or prohibit misuse.
- Ensure other relevant policies, such as computer use, privacy, confidentiality, and harassment/discrimination, and cyber bullying are aligned.
- Ensure policy covers how policy is applied when employee uses own devices for work purposes.
- Consistently apply policy.
- Clearly specify anything prohibited, such as certain Internet sites or file sharing.
- Clearly specify use or non-use of social media sites and whether usage on company equipment will be monitored, including any impact on work productivity.
- Communicate consequences of breaches of policy.
- Through the organization's systems, block any sites the organization does not want employees to access.
- Inform employees that any confidential information is not to be shared or sent electronically.
- Advise employees that e-mail and computer use, including any personal information stored on computer, is not private and therefore may be reviewed by others.
- As technology changes, review, update, and communicate policy changes.

Sources: Adapted from materials presented at a seminar presented by Fasken Martineau, October 1, 2014; Jeffrey R. Smith, "Mobile Technology Blurs Privacy Lines," *Canadian HR Reporter*, July 22, 2014, accessed April 4, 2015, **www.hrreporter.com/blog/Employment-Law/archive/2014/07/22/mobile-technology-blurs-privacy-lines**; Bernhard Warner, "Keeping Your Social-Media Policy in the Workplace and Out of the Courtroom," *Inc.com*, accessed April 4, 2015, **www.inc.com/magazine/201407/bernhard-warner/how-to-keep-up-with-social-media-policy-in-the-workplace.html**; Imogen Reseigh and Nicola Ihnatowic, "Think Before You Tweet: A Lawyers' Guide to Using Social Media at Work," *The Guardian*, November 25, 2014, accessed April 4, 2015, **www.theguardian.com/public-leaders-network/2014/nov/25/lawyers-guide-social-media-work-public-sectorguide to using social media at work**; and University of Bergen, "Use of Private Social Media Affects Work Performance," November 13, 2014, *Science Daily*, accessed April 4, 2015, **www.sciencedaily.com/releases/2014/11/141113085146.htm**.

AT WORK WITH HRM 9.3 WHAT HAPPENS WHEN YOU IMPERSONATE SOMEONE?

Is impersonating someone illegal? It depends on the circumstances. People often go to costume parties and pretend they are someone else and we don't get concerned. But what if the person were dressed as a member of the armed forces? That is a different story. Impersonating a public officer and falsely displaying badges on a uniform is illegal.

During Remembrance Day events in Ottawa, a person dressed in full uniform was interviewed by several news agencies about what the occasion meant to him. He went on to describe what it was like to serve in the military. Unfortunately, none of the story and only some of the items on his uniform were real. Whether or not he would have been detected if he hadn't been on news reports, no one knows.

What we do know is that he worked for a construction company and had told his co-workers for some time that he was a veteran. He was never doubted until the news report and various people started informing appropriate agencies that the man was impersonating a service person.

The construction company immediately suspended him, with pay, and commenced an investigation into the situation. In the meantime, the employee was arrested and

continued

faces many charges under the *Criminal Code*. The company is being careful with the investigation, including determining whether the actions are detrimental to the company's reputation and its ability to conduct business. While the actions and behaviour were considered disrespectful to many, the company needs to determine whether the employee thought he was doing something thoughtful, like paying respect to the people in the armed forces.

During the court hearing in early 2015, he pleaded guilty to various charges and apologized for his actions. He said all he wanted to do by wearing the uniform was honour the people who made sacrifices.

CRITICAL THINKING QUESTION:

Do you think the employee ought to have been terminated? Why or why not?

Sources: Adapted from Sarah Dobson, "Should 'Fake' Veteran Be Fired?" *Canadian HR Reporter*, December 15, 2014, accessed April 4, 2015, **www.hrreporter.com/articleview/23103-should-fake-veteran-be-fired**; Jeffrey R. Smith, "Worker's Off-Duty Misconduct One to 'Remember,'" *Canadian HR Reporter*, November 17, 2014, accessed April 4, 2015, **www.hrreporter.com/blog/Employment-Law/archive/2014/11/17/workers-off-duty-misconduct-one-to-remember**; "Man Accused of Impersonating Soldier Pleads Guilty to Wearing Medals, Uniform," *The Globe and Mail*, March 4, 2015, accessed April 4, 2015, **www.theglobeandmail.com/news/national/man-accused-of-impersonating-soldier-pleads-guilty-to-wearing-medals-uniform/article23297320**.

Stephen Simpson/Iconica/Getty Images

Given the use of computers throughout the world, users need to be vigilant about protecting and securing information.

DISCIPLINARY POLICIES AND PROCEDURES

LO3

What is the process of establishing disciplinary practices?

The rights of managers to discipline and discharge employees are increasingly limited. There is thus a great need for managers at all levels to understand discipline procedures. Disciplinary action taken against an employee must be for justifiable reasons, and there must be effective policies and procedures to govern its use. Such policies and procedures serve to assist those responsible for taking disciplinary action and help to ensure that employees receive fair and constructive treatment. Equally importantly, these guidelines help to prevent disciplinary action from being voided or from being reversed through the appeal system.

If an organization has an HR department, it will have a major responsibility in developing the disciplinary policies and procedures. While the HR department will get top-management approval, it is also critical that supervisors and managers be involved in the development of the policies and procedures. It will be the supervisors and managers who carry out the policies; their experiences can contribute to more effective coordination and consistency of disciplinary action throughout the organization. As part of the manager–HR partnership, the HR department will work with the manager to ensure that any actions taken against employees are consistent with any collective agreements and conform to current law.

The primary responsibility for preventing or correcting disciplinary problems rests with an employee's immediate supervisor. This person is best able to observe evidence of unsatisfactory behaviour or performance and to discuss the matter with the employee. Discussion is frequently all that is needed to correct the problem, and disciplinary action becomes unnecessary. However, when disciplinary action is needed, the supervisor should strive to use a problem-solving attitude. Causes underlying the problem are as important as the problem itself, and any attempt to prevent recurrence will require an understanding of them.

Admittedly, it is often difficult for supervisors to maintain an objective attitude toward employee infractions. But if supervisors can maintain a problem-solving stance, they are likely to come up with a diagnosis nearer the truth than if they used the approach of a trial lawyer. For example, if an employee is late for work several days in a row, the supervisor needs to discuss the situation with the employee and try to determine the reasons for the lateness. The supervisor needs to remember that the objective is to get the employee to work on time, not to discipline the individual. Therefore, by attempting to find out the reasons, the supervisor is in a better position to work with the employee to find an acceptable solution.

About.com
www.humanresources.about.com

HR Council
www.hrcouncil.ca

For additional resources about disciplining employees, see About.com (**www.humanresources.about.com**) and HR Council (**www.hrcouncil.ca**; access the HR Toolkit link).

Setting Organizational Expectations

Clearly stating expectations of performance and behaviour is the foundation for an effective disciplinary system. These expectations govern the type of behaviour expected of employees. Since employee behaviour standards are established through the setting and communicating of organizational procedures and rules, the following suggestions may help reduce problems in this area:

1. Information about rules should be widely distributed and known to all employees. It should not be assumed that employees know what is expected of them.
2. Rules, especially those critical to work success, should be reviewed periodically, perhaps annually.
3. The reasons for rules concerning performance and behaviour should always be explained. Acceptance is greater when employees understand the reasons behind rules.
4. Organization policies and rules should always be written. Ambiguity should be avoided, since this can result in different interpretations by different supervisors.
5. Rules must be reasonable and relate to the safe and efficient operation of the organization. They should not be made simply because of personal likes or dislikes.
6. If management has been lax in the enforcement of a policy or rule, it must be restated, along with the consequences for its violation, before disciplinary action can begin.
7. Have employees sign a document indicating that they have read and understood the organizational rules regarding their behaviour and performance.

When seeking reasons for unsatisfactory performance, supervisors must keep in mind that employees may not be aware of certain expectations. Before initiating any disciplinary action, therefore, it is essential that supervisors determine whether they have given their employees careful and thorough orientation in what is expected of them in relation to their jobs.

It is worth noting that organizations will change expectations if a significant crisis has undermined employee trust and that there is a culture that is no longer appropriate. This is what occurred after the Ghomeshi scandal and subsequent investigative report. The credibility of CBC was significantly damaged and new expectations around behaviour were developed and widely communicated to all employees.[28]

Defining Discipline

LO4

What is discipline and how do you investigate a disciplinary problem?

In dictionaries, **discipline** normally has one of three meanings:

1. treatment that punishes
2. orderly behaviour in an organizational setting
3. training that moulds and strengthens desirable conduct—or corrects undesirable conduct—and develops self-control

Discipline
(1) Treatment that punishes, (2) orderly behaviour in an organizational setting, or (3) training that moulds and strengthens desirable conduct—or corrects undesirable conduct—and develops self-control

To some managers, discipline is synonymous with force. They equate the term with the punishment of employees who violate rules or regulations. Other managers think of discipline as a general state of affairs—a condition of orderliness in which employees conduct themselves according to standards of acceptable behaviour. Discipline, viewed in this manner, can be considered positive when employees willingly practise self-control and respect organizational values and expectations.

The third definition considers discipline a management tool used to correct undesirable employee performance or behaviour. Discipline is applied as a constructive means of getting employees to conform to acceptable standards of behaviour and performance. Figure 9.2 provides examples of common disciplinary problems.

Many organizations, such as Goodyear Aerospace, define the term "discipline" in their policy manuals as training that "corrects, moulds, or perfects knowledge, attitudes, behaviour, or conduct." Discipline is thus viewed as a way to correct poor employee performance rather than simply to punish for an offence. As these organizations emphasize, discipline should be seen as a method of training employees to perform better or to improve their job attitudes or work behaviour. It is also interesting to note that the word "discipline"

FIGURE 9.2 Common Disciplinary Problems

Attendance Problems
- unexcused absence
- chronic absenteeism
- unexcused or excessive tardiness
- leaving without permission

Dishonesty and Related Problems
- theft
- falsifying employment application
- willfully damaging organizational property
- punching another employee's time card
- falsifying work records

Work Performance Problems
- failure to complete work assignments
- producing substandard products or services
- failure to meet established production requirements

On-the-Job Behaviour Problems
- intoxication at work
- insubordination
- horseplay
- smoking in unauthorized places
- fighting
- gambling
- failure to use safety devices
- failure to report injuries
- carelessness
- sleeping on the job
- using abusive or threatening language with supervisors
- possession of narcotics or alcohol
- possession of firearms or other weapons
- all forms of harassment, such as sexual innuendo or actions, teasing, racial slurs, inappropriate jokes, and bullying

is derived from the word "disciple," which means follower or pupil. Figure 9.3 shows one disciplinary model, which consists of several steps that must be carried out to ensure that the termination is justifiable.

Investigating the Disciplinary Problem

It's a rare manager who has a good, intuitive sense of how to investigate employee misconduct. Too frequently, investigations are conducted in a haphazard manner; worse, they overlook one or more investigative concerns. In conducting an employee investigation, it is important to be objective and to avoid the assumptions, suppositions, and biases that often surround discipline cases.

Toolkit 9.3 lists things that need to be considered when doing workplace investigations. Paying attention to each item will help ensure a full and fair investigation while providing reliable information free from personal prejudice. And as mentioned in Chapter 2, many actions an organization would take in relation to an employment issue require a careful and full investigation. Further, some employment concerns, such as absences, may need "reasonable accommodation" (see Chapter 2), and therefore discipline would be an inappropriate action.[29]

When preparing documentation, it is important that the manager record the incident immediately after the infraction takes place. Then, the memory of the incident is still fresh, and the manager can ensure that the record is complete and accurate. It is critical that the documentation be complete. This information will include whether there had been any previous warnings with an opportunity to improve. These documents are necessary to prove that the employer had the right to discipline.[30]

The Investigative Interview

Before any disciplinary action is initiated, an investigative interview should be conducted to make sure employees are fully aware of the offence. This interview is necessary because the supervisor's perceptions of the employee's behaviour may not be entirely accurate. The interview should concentrate on how the offence violated the performance standards of the job. It should avoid getting into personalities or areas unrelated to job performance. Most importantly, the employee must be given a full opportunity to explain so that any deficiencies for which the organization may be responsible are revealed. In fact, it is critical to the outcome of any discipline to conduct a careful investigation as quickly as possible and to ensure that the investigation is approached thoughtfully and independently.[31]

Approaches to Disciplinary Action

LO5

What are the differences between progressive and positive discipline?

When taken against employees, disciplinary action should never be thought of as punishment. Discipline can embody a penalty as a means of obtaining a desired result; however, punishment should not be the intent of disciplinary action. Rather, discipline

FIGURE 9.3 A Disciplinary Model

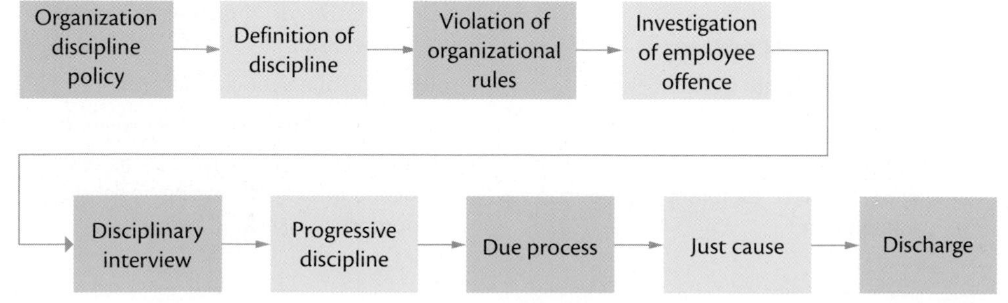

must have as its goal the improvement of the employee's future behaviour. To apply discipline in any other way—as punishment or as a way of getting even with employees—can invite only problems for management, including possible wrongful-dismissal suits. If a thorough investigation shows that an employee has violated some organization rule, disciplinary action must be imposed. Two approaches to disciplinary action are progressive discipline and positive discipline.

Progressive Discipline

Generally, discipline is imposed in a progressive manner. By definition, **progressive discipline** is the application of corrective measures by increasing degrees. Progressive discipline is designed to motivate employees to correct their misconduct voluntarily. The technique is aimed at correcting unacceptable behaviour as soon as it starts, using only enough corrective action to remedy the shortcoming. However, the sequence and severity of the disciplinary action vary with the type of offence and the circumstances surrounding it. Since each situation is unique, a number of factors must be considered in determining how severe a disciplinary action should be.

Progressive discipline
Application of corrective measures by increasing degrees

To highlight the uniqueness of situations, a recent case involved an employee who was disciplined for going to the restroom too often.[32] Before any action is taken, it is important that the incident be investigated. It is also key to remember that the investigation can have an impact on the organization and careful planning needs to take place. Therefore, creating a plan can help in identifying what steps have to be taken, by whom, and when. For example, with the rise of social media, confidentiality and privacy for those involved must be clearly spelled out.[33] Some of the factors to consider when conducting an investigation are listed in Toolkit 9.3.

The typical progressive discipline procedure includes four steps: (1) an oral warning (or counselling) that subsequent unsatisfactory behaviour or performance will not be tolerated, (2) a written warning, (3) a suspension without pay, and (4) termination.

The progressive discipline used by several organizations is described in At Work with HRM 9.4. The "capital punishment" of discharge is utilized only as a last resort. Organizations normally use lower forms of disciplinary action for less severe performance problems. It is important for organizations to follow "best practices" when documenting discipline:

- Complete the documentation in a timely manner.
- Ensure all documents are dated.
- Ensure the documentation clearly identifies what occurred and what was expected.
- Ensure the investigation is documented, including an opportunity for the employee to provide their perspective.
- Share the outcome of investigation with the employee.
- Share a copy of the investigative conclusions with the employee and the supervisor.[34]

TOOLKIT 9.3 WHAT MAKES AN EFFECTIVE INVESTIGATION?

1. Plan the investigation before starting investigation that includes whether a particular process must be followed and whether the situation is serious enough to result in discipline.
2. Arrange for the investigation to be conducted by an individual who is trained and experienced.
3. Ensure that the investigator is as independent as possible.
4. Identify all relevant issues and explore them as appropriate.
5. Ensure that the accused is informed and provided an opportunity to give their side of the story.
6. Ensure all appropriate individuals are interviewed to gain their perspective of the situation.

continued

7. Ensure that the investigation has sufficient resources to be completed.
8. Have the investigator prepare a full written report with conclusions.
9. Share the results of the investigation with the parties involved.
10. If situation is serious, ensure steps are taken to prevent from occurring again, including training and counselling.
11. If the claim is not validated, explain to the parties how the conclusion was reached.
12. Ensure there is closure for all involved, including any witnesses.

Sources: Adapted from Ruth Mayhew, "How to Conduct an Effective Disciplinary Interview," *The Houston Chronicle*, 2015, accessed April 5, 2015, **http://smallbusiness.chron.com/conduct-effective-disciplinary-interview-10327.html**; Kellie Auld, "Handle with Care: The Impact of Workplace Investigations," *PeopleTalk*, Summer 2015, 32–33; and Michael Richards and Nicholas Sharratt, "Workplace Investigations Need to Be Thorough, Unbiased," *Canadian HR Reporter*, July 14, 2014, accessed April 4, 2015, **www.hrreporter.com/articleview/21715-workplace-investigations-need-to-be-thorough-unbiased**.

AT WORK WITH HRM 9.4

PROGRESSIVE DISCIPLINE APPROACHES

A number of organizations have readily available guidelines aimed at changing unwanted employee behaviour. Before discipline begins, it is expected that the supervisor can show that the employee is aware of desired behaviour and that he or she is choosing to act otherwise. Frequently, all that is needed is to let employees know that a particular behaviour inappropriate. Employees usually react positively to this. Progressive discipline definitely is not used as a way of punishing an employee. Typical steps in a discipline process are the following:

Step 1: Establish cause for action. Employer needs to determine that an incident that warrants discipline has occurred. If for performance, the employer must be able to prove to an arbitrator or judge that the employee knew of expectations and that supervision occurred to ensure the standard.

Step 2: Coaching. This is a supportive discussion in which the supervisor reinforces expectations of either performance or behaviour. It is important that this conversation is noted in the supervisor's calendar.

Step 3: Verbal warning. This is a private discussion between the employee and the supervisor that takes place if there has been a repeat after the coaching session. The supervisor describes the incident and ensures that all sides of the story are heard. Human Resources and Skills Development Canada's verbal warning step also states that the supervisor needs to be very clear on outlining the consequences if expectations are not met.

Step 4: Written warning. If the employee's behaviour continues, a meeting is held with the supervisor and the employee. At the meeting the supervisor describes the events, reviews expectations as discussed in step 1, seeks solutions from the employee, and indicates what will happen if unacceptable behaviour continues. The meeting is summarized in writing and placed in the employee's personnel file. It is also helpful if the written warning includes a plan to ensure that the employee has sufficient time to improve.

Step 5: Suspension. If the inappropriate behaviour continues, the supervisor will next consider suspension. A meeting is held, similar to the meeting in step 2. At the conclusion of the meeting, a suspension may be imposed of a duration linked to the nature of the problem—it might be one day or several days. A letter of suspension is written and placed in the employee's file.

Step 6: Dismissal. This is a very serious step, taken only when all other options have been exhausted. Again, a meeting is held to review facts and expectations and to summarize previous meetings and actions. Even at this meeting, it is important to provide an opportunity for the employee to explain. At the end of the meeting, a letter of dismissal is presented. One copy is given to the employee, and one copy is put in the employee's file.

CRITICAL THINKING QUESTION:

Are there any other steps that ought to be taken in corrective discipline? Describe and explain.

Sources: Adapted from Jeffrey R. Smith, "Misconduct or Miscommunication?" *Canadian HR Reporter*, September 16, 2014, accessed April 5, 2015, **www.hrreporter.com/blog/Employment-Law/archive/2014/09/16/misconduct-or-miscommunication**; "Progressive Discipline," HR Council, accessed April 4, 2015, **http://hrcouncil.ca/hr-toolkit/keeping-people-discipline.cfm#_secA2**; "Progressive Discipline," go2HR, accessed April 5, 2015, **www.go2hr.ca/articles/progressive-discipline**; and Jeffrey R. Smith, "Word of Warning," *Canadian HR Reporter*, December 16, 2014, accessed April 5, 2015, **www.hrreporter.com/blog/Employment-Law/archive/2014/12/16/word-of-warning**.

Positive Discipline

Although progressive discipline is the most popular approach to correcting employee misconduct, some managers have questioned its logic. They have noted that it has certain flaws, including its intimidating and adversarial nature, which prevent it from achieving the intended purpose. For these reasons, some organizations are using an approach called **positive**, or **nonpunitive**, **discipline**. Positive discipline is based on the concept that employees must assume responsibility for their personal conduct and job performance.[35]

Positive, or nonpunitive, discipline
System of discipline that focuses on the early correction of employee misconduct, with the employee taking total responsibility for correcting the problem

Positive discipline requires a co-operative environment in which the employee and supervisor engage in joint discussion and problem solving to resolve incidents of employee irresponsibility. It also requires that the supervisor takes a coaching and supportive role.[36] The approach focuses on the early correction of misconduct, with the employee taking total responsibility for resolving the problem. Management imposes nothing; all solutions and affirmations are jointly reached. While positive discipline appears similar to progressive discipline, its emphasis is on giving employees reminders rather than reprimands as a way to improve performance. Figure 9.4 illustrates the procedure for implementing the three-step positive discipline procedure.

Compiling a Disciplinary Record

In applying either progressive or positive discipline, it is important for managers to maintain complete records of each step of the procedure. When employees fail to meet the obligation of a disciplinary step, they should be given a warning, and their manager should document the warning. A copy of this warning is usually put in the employee's personnel file. After an established period—frequently six months—the warning is usually removed,

FIGURE 9.4 Positive Discipline Procedures

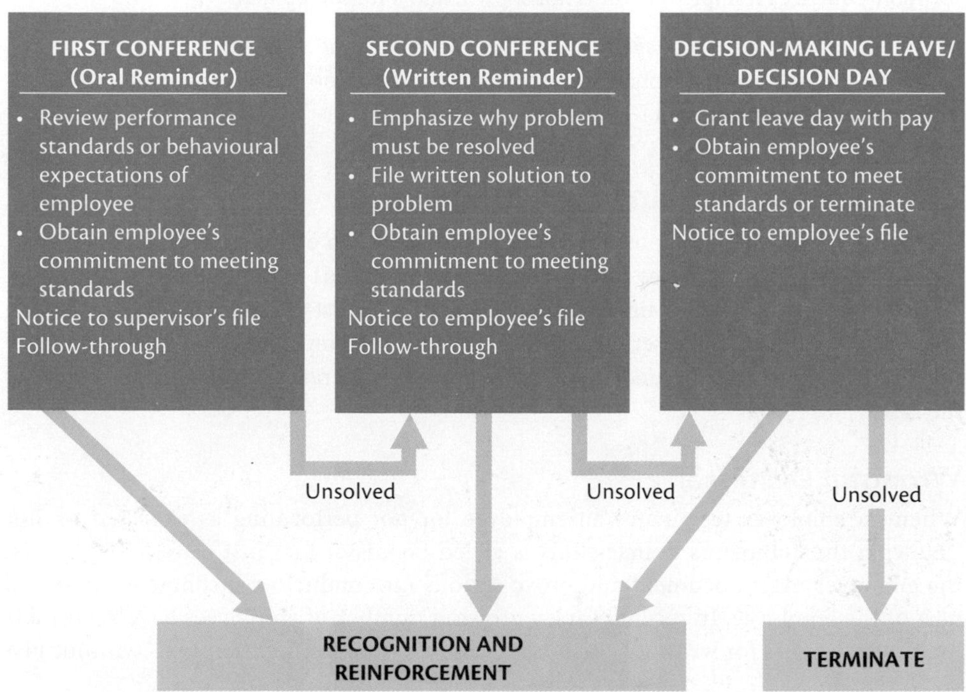

provided it has served its purpose; otherwise, it remains in the file to serve as evidence should a more severe penalty become necessary.

An employee's personnel file contains the employee's complete work history. It serves as a basis for determining and supporting disciplinary action and for evaluating the organization's disciplinary policies and procedures. Maintenance of proper records also provides management with valuable information about the soundness of its rules and regulations. Those rules that are violated most frequently should get particular attention, because the need for them might no longer exist, or some change might be required to facilitate their enforcement. If the rule is shown to have little or no value, it should be revised or rescinded. Otherwise, employees are likely to feel they are being restricted unnecessarily.

Documentation of Employee Misconduct

"It's too complicated." "I just didn't take time to do it." "I have more important things to do." These are some frequent excuses used by managers who have failed to document cases of employee misconduct. The most significant cause of inadequate documentation, however, is that managers have no idea what constitutes good documentation. Unfortunately, the failure of managers to record employee misconduct accurately can result in the reversal of any subsequent disciplinary action. Written records are key in discipline.[37] For documentation to be complete, the following nine items should be included:

1. employee's name and job title
2. names of others involved or who witnessed the incident
3. date, time, and location of the incident(s)
4. creation of a factual account of what happened and why it is a problem
5. identification of which policies were broken
6. notation of the impact of the behaviour on other employees
7. identification of changes required to correct the problem and by what date
8. prior discussion(s) with the employee about the problem
9. consequences if improvement is not shown, and a follow-up date[38]

About Human Resources
humanresources.about.com

It is critical that managers at all levels understand the guidelines for appropriate discipline. For additional resources on discipline, do a search on "discipline" at **humanresources.about.com**.

Grounds for Termination

No matter how helpful and positive a supervisor is with an employee who is not abiding by the organization's policies and expectations, or doesn't fit into the organizational culture, there may come a time when the employee must be terminated (dismissed). Since termination has such serious consequences for the employee—and possibly for the organization—it should be undertaken only after a deliberate and thoughtful review of the case.

Wrongful Dismissal

Wrongful dismissal
Terminating an employee's employment without just cause

When an employer terminates an employee for not performing as expected or not following the company's policies, this is called dismissal for "just cause." To do this, the employer must document and prove serious misconduct or incompetence on the part of the employee. In recent years, a growing number of employees have sued their former employers for **wrongful dismissal**, claiming the termination was "without just or sufficient cause," implying a lack of fair treatment by management or insufficient reasons for the termination. Termination for cause also expects that the employee been informed of this prior to termination and had an opportunity to change their behaviour or improve their performance. This means that a termination resulting from a job redefinition/redesign, downsizing, restructuring, or lack of organizational fit is not just cause. However, poor performance, poor interpersonal relationships, and technical incompetence might be just cause if the employee had been informed of expectations and had been given a chance to improve but failed to conform. Figure 9.5 lists some "just cause" reasons.

Many managers are faced with having to terminate someone when there are sufficient and legitimate grounds for doing so. Some companies may suggest that just cause includes the organization's financial difficulties. It is important for managers and supervisors to know that the economic hardship of the company is not a justifiable reason to terminate someone's employment. HRM and the Law 9.1 gives two examples of wrongful dismissal cases. For additional information on wrongful dismissals, see **www.duhaime.org**.

Duhaime Law
www.duhaime.org

Managers must be able to document that any performance problems have been brought to the attention of the employee and that sufficient time, training, and assistance have been given to improve the weak performance. If the organization has an HR professional, the line manager needs to work closely with the HR person to ensure that the appropriate type of documentation occurs. Other tips to prevent a challenge by a terminated employee are discussed later in the chapter.

If an employee termination is to be upheld for just cause, what constitutes fair employee treatment and valid reasons? This question is not easily answered, but standards governing just-cause dismissal have evolved from the field of labour arbitration. These standards are applied by arbitrators in dismissal cases to determine whether management had just cause. These guidelines are normally set forth in the form of questions, as provided in Toolkit 9.4. For example, before dismissing an employee, did the manager warn the person of possible disciplinary action in the past? A "no" answer to any of the seven questions generally means that just cause was not established and that management's decision to terminate was arbitrary, capricious, or discriminatory. These guidelines are being applied not only by arbitrators in dismissal cases but also by judges in wrongful-dismissal suits.

Even when guidelines are used, the employer might not be able to prove just cause. For example, a Toronto city employee was terminated in 2009 but a decision made by an arbitrator in 2014 reinstated the employee as the employer hadn't been able to prove just cause. Even though the arbitrator did not order back pay, the employee has stated that they will pursue this through the courts.[39]

FIGURE 9.5 Sample "Just Cause" Reasons

- excessive lateness or absenteeism
- theft from the company
- improper or wrong conduct, such as fighting with a co-worker

Depending on the seriousness of the wrongdoing, the individual may be terminated immediately, bypassing the steps of progressive discipline. For example, a hotel concierge who makes threatening statements to a guest could be terminated right away.

Termination is the final stage of the discipline process.

vadimguzhva/Thinkstock

HRM AND THE LAW 9.1 WHAT DO COURTS SAY ABOUT WRONGFUL DISMISSALS?

Can someone be terminated for being dishonest? Like so many other court decisions, the answer is "it all depends." And in the case of dishonesty, a recent court decision indicated that while there might be cause for termination if an employee is dishonest, it will depend on the whole situation and what is determined through an investigation.

This particular case revolved around a ferry service that fired one of its managers for giving about $200 worth of vouchers for food and beverages to their daughter's hockey team. The manager was authorized to provide vouchers if passengers were inconvenienced in any way. The ferry company stated at trial that the action violated its code of business conduct and ethics and that breached the fundamental relationships of trust and good faith. An earlier court decision had reinforced that the context of the incident had to be considered to determine whether the misconduct was so bad that termination was the only option. Among the factors considered for the context were the nature of the dishonesty, the circumstances, and the position of the employee. On appeal, the judge determined that the original trial judge had not taken the context of the incident into consideration and that the evidence didn't support a termination with cause. It is important to remember that there is no single approach to doing a termination.

In another case involving good faith and loyalty, a Quebec employer terminated a long-service employee for being disloyal. The employee was a cashier in a grocery store and repeated told customers that prices were lower at other stores. When the owner was informed of this conduct, the person was terminated for being disloyal—a breach of trust. The union grieved the action and the arbitrator upheld the termination saying that the conduct was disloyalty and termination was an appropriate action by the employer.

CRITICAL THINKING QUESTIONS:

1. Do you think the decisions were correct?
2. How would you have ruled in these two situations?

Sources: Adapted from Lindsey Taylor, "When Is Dishonesty Just Cause for Dismissal?" *The HR Space*, February 10, 2015; *Roe v. British Columbia Ferry Services, Ltd.* (2015), BCCA1, CA041674, January 6, 2015; Mohamed Badreddine, "Disloyal Conduct May Justify Termination," *The HR Space*, August 30, 2014; and *Provigo (Alimentation D.M. St-Georges Inc.—Saint-Michel-des-Saints) and Travailleuses et travailleurs unis de l'Alimentation et du commerce, Local 500 (Nancy Beaulieu)*, March 13, 2014.

TOOLKIT 9.4 "JUST-CAUSE" DISMISSAL GUIDELINES

1. Did the organization forewarn the employee of the possible disciplinary consequences of his or her action?
2. Were management's requirements of the employee reasonable in relation to the orderly, efficient, and safe operation of the organization's business?
3. Did management, before changing the working conditions or discharging the employee, make a reasonable effort to establish that the employee's performance was unsatisfactory?
4. Was the organization's investigation conducted in a fair and objective manner?
5. Did the investigation produce sufficient evidence or proof of guilt as charged?
6. Has management treated this employee under its rules, orders, and penalties as it has other employees in similar circumstances?
7. Did the discharge fit the misconduct, considering the seriousness of the proven offence, the employee's service record, and any mitigating circumstances?

Constructive Dismissal

Another type of dismissal is **constructive dismissal**, which occurs when an employer changes an employee's working conditions such that compensation, status, or prestige is reduced. While employers have the right to make changes to employment conditions, there is an expectation that the employer provide appropriate notice. Even if the employee agrees to the changed conditions (the only other option might be unemployment) or resigns, the court may consider the employee to have been dismissed.[40]

Constructive dismissal Changing an employee's working conditions such that compensation, status, or prestige is reduced

Two cases illustrate the concept. One involved an employer in Ontario who changed the hours of work for an overnight shift from 8:00 p.m.–4:30 a.m. to 10:00 p.m.–5:30 a.m. The employee didn't agree to the change and decided to resign. When the employer received the resignation, it decided not to implement the change. The employee responded by saying that a written guarantee of no change in hours was needed for the employee to return. The employer refused and the employee filed a claim for constructive dismissal. It was the Ontario Labour Relations Board that decided there was no validity to the claim on two bases: (1) the change in hours was minor and (2) the employer never implemented the change.[41]

In another case, also in Ontario, a company that developed engineering solutions for office printing reduced its staff and added the duties and responsibilities of an IT administrator to a technician who had been employed for about 10 years. The employee took on the extra responsibilities, at no increase in pay, but after a year indicated that the work was too much and would like a raise. The company said no, and the employee stated that the IT administrator work would no longer be done. The employer responded by hiring a contractor and told the employee they would be terminated in 12 months. The company expected that the employee would work those 12 months but denied access to the company's computer system that was necessary to perform the regular technician duties. At trial, the court decided that the company had constructively dismissed the employee when the original extra duties were added without additional compensation.[42]

These two different cases both deal with changes to working conditions yet have different outcomes. To access the latest information on constructive dismissals, Carswell's *The Wrongful Dismissal Handbook* is a helpful resource.

In a non-union setting, employers can give notice of future changes in compensation (wages and benefits), working hours, location, and other similar items so long as they provide notice equivalent to that given for dismissal. For example, if the company wished to reduce the amount of paid sick leave, it could do so with sufficient notice.

Terminating Employees

Regardless of the reasons for a termination, it should be done with personal consideration for the employee affected. Every effort should be made to ease the trauma a dismissal creates. The employee must be informed honestly, yet tactfully, of the exact reasons for the action. Such candour can help the employee face the problem and adjust to it in a constructive manner.

Managers need to discuss, and even rehearse, with their peers the upcoming termination meeting. This practice can ensure that all important points are covered while giving confidence to the manager. Although managers agree that there is no single right way to conduct the dismissal meeting, the following guidelines will help to make the discussion more effective:

1. Hold the meeting as early in the week as possible and in a neutral meeting place.
2. Come to the point within the first two or three minutes, and list in a logical order all reasons for the termination.
3. Be straightforward and firm, yet tactful, and remain resolute in the decision; avoid debating reasons and decisions.
4. Make the discussion private, businesslike, and fairly brief; make notes of the meeting.
5. Avoid making accusations against the employee and injecting personal feelings into the discussion; be courteous and respectful at all times.
6. Avoid bringing up any personality differences.
7. Provide any information concerning severance pay and the status of benefits and coverage.
8. Explain how employment inquiries from future employers will be handled.
9. Arrange a mutually-agreed-upon time for the employee to clear out personal belongings and for the return of any company property.
10. Have another manager present as a witness.

Termination meetings should be held in a neutral location, such as a conference room, so that the manager can leave if the meeting gets out of control. The prudent manager will also have determined, prior to the termination decision, that the dismissal does not violate any legal rights the employee may have.

Finally, when terminated employees are escorted off the premises, the removal must not serve to defame the employee. Managers should not give peers the impression that the terminated employee was dishonest or untrustworthy. Furthermore, managers are advised never to discuss the discharge with other employees, customers, or any other individual.

Providing Career Transition Assistance

Employers often use career transition or outplacement services to assist employees who are being dismissed. Assistance is especially likely to be provided for employees of long tenure. While terminations do not have the negative stigma they once did, they are still traumatic for the employee.

And not just the usual organizations we think of provide help. For example, with the return of soldiers from fighting in the Middle East, career transition services are being offered to veterans to help them secure work in an evolving economic environment.[43] These services are especially helpful for people who have spent much time in the military and may not know how to define and market their skill sets.[44]

Managers cite the following reasons for providing outplacement services: concern for the well-being of the employees, protection against potential lawsuits, and the psychological effect on remaining employees. Outplacement consultants assist employees being terminated by reducing their anger and grief, and helping them regain self-confidence as they begin searching in earnest for a new job. Since many terminated workers have been out of the job market for some time, they may lack the knowledge and skills needed to look for

anyaberkut/Thinkstock

Web-based learning is part of career transition as people learn new skills.

a new job. Outplacement specialists can coach them in how to develop contacts, probe for job openings through systematic letter and telephone campaigns, and handle employment interviews and salary negotiations.

The Results of Inaction

Failure to act implies that the performance or behaviour of the employee concerned is acceptable. If disciplinary action is eventually taken, the delay will make it more difficult to justify the action, if appealed. In defending against such an appeal, the employer is likely to be asked why an employee who had not been performing or behaving satisfactorily was kept on the payroll. An even more probing question might be "Why did that employee continue to receive pay adjustments if there was a question about the performance?"

Such contradictions in practice can only aid employees in successfully challenging management's corrective actions. Unfortunately, some supervisors try to build a case to justify their corrective actions only after they have decided that a particular employee should be dismissed. The following are common reasons given by supervisors for their failure to impose a disciplinary penalty:

1. The supervisor had failed to document earlier actions, so no record existed on which to base subsequent disciplinary action.
2. Supervisors believed they would receive little or no support from higher management for the disciplinary action.
3. The supervisor was uncertain of the facts underlying the situation requiring disciplinary action.
4. Failure by the supervisor to discipline employees in the past for a certain infraction caused the supervisor to forgo current disciplinary action in order to appear consistent.
5. The supervisor wanted to be seen as a likable person.

It is critical to remember that any grounds for discipline must be well documented. Failure to do so can result in the disciplinary action being invalid.

APPEALING DISCIPLINARY ACTIONS

With growing frequency, organizations are taking steps to protect employees from arbitrary and inequitable treatment by their supervisors. A particular emphasis is put on creating a climate in which employees are assured they can voice their dissatisfaction with their superiors without fear of reprisal. This safeguard can be provided through the implementation of a formal procedure for appealing disciplinary actions.

Alternative Dispute-Resolution Procedures

LO6

What are the different types of alternative dispute-resolution procedures?

Alternative dispute resolution (ADR)
Term applied to different types of employee complaint or dispute-resolution procedures

In unionized workplaces, grievance procedures are stated in virtually all collective agreements. In non-union organizations, however, processes of **alternative dispute resolution (ADR)** are increasingly being used to keep employers out of court. The employer's interest stems from the desire to meet employees' expectations for fair treatment in the workplace while guaranteeing them due process—in the hope of minimizing discrimination claims or wrongful-dismissal suits.

Some organizations prefer these procedures as an avenue for upward communication for employees and as a way to gauge the mood of the workforce. Others view these systems as a way to resolve minor problems before they mushroom into major issues, thus leading to improved employee morale and productivity.

The appeal procedures described in this chapter are mediation, step-review systems, the use of a hearing officer, the open-door policy, an ombudsperson, and arbitration. Helpful resources for additional information on ADR can be found at **www.amic.org** and **www.crnhq.org**.

ADR Institute of Canada
www.amic.org

Conflict Resolution Network
www.crnhq.org

Mediation

Mediation
The use of an impartial third party to help facilitate a resolution to employment disputes

Mediation is fast becoming a popular way to resolve employee complaints and labour disputes involving unions. The essence of mediation is facilitating face-to-face meetings so that the employee and manager can reach an agreement. It is a flexible process shaped by the interests of the two parties.[45] It can also be used to resolve a wide range of employee complaints in a cost-effective and fairly quick process.[46] Employees like the process because of its informality. Settlements fashioned through mediation are readily accepted by the parties, thus promoting a favourable working relationship.

Conciliation is another form of mediation. It is used in labour relations, primarily in disputes involving governments as the employer or with federally regulated employers. For example, in late 2014, both the Teamsters Canada Rail Conference and VIA Rail asked that a conciliator be appointed to help with negotiations. In doing so, both parties were able to prevent a service disruption.[47]

Step-Review Systems

Step-review system
System for reviewing employee complaints and disputes by successively higher levels of management

As Figure 9.6 illustrates, a **step-review system** is based on a pre-established set of steps—normally four—for the review of an employee complaint by successively higher levels of management. These procedures are patterned after the union grievance systems, which will be discussed in Chapter 10. For example, they normally require that the employee's complaint be formalized as a written statement. Managers at each step are required to provide a full response to the complaint within a specified time period, perhaps three to five working days.

Use of a Hearing Officer

Hearing officer
Person who holds a full-time position with an organization but assumes a neutral role when deciding cases between management and aggrieved employees

This procedure is ordinarily confined to large organizations, where unions may represent employees. The **hearing officer** holds a full-time position with the organization but assumes a neutral role when deciding cases between an aggrieved employee and management.

FIGURE 9.6 Step-Review Appeal Procedure

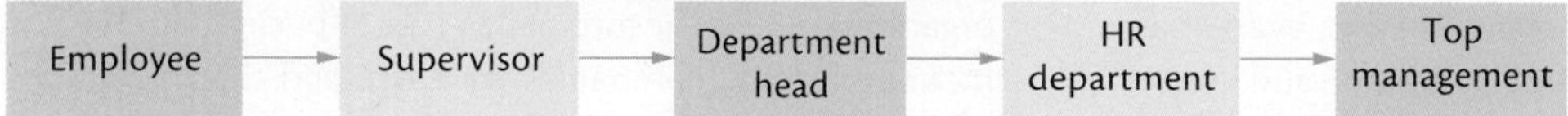

Hearing officers are employed by the organization; however, they function independently from other managers and occupy a special place in the organizational hierarchy. Their success rests on being perceived as neutral, highly competent, and completely unbiased in handling employee complaints. They hear cases upon request, almost always made by the employee. After considering the evidence and facts presented, they render decisions or awards that are normally final and binding on both sides.

Open-Door Policy

The open-door policy is an old standby for settling employee complaints. In fact, most managers, regardless of whether their organization has adopted a formal open-door policy, profess to maintain one for their employees. The traditional **open-door policy** identifies various levels of management above the immediate supervisor that an aggrieved employee may contact; the levels may extend as high as a vice-president, president, or chief executive officer. Typically, the person who acts as "the court of last resort" is the HR director or a senior staff official.

Open-door policy
Policy of settling grievances that identifies various levels of management above the immediate supervisor for employee contact

Ombudsperson System

An **ombudsperson** is a designated individual from whom employees may seek counsel for the resolution of their complaints. The ombudsperson listens to an employee's complaint and attempts to resolve it by mediating a solution between the employee and the supervisor. This individual works co-operatively with both sides to reach a settlement, often employing a clinical approach to problem solving. Since the ombudsperson has no authority to finalize a solution, compromises are highly possible, and all concerned tend to feel satisfied with the outcome. To function successfully, an ombudsperson must be able to operate in an atmosphere of confidentiality that does not threaten the security of the managers or subordinates involved in a complaint. Such a system also allows the ombudsperson to make recommendations to improve workplace practices.[48]

Ombudsperson
Designated individual from whom employees may seek counsel for the resolution of their complaints

Arbitration

Private employers may require that employees submit their employment disputes for a binding resolution through arbitration. (Arbitration is fully explained in Chapter 10.) Arbitration can save court costs and avoid time delays and unfavourable publicity.

For trends in the areas covered in this chapter, see Emerging Trends 9.1.

EMERGING TRENDS 9.1

1. ***Employers making more use of alternative dispute resolutions.*** With the negative consequences of workplace conflicts, and with the increasing costs of litigation, employers are making more use of mediation to help resolve conflicts.
2. ***Improving organizational transparency.*** While organizations who strive to be as transparent as possible are seen as progressive, there is a fine line between people feeling watched and the need for transparency. It is commonly understood that people change behaviours

continued

when being observed and therefore having everyone work in open space to increase collaboration and innovation may be counterproductive if people feel they are being watched.

3. ***More attention to privacy issues.*** Companies have legitimate rights to protect their products and their employees through monitoring. However, recent incidents have highlighted the need to ensure both customer and employee information is protected from inappropriate access and use. Further, concerns are being raised about accessing one's social media as part of a screening step when considering someone for employment.
4. ***Better use of social media.*** Not too many years ago, organizations were creating very restrictive practices for use of Internet access on work time. Now as many organizations use the Internet as part of business information retrieval, companies have decided that social media sites might provide helpful contacts and that the benefits can outweigh the risks of people wasting time. Social media is also being used to help bridge relationships between Boomers and Millennials in the workplace.
5. ***More attention to after-work behaviour.*** Because of situations like the CBC case, more employers are willing to discipline employees, including termination, for off-duty behaviour that is considered inappropriate. Other real examples include a person working at a retail clothier who posted derogatory comments on Facebook and was fired and two individuals in Quebec schools terminated for having been porn stars when they were younger.

Sources: Adapted from David Brubaker, Cinnie Noble, Richard Fincher, Susan Kee-Young Park, and Sharon Press, "Conflict Resolution in the Workplace: What Will the Future Bring?" *Conflict Resolution Quarterly* 31, no. 4 (Summer 2014): 357–386; Brian Kreissl, "Managing a Multigenerational Workforce," *Canadian HR Reporter*, April 6, 2015, accessed April 11, 2015, **www.hrreporter.com/articleview/23960-managing-a-multigenerational-workforce-toughest-hr-question**; Sarah Dobson, "Health-Care Privacy Breaches Highlight Staff Challenges," *Canadian HR Reporter*, March 9, 2015, accessed April 11, 2015, **www.hrreporter.com/articleview/23748-health-care-privacy-breaches-highlight-staff-challenges**; Lorenzo Lisi, "Checking a Job Applicant's Online Presence," *Canadian HR Reporter*, February 9, 2015, **www.hrreporter.com/articleview/23461-checking-a-job-applicants-online-presence-toughest-hr-question**; "5 cases of People Who Lost Jobs over Off-Hours Conduct," *Canadian Employment Law Today*, May 14, 2015, accessed July 7, 2015, **www.employmentlawtoday.com/articleview/24350-5-cases-of-people-who-lost-jobs-over-off-hours-conduct?utm_medium=Email&utm_campaign=HRNewswire_20150520&utm_source=Act-On%20Software**; Liz Bernier, "When Workers Feel Watched," *Canadian HR Reporter*, November 3, 2014, accessed April 11, 2015, **www.hrreporter.com/articleview/22674-when-workers-feel-watched**; and Sarah Dobson, "Bad Behaviour, Zero Tolerance," *Canadian HR Reporter*, Jun 1, 2015, 1.

Summary

1. Describe statutory rights, contractual rights, due process, and legal implications of those rights.
   - Statutory rights derive from legislation, such as human rights legislation.
   - Contractual rights are derived from contracts, such as an employment contract.
   - Due process is the employee's right to be heard through a complaint process.
   - Legal implications flow from how the employee is treated.
2. Identify the job expectancy rights of employees.
   - Fair and equitable treatment
   - A workplace that is safe and drug-free
   - Reasonable treatment regarding privacy
   - Access to one's own personnel files
   - Not being subject to discipline for off-duty behaviour
   - Being notified of any plant closings
3. Explain the process of establishing disciplinary practices, including the proper implementation of organizational expectations.
   - The primary purpose of having disciplinary procedures is to prevent or correct discipline problems.
   - Failure to take disciplinary action serves only to aggravate a problem that eventually must be resolved.
   - Organizations need to clearly outline rules and expectations regarding performance and behaviour.

4. Discuss the meaning of discipline and how to investigate a disciplinary problem.
   - Discipline is action that results in desirable conduct or performance.
   - If a problem occurs, the supervisor needs to determine when the situation occurred and to have a full discussion with the employee to get the employee's view of the situation.
5. Outline the differences between progressive and positive discipline.
   - Progressive discipline is the application of corrective measures by increasing degrees.
   - Progressive discipline is designed to motivate an employee to correct misconduct.
   - Positive discipline is based on the concept that the employee must assume responsibility for personal conduct and job performance.
   - Positive discipline requires a co-operative environment for joint discussion and problem solving between the supervisor and the employee.
6. Identify the different types of alternative dispute-resolution procedures.
   - Step-review systems
   - Peer-review systems
   - Use of hearing officers
   - Open-door system
   - Ombudsperson system
   - Arbitration

Need to Know

- Definition of termination with cause, and wrongful dismissal
- Types of disciplinary approaches
- Types of discipline appeal mechanisms for non-union staff
- Definition of discipline

Need to Understand

- How employee rights are protected
- How to conduct a discipline investigation
- How to dismiss an employee
- Factors used to determine if termination was for cause

KEY TERMS

alternative dispute resolution (ADR) 308
constructive dismissal 305
contractual rights 285
discipline 297
due process 286
employee rights 283
hearing officer 308
mediation 308
negligence 283
ombudsperson 309
open-door policy 309
positive, or nonpunitive, discipline 301
progressive discipline 299
statutory rights 284
step-review system 308
wrongful dismissal 302

REVIEW QUESTIONS

1. What is the definition of management rights and employee rights?
2. Explain statutory rights and contractual rights.
3. What are some of the guidelines for developing a policy on employee searches?
4. List some of the guidelines employers ought to use when developing policies for e-mail, Internet, voice mail, and social media usage.

5. Why is documentation so important in the disciplinary process?
6. Explain the differences and similarities between progressive and positive discipline.
7. Explain "just cause" dismissal and "wrongful" dismissal.
8. What is mediation?

CRITICAL THINKING QUESTIONS

1. What does John Jacak in the HRM Close-up say are the most important aspects in a privacy policy?
2. Suki frequently posts tweets about her unhappiness at work and makes derogatory comments about her supervisor. Does her employer have the right to control what she tweets? Why? What might the employer do?
3. Pardeep works as a millwright in a sawmill. The company is considering redesigning its discipline procedures to be oriented toward positive discipline. What would be the advantages and disadvantages of this change? What would the company want to include in the new procedure?
4. You have recently been promoted to a supervisory position. One of your first tasks is to discipline one of your staff for an ongoing tardiness problem. What information do you need prior to the discipline meeting and how would you conduct the meeting?
5. Your professor is dealing with a case where a student was alleged to have cheated on the final exam. Would documentation be important? If so, what type of documentation would be necessary?

DEVELOPING YOUR SKILLS

1. Individually read the following scenarios. Then in groups of four to five students, determine if the situations are or are not fair. Explain your reasons. Be prepared to share your information with the rest of the class.
   A. Jane was using the company network system to locate childcare facilities in her local community. Her supervisor observed this and then sought confirmation from the IT unit. Jane was given a written reprimand. Meanwhile, John used his desk telephone to do his personal banking and bill paying. John was not reprimanded.
   B. Sonita spent her lunch hour at the gym; she is following a strenuous workout program as she prepares for a triathlon event in the next several weeks. Meanwhile, Anthony met his friends for lunch, sharing several beers at the local pub. Both employees felt fatigued in the afternoon, and their work performance decreased, which was noted by their supervisor. Anthony was asked to meet with his supervisor to review performance expectations and received a verbal warning. Sonita did not.
2. Working in groups of 3 or 4, discuss the following questions:
   A. What would you do if you discovered that your employer was regularly following your tweets?
   B. Do you object to monitoring of employees? Why or why not?
   C. Would you object to being monitored? Why or why not?
3. On an individual basis, access the website of the Office of the Privacy Commissioner of Canada (**www.priv.gc.ca**). Click the "Privacy Quiz for Organizations" and take the quiz. Would you recommend that your employer look at the quiz? Why?
4. Access the following sites, which discuss employee privacy rights in the workplace. Prepare a one-to-two-page report summarizing what each site has to offer. Indicate if there are any areas of the site that might be more helpful to an employee rather than an employer.
   - **www.priv.gc.ca**
   - **www.epic.org**
   - **www.cippic.ca/workplace-privacy**

Privacy Commissioner of Canada
www.priv.gc.ca

Electronic Privacy Information Centre
www.epic.org

Electronic Frontier Foundation
www.eff.org/issues/privacy

Canadian Internet Policy and Public Interest Clinic
www.cippic.ca/workplace-privacy

5. Conduct your own Internet search, using any search engine, under the heading of "employee discipline." Share with your classmates what you learned and provide at least two URLs you found helpful.

CASE STUDY 1

What About My Privacy?

There are two sides to the issue of workplace privacy. The employee side holds that employees have the right to privacy and that employers should respect and trust their employees. The employer side holds that the workplace is a public environment and that the organization is responsible for the actions of its employees, and for their interactions with clients, visitors, and other employees.

Many companies monitor e-mail, voice mail, and employee computer use. Most employee monitoring is perfectly legal. The general legal view is that computers, telephones, and so on are company property, and that employees should not be using them for personal reasons. Companies can trace deleted e-mails and voice mails, special software can track Internet use, and wireless video cameras are small enough to look like pagers. More and more employees are using technology, and this makes it even easier to monitor their work. Even Bill Gates was caught: his private e-mails were used in the Microsoft antitrust hearings in the United States. Organizations monitor employees in order to deter crime, protect business secrets, and ensure a safe and equitable workplace.

A major reason for monitoring is to ensure that employees are actually working. Most employees waste at least a little time each day, however innocently. One company used a software tracking system to identify a group of employees who were selling Amway products from work. Another manager watched in horror as one of his top employees was led away by police, who had tracked his illegal activity (child pornography) through his e-mail address, which contained the company name.

Some employers have abused their right to monitor employees—for example, by videotaping them in washrooms, or hiring investigators to follow them. Another problem is the inferential misuse of the information obtained. For example, an employee may be visiting sites on suicide, AIDS, or substance abuse while doing research for a university paper. Employers may falsely infer from this that these issues personally affect the individual.

And now there is the popularity of social media sites such as Facebook, Twitter, MySpace, etc. Employers will sometimes to monitor employees as they post information to see what is being communicated about the company or whether the employee is doing that may create issues for the company.

Questions:

1. Employers usually do not have policies on using the telephone at work. Why, then, do employers need to develop policies on monitoring the use of e-mail and other forms of technology?
2. Few studies have considered the impact of monitoring on employee behaviour. Does it reduce crime, and make workplaces safer and more productive? Or does it increase stress, and result in an adversarial relationship? What do you think and why?

CASE STUDY 2

Can't the Absence Be Ignored?

Most organizations have policies and practices regarding absence from the workplace. And these same organizations usually track and monitor attendance and will take action when absence appears to be excessive. But what does the company do if a superior performer is frequently absent?

Caleb has been with a sales organization for about 10 years and has consistently met and exceeded his objectives each year. The company feels that its success and growth have been accomplished partially through Caleb's good work.

Over the past several months, Caleb's manager, Soon Lee, has noticed that the times Caleb is late or absent have been increasing. The manager asked that an analysis be done of Caleb's attendance over the previous 12 months and discovered a consistent pattern of Caleb being absent on either a Friday or a Monday every couple of weeks. This information only provided full-day absences and didn't identify the number of times he was late. Soon-Lee only had her anecdotal memories of the tardiness. And with his superior performance, she was reluctant to bring it up with him.

After several months, other employees spoke to Soon-Lee about Caleb's absences and the increased pressure it was putting on them to handle his clients. Soon-Lee knew she had to do something, as tensions in the work environment were increasing.

When Soon-Lee met with Caleb about it, he immediately went on the defensive and explained that he wasn't absent very often and even if he was that it shouldn't matter given his superior performance. Soon-Lee decided it was important to clarify expectations about his attendance even with superior performance. Caleb wasn't happy but said he did understand and would improve.

However, the attendance didn't change and Soon-Lee had another discussion with him. She warned Caleb that any further patterns of absenteeism would result in his termination.

Unfortunately, Caleb's pattern of absences continued and, after another three months of repeated warnings Soon-Lee terminated him.

Questions:

1. Do you think Soon-Lee was correct in deciding to terminate Caleb when she did? Why or why not?
2. Was there something else Soon-Lee could have done? If so, what?
3. If you were Soon-Lee, what would you have done?

NOTES AND REFERENCES

1. "Pre-employment Screening Services," accessed March 28, 2015, www.dataresearch.com/frame.htm.
2. "Twitterverse Strikes Again," *Canadian HR Reporter,* March 9, 2015, accessed March 28, 2015, www.hrreporter.com/articleview/23738-weird-workplace.
3. Stuart Rudner, "Proper, Consistent Hiring Practices Crucial," *Canadian HR Reporter,* March 24, 2014, accessed March 28, 2015, www.hrreporter.com/blog/Canadian-HR-Law/archive/2014/03/24/proper-consistent-hiring-practices-crucial.
4. "Criminal Charges Laid in Deadly Lac-Mégantic Railway Disaster," *Canadian HR Reporter,* May 13, 2014, accessed March 28, 2015, www.hrreporter.com/articleview/21111-criminal-charges-laid-in-deadly-lac-megantic-railway-disaster.
5. *Wallace v. United Grain Growers* (1997), 152 DLR (4th) 1 (SCC); *BC(PSERC) v. BCGEU* (1999), SCJ No. 46 (SCC).
6. Jeffrey Smith, "B.C. Employer Puts an End to Worker's Ongoing Harassment," *Canadian HR Reporter*, February 23, 2015, 5.
7. Todd Humber, "Hefty Bill Is in on Unpaid Overtime," *Canadian HR Reporter*, September 8, 2014, accessed March 28, 2015, www.hrreporter.com/articleview/22183-hefty-bill-is-in-on-unpaid-overtime.
8. Ibid.

9. Colon Gibson, "Ensuring Termination Clauses Remain Valid in Fixed Contracts," *Canadian HR Reporter*, March 10, 2014, accessed April 2, 2015, www.hrreporter.com/articleview/20469-ensuring-termination-clauses-remain-valid-in-fixed-employment-contracts-toughest-hr-question.
10. "Refusing to Collaborate in an Employer's Psychological Harassment Investigation Can Be Grounds for Dismissal," *The HR Space*, Fasken Martineau, March 24, 2015.
11. *Business Dictionary*, accessed April 2, 2015, www.businessdictionary.com/definition/due-process.html.
12. Canada, Department of Justice, "About Canada's System of Justice," accessed April 2, 2015, www.justice.gc.ca/eng/csj-sjc/just.
13. Canadian Centre for Occupational Health and Safety, "Substance Abuse in the Workplace," accessed April 3, 2015, www.ccohs.ca/oshanswers/psychosocial/substance.html.
14. "Canadian Human Rights Commission's Policy on Alcohol and Drug Testing," accessed April 3, 2015, www.chrc-ccdp.gc.ca/sites/default/files/padt_pdda_eng.pdf.
15. Statistics Canada, "Heavy Drinking" accessed April 5, 2015, www.statcan.gc.ca/tables-tableaux/sum-som/l01/cst01/health79b-eng.htm.
16. Dr. Anita Teslak, "Benefits Trend: How HR Can Help with Substance Abuse," *Benefits Canada*, January 16, 2015, accessed April 3, 2015, www.benefitscanada.com/benefits/health-wellness/benefits-trends-how-hr-can-play-a-role-in-mental-health-issues-61152, and Nadine Wentzell, "Dealing with Prescription Drug Abuse in the Workplace," *Canadian HR Reporter*, September 8, 2014, accessed April 3, 2015, www.hrreporter.com/articleview/22175-dealing-with-prescription-drug-abuse-in-the-workplace.
17. Ibid.
18. "Connecticut Catering Company CEO Resigns over Dog-Kicking Incident," *Canadian HR Reporter*, September 2, 2014, accessed April 3, 2015, www.hrreporter.com/articleview/22122-connecticut-catering-company-ceo-resigns-over-dog-kicking-incident.
19. FairWork Ombudsman, "Workplace Privacy," accessed April 5, 2015, www.fairwork.gov.au/about-us/policies-and-guides/best-practice-guides/workplace-privacy; and Christin Choi, "5 Best Practices for Lawfully Monitoring Your Employees' Social Media Activities," *Philadelphia Business Journal*, October 27, 2014, accessed April 3, 2015, www.bizjournals.com/philadelphia/blog/guest-comment/2014/10/5-best-practices-for-lawfully-monitoring-your.html?page=all.
20. Sarah Dobson, "Health-Care Privacy Breaches Highlight Staff Challenges," *Canadian HR Reporter*, March 9, 2015, 1.
21. Office of the Privacy Commissioner of Canada, *Privacy and Social Networking in the Workplace*, accessed April 3, 2015, www.priv.gc.ca/resource/fs-fi/02_05_d_41_sn_e.asp.
22. Susan M. Heathfield, "Medical File and Medical File Contents," *About.com*, accessed April 4, 2015, http://humanresources.about.com/od/glossarym/g/medical-file-contents.htm.
23. Neil Kokemuller, "The Importance of Electronic Communication in Workplace Collaboration," *The Houston Chronicle*, April 4, 2015, http://work.chron.com/importance-electronic-communication-workplace-collaboration-4081.html.
24. Jeffrey R. Smith, "Mobile Technology Blurs Privacy Lines," *Canadian HR Reporter*, July 22, 2014, accessed April 4, 2015, www.hrreporter.com/blog/Employment-Law/archive/2014/07/22/mobile-technology-blurs-privacy-lines.
25. Fasken Martineau, "Blockbuster Annual Update on Labour, Employment, Human Rights and Privacy," October 1, 2014.
26. Leah Eichler, "What You Do After Hours Matters Too," *The Globe and Mail*, October 31, 2014, accessed April 4, 2015, www.theglobeandmail.com/report-on-business/careers/career-advice/life-at-work/when-work-and-your-private-life-collide/article21405962.
27. Jeffrey R. Smith, "Word of Warning," *Canadian HR Reporter*, December 16, 2014, accessed March 15, 2015, www.hrreporter.com/blog/employment-law/postprint/2014/12/16/word-of-warning.
28. Liz Bernier, "Picking Up the Pieces After a Workplace Scandal," *Canadian HR Reporter*, June 1, 2015, 8.
29. Jeffrey R. Smith, "Bad Breads for Employees and Employers," *Canadian HR Reporter*, January 27, 2015, accessed April 4, 2015, www.hrreporter.com/blog/Employment-Law/archive/2015/01/27/bad-breaks-for-employees-and-employers.
30. Stuart Rudner, "Learn the Art of Negative Feedback," *Canadian HR Reporter*, January 27, 2014, accessed April 4, 2015, www.hrreporter.com/blog/Canadian-HR-Law/archive/2014/01/27/learn-the-art-of-negative-feedback.
31. Michael Richards and Nicholas Sharratt, "Workplace Investigations Need to Be Thorough, Unbiased," *Canadian HR Reporter*, July 14, 2014, accessed April 4, 2015, www.hrreporter.com/articleview/21715-workplace-investigations-need-to-be-thorough-unbiased.
32. Jon Hyman, "Pull Over the Potty Police," *Workforce*, September 3, 2014, accessed April 4, 2015, www.workforce.com/articles/20751-pull-over-the-potty-police.
33. Kellie Auld, "Handle with Care: The Impact of Workplaces Investigations," *PeopleTalk*, Summer 2015, 32–33.
34. Jeffrey Kadlic, "Employee Discipline & Discharge Best Practices," Evolution Capital Partners, February 3, 2014, accessed April 4, 2015, www.evolutioncp.com/blog/entrepreneurship/employee-discipline-discharge-best-practices.
35. Readers interested in the pioneering work on positive discipline should see James R. Redeker, "Discipline, Part 1: Progressive Systems Work Only by Accident," *Personnel* 62, no. 10 (October 1985): 8–12; James R. Redeker, "Discipline, Part 2: The Nonpunitive Approach Works by Design," *Personnel* 62, no. 11 (November 1985): 7–14. See also Alan W. Bryant, "Replacing Punitive Discipline with a Positive Approach," *Personnel Administrator* 29, no. 2 (February 1984): 79–87; and Chimezie A. B. Osigweh Yg and William R. Hutchison, "Positive Discipline," *Human Resource Management* 28, no. 3 (Fall 1989): 367–383.
36. Brian Kreissl, "Moving Towards a More Collaborative Labour Relations Climate," *Canadian HR Reporter*, March 24, 2015, www.hrreporter.com/blog/HR-Policies-Practices/archive/2015/03/24/moving-towards-a-more-collaborative-labour-relations-climate.
37. HR Council for the Nonprofit Sector, "Keeping the Right People: Discipline," accessed April 5, 2015, http://hrcouncil.ca/hr-toolkit/keeping-people-discipline.cfm#top.
38. Ibid.
39. "Six Years Lost to Dismissal Dispute, but Employee Vows to Extend It," *HRM Online*, June 24, 2015, accessed July 7, 2015, www.hrmonline.ca/hr-news/six-years-lost-to-dismissal-dispute-but-employee-vows-to-extend-it-192677.aspx.
40. "Constructive Dismissal," accessed April 11, 2015, www.duhaime.org/LegalDictionary/C/ConstructiveDismissal.aspx.
41. Jeffrey R. Smith, "We Didn't Really Mean It," *Canadian HR Reporter*, February 3, 2015, accessed April 11, 2015, www.hrreporter.com/blog/Employment-Law/archive/2015/02/03/we-didnt-really-mean-it.
42. Jeffrey R. Smith, "When Fewer People Must Do More," *Canadian HR Reporter*, August 12, 2014, accessed April 11, 2015, www.hrreporter.com/blog/Employment-Law/archive/2014/08/12/when-fewer-people-must-do-more.
43. Sarah Sipek, "Deloitte Offers CORE Training for Veterans," *Workforce*, November 10, 2014, accessed April 11, 2015, http://www.workforce.com/articles/20903-core-training.
44. Ibid.

45. Michael Roberts, "Resolving Disputes Through Employment Mediation," Mediate.com, accessed April 11, 2015, www.mediate.com/articles/roberts2.cfm.
46. Ibid.
47. "Negotiations at VIA Rail: The Teamsters Union and the Employer Have Requested a Conciliator," *Newswire.ca*, December 19, 2014, accessed April 11, 2015, www.newswire.ca/en/story/1466275/negotiations-at-via-rail-the-teamsters-union-and-the-employer-have-requested-a-conciliator.
48. Sarah Dobson, "Poor HR Practices Under Microscope," *Canadian HR Reporter*, May 19, 2014, accessed April 11, 2015, www.hrreporter.com/articleview/21206-poor-hr-practices-under-microscope.

10 Understanding Labour Relations and Collective Bargaining

LEARNING OUTCOMES

After studying this chapter, you should be able to

1. Explain the federal and provincial legislation that provides the framework for labour relations.
2. Cite the reasons employees join unions.
3. Outline the process by which unions organize employees and gain recognition as their bargaining agent.
4. Illustrate the functions labour unions perform at international, national and local levels.
5. Describe the bargaining process and the bargaining goals and strategies of a union and an employer.
6. List the forms of bargaining power that a union and an employer may utilize to enforce their bargaining demands.
7. Identify the major provisions of a collective agreement, including the issue of management rights.
8. Describe a typical grievance procedure, and explain the basis for arbitration awards.

OUTLINE

(*Continued*)

HRM CLOSE-UP

"Transparency, understanding, making sure that you're focused on not just the interests of the company, but the interests of all involved are key."

In early 2015, Jazz Aviation reached an 11-year agreement with its almost 1,200 unionized pilots. In a field as ever-changing as the airline industry, a contract of that duration was practically unheard of, but it was merely the latest in a history of labour accomplishments by one of the largest regional airlines in the world.

Established in 2001 after Air Canada merged its 4 regional airlines into 1 single entity initially known as Air Canada Regional, the wholly-owned subsidiary was renamed, rebranded, and unveiled as Air Canada Jazz the following year.

The procedure had been a long and complex one that had involved no fewer than 20 collective agreements with unions representing everyone from pilots to maintenance staff. One of those most heavily involved in the process was Colin Copp, now Jazz's president.

"I had the responsibility to merge all these carriers from a labour relations perspective," he explains. "One of the things we started to do back then was to really look at ... building a relationship with the unions that would be supportive of some of their interests and needs."

Having attended Trinity Western University's aviation program and holding a pilot's licence, Copp had entered the airline industry as a flight dispatcher in 1989 and worked his way up to director of operations at AirBC. Although originally drawn by an interest in aviation, he soon found himself equally captivated by labour relations.

"Once I was in the business what got me interested in labour relations and senior management were the challenges," Copp explains. "The need for change and how you get through change; how you manage change; how you execute change; how you strategize around change. That's what has driven me into the labour relations world and then from there into the executive world where we're really dealing with trying to find solutions around large global problems that are typically always related in some way to employees."

While many may think of aircraft as the backbone of any airline, Copp quickly realized that the single biggest and most important asset was its people. "You really are dealing with a commodity product that's dependent on labour in all ways so you're dependent on pilots, you're dependent on flight attendants, you're dependent on maintenance," he says.

"When you really look at it, all the airlines run basically the same type of business. There's very little difference except for employees and culture. Those are the 2 key differentiators that really make or break a business."

Colin Copp, President, Jazz Aviation LP.

In 2006 Air Canada sold their Jazz assets and the airline became an independent company trading on the Toronto Stock Exchange. Today, in addition to offering private charters and general services to other airline operators, Air Canada purchases all of Jazz's seat capacity which is then operated under the name Air Canada Express.

"We have several masters," Copp explains of Jazz's structure. "We have Air Canada as a master, they're our customer; we have our unions who are pretty much a key stakeholder for us; and as a subsidiary of our parent company, Chorus Aviation, we indirectly have a shareholder group that have a big say in things. So we're working with multiple stakeholders and ... making sure that ... it's important to understand their interests as well as our own in these things."

The historic agreement with the Air Line Pilots Association in January 2015 had not been accomplished overnight. Jazz and the pilots had spent 2 years discussing the plan for the company and the changes and challenges that lay ahead. Once direct negotiations on the contract began, it had taken a further 2 months to reach a deal acceptable to both sides, but ultimately Copp attributes the completion of that agreement to understanding.

"Transparency, understanding, making sure that you're focused on not just the interests of the company, but the interests of all involved are key. Whoever the stakeholders are, you have to make sure you understand what's important to them. I would say that most of the success of the agreement can be attributed to the fact that the relationship was very strong and there was good understanding of what was important to both sides."

Source: Used by permission of Colin Copp

INTRODUCTION

Mention the word "union" and most people will have some opinion, positive or negative. To some, the word evokes images of labour–management unrest—grievances, strikes, picketing, and boycotts. To others, the word represents fairness, opportunity, equal representation, and someone who will look after them. Many think of unions as simply creating an adversarial relationship between employees and managers, while others feel that unions are necessary to counterbalance the power employers have.

Regardless of how people feel about them, unions have been an important force shaping organizational practices, legislation, and political thought in Canada since the mid-1800s. Consider Colin Copp's statements in the HRM Close-up. Some people might say that fears about unionization have helped employers become better at managing people. Today, unions remain of interest because of their influence on organizational productivity and competitiveness, the development of labour law, and HR policies and practices. Like business organizations themselves, unions are undergoing changes in both operation and philosophy. Labour–management co-operative programs, company buyouts by unions, and labour's increased interest in global trade are examples of labour's new role in society. Currently, of the 17.9 million people employed, approximately 4.7 million are unionized, of which the majority are in the public sector.[1]

In spite of the long history of unions, the intricacies of labour relations are unfamiliar to many individuals. Therefore, this chapter describes government regulation of labour relations, the labour relations process, the reasons workers join labour organizations, the structure and leadership of labour unions, contemporary challenges to labour organizations, and the role a supervisor or manager plays in labour relations.

Unions and other labour organizations can significantly affect the ability of managers to direct and control the various HR processes. For example, union seniority provisions in the labour contract may influence who is selected for job promotions or training programs. Pay rates may be determined through union negotiations, or unions may impose restrictions on management's employee evaluation methods. Therefore, it is essential that managers understand how unions operate and familiarize themselves with the growing body of laws governing labour relations. It is also important for the supervisor to understand how unionization affects the actions of the union and those of the HR professional.

THE LAWS GOVERNING LABOUR RELATIONS

Unions have a long history in North America, and the regulations governing labour relations have evolved over time. Initially, employers strongly opposed union growth, using court injunctions (e.g., court orders forbidding various union activities, such as picketing and strikes) and devices, such as the "yellow-dog contract"—an employers' anti-union tactic by which employees had to agree not to join a union while working for the employer's organization. Using strikebreakers, blacklisting employees (e.g., circulating the names of union supporters to other employers), and discriminating against those who favoured unionization were other anti-union tactics.

Today, the laws governing labour relations seek to create an environment in which both unions and employers can exercise their respective rights and responsibilities. Chapter 2 provided an overview of the various employment laws, including those governing labour relations. This chapter now looks at the laws in more detail.

Labour Relations Legislation

LO1

Which laws govern federal and provincial labour relations?

The first labour relations legislation, the *Trades Unions Act*, was passed by the federal Parliament in 1872. This act exempted unions from charges of criminal conspiracy, allowed them to pursue goals of collective bargaining without persecution, and gave them the ability to strike. Between 1872 and 1900, legislation to settle industrial disputes was enacted in a number of provinces, including Quebec, Ontario, British Columbia, and Nova Scotia. Although these acts are no longer in effect, they did mark Canada's early recognition of the rights of unions.

Several different laws at the federal and provincial levels currently regulate labour relations. These laws make up a labour relations "system" consisting of government, unions, and employers. The government makes the laws that regulate how unions and employers behave with each other.[2] In making laws, the government will determine who can unionize and where they can unionize. There are specific laws, or acts, for different sectors, industries, and workers.

Canada's labour relations system is highly decentralized, whereas the U.S. system is highly centralized. For example, in Canada, the federal law governs interprovincial transportation and communications, while provincial legislation governs manufacturing and mining. However, 90% of the workforce is governed by provincial legislation. As mentioned earlier in this book, the *Canada Labour Code* governs federally regulated companies such as Bell, Rogers, Canadian National Railway, and Telus, whereas the province in which they operate governs companies such as Molson Breweries. All labour legislation, whether federal or provincial, has certain features in common:

- the right of people to join unions
- the requirement that employers recognize a certified union as the rightful and exclusive bargaining agent for that group of employees
- the identification of unfair labour practices
- the right of unions to strike and right of employers to lock out workers[3]

The Canada Industrial Relations Board (CIRB) was established to administer and enforce the *Canada Labour Code*. Similarly, each province has a labour relations board (LRB) whose members are appointed by the provincial government and who administer the labour law. (The exception is Quebec, which has a labour court and commissioners.) The LRB is generally separate from the government and is composed of representatives from labour and management. The duties of the LRB include, but are not limited to,

- processing union applications to represent employees
- processing applications to terminate union bargaining rights
- hearing unfair-labour-practice complaints
- hearing complaints and issuing decisions regarding strikes, lockouts, and picketing[4]

It is important to remember that the administrative regulations are greatly influenced by the politics of any provincial government. Therefore, the legislation can be relatively similar, but the interpretation of the law can vary greatly from one province to another. The law typically gets interpreted by the decisions made by the respective labour boards that then influence the actions a union or company can take in the future. To learn more about the administration of labour relations, see Toolkit 10.1, which lists the websites of the labour relations boards.

LO2

What are some of the reasons employees give for unionizing?

WHY EMPLOYEES UNIONIZE

Employees frequently feel that individually, they will be unable to exercise power regarding their employment conditions at any particular employer. The treatment and benefits they receive depend in large part on how their employers view their worth to the organization. Of course, if they believe they are not being treated fairly, they have the choice of quitting. However, another way to correct the situation is to organize and bargain with the employer collectively. When employees pursue this direction, the labour relations process begins. As Figure 10.1 illustrates, the **labour relations process** consists of a logical sequence of 4 events: (1) employees desire collective representation, (2) union organizers or employees begin the organizing campaign, (3) collective negotiations lead to a collective agreement, and (4) the collective agreement is administered. Laws and administrative rulings influence each of the separate events by granting special privileges to, or imposing defined constraints on, employees, employers, and union officials.[5]

Labour relations process
Logical sequence of 4 events: (1) workers desire collective representation, (2) the union begins its organizing campaign, (3) collective negotiations lead to a contract, and (4) the contract is administered

TOOLKIT 10.1 LABOUR RELATIONS BOARDS

Labour relations boards are making it easier for employers and employees to access information. The following websites are a valuable resource for the supervisor and HR professional.

Jurisdiction	Name	Web site
Federal government	Canada Industrial Relations Board	**www.cirb-ccri.gc.ca**
Alberta	Alberta Labour Relations Board	**www.alrb.gov.ab.ca**
British Columbia	Labour Relations Board	**www.lrb.bc.ca**
Manitoba	Manitoba Labour Board	**www.gov.mb.ca/labour/labbrd**
New Brunswick	Labour and Employment Board	**www.gnb.ca/LEB-CTE/index-e.asp**
Newfoundland and Labrador	Labour Relations Board	**www.hrle.gov.nl.ca/lrb**
Nova Scotia	Labour Relations Board	**www.novascotia.ca/lae/labourboard**
Ontario	Ontario Labour Relations Board	**www.olrb.gov.on.ca**
Prince Edward Island	Labour Relations Board	**www.gov.pe.ca/labour/index.php3?number=1006679&lang=E**
Quebec	*Labour Code* administered through investigations and commissions created at the time of a complaint	
Saskatchewan	Labour Relations Board	**www.sasklabourrelationsboard.com**

FIGURE 10.1 Labour Relations Process

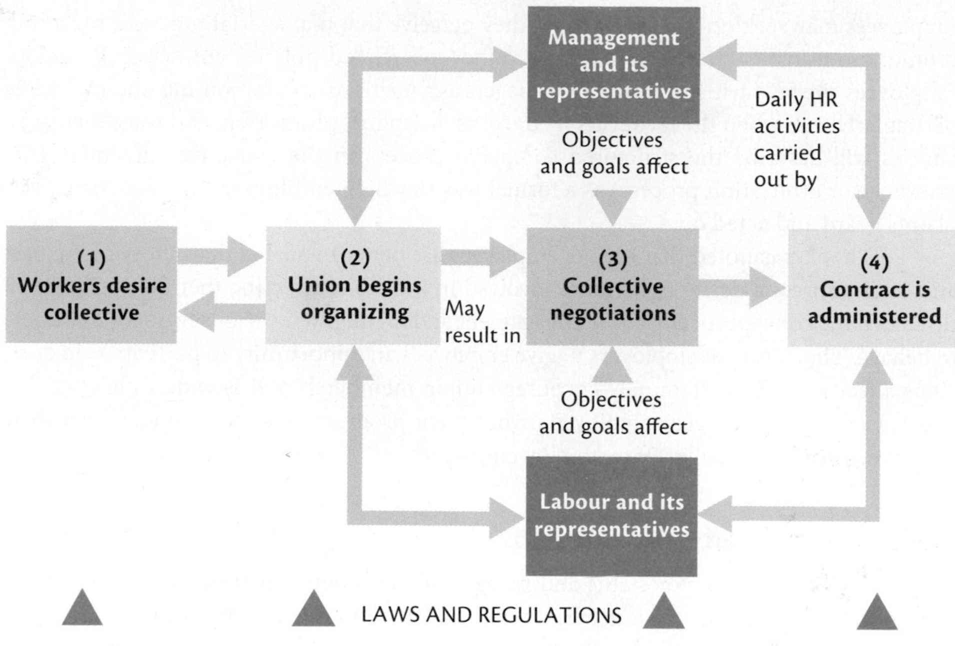

The majority of research on why employees unionize comes from the study of blue-collar employees in the private sector. These studies generally conclude that employees unionize as a result of

1. economic need
2. general dissatisfaction with managerial practices
3. a desire to fulfill social and status needs

It should be pointed out that some employees join unions because of the **union shop** provisions of the collective agreement that require employees to join as a condition of their employment. Others join because the employer is a **closed shop**—only members of a union will be hired—or because they choose to under an **open shop** provision. Even when forced to join, many employees eventually accept the concept of unionism. The sections that follow look at some of the more specific reasons people unionize and what role the supervisor and/or organization plays in the unionization process.

Union shop
Provision of the collective agreement that requires employees to join the union as a condition of their employment

Closed shop
Provision of the collective agreement that requires employers to hire only union members

Open shop
Provision of the collective agreement that allows employees to join or not join the union

Pay, Benefits, and Working Conditions

Whether or not a union can become the bargaining agent for a group of employees will be influenced by the employees' degree of dissatisfaction, if any, with their overall employment conditions. For example, employees may feel their concerns about health and safety are ignored or they may be required to wear uniforms without being reimbursed for the cost. It will also depend on whether the employees perceive the union as likely to be effective in improving these conditions. However, unhappiness with wages, benefits, and working conditions appear to be the strongest reasons to join a union. Unions will generally try to convince potential members that they can deliver pay increases and benefits. Other issues that have concerned unions include changes in business practices such as using contract workers, outsourcing, and paying much lower wages to immigrant workers.[6]

Dissatisfaction with Supervisors and Managers

Employees may seek unionization when they perceive that managerial practices regarding promotion, transfer, shift assignment, or other job-related policies are decidedly unfair. Employees cite favouritism shown by managers as a major reason for joining unions. This is particularly true when the favouritism concerns discipline, promotion, and wage increases. Unions will describe the structured complaint process in the collective agreement (the grievance or arbitration process) as a formal way in which employees can have their complaints heard and acted on.

This book has noted that today's employees are better educated than those of the past and often express a desire to be more involved in decisions affecting their jobs. Chapter 3 discussed the concepts of employee engagement and highlighted various ways for managers to behave. The failure of employers to give employees an opportunity to participate in decisions affecting their welfare may encourage union membership. It is widely believed that one reason managers begin employee involvement programs and seek to empower their employees is to avoid collective action by employees.

Social and Status Concerns

Employees whose needs for status and recognition are being frustrated may join unions as a means of satisfying these needs. Through their union, they have an opportunity to fraternize with other employees who have similar desires, interests, and problems. Joining the union also enables them to put to use any leadership talents they may have. In the final analysis, the deciding factor is likely to be whether employees perceive that the benefits of joining a union outweigh the costs associated with membership.

Sometimes, employees in similar industries may feel that they can improve their pay and working conditions only by joining a union. At Work with HRM 10.1 describes a number of employee categories at Porter Airlines that have joined a union. Porter is a relatively new airline that competes directly with both Air Canada and WestJet.

Toronto Star

Metal workers started the Winnipeg Strike of 1919 to force their employers to improve their working conditions.

AT WORK WITH HRM 10.1

PORTER AIRLINES

Is it easy to organize workers now? Not very, said Unifor union president, Jerry Dias. However, he indicated that unionizing the baggage handlers at Porter Airlines was huge as the current organizing drive lasted 6 months.

Porter Airlines, operating out ofl Toronto, has been mainly non-union except for a few refuelling employees. This changed when Unifor was certified by the Canadian Labour Relations Board to represent 80 baggage handlers, 70 ramp operations workers at Porter's Billy Bishop Airport, and about 125 customer service representatives.

Porter's success in the market has been its relatively low operating costs. It has stated that it may now have higher labour costs even though it has a high level of efficiency. Prior to certification, the handlers earned between $12 and $16 per hour, whereas the average for baggage handlers in the industry is $24 per hour according to Unifor.

Unifor and Porter Airlines successfully negotiated a first collective agreement for these members in early May 2015. While little information was publicly disclosed about the terms and conditions, both parties indicated that the agreement was substantive. The negotiating process and the outcome was recognized by the federal Minister of Labour as an example of working constructively together to achieve the best solution for each party.

CRITICAL THINKING QUESTION:

Why do you think these employees unionized at Porter?

Sources: Adapted from Greg Keenan, "Porter's Baggage Handlers Join Unifor," *The Globe and Mail*, September 26, 2014, B6; "Ramp Agents at Porter Airlines Choose Unifor," November 3, 2014, accessed May 21, 2015, **www.unifor2002.org/NewsRoom/ramp-agents-at-porter-airlines-choose-unifor.aspx**; "First Agreement Reflects Fairness and Respect for Members at Porter," April 28, 2015, accessed May 21, 2015, **www.unifor2002.org/NewsRoom/first-agreement-reflects-fairness-and-respect-for-members-at-porter.aspx**; "Porter Airlines Customer Service Agents to Be Represented by Unifor," December 3, 2014, accessed May 21, 2015, **www.680news.com/2014/12/03/porter-airlines-customer-service-agents-to-be-represented-by-unifor/#__federated=1**; and "Porter Airlines and Unifor Local 2002 Negotiate Their First Collective Agreements," Government of Canada, May 6, 2015, **http://news.gc.ca/web/article-en.do?nid=971229**.

HOW EMPLOYEES ORGANIZE

Once employees desire to unionize, a formal organizing campaign may be started either by a union organizer or by employees acting on their own behalf. Contrary to popular belief, most organizing campaigns are begun by employees rather than by union organizers. Large national unions such as the Unifor, the United Brotherhood of Carpenters, the United Steelworkers, and the Teamsters, however, have formal organizing departments whose purpose is to identify organizing opportunities and launch organizing campaigns. It has been no secret that the labour movement has targeted certain types of employers. Larger unions have moved out of their traditional industries into other areas. This has been due to changes from a goods-producing society to a service-based society and an overall decline in union membership. This last has also created new opportunities for unions. One opportunity led to the creation of Unifor—the merger of the Canadian Auto Workers (CAW) and the Communication, Energy and Paperworkers Union of Canada (CEP)—2 large and influential labour unions.[7]

One of the more interesting unionization cases for the last several years relates to the attempted unionization of Walmart Canada. While Walmart has had stores in Canada for over 20 years, none are currently organized. A store that unionized in Quebec about ten years ago was closed shortly after the employees joined a union. And that started a lengthy legal battle initiated by the United Food and Commercial Workers of Canada—the union that was certified. Even though Walmart stated that the store was closed as it was unprofitable, the union challenged that rationale. The Supreme Court of Canada finally heard the case in 2014 and concluded that Walmart had violated Quebec labour law by modifying the working conditions of the employees—that is, shutting the store.[8] Unfortunately, there really is no recourse; the court cannot order employees to be rehired. It did instruct an arbitrator to determine if there might be damages.

Since organizing campaigns can be expensive, union leaders carefully evaluate their chances of success and the possible benefits to be gained from their efforts. Important in this evaluation is the employer's vulnerability to unionization. Union leaders also consider the effect that allowing an employer to remain non-union might have on the strength of their union within the area. A non-union employer can impair a union's efforts to standardize employment conditions within an industry or geographic area, and weaken the union's bargaining power with employers it has unionized. Unions will also assess whether there is a possibility that future employees may wish to decertify. Just as the costs of unionizing can be high, so can the challenges coming from employees wanting to cease having the union represent them.

Organizing Steps

LO3

What is the process to unionize?

The typical organizing campaign follows a series of progressive steps that can lead to employee representation. The organizing process normally includes the following steps:

1. employee–union contact
2. initial organizational meeting
3. formation of in-house organizing committee
4. application to labour relations board
5. issuance of certificate by labour relations board
6. election of bargaining committee and contract negotiations

Step 1. The first step begins when employees and union officials make contact to explore the possibility of unionization. During these discussions, employees will investigate the advantages of representation, and union officials will begin to gather information on employee needs, problems, and complaints as well as information on the employer's financial health and supervisory styles. To win employee support, union organizers must build a case against the employer and for the union.

Supervisors and managers can become familiar with the questions unions ask employees during organizing drives and therefore better assess the effectiveness of their management practices. Toolkit 10.2 presents these questions.

When employees feel dissatisfied, they will often think about joining a union.

© Richard Baker/In Pictures/Corbis

TOOLKIT 10.2 FREQUENTLY ASKED QUESTIONS

Many organizations find themselves unionized and are surprised that it has happened. There is also a mistaken belief that unions do not actively recruit new members. The following are the questions union organizers usually ask employees:

1. Do you think people get paid more in other organizations? (Unions will know how much people are paid in the industry and geographic area.)
2. Are decisions about how much employees are paid based on logic or favouritism? (Usually, unions will have received information that supervisors make decisions in an arbitrary fashion.)
3. Are decisions about promotions based on merit or favouritism? (Unions usually have information about a particular individual who was promoted for reasons other than merit.)
4. If something happens that you feel is unfair, do you have recourse? Can you get your complaint heard? Who will hear it? Can they fix it? (Many small companies do not have a way to handle employee complaints. Unions will talk about the formal grievance procedure and the protections that can be provided to employees who feel helpless in dealing with a problem.)
5. How are shift schedules determined? (Unions will say that shifts ought to be determined by seniority.)
6. How are performance problems handled? (Unions will convince potential members that a union can ensure that people are treated fairly if there are performance issues.)
7. Do you feel that your manager criticizes you unfairly? (Unions will describe the processes that can be used if employees feel that they have not been treated fairly.)
8. Does your boss treat you with respect? (Unions will indicate that the power of a collective group of people will make the employer treat everyone respectfully.)

Step 2. As an organizing campaign gathers momentum, the organizer will schedule an initial union meeting to attract more supporters. The organizer will use the information gathered in step 1 to address employee needs and explain how the union can secure these goals.

Step 3. The 3rd important step in the organizing drive is to form an in-house organizing committee composed of employees willing to provide leadership to the campaign. The committee's role is to interest other employees in joining the union and in supporting its campaign. An important task of the committee is to have employees sign a **membership card** (or authorization card), indicating their willingness to be represented by a labour union in collective bargaining with their employer. The number of signed membership cards demonstrates the potential strength of the labour union. Legislation across Canada states that unions must have a majority of employees as members in a bargaining unit before they can apply for certification election. However, most jurisdictions now interpret this to mean that at least 50% of those voting constitute a majority. In other words, those who do not cast ballots are not assumed to be voting against the certification of the union. The union membership card, once signed, is confidential, and only the labour relations board has access to the cards.

Membership card
A statement signed by an employee authorizing a union to act as a representative of the employee for purposes of collective bargaining

Step 4. Application is made to the appropriate labour relations board. In Canada, a majority of unions are certified without a vote if the labour relations board finds that the union has the support of the majority of the employees, on the basis of the number of signed cards. However, in Ontario, if 40% or more of the employees sign membership cards, a vote can be requested.

Step 5. The labour relations board reviews the application and initially informs both the employer and the employees about the application. This application is posted so that either employees or the employer have an opportunity to challenge.

Step 6. Once the labour relations board determines that the union is certified, a bargaining committee is put in place to start negotiating a collective agreement. If the union is a national union, such as the Unifor, usually a national representative works with the bargaining committee to negotiate the collective agreement with the company.

Employer Tactics

Employers must not interfere with the certification process. They are prohibited by law from dismissing, disciplining, or threatening employees for exercising their rights to form a union. Employers cannot promise better conditions, such as increased vacation days, if the employees vote for no union or choose one union over another. Employers cannot unilaterally change wages and working conditions during certification proceedings or during collective bargaining. Like unions, they must bargain in good faith, meaning that they must demonstrate a commitment to bargain seriously and fairly. In addition, they cannot participate in the formation, selection, or support of unions representing employees.

None of these prohibitions prevents an employer from making the case that the employees have a right not to join a union or that they can deal directly with the employer on any issue. Employer resistance to unionization is the norm in Canada; however, employers need to recognize that they cannot intimidate or coerce employees but employers can express opinions of opposition to any union drive.[9] Attempts by employers to influence employees are scrutinized closely by officials of the organizing unions and the labour relations board.

Union Tactics

Unions also have a duty to act in accordance with labour legislation. Unions are prohibited from interfering with the operation of an employer's organization. They cannot intimidate or coerce employees to become or remain members of a union. Nor can they force employers to dismiss, discipline, or discriminate against non-union employees. They must provide fair representation for all employees in the **bargaining unit**, whether in collective bargaining or in grievance procedure cases. Unions cannot engage in activities such as strikes before the expiration of the union contract.

Bargaining unit
Group of 2 or more employees who share common employment interests and conditions and may reasonably be grouped together for purposes of collective bargaining

Unfair labour practices
Specific employer and union illegal practices that operate to deny employees their rights and benefits under labour law

Any of the prohibited activities discussed above for both employers and unions are considered **unfair labour practices**. Charges of unfair labour practices are made to the labour relations board, whose duty is to enforce the applicable labour laws and decide if an unfair labour practice occurred. An example of an unfair labour practice by an employer would be to threaten to fire people who wanted to join a union. Similarly, a union cannot threaten harm to employees if they don't join the union. Figure 10.2 provides a list of unfair labour practices on both the union and the management sides.

FIGURE 10.2 Unfair Labour Practices

Unfair labour practices by employers include the following:

- helping to establish or administer a union
- altering the working conditions of the employees while a union is applying for certification without the union's consent
- using intimidation, coercion, threats, promises, or exercising undue influence while a union is being organized
- failing to recognize or bargain with the certified union
- hiring professional strike breakers

Unfair labour practices by unions include the following:

- contributing financial or other support to an employees' organization
- not representing fairly the employees in the bargaining unit
- bargaining or negotiating a collective agreement with an employer while another union represents the employees in the bargaining unit
- calling or authorizing an unlawful strike, or threatening to do so

CERTIFICATION PROCEDURES

The procedures for union **certification** vary across Canadian jurisdictions. As mentioned earlier, if an applicant union can present documentation that it has sufficient support in the proposed bargaining unit, labour boards will grant certification to the union or grant a vote. The labour relations board must certify a union before it can act as a bargaining unit for a group of employees. The union normally provides evidence by submitting signed authorization cards and proof that initiation dues or fees have been paid.[10] Recognition of a union may be obtained through voluntary recognition, regular certification, or a prehearing vote.

Certification
Acquisition of exclusive rights by union to represent the employees

However, there can be a situation in which the legal framework of labour relations forces a person to join a particular union if the person wants to work. For example, the government of Quebec has legislation that requires all construction workers to belong to 1 of 5 unions. This also means that any construction company must hire only unionized workers.

Voluntary Recognition

All employers, except those in the province of Quebec, may voluntarily recognize and accept a union. This has not happened often, except in the construction industry where there is a great reliance on union hiring halls. Recently, however, some university faculty members at major B.C. universities organized into trade unions, leaving the University of British Columbia as the only institution that had "voluntarily" recognized its faculty some years earlier.[11]

Regular Certification

The regular certification process begins with the union submitting the required minimum membership evidence to the labour relations board. Generally, if an applicant union can demonstrate that it has sufficient support in the proposed bargaining unit, labour boards may grant certification on that basis. (However, with changes in government, labour relations legislation is often reformed. Therefore, requirements for granting certification may change.) The labour relations board may order a representative vote if a sizable minority of workers have indicated either support for or opposition to the unionization.

There are times that employee associations eventually seek certification. For example, in late June 2015, a group of WestJet pilots made an application to the Canada Industrial Relations Board to certify its 1,200 pilots. If approved, the Board will conduct a secret ballot to determine if the majority of pilots wish to be unionized.[12]

Prehearing Votes

If there is evidence of irregularities, such as unfair labour practices taking place during the organizing drive, a prehearing vote may be taken. The purpose of this vote is to establish the level of support among the workers. Depending on the particular labour relations legislation, votes can be called if less than 50% of the employees indicate support for a union.

Once a union has been certified, employees are part of a collective and can no longer individually make special arrangements on pay, hours of work, and so on. Likewise, this means that the manager and supervisor can no longer treat individuals differently—that is, they can't make individual deals.

Contract Negotiations

Once a bargaining unit has been certified by the labour relations board, the employer and the union are legally obliged to bargain in good faith over the terms and conditions of a collective agreement. The collective agreement is for at least 1 year. As the contract expiry date approaches, either party must notify the other of its intention to bargain for a renewal collective agreement or contract negotiation.

Unifor is the merger of 2 influential unions creating the largest private-sector union, with over 305,000 members.

© Douglas MacLellan/Demotix/Corbis

Decertification

All legislation allows for decertification of unions under certain conditions. If the majority of employees indicate that they do not want to be represented by the union or that they want to be represented by another union, or if the union has failed to bargain, an application for decertification can be made to the labour relations board. If a collective agreement has been reached with the employer, this application can be made only at specified times, such as a few months before the agreement expires. Either employees or the employer can initiate the application for decertification if the union fails to bargain.

One of the more unusual decisions regarding decertification occurred in British Columbia when seasonal farm workers from Mexico wanted to decertify. The union charged that the Mexican government and Vancouver consulate had interfered; the labour board concurred. However, the Mexican government launched a lawsuit saying that the Mexican government had immunity. While the Mexican government lost the case at the appeal court, it was concerned that employers would feel that Mexican workers were too much trouble and that workers from other Latin countries would be hired instead of from Mexico.[13]

Impact of Unionization on Managers

The unionization of employees can affect managers in many ways. Perhaps most significant is the effect it can have on the ability of managers to make decisions about employees. A union can assist employees if they believe they haven't been treated in accordance with the agreed-on employment conditions. As an example, if a company doesn't have a formal complaint mechanism, there is now a structured grievance procedure. And the decisions of a structured grievance procedure can be enforced through the courts (as will be discussed later in this chapter). Unionization also restricts the freedom of management to formulate HR policy and practices unilaterally.

Challenges to Management Decisions

Unions typically attempt to achieve greater participation in management decisions that affect their members. Specifically, these decisions may often involve such issues as the subcontracting of work, productivity standards, and job content. Employers quite naturally seek to claim many of these decisions as their exclusive **management rights** (discussed more fully later in this chapter). However, these rights are subject to challenge and erosion by the union. They may be challenged at the bargaining table, through the grievance procedure, through strikes and through illegal actions. Read At Work with HRM 10.2 to gain a fuller understanding of this.

Management rights
Decisions regarding organizational operations over which management claims exclusive rights

Loss of Supervisory Flexibility

At a labour–management conference, a union official commented, "Contract terms covering wages, benefits, job security, and working hours are of major importance to our membership." However, for managers and supervisors, the focal point of the union's impact is at the operating level (the shop floor or office facility), where the terms of the collective agreement are implemented on a daily basis. For example, these terms can determine what corrective action is to be taken in directing and disciplining employees. When disciplining employees, supervisors must be certain that they can demonstrate just cause (see Chapter 9) for their actions because these actions can be challenged by the union, and a supervisor can be called as defendant during a grievance hearing. If the challenge is upheld, the supervisor's effectiveness in coping with subsequent disciplinary problems may be impaired. Specific contract language can also reduce the supervisor's flexibility to manage in such areas as scheduling, training, performance evaluation, and promotions, to name a few.

The list provided in Toolkit 10.3 offers guidelines to help managers and supervisors understand what they can do to create a work environment in which employees will see no need to unionize. You will note that these are all similar to the ideas presented in Chapter 3 about creating a culture of well-being.

AT WORK WITH HRM 10.2

MONTREAL HAS SAID "ENOUGH!"

While employers are often blamed for poor relationships with its unions, what should happen when unionized firefighters get angry and vandalize municipal property?

Quebec has a long history of militant unions and allowing unions to be disruptive—even when the disruption is illegal—with no consequences. However, the city of Montreal decided that this type of behaviour had to stop. And city council decided it had to take decisive action.

In late summer 2014, firefighters stormed Montreal city hall and went on a rampage—broken windows, hurled water glasses and reams of paper, and blasted sirens and air horns. Council members were frightened enough to seek safety under their desks. While actions similar to this would have gone unpunished in another time, the city fired 6 firefighters and suspended another 57 unionized workers. All the actions were caught on camera. Firefighters were protesting Quebec legislation that would restructure municipal pension plans and supersede anything in any collective agreement.

The Quebec Municipal Affairs Minister stressed that authorities will not tolerate such illegal actions in a free and democratic society and that future illegal acts will have consequences. In addition, the province of Quebec criminally charged other firefighters and city workers for illegal assembly and interfering with city work. The firefighters union downplayed the damage and said that it was just a protest.

The union also said that it was very disappointed in how the city responded, calling it a political action even though the union's dispute is with the provincial government.

CRITICAL THINKING QUESTIONS:

1. Do you think the city responded appropriately by firing and/or suspending those who vandalized city hall? Explain your answer.
2. Do you think the province acted fairly by laying criminal charges? Why or why not?
3. What would you have done?

Sources: Adapted from Graeme Hamilton, "Fighting Union Fire with Firings," *The National Post*, October 3, 2014, A1; "Montreal's Mayor Lashes Out at Firefighters Who Ransacked City Hall," *The Toronto Sun*, August 19, 2014, accessed May 22, 2015, **www.torontosun.com/2014/08/19/fire-fighters-storm-montreal-council-chambers-shower-it-with-papers**; and James Mennie, "Firefighters to Be Fired for Rampage," *Montreal Gazette*, October 2, 2014, access May 22, 2015, **http://montrealgazette.com/news/local-news/gazette-midday-firefighters-to-be-fired-for-rampagepkp-re-invents-himself**.

TOOLKIT 10.3 CREATING A POSITIVE WORK ENVIRONMENT

1. If you have something to say to one of your employees, say it directly—and soon.
2. Praise employees publicly; criticize in private.
3. Remember that actions speak louder than words. Be sure your actions "say" what you want them to.
4. Be respectful of all your employees—even the poor performers.
5. Set up a file system for employee information, where you can keep documentation on pay raises, performance reviews, and the like. Allow employees access to their files, and encourage them to review their files.
6. Create performance goals with each employee—goals that are challenging but attainable; monitor performance and provide feedback.
7. Share business information.
8. Seek input from employees when making changes that will affect them.
9. Ask employees for suggestions on how to improve business operations.

HOW UNIONS OPERATE

International Brotherhood of Electrical Workers
www.ibew.org

International Brotherhood of Boilermakers
www.boilermakers.org

Canadian Union of Postal Workers
www.cupw.ca

Ontario Secondary School Teachers' Federation
www.osstf.on.ca

Unions that represent skilled craft workers, such as carpenters or masons, are called craft unions, such as the International Brotherhood of Electrical Workers (IBEW) (**www.ibew.org**) and the Brotherhood of Boilermakers (**www.boilermakers.org**). Unions that represent unskilled and semiskilled workers employed along industry lines are known as industrial unions—for example, the Canadian Union of Postal Workers (**www.cupw.ca**) and the Ontario Secondary School Teachers' Federation (**www.osstf.on.ca**). While the distinction between craft and industrial unions still exists, technological changes and competition among unions for members have weakened it. Today, skilled and unskilled workers, white-collar and blue-collar workers, and professional groups are being represented by both types of union.

Besides unions, there are also employee associations representing various groups of professional and white-collar employees. Examples of employee associations are the Federation of Quebec Nurses and the Alberta Teachers' Association. In competing with unions, these associations may function as unions and become just as aggressive as unions in representing members. These associations are non-union; however, if the employee association met the necessary criteria under labour legislation, the association could become certified as a union.

Regardless of their type, labour organizations are diverse, each with its own method of governance and objectives. And it is important to remember that unions are primarily political organizations. That is, they have elected leaders who can be voted out of office if the wishes of the members are not met. And there can be situations in which unions are antagonistic toward each other, such as the United Brotherhood of Carpenters and the Labourers International Union of North America (LIUNA). Both are Ontario labour unions attempting to increase each of their "market share" of construction work and in some situations to raid each other.[14]

Because of the political nature of unions, many have come together under an umbrella organization, called the Canadian Labour Congress (CLC). Through this organization, the CLC (**www.canadianlabour.ca**) attempts to influence government policy by commenting on economic conditions, such as the unemployment rate. Also, since most of the major unions in Canada are members of the CLC, the CLC also helps to referee between unions if they are seeking to organize the same group of workers. Because of its size and resources, the CLC is a very influential organization in Canada, and globally as well. In addition to the CLC, most provinces have umbrella organizations, one of which is the B.C. Federation of Labour (**www.bcfed.ca**). Both these organizations went through a change of leadership in 2014. Read At Work with HRM 10.3 to learn more about these changes.

Canadian Labour Congress
www.canadianlabour.ca

B.C. Federation of Labour
www.bcfed.ca

Canada's rate of unionization continues to fall, and is currently at 28.8%.[15] The decline is most notable among men and younger employees.[16] Part of the reason or the decline is the shift in the Canadian economy from manufacturing and construction to professional services and retail trade.[17] Rates of unionization vary across the world, from almost 70% in Sweden to 4% in Turkey, 26% in the United Kingdom, and 11% in the United States.[18]

Structure, Functions, and Leadership of International and National Unions

International unions tend to be affiliates of American unions, with headquarters in the United States. In Canada, there are 39 international unions (with membership of about 1.3 million workers) and 179 national unions (with membership of more than 3 million).[19] There are about the same number of international and national unions as there has been for many years, although the size and composition have changed.

LO4

What are the functions of unions at international, national and local levels?

Both international and national unions are made up of local unions. The objectives of these unions are to help organize local unions, to provide strike support, and to assist local unions with negotiations, grievance procedures, and the like. These unions also represent membership interest with internal and external constituents. By ensuring that all employers pay similar wages to their unionized workers, they fulfill the additional role of removing higher wages as a competitive disadvantage.

Structure and Functions of Local Unions

Employees of any organization can form their own union, with no affiliation to a national or international union. In this case, the local is the union. However, most local unions are members of national or international unions or the Canadian Labour Congress, which make available to them financial resources and advice. There are approximately 14,700 locals in Canada—less than in previous years.[20] Some of the reduction is due to mergers between unions. For example, the merger of the Canadian Auto Workers (CAW) and Communications, Energy, and Paperworkers Union (CEP) created the 3rd-largest union in Canada—Unifor—with over 308,000 members (**www.unifor.org**).[21]

Unifor
www.unifor.org

Unionized employees pay union dues that finance the operation of the local union. The officers of a local union are usually responsible for negotiating the local collective agreement, for ensuring that the agreement is adhered to, and for investigating and processing member grievances. Read Ethics and HRM 10.1 to understand what can happen if a national union has a concern about the operation of a local.

ETHICS IN HRM 10.1

ETHICS APPLY TO ALL!

Much attention is paid to business ethics in today's global economy. But does that also apply to union organizations? The answer is yes.

An issue arose recently in a CUPE (Canadian Union of Public Employees) local regarding its spending during a strike. The union represents the teaching assistants at York University and spent about $300,000 on food and beverages as well as paying hundreds of thousands of dollars in strike pay, leaving the local with an $800,000 debt after a 3-month strike. The national union requested the audit and also put the local under "administration"—a highly unusual step. However, it did so given the severity of the financial issues. Further, the executive of the local at the time was dismissed by the national union.

The most problematic expense during the forensic audit was a single bill for coffee, soup, bread, and cookies that totalled $56,500. Those on the picket line were also allowed to order food for delivery. Further, other food items were

continued

purchased from a university restaurant instead of getting from bulk-food stores. Lastly, 1 restaurant appeared to have only 1 customer—the local union during the strike.

The forensic audit confirmed that union officials didn't take their fiduciary responsibilities seriously and didn't appear to attempt any type of efficiencies. The annual dues for this local's members are 2.5%.

CRITICAL THINKING QUESTIONS:

1. Do you think the national union did the right thing to order an audit and dismiss the executive? Explain your answer.
2. During a strike, do you think those on picket lines should receive food and beverages? Why or why not?

Source: Adapted from "Simona Chiose, "Union overspent in last strike, audit says," *The Globe and Mail*, March 31, 2015, A12.

Role of the Union (Shop) Steward

Union (shop) steward
Employee who, as an unpaid union official, represents the interests of members in their relations with management

The **union (shop) steward** represents the interests of union members in their relations with their immediate supervisors and other members of management. Union stewards are employees of the company and are normally selected by union members within their department. They serve without union pay.

A union steward can be viewed as a "person in the middle," caught between conflicting interests and groups. It cannot be assumed that stewards will always champion union members and routinely oppose managerial objectives. Union stewards are often insightful individuals working for the betterment of employees and the organization. Therefore, supervisors and managers at all levels are encouraged to develop a positive working relationship with stewards and all union officials. This relationship can have an important bearing on union–management co-operation and on the efficiency and morale of the workers.

Role of the Business Agent

Business agent
Normally a paid labour official responsible for negotiating and administering the collective agreement and working to resolve union members' problems

Negotiating and administering the collective agreement and working to resolve problems arising in connection with it are major responsibilities of the **business agent**. In performing these duties, business agents must be all things to all people within their unions. They frequently are required to assume the role of counsellor in helping union members with both personal and job-related problems. They are also expected to satisfactorily resolve grievances that cannot be settled by the union stewards. Administering the daily affairs of the local union is another significant part of the business agent's job.

Union Leadership Approaches and Philosophies

To evaluate the role of union leaders accurately, one must understand the nature of their backgrounds and ambitions, and recognize the political nature of the offices they occupy. The leaders of many national unions have been able to develop political machines that enable them to defeat opposition and to perpetuate themselves in office. Tenure for the leaders of a local union, however, is less secure. If they are to remain in office, they must be able to convince a majority of the members that they are serving them effectively.

Although it is true that union leaders occupy positions of power within their organizations, rank-and-file members can and often do exercise a strong influence over these leaders, particularly with respect to the negotiation and administration of the collective agreement. It is important for managers to understand that union officials are elected to office and, like any political officials, must be responsive to the views of their constituency. The union leader who ignores the demands of union members may risk (1) being voted out of office, (2) having members vote the union out as their bargaining agent, (3) having members refuse to ratify the union agreement, or (4) having members engage in wildcat strikes or work stoppages.

To be effective leaders, union officials must also pay constant attention to the general goals and philosophies of the labour movement. Unions also have historically been politically active, backing such parties as the NDP. However, at times a union will comment on government policy. For example, the United Steelworkers union, along with the Ontario government, challenged the handling of the financing restructuring of United States Steel Canada Inc. when it filed for bankruptcy in late 2014.[22] Subsequently, the Steelworkers argued in court that the U.S. parent (U.S. Steel Corporation) should not be allowed to be listed as the debtor, as it is in conflict with the current situation.[23]

One success story of union philosophy is a worker-owned pulp mill in British Columbia. Harmac Pacific, located in Nanaimo, was declared insolvent in 2008 and then put into receivership. A group of employees, including members of the then Pulp, Paper and Woodworkers of Canada, with the help of investors, put together an offer to take over the operation. The employees also agreed to buy into the mill at $25,000 per person, with employee ownership now at 25%.[24] The mill not only survived, but has been upgraded so that it is now producing 365,000 tonnes of pulp per year. Its success is based on a new business model that is both responsive and adaptable to changing global conditions.

AT WORK WITH HRM 10.3

CHANGING OF THE GUARD

Throughout this textbook readers have been learning about the changes impacting employers. But does that happen to unions too? The answer is "Absolutely!"

The year 2014 saw significant change for both the Canadian Labour Congress (CLC) and the B.C. Federation of Labour. Both organizations had been led by very senior union leaders for many years. Both organizations also have a strong history of being constructive advocates for unions and their members and the issues they believe are important to members and to society at large.

The new head of the CLC, Hassan Yussuff, became president when he was elected over the incumbent president, Ken Georgetti, president for 15 years. His election may also mark a change in how the CLC goes about its work, as Yussuff has openly criticized the CLC for being too passive. He was also instrumental in the merger of the former CAW and CEP into the 3rd-largest Canadian union—Unifor. Yussuff also states that public policy reform is a priority for the CLC—particularly expanding the Canadian Pension Plan which could provide more income to people when they retire. He also acknowledges that much of the public is resentful of the high wages unionized employees receive; but he believes that more needs to be done to help people understand the value of unions in Canada. He also plans to be more visible to unionized and non-unionized workers than his predecessor.

Jim Sinclair, the outgoing head of the B.C. Federation of Labour, takes great pride in having run an organization that has a strong public profile with good working relations with the provincial government. He also is pleased with the successful outcome of lobbying for a higher minimum wage. Others in the labour movement acknowledge that Sinclair played a large role in providing a voice for the families of farm workers who died from toxic fumes on a mushroom farm. He is well known for having had to balance between being militant and negotiating deals with some provincial governments that weren't favourable toward unions. On his departure, he says that he survived 6 different provincial governments!

Part of the message that both organizations promote is that unions not only train members but are another avenue for mentoring younger workers and for benchmarking best practices. And of course, the message also includes the fact that unions provide a voice for the advancement of our society in general.

CRITICAL THINKING QUESTIONS:

1. What are some of the challenges and opportunities facing both these organizations? Explain your answer.
2. Do you think union wages are too high? Why or why not?
3. Should Hassan Yussuff take a more militant approach to push public policy? Explain your answer.

Sources: Adapted from Rob Shaw, "Changing of the Labour Guard in B.C. as Sinclair Signs Off," *The Vancouver Sun*, November 15, 2014, H1; Janet McFarland, "Union Roots Run Deep for New Face of Labour," *The Globe and Mail*, June 21, 2014, B3; "Unionized Labour," accessed May 31, 2015, **www.unionizedlabour.ca**; and "Organized Labour in B.C.," *The Vancouver Sun*, July 1, 2014, 1–8.

Labour Relations in the Public Sector

Canadian Union of Public Employees
http://cupe.ca

National Union of Public and General Employees
www.nupge.ca

Public Service Alliance of Canada
http://psacunion.ca

Collective bargaining among federal, provincial, and municipal government employees, and among employees in parapublic agencies (private agencies or branches of the government acting as extensions of government programs) has increased dramatically since the 1960s. Over 71% of all public employees are now unionized in contrast to 16% for the private sector.[25] The 3 largest unions in Canada represent public-sector employees. The Canadian Union of Public Employees (CUPE) **(http://cupe.ca)** is the largest union in Canada, representing more than 600,000 members. The 2nd-largest union, with 340,000 members, is the National Union of Provincial Government Employees (NUPGE) **(www.nupge.ca)**, which represents employees at the provincial level. The largest union representing employees at the federal level is the Public Service Alliance of Canada (PSAC) **(http://psaunion.ca)**, with more than 188,000 members.[26] Growth in these unions is threatened by increased cost-cutting efforts of governments at all levels, resulting in employee reductions.

While public- and private-sector collective bargaining have many features in common, a number of factors differentiate them. Two key distinctions are the political nature of the labour–management relationship and public-sector strikes.

Political Nature of the Labour–Management Relationship

Government employees are not able to negotiate with their employers on the same basis as their counterparts in private organizations. It is doubtful that they will ever be able to do so, because of inherent differences between the public and private sectors.

One significant difference is that labour relations in the private sector have an economic foundation, whereas in government their foundation tends to be political. Since private employers must stay in business in order to sell their goods or services, their employees are not likely to make demands that could bankrupt them. Governments, on the other hand, must stay in business because alternative services are usually not available. This assumption was recently challenged when the Supreme Court of Canada determined that the right to strike was a fundamental right protected by the Constitution.[27] Further, another Supreme Court of Canada decision now allows the RCMP to unionize—something not allowed by federal legislation. Again, the court determined that the law violated the fundamental right to freedom of association.[28] With these changes, there may be less ability for governments to legislate certain restrictions.

Provincial governments will sometimes look at reaching a type of compromise with unions to further economic goals. This certainly happened in British Columbia when an alliance of building trade unions threatened to encourage construction workers to say away from the Site C megaproject. The Crown corporation responsible for the new dam, BC Hydro, wanted to change the decades-old agreement to open the construction to people who weren't required to belong to a union.[29] Eventually, the government intervened and helped reach an agreement in which BC Hydro will give a higher priority to using contractors who recruit workers from the building trade unions.[30]

Strikes in the Public Sector

Strikes by government employees create a problem for lawmakers and for the general public. Because the services that government employees provide, such as police work and firefighting, are often considered essential to the well-being of the public, public policy is opposed to such strikes. However, various provincial legislatures have granted public employees the right to strike. Where striking is permitted, the right is limited to specific groups of employees—those performing nonessential services—and the strike cannot endanger the public's health, safety, or welfare.

Public-sector unions contend, however, that denying them the same right to strike as employees in the private sector greatly reduces their power during collective bargaining.

THE CANADIAN PRESS IMAGES/Dominic Chan

Canada Post workers strike to make people aware of the dispute.

Public employees who perform essential services do, in fact, strike. Teachers, sanitation employees, police, transit employees, firefighters, and postal employees have all engaged in strike action. To avoid a potentially critical situation, various arbitration methods are used for resolving collective-bargaining deadlocks in the public sector. One is compulsory binding arbitration for employees such as police officers, firefighters, and others in jobs in which strikes cannot be tolerated. Another method is final-offer arbitration, under which the arbitrator must select one or the other of the final offers submitted by the disputing parties. With this method, the arbitrator's award is more likely to go to the party whose final bargaining offer has moved the closest to a reasonable settlement. The government can also enact back-to-work legislation, an option being used more and more when concerns arise about public health or safety.

On the other hand, when teachers do strike, there are times the public isn't supportive and governments have to intervene. This occurred in Ontario when the provincial government agreed to certain demands by the teachers' union that were subsequently determined to have cost the taxpayers $468 million more than necessary.[31]

THE COLLECTIVE BARGAINING PROCESS

LO5

What are the key activities in the bargaining process?

Once a union wins bargaining rights for employees, its 2 primary functions are to negotiate the collective agreement and resolve member complaints, usually through the grievance-arbitration process. Interestingly, according to labour law, once the union is certified to negotiate for bargaining-unit members, it must represent everyone in the unit equally, regardless of whether employees subsequently join the union or elect to remain non-members. The collective agreement ultimately negotiated establishes the wages, hours, employee benefits, job security, and other conditions under which represented employees agree to work.

Those unfamiliar with contract negotiations often view the collective bargaining process as an emotional conflict between labour and management, complete with marathon sessions and fist pounding. In reality, negotiating a collective agreement entails long hours of extensive preparation combined with diplomatic manoeuvring and the development of bargaining strategies. Furthermore, negotiation is only one part of the collective bargaining process. Collective bargaining may also include the use of economic pressures in the form of strikes and boycotts by a union. Lockouts, plant closures, and the replacement of strikers are similar pressures used by an employer. In addition, either or both parties may seek support from the general public or from the courts as a means of pressuring the opposing side. For an overview of the collective bargaining process, review Figure 10.3.

Good-Faith Bargaining

Once a union has been recognized as the representative for employees, an employer is obligated to negotiate in good faith with the union's representatives over conditions of employment. Good faith requires the employer's negotiators to meet with their union counterparts at a reasonable time and place to discuss these conditions. In discussing the other party's proposals, each side will put forward their demands and attempt to justify their position.[32] Finally, at the conclusion of negotiations, a written document—the collective agreement—is produced, which governs the day-to-day employment relationship.[33] Furthermore, an employer cannot override the bargaining process by making an offer directly to the employees. Figure 10.4 illustrates several common examples of bad-faith employer bargaining.

Preparing for Negotiations

Preparing for negotiations includes planning the strategy and assembling data to support bargaining proposals. It will permit collective bargaining to be conducted in an orderly fashion and on a factual and positive basis with a greater likelihood of achieving desired

FIGURE 10.3 The Collective Bargaining Process

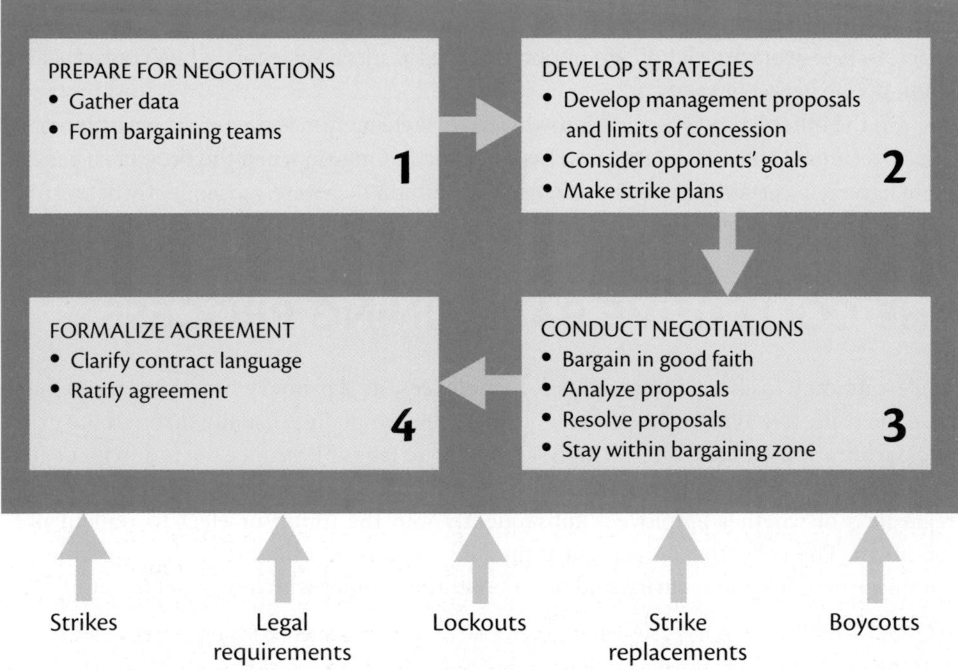

FIGURE 10.4 Examples of Bad-Faith Bargaining

Employer

- using delaying tactics, such as frequent postponements of bargaining sessions
- insisting that the union stop striking before resuming negotiations
- unilaterally changing bargaining topics
- negotiating with individual employees other than authorized union representatives
- going through the motions of bargaining rather than conducting honest negotiations
- refusing to meet with authorized union representatives

Union

- using delaying tactics, such as frequent postponements of bargaining sessions
- withdrawing concessions previously granted
- unilaterally changing bargaining topics
- going through the motions of bargaining rather than conducting honest negotiations
- refusing to meet with authorized employer representatives

goals. Negotiators often develop a bargaining book that serves as a cross-reference file to determine which contract clauses would be affected by a demand. Assuming that the collective agreement is not the first to be negotiated by the parties, preparation for negotiations ideally should start soon after the current agreement has been signed. This practice will allow negotiators to review and diagnose weaknesses and mistakes made during the previous negotiations while the experience is still current in their minds.

Gathering Bargaining Data

Internal data relating to grievances, disciplinary actions, transfers and promotions, layoffs, overtime, former arbitration awards, and wage payments are useful in formulating and supporting the employer's bargaining position. In addition, information can be obtained from other collective agreements negotiated in the company's industry. These agreements are usually available through the labour relations boards.

The supervisors and managers who must live with and administer the collective agreement are the key sources of ideas and suggestions concerning changes that are needed in the next agreement. Their contact with union members and representatives provides them with a firsthand knowledge of the changes that union negotiators are likely to propose. Any concerns that supervisors and managers might have with the collective agreement should be thoroughly understood, considered, and incorporated as appropriate into the overall bargaining approach. And since supervisors work with the collective agreement on a daily basis, it is important that the supervisors and managers be involved in the data-collection process so that they understand and feel part of the bargaining process.

Developing Bargaining Strategies

It is critical that the organization develop a strategy for negotiations. Without adequately planning what it wants to achieve, a company might end up with an unwanted outcome. Negotiators for an employer should develop a written plan covering their bargaining strategy. The plan should consider the proposals that the union is likely to submit, based on the most recent agreements with other employers and the demands that remain unsatisfied from previous negotiations. The plan should also consider the goals the union is striving to achieve and the extent to which it may be willing to make concessions or resort to strike action to achieve these goals. Likewise, it is essential that the company identify the point at which it is willing to let the employees strike or to lock out the employees. Not knowing the organization's limits can create difficulties at negotiations and perhaps incur job action that could have been avoided.

At minimum, the employer's bargaining strategy must address these points:

- Identify the likely union objectives, including specific proposals and management responses to them.
- Develop a list of organizational objectives, including management demands, limits of concessions, and anticipated union responses.
- Identify the nature of the union–management relationship and the relationship the union has with its members.
- Determine whether the company is prepared to lock out or take a strike.
- Develop a database to support management bargaining proposals and to counteract union demands.
- Determine whether the company will operate if employees strike and prepare a contingency operating plan.

Certain elements of strategy are common to both the employer and the union. Generally, the initial demands presented by each side are greater than those it may hope to achieve. This approach is taken in order to provide room for compromise. Moreover, each party will usually avoid giving up the maximum it is capable of conceding in order to allow for further compromise that may be needed to break a bargaining deadlock.

Forms of Collective Bargaining

Traditionally, the collective bargaining relationship between an employer and a union has been adversarial. The union has held the position that, while the employer has the responsibility for managing the organization, the union has the right to challenge certain actions of management. Unions also have taken the position that the employer has an obligation to operate the organization in a manner that will provide adequate compensation to employees. Moreover, unions maintain that their members should not be expected to subsidize poor management by accepting less than their full entitlement.

With adversarial bargaining, negotiators start with defined positions and through deferral, persuasion, trade, or power, the parties work toward resolving individual bargaining demands. In traditional bargaining, with its give-and-take philosophy, the results may or may not be to the complete satisfaction of one or both parties. In fact, when one side feels it has gotten "the short end of the stick," bitter feelings may persist for the life of the agreement.

To overcome these negative feelings, labour and management practitioners may follow a nonadversarial approach. **Interest-based bargaining** (IBB), or interest-based negotiations, is based on the identification and resolution of mutual interests rather than the resolution of specific bargaining demands. IBB is "based on relationships of mutual respect and trust among the parties, in lieu of the adversarial nature of traditional collective bargaining."[34] The focus of bargaining strategy is to discover mutual bargaining interests with the intent of formulating options and solutions for mutual gain.

Interest-based bargaining
Problem-solving bargaining based on a win-win philosophy and the development of a positive long-term relationship

Interest-based bargaining is novel in both its philosophy and its process. Also distinct are the bargaining tools used to expedite a successful nonadversarial negotiating experience. Rather than using proposals and counterproposals to reach agreement (as with adversarial negotiations), participants use brainstorming, consensus decision making, active listening, process checking, and matrix building to settle issues. This style of negotiation was pioneered by Roger Fisher and William Ury, 2 professors at the Harvard Business School, and published in their highly successful book *Getting to Yes*. Fry and Ury stressed the need to focus on the problem (not the positions of the parties), to separate the people from the problem, and to create options for mutual benefit. In this fashion, the parties strive to find solutions and thus improve their overall relationship.[35]

Conducting the Negotiations

Among the factors that tend to make each bargaining situation unique are the economic conditions under which negotiations take place, the experience and personalities of the negotiators on each side, the goals they are seeking to achieve, and the strength of the relative positions. Some collective agreements can be negotiated informally in a few hours, particularly if the contract is short and the terms are not overly complex. Other agreements, such as those negotiated with large organizations, such as Air Canada and CP Rail, require months before settlements are reached.

Bargaining Teams

The composition and size of bargaining teams are often a reflection of the desires and practices of the parties. Normally, each side will have 4 to 6 representatives at the negotiating table. The chief negotiator for management is usually the senior HR person; the chief negotiator for the union is usually the local union president or union business agent. Others making up management's team may include representatives from accounting or finance, operations, and other HR staff. The local union president is likely to be supported by the chief steward, various local union vice-presidents, and a representative from the national union. In some cases, the representative from the national union will be the chief negotiator for the local union.

Labour negotiations have become increasingly complex and legalistic. Therefore, it is advisable that the parties have an experienced negotiator.

The initial meeting of the bargaining teams is particularly important because it establishes the climate that will prevail during the negotiations that follow. A cordial attitude, with perhaps the injection of a little humour, can contribute much to a relaxation of tensions and help the negotiations to begin smoothly.

Analyzing the Proposals

The negotiation of a collective agreement can have some of the characteristics of a poker game, each side attempting to determine its opponent's position while not revealing its own. Each party will normally try to avoid disclosing the relative importance that it attaches to a proposal so that it will not be forced to pay a higher price than is necessary to have the proposal accepted. As with sellers who will try to get a higher price for their products if they think the prospective buyer strongly desires them, negotiators will try to get greater concessions in return for granting those their opponents want most.

As they develop their collective bargaining proposals, astute negotiators know that some demands are more important to their side than others—either for economic or for political reasons. Therefore, the proposals that each side submits generally may be divided into those it feels it must achieve, those it would like to achieve, and those it is submitting primarily for trading purposes. As bargainers discuss the proposals from each side, they are constantly trying to determine the intensity with which each side is committed to its demands. The ability to accurately gauge "commitment" to various proposals can spell the difference between an agreement and an impasse.

Resolving the Proposals

For each bargaining issue to be resolved satisfactorily, the point at which agreement is reached must be within limits that the union and the employer are willing to accept. The area within these 2 limits is called the "bargaining zone." In some bargaining situations, the solution desired by one party may exceed the limits of the other party. Thus, that solution is outside the bargaining zone. If that party refuses to modify its demands sufficiently to bring them within the bargaining zone, or if the opposing party refuses to extend its limit to accommodate the demands of the other party, a bargaining deadlock will result.[36] For example, when bargaining a wage increase for employees, if the union's lowest limit is a 2% increase and management's top limit is 3%, an acceptable range—the bargaining zone—is available to both parties. If management's top limit is only 1%, however, a bargaining zone is not available to either side and deadlock is likely.

LO6

What forms of bargaining power do unions and employers have?

The Union's Power in Collective Bargaining

During negotiations, it is necessary for each party to retreat sufficiently from its original position to permit an agreement to be achieved. If this does not occur, the negotiations will become deadlocked, and the union may resort to the use of economic power to achieve its demands. Otherwise, its only alternative will be to have members continue working without a collective agreement once the old one has expired. The economic power of the union may be exercised by striking, picketing, or boycotting the employer's products and encouraging others to do likewise. As managers know well, the ability to engage in or even threaten to engage in such activities also can serve as a form of pressure. And in some cases, employees do not actually strike, but slow down their work and create pressure on the company. Or the employees will "work to rule"—strictly follow the terms of the collective agreement. This means that if the collective agreement specifies that employees will have a 45-minute lunch break, yet most employees take only 30 and work the other 15 minutes, in a work-to-rule, the employees would take the full 45 minutes.

Striking

Strike
A situation in which unionized workers refuse to perform their work during labour negotiations

A **strike** is the refusal of a group of employees to perform their jobs. It is legal only during negotiations after the collective agreement has expired. Employees cannot strike during the collective agreement as proscribed by labour legislation. Although strikes account for only a small portion of total workdays lost in industry each year, they are a costly and emotional event for all concerned. For example, in early 2015, CP Rail went on strike. Because of the potential economic fallout from a lengthy transportation strike, the federal government was planning back-to-work legislation even before the strike started. Fortunately, after only 1 day, the union (Teamsters Canada) and CP Rail agreed to mediated arbitration.[37]

Unions usually will seek strike authorization from their members to use as a bargaining ploy to gain concessions, making a strike unnecessary. A strike vote by the members does not mean they want or expect to go out on strike. Rather, it is intended as a vote of confidence to strengthen the position of their leaders at the bargaining table. The threat of a strike creates as much of a problem as an actual strike.

Since a strike can have serious effects on the union and its members, the union must analyze the prospects for its success carefully. For example, the elementary/secondary school teachers' strike in British Columbia in 2014 created issues for parents and students. Parents were concerned about how to have their children both educated and cared for during the strike while students, particularly those graduating, were concerned about getting marks for entrance into postsecondary schools. While in previous strikes the government had legislated teachers back to work, it didn't do so this time. The strike continued for many weeks before a negotiated settlement occurred. Many people were critical of both the union and the government for allowing the strike to continue for as long as it did.[38]

Work stoppages continue to create issues for the Canadian economy. The federal government is now publishing monthly statistics, and for the year 2014 there were almost 1.7 million person-days lost, of which 70% were in the public sector.[39] Strikes can be disruptive and challenging to the organizations struck. Of critical importance is whether the employer will be able to continue operating using supervisory and nonstriking personnel and replacement workers. In organizations with high levels of technology and automation, and consequently fewer employees, continuing service with supervisors and managers is more likely. For example, among the highly automated telecommunications companies, supervisors can maintain most services during a strike. The greater the ability of the employer to continue operating the company's services, the smaller the union's chances of achieving its demands through a strike.

To understand more about the issues over which unions will strike, check out the websites of the International Association of Machinists and Aerospace Workers (**www.iamaw.ca**), the Canadian Union of Public Employees (**cupe.ca**), and the International Brotherhood of Electrical Workers (IBEW) (**www.ibew.org**).

International Association of Machinists and Aerospace Workers
www.iamaw.ca

Canadian Union of Public Employees
http://cupe.ca

International Brotherhood of Electrical Workers
www.ibew.org

Picketing

When a union goes on strike, it will picket the employer by placing persons at business entrances to advertise the dispute and to discourage people from entering the premises. Even when the strikers represent only a small proportion of the employees within the organization, they can cause shutdown of an entire organization if enough of the organization's remaining employees (i.e., sympathy strikers) refuse to cross their picket line. Furthermore, because unions often refuse to cross other unions' picket lines, the pickets may serve to prevent trucks and railcars from entering the business to deliver and pick up goods.

Striking workers use pickets to advertise breakdown in collective bargaining.

If a strike fails to stop an employer's operations, the picket line may serve as more than a passive weapon. Employees who attempt to cross the line may be subjected to verbal insults and even physical violence. Mass picketing, in which large groups of pickets try to block the path of people trying to enter an organization, may also be used. However, the use of picket lines to exert physical pressure and incite violence is illegal and may harm more than help the union cause.

Boycotting

Another economic weapon of unions is the boycott, which is a refusal to patronize the employer. For, example, production employees on strike against a hand-tool manufacturer might picket a retail store that sells the tools made by the struck employer. Unions will also use handbills, radio announcements, and notices in newspapers to discourage purchase of the employer's product or service.

The Employer's Power in Collective Bargaining

The employer's power in collective bargaining largely rests in being able to shut down the organization or certain operations within it. The employer can transfer these operations to other locations or can subcontract them to other employers through outsourcing. General Motors outsources to foreign manufacturers many parts used in the assembly of North American cars. In exercising their economic freedom, however, employers must be careful that their actions are not interpreted by the provincial labour relations board to be an attempt to avoid bargaining with the union.

Operating During Strikes

When negotiations become deadlocked, typically it is the union that initiates action and the employer that reacts. In reacting, employers must balance the cost of taking a strike against the long- and short-term costs of agreeing to union demands. They must also consider how long operations might be suspended and the length of time that they and the unions will be able to endure a strike. An employer who chooses to accept a strike must then decide whether to continue operating if it is possible to do so. As mentioned earlier in this chapter, CP Rail and the Teamsters were in arbitration, but in preparation for another strike CP Rail was asking all its office staff to become qualified conductors and engineers so that trains could continue to run.[40]

Should employees go on strike, employers in certain jurisdictions are limited in their ability to hire replacement workers. Quebec and British Columbia have passed "anti-scab" laws, forbidding the use of replacement workers during a strike. Employers have the right to dismiss workers who engage in sabotage or violence during a strike.

Workers are entitled to return to their jobs, but not necessarily their previous position, once a strike is settled. The right to return to work is often an issue to be negotiated. Although laws vary, in many cases employees must submit, in writing, their intention to return to their job once a strike is finalized.

Using the Lockout

Lockout
Strategy by which the employer denies employees the opportunity to work by closing its operations

Although not often used, a **lockout** occurs when an employer takes the initiative to close its operations. Besides being used in bargaining impasses, lockouts may be used by employers to combat union slowdowns, damage to their property, or violence within the organization that may occur in connection with a labour dispute.

While this approach hasn't been used often, the Chronicle Herald in Halifax locked out its pressroom workers for almost three weeks in early 2015 before an agreement was reached.[41]

Under Labour Relations Board provisions, an employer cannot enforce a lockout within a prescribed number of hours (48 to 72) of a strike vote. Lockouts affect nonstriking workers. For example, when miners at Inco are locked out, administrative work ceases, and office staff are also locked out or laid off. Employers may be reluctant to resort to a lockout because of their concern that denying work to regular employees might hurt the organization's image.

Resolving Bargaining Deadlocks

When a strike or a lockout occurs, both parties are soon affected by it. The employer will suffer a loss of profits and customers, and possibly of public goodwill. The union members suffer a loss of income that is likely to be only partially offset by strike benefits or outside income. The union's leaders risk the possibility of losing members, of being voted out of office, of losing public support, or of having the members vote to decertify the union as their bargaining agent. As the losses to each side mount, the disputing parties usually feel more pressure to achieve a settlement.

Mediation and Arbitration

When the disputing parties are unable to resolve a deadlock, a 3rd party serving in the capacity of a conciliator, a mediator, or an arbitrator may be called on to provide assistance. In many jurisdictions, conciliation is compulsory before a legal strike or lockout. The conciliator, appointed by the provincial ministry of labour, helps the parties reconcile their differences in an attempt to reach a workable agreement. If the conciliation effort is unsuccessful, a report is filed with the ministry of labour, which, in rare instances, may appoint a conciliation board that accepts presentations from both parties and makes non-binding formal recommendations. If a settlement cannot be reached at this stage, a strike is permitted, except in Manitoba, Alberta, Saskatchewan, and Quebec where strikes are permissible during conciliation. This two-stage conciliation process is normally reserved for high-profile cases in which significant social and economic consequences would result from a strike.

Mediator
Third party in a labour dispute who meets with one party and then the other in order to suggest compromise solutions or to recommend concessions from each side that will lead to an agreement

Mediation is similar to conciliation except that it is voluntary (the 2 parties contract a neutral 3rd party to help them), and the mediator assumes a more active role as a negotiator. A **mediator** serves primarily as a fact finder and someone to open up a channel of communication between the parties. Recent research has demonstrated that early intervention not only resolves disputes sooner but saves money.[42] Typically, the mediator meets with one party and then the other in order to suggest compromise solutions or to recommend concessions from each side that will lead to an agreement without causing either to lose face. Mediators have no power or authority to force either side toward an agreement. They must have exceptional communication skills (listening and handling strong emotions), a variety of assessment skills to identify causes of conflict, and the ability to respond to cultural and power issues.[43]

Mediate.com
www.mediate.com/odr

ADR Resources
www.adrr.com

ADR Institute of Canada
www.adrcanada.ca

One of the newer forms of mediation is online mediation. Through using Internet-based help, ways can be found to use experts in helping solve the dispute without having the expert present. Check out some of these resources by visiting the following sites: Mediate.com (**www.mediate.com/odr**), ADR Resources (**www.adrr.com**), and ADR Institute of Canada (**www.adrcanada.ca**).

Arbitrator
Third-party neutral who resolves a labour dispute by issuing a final and binding decision in an agreement

Interest arbitration
A mechanism to renew or establish a new collective agreement for parties

Arbitration is the only 3rd-party resolution form that results in binding decisions. An **arbitrator** assumes the role of a decision maker and determines what the settlement between the 2 parties will be. In other words, arbitrators write a final contract that the parties must accept. Compared with mediation, arbitration is not often used to settle private-sector bargaining disputes. In those essential-service areas within the public sector where strikes are prohibited, the use of **interest arbitration** is a common method to resolve bargaining deadlocks. Because 1 or both parties are generally reluctant to give a 3rd party the power to make the settlement for them, a mediator typically is used to break a deadlock and assist the parties in reaching an agreement. Once an agreement is concluded, an

Rights arbitration
A mechanism to resolve disputes about the interpretation and application of a collective agreement during the term of that collective agreement

arbitrator may be called on to resolve disputes arising in connection with the administration of the agreement. This type of arbitration is called grievance arbitration, or **rights arbitration**.

THE COLLECTIVE AGREEMENT

At the conclusion of negotiations, a collective agreement is put in writing and ratified by the union membership. The union typically does this by asking that the members vote on the new terms. The representatives of both parties then sign the agreement—a legal, binding contract. The scope of the agreement (and the length of the written document) will vary with the size of the employer and the length of the bargaining relationship. Toolkit 10.4 shows some of the major articles in a collective agreement and also provides examples of some new and progressive contract clauses.

Two important items in any collective agreement pertain to the issue of management rights and the forms of security afforded the union.

The Issue of Management Rights

LO7

What are the major provisions of a collective agreement?

Management rights have to do with conditions of employment over which management is able to exercise exclusive jurisdiction. Since virtually every management right can and has been challenged successfully by unions, the ultimate determination of these rights will depend on the relative bargaining power of the 2 parties. Furthermore, to achieve union co-operation or concessions, employers have had to relinquish some of these time-honoured rights.

Residual Rights

Residual rights
Concept that management's authority is supreme in all matters except those it has expressly conceded to the union in the collective agreement

In the collective agreement, management rights may be treated as **residual rights** or as defined rights. The residual rights concept holds that management's authority is supreme in all matters except those it has expressly conceded in the collective agreement, or in those areas where its authority is restricted by law. Put another way, management does not look to the collective agreement to ascertain its rights; it looks to the agreement to find out which and how much of its rights and powers it has conceded outright or agreed to share with the union.[44]

Residual rights might include the right of management to determine the product to produce or to select production equipment and procedures. Employers who subscribe to the residual rights concept prefer not to mention management rights in the collective agreement on the grounds that they possess such rights already. To mention them might create an issue with the union.

TOOLKIT 10.4 TYPICAL ITEMS IN A COLLECTIVE AGREEMENT

Typical clauses will cover:

- wages
- vacations
- holidays
- work schedules
- management rights
- union security
- transfers
- discipline
- grievance procedures
- no strike/no lockout clause
- overtime

continued

- safety procedures
- severance pay
- seniority
- pensions and benefits

Progressive clauses will cover:

- employee access to records
- limitations on use of performance evaluation
- eldercare leave
- flexible medical spending accounts
- protection against hazards of technology (repetitive strain injuries or chemicals, such as PCBs)
- limitations against electronic monitoring
- procedures governing drug testing (or other substances)
- bilingual stipends
- domestic partnership benefits (same-sex benefits)

Defined Rights

The **defined rights** concept, on the other hand, is intended to reinforce and clarify which rights are exclusively those of management. This concept means that the employer has only those rights that are written into the collective agreement. It serves to reduce confusion and misunderstanding and to remind union officers, union stewards, and employees that management never relinquishes its right to operate the organization. For example, a defined right would include the right of management to take disciplinary action against problem employees. The great majority of collective agreements contain provisions covering management rights. The following is an example of a general statement defining management rights in 1 collective agreement:

Defined rights
Concept that management's authority should be expressly defined and clarified in the collective agreement

ARTICLE 6—MANAGEMENT RIGHTS

6.01 The Union agrees that it is the exclusive function of the Employer to perform the usual functions of management, including, but not so as to restrict the generality, of the foregoing:

a. conduct its business in all respects in accordance with its commitments and responsibilities, including the right to maintain and improve order, discipline, and efficiency;
b. to make, alter from time to time, and enforce reasonable rules of conduct and procedure to be observed by the employees.

6.02 It is agreed that the functions set forth in Article 6.01 shall not be exercised in a manner inconsistent with the express provisions of this Agreement.

6.03 Notwithstanding anything to the contrary within this Agreement, a claim that an employee has been unjustly discharged or disciplined may be the subject of a grievance and dealt with in accordance with the grievance procedure.[45]

Forms of Union Security

When a labour organization is certified by a labour relations board as the exclusive bargaining representative of all employees in a bargaining unit, it must, by law, represent all employees in the unit, non-union and union members alike. In exchange for its obligation to represent all employees equally, union officials will seek to negotiate some form of compulsory membership as a condition of employment. Union officials argue that compulsory membership prevents the possibility that some employees will receive the benefits of unionization without paying their share of the costs. A standard union security provision is dues checkoff, which gives the employer the responsibility of withholding union dues from the paycheques of union members who agree to such a deduction.

The more common forms of union security found in collective agreements are the following:

1. The *closed shop* states that employers will hire only union members.
2. The *union shop* provides that any employee not a union member upon employment must join the union within 30 days or be terminated.
3. The *agency shop* states that union membership is voluntary yet all bargaining unit members must pay union dues and fees.
4. The *open shop* allows employees to join the union or not. Nonmembers do not pay union dues. This is the rarest form of union security.

Few issues in collective bargaining are more controversial than the negotiation of these agreements. Though rare, closed-shop clauses are perhaps the most adversarial because they require employers to recruit employees from a union hiring hall.

Working in conjunction with the union-shop clause are the various seniority provisions of the collective agreement. Unions prefer that many personnel decisions (e.g., promotions, job transfers, shift assignments, vacations) be based on seniority, a criterion that limits the discretion of managers to make such decisions on the basis of merit.

Administration of the Collective Agreement

Negotiation of the collective agreement, as mentioned earlier, is usually the most publicized and critical aspect of labour relations. Strike deadlines, press conferences, and employee picketing help create this image. Nevertheless, as managers in unionized organizations know, the bulk of labour relations activity comes from the day-to-day administration of the agreement. Once the collective agreement is signed, each party frequently will interpret clauses differently. These differences are traditionally resolved through the grievance procedure.

Sometimes the administration of the collective agreement has to be done through the union itself. For example, the Windsor police were called in to investigate a hate crime when a worker at Fiat Chrysler found nooses around his work stage. Since this is considered a hate crime, the union met with all its members to remind them that this is totally unacceptable and that if caught, one will lose union membership.[46]

Toolkit 10.5 provides examples of clauses from collective agreements.

TOOLKIT 10.5 CLAUSES FROM COLLECTIVE AGREEMENTS

1. Leave With or Without Pay for Other Reasons

At its discretion, the Employer may grant:

a. leave with pay when circumstances not directly attributable to the employee prevent his or her reporting for duty; such leave shall not be unreasonably withheld;
b. leave with or without pay for purposes other than those specified in this Agreement. (Between Canada Revenue Agency and the Public Service Alliance of Canada)

2. Layoffs

The Employer shall give all permanent Employees with one (1) or more years of service, two (2) consecutive working days' notice of lay off or two (2) days' pay.

(Between Communications, Energy, and Paperworkers Union and A.B.C. Press [1979] Limited)

3. Seniority

SENIORITY LIST The Company shall at least once every six (6) months, post in a conspicuous place on its premises an

continued

up-to-date list of all employees covered by this Agreement showing the date when each commenced his employment with the Company. The Company shall forward to the Union a copy of each list on the date of its posting.

LAYOFFS In the event of layoffs, seniority shall be recognized. The principle of last man on, first man off, shall prevail, subject to job classification. The Company shall give at least forty-eight (48) hours' notice on layoffs, exclusive of Saturdays, Sundays, and General Holidays.

(Between Robinson Rentals and Sales and International Union of Operating Engineers.)

GRIEVANCE PROCEDURES

LO8

How does a grievance procedure work?

Grievance procedure
Formal procedure that provides the union a way to process a complaint that something within the collective agreement has been violated

The **grievance procedure** typically provides for the union to represent the interests of its members in processing a complaint that something in the collective agreement has been violated. It is considered by some authorities to be the heart of the collective agreement—the safety valve that gives flexibility to the whole system of collective bargaining.[47] Further, a grievance procedure by law precludes a union from striking during the term of a collective agreement. And if a union decides to conduct an illegal strike, there can be financial consequences. This happened to the Canadian Union of Postal Workers that conducted an illegal strike and was ordered by an arbitrator to pay Canada Post $35,000 in damages and $29,000 for legal costs.[48] When negotiating a grievance procedure, one important concern for both sides is how effectively the system will serve the needs of employees and management. A well-written grievance procedure will allow grievances to be processed quickly and with as little red tape as possible. Furthermore, it should serve to foster co-operation, not conflict, between the employer and the union.

The operation of a grievance procedure is unique to each individual collective bargaining relationship but is required under Canadian labour relations codes. Grievance procedures are negotiated to address the organization's structure and labour–management philosophy and the specific desires of the parties.

Although each procedure is unique, there are common elements among systems. For example, grievance procedures normally specify how the grievance procedure is to be initiated, the number and timing of steps that are to compose the procedure, and the identity of representatives from each side who are to be involved in the hearings at each step (see Figure 10.5). The purpose of this multistep process is to allow higher levels of union and management representatives to look at the issue from different perspectives. When a grievance cannot be resolved at one of the specified steps, most agreements provide for the grievance to be submitted to a 3rd party—usually an arbitrator—whose decision is final and binding. It is not the function of an arbitrator to help the 2 parties reach a compromise solution. Rather, it is the arbitrator's job to mandate how the grievance is to be resolved.

Initiating the Formal Grievance

In order for an employee's grievance to be considered formally, it must be expressed orally and/or in writing—ideally to the employee's immediate supervisor. If the employee feels unable to communicate effectively with the supervisor, the grievance may be taken to the union steward, who will discuss it with the supervisor. Since grievances are often the result of an oversight or a misunderstanding, many of them can be resolved at this point. Whether it is possible to resolve a grievance at the initial step will depend on the supervisor's ability and willingness to discuss the problem with the employee and the steward. Supervisors should be trained formally in resolving grievances. This training should include

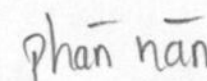

FIGURE 10.5 Grievance Procedure

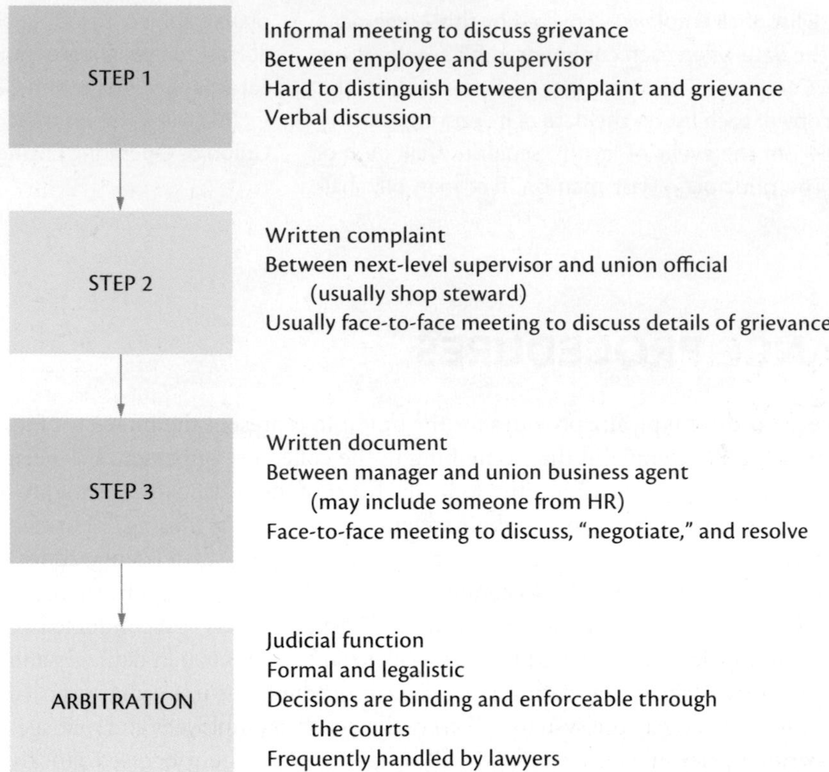

familiarization with the terms of the collective agreement and the development of counselling skills to facilitate a problem-solving approach.

In some instances, a satisfactory solution may not be possible at the first step, because there are legitimate differences of opinion between the employee and the supervisor or because the supervisor does not have the authority to take the action required to satisfy the griever. Personality conflicts, prejudices, emotionalism, stubbornness, or other factors may also be barriers to a satisfactory solution at this step.

Grievance Resolution

If a grievance is to be resolved successfully, representatives of both management and the union must be able to discuss the problem in a rational and objective manner. A grievance should not be viewed as something to be won or lost. Rather, both sides must view the situation as an attempt to solve a problem. Throughout the process, both parties will try to resolve the issue. However, if the conflict cannot be resolved through discussion and compromise, all collective agreements in Canadian jurisdictions contain a provision for arbitration, or **grievance resolution**. An arbitrator (usually a lawyer or professional skilled in the arbitration process) or a board or panel (consisting of a union nominee, a management nominee, and a neutral chair) hears the case and submits a decision, including the rationale. The decision is final, and the parties are legally bound to accept the decision unless there is serious concern over the arbitrator's competence or integrity.

Grievance resolution
Process in which a neutral 3rd party assists in the resolution of an employee grievance

One criticism of the arbitration process is that it is slow (up to 2 years) and costly. One solution is expedited arbitration, which is an agreement to bypass some steps in the grievance process when the issue is particularly important or urgent, as in the case of employee dismissals or layoffs of employees.

Rights Arbitration

The function of rights (or grievance) arbitration is to provide the solution to a grievance that a union and an employer have been unable to resolve by themselves. As mentioned earlier, arbitration is performed by a neutral 3rd party (an arbitrator or impartial umpire). This 3rd party's decision dictates how the grievance is to be settled. Both parties are obligated to comply with the decision. Even if one of the parties believes the arbitrator's award is unfair, unwise, or inconsistent with the collective agreement, that party may have no alternative but to comply. Read HRM and the Law 10.1 for two different outcomes when employees were terminated.

The Decision to Arbitrate

If a grievance cannot be resolved through the grievance procedure, each disputing party must decide whether to use arbitration to resolve the case. The alternatives would be for the union to withdraw the grievance or for the employer to agree to union demands.

HRM AND THE LAW 10.1 FIRED!

You might think that terminating an employee's work is an action that ought not to be challenged by a union, but that is rarely the case. Even if a union agrees that the person was appropriately terminated, it will usually always launch a grievance to challenge the employer's action. Employers want to be sure that they have the evidence to prove that wrongdoing occurred, as an arbitrator might decide that termination was too severe and reinstate the employee with full back pay.

Two recent cases had different outcomes: in one case the arbitrator decided that the employer had been wrong in the termination, and in the other decided that the termination was appropriate.

A lifeguard at a health spa in Saskatchewan was terminated for failing to report to work at the end of an approved leave. The employee had requested an extension that was denied due to the short notice of the request. Further, the spa said that if the employee didn't return by the original date their employment might be in jeopardy. During the arbitration hearing, the spa felt that the employee was being dishonest and hadn't intended to return on time. The arbitrator determined that the employer suffered no economic loss, the employee was not being dishonest, and was wrong in terminating the employee. Further, although the spa had every right to discipline the employee for not reporting to work as agreed, termination was too severe. The arbitrator ordered reinstatement with full back pay and a warning about any future absences.

In another case, a heavy-duty mechanic in Edmonton was terminated for verbal harassment of a co-worker. The mechanic, from Europe, had been hired in 2009 and went through respectful workplace training that included awareness of the employer's code of conduct. The mechanic, who spoke little English, made friends with another co-worker from Africa who also spoke little English. However, over time, the friendship experienced tensions and the mechanic began to make more and more derogatory comments about the person's skin colour and inability to speak English. He also used profanity and made inappropriate comments about his friend's mother. After many warnings, the employer terminated the mechanic's employment for violating the respectful workplace and violence policies. During the arbitration, even though the employee denied any wrongdoing, the arbitrator determined that the mechanic lacked credibility and was evasive during testimony. It was proven that the mechanic had clearly made frequent racist comments and slurs and that co-workers were uncomfortable. The termination was upheld.

CRITICAL THINKING QUESTIONS:

1. If you were the arbitrator, what decisions would you make? Explain your answers.
2. Is there any other information you would want before a decision was made? If so, what?

Sources: Adapted from Jeffrey Smith, "Fired Lifeguard Rescued in Arbitration," *Canadian HR Reporter*, October 6, 2014, 7; and Jeffrey Smith, "Firing for Racist Comments Upheld," *Canadian HR Reporter*, March 9, 2015, 5.

In deciding whether to use arbitration, each party must weigh the costs involved against the importance of the case and the prospects of gaining a favourable award. It would seem logical that neither party would allow a weak case to go to arbitration if there were little possibility of gaining a favourable award. But there may be other reasons for advancing a grievance. For example, it is not unusual for a union to take a weak case to arbitration in order to demonstrate to the members that the union is willing to exhaust every remedy in looking out for their interests. Union officers also are not likely to refuse to take to arbitration the grievances of popular or politically powerful members, even if the cases are weak. Moreover, unions have a legal obligation to provide assistance to members who are pursuing grievances. Because members can bring suit against their unions for failing to process their grievances adequately, many union officers are reluctant to refuse taking even weak grievances to arbitration.

Management, on the other hand, may allow a weak case to go to arbitration to demonstrate to the union officers that management "cannot be pushed around." Managers at lower levels may also be reluctant to risk the displeasure of top management by stating that a certain HR policy is unworkable or unsound. Stubbornness and mutual antagonism may force many grievances into arbitration because neither party is willing to make concessions to reach an agreement—even if it knows it is in the wrong.

The Arbitration Process

The issues to be resolved through arbitration may be described formally in a statement. Each party makes a joint submission to the arbitrator, indicating the rationale for the grievance. The submission to arbitrate must state the nature of the dispute with reference to the section of the collective agreement that has allegedly been breached. Such a statement might read: "Was the three-day suspension of Alex Hayden for just cause? If not, what is the appropriate remedy?" However, the two parties at the beginning of the hearing also present grievable issues orally to the arbitrator. The purpose of an arbitration hearing is to provide a full and fair hearing of the matter in dispute. If minutes and memoranda covering the meetings held at earlier stages of the grievance procedure have been prepared, these are sometimes submitted prior to the formal hearing to acquaint the arbitrator with the issues.

In arbitrating a dispute, the arbitrator is responsible for ensuring that each side receives a fair hearing, during which it may present all the facts it considers pertinent to the case. The procedures for conducting arbitration hearings and the restrictions governing the evidence that may be introduced during these hearings are more flexible than those permitted in a court of law. Hearsay evidence, for example, may be introduced, provided it is considered as such when evaluated with the other evidence presented. The primary purpose of the hearing is to assist the arbitrator in obtaining the facts necessary to resolve a human resources problem rather than a legal one. The arbitrator, therefore, has a right to question witnesses or to request additional facts from either party.

Depending on the importance of the case, the hearings may be conducted either in an informal way or in a very formal way not unlike that of a court trial. If the proceedings have witnesses who will testify, they are sworn in. After conducting the hearing and receiving all written evidence, or any other submissions allowed, the arbitrator customarily has 30 days to consider the evidence and to prepare a decision. In the majority of labour contracts, the parties share the costs of arbitration equally. In all grievance arbitrations except those involving any form of discipline, the "burden of proof" rests with the union—that is, the union must prove that the employer violated the written collective agreement.

The Arbitration Award

Arbitration award
Final and binding award issued by an arbitrator in a labour–management dispute

The **arbitration award** should include not only the arbitrator's decision but also the rationale for it. The reasoning behind the decision can help provide guidance concerning the interpretation of the collective agreement and the resolution of future disputes arising from its administration. In pointing out the merits of each party's position, the reasoning that underlies the award can help lessen the disappointment and protect the self-esteem of those representing the unsuccessful party. In short, tact and objective reasoning can help to reduce disappointment and hard feelings.

The foundation for an arbitrator's decision is the collective agreement and the rights it establishes for each party. In many instances, the decision may hinge on whether management's actions were justified under the terms of this agreement. Sometimes, it may depend on the arbitrator's interpretation of the wording of a particular provision. Established HR policies and past practices can also provide the basis for determining the award. And it must be remembered that an arbitration decision, if need be, is enforceable through the courts.

In many grievances, such as those involving employee performance or behaviour on the job, the arbitrator must determine whether the evidence supports the employer's action against the griever. The evidence must also indicate whether the employee was accorded the right of due process, which is the employee's right to be informed of unsatisfactory performance and to have an opportunity to respond to these charges. Under most collective agreements, an employer is required to have just cause (i.e., a good reason) for the action it has taken, and such action should be justified by the evidence presented.

If the arbitration hearing indicates that an employee was accorded due process and the disciplinary action was for just cause, the severity of the penalty must then be assessed. Where the evidence supports the discipline imposed by the employer, the arbitrator will probably let the discipline stand intact. However, it is within the arbitrator's power, unless denied by the submission agreement, to reduce the penalty. It is not uncommon, for example, for an arbitrator to reduce a discharge to a suspension without pay for the period the griever has been off the payroll.

Because of the importance and magnitude of arbitration in grievance resolution, the process by which arbitrators make decisions and the factors that influence those decisions are of continuing interest to managers. Typically, arbitrators use 4 factors when deciding cases:

1. the wording of the collective agreement
2. the submission agreement as presented to the arbitrator
3. testimony and evidence offered during the hearing about how the collective agreement provisions have been interpreted
4. arbitration criteria or standards (i.e., similar to standards of common law) against which cases are judged

When deciding the case of an employee discharged for absenteeism, for example, the arbitrator would consider these factors separately and/or jointly. Arbitrators are essentially constrained to decide cases on the basis of the wording of the collective agreement and the facts, testimony, and evidence presented at the hearing. For example, in a recent termination case, the employee (a labourer at a potash mine) was terminated for taking sick leave when a vacation request for the same time was denied. Even though the employee had had no discipline record, the employer believed the employee was not telling the truth about the reason for the absence. The employer hired an investigator that obtained video footage of the employee working in his side business of landscaping. The employee eventually returned to work and provided medical documentation of the absence. The employer wanted to see all business records of his landscaping company during the work absence. The employee complied, but the company still determined that the medical documentation didn't support the absence and that the employee was really working at another job—something prohibited under the terms of the collective agreement. The employee was terminated for being dishonest. The arbitration panel determined through the facts, testimony, and evidence presented that the employer only got information to support its suspicions and didn't get the employee's side of the story. Further, evidence during the arbitration demonstrated that the employee was suffering from mental stress that the employee felt would put other employees at risk in the mine. The arbitrator found that the company did not have just cause to terminate and ordered reinstatement with full back pay.[49]

Given the ongoing economic climate, labour relations and collective bargaining continue to undergo many changes. See Emerging Trends 10.1 for some of the more important ones.

A grievance can be concluded through the formal process of arbitration.

vm/E+/Getty Images

EMERGING TRENDS 10.1

1. ***Changes in bargaining rights.*** With recent Supreme Court of Canada decisions, labour law is changing bargaining rights for certain workers whether or not the provincial or federal legislation allows it. Both the RCMP and the Ontario Mounted Police received decisions that stated the right to unionize was a fundamental right under the *Charter of Rights and Freedoms*.
2. ***Labour push in the auto industry.*** While the auto industry in Canada is still weak, Chrysler recently decided to invest $2 billion in its Windsor plant, and in doing so found that Unifor wanted to return to pattern bargaining. In addition, Unifor was successful in organizing a Toyota plant in Ontario—something that had been resisted for years. Unifor has also identified that it has a priority of encouraging Ford to invest it its engine factory in Windsor.
3. ***Change in labour–management relations.*** Even though there is unrest and tougher negotiations, organizations are developing new relationships with their unions. As organizations continue to change and evolve, unions can be helpful in providing the employer with insights into how the employees are feeling. For example, U.S. Steel Canada in Hamilton negotiated the collective agreement with the United Steelworkers for the first time without locking out workers. Further, in late summer 2015, WestJet pilots rejected another attempt to become unionized.
4. ***Decline in unionization.*** Union density in Canada continues to decline—currently it is about 30%. Much of the decline is due to the shift from an industrial economy to one of service and knowledge. People in these sectors are usually more educated and therefore tend to resist collective action. Further, some provinces have enacted labour legislation that restricts the union certification process. Beyond that, Gen X and Y, as well as Millennials, have different expectations and views of their role in

continued

the workplace. These younger workers see themselves as more independent and able to make their own way, and they expect to be encouraged to contribute. They also see the unionized workplace as adversarial and do not want to be associated with that type of environment.

5. ***Changing dynamics in labour negotiations.*** Since more disruption during labour negotiations occurs in the public sector, some governments are attempting to find different ways to ensure labour peace. For example, the Ontario government recently offered both Hydro One and Ontario Power Generation workers stock in Hydro One as the government considers moves to sell 60% of Hydro One to the private sector. However, in other sectors of the economy, employers are focusing on increased productivity in any negotiations with their unions. Likewise, GM is pushing its union, Unifor, to eliminate certain pension provisions for new employees.

Sources: John D.R. Craig, Christopher Pigott, and Brandon Wiebe, "The New Labour Trilogy: The Supreme Court of Canada Reshapes Labour Law," *The HR Space*, Fasken Martineau 2015; Sabrina Nanji, "Auto Industry Retools," *Canadian HR Reporter*, February 23, 2015, 17; Greg Keenan, "Unifor Urges Ford to Spend in Windsor," *The Globe and Mail*, February 27, 2015, B3; Greg Keenan, "Oshawa's GM Plant Sitting in Labour Limbo," *The Globe and Mail*, January 29, 2015, B3; Greg Keenan, "U.S. Steel, Hamilton Workers Reach Tentative Agreement," *The Globe and Mail*, October 15, 2014, B4; "Union Coverage in Canada, 2013," Employment and Social Development Canada, April 2014; Adrian Morrow, "Ontario to Give Power Workers Shares in Privatized Hydro One," *The Globe and Mail*, May 1, 2015, A1; Bryce Swerhun and David Shepherdson, "Industrial Relations Outlook 2015," Conference Board of Canada, December 24, 2014; Kristine Owram, "WestJet Pilots Reject Union," *Financial Post*, August 6, 2015, FP1; and Greg Keenan, "GM Pushes Unifor to Drop Pension Plan's Key Pillar," *The Globe and Mail*, April 9, 2015, B1.

Summary

1. Explain the federal and provincial legislation that provides the framework for labour relations.
   - Laws determine who can unionize.
   - Laws require that unions and employers bargain in good faith.
   - Laws provide for unions to strike and for employers to lock out.
2. Cite the reasons employees join unions.
   - Dissatisfaction with pay and benefits
   - Dissatisfaction with managerial practices.
   - Desire for recognition and status.
3. Outline the process by which unions organize employees and gain recognition as their bargaining agent.
   - Employees make contact with a union representative.
   - Union schedules meeting with other employees.
   - Application is made to labour relations board.
   - Labour relations board grants bargaining rights.
4. Illustrate the functions labour unions perform at international, national and local levels.
   - National unions help organize local unions.
   - National unions help train and educate local unions.
   - Local unions negotiate collective agreements and process member grievances.
5. Describe the bargaining process and the bargaining goals and strategies of a union and an employer.
   - Each side will prepare a list of goals it wishes to achieve while additionally trying to anticipate the goals desired by the other side.
   - Both employer and union negotiators will be sensitive to current bargaining patterns within the industry, general cost-of-living trends, and geographical wage differentials.
   - The collective bargaining process includes not only the actual negotiations but also the power tactics used to support negotiating demands.
6. List the forms of bargaining power that a union and an employer may utilize to enforce their bargaining demands.
   - The union's power in collective bargaining comes from its ability to picket, strike, or boycott the employer.

- The employer's power during negotiations comes from its ability to lock out employees or to operate during a strike by using managerial or replacement employees.

7. Identify the major provisions of a collective agreement, including the issue of management rights.
   - Typical collective agreements will contain numerous provisions governing the labour–management employment relationship.
   - Major areas of interest concern wages (rates of pay, overtime differentials, holiday pay), hours (shift times, days of work), and working conditions (safety issues, performance standards, retraining).
   - Management rights refers to the supremacy of management's authority in all issues except those shared with the union through the collective agreement.
8. Describe a typical grievance procedure and explain the basis for arbitration awards.
   - The procedure will consist of 3 to 5 steps—each step having specific filing and reply times.
   - Higher-level managers and union officials will become involved in disputes at the higher steps of the grievance procedure.
   - The final step of the grievance procedure may be arbitration.
   - Arbitrators render a final decision for problems not resolved at lower grievance steps.
   - Arbitrators consider the wording of the collective agreement, testimony, and evidence offered during the hearing, including how the parties have interpreted the collective agreement.

Need to Know

- Legislation in your province governing labour relations
- Steps employees go through to unionize
- Definition of collective bargaining
- Definition of grievance
- Difference between mediation and arbitration
- Definition of defined rights and residual rights

Need to Understand

- Relationship of supervisory actions and behaviours in employees unionizing
- Expected behaviours from employers and unions during organizing drive
- Impact of unionization on supervisory actions
- Steps and importance of preparation for negotiations
- Steps in grievance process

KEY TERMS

arbitration award 352
arbitrator 345
bargaining unit 328
business agent 334
certification 329
closed shop 323
defined rights 347
grievance procedure 349
grievance resolution 350
interest arbitration 345
interest-based bargaining 340
labour relations process 322
lockout 344
management rights 331
mediator 345
membership card 327
open shop 323
residual rights 346
rights arbitration 346
strike 342
unfair labour practices 328
union shop 323
union (shop) steward 334

REVIEW QUESTIONS

1. Explain how labour relations are regulated at both the federal and the provincial level.
2. What are some of the unfair labour practices that apply to employers? Do these same practices apply to unions? Explain any differences.
3. Describe the impact on supervisors of employees becoming unionized.
4. What is the role of a union business agent and a union shop steward?
5. Describe the collective bargaining process.
6. What is a strike and a lockout?
7. What is mediation and arbitration?
8. What are some of the employment conditions covered in a collective agreement?
9. Explain a rights (or grievance) arbitration.

CRITICAL THINKING QUESTIONS

1. In the HRM Close-up, what are the reasons for success in Jazz reaching a long-term collective agreement with its pilots?
2. A few employees in your company have approached you to work with them in organizing the staff into a union. You are surprised at their feelings as you felt that employees were treated fairly. What arguments might they give you to join the union? What arguments might you give for not joining?
3. One of your friends is a supervisor in a fast-food restaurant. The restaurant has just become unionized and your friend is not sure how to treat the staff. What advice would you give?
4. What approach might an employer take to discourage employees from joining a union? What response might a union make?
5. Since provincial labour laws do not typically cover individuals who are self-employed, what might be some of the arguments to change the law? What arguments would you use to leave as is?
6. Your best friend has recently been appointed a shop steward of their work unit. You know the friend's supervisor and feel that the supervisor has always been fair in dealing with staff. What advice might you give your friend in their new role?
7. The negotiations between Pivotal Construction Services International and its union have become deadlocked. What form of bargaining power does each side possess to enforce its bargaining demands? What are the advantages and disadvantages of each form of bargaining power for both the union and the employer?
8. Sam Wong has decided to file a grievance with the union steward, alleging that he was not promoted and a more junior (in seniority) employee was. Describe the steps in the grievance process and what information would be necessary.

DEVELOPING YOUR SKILLS

1. *Unionized Postal Workers Support Woman*, a news story produced by CTV, tells the story of unionized workers demonstrating in Ottawa regarding a community mailbox. Watch the YouTube clip at **www.youtube.com/watch?v=FLDroUW_WBU**, and then in groups of 3 or 4 determine whether you support this type of demonstration. Give reasons for your response.
2. Access to technology has been changing the dynamics in bargaining. Go to UNI Global Union at **www.uniglobalunion.org** and explore the various items in a global union that represents 900 unions and 20 million workers worldwide. Prepare a 2-or-3-page summary explaining how the use of social media and Web technology, can affect people's perspectives on labour relations.
3. A group of students wants a health-food restaurant on their college campus. College administrators want a Subway food franchise. Resources allow for only 1 food outlet.

Divide the class into bargaining teams, with 1 team representing the students, and the other team representing the college administrators. The objective is for each side to negotiate from that perspective and reach an agreement. (If there is another issue on your campus use the real and current issue instead.)

National Union of Public and General Employees
www.nupge.ca

Canadian Union of Public Employees
www.cupe.ca

United Food and Commercial Workers Canada (UFCW)
www.ufcw.ca

Public Service Alliance of Canada
www.psacunion.ca

Teamsters
www.teamsters.ca

4. During a union organizing drive, labour and management will develop a plan to present their positions to employees. A goal of each side will be to collect information on the other that can be used to build a case for or against the union. In addition, each side will seek to avoid committing unfair labour practices. Working in teams of union and management representatives, answer the following questions, and be prepared to present your findings during a discussion period.
   A. What methods might the union use to contact employees?
   B. What information might the union collect on management in order to obtain employee support?
   C. What information might management want to collect on the union?
   D. What methods might unions and management use to tell their story to employees? What illegal actions will the union and management want to guard against?
5. Access the following union websites:
   - **www.nupge.ca**
   - **www.cupe.ca**
   - **www.unifor.org**
   - **www.ufcw.ca**
   - **www.psacunion.ca**
   - **www.teamsters.ca**

   Review the profile of the union and the current issues it supports. Compare each union with regard to membership and issues. Bring your information to class and share it in groups of 4 or 5. Identify at least 1 aspect of the site that surprised you and 1 that impressed you.
6. Access the Canadian Industrial Relations Board website (**www.cirb-ccri.gc.ca/eic/site/047.nsf/eng/h_00003.html**), where summaries of cases can be found. Access, too, the site of your provincial labour relations board (see Toolkit 10.1 above) and access the link to decisions. Retrieve 1 or 2 decisions from each site. Prepare a 2-to-3-page report comparing the decisions.

Canadian Industrial Relations Board
www.cirb-ccri.gc.ca/eic/site/047.nsf/eng/h_00003.html

Unionized postal workers support woman
www.youtube.com/watch?v=FLDroUW_WBU

UNI Global Union
www.uniglobalunion.org

CASE STUDY 1

What Should the Union Do?

Perhaps the biggest story about unionized employees and the work environment in 2015 was the fallout from the behaviours of a former CBC host, Jian Ghomeshi.

Ghomeshi was host of CBC's popular radio show Q until he was suspended and eventually fired in the fall of 2014 for alleged workplace harassment. While some of the accusations involved actions and behaviours outside the workplace, CBC was concerned about the popularity of Ghomeshi and the messages his actions and behaviours conveyed.

CBC decided that since there were suggestions that workplace harassment was a common occurrence, it retained an independent investigator to interview employees and make recommendations to prevent anything similar in the future. And since the employees are unionized, including Ghomeshi, it put the union in a difficult position during the actual investigation. The union noted that while it believed any wrongdoing ought to be investigated, it also cautioned its members not to expose themselves to any discipline from the information gathered.

The investigator concluded the work and in April 2015 released the report that clearly stated CBC management had ignored what was going on for years, and so by doing nothing condoned the inappropriate behaviour. The report further identified that the union, Canada Media Guild (CMG), was aware of complaints from employees about workplace harassment. The investigator, however, could find no evidence that any formal action by either CBC or the union had occurred in relation to Ghomeshi's behaviours, even though the collective agreement states that it is "the right of employees to work in an environment free of harassment." The report did state that Ghomeshi was a "star" and was allowed to exhibit inappropriate behaviour with no consequences. As a result of the conclusions, 2 executives were terminated. Further, the union, Canadian Media Guild, issued a statement that it welcomes the recommendations in the report and that it supported workplaces that are free from harassment.

Sources: Adapted from Paola Loriggio, "CBC Union Warns Members About Investigation into Ghomeshi Allegations," *Canadian HR Reporter*, December 8, 2014, accessed June 13, 2015, **www.hrreporter.com/articleprint.aspx?articleid=23031**; Jacques Gallant, "Jian Ghomeshi Scandal Leads to CBC 'Severing Ties" with Ex-Head of Radio, HR Director," *The Toronto Star*, April 16, 2015, accessed June 13, 2015, **www.thestar.com/news/gta/2015/04/16/jian-ghomeshi-scandal-report-leads-to-cbc-severing-ties-with-ex-head-of-radio-hr-director.html**; Janice Rubin and Parisa Nikfarjam, "Report: CBC Workplace Investigation Regarding Jian Ghomeshi," April 13, 2015; and "The Canadian Media Guild Committed to Working with CBC to Ensure a Safe and Harassment-Free Workplace," Canadian Media Guild, April 16, 2015, accessed June 13, 2015, **www.cmg.ca/en/2015/04/16/the-canadian-media-guild-committed-to-working-with-cbc-to-ensure-a-safe-and-harassment-free-workplace**.

Questions:

1. What might the union have done when its members complained about harassment? Explain your answer.
2. What should the CBC management and union do now? Explain your answer.

CASE STUDY 2

What's Wrong with Tattoos?

With the variety of tattoos and body piercings on many people, one would think that it is OK to have and display in any work environment. However, this was recently challenged by a case involving the Canadian Union of Public Employees (CUPE).

The policy grievance went to arbitration involving the Ottawa Hospital regarding a new dress code policy. The new code specifically stated that clothing needed to be able to cover any tattoos and piercings. The hospital argued that the policy was necessary due to the number of elderly patients who were uncomfortable around individuals with piercings and tattoos.

For 50 years, in a unionized workplace, arbitrators have held that any dress code must be "reasonable." And, of course, what was "reasonable" in 1965 when the first ruling was made may not be reasonable in 2015. The original arbitration had a number of tests for any new policy: (1) it must not be inconsistent with terms of collective agreement, (2) it must not be unreasonable, (3) it must be clear, (4) it must be made known to the employees, (5) employees must be notified of any breach of policy, and (6) policy must be consistently enforced.

During the arbitration hearing, the union argued that these tests were not met. The hospital also argued that the tests were outdated and need to be revised, particularly in a hospital setting.

The arbitrator did acknowledge that some patients might not have positive impressions of body piercings or tattoos but that they also might not have positive impressions of any other particular staff member. Further, the arbitration determined that there was no human rights issue but a simple one of an employer wanting to prevent any complaints.

The arbitrator ruled in favour of the union indicating that there was no business case or evidence for the policy. The arbitrator also stated that there was no apparent connection between look of a staff member and any health outcomes.

Sources: Adapted from Dr. D. Doorey, "Should Employers Be Permitted to Discriminate on the Basis of Appearance?" October 14, 2014, accessed June 14, 2015, http://**lawofwork.ca/?p=7688**; and *In the Matter of an Arbitration Between: The Ottawa Hospital and Canadian Union of Public Employees*, Local 4000, January 14, 2013.

Questions:

1. Do you think an employer ought to be able to institute any type of dress code, including one dealing with body piercings and/or tattoos? Why or why not?
2. Since the "tests" for implementing a policy is only applicable to unionized work environments, do you think "personal appearance" ought to be a prohibited ground in human rights legislation? Why or why not?

NOTES AND REFERENCES

1. Statistics Canada, "Distribution of Employed People, by Industry, by Province," accessed May 20, 2015, www.statcan.gc.ca/tables-tableaux/sum-som/l01/cst01/labor21a-eng.htm; "Union Coverage in Canada," June 14, 2014, Employment and Social Development.
2. For a more complete understanding of the labour relations system in Canada, refer to Morley Gunderson and Daphne G. Taras, *Canadian Labour and Employment Relations*, 6th ed. (Toronto: Pearson, 2009); Larry Suffield, *Labour Relations*, 3rd ed. (Toronto: Pearson, 2012); and William H. Holley, Kenneth M. Jennings, and Roger S. Wolters, *The Labor Relations Process* (Toronto: Nelson Education, 2012).
3. Labour Canada, "Labour Law," accessed May 20, 2015, www.labour.gc.ca/eng/resources/laws/index.shtml.
4. Suffield, *Labour Relations*, 82.
5. To read more about the labour relations process, consult Gunderson and Taras, *Canadian Labour and Employment Relations*; Suffield, *Labour Relations*; Lex Borghans, Bas Ter weel, and Bruce A. Weinberg, "People Skills and the Labor-Market Outcomes of Underrepresented Groups," *Industrial and Labor Relations Review* 67, no. 2 (April 2014): 287–334.
6. Joseph Bonney, "A Win for Unionization: *Journal of Commerce* 16, no. 3 (February 2015): 20; and Victor Silverman," "Victory at Pomona College: Union Strategy and Immigrant Labor," *Labor Studies Journal* 40, no. 1 (March 2015): 8–31.
7. "Unifor History and Mission," accessed May 21, 2015, www.unifor.org/en/about-unifor/history-mission.
8. Holly Shaw, "Quebec Ruling Against Wal-Mart Canada Closing Unionized Store Hollow Victory," *Financial Post*, June 27, 2014, accessed May 21, 2015, http://business.financialpost.com/news/retail-marketing/wal-mart-violated-quebecs-labour-code-by-closing-store-after-worker-unionization-attempt-court-rules.
9. Colin Gibson, "Public Opposition to Union Organizing," *Canadian HR Reporter*, July 14, 2014, accessed May 22, 2015, www.hrreporter.com/articleview/21719-public-opposition-to-union-organizing.
10. Canada Industrial Relations Board Regulations and *Ontario Labour Relations Act*.
11. Garrett Hinchley, "University of Victoria Faculty Members Embrace Union," *The Globe and Mail*, February 27, 2014, www.theglobeandmail.com/news/british-columbia/university-of-victoria-faculty-members-embrace-union/article16929085.
12. Greg Keenan, "WestJet Pilots' Association Seeks Union Certification," *The Globe and Mail*, June 25, 2015, B1.
13. Sunny Dhillon, "B.C. Court Rules Against Mexico in Dispute over Seasonal Farm Workers," *The Globe and Mail*, February 3, 2015, accessed May 22, 2015, www.theglobeandmail.com/news/british-columbia/bc-court-rules-against-mexico-in-dispute-over-seasonal-farm-workers/article22777687.
14. Adrian Humphreys, "War of the Unions," *National Post*, December 20, 2014, A9.
15. Nicola Middlemiss, "Unionization Rates Falling in Canada," *HRM Online*, June 17, 2015, accessed July 13, 2015, www.hrmonline.ca/hr-news/unionization-rates-falling-in-canada-192441.aspx; and Statistics Canada, "Unionization Rates Falling," *Canadian Megatrends*, May 28, 2015, accessed July 13, 2015, www.statcan.gc.ca/pub/11-630-x/11-630-x2015005-eng.htm.
16. Ibid.
17. Ibid.
18. "Trade Union Density," OECD.StatExtracts, accessed May 23, 2015, https://stats.oecd.org/Index.aspx?DataSetCode=UN_DEN.
19. Strategic Policy, Analysis, and Workplace Information Directorate, Labour Program, Human Resources and Skills Development Canada, *Union Membership in Canada—2010*, 6.
20. *Union Membership in Canada—2010*, 7.
21. *Union Coverage in Canada*, Employment and Social Development Canada, Labour, June 2014, 4.
22. Greg Keenan, "Union Pushes to Part U.S. Steel, Canadian Arm," *The Globe and Mail*, B3.
23. Greg Keenan and Adrian Morrow, "U.S. Steel, Ontario in Test of Wills over Canadian Restructuring," *The Globe and Mail*, October 4, 2014, B1.
24. Robert Barron, "Six Years On, Harmac Remains a Success Story," *Nanaimo Daily News*, October 3, 3014, accessed June 1, 2015, www.nanaimodailynews.com/news/nanaimo-region/six-years-on-harmac-remains-a-success-story-1.1412901; Harmac Pacific, "Employees," www.harmacpacific.com, accessed June 1, 2015; and "Harmac Pacific: Mill Has Evolved over Six Decades," *Nanaimo Business News*, April 2, 2015, accessed June 1, 2015, http://nanaimobusinessnews.ca/2015/04/02/harmac-pacific-mill-has-evolved-over-six-decades.
25. David Doorey, "Some Thoughts on Canadian Unionization Rates," June 1, 2015, http://lawofwork.ca/?p=52.
26. *Union Membership in Canada—2010*, 3.
27. Sean Fine, "Court Protects Public-Sector Workers' Right to Strike," *The Globe and Mail*, January 31, 2015, A14.

28. Douglas Quan, "Mounties Keenly Await Decision on Union Bid," *The Vancouver Sun*, January 14, 2015, B2, and James Fiz-Morris, "RCMP Officers Have Right to Collective Bargain, Supreme Court Rules," *CBC News*, January 16, 2015, accessed June 1, 2015, www.cbc.ca/news/politics/rcmp-officers-have-right-to-collective-bargaining-supreme-court-rules-1.2912340.
29. Justine Hunter, "Alliance of Unions Threatens Site C Labour," *The Globe and Mail*, March 31, 2015, S1.
30. Justine Hunter, "BC Hydro Finds Compromise with Unions," *The Globe and Mail*, May 28, 2015, S3.
31. Adrian Morrow, "Wynne's Peach Deal with Teachers Had Hidden Costs," *The Globe and Mail*, November 14, 2014, A7.
32. Suffield, *Labour Relations*, 201–218.
33. Gunderson and Taras, *Canadian Labour and Employment Relations*, 294–300.
34. Peter Lucas Stockli and Carmen Tanner, "Are Integrative or Distributive Outcomes More Satisfactory?" *European Journal of Social Psychology* 44, no. 3 (January 2014): 202–208.
35. Roger Fisher and William Ury, *Getting to Yes* (Toronto: Penguin Books, 1991).
36. Ross Stagner and Hjalmar Rosen, *Psychology of Union–Management Relations* (Belmont, CA: Wadsworth, 1965), 95–97. This is another classic in the field of labour–management relations.
37. Leah Schnurr, "CP Rail Strike Ends as 2 Sides Agree to Arbitration," *Canadian HR Reporter*, February 17, 2015, accessed June 1, 2015, www.hrreporter.com/articleview/23529-cp-rail-strike-ends-as-2-sides-agree-to-arbitration.
38. "B.C. Teachers' Strike Is Over, 86% Vote 'Yes' to Accept Deal," *CBC News*, September 18, 2014, accessed June 1, 2015, www.cbc.ca/news/canada/british-columbia/b-c-teachers-strike-is-over-86-vote-yes-to-accept-deal-1.2771202; Stephen Smart, "B.C. Teachers' Strike: Could It Have Ended Much Sooner, asks Stephen Smart," *CBC News*, September 19, 2014, accessed June 1, 2015, www.cbc.ca/news/canada/british-columbia/b-c-teachers-strike-could-it-have-ended-much-sooner-asks-stephen-smart-1.2771061; and Andrea Woo, "'Disillusioned' B.C. Teachers Grudgingly Voting on New Contract," *The Globe and Mail*, September 18, 2014, accessed June 1, 2015, www.theglobeandmail.com/news/british-columbia/many-disillusioned-bc-teachers-grudgingly-vote-to-end-strike/article20685888.
39. "Work Stoppages by Sector and Year," Labour Program, Government of Canada, May 5, 2015, accessed June 1, 2015, www.labour.gc.ca/eng/resources/info/datas/work_stoppages/work_stoppages_year_sector.shtml.
40. Kyle Bakx, "CP Rail Training More Office Workers to Operate Trains in Case of Strike," *CBC News*, May 14, 2015, accessed June 1, 2015, www.cbc.ca/news/canada/calgary/cp-rail-training-more-office-workers-to-operate-trains-in-case-of-strike-1.3074535.
41. Robert Devet, "Locked Out Herald Workers Reach Tentative Agreement," *Halifax Media Co-op*, March 6, 2015, accessed June 1, 2015, http://halifax.mediacoop.ca/fr/story/locked-out-herald-workers-reach-tentative-agreemen/33226.
42. Laurie Anstis, "Keeping the peace," *Employers Law*, May 2014, 18–19.
43. Queen's University, Industrial Relations Centre, "Dispute Resolution Skills," June 1, 2015.
44. For an expanded discussion of management's residual rights, termed "reserved rights" in the United States, see Paul Prasow and Edward Peters, *Arbitration and Collective Bargaining*, 2nd ed. (New York: McGraw-Hill, 1983): 33–34. This book is considered an authority on management rights issues.
45. Collective Agreement, Hospital Employee's Union and Amica at Arbutus Manor, April 1, 2011 to March 31, 2015.
46. Dave Battagello, "Police Investigate Hate Crime at Auto Plant," *The Vancouver Sun*, March 31, 2015, B2.
47. "The Steward and Grievance Procedures," Unifor Local 506, accessed June 1, 2015, http://unifor506.ca/information/education/the-steward-and-grievance-procedures.
48. "Arbitrator Orders Union to Pay Punitive Damages and Legal Costs of Employer Following Union's Involvement in Illegal Strike," *The HR Space*, Fasken Martineau, 2014.
49. Jeffrey Smith, "Mosaic Potash Too Suspicious of Timing Around Medical Leave: Arbitrator," *The Canadian HR Reporter*, August 11, 2014, 5.

11 Learning About International Human Resources Management

LEARNING OUTCOMES

After studying this chapter, you should be able to

1. Identify the types of organizational forms used for competing internationally.
2. Explain the economic, political-legal, and cultural factors in different countries that need to be considered from an HR perspective.
3. Illustrate how Canadian and international HRM differ.
4. Describe the staffing process for individuals working internationally.
5. Discuss the unique training needs of employees that work internationally.
6. Outline the characteristics of a good international recognition and rewards program.
7. Reconcile the difficulties of home- and host-country performance management systems.
8. Explain how labour relations differ around the world.

OUTLINE

HRM CLOSE-UP

"It is very important when you have international business ... to understand how they work, to understand the way they do things, because if you stay in your head office and you do everything from there, you'll miss some parts."

An unusual group of performers appeared in the small city of Baie-Saint-Paul, Quebec, in the early 1980s. The young entertainers juggled, danced and breathed fire, walked on stilts, and played music. It was reminiscent of the entertainment that had travelled around Europe in medieval times, only now with a decidedly modern twist.

Several years later, the fledgling troupe toured Quebec as part of celebrations for the 450th anniversary of Jacque Cartier's arrival in Canada. By then they were known as Cirque du Soleil, and in the 30 years since, more than 160 million people around the world have been treated to their spectacle.

From those humble beginnings, Cirque du Soleil now employs 4,000 people across the globe. While their Montreal head office is home to 1,500 employees, the remainder are spread throughout almost 20 residential and travelling shows that in any given year can be seen everywhere from Thailand and Israel to Mexico and Australia.

While such a global presence has been key to the company's international acclaim, having staff from all over the world spread across the world can also be a corporate challenge, not just logistically and organizationally but also in maintaining a core identity and a unity of spirit among employees.

"The way it works is that even though people are all over the world, we make sure they have the soul of Cirque du Soleil everywhere they go because it's very important for us" explains Marie-Josée Guilbault, Cirque du Soleil's Senior Vice-President, Organization and Culture.

That soul has been present from the very beginning, even when there were only 73 people in Baie-Saint-Paul. Today, each individual production, whether travelling or residential, has approximately 100 people and yet the feeling whether in Asia or Las Vegas remains true to the company's origins.

"It's different because we're much bigger," says Guilbault. "But within the shows, honestly, I think it's still very much there."

Right from the start, Cirque had performers from outside Canada, but today they boast more than 50 different nationalities speaking more than 25 languages and yet they've managed to achieve a harmony that would be the envy of the United Nations.

"For us, everyone at Cirque is a Cirquassier," Guilbault explains. "It's a very open-minded place and everybody just comes in and does what they have to do and we respect them a lot, they respect each other a lot, and it's a very natural thing for us."

While many businesses periodically bring their out-of-town or overseas staff to head office, Cirque takes head office to the staff.

"What we used to have was called a President's Tour where the president would visit all of the shows, give them news and talk to them," explains Guilbault. But now, with so many shows spread throughout the world, the task has been handed to the vice-presidents, including Guilbault.

"We're there for a few days and we give them information and we're available, but we also take part in the day-to-day work that they do. I was recently on a tour and I went under the stage with the technicians and did the work with them. They know that we care, and they know that we understand what they do, because one of the things that is very important when you have an international business like that is to understand how they work, to understand the way they do things. If you stay in your head office and you do everything from there, you'll miss some parts. They know that we understand their work. They know that we know the differences, and I think that's a key thing in having success when you have so many sites."

Used by permission of Marie-Josée Guilbault

Marie-Josée Guilbault, Senior Vice-President, Organization and Culture, Cirque du Soleil.

It's that personal contact and reinforcement that has helped maintain Cirque's sense of identity and team spirit, and Guilbault believes it is Cirque du Soleil's international presence that has in turn ultimately made it the unrivalled success it is.

"I don't think Cirque would be as successful or such a major company as we are today if we had stayed in Canada and the States. Our shows are international. They're conceived to be international, and honestly, for me it's not an advantage, it's a must."

Source: Used by permission of Marie-Josée Guilbault

INTRODUCTION

Even with the continuing slow growth globally, there are many examples of companies competing in a global environment. These examples might include acquisitions of international companies, such as in 2014 Burger King acquiring Canada's iconic Tim Hortons. Or they might highlight companies expanding into other markets, such as Hitachi in Canada, Bombardier in Asia, BMO in the United States, or Cirque du Soleil as mentioned in the HRM Close-up. Or examples might focus on international companies gaining dominance here in Canada, such as Starbucks, Walmart, and Lowes. Lastly, the examples might include companies acquiring a Canadian company and shutting it down, such as the acquisition of Future Shop by Best Buy and then shutting down all Future Shops in 2015.

Whatever the angle, we see clearly that globalization is a chief factor driving Canadian business. Nearly all organizations today are influenced by international competition. Some handle the challenge well, while others fail miserably when they try to manage across borders. More often than not, the difference boils down to how people are managed, the adaptability of cultures, and the flexibility of organizations. Because of this, many organizations are focusing on their human resources management practices.[1]

The importance of globalization notwithstanding, we have—for the most part—emphasized HRM practices and systems, as they exist in Canada. This is not so much an oversight on our part as a deliberate decision to explain the HR practices in the most fundamental way. However, the topic of international HRM is so important that we wanted to dedicate an entire chapter to its discussion. Our thinking is that now after you have read (and, we hope, discussed) some of the best practices for managing people at work, it might be appropriate to see how some of these practices may change as we enter into the international arena.

MANAGING ACROSS BORDERS

LO1

What types of organizational forms are used internationally?

International business operations can take several different forms. A large percentage of them carry on their international business with only limited facilities and minimal representation in foreign countries. Others, particularly Fortune 500 corporations, have extensive facilities and personnel in various countries of the world. For example, Dell employs more people outside the United States than within it. Managing these resources effectively, and integrating their activities to achieve global advantage, is a challenge to the leadership of these companies.

International corporation
Domestic firm that uses its existing capabilities to move into overseas markets

Multinational corporation (MNC)
Firm with independent business units operating in several countries

Figure 11.1 shows 4 basic types of organizations and how they differ in the degree to which international activities are separated to respond to the local regions and integrated to achieve global efficiencies. The **international corporation** is essentially a domestic firm that builds on its existing capabilities to penetrate overseas markets. Companies such as Honda, General Electric, and Procter & Gamble used this approach to gain access to Europe—they essentially adapted existing products for overseas markets without changing much else about their normal operations. One such adaptation, for example, was P&G's extremely successful introduction of a detergent brick used on washboards in India.

A **multinational corporation (MNC)** is a more complex form that usually has fully autonomous units operating in several countries. Shell, Philips, and ITT are 3 typical MNCs. These companies have traditionally given their foreign subsidiaries a great deal of latitude to address local issues such as consumer preferences, political pressures, and economic trends in different regions of the world. There is even a criticism of many universities in the United States that have opened campuses in other countries, thus becoming multinational.[2] However, while there has been criticism of U.S. universities, Canadian institutions are actively, and with encouragement, starting campuses in other countries such as India and China.[3] Frequently, these subsidiaries are run as independent companies,

FIGURE 11.1 Types of Organizations

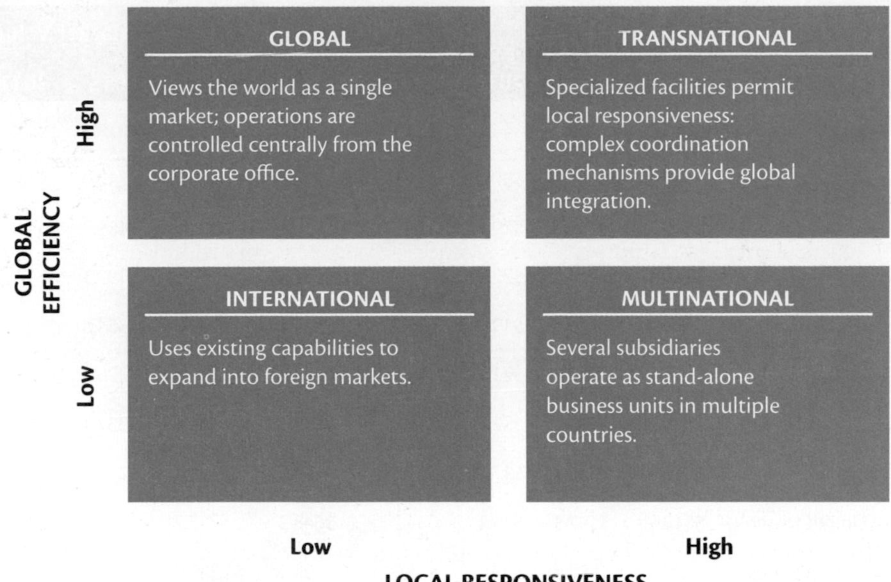

without much integration. The **global corporation**, on the other hand, can be viewed as a multinational firm that maintains control of operations back in the home office. Japanese companies such as Matsushita and NEC, for example, tend to treat the world market as a unified whole and try to combine activities in each country to maximize efficiency on a global scale. These companies operate much like a domestic firm, except that they view the whole world as their marketplace.

Global corporation
Firm that has integrated worldwide operations through a centralized home office

Finally, a **transnational corporation** attempts to achieve the local responsiveness of an MNC while achieving the efficiencies of a global firm. To balance this "global/local" dilemma, a transnational uses a network structure that coordinates specialized facilities positioned around the world. By using this flexible structure, a transnational provides autonomy to independent country operations but brings these separate activities together into an integrated whole. For most companies, the transnational form represents an ideal rather than a reality. Barrick Gold Corporation, the world's leading gold mining company, is headquartered in Canada and is considered a transnational company.[4]

Transnational corporation
Firm that attempts to balance local responsiveness on a global scale via a network of specialized operating units

Although various forms of organization exist, in this chapter we will generally refer to any company that conducts business outside its home country as an international business. Canada, of course, has no monopoly on international business. International enterprises are found throughout the world. In fact, some European and Pacific Rim companies have been conducting business on an international basis much longer than their Canadian counterparts. The close proximity of European countries, for example, makes them likely candidates for international trade. Figure 11.2 shows a list of the top global companies, measured by sales, profits, assets, and market value.[5] You will note significant changes in the composition of the lists between 2015 and 2012 that demonstrates the rise of China as a global economic force.

These companies are in a strong position to affect the world economy in the following ways:

1. Production and distribution extend beyond national boundaries, making it easier to transfer technology.
2. They have direct investments in many countries, affecting the balance of payments.
3. They have a political impact that leads to co-operation among countries and to the breaking down of barriers of nationalism.

Although Figure 11.2 is showing financial measures to demonstrate "top" or "best" there are other lists. For example, there is the world's "Most Admired Companies" list. This

FIGURE 11.2 Top International Companies—2015 and 2012 (all figures in billions)

2015 Rank	2012 Rank	Company	Country	Sales 2015	Sales 2012	Profits 2015	Profits 2012	Assets 2015	Assets 2012	Market Value 2015	Market Value 2012
1	5	ICBC	China	$166.8	$69.2	$44.8	$25.1	$3,322	$2039.1	$278.3	$237.4
2	*	China Construction Bank	China	$130.5	$143.7	$37	$10.3	$2,698.9	$392.6	$212.9	$202.2
3	*	Agricultural Bank	China	$129.2		$29.1		$2,574.8		$189.9	
4	*	Bank of China	China	$120.3		$27.5		$2,458.3		$199.1	
5	8	Berkshire Hathaway	United States	$194.7		$19.9		$534.6		$354.8	
6	2	JP Morgan Chase	United States	$97.8	$220.8	$21.2	$19	$2,593.6	$2,265.8	$225.5	$170.1
7	1	ExxonMobil	United States	$376.2	$433.5	$32.5	$41.1	$349.5	$331.1	$357.1	$407.4
8	7	PetroChina	China	$333.4	$310.1	$17.4	$20.6	$387.7	$304.7	$334.6	$294.7
9	3	General Electric	United States	$148.5	$147.3	$15.2	$14.2	$648.3	$717.2	$253.5	$213.7
10	9	Wells Fargo	United States	$90.4	$87.6	$23.1	$15.9	$1,701.4	$1,313.9	$278.3	$178.7

*Company didn't make list in 2012.
Source: From Forbes Magazine, "The World's Largest Companies 2015, May 6, 2015, accessed June 14, 2015, http://www.forbes.com/global2000/list/#tab:overall and Forbes Magazine, "The World's Biggest Companies," April 18, 2012, www.forbes.com/global2000/ (accessed April 22, 2012).

list, conducted jointly by *Fortune* and Hay Group, was determined by surveying executives, directors, and industry analysts in a methodological "peer review" of reputation. It was done this way because of a belief that a company's reputation is positively related to measurable outcomes, such as innovation, social responsibility, financial soundness, and global competitiveness. Interestingly enough, the top 3 on the Most Admired list—Apple, Google, and Amazon—had only recently started when the list was originally compiled 15 years ago.[6] *Fortune* also prepared the list "The 100 Best Companies to Work For," which identified Google as the top company, primarily for its unique benefits program which includes 12 weeks of fully paid baby-bonding time and $500 "bonding bucks" to all new parents.[7] Google has held the top spot several years in a row.

Another, more recent list measures the world's most sustainable organizations—those equipped to prosper in the long term because of their approach to relationship building with all the various stakeholders. This 2015 list included the following Canadian companies: Tim Hortons, Teck Resources, Telus, Bombardier, Enbridge Inc., Toronto-Dominion Bank, Celestica, Bank of Montreal, Encana Corporation, Suncor Energy, and Intact Financial.[8] It is important to remember that Canada is an export nation, and therefore most of our major companies do business outside Canada. For example, Hudson Bay announced in June 2015 that it was buying a very profitable German department store chain both for its name in Germany but for its vast real estate holdings.[9] It sees this acquisition as a method to launch its other high-profile store, Saks Fifth Avenue, in Europe.[10] It is listed as one of Canada's top companies.[11]

So how do Canadian companies compare to those on the world lists? Figure 11.3 lists the top 10 most profitable Canadian companies in 2014. It is interesting to note that 6 of the 10 were financial institutions.

Society for Human Resource Management
www.shrm.org

The Society for Human Resource Management provides current news updates on issues concerning HRM from around the world. Currently, the information can be found at "Global HR" under its HR Topics & Strategy category.

FIGURE 11.3 Top 10 Canadian Companies

Rank	Company	2015 Profits (billions US$)	2015 Revenues (billions US$)
1	Royal Bank of Canada	3.910	42.011
2	Toronto-Dominion Bank	7.776	36.305
3	Bank of Nova Scotia	7.071	30.839
4	Bank of Montreal	4.277	21.298
5	Canadian Natural Resources	3.929	22.245
6	Imperial Oil	3.785	36.966
7	Encana	3.392	11.445
8	Manulife Financial	3.501	54.687
9	Brookfield Asset Management	3.110	20.148
10	CIBC	3.218	17.394

Source: "Top 1000: Exclusive Rankings of Canada's Most Profitable Companies," *The Globe and Mail Report on Business*, July/August 2015, 54.

How Does the Global Environment Influence Management?

LO2

What factors need to be considered from an HR perspective in different countries?

In Chapter 1, we highlighted some of the challenges facing business and therefore affecting human resources management. One of the major economic issues we discussed was the creation of free trade zones within Europe, North America, and the Pacific Rim. As of June 2015, there were 20 member countries within the European Union (EU), whose goal is to have a single market for the movement of goods, services, people, and money across certain national borders.[12] However, there has been ongoing concern with some of the economic health of some of the members, particularly Greece, which has been on the verge of bankruptcy for a number of years.[13] A similar transition has been occurring within North America since the passage of NAFTA (discussed in Chapter 1). While there had been fears that NAFTA would lead to a loss of jobs for companies in the 3 countries, just the opposite has occurred. In the 20 years since NAFTA was created, trade has totalled over $1.1 trillion.[14] The United States is Canada's largest partner; the EU is Canada's 2nd-largest economic partner; and China is now the 3rd-largest trading partner.[15]

Similarly to NAFTA, numerous trade associations, including the Association of Southeast Asian Nations (ASEAN), East Asia Economic Group, and Asia-Pacific Economic Cooperation (APEC), have significantly facilitated trade among Asian countries, making Asia the fastest-growing region in the world. China—Asia's fastest-growing country—has emerged as a dominant trade leader since instituting trade reforms in the late 1970s. In the past 15 years, China's economy has grown fourfold, drastically altering political and trading relations among nations. Some industry analysts estimate that the country now produces 50% of the world's cameras, 30% of air conditioners and televisions, 25% of washing machines, and 20% of refrigerators worldwide. In addition, China's 1.4 billion people represent a massive, largely untapped consumer market for global companies. Even with slow global growth, China's GDP still expanded by 7.4% in 2014.[16] Today more cars are sold in China than in Europe. Driving this trend are multinational corporations, such as General

Electric, Toyota, and Intel, which are building or expanding their manufacturing units in the country.

And in the summer of 2015, U.S. lawmakers approved a very large Pacific Rim trade arrangement called the Trans-Pacific Partnership.[17] This agreement is the biggest trade agreement since NAFTA and may create some pressure for Canada. Specifically, the trade deal is expected to allow duty-free dairy and poultry, and since Canada protects those industries through a production quota system, the agreement could cause problems for farms in Quebec and Ontario.[18]

The auto industry has undergone tremendous global change. Fiat, which purchased a portion Chrysler automaker a few years ago, recently acquired the remaining 42%.[19] Likewise, a German transmission maker acquired a Livonia-based automotive company and Volkswagen acquired the remaining shares of Scania, a truck manufacturer in Sweden.[20] More recently, General Motors and Isuzu (Japan) entered into an agreement to collaborate on the production of medium-duty trucks.[21]

In addition to China, other key countries for trade are Brazil, Russia, India, and South Africa. With China, these countries are called "BRICS." and are considered to have the fast-growing economies, capturing about 27% of the world's $73 billion GDP.[22] Currently, India is planning to be the 2nd-largest employer in the world by 2019 with the tourism and hospitality sector reaching $418 billion.[23]

Canada signed a free-trade agreement with South Korea in early 2015.[24] The agreement is credited with inBay Technologies of Ottawa entering into a distribution agreement with AirCUVE which provides systems for cell-phone users in South Korea.[25] On the other hand, Panasonic, headquartered in Japan, wants to sell its health-care subsidiary to have a more focused corporation.[26]

The fact that international corporations can choose the countries in which they do business or relocate operations generally results in the selection of countries that have the most to offer. For example, several Canadian forestry companies have bought mills in the United States, as lumber in Canada is being devastated by a pest infestation.[27] In addition to economic factors, political-legal factors are a huge consideration. In many countries, particularly those in Africa, governments poorly protect property rights. Whoever has the political power or authority can seize others' property with few or no consequences. Civil unrest can also lead to the poor enforcement of property rights. This situation gives companies less incentive to locate factories or invest in those countries. Another issue relates to intellectual property rights—rights related to patents, trademarks, and so forth. Despite the fact that private property rights are now generally enforced in China, intellectual property rights have seen little protection. For example, when General Motors formed a joint venture with a Chinese company to produce and sell a new automobile in the country, a knockoff version of the car could be seen on China's streets even before GM and its partner were able to manufacture their first car.

Cultural environment
Communications, religion, values and ideologies, education, and social structure of a country

Beyond the economic and political-legal issues just mentioned, a country's **cultural environment** (communications, religion, values and ideologies, education, and social structure) also has important implications when it comes to a company's decision about when and how to do business in another country. Because of language and culture similarities, many Canadian companies are finding the United States, Ireland, and the United Kingdom attractive places to locate their facilities, particularly call centres. Eastern Europe has also begun to attract interest because citizens there are well educated and, for the most part, possess English-speaking skills. Figure 11.4 summarizes the complexity of the cultural environment in which HR must be managed.

Culture is an integrated phenomenon. By recognizing and accommodating taboos, rituals, attitudes toward time, social stratification, kinship systems, and the many other components listed in Figure 11.5, managers stand a better chance of

FIGURE 11.4 The Cultural Environment of International Business

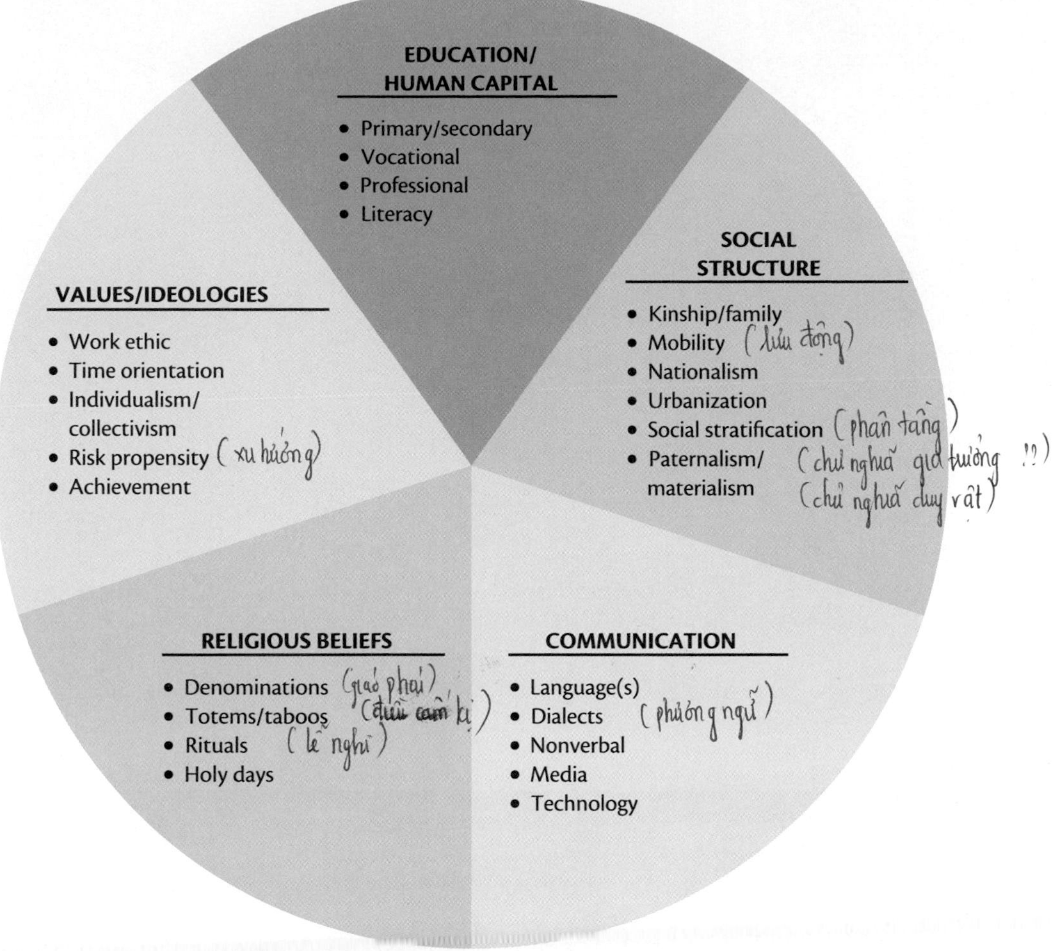

Source: Top 1000: Exclusive rankings of Canada's most profitable companies," *The Globe and Mail Report on Business*, July/August 2015, 54. © The Globe and Mail Inc. All Rights Reserved.

understanding the culture of a **host country**—a country in which an international business operates. Different cultural environments require different approaches to human resources management.

Strategies, structures, and management styles appropriate in one cultural setting may lead to failure in another. Even in countries that have close language or cultural links, HR practices can be dramatically different. In some countries night shifts are taboo. In other countries employers are expected to provide employees with meals and transportation between home and work. In India, workers generally receive cash bonuses on their wedding anniversaries with which to buy gifts for their spouses, and dating allowances are provided to unmarried employees. Also in India, promotional opportunities are more highly valued than compensation. And Japan recently introduced a 4-day workweek to motivate employees so that businesses outcomes can improve.[28] Read At Work with HRM 11.1 to learn more about the cultural implications of doing business in another country.

For more information on the various trade agreements and doing business in other countries, check out NAFTA (**www.nafta-sec-alena.org**), Europa (**europa.eu**), ASEAN (**www.aseans.org**), TPP (**https://ustr.gov/tpp**) and Foreign Affairs and International Trade Canada (**international.gc.ca**).

Host country
Country in which an international corporation operates

NAFTA
www.nafta-sec-alena.org

Europa
europa.eu

ASEAN
www.asean.org

TPP
https://ustr.gov/tpp

Foreign Affairs and International Trade Canada
international.gc.ca

FIGURE 11.5 Changes in International Staffing over Time

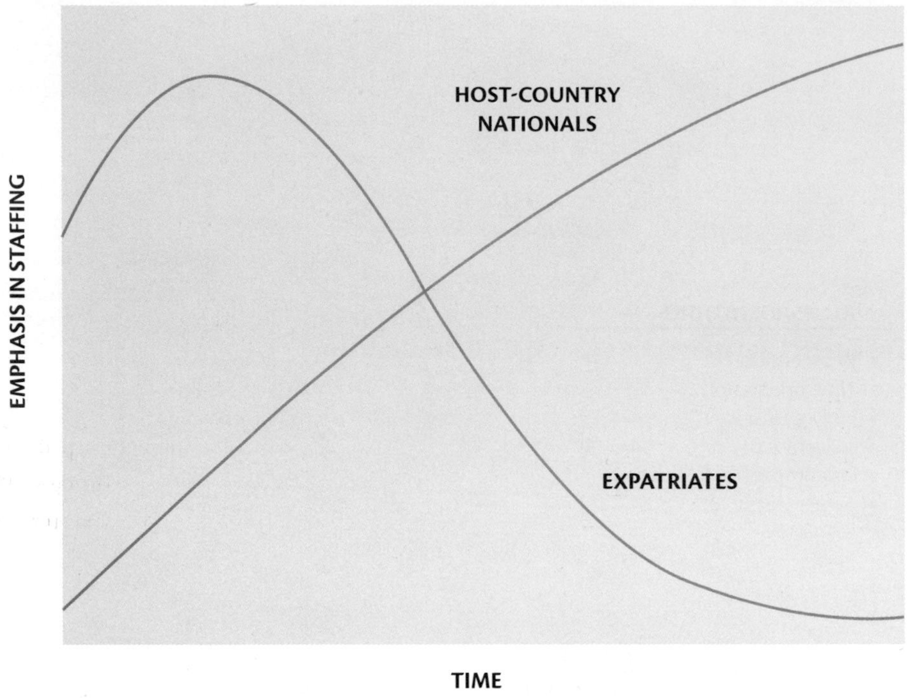

AT WORK WITH HRM 11.1

NOT AMAZON!

With the worldwide presence of Amazon, it is hard to imagine it might not understand that the cultural environment in any country makes a big difference in how business is conducted.

In late 2014, just before the holiday shopping rush, Amazon learned the hard way that Germany has certain expectations regarding who speaks for employees. Amazon, as part of its operating style, is used to dealing directly with its employees—and not through a union. However, in Germany, unions are very powerful and used to having a collaborative relationship with companies that has led to sector-wide labour agreements.

While there had been a series of walkouts at the Amazon warehouse for almost a year, the action escalated when the employees staged a strike in Amazon's busiest shopping season. The union, Verdi, wanted to begin collective bargaining to establish a collective agreement that would result in wages higher than in other retail sectors. Amazon, however, believed its wages were in line and competitive for the type of work being done in the warehouse.

Amazon had been doing business in Germany for almost 20 years and didn't see the need to make changes in how it dealt with its employees. The company felt that anything coming between it and its staff slowed down operations and innovation. Amazon has about 10,000 German workers in its distribution centres throughout the year and then hires an additional 10,000 during seasonal activity.

The union, on the other hand, felt there is a social partnership between unions and employers and that Amazon was being unreasonable.

All this was particularly troubling because Germans tend to be eager online shoppers, and Germany is Amazon's largest market after the United States. Many experts saw it as a clash of German society and U.S. arrogance.

CRITICAL THINKING QUESTIONS:

1. Do you think Amazon ought to conform to the culture of relationships with unions in Germany? Why or why not?
2. What might happen if the strikes and confrontation continue? Explain your answer.

Source: Adapted from Joanna Slater, "Amazon.com's German Culture Clash," *The Globe and Mail*, December 23, 2014, B1.

Canadian vs. International HRM

International HRM differs from domestic HRM in several ways. In the first place, it necessarily puts more emphasis on functions and activities such as relocation, orientation, and translation services to help employees adapt to new and different environments outside their own countries and to help newly hired employees in foreign countries adapt to working for companies headquartered outside their borders. Because of the complexity of HR when doing business in other countries, larger companies will have HR professionals devoted solely to assisting with the globalization process. Further, some companies will also hire international staffing firms, such as Boston Global Consulting. These firms have expertise when it comes to relocating employees, establishing operations abroad, and helping with import/export and foreign tax issues.

LO3

How do Canadian HRM and international HRM differ?

HR management systems have come a long way in terms of helping firms improve their international coordination. A good HR management system can facilitate communication, record keeping, and a host of other activities worldwide. Some HRMSs are designed to track the whereabouts of employees travelling or on assignment. This can be important in the event of a transportation accident, a natural disaster such as a tsunami, a terrorist attack, or civil strife when evacuation plans may have to be implemented.

HR PLANNING, RECRUITING, AND SELECTING

International Staffing

International management poses many problems in addition to those faced by a domestic operation. Because of geographic distance and a lack of close, day-to-day relationships with headquarters in the home country, problems must often be resolved with little or no counsel or assistance from others. It is essential, therefore, that special attention be given to the staffing practices of overseas units. In fact, a recent study suggests that the inability to successfully integrate cultural differences is a major reason global mergers and acquisitions fail.[29]

LO4

What is the staffing process for individuals working internationally?

There are 3 sources of employees with whom to staff international operations. First, the company can send people from its home country. These employees are often referred to as **expatriates**, or **home-country nationals**. Second, it can hire **host-country nationals**, natives of the host country, to do the managing. Third, it can hire **third-country nationals**, natives of a country other than the home or host country.

Expatriates or home-country nationals Employees from the home country who are on international assignment

Host-country nationals Employees who are natives of the host country

Third-country nationals Employees who are natives of a country other than the home country or the host country

Each of these provides certain advantages and certain disadvantages. Most corporations, such as the Four Seasons Hotels (described in At Work with HRM 11.2), use all 3 sources for staffing multinational operations.

As shown in Figure 11.5, at early stages of international expansion, organizations often send home-country expatriates to establish activities (particularly in less-developed countries) and to work with local governments. Doing this is generally very costly. Expatriate assignments cost companies, on average, $1 million over a 3-year period, which can be 3 to 5 times what a domestic assignment costs. As a result, many companies are taking greater pains to more clearly outline the overall goal of the foreign assignment and its timetable for completion. To reduce the costs some companies are considering short-term and "commuter" assignments. A short-term assignment lasts 6 to 12 months, with the employee remaining under a home-country employment contract. Companies will also take into account the "quality of life" in another country when deciding whether to use local talent or an expatriate.[30]

AT WORK WITH HRM 11.2

WORLD-CLASS HIRING

Four Seasons Hotels, with a staff of 44,000, has grown in 50 years to 94 hotels in 39 countries. The Four Seasons brand is synonymous with luxury and first-class service standards. The execution of the strategy of being the best in the world starts with leaders who are passionate about the corporation's customer service and employee relations' values. These leaders can take a concept such as "We have chosen to specialize within the hospitality industry by offering only experiences of exceptional quality" and paint a picture for employees that is clear and motivational, and that results in the delivery of that exceptional personal service.

Does the perception of service excellence depend on the country or culture in which Four Seasons operates? Four Seasons trains service staff to be sensitive to guests' needs and to minimize or avoid culture and language problems. It also has an ethical culture that focuses on doing business according to the applicable laws in the country in which it has hotels.

So that employees can meet these high performance expectations, Four Seasons selects employees based on their service attitudes. Candidates for employment must undergo 4 behaviourally based interviews (including 1 with the general manager) to determine their service attitudes and current skills and knowledge.

Four Seasons does not have a rigid formula for selecting home-country nationals or expatriates for any given country. The ratios depend on 3 factors: regulations, economics, and corporate management development needs. For example, Indonesia used to have a rule that no more than 3 expatriates could be employed per hotel and it set expatriate reduction targets to meet this regulation. Economically, it made sense, since an expatriate general manager could cost as much as 75 or 80 local employees. And finally, it will choose candidates on the basis of their need for global exposure and professional development, to match our targeted needs for international expansion.

The biggest challenge in international HR is management development. Four Seasons needs to develop culturally appropriate leadership in preparation for specific new locations on a defined timeline. If managers cannot be found who can speak the language, and understand the culture, the ability to grow is limited.

This attention to the selection and development of high-performance employees has resulted in *Fortune* magazine naming Four Seasons one of the 100 best employers in the world for many years. Consequently, Four Seasons is now able to attract more and better applicants. Four Seasons is also widely recognized as the best luxury hotel chain in the world. Furthermore, the turnover rate at Four Seasons is one of the lowest in the hospitality sector. Even those employees who have left are often recaptured as they elect to return to the kind of culture that treats them as they treat the guests.

CRITICAL THINKING QUESTION:

Do you think Four Seasons ought to focus more on developing local managers? Why or why not?

Sources: Adapted from "The 100 Best Companies to Work For," *Fortune*, March 15, 2015, 148; "About Four Seasons," Four Seasons, accessed June 16, 2015, **www.fourseasons.com/about_four_seasons/service-culture**; and "Supporting Sustainability," Living Values Four Seasons, accessed June 16, 2015, **http://livingvalues.fourseasons.com/category/supporting-sustainability/#**.

Given the ever-expanding global environment, more and more people appear to be open to working in another country. Many individuals, especially in Canada, feel that such work experience is an asset to their future career opportunities.[31]

At later stages of internationalization, there is typically a steady shift toward the use of host-country nationals. This move has three main advantages:

1. Hiring local citizens is less costly than relocating expatriates.
2. Since local governments usually want good jobs for their citizens, foreign employers may be required to hire them.
3. Most customers want to do business with companies (and people) they perceive to be local versus foreign.

Because Canadian companies want to be viewed as true international citizens, there has also been a trend away from hiring expatriates to head up operations in foreign countries, particularly European countries. Bombardier and Four Seasons, which have strong regional organizations, tend to replace their expatriate managers with local managers as quickly as possible. In addition to hiring local managers to head their foreign divisions and plants, more companies are using third-country nationals. Third-country nationals are often multilingual and already acclimated to the host country's culture—perhaps because they live in a nearby region. Thus, they are also less costly to relocate and sometimes better able to cope culturally with the foreign environment. At Work with HRM 11.3 tells the story of a B.C. company entering into a partnership with a Chinese conglomerate.

Companies tend to continue to use expatriates only when a specific set of skills is needed or when individuals in the host country require development. It is important to note, however, that while top managers may prefer one source of employees to another, the host country may put pressure on them that restricts their choices. Such pressure takes the form of sophisticated government persuasion through administrative or legislative decrees designed to employ host-country individuals. To encourage local hiring, the host country frequently implements tax incentives, tariffs, and quotas.

Canadian employers wishing to assess thousands of academic credentials for foreign-born employees can consult the not-for-profit World Education Services at **www.wes.org**.

Recruiting Internationally

Improved telecommunications and travel have made it easier to match up employers and employees of all kinds worldwide. Rolls-Royce, headquartered in the United Kingdom, hires 25% of its 25,000 employees abroad. Because its customers come from around the globe, Rolls-Royce figures its workforce should as well. Airbus, the European commercial jet maker, recruits engineers from universities and colleges all over Europe. American-based Boeing's need for engineers

AT WORK WITH HRM 11.3 THE FLOAT PLANE LANDS!

Doing business with Chinese companies is not simple, nor does it happen quickly. Take Harbour Air, a Vancouver-based float plane company that has undertaken a strategic partnership with a large Chinese firm to provide float-plane services and knowledge in a new venture.

The firm will help Zongshen Industrial Group set up the first float-plane operation in China. Given the 1.4 billion people in China and the many waterways, it is hard to image there are no planes in operation. The expertise Harbour Air brings to the relationship will provide a solid launching pad for services in Shanghai and other South Asia places.

Part of the deal allows for the purchase of 49% of shares of Harbour Air from its current owner and CEO, Greg McDougall. McDougall indicated that he had been approached for a number of years to export the expertise, but resisted for fear of bureaucracy and lethargy as regulators dealt with expansion of low-flying aircraft. However, he felt that the time was now to move into another market. There is a need to have fast and efficient transportation services along China's coastal routes and Zongshen indicated that local governments are strongly supporting the new endeavour.

Besides the expertise and knowledge Harbour Air will bring, the new company will be called Harbour Air China. Another reason for utilizing this approach is to generally introduce more aviation into China. Part of the long-term plan is to build its own seaplanes as the business expands into Malaysia and Vietnam.

This relationship will also allow Harbour Air to expand into the northern area of British Columbia, where the oil and gas development is creating more demand for coastal plane services.

CRITICAL THINKING QUESTIONS:

1. Besides expertise, what other advantages might Harbour Air have in partnering with Zongshen?
2. What might be some disadvantages for Harbour Air in the future with the current ownership arrangement?

Sources: Adapted from Iain Marlow, "Harbour Air's Commuter Seaplanes Soon to be Tried in Chinese Market," *The Globe and Mail*, June 18, 2015, B2; Jeff Lee, "Harbour Air Partners with Chinese Company," *The Vancouver Sun*, June 17, 2015, A1; and Jeff Lee, "Harbour Air Deal with Zuo Zongshen Larger Than First Thought," *The Vancouver Sun*, June 17, 2015, accessed June 20, 2015, **http://blogs.vancouversun.com/2015/06/17/harbour-air-deal-with-zuo-zongshen-%e5%b7%a6%e5%ae%97%e7%94%b3-larger-than-first-thought**.

is so great that it also recruits internationally and has even opened a design centre in Moscow. The trend is likely to continue as the populations in developed countries age, and companies search for talent elsewhere. Even China, despite its massive population, will face labour shortages because laws there prohibit couples from having more than one child.

Companies must be particularly responsive to the cultural, political, and legal environments both domestically and abroad when recruiting internationally. For example, Starbucks and Honeywell have made a special effort to create codes of conduct for employees throughout the world to ensure that standards of ethical and legal behaviour are known and understood. PepsiCo has taken a similar approach to ensuring that company values are reinforced (even while recognizing the need for adapting to local cultures). The company has 4 core criteria viewed as essential in worldwide recruiting efforts: (1) personal integrity, (2) a drive for results, (3) respect for others, and (4) capability. However, it is important to recognize local cultures in relation to implementing ethical codes in other countries.

In general, however, employee recruitment in other countries is subject to more government regulation than it is in Canada. Regulations range from those that cover procedures for recruiting employees to those that govern the employment of foreign workers or require the employment of the physically disabled, war veterans, or displaced persons. Many Central American countries, for example, have stringent regulations about the number of foreigners that can be employed as a percentage of the total workforce. Virtually all countries have work-permit or visa restrictions that apply to foreigners. A **work permit**, or **visa**, is a document issued by a government granting authority to a foreign individual to seek employment in that government's country.

Work permit or visa
A government document granting a foreign individual the right to seek employment

Multinational companies (MNCs) tend to use the same kinds of internal and external recruitment sources as are used in their home countries. At the executive level, companies use search firms such as Korn/Ferry in Canada or Spencer Stuart in the United Kingdom. At lower levels, more informal approaches tend to be useful. While unskilled labour may be readily available in a developing country, recruitment of skilled workers may be more difficult. Many employers have learned that the best way to find workers in these countries is through referrals and radio announcements; that's because many people lack sufficient reading or writing skills. Other firms use international recruiting firms to find skilled labour abroad. Some countries require the employment of locals if adequate numbers of skilled people are available. Specific exceptions are sometimes granted (officially or unofficially) for difficult situations such as farm workers from Mexico in Canada or for Italian, Spanish, Greek, and Turkish workers in Germany and the Benelux countries (Belgium, the Netherlands, and Luxembourg). Foreign workers invited to come to perform needed labour are usually referred to as **guest workers**. Although hiring non-nationals may result in lower direct labour costs for a company, the indirect costs—those related to housing, language training, health services, recruitment, transportation, and so on—can be substantial. Some organizations, such as health authorities recruiting nursing staff, are nonetheless finding the expenditures worthwhile.[32]

Guest workers
Foreign workers invited to perform needed labour

However, even though international recruitment is still strong, there are restrictions in some countries about the number of non-resident hirings. For example, the United Kingdom in late 2014 changed its regulations for hiring skilled workers so that there was more opportunity for residents before immigrants were brought in specifically for certain jobs.[33] With situations like this and the increasing complexity in the world, companies are using a number of different approaches to have the talent they need.[34]

In order to ensure that global talent is attracted and retained in other countries, organizations need to focus on the following:

1. brand—having a reputation for where people can excel
2. compensation—ensuring that the rewards program is competitive and fits the local circumstances as well as what applies in the home country
3. development—increasing employees' skills and competencies
4. culture—understanding the local environment and what additional supports might be necessary to attract and retain employees[35]

Apprenticeships

A major source of trained labour in European nations is apprenticeship-training programs (described in Chapter 6). On the whole, apprenticeship training in Europe is superior to that in Canada. In Europe, a dual-track system of education directs a large number of youths into vocational training. The German system of apprenticeship training, one of the best in Europe, provides training for office and top jobs under a 3-way responsibility contract between the apprentice, the parents, and the organization. At the conclusion of their training, apprentices can work for any employer but generally receive seniority credit with the training firm if they remain in it. France has been able to draw on its "Grandes Écoles" for centuries. Created during the Renaissance to fulfill a need that universities weren't meeting, the Grandes Écoles educate prospective engineers up to the equivalent level of Master of Engineering. It is said that people who have graduated from the various institutions in the Grandes Écoles run France—even the former French president.[36]

Staffing Transnational Teams

In addition to focusing on individuals, it is also important to note that companies are increasingly using transnational teams to conduct international business. **Transnational teams** are composed of members of multiple nationalities working on projects that span multiple countries. Recent research has indicated that the ability to communicate effectively between different nationalities is critical to the success of the team.[37]

Transnational teams
Teams composed of members of multiple nationalities working on projects that span multiple countries

Sometimes, companies send employees on temporary assignments abroad as part of transnational teams that last a few months. They might do so to break down cultural barriers between international divisions or disseminate new ideas and technology to other regions. The fundamental task in forming a transnational team is assembling the right group of people who can work together effectively to accomplish the goals of the team. Many companies try to build variety into their teams in order to maximize responsiveness to the special needs of different countries. For example, when Heineken formed a transnational team to consolidate its production facilities, it ensured that team members were drawn from each major region within Europe. Team members tended to have specialized skills, and members were added only if they offered some unique skill that added value to the team.

Selecting Employees Internationally

As you might imagine, selection practices vary around the world. In Canada, managers tend to emphasize merit, with the best-qualified person getting the job. In other countries, however, firms tend to hire on the basis of family ties, social status, language, and common origin. The candidate who satisfies these criteria may get the job even if otherwise unqualified. Much of this is changing—there has been a growing realization among organizations in other nations that greater attention must be given to hiring those most qualified. In addition to a person's qualifications, various other hiring laws are enforced around the world. Labour union restrictions, which will be discussed later in this chapter, can also have an impact on hiring.

The Selection Process

The selection process for international assignments should emphasize different employment factors, depending on the extent of contact that one would have with the local culture and the degree to which the foreign environment differs from the home environment. For example, if the job involves extensive contacts with the community, as with a chief executive officer, this factor should be given appropriate weight. In addition, other factors that might be different in a foreign environment include the way in which business is conducted.[38]

If a candidate for expatriation is willing to live and work in a foreign environment, an indication of the person's tolerance of cultural differences should be obtained. On the other hand, if local nationals have the technical competence to carry out the job successfully, they should be carefully considered for the job before the firm launches a search (at home) for a candidate to fill the job. As stated previously, most corporations realize the advantages to be gained by staffing international operations with host-country nationals wherever possible.

Selecting home-country and third-country nationals requires that more factors be considered than in selecting host-country nationals. While the latter must, of course, possess managerial abilities and the necessary technical skills, they have the advantage of familiarity with the physical and cultural environment and the language of the host country. And depending on the country, certain factors in the environment may be key as to whether or not the person is an "expat." One tool in our world of technology to help locate and source applicants is mobile applications that are multilingual.[39] Using such technology allows a more focused and targeted approach. The discussion that follows will focus on the selection of expatriate managers from the home country.

Selecting Expatriate Managers

One of the toughest jobs facing many organizations is finding employees who can meet the demands of working in a foreign environment. There are several steps involved in selecting individuals for an international assignment. The sequencing of these activities can make a big difference.

Step 1: Begin with self-selection. Employees should begin the process years in advance by thinking about their career goals and interest in international work. By beginning with self-selection, companies can more easily avoid the problems of forcing otherwise promising employees into international assignments where they would be unhappy and unsuccessful. In cases where individuals have families, the decisions about relocation are more complicated. Employees should seek out information to help them predict their chances of success in living abroad. Companies such as EDS and Deloitte & Touche give the self-selection instruments to their employees to help them think through the pros and cons of international assignments.

Step 2: Create a candidate pool. After employees have self-selected, organizations can put together a database of candidates for international assignments. Information on the database might include availability, languages, country preferences, and skills. While there have not been many women in managerial positions in the Middle East, this is changing in Gulf Cooperation Council states where companies are increasingly see social attitudes changing and that women are now being actively sought for leadership roles.[40]

FIGURE 11.6 Expatriate Selection Criteria

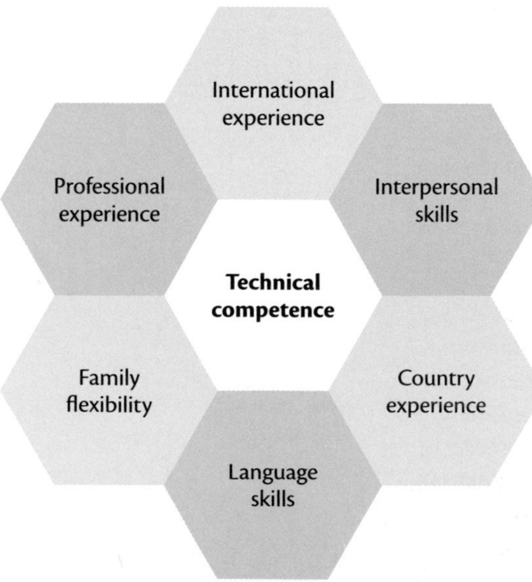

Step 3: Assess core skills. From the short list of potential candidates, managers can assess each candidate on technical and managerial readiness relative to the needs of the assignment. Although many factors determine success abroad, the initial focus should be on the requirements of the job. One of the key skills that can create success is language skills of the host country.[41]

Step 4: Assess augmented skills and attributes. As shown in Figure 11.6, expatriate selection decisions are typically driven by technical competence as well as professional and international experience. In addition, however, an increasing number of organizations have also begun considering an individual's ability to adapt to different environments. Participating in a variety of different activities, such as athletic or social programs, can be very helpful in assisting the person in adapting to the host country.[41]

To be more specific, companies such as Colgate-Palmolive, Whirlpool, and Dow Chemical have identified a set of **core skills** that they view as critical for success abroad and a set of **augmented skills** that help facilitate the efforts of expatriate managers. For example, decision making, team building, and adaptability are some of the core skills; negotiation skills and change management are two of the augmented skills. It is worth noting that many of these skills are not significantly different from those required for managerial success at home.

Core skills
Skills considered critical to an employee's success abroad

Augmented skills
Skills helpful in facilitating the efforts of expatriate managers

Failure rate
Percentage of expatriates who do not perform satisfactorily

Even companies that believe they have selected the best candidates frequently experience high expatriate **failure rates**. The primary reason for an assignment failure is the person's family—spouse and children. In studies on this topic, it was determined that inadequate attention was paid to ensuring that the family could adapt to the new conditions. Besides family issues, failures also occurred due to the person's lack of job knowledge, poor relational leadership skills, and lack of cultural openness and adaptability.[42] Samsung, another global electronics manufacturing company, has found that the most common reasons for an unsuccessful foreign assignment were inability to adapt to the different culture, lack of appropriate skills, and lack of communication skills.[43]

There are a number of ways to improve the success of expatriate assignments. One important step is to involve spouses early in the process. In addition, training and development for both expatriates and their families can have a big impact. (This matter will be discussed next.) As an example of how companies can prepare employees and their families, consider Shell, which created an online information centre called the Outpost Expatriate Support Network (**www.outpostexpat.nl**).

Outpost Expatriate Support Network
www.outpostexpat.nl

TRAINING AND DEVELOPMENT

LO5

What are the training needs for employees working internationally?

Although companies try to recruit and select the very best people for international work, it is usually necessary to provide some type of training. Not only is this type of training important to expatriate managers; it is also important for the foreign employees they will ultimately supervise. To know and understand how the Japanese or Chinese negotiate contracts or how businesspeople from Latin America view the enforcement of meeting times, for example, can help expatriate managers and their employees deal with each other more successfully. To illustrate this latter point, Finning International, in its desire to provide global exposure to its key staff, has had to ensure that the Canadian managers understand that the concept of time is very relaxed in the operations in Chile.[42] The biggest mistake managers can make is to assume that people are the same everywhere. Corporations that seriously desire to succeed in global business are tackling these problems head-on by providing intensive training.

Content of Training Programs

Lack of training is one of the principal causes of failure among employees working internationally. Those working internationally need to know as much as possible about (1) the country where they are going, (2) that country's culture, and (3) the history, values, and dynamics of their own organizations. Figure 11.7 gives an overview of what one needs to study for an international assignment. In many cases, the employee and the family can obtain a great deal of general information about the host country, including its culture, geography, social and political history, climate, food, and so on, through the Internet, books, lectures, and DVDs. The knowledge gained will at least help the participants have a better understanding in their assignments. Sensitivity training can also help expatriates overcome ethnic prejudices they might harbour. Expatriates can simulate a field experience in sensitivity training by visiting a nearby subculture in their native countries or visiting a foreign country before relocating there. Other types of training can include fundamentals of the international business and its strategy, as DHL Express has done to ensure a common understanding of the business throughout the world.[43]

FIGURE 11.7 Preparing for an International Assignment

To prepare for an international assignment, one should become acquainted with the following aspects of the host country:

1. social and business etiquette
2. history and folklore
3. current affairs, including relations between the host country and Canada
4. cultural values and priorities
5. geography, especially its major cities
6. sources of pride and great achievements of the culture
7. religion and the role of religion in daily life
8. political structure and current players
9. practical matters, such as currency, transportation, time zones, and hours of business
10. the language

Language Training

Communication with individuals who have a different language and a different cultural orientation is extremely difficult. Most executives agree that it is among the biggest problems for the foreign business traveller. Students who plan careers in international business should start instruction in one or more foreign languages as early as possible. The top-ranked China Europe International Business School (CEIBS), jointly founded by the Chinese government and the European Union, also offers language training. Some companies do their own language training. Multinational companies, and businesses that outsource work abroad, stand to benefit from this type of training.

Fortunately for most Canadians, English is almost universally accepted as the primary language for international business. Particularly when many people from different countries are working together, English is usually the designated language for meetings and formal discussions. Many companies also provide instruction in English for those who have to use it in their jobs.

Learning the language is only part of communicating in another culture, though. The following list illustrates the complexities of the communication process in international business.

1. In England, to "table" a subject means to put it on the table for current discussion. In Canada, it means to postpone discussion of a subject, perhaps indefinitely.
2. In Canada, information flows to a manager. In cultures where authority is centralized (such as Europe and South America), the manager must take the initiative to seek out the information.
3. Getting straight to the point is uniquely North American. Many Europeans, Arabs, and others resent this directness in communication.
4. In Japan, there are 16 ways to avoid saying "no."
5. When something is "inconvenient" to the Chinese, it is most likely downright impossible.
6. In most foreign countries, expressions of anger are unacceptable; in some places, public display of anger is taboo.
7. The typical North American must learn to treat silences as "communication spaces" and not interrupt them.
8. In general, North Americans must learn to avoid gesturing with the hand. Nonverbal communication training can help businesspeople avoid some of these communication pitfalls.[44]

michaeljung/Shutterstock.com

Both the individual and the company benefit from experiences gained from international assignments.

Cultural Training

Cross-cultural differences represent one of the most elusive aspects of international business. Brazilians tend to perceive North Americans as always in a hurry, serious, reserved, and methodical, whereas the Japanese view North Americans as relaxed, friendly, and impulsive. Why do these different perceptions exist, and how do they affect the way we do business across borders?

Managerial attitudes and behaviours are influenced, in large part, by the society in which managers have received their education and training. Similarly, reactions of employees are the result of cultural conditioning. Every culture has its expectations for the roles of managers and employees. On her first day on the job abroad, one expatriate manager recalls her boss ordering a bottle of wine to split between the two of them at lunch. Although this practice is common in Britain, the expatriate manager was initially taken aback. Being successful as a manager depends on one's ability to understand the way things are normally done and to recognize that changes cannot be made abruptly without considerable resistance, and possibly antagonism, on the part of local nationals. Some organizations are finding that by developing a global mindset and encouraging self-training, people are better equipped for an international assignment.[45]

Studying cultural differences can help managers identify and understand work attitudes and motivation in other cultures. When compared with the Japanese, North Americans may feel little loyalty to their organization. In Japan, for example, employees are more likely to feel a strong loyalty to their company, although recent reports show that this may be changing. Japanese companies no longer universally guarantee an employee a job for life, and layoff decisions are increasingly being made on the basis of merit, not seniority—a practice unthinkable in the country in the past. Latin Americans tend to view themselves as working not only for a particular company but also for an individual manager. Thus, managers in Latin American countries can encourage performance only by using personal influence and working through individual members of a group. You may wish to review the information about culture in Chapter 3 and also re-examine the Hofstede model of national culture (**http://geert-hofstede.com/national-culture.html**).

The Hofstede Centre
http://geert-hofstede.com/national-culture.html

One important dimension of leadership, whether we are talking about international or domestic situations, is the degree to which managers invite employee participation in decision making. While finding hard data on employee participation across different countries is difficult, careful observers report that Canadian managers are about in the middle on a continuum of autocratic to democratic decision-making styles. Scandinavian and Australian managers also appear to be in the middle. South American and European managers, especially those from France, Germany, and Italy, are toward the autocratic end of the continuum; Japanese managers are at the most participatory end. Additional information about living, relocating, and working globally, as well as daily news, can be found at EscapeArtist.com (**www.escapeartist.com**).

EscapeArtist.com
www.escapeartist.com

Assessing and Tracking Career Development

International assignments provide some definite developmental and career advantages. For example, working abroad tends to increase a person's responsibilities and influence within the corporation. In addition, it provides a person with a set of experiences that are uniquely beneficial to both the individual and the firm. International assignments can expand a person's career prospects—both in the existing company and possibly elsewhere.

To maximize the career benefits of a global assignment, a candidate should ask two key questions before accepting an international position:

1. Do the organization's senior executives view the firm's international business as a critical part of its operation? Research shows that expatriates with clear goals that truly need to be accomplished are likely to find their assignments more rewarding. Realizing this, fewer companies are sending expatriates abroad for career development purposes only.
2. Within top management, how many executives have a foreign-service assignment in their background, and do they feel it important for one to have overseas experience? Colgate-Palmolive sees a foreign assignment as part of an extended career track rather than as a one-off assignment. A successful international assignment tends to lead to another and another. "Our top priority is to identify, develop, and retain the next two to three generations of leaders," said one Colgate-Palmolive manager. Part of that strategy includes directly using the knowledge of the company's current and former expatriates.

Companies such as SAP inform candidates when they are first employed that a global assignment may be part of their overall career development; it then seeks specific information at the appropriate time about interests and what the employee wants out of the global assignment.[46]

Managing Personal and Family Life

Culture shock
Perpetual stress experienced by people who settle overseas

As noted previously, one of the most frequent causes of an employee's failure to complete an international assignment is personal and family stress. **Culture shock**—a disorientation that causes perpetual stress—is experienced by people who settle overseas for extended periods. The stress is caused by hundreds of jarring and disorienting incidents such as being unable to communicate, having trouble getting the telephone to work, being unable to read the street signs, and a myriad of other everyday matters that are no problem at home. Soon minor frustrations become catastrophic events, and one feels helpless and drained, emotionally and physically.

In Chapter 5, it was noted that more and more employers are helping dual-career couples to find suitable employment in the same location. To accommodate such partnerships, some employers are providing informal help finding jobs for the spouses of international transferees. Many industry studies have indicated that the #1 reason people refuse international assignments or the assignment fails is partner/spousal issues.[47] To improve this, some companies are establishing more formal programs to assist expatriate couples. These include career- and life-planning counselling, continuing education, intercompany networks to identify job openings in other companies, and job-hunting/fact-finding trips.

Repatriation

An increasing number of companies such as Enbridge are developing programs specifically designed to facilitate **repatriation**—that is, helping employees make the transition back home. Coming back is often difficult. An employee recently repatriated from Colombia walked outside his Edmonton office and waited for his driver, not remembering that he had driven his own car to work. Another family, repatriated from Kazakhstan, had to be restrained from purchasing all the fresh vegetables at the supermarket, because over there, if there was fresh produce you hoarded it because it might not be there next week. Repatriation programs are designed to prepare employees for adjusting to life at home (which at times can be more difficult than adjusting to a foreign assignment). ExxonMobil employees are given a general idea of what to expect following a foreign assignment even before they leave home. Unfortunately, not all companies have career development programs designed for repatriating employees. A recent study by the Canadian Employee Relocation Council (CERC, **www.cerc.ca**) found that few organizations have a structured program to repatriate employees. This can be quite problematic if a situation arises in which the person on a global assignment has to be terminated.[48] The company may have to take into consideration host country labour laws and not just rely upon the contractual terms of the global assignment.[49]

Repatriation
Process of employee transition home from an international assignment

Canadian Employee Relocation Council
www.cerc.ca

A recent survey undertaken by CERC indicated that the top reasons employees decline such an assignment are family issues, concerns over spouse/partner career, and the housing costs in a new location. It further identified that the average age of the employee on an international assignment is 26 to 40.[50]

Employees often lament that their organizations are vague about repatriation, about their new roles within the company, and about their career progression. In many cases, employees abroad have learned how to run an entire international operation—or at least significant parts of it. When they return home, however, their responsibilities are often significantly diminished. In fact, the evidence suggests that only a fraction of them are promoted. It is also not uncommon for employees to return home after a few years to find *no* position for them in the firm and no one they know who can help them. Employees often feel that their firms disregard their difficulties in adjusting to life back in Canada.

Even when employees are successfully repatriated, their companies often do not fully utilize the knowledge, understanding, and skills developed on these global assignments. This hurts the employee, of course, but it may hurt equally the firm's chances of using that employee's expertise to gain competitive advantage. Not surprisingly, expatriates sometimes leave their company within a year or two of coming home. Since as many as 50% of returning employees leave the company soon after their return, one global expert suggests that the key to making the repatriation successful is communication—constantly so that the employees will have good information about what to expect on the return.

At companies with good repatriation processes, employees are given guidance about how much the expatriate experience may have changed them and their families. Some firms introduce former expatriates and their spouses to other former expatriates at special social events. And more companies are making an effort to keep in touch with expatriates while they are abroad, which has been made easier by e-mail, instant messaging, and video conferencing. Colgate's division executives and other corporate staff members frequently visit international transferees. Dow appoints a high-level manager who serves as a home-country contact for information about organizational changes, job opportunities, and anything related to compensation. However, a recent report indicated that many firms are now spending less on international assignments that over time could influence the number of people willing to accept such work.[51]

REWARDS AND RECOGNITION

LO6

What are the characteristics of a good international rewards and recognition program?

One of the most complex areas of international HRM is compensation. Different countries have different norms for employee compensation. Managers should consider carefully the motivational use of incentives and rewards in foreign countries. For North Americans, while nonfinancial incentives such as prestige, independence, and influence may be motivators, money is likely to be the driving force. And the concern is not just for larger organizations.

Other cultures are more likely to emphasize respect, family, job security, a satisfying personal life, social acceptance, advancement, or power. Since there are many alternatives to money, the rule is to match the reward with the values of the culture. In individualistic cultures, such as Canada, pay plans often focus on individual performance and achievement. However, in collectivist societies such as Asian and South American societies, people may value group relationships more than promotions.[52]

In general, a guiding philosophy for designing pay systems might be "think globally and act locally." That is, executives should normally try to create a pay plan that supports the overall strategic intent of the organization but provides enough flexibility to customize particular policies and programs to meet the needs of employees in specific locations.

After a brief discussion of compensation practices for host-country employees and managers, the focus will be on the problems of compensating expatriates.

Compensation of Host-Country Employees

As shown in Figure 11.8, hourly compensation can vary dramatically from country to country, from about $67 in Norway to $22 in Israel and South Korea.[53] Host-country employees are generally paid on the basis of productivity, time spent on the job, or a combination of these factors. In industrialized countries, pay is generally by the hour; in developing countries, by the day. The piece-rate method is also quite common. In some countries, including Japan, seniority is an important element in determining employees' pay rates. When companies commence operations in a foreign country, they usually set their wage rates at or slightly higher than the prevailing wage for local companies. Eventually, though, they are urged to conform to local practices to avoid "upsetting" local compensation practices.

Large companies such as McDonald's or Walmart can almost dictate what they pay. For example, McDonald's U.S. decided in April 2015 to raise pay by more than 10% and include some additional benefits.[54] It should also be noted that there was a protest by its workers in late 2014, some of whom were arrested for a sit-in in Times Square, demanding higher wages.[55] However, at the same time, Walmart was cutting health insurance for part-time employees as a way to manage costs.[56] And then you have companies like IKEA, which is planning to increase its minimum wage in the United States to $11.87.[57]

Employee benefits can range dramatically from country to country as well. And more companies are now creating targeted benefits packages for people working in global assignments so that costs can be better managed such as using hired drivers in Singapore since the cost of drivers' licenses are so expense.[58] In Sweden, for example, paid maternity leave remains at 480 days while some countries such as the United Kingdom and Greece have reduced benefits due to economic concerns.[59] Then you have situations in India where 45 law officers in Chandigarh (a city in northern India) had not been paid for almost a year as the government had no money while other parts of India reduced the retirement age from 60 to 58.[60]

Labour costs are one of the biggest motivators for international expansion, but many managerial and administrative issues must be addressed when an organization establishes operations overseas. For example, bad press can be generated for charging hundreds of dollars for individual products while the people who make them—sometimes children in developing countries working under poor conditions—earn only a few cents. Bad press can also be generated when an organization is accused of paying people inappropriately. See Ethics in HRM 11.1 for the story of a government department in India.

FIGURE 11.8 Hourly Compensation Costs in Different Countries for Workers in Manufacturing

Country	$/Hour (U.S. dollars)
Norway	65.86
Switzerland	63.23
Belgium	54.88
Sweden	51.10
Denmark	51.07
Germany	48.98
Australia	47.09
Finland	44.57
Austria	44,36
France	42.85
Netherlands	42.26
Ireland	41.98
Italy	36.92
United States	36.34
Canada	**36.33**
United Kingdom	31.00
Japan	29.13
Spain	28.09
New Zealand	25.85
Singapore	23.95
Israel	22.25
South Korea	21.96

Source: The Conference Board, "International Comparisons of Hourly Compensation Costs in Manufacturing, 2013," December 2014.

Compensation of Host-Country Managers

In the past, remuneration of host-country managers has been ruled by local salary levels; however, increased competition among different companies with subsidiaries in the same country has led to a gradual upgrading of host-country managers' salaries. Overall, international firms are moving toward a narrowing of the salary gap between the host-country manager and the expatriate. For example, the expected salary for a warehouse manager in either Shanghai or Beijing ranges from $3,000–$6,000 per month.[61] There is a recognition that talent is scarce and competition is intense.

The ongoing global economic challenges are putting pressure on companies to attract and retain the top talent. A number of studies have suggested that this translates into a better link between global performance expectations—both of the company and the individual—and an appropriate rewards package. Talent is mobile, and organizations are learning there is a wide spectrum of approaches for compensating people in an international environment.[62]

ETHICS IN HRM 11.1 FOR HOW MANY YEARS?

While investigations into employee conduct can take many months, in North America we certainly don't expect an investigation to take years and continue paying the employee.

The Central Public Works Department in New Delhi, India, was concerned about the unauthorized leave that an employee in its architectural section. The employee originally was authorized to take a 30-day leave in 1990 for a trip to the U.S. However, the person never returned to work but continued to be an employee and accrue benefits, including pension entitlement, until May 2012! During the intervening years, the employee on several occasions requested leave extensions but none were granted. However, in 1992, an investigation commenced and the employee was asked to appear at a hearing to tell their story before any discipline was determined. But the person never appeared, and the government official doing the investigation left. Other people took over the file but nothing ever happened. Then in May 2012, the person was eligible to retire and did so, and the investigation concluded with a decision that the person ought to have the pension reduced to compensate for everything that had gone on for all those years.

CRITICAL THINKING QUESTIONS:

1. Do you think other people involved in this situation ought to be disciplined? Explain your answer.
2. Do you think something like this could happen in a government department in Canada? Why or why not?

Source: Adapted from Dipak Dash, "CPWD Staff Retires After 22-Year Leave, Probe Drags On," *The Times of India*, November 28, 2014, 6.

Compensation of Expatriate Managers

If the assignment is going to be successful, the expatriate's compensation plan must be competitive, cost-effective, motivating, fair, easy to understand, consistent with international financial management, easy to administer, and simple to communicate.

For short-term assignments, usually those that are project-based, expatriates are frequently given *per diem* (per-day) compensation. These managers might reside in hotels and service apartments instead of leasing houses. They are also less likely to bring their family members with them. The assignment becomes more like a commuting assignment in which the expatriate spends the week in the host country and returns home on the weekend.

For longer-term assignments, there are two basic types of compensation systems. The first is home-based pay, which is based on the compensation practices of the expatriate's home country. For example, an airline pilot working for KLM Dutch Airlines and living in Vancouver is paid in euros. The second type of compensation system is host-based pay. Companies are under pressure to move expatriates to this type of pay because it is generally less costly. Host-based pay is compensation equivalent to that earned by employees in the country in which the expatriate is on assignment. It is given in the local currency, along with the local benefits, which means that fluctuations in currency exchange can affect the expat manager.[63]

Whether a company uses home-based or host-based pay depends on whether the employee may also depend on the cost of living within a particular country. For example, Switzerland and Norway are very expensive countries, whereas India and Serbia are the least expensive.[64]

A serious issue related to expatriate compensation is medical care when a major event, such as the Ebola crisis in 2014 in West Africa or the ongoing political unrest in the Middle East, occurs. Employees are unlikely to consent to a global assignment if they cannot get health care comparable to what's available in their home countries, including medical evacuation if that is necessary.[65] Often, Canadian-based plans can't cover expatriate employees or efficiently deal with claims that need to be reimbursed in foreign currency. One solution is to transfer the employee to a global employment company that can provide these types of benefits.

PERFORMANCE MANAGEMENT

As we noted earlier, individuals frequently accept international assignments because they know they can acquire skills and experiences that will make them more valuable to their companies. Frequently, however, it can be difficult for the home office to assess the performance of employees working abroad. Even the notion of performance assessment is indicative of a North American management style that focuses on the individual, something that can cause problems in Asian countries such as China, Japan, and Korea and Eastern European countries such as Hungary and the Czech Republic.

LO7

What are the difficulties with managing performance internationally?

Who Should Be Involved?

In many cases, an individual working internationally has at least 2 allegiances: one to his or her home country (the office that made the assignment) and the other to the host country in which the employee is currently working. Superiors in each location frequently have different information about the employee's performance and may also have very different expectations about what constitutes good performance. For these reasons, the multiple-rater (360-degree) review discussed in Chapter 7 is finding favour among global firms.

Home- vs. Host-Country Reviews

Domestic managers are frequently unable to understand expatriate experiences, value them, or accurately measure their contribution to the organization. Geographical distances create communication problems for expatriates and home-country managers even with the use of technology such as e-mail and instant messaging. And although local managers with daily contact with expatriates are more likely to have an accurate understanding of their performance, there can still be problems. First, local cultures may influence one's perception of how well an individual is performing. As noted earlier in the chapter, participative decision making may be viewed either positively or negatively, depending on the culture. Such cultural biases may not have any bearing on an individual's true level of effectiveness. In addition, local management frequently does not have enough perspective on the entire organization to know how well an individual is contributing to the firm as a whole.

Given the pros and cons of home-country and host-country reviews, most observers agree that performance reviews should try to balance the 2 sources of performance information. Although host-country employees are in a good position to view day-to-day activities, in many cases the individual is still formally tied to the home office. Promotions, pay, and other administrative decisions are connected there, and as a consequence, the home-country manager usually handles the written evaluation. Nevertheless, the review should be completed only after vital input has been gained from the host-country manager.

Performance Criteria

Because expatriate assignments are so costly, organizations are increasingly under pressure to calculate the return on investment of these assignments. What did the firm get for the $1 million it spent to send an expatriate abroad? Has the expatriate achieved the goals set forth in the assignment in the appropriate time frame? Obviously, the goals and responsibilities inherent in the job assignment are among the most important criteria used to assess an individual's performance, and different goals necessitate measuring different criteria. Using a return-on-investment (ROI) approach, similar to what was discussed in Chapter 6, for determining the value of training and development, can be lacking. Productivity, profits,

Using video conferencing is a good way to have contact with staff working in other countries.

Blend Images/Shutterstock.com

and market share, while valid, may not capture the full range of an expatriate's responsibility. Leadership development, for example, involves a much longer-term value proposition. In many cases, an expatriate is an ambassador for the company, and a significant part of the job is cultivating relationships with citizens of the host country. As discussed at the beginning of this chapter, an individual's success or failure is affected by a host of technical and personal factors. For example, as one might guess, it is much easier to adjust to similar cultures than to dissimilar ones. A Canadian can usually travel to the United Kingdom or Australia and work with locals almost immediately. Send the same individual to Hungary or Malaysia, and the learning curve is steeper.

Providing Feedback

Performance feedback in an international setting is clearly a 2-way street. Although the home-country and host-country superiors may tell expatriates how well they are doing, it is also important for expatriates to provide feedback regarding the support they are receiving, the obstacles they face, and the suggestions they have about the assignment. More than in almost any other job, expatriates are in the best position to evaluate their own performance.

In providing feedback to expatriates, here are some tips:

1. Create and maintain a trusting relationship between the employee and supervisor.
2. Help employees identify and focus on most important objectives.
3. Be involved in all aspects of employees' lives to ensure no external issues are creating problems.
4. Establish regular meetings, whether in person or via technology.
5. Hold employees accountable for outcomes.[66]

If the performance is not successful after review and coaching, careful attention needs to be paid to the local environment before terminating an employee. In some cases, such as China, employees can be terminated only for cause (discussed in Chapter 9); in other cases, such as in France, a prescribed procedure must be followed.[67] Read HRM and the Law 11.1 to learn what a U.S. company did in relation to its CEO.

HRM AND THE LAW 11.1 FIRING A CEO FOR SEXUAL HARASSMENT?

Many organizations throughout the world would not tolerate any form of sexual harassment. Why, then, would a successful company in the United States allow inappropriate behaviour of its CEO toward women for many years?

There is no easy answer to the dilemma. American Apparel, a very successful clothing manufacturer headquartered in Los Angeles, California, fired its CEO in late 2014 for ongoing inappropriate conduct. Depending on whom you ask, the issues began to surface in 2004 when the CEO was accused of wrong conduct during an interview for a magazine. The following year a number of sexual harassment lawsuits began accusing him of everything from sexist comments to walking around in his office in his underwear. He continued in his role as CEO even after a 2010 decision by the Equal Employment Opportunity Commission that he had discriminated against women.

For many years, men in positions of power have been allowed to behave inappropriately to women, in particular. With the rise of social media and easy communication of information, tolerance of this type of behaviour is being dealt with.

What may have been the CEO's downfall was a video of him walking around naked at work that appeared online in early 2014. It is also possible that as the situation became more and more public the board of directors had no other choice but to terminate to ensure that the business—which caters to women's apparel—was not put in jeopardy. The termination also included allegations that funds were used improperly for family travel.

In addition to the termination, the board approved a new sexual harassment policy that includes a prohibition of dating even casually. This approval occurred after the board had reorganized the company's management and added a woman to the board.

CRITICAL THINKING QUESTIONS:

1. Why do you think the board waited so long to take action? Explain your answer.
2. If you were on the board, what would you have done, when, and why?

Sources: Adapted from Matt Townsend, "American Apparel Strengthens Sexual Harassment Rules," *The Vancouver Sun*, January 10, 2015, D5; Frank Bruni, "A Grope and a Shrug," *The New York Times*, June 30, 2014, accessed June 27, 2015, **www.nytimes.com/2014/07/01/opinion/frank-bruni-dov-charney-american-apparel-and-sexual-harassment.html?_r=0**; and Hayley Peterson and Ashley Lutz, "How the Founder and CEO of American Apparel Went from Mega-Mogul to Sleeping on a Friend's Couch," *Financial Post*, December 23, 2014, accessed June 27, 2015, **http://business.financialpost.com/business-insider/how-the-founder-and-ceo-of-american-apparel-went-from-mega-mogul-to-sleeping-on-a-friends-couch**.

THE LABOUR ENVIRONMENT WORLDWIDE

LO8

How do labour relations differ around the world?

Labour relations in countries outside Canada differ significantly from those here. Differences exist not only in the collective bargaining process but also in the political and legal conditions. For example, the EU prohibits discrimination against workers in unions, but in many countries labour unions are illegal. China has only one officially recognized organization of workers, the All-China Federation of Trade Unions, but as China's economy slows, more workers, foreign companies are seeing more labour unrest and more aggression on the part of workers.[68]

Other examples of the labour environment in other countries include the investigation into the deaths of over 1,000 people at a Bangladesh factory. What is unusual is that owner of the factory has now been formally charged with murder.[69] Further, the labour laws in India are being blamed for poor economic performance, as it is almost impossible to fire anyone without agreement between its unions and the company.[70] To gain a basic idea about labour–management relations in an international setting, we will look at 4 primary areas: (1) the role of unions in different countries, (2) collective bargaining in other countries, (3) international labour organizations, and (4) the extent of labour participation in management.

The Role of Unions

The role of unions varies from country to country and depends on many factors, such as the level of employee participation, per capita labour income, mobility between management and labour, homogeneity of labour (racial, religious, social class), and unemployment levels. These and other factors determine whether the union will have the strength it needs to represent labour effectively. Nearly all of Sweden's workers are organized, giving the unions in this country considerable strength and autonomy. By contrast, in countries with relatively high unemployment, low pay levels, and no union funds with which to support social welfare systems, unions are driven into alliance with other organizations: political party, church, or government. This kind of relationship is in marked contrast to Canada, where the union selected by the majority of employees bargains only with the employer, not with other institutions. As mentioned earlier in this section, China has a central union that is more aligned with employers than the employees.

There are many examples of union unrest in the global economy. For example, the rail union in Germany, GDL, shut the entire system down in early May 2015, which is estimated to have cost the German economy many hundred million euros.[71] Likewise, there have been ongoing disputes between Greece and its creditors to reform pension and labour laws—something that the Greek government knows would create shutdowns by unionized workers.[72] On the other hand, Chile boosted the power of its unions to ensure that there is no labour unrest and improve its income inequality.[73] Unions in India decided not to stage a sit-in at a state legislature protesting the decision to remove a tax on natural gas when the companies decided to restart the gas plants and bring people back to work.[74] As well, unions in the United States are targeting fast-food franchisers in a bid to help the franchise owner have more protection from the corporation.[75] And lastly, union activists in France physically attacked 2 managers at Air France when an announcement was made that the company would be laying off 3,000 staff as it restructured.[76]

Collective Bargaining in Other Countries

In Chapter 10, you studied the collective bargaining process as typically carried out in companies operating in Canada. In other countries, the whole process can vary widely, especially with regard to the role of government. In Australia and New Zealand, for most of the 20th century, labour courts had the authority to impose wages and other employment conditions on a broad range of firms. In the United Kingdom and France, the government intervenes in all aspects of collective bargaining. Government involvement is only natural where parts of industry are nationalized. Also, in countries where nationalization is heavy, government involvement is more likely to be accepted, even in the non-nationalized companies.

International Labour Organizations

International Confederation of Free Trade Unions
www.icftu.org

European Trade Union Confederation
www.etuc.org

International Labor Organization
www.ilo.org

The most active of the international union organizations has been the International Confederation of Free Trade Unions (ICFTU, **www.icftu.org**), which has its headquarters in Brussels. Co-operating with the ICFTU are numerous International Trade Secretariats (ITSs), which are really international federations of national trade unions operating in the same or related industries. In addition to the ITSs, the ICFTU also co-operates with the European Trade Union Confederation (ETUC, **www.etuc.org**) that represents over 90 national trade organizations in 39 countries plus 10 EU trade union federations and is focused on defending fundamental social values such as equality.[77] Another active and influential organization is the International Labor Organization (ILO, **www.ilo.org**), a specialized agency of the United Nations. The ILO perhaps has had the greatest impact on the rights of workers throughout the world. It promotes the rights of workers to organize, the eradication of forced and child labour, and the elimination of discrimination. Read At Work with HRM 11.4 to learn more about the ILO from one of Canada's representatives.

Labour Participation in Management

In many European countries, law establishes provisions for employee representation. An employer may be legally required to provide for employee representation on safety and hygiene committees, worker councils, or even on boards of directors. While their responsibilities vary from country to country, worker councils basically provide a communication channel between employers and workers. The legal codes that set forth the functions of worker councils in France are very detailed. Councils are generally concerned with grievances, problems of individual employees, internal regulations, and matters affecting employee welfare.

A higher form of worker participation in management is found in Germany, where law requires representation of labour on the board of directors of a company. This arrangement is known as **codetermination** and often by its German word, *Mitbestimmung*. While sometimes puzzling to outsiders, the system is fairly simple: company shareholders and employees are required to be represented in equal numbers on the supervisory boards of all corporations with more than 2,000 employees.

Codetermination
Representation of labour on the board of directors of a company

Concluding Comments

Each of these differences makes managing human resources in an international context more challenging. But the crux of the issue in designing HRM systems is not choosing one approach that will meet all the demands of international business. Instead, organizations facing global competition must balance several approaches and make their policies flexible enough to accommodate differences across national borders. Throughout this book we have noted that different situations call for different approaches to managing people, and nowhere is this point more clearly evident than in international HRM.

As the discussion on international HRM draws to a close, remember that whether the world is less volatile or not, today's organizations will need to be vigilant about employee engagement in a global context. There is, and will continue to be, competition for global talent, and companies will need to monitor and take actions to motivate and engage

AT WORK WITH HRM 11.4

WHAT A PRIVILEGE!

What's it like being one of Canada's representatives to the International Labour Organization (ILO)? Just ask John Beckett, Vice-President, Training, Safety and Recruitment for the B.C. Maritime Employers Association, and he will describe the privilege it is to be one of Canada's employer representatives on one of the ILO's committees.

The ILO, as an agency of the United Nations, is funded by the United Nations, which is funded by member countries. The ILO is considered to be the "house of labour," with labour, employer, and government representatives. While it started in the early 1900s, it wasn't until after World War II that it really took off. As John states, "The primary mandate is for continuous improvement on social issues throughout the world." Much of its focus has been on labour issues.

Typically, the ILO identifies 3 or 4 areas every year in which active work occurs by the members. John, as a representative of Canada, sits on one of the ILO's subcommittees. This particularly committee, labour inspection protocols, has about 400 members. While it might seem that this is quite a few for getting things done, in fact things do get done, and new standards called "conventions" are agreed to. Then each member country can choose to adopt or accept the convention and develop legislation to support it. Canada has a good track record of adopting the various conventions over the years.

What's the most interesting aspect of John's work? "It is the international reach of the ILO in social programs and reforms," says John. "And it is great being part of the changes that happen."

CRITICAL THINKING QUESTION:

Why else might John Beckett consider his role privilege? Explain.

employees all over the world.[78] Furthermore, as already demonstrated, multinational companies will relocate operations that provide a competitive advantage—whether in terms of natural resources, cost of labour, or inducements by governments.

Are the factors in employee engagement different for global assignments than for domestic ones? No, all organizations are concerned with the attraction and retention of talent.[79] After that, the differences depend on the country although flexibility and appropriate compensation for the assignments are also important.[80]

Moving forward with a still struggling global economy, organizations will have to continue with an emphasis on talent management in order to succeed in what is now a solid global economy. Consider the other areas to watch in Emerging Trends 11.1.

EMERGING TRENDS 11.1

1. ***Advances of technology.*** With ongoing technological advancements in communication, it is easier to have a global workforce feel and act more connected.
2. ***Global talent attraction and retention.*** The global workforce is changing and employers need to understand. For example, there are multigenerational workforces and more women entering the workforce in some countries. Likewise, there are certain skill gaps throughout the world.
3. ***Changes in cultural diversity.*** As more women move through the employment ranks, even in countries where women have not been traditionally been highly respected, there is pressure to develop and promote women to higher levels.
4. ***Aligning HR practices throughout global companies.*** Although there is always a need to customize HR practices to a specific geographic environment, there is a desire to align practices such as tracking employees, managing performance, and identifying future leaders.
5. ***Focusing on employee engagement.*** Even global companies have concerns about employee engagement and therefore develop strategies for its international operations to keep employees engaged and operating at their peak.
6. ***Reforming pensions.*** With the continual sluggish world economy, more countries are examining public pensions, and pensioners are becoming more vocal when their funds have been invested in organizations that appear to have excessive pay for executives.

Sources: Adapted from "What's Next: Future Global HR Trends," *Society of Human Resource Management Foundation*, accessed June 28, 2015, **http://futurehrtrends.eiu.com/report-2014/challenges-human-resource-management**; Kris Dunn, "Adding Up the Asian Equation at Google," *Workforce*, August 5, 2014, accessed June 28, 2015, **www.workforce.com/articles/20650-adding-up-the-asian-equation-at-google**; Tari Ellis, Chiara Marcati, and Julia M. Sperling, "Promoting Gender Diversity in the Gulf," *McKinsey Insights*, February 2015, **www.mckinsey.com/insights/organization/promoting_gender_diversity_in_the_gulf?cid=other-eml-alt-mkq-mck-oth-1502&p=1**; Takeo Yamaguchi, "Standardizing HR Practices Around the World," *Harvard Business Review*, September 2014, 5; Nicola Middlemiss, "Xerox CEO Says Gender Quotas Won't Work," *HRM Online*, February 10, 2015, accessed February 14, 2015, **www.hrmonline.ca/hr-news/xerox-ceo-says-gender-quotas-wont-work-187990.aspx**; "Driving Success Through Employee Engagement," Towers Watson, 2014; Josephine Cumbo, "Warning Over 'Myopic Behaviour' in Retirement," *Financial Times*, December 8, 2014, 4; and Chris Flood, "Pensions Group Calls for Shareholder Action," *Financial Times*, December 8, 2014, 2.

Summary

1. Identify the types of organizational forms used for competing internationally.
   - International—domestic firm that uses existing capabilities to move into global markets
   - Multinational—fully autonomous units operating in multiple countries
   - Global—multinational firm that maintains control back in the home office
   - Transnational—, firm that attempts to balance local responsiveness with efficiencies of global firm
2. Explain the economic, political-legal, and cultural factors in different countries that need to be considered from an HR perspective.
   - Trade agreements can shift jobs from one location to another.
   - Companies will move or expand operations depending on which country provides best economic return.

- Property rights and intellectual property rights will determine which countries companies do business in.
- Cultural factors include language, religion, values, education, and social structure.

3. Illustrate how Canadian and international HRM differ.
   - Functions such as relocation, orientation, and translation services become more important for global assignments.
   - Decisions need to be made regarding the currency of compensation.
   - More attention is paid to the security of international staff, particularly if the geographic area is high risk.
4. Describe the staffing process for individuals working internationally.
   - Companies can send people from the home country (expatriates).
   - Firms can hire employees who are natives to the host country.
   - Employee recruitment in other countries is subject to more government regulation than in Canada.
5. Discuss the unique training needs for employees who work internationally.
   - Content needs to have information about the country and the country's culture.
   - Language training may be necessary.
   - Special attention needs to be paid to helping the employees manage personal and family life.
   - Some development programs are designed to facilitate repatriation.
6. Outline the characteristics of a good international recognition and rewards program.
   - Different cultures value recognition and rewards differently.
   - Determine whether the employee will be paid through the policies of home or host country and in what currency.
7. Reconcile the difficulties of home- and host-country performance management systems.
   - Decisions need to be made on who will be involved in performance process.
   - Domestic managers may not fully understand the expatriate experiences, so it is a good idea to involve the host-country manager.
   - Performance criteria need to include more than just financial goals.
   - It is important to provide feedback regularly to the expatriate.
8. Explain how labour relations differ around the world.
   - Labour laws are different from one country to another.
   - Government may be more involved in determining wage rates even with unionized staff.
   - Some countries, such as Germany, have a high degree of worker participation.

Need to Know

- Definition of international, multinational, global, and transnational corporation
- Definition of expatriate
- Definition of culture shock

Need to Understand

- Role of economic, political-legal, and cultural issues in global assignments
- Advantages of using home- or host-country nationals
- Contents of training program when someone is taking on global assignment
- Different components of recognition and rewards in an international assignment
- Role home-country manager plays in supporting expatriate
- Differences in international labour relations

KEY TERMS

augmented skills 377
codetermination 389
core skills 377
cultural environment 368
culture shock 380
expatriates, or home-country nationals 371
failure rate 377
global corporation 365
guest workers 374
host country 369
host-country nationals 371
international corporation 364
multinational corporation (MNC) 364
repatriation 381
third-country nationals 371
transnational corporation 365
transnational teams 375
work permit or visa 374

REVIEW QUESTIONS

1. What are the types of organizational forms used for competing internationally?
2. Explain the factors in different countries that need to be considered from an HR perspective.
3. Identify if, and then describe any differences in Canadian and international HR.
4. Describe the staffing process for individuals working abroad.
5. Explain the unique training needs for an individual working internationally.
6. Describe the characteristics of a good international recognition and rewards program.
7. Identify the difficulties between home- and host-country performance management systems.
8. Describe the differences in labour relations around the world.

CRITICAL THINKING QUESTIONS

1. Cirque du Soleil, as described in the HRM Close-up at the beginning of this chapter, and in Case Study 1, is a Canadian icon. What is the challenge and the way Cirque manages that challenge as described by Marie-Josée Guilbault?
2. Examine Figures 11.2 and the list of "Most Admired Companies" at **http://fortune.com/worlds-most-admired-companies**. What reasons would firms from China be in the top 4 on Figure 11.2? What might be some of the reasons the firms on the list of "Most Admired Companies are all from the United States?
3. RBC operates in over 40 countries and employs both Canadians and local staff. What are the advantages of employing Canadians with roots in the host country? Would you use expatriate managers or host-country nationals to staff RBC offices? Explain.
4. How can Canadian managers minimize any difficulties in relationships with employees in a foreign operation?
5. How can learning about different cultures be incorporated into a manger's professional development plan and how could the organization assess the learning?
6. If the cost of living is higher in a foreign country than in Canada, would the expatriate be paid more or less than in Canada? Explain.
7. Bombardier Inc. recently fired an employee for accepting confidential information about a Dutch train contract in which the Dutch company was going to purchase a new fleet of trains. Since selling and receiving confidential information occurs throughout the world, do you think the employee ought to have been fired? Why or why not?

DEVELOPING YOUR SKILLS

The Globe and Mail Top Publicly Traded Companies
www.theglobeandmail.com/report-on-business/rob-magazine/top-1000

1. Access the archives of *The Globe and Mail* rankings of the top Canadian companies at **www.theglobeandmail.com/report-on-business/rob-magazine/top-1000**. Access the 2014 or 2013 list in the archives. What differences do you notice? What might be some of the reasons?

2. Using any search engine, do a search on "resources for expatriates." Examine the top 5 different resources? What might be the most useful if you were thinking of working in another country?
3. Access the Expatriate Foundation (**http://expatriatefoundation.org**) and click on the "Resources" link. Pick one of the resources and examine more closely. How useful was it? Why?
4. Access WageIndicator.org (**www.wageindicator.org/main**), find a country that is of interest to you for possible work. Think of a type of work you are interested in and see what the wages are for that work in that country. Is it what you thought? Explain.

Expatriate Foundation
http://expatriatefoundation.org

WageIndicator.org
www.wageindicator.org

CASE STUDY 1

And the Show Goes On!

What happens when the creative force that started Cirque du Soleil sells 60% of his company to a U.S. investment group and 20% to a Chinese investment group? An increase in the Chinese market for its shows, is what Guy Laliberté is expecting.

Cirque du Soleil is certainly one of Canada's foremost known exports, with shows in many parts of the world, including Germany, Australia, Singapore, and Israel, to name a few. With more than 4,000 employees worldwide, the employee base represents over 50 different nationalities that speak 25 different languages. Also of note is that over 150 million people have seen one of its shows since it was started in 1984 by Laliberté, a street performer who had a vision of a different form of entertainment. For anyone who has seen a Cirque performance, it is truly memorable—not anything like a circus!

There has been consideration for a number of years of expanding shows in China. However, since China is a somewhat complex market, careful research is a must before any expansion even with a new financial partner. Laliberté is confident that the Chinese partner knows China well and will assist in both planning and execution of any expansion plans.

While it wasn't clear why the founder and sole owner of the company decided to sell all but 10% of the company, he did indicate that the U.S. private equity firm, TPG, has strong relationships with both media and entertainment that might provide new revenue opportunities for Cirque. Laliberté, however, is planning to main some amount of creative control over Cirque for the time being.

Part of the sale includes an agreement that the headquarters would remain in Montreal—at least as long as TPG is the majority owner. As the new chair of the company states, "The DNA of the company is in its Quebec-based creativity." Its success is attributed to the organizational culture that is maintained by paying attention to it and its values. Also key has been ensuring that business decisions aren't getting in the way of creativity.

Sources: Adapted from Jaela Bernstein, "Cirque du Soleil Selling Majority Stake to Investor TPG," *CBC News*, April 20, 2015, accessed June 29, 2015, **www.cbc.ca/news/canada/montreal/cirque-du-soleil-selling-majority-stake-to-investor-tpg-1.3040202**; "Cirque du Soleil at a Glance," accessed June 29, 2015, **www.cirquedusoleil.com/en/home/about-us/at-a-glance.aspx**; Damon Van der Linde, "Cirque du Soleil Headquarters to Remain in Montreal After Sale to U.S. Firm," *Montreal Gazette*, April 20, 2015, accessed June 29, 2015, **http://montrealgazette.com/business/local-business/cirque-du-soleil-sells-majority-stake-to-u-s-private-equity-firm**; and Jared Lindzon, "For the Cirque's Operational Ringmaster, Creativity Rules," *The Globe and Mail*, March 3, 2015, accessed June 29, 2015, **www.theglobeandmail.com/report-on-business/careers/management/for-the-cirques-operational-ringmaster-creativity-rules/article23263370**.

Questions:

1. What are some of the reasons, besides financial, that Laliberté decided to sell? Explain.
2. What are some concerns Laliberté might have with the new equity partner?
3. What cultural factors may Cirque need to consider when developing and producing shows in China?

CASE STUDY 2

Is Global Competition Good?

What happens when two entrepreneurs start selling coconut water at the same time in the same place? Two great companies competing internationally 10 years later.

Vita Coco, founded by Michael Kirban, and Zico, founded by Mark Rampolla discovered quite accidentally that both started selling coconut water in Manhattan in 2004. Both men were athletically active and found that coconut water was useful in rehydrating. But at the time, this was not friendly competition and soon the tactics that each used garnered the name "coconut wars." Each started out simply: Kirban going around on in-line skates with samples in a backpack and Rampolla driving around in an old van with samples to stores. The reason both picked Manhattan is that it has a very large number of independent stores where the owners can quickly make decisions.

When each discovered that there was a competitor, both entrepreneurs were in shock. Kirban had discovered coconut water in Brazil and was anxious to bring to the U.S.; Rampolla discovered coconut water in Costa Rica and also wanted to build a business selling it in the U.S. With consumers not only being exposed to coconut water for the first time, but also having choices of brands, competition soon became quite visible. Some salespeople learned phrases in Spanish, Arabic, Korean, and Hebrew to pitch to certain audiences.

This competition went on until 2009 when Coca-Cola bought 20% of Zico. Vita Coco responded by selling 10% of its company to a group of celebrities that included Madonna and Demi Moore. Both investments created much media attention and sales were expected to rise.

But like any deal, the outcomes depend on the details. For Vita Coco, it was able to continue accessing distributors that it felt could make a difference. On the other hand, Zico was restricted to how Coke handled distribution—which did not include sales staff that were focused on only Zico.

Where are things today? Rampolla sold all the remaining shares to Coke in late 2014 but it still seen as the face of Zico. Vita Coco continues as a strong independent brand with sales in dozens of countries over the world. Vita Coco also recently announced that it was getting rid of the celebrity ambassadors. Both are embarking on large marketing campaigns as the trend for increased sales continues. Kirban would like to have strong competition, which he believes is good for business, but without the wars, as he did in the beginning.

Sources: Adapted from K. Divan, "The Coconut Wars," *Gladrags Magazine*, December 2014, 88–90; "Our Story," Vita Coco, accessed June 29, 2015, **http://vitacoco.com/our-story**; "Our Story," Zico, accessed June 29, 2015, **http://zico.ca/our-story**; Seth Stevenson, "Gatorade Is the Antichrist," *Slate*, accessed June 29, 2015, **www.slate.com/articles/business/branded/2011/11/coconut_water_why_is_it_suddenly_so_popular_.html**; and Declan Harty, "Jessica Alba Returns for Zico as Vita Coco Ditches Celebs," *Advertising Age*, June 6, 2015, accessed June 29, 2015, **http://adage.com/article/advertising/zico-coconut-water-vita-coco-launch-summer-campaigns/298899**.

Questions:

1. What helped to make this a global success?
2. If you were asked to become a sales representative for either company in Asia, what might you need to know about the national culture?

NOTES AND REFERENCES

1. Liz Bernier, "Canada Tops in Attracting Talent," *Canadian HR Reporter*, November 3, 2014, 1; M Rajendran, "More Indians to Head Global Cos: Top Headhunter," *Hindustan Times*, November 25, 2014, 13; and Sarah Dobson, "Following a Not-So-Linear Path," *Canadian HR Reporter*, May 4, 2015, 19.
2. Jason Lane and Kevin Kinser, "Have Our Universities Become Multinational Corporations?" *Newsweek*, June 14, 2015, accessed June 14, 2015, www.newsweek.com/have-our-universities-become-multinational-corporations-342346.

3. Daina Lawrence, "Canadian Schools Are Taking the Classroom to Where The Students Live," *The Globe and Mail*, June 16, 2015, B10.
4. "About Barrick," Barrick Gold, accessed June 14, 2015, http://barrickbeyondborders.com/search-results/?q=global+overview.
5. Forbes staff, "2015 Global 2000: Methodology," *Forbes*, May 6, 2015, accessed June 14, 2015, www.forbes.com/sites/andreamurphy/2015/05/06/2015-global-2000-methodology.
6. "Methodology: World's Most Admired Companies," *Fortune*, accessed June 14, 2015, http://fortune.com/worlds-most-admired-companies.
7. "The 100 Best Companies to Work For," *Fortune*, March 15, 2015, 143.
8. Richard Blackwell, "A Dozen Canadian Firms Crack List of World's Top 100 Sustainable Companies," *The Globe and Mail*, January 21, 2015, accessed June 15, 2015, www.theglobeandmail.com/report-on-business/a-dozen-canadian-firms-crack-list-of-worlds-top-100-sustainable-companies/article22554162; and "2015 Global 100 Most Sustainable Corporations in the World," January 21, 2015, accessed June 15, 2015, www.corporateknights.com/reports/global-100/2015-global-100-results-14218559.
9. Marina Strauss, "Hudson's Bay Set to Buy German Chain," *The Globe and Mail*, June 15, 2015, B1.
10. Marina Strauss, "HBC Eyes European Launch for Saks," *The Globe and Mail*, June 16, 2015, B1.
11. "Canada's 100 Biggest Companies by Revenue," *The Globe and Mail*, June 24, 2014, www.theglobeandmail.com/report-on-business/rob-magazine/top-1000/rankings/canadas-100-biggest-companies-by-revenue/article19312502.
12. "Countries," accessed June 15, 2015, http://europa.eu/about-eu/countries/index_en.htm.
13. James Kanter, Alison Smale, and Niki Kitsantonis, "EU Urged to Plan for Greece to Default," *The Globe and Mail*, June 16, 2015, B9.
14. "NAFTA @ 20—Fast Facts," Foreign Affairs and International Trade Canada, accessed June 15, 2015, www.international.gc.ca/trade-agreements-accords-commerciaux/agr-acc/nafta-alena/facts.aspx?lang=eng.
15. *International Commerce—By Country*, Foreign Affairs and International Trade Canada, 2011, accessed June 15, 2015, www.international.gc.ca/Commerce_International/Commerce_Country-Pays.aspx?lang=eng.
16. "GDP Growth in China 1952-2014," accessed June 15, 2015, http://chinability.com/GDP.htm.
17. Paul Koring, "Obama Nears Landmark Trade Pact," *The Globe and Mail*, June 24, 2015, A1.
18. Barrie McKenna and John Ibbitson, "TPP Pact Will Put Pressure on Canadian Dairy, Poultry Industries," *The Globe and Mail*, June 25, 2015, A1.
19. Brent Snavely, "Pace of Auto Industry Mergers Hits Seven-Year High," *Detroit Free Press*, November 4, 2014, accessed June 15, 2015, www.freep.com/story/money/cars/2014/11/04/automotive-merger-acquisition-pricewaterhousecoopers-fiat-chrysler/18487615.
20. Ibid.
21. "GM, Isuzu Partner on Truck Line," *The Vancouver Sun*, June 17, 2015, C1.
22. "GDP (Current US$)," The World Bank, 2014, accessed June 15, 2015, http://data.worldbank.org/indicator/NY.GDP.MKTP.CD; and "BRICS in Numbers," June 10, 2015, accessed June 15, 2015, http://en.brics2015.ru.
23. Gauri Kohli, "Potential for Hospitality," *Hindustan Times*, November 25, 2014, 17.
24. "Canada–Korea Free Trade Agreement (CKFTA)," Foreign Affairs and International Trade Canada, January 1, 2015, accessed June 15, 2015, www.international.gc.ca/trade-agreements-accords-commerciaux/agr-acc/korea-coree/index.aspx?lang=eng&utm_source=dfatd-maecd&utm_medium=dfatd-maecd&utm_campaign=ckfta-alecc; and Bill Curry, "Canada-South Korea Free-Trade Deal Shows Small Gains for Both Sides: Report," *The Globe and Mail*, January 15, 2015, www.theglobeandmail.com/news/politics/canada-south-korea-free-trade-deal-shows-small-gains-for-both-sides-report/article22455748.
25. David Israelson, "South Korea Trade Agreement Helped Ink Tech Deal," *The Globe and Mail*, May 12, 2015, accessed June 16, 2015, www.theglobeandmail.com/report-on-business/international-business/south-korea-trade-agreement-helped-ink-tech-deal/article24379088.
26. Ben McLannahan, "Titans Slim Down and Fight Back," *Financial Times*, December 8, 2014, 1.
27. Christopher Donville and Willem Marx, "Beetle Plague Pushes Canadian Firms to buy U.S. Mills," *The Globe and Mail*, June 24, 2015, B7.
28. "Japanese Firms are Improving Results by Boosting Motivation," *The Vancouver Sun*, January 17, 2015, F6.
29. Iulian Warter and Liviu Warter, "The New Face of Global M & A: Intercultural Issues in the Banking Industry," *Forum Scientiae Oeconomia* 3, no. 1 (2015): 127–138.
30. Sarah Dobson, "A Tale of 2 Cities," *Canadian HR Reporter*, July 14, 2014, accessed June 16, 2015, www.hrreporter.com/articleview/21712-a-tale-of-2-cities.
31. Brenda Bouw, "The Growing Appeal of Working Abroad," *The Globe and Mail*, July 2, 2014, B10.
32. Anne Harvey, vice-president, Employee Engagement, Vancouver Coastal Health Authority, interview by author, June 2015.
33. Lubna Kably, "Strict UK Laws Seek to Scan Migrants' Job Role," *The Times of India*, December 8, 2014, 17.
34. "Employers Worldwide Explore Alternative Mobility Strategies," Mercer, 2014, accessed June 20, 2015, www.mercer.ca/content/mercer/north-america/ca/en/insights/view/2014/employers-worldwide-explore-alternative-mobility-strategies.html.
35. Luc Minguet, "Creating a Culturally Sensitive Corporation," *Harvard Business Review*, September 2014, 101–103; Charles Doucot, "Mining for Talent," *Canadian HR Reporter*, February 9, 2015, accessed June 20, 2015, www.hrreporter.com/articleview/23466-mining-for-talent; Sarah Dobson, "Following a Not-So-Linear Path," *Canadian HR Reporter*, May 4, 2015, accessed June 20, 2015, www.hrreporter.com/articleview/24230-following-a-not-so-linear-path; Colette O'Neill, "Employer Brand: A New Weapon in the Recruitment Arsenal," *Canadian HR Reporter*, February 12, 2015, accessed June 20, 2015, www.hrreporter.com/articleview/23520-employer-brand-a-new-weapon-in-the-recruitment-arsenal; and Claudine Kapel, "Rise in Hiring Activity Puts Retention Back in Spotlight," *Canadian HR Reporter*, August 25, 2014, accessed June 20, 2015, www.hrreporter.com/blog/Compensation-Rewards/archive/2014/08/25/rise-in-hiring-activity-puts-retention-back-in-spotlight.
36. "Facts on Education in France: Understanding the Grandes Écoles," accessed June 20, 2015, www.understandfrance.org/France/Education.html#ancre32799.
37. Ana Langovic Milicevic, Vladimir Tomasevic, and Smiljka Isakovic, "The Importance of Successful Project Team Communication in Agribusiness," *Economies of Agriculture*, 2014: 367–379.
38. Eduardo Caride, "Diversifying Talent to Suit Market," *Harvard Business Review*, September 2014, 4–5.
39. Andrea Park, "Found in Translation: Job Applications Go Mobile, Multilingual," *Workforce*, July 14, 2014, accessed June 20, 2015, www.workforce.com/articles/20624-found-in-translation-job-applications-go-mobile-multilingual.
40. Tari Ellis, Chiara Marcati, and Julia M. Sperling, "Promoting Gender Diversity in the Gulf," *McKinsey Quarterly*, February 2015, accessed June 20, 2015, www.mckinsey.com/insights/organization/promoting_gender_diversity_in_the_gulf.

41. Jan Seimer and Jakob Lauring, "Host Country Language Ability and Expatriate Adjustment: The Moderating Effect of Language Difficulty," *The International Journal Of human Resource Management* 26, no. 3 (2015): 401–420.
42. Information supplied to current author by Doug Whitehead, chair of the board of directors, April 2015.
43. "Happy Staff, Happy Customers," *New Zealand Management*, December 1, 2014, 3.
44. Managers who are interested in setting up a language-training program, wish to evaluate commercially available language-training programs, or wish to find appropriate cross-cultural training can use the following resources: Rosetta Stone, www.rosettastone.com; Berlitz, www.berlitz.com; Global Integration, www.global-integration.com; and DFA Intercultural Global Solutions, www.deanfosterassociates.com. Additional resources can be found through continuing education at many local universities or community colleges.
45. Elaine M. Walker, "Expatriate Management," October 13, 2014, accessed June 21, 2015, www.slideshare.net/JaelynBai/expatriate-management-40222453.
46. Sarah Fister Gale, "High-Po's Say: We Won't Go," *Workforce*, January 14, 2015, accessed June 21, 2015, www.workforce.com/articles/21029-high-pos-say-we-wont-go.
47. Dawn S. Onley, "Avert Assignment Failure: Support Spouses in Overseas Relocations," Society of Human Resource Management, March 13, 2014, accessed June 21, 2015, www.shrm.org/hrdisciplines/global/articles/pages/spouses-overseas-relocations.aspx.
48. Julie Lessard, "Avoiding a Long and Costly Journey," *Canadian HR Reporter*, September 8, 2014, 15.
49. Ibid.
50. "2015 Employee Relocation Survey," Canadian Employee Relocation Council, June 21, 2015, https://c.ymcdn.com/sites/www.cerc.ca/resource/resmgr/Research/CERC_2015_Survey_by_the_numb.pdf.
51. Kate Everson, "Special Report: Relocation Sector Keeps Moving Right Along," *Workforce*, July 3, 2014, accessed June 21, 2015, www.workforce.com/articles/20593-special-report-relocation-sector-keeps-moving-right-along.
52. "Cultural Differences," Iowa State University, Center for Excellence in Learning and Teaching, June 21, 2015, www.celt.iastate.edu/celt-resources/international-resources/cultural-differences.
53. Those students interested in how quickly these costs have increased may either look at the 4th edition of this textbook, Figure 11.9 on page 364, or access the U.S. Department of Labor, "International Comparison" for 2008. You'll notice that most of the costs have increased substantially.
54. "McDonald's to Offer Raises, Paid Time Off," *The Globe and Mail*, April 2, 2015, B4.
55. Steven Greenhouse, "Fast-Food Workers Seeking Higher Wages Arrested During Protest," *The Globe and Mail*, September 5, 2014, A9.
56. Shelly Banjo and Stephanie Armour, "Wal-Mart to Cut Health Coverage for More Workers," *The Globe and Mail*, October 5, 2014, B10.
57. Anne D'Innocenzio, "IKEA to Increase Minimum Wage in U.S.," *The Globe and Mail*, June 25, 2015, B11.
58. Karen Pallarito, "Assignments to Asia Present Foreign Benefits Challenges," *Benefits Outlook*, June 22, 2014, accessed June 21, 2015, www.crainsbenefitsoutlook.com/article/20140622/CBO/140619882/assignments-to-asia-present-foreign-benefits-challenges.
59. "Quick Facts: Sweden," accessed June 21, 2015, https://sweden.se/quickfact/parental-leave; *Maternity and Paternity at Work*, International Labour Organization, 2014, 66, and "Paternity Leave Around the World," *HRM Online*, June 16, 2014, accessed June 25, 2015, www.hrmonline.ca/hr-news/paternity-leave-around-the-world.
60. Ajay Sura, "$5 Law Officers Not Paid Salaries Since Last Year," *The Times of India*, November 28, 2014, P3; and Geentanjali Gayatri, "Haryana Staff Retirement Age Back at 58," *The Tribune*, November 26, 2014, 1.
61. "Guide to China Market Salaries 2nd Quarter 2015," J.M. Gemini Personnel Ltd.
62. "5 Important Considerations for Your Global Mobility Program," Mercer, 2015, 20.
63. "Compensating Your Employees for Change," ECA International, February 9, 2015, accessed June 25, 2015, www.eca-international.com/news/articles/8141/Compensating_your_employees_for_change_?HighlightText=host-based+pay#.VYyCDmAseEk.
64. "Cost of Living Index, Updated June 2015," Expatistan, accessed June 25, 2015, www.expatistan.com/cost-of-living/index.
65. Saliou Samb and Stephanie Nebehay, "Miners in Lockdown in Guinea as Ebola Death Toll Hits 84," *Canadian HR Reporter*, April 3, 2014, accessed June 26, 2015, www.hrreporter.com/articleview/20716-miners-in-lockdown-in-guinea-as-ebola-death-toll-hits-84.
66. Jane F. Maley and Miriam Moeller, "Global Performance Management Systems: The Role of Trust as Perceived by Country Managers," *Journal of Business Research* 67, no. 1 (2014): 2803–2810; and Annamarie Mann and Ryan Darby, "Should Managers Focus on Performance or Engagement?" *Gallup Business Journal*, August 2014, 1.
67. Grace Yang, "Terminating China Employees: The Basics," *China Law Blog*, April 17, 2015, accessed June 26, 2015, www.chinalawblog.com/2015/04/terminating-china-employees-the-basics.html; and "The Employment Relationship," Worldwide Consulting Group, accessed June 26, 2015, www.worldwideconsulting.com/france.htm.
68. Kent D. Kedl, "Forbes: With Labor Disputes in China on the Rise, Companies Must Tread Carefully," *China Labour Bulletin*, March 24, 2015, accessed June 26, 2015, www.clb.org.hk/en/content/forbes-labor-disputes-china-rise-companies-must-tread-carefully.
69. "Murder Charges Filed in 2013 Factory Collapse," *The Globe and Mail*, June 2, 2015, B8.
70. Unni Krishnan, "How Decades-Old Labour Laws Strangle Growth," *The Vancouver Sun*, August 18, 2014, A14.
71. Joanna Slater, "Rail Strike Brings Germany to a Halt," *The Globe and Mail*, May 6, 2015, A3.
72. Renee Maltezou and Jan Strupczewski, "Pension, Labour Disputes Dog Greek Talks as Cash Dwindles," *The Globe and Mail*, May 5, 2015, B9.
73. "Chile Boosts Power of Unions, Leaders," *The Vancouver Sun*, December 31, 2014, B1.
74. "FACT Unions Withdraw Plans for Protest in State Capital," *The Hindu*, December 1, 2014, 3.
75. Candice Choi, "Unions Woo Fast-Food Franchisees," *The Vancouver Sun*, May 1, 2015, D5.
76. Lori Hinnant, "Union Attacks Air France Bosses," *The Globe and Mail*, October 6, 2015, A15.
77. European Trade Union Confederation, accessed June 28, 2015, www.etuc.org.
78. Ibid.
79. "5 Important Considerations for Your Global Mobility Program," Mercer, 2015, 5.
80. Ibid.

Glossary

Achievement tests
Measures of what a person knows or can do right now (page 157)

Alternative dispute resolution (ADR)
Term applied to different types of employee complaint or dispute-resolution procedures (page 308)

Apprenticeship training
System of training in which a worker entering the skilled trades is given thorough instruction and experience, both on and off the job, in the practical and theoretical aspects of the work (page 184)

Aptitude tests
Measures of a person's capacity to learn or acquire skills (page 157)

Arbitration award
Final and binding award issued by an arbitrator in a labour–management dispute (page 352)

Arbitrator
Third-party neutral who resolves a labour dispute by issuing a final and binding decision in an agreement (page 345)

Augmented skills
Skills helpful in facilitating the efforts of expatriate managers (page 377)

Balanced Scorecard
A measurement framework that helps managers translate strategic goals into operational objectives (page 227)

Bargaining unit
Group of two or more employees who share common employment interests and conditions and may reasonably be grouped together for purposes of collective bargaining (page 328)

Behaviour modification
Technique that if behaviour is rewarded it will be exhibited more frequently in the future (page 183)

Behavioural description interview (BDI)
Question about what a person did in a given situation (page 153)

Behaviourally anchored rating scale (BARS)
A behavioural approach to performance review that consists of a series of vertical scales, one for each important dimension of job performance (page 224)

Benchmarking
(1) Finding the best practices in other organizations that can be brought into a company to enhance performance (page 16); (2) process of measuring one's own services and practices against the recognized leaders in order to identify areas for improvement (page 190)

Bona fide occupational qualification (BFOQ)
A justifiable reason for discrimination based on business reasons of safety or effectiveness (page 42)

Business agent
Normally a paid labour official responsible for negotiating and administering the collective agreement and working to resolve union members' problems (page 334)

Certification
Acquisition of exclusive rights by union to represent the employees (page 329)

Closed shop
Provision of the collective agreement that requires employers to hire only union members (page 323)

Codetermination
Representation of labour on the board of directors of a company (page 389)

Competency-based pay
Pay based on how many capabilities employees have or how many jobs they can perform (page 258)

Constructive dismissal
Changing an employee's working conditions such that compensation, status, or prestige is reduced (page 305)

Consumer price index (CPI)
Measure of the average change in prices over time in a fixed "market basket" of goods and services (page 252)

Contractor
A person who is hired by contract to perform a specific job and is not considered part of the employee base (page 12)

Contractual rights
Rights that derive from contracts (page 285)

Co-operative training
Training program that combines practical on-the-job experience with formal education (page 185)

Core competencies
A combination of knowledge, skills, and characteristics needed to effectively perform a role in an organization (page 18)

Core skills
Skills considered critical to an employee's success abroad (page 376)

Cultural environment
Communications, religion, values and ideologies, education, and social structure of a country (page 368)

Culture
Consistent and observable pattern of behaviours in organizations (page 20)

Culture shock
Perpetual stress experienced by people who settle overseas (page 380)

Cumulative trauma disorders
Injuries involving tendons of the fingers, hands, and arms that become inflamed from repeated stresses and strains (page 89)

Customer input
Performance review that, like team review, is based on TQM concepts and seeks information from both external and internal customers (page 220)

Cyber bullying
Bullying by using communication technology and information (page 92)

Defined rights
Concept that management's authority should be expressly defined and clarified in the collective agreement (page 347)

Designated groups
Women, visible minorities, First Nations peoples, and persons with disabilities who have been disadvantaged in employment (page 53)

Development
The acquisition of skills, behaviours, and abilities to perform future work

or to solve an organizational problem (page 174)

Direct compensation
Employee wages and salaries, incentives, bonuses, and commissions (page 244)

Disability management
Integrated approach to managing disability-related benefits (page 96)

Discipline
(1) Treatment that punishes, (2) Orderly behaviour in an organizational setting, or (3) Training that moulds and strengthens desirable conduct—or corrects undesirable conduct—and develops self-control (page 297)

Diversity management
The optimization of an organization's multicultural workforce in order to reach business objectives (page 58)

Downsizing
The planned elimination of jobs (page 11)

Due process
Employee's right to a fair process in making a decision related to employment relationship (page 286)

Eldercare
Care provided to an elderly relative by an employee who remains actively at work (page 269)

E-learning
Learning that takes place through electronic media (page 186)

Employee assistance program (EAP)
Program to provide short-term counselling and referrals to appropriate professionals (page 97)

Employee empowerment
Granting employees power to initiate change, thereby encouraging them to take charge of what they do (page 120)

Employee engagement
Amount of commitment and dedication an employee has toward organization (page 76)

Employee rights
Expectations of fair treatment from employers (page 283)

Employee teams
An employee-contributions technique in which work functions are structured for groups rather than for individuals, and team members are given discretion in matters traditionally considered management prerogatives, such as process improvements, product or service development, and individual work assignments (page 122)

Employment branding
An organization's reputation as an employer (page 139)

Employment equity
A distinct Canadian process for achieving equality in all aspects of employment (page 53)

Equitable compensation
Compensation received is perceived to be equal to the value of the work performed (page 247)

Ethics
Set of standards of conduct and moral judgments that help to determine right and wrong behaviour (page 61)

Expatriates or home-country nationals
Employees from the home country who are on international assignment (page 371)

Failure rate
Percentage of expatriates who do not perform satisfactorily (page 377)

Global corporation
Firm that has integrated worldwide operations through a centralized home office (page 365)

Globalization
Moving local or regional business into global marketplace (page 10)

Graphic rating scale
A trait approach to performance review whereby each employee is rated according to a scale of characteristics (page 223)

Grievance procedure
Formal procedure that provides for the union to represent members and nonmembers in processing a grievance (page 349)

Grievance resolution
Process in which a neutral third party assists in the resolution of an employee grievance (page 350)

Guest workers
Foreign workers invited to perform needed labour (page 374)

Harassment
Any unwanted physical or verbal conduct that offends or humiliates the individual (page 45)

Hearing officer
Person who holds a full-time position with an organization but assumes a neutral role when deciding cases between management and the aggrieved employees (page 308)

Host country
Country in which an international corporation operates (page 369)

Host-country nationals
Employees who are natives of the host country (page 371)

Hourly work
Work paid on an hourly basis (page 249)

Human capital
The individual's knowledge, skills, and abilities that have economic value to an organization (page 18)

Human resource planning
Process that the people required to run the company are being used as effectively as possible, where and when they are needed, in order to accomplish the organization's goals (page 134)

Human resources management (HRM)
An integrated set of processes, programs, and systems in an organization that focuses on the effective deployment and development of its employees (page 4)

Human resources management strategy
Identifying key HR processes and linking those to the overall business strategy (page 28)

Inclusion
Putting concepts of diversity into action (page 58)

Indirect compensation
All other forms of rewards such as extended health and dental plans, and other, similar programs and plans (page 244)

Industrial disease
A disease resulting from exposure relating to a particular process, trade, or occupation in industry (page 78)

Instructional objectives
Desired outcomes of a training program (page 181)

Interest arbitration
A mechanism to renew or establish a new collective agreement for parties (page 345)

Interest-based bargaining
Problem-solving bargaining based on a win-win philosophy and the development of a positive long-term relationship (page 340)

Internal job posting
Method of communicating information about job openings (page 140)

International corporation
Domestic firm that uses its existing capabilities to move into overseas markets (page 364)

Internship programs
Programs jointly sponsored by colleges, universities, and other organizations that offer students the opportunity to gain real-life experience while allowing them to find out how they will perform in work organizations (page 185)

Job
A group of related activities and duties (page 108)

Job analysis
Process of obtaining information about jobs by determining the duties, tasks, or activities and the skills, knowledge, and abilities associated with the jobs (page 109)

Job characteristics model
An approach to job design that recognizes the link between motivational factors and components of the job to achieve improved work performance and job satisfaction (page 120)

Job description
A document that lists the tasks, duties, and responsibilities of a job to be performed along with the skills, knowledge, and abilities or competencies needed to successfully perform the work (page 110)

Job design
Process of defining and organizing tasks, roles, and other processes to achieve employee goals and organizational effectiveness (page 118)

Job evaluation
Systematic process of determining the relative worth of jobs in order to establish which jobs should be paid more than others within an organization (page 250)

Job incumbent
The employee hired to do a job (page 109)

Job specifications
Statement of the needed knowledge, skills, and abilities of the person who is to perform the position. The different duties and responsibilities performed by only one employee (page 110)

Labour market
Area from which applicants are recruited (page 142)

Labour relations process
Logical sequence of 4 events: (1) workers desire collective representation, (2) the union begins its organizing campaign, (3) collective negotiations lead to a contract, and (4) the contract is administered (page 322)

Lean
Organizational system of improvements that maximize customer value and minimize waste (page 16)

Lockout
Strategy by which the employer denies employees the opportunity to work by closing its operations (page 344)

Management forecasts
Opinions and judgments of supervisors or managers and others knowledgeable about the organization's future employment needs (page 136)

Management rights
Decisions regarding organizational operations over which management claims exclusive rights (page 331)

Manager and/or supervisor review
Performance review done by the employee's supervisor (page 218)

Markov analysis
Method for tracking the pattern of employee movements through various jobs (page 136)

Material Safety Data Sheet (MSDS)
Documents that contain vital information about hazardous substances (page 87)

Mediation
The use of an impartial third party to help facilitate a resolution to employment disputes (page 308)

Mediator
Third party in a labour dispute who meets with one party and then the other in order to suggest compromise solutions or to recommend concessions from each side that will lead to an agreement (page 345)

Membership card
A statement signed by an employee authorizing a union to act as a representative of the employee for purposes of collective bargaining (page 327)

Mentors
Managers who coach, advise, and encourage less experienced employees (page 197)

Multinational corporation (MNC)
Firm with independent business units operating in several countries (page 364)

Negligence
Failure to provide reasonable care where such failure results in injury to consumers or other employees (page 283)

Occupational illness
Abnormal condition or disorder resulting from exposure to environmental factors in the workplace (page 78)

Occupational injury
Any cut, fracture, sprain, or amputation resulting from a workplace accident (page 78)

Ombudsperson
Designated individual from whom employees may seek counsel for the resolution of their complaints (page 309)

On-the-job training (OJT)
Method by which employees are given hands-on experience with instructions from their supervisor or other trainer (page 184)

Open-door policy
Policy of settling grievances that identifies various levels of management above the immediate supervisor for employee contact (page 309)

Open shop
Provision of the collective agreement that allows employees to join or not join the union (page 323)

Organizational culture
Collective understanding of beliefs and values that guide how employees act and behave (page 74)

Orientation
Formal process of familiarizing new employees with the organization,

their jobs, and their work unit; critical to socialization which is the embedding of organizational values, beliefs, and accepted behaviours (page 174)

Outsourcing
Contracting outside the organization for work formerly done by internal employees. The small-business owner saves money, time, and resources by outsourcing tasks such as accounting and payroll (page 12)

Panel (group) interview
An interview in which a board of interviewers questions and observes a single candidate (page 152)

Pay equity
The practice of equal pay for work of equal value (page 56)

Pay grades
Groups of jobs within a particular class that are paid the same rate or rate range (page 257)

Pay-for-performance standard
Standard by which managers tie compensation to employee effort and performance (page 247)

Peer review
Performance reviews done by one's fellow employees, generally on forms compiled into a single profile for use in the performance interview conducted by the employee's manager (page 219)

Performance management system
A set of integrated management practices (page 208)

Piecework
Work paid according to the number of units produced (page 249)

Position
Specific duties and responsibilities performed by only one employee (page 108)

Positive, or nonpunitive, discipline
System of discipline that focuses on the early correction of employee misconduct, with the employee taking total responsibility for correcting the problem (page 301)

Progressive discipline
Application of corrective measures by increasing degrees (page 299)

Promotion
Change of assignment to a job at a higher level in the organization (page 197)

Psychological harassment
Repeated and aggravating behaviour that affects an employee's dignity, psychological or physical integrity that results in a harmful work environment (page 48)

Real wages
Wage increases larger than rises in the consumer price index; that is, the real earning power of wages (page 253)

Reasonable accommodation
Attempt by employers to adjust the working conditions and employment practices of employees to prevent discrimination (page 43)

Recruitment
The process of locating and encouraging potential applicants to apply for jobs (page 138)

Reliability
The degree to which interviews, tests, and other selection procedures yield comparable data over time and by alternative measures (page 149)

Repatriation
Process of employee transition home from an international assignment (page 381)

Residual rights
Concept that management's authority is supreme in all matters except those it has expressly conceded to the union in the collective agreement (page 346)

Reverse discrimination
Giving preference to members of certain groups such that others feel they are the subjects of discrimination (page 44)

Rights arbitration
A mechanism to resolve disputes about the interpretation and application of a collective agreement during the term of that collective agreement (page 346)

Role
The part played by an employee within an organization and the associated expected behaviours (page 108)

Selection
The process of choosing individuals who have relevant qualifications and who will best perform on the job to fill existing or projected job openings (page 148)

Self-review
Performance review done by the employee being assessed, generally on a form completed by the employee prior to the performance interview (page 219)

Situational question
Question in which an applicant is given a hypothetical incident and asked how he or she would respond to it (page 154)

Six Sigma
A process used to translate customer needs into a set of optimal tasks that are performed in concert with one another (page 16)

Skills inventory
Information about the education, experiences, skills, etc. of staff (page 136)

Staffing table
Graphical representations of organizational jobs along with the numbers of employees currently occupying those jobs and future employment needs (page 136)

Standards of performance
Set out the expected results of the job (page 115)

Statutory rights
Rights that derive from legislation (page 284)

Step review system
System for reviewing employee complaints and disputes by successively higher levels of management (page 308)

Stress
Any adjustive demand caused by physical, mental, or emotional factors that requires coping behaviour (page 92)

Strike
A situation in which unionized workers refuse to perform their work during labour negotiations (page 342)

Subordinate review
Performance review of a superior by an employee, which is more appropriate for developmental than for administrative purposes (page 219)

Systemic discrimination
The exclusion of members of certain groups through the application of employment policies or practices based on criteria that are not job-related (page 41)

Talent management
Leveraging competencies to achieve high organizational performance (page 19)

Team review
Performance review, based on TQM concepts, that recognizes team accomplishment rather than individual performance (page 220)

Telecommuting
Conducting work activities in different locations through the use of technology (page 14)

Third-country nationals
Employees who are natives of a country other than the home country or the host country (page 371)

Total rewards
Everything that the employee feels is of value in the employment relationship (page 245)

Trainee readiness
The consideration of a trainee's maturity and experience when assessing him or her (page 182)

Training
The acquisition of skills, behaviours, and abilities to perform current work (page 174)

Transfer
Placement of an individual in another job for which the duties, responsibilities, status, and remuneration are approximately equal to those of the previous job (page 196)

Transfer of training
Effective application of principles learned to what is required on the job (page 189)

Transnational corporation
Firm that attempts to balance local responsiveness and global scale via a network of specialized operating units (page 365)

Transnational teams
Teams composed of members of multiple nationalities working on projects that span multiple countries (page 375)

Trend analysis
Quantitative approach to forecasting labour demand on an organizational index (page 136)

Unfair labour practices
Specific employer and union illegal practices that operate to deny employees their rights and benefits under labour law (page 328)

Union shop
Provision of the collective agreement that requires employees to join the union as a condition of their employment (page 323)

Union (shop) steward
Employee who, as an unpaid union official, represents the interests of members in their relations with management (page 334)

Validity
How well a test or selection procedure measures a person's attributes (page 149)

Virtual team
A team with widely dispersed members linked through computer and telecommunications technology (page 123)

Wage and salary survey
Survey of the wages paid to employees of other employers in the surveying organization's relevant labour market (page 256)

Whistleblowing
Reporting unethical behaviour outside the organization (page 62)

Work
Tasks or activities that need to be completed (page 108)

Work permit or visa
A government document granting a foreign individual the right to seek employment (page 374)

Workplace stressor
A workplace event, process, or practice that has the potential to cause worker stress (page 94)

Wrongful dismissal
Terminating an employee's employment without just cause (page 302)

Name Index

Subject Index